CRUSADER IN CRINOLINE

CRUSADER IN CRINOLINE

The Life of Harriet Beecher Stowe

By Forrest Wilson

A great picture of the 19th century, an era that strangely parallels our own. The tumultuous life of the author of *Uncle Tom's Cabin* is thrown in sharp relief against the crowded screen of her times in this lively yet scholarly portrayal. Here is a pulsating, entertaining story of America at one of its most critical moments and of the woman—passionate, intelligent, indomitable—who stood at the vortex of the whirlwind that blew through the States.

Opening in the beautiful airy town of Litchfield, with its crown of New England culture, the story follows the various members of the Beecher family through their restless stages in Boston, Hartford, and New York until the fateful trek to Cincinnati by which Dr. Lyman Beecher hoped to win the West for Christ.

When Lyman Beecher one day in 1811 called on his old friend Judge Reeve to tell him of the birth of his latest child, gently deprecating the fact that it was a girl, neither of these leading Federalists could have dreamed that this tiny girl would one day preach a sermon which would have a more far-reaching effect than any New England divine could possibly have conceived. Daughter of gentle, intellectual Roxana and the mercurial preacher, Lyman Beecher, Harriet was one of a family of eleven, all of whom were extraordinary and two pre-eminent. She grew up in a family at once emotional and intellectual, kept in constant ferment by Lyman Beecher's "evangelical man-hunts." The growth of this strange little girl, bright, odd, laughing, with her penchant for books and her worries about sin and salvation, is brilliantly described. The lonely years of her young womanhood when she taught in her sister's female seminary and the por-

(Continued on back flap)

Crusader in Crinoline

THE LIFE OF
HARRIET BEECHER STOWE

by

FORREST WILSON

30 ILLUSTRATIONS

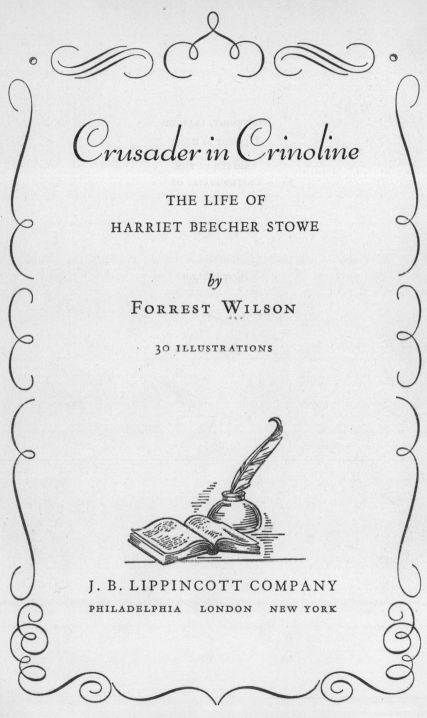

J. B. LIPPINCOTT COMPANY
PHILADELPHIA LONDON NEW YORK

First Edition

To

MARIE HUMPHREYS WILSON

REMARKS IN RETROSPECT

About People with Lanterns, and Others

The explorer who steps from the sunlight of the present into the mouth of that Mammoth Cave which immures the past soon finds himself upon a rare adventure. At first, with eyes yet unaccustomed to the shadows of history's retreat, he gropes ahead in some confusion, but not for long. Presently down the dark incline he sees the flicker of a lantern. He stumbles toward it and then meets the first of that devoted band of custodians of our national memories, the keepers of the American historical collections.

From that moment the explorer's path will be made easy for him. He need only follow the counsel of the great Sermon: "Ask, and it shall be given you; seek, and ye shall find; knock, and it shall be opened unto you."

But how exciting are the asking and seeking, when one begins to uncover the traces of a life lived and gone so irrevocably, it would seem from without, into oblivion! The pursuit becomes a fever, a sport, the trophies of which are apt to be exaggerated out of proportion to their true value. Millions of lives lived, yet one of ordinary skill can, if he tries, follow the footsteps of a single individual on the sands of time! The merest fact, if only hitherto lost and forgotten, is bagged with a satisfaction peculiarly immense, whereas a really major discovery may give the exulting hunter a sleepless night.

This hunt is now over, its spoils have been assembled, and what the assembler remembers most warmly and gratefully is the help given him by the librarians—sympathetic and even anxious help rendered voluntarily by men and women whose only interest in the work is their passion to have history written. An example occurred in the Library of Congress, where Dr. T. P. Martin, acting chief of the Division of Manuscripts, whose special field is Anglo-American commercial relations in the early years of the Republic, remembered a reference to Mrs. Stowe in the private correspondence of James Buchanan, when he was our Minister to the Court of St.

7

James. This clue uncovered the important but suppressed fact that Queen Victoria had refused to receive the most celebrated American woman who ever visited the British Isles.

Without such help no researcher, unless he has a lifetime at his disposal, can hope to glean from any great stack of source-material all of the grain that is grist for his particular mill. It is impracticable to index a large collection of manuscripts, for example, so that the cards will tell the outsider in any great detail what the manuscripts contain. But the librarians know their own libraries pretty well and by handling the manuscripts year after year fill their heads with remembered details of the contents. Often they can bring out treasures from the most unexpected files.

This sort of coöperation I had from the beginning to the end of the research on which this biography is based. It began in St. Augustine, Fla., where Mrs. E. W. Lawson, in charge of the Webb Memorial Library, ransacked shelves and cabinets and in particular unearthed the sprightly comments on Mrs. Stowe in Florida by "Silvia Sunshine," a Kentucky woman, who, as Mrs. Amanda M. Brooks, ended her days in St. Augustine. Over at near-by Mandarin was Miss Mary B. Graff, who teaches high-school classes in Jacksonville five days a week and seems to spend her Saturdays rummaging in Mandarin attics for historical lore. She most generously gave me the use of her file cards; and at Mandarin, in Mrs. Harry Nicholl, I met perhaps the only person now alive who could give me intimate, first-hand recollections of Mrs. Stowe in her active days.

That great repository of history in its documents, the Henry E. Huntington Library at San Marino, Calif., afforded the richest hunting of all. Its air-conditioned, fireproof, and earthquake-proof vaults gave up not the dozen or score of Harriet Beecher Stowe's letters I hoped to find there, but nearly two hundred of them, at least half of which had never been published. Here with an exception or two were all the letters which Annie Fields quoted in whole or in part in her 1898 "official" biography of Mrs. Stowe, and a great many others besides. Among them was the complete file of letters which Mrs. Stowe sent to her publishers during the troubled and beset weeks when she was writing her *Lady Byron Vindicated*. Even Mrs. Fields never saw these letters, which in themselves write a vivid chapter in Mrs. Stowe's life. At San Marino, too, were about twenty unpublished letters of Calvin Ellis Stowe, all as pertinent to this biography as Mrs. Stowe's own.

Captain R. B. Haselden, curator of manuscripts at the Huntington Library, and his assistants showed this same concern I have mentioned that I take the fullest advantage of the collection's resources—and I should especially name Miss Ethel Pearce, under whose monitory eye I spent a busy fortnight copying the letters. As part of his equipment Captain Haselden maintains a laboratory for the detection of forgeries, palimpsests, &c., and during my visit submitted several of Mrs. Stowe's letters to his handwriting experts. They made the interesting discovery that her "autograph" letters, though apparently all alike, are actually written in three handwritings, the other two, besides her own, no doubt being those of her twin daughters, Harriet and Eliza Stowe, who served their mother as amanuenses. It would take a special study to determine which of Mrs. Stowe's letters she actually wrote with her own pen, though of course all have the value of autographs.

Miss Eleanor S. Wilby, librarian of the Historical and Philosophical Society of Ohio, which occupies quarters in the Library Building of the University of Cincinnati, was so patient and thorough about unearthing old files of Cincinnati newspapers that it took me six weeks to work through them. Miss Wilby found for me what remain of the "Semi-Colon Papers," including Calvin Stowe's letters from Germany in 1836. But her interest did not end with my departure. Since then, in going through the Society's autograph letters she has kept this book in mind and as a result has been able to send me copies of several additional Stowe letters of interest.

And so it went. At the Library of Congress, besides Dr. Martin I should mention Mr. David C. Mearns, acting superintendent of the reading rooms, who took a personal interest in my work and gave me every facility at his command for accomplishing it, including the use of one of the research offices in the new, air-conditioned, and sound-proof Library of Congress Annex—and anyone who knows Washington's July appreciates air-conditioning.

Miss Mary G. Gilman, librarian of the Brunswick (Me.) Public Library, made the local histories available for me. Rather strangely, the Bowdoin College Library contains no unique Stowe material; but Robert Peter Tristram Coffin, the poet and Bowdoin professor, gave up a summer afternoon to tell me what he knew about Mrs. Stowe at Brunswick and on the islands and shores of Casco Bay. And I must bow to the young summer-vacation librarians of the

Phillips (Andover) Academy's excellent library for spreading before me a great deal of interesting material elsewhere unavailable.

The librarians of the Harvard University Library prefer anonymity, as do those of the Yale Library; but in both institutions I found a ready desire to help my research, and from both I took much treasure. Though at Yale, the traditional Beecher college, the Stowe letters are not so numerous as at Harvard, they nearly all happen to be of paramount importance to a biographer of Mrs. Stowe. Here was the early correspondence of Harriet Beecher and her sister Catharine with Mary Dutton, and here also I found a veritable answer to prayer—a letter from Mrs. Stowe in which she told at length exactly how she felt about the Beecher-Tilton scandal of the 1870's.

The Boston Public Library holds the largest cache of Mrs. Stowe's letters that exists outside the great collection in the Huntington Library; and Miss Harriet Swift, the assistant in charge of the Rare Book Department, took personal pains to see that it was all placed at my disposal. Here, among the Garrison Papers, was a copy of the letter in which Mrs. Stowe outlined to Dr. Gamaliel Bailey, editor of the *National Era,* her plans for *Uncle Tom's Cabin.* This document is unique, the original letter having disappeared. Mrs. Stowe herself did not know of its existence; and at the end of her life, when gathering her biographical material, she relied on her memory for what she had told Dr. Bailey. The Garrison copy shows that her memory was accurate. Another unique item brought out by Miss Swift was a copy of the Fields 1898 biography annotated by a Boston journalist of the last generation, Elizabeth Porter Gould, which gave me information of value.

At Hartford the secretary of the Connecticut Historical Society, Mr. Albert C. Bates, produced the astonishing and recently rediscovered diary of Isabella Beecher Hooker. In the absence of a dispersed board of managers, Mrs. Anne Cole Wilson, the curator, nevertheless arranged immediate permission for me to examine the records and books of the Litchfield Historical Society. Mr. W. R. Leech, first assistant in charge of manuscripts at the New York Public Library, and the librarians of the Presbyterian Historical Society and the Pennsylvania Historical Society, both in Philadelphia, were all coöperative. In the Presbyterian Historical Society's library I found two years of the file of the Cincinnati *Journal* which I had given up for lost. Mrs. Edith Very Sherwood, librarian of the Westport (Conn.) Public Library, has procured numerous volumes for me on loan from the Library of Congress and has given me the unrestricted use of the collection in her charge.

To all these benefactors my sincere thanks.

A more personal kind of encouragement has come from my literary representative, Mr. William C. Lengel, of New York; Mr. J. Jefferson Jones, managing editor of J. B. Lippincott Company; Mr. George Stevens, of Lippincott's New York office; my niece Carolyn, who helped me with my files; and my friend Mr. Claude Watts, of Washington, D. C., who has read the manuscript editorially.

My gratitude to them, too.

Finally I must say a word about Mrs. Stowe's grandson, Mr. Lyman Beecher Stowe, who has not only read the manuscript, incidentally saving me from making several blunders, but has also lent me various items from his Memorabilia for use as illustrations. In the main, he has approved of the book insofar as it pertains to his grandmother, while rather emphatically dissociating himself from any necessary agreement with my statements about or attitudes toward other members of the Beecher family.

Weston, Conn.   FORREST WILSON.

ACKNOWLEDGMENT

The poem, *At The Summit,* by Oliver Wendell Holmes, originally published in *The Atlantic Monthly* for August, 1882, and the unnamed poem read by Holmes at the celebration of Harriet Beecher Stowe's seventieth birthday, and also the birthday poem, untitled, by John Greenleaf Whittier, read on the same occasion, are used in this book by permission of Houghton Mifflin Company. The sonnet, *Harriet Beecher Stowe,* by Paul Laurence Dunbar, first published in *The Century Magazine* for November, 1898, reprinted at the end of this book, is used by permission of D. Appleton-Century Company and of Dodd, Mead & Company, the latter being the publishers of Paul Laurence Dunbar's complete poems.

CONTENTS

I

LITCHFIELD, 1811–1824

II

HARTFORD, 1824–1832

III

CINCINNATI, 1832–1850

IV

BRUNSWICK, 1850–1852

V
ANDOVER, 1852–1864

VI
HARTFORD, 1864–1896

ILLUSTRATIONS

I

LITCHFIELD

1811-1824

Birthplace at Litchfield, Conn.

BEECHER-STOWE FAMILY

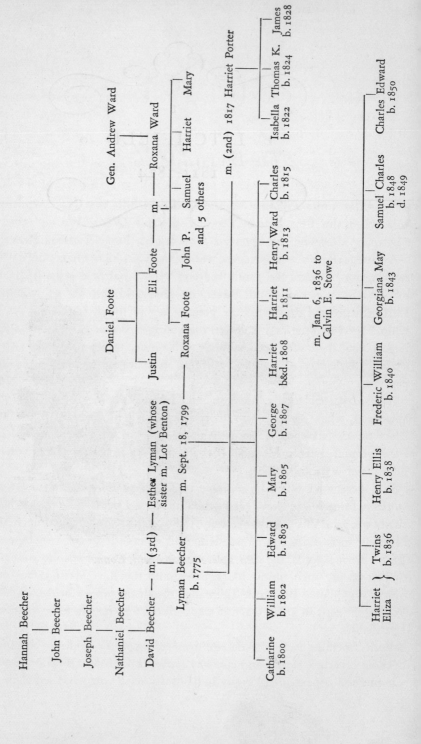

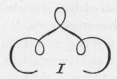

The Blessed Village

COLONIAL times still slept on the Litchfield hills that June day in 1811 when the Rev. Lyman Beecher—not yet *Doctor* Beecher—paid his customary afternoon call upon his great friend, Judge Tapping Reeve.

As Judge Reeve welcomed the ruddy, nervous clergyman, the day was wearing on. Already the gaudy red and yellow Fairfield stage had rattled in over the stones of South Street, its driver, Hiram Barnes, whom the Litchfield urchins considered the greatest wit in town, flourishing his long whip. Piped by flute and flageolet, the young ladies of Miss Pierce's school were taking their prescribed evening walk under the elms, two by two and making a display of the last fashions in bonnets, spencers and dimity pantalets.

A display, incidentally, not lost upon Judge Tapping Reeve. The venerable jurist, whose portly figure stooped over his gold-headed staff and whose silver tresses fell upon his shoulders in a style all his own, confessed to an eye for female beauty. He never saw a girl he did not want to kiss nor a boy he did not want to thrash.

But there were other appreciative beholders of the procession. Knots of students from Judge Reeve's law school made it a point to be on Litchfield's shady streets at this hour to exchange the banter of young courtship with the blushing girls. Both sets of pupils looked reverently at the two figures on Judge Reeve's porch, the girls with modest sidelong glances, the young gentlemen baring their heads. Judge Reeve and the Rev. Mr. Beecher shared only with Colonel Benjamin Tallmadge the distinction of being Litchfield's leading citizens in a day when it was a distinction merely to be a citizen of Litchfield.

Both worthies wore the decent dress of good Federalists—boots, hose, buckled breeches, stocks, and cutaway coats—though Mr. Beecher presented a homespun appearance. Already in his thirty-sixth year possessed of the best

theological brain in America, he left to lesser men of the established clergy
the affectations of queue, cocked hat, and ebony cane. The law students,
too, clung to the eighteenth-century garb. Whatever his private political
opinions, in this atmosphere a young man could scarcely risk the competing
fashion of tight trousers, then called pantaloons. Trousers had been spewed
out of the French Revolution and were the badge of Sabbath-breakers, rum-
selling tippling folk, infidels, and ruff-scuff generally. In one word, of
Democrats.

As they stepped into the house Mr. Beecher had to inform his friend of a
new birth into his teeming household at the parsonage. Roxana Beecher's
accouchement that day could scarcely have been news to the judge, whose
vast wife—the largest woman Catharine Beecher ever saw—with her silvery
voice, her great culture, and her droll wit, was so intimate with Roxana as
to be a second mother to the Beecher children. Her chaise (for she was too
stout to walk the short distance up the North Street to the parsonage) stood
as often at the Beechers' hitching post as the minister's old carryall itself.

What may have been news to Judge Reeve was the babe's sex..Previously
Roxana Beecher had given birth to six children—three boys and three girls.
And now this seventh, born June 14, 1811, was another daughter.

"Wisht it had been a boy," lamented Lyman Beecher. Such clipped lacon-
ics were part of his professional merchandise. Profound in the Calvinistic
fathers, his wit already becoming legendary, he could recognize Byron's
genius ahead of most Americans, a reading of *Ivanhoe* made him rescind
the puritanical ban on novels in his house, he loved music, played the fiddle
(execrably), and mourned that he had never heard Paganini (which he
pronounced Padge-a-nigh-nigh); yet he always said *creetur'* and *natur'*. The
backwoods flavour he preserved in his speech gave it something of its
strange, electrical power in the pulpit.

Judge Reeve whispered some humorous consolation for his friend. He
had long since lost his voice but had so developed whispering that a class of
a hundred could take his lectures without difficulty. The judge could appreciate Brother Beecher's chagrin. In the Beecher family boys meant future
preachers; and the head of the most celebrated law school in the United
States could not gainsay that preachers—Congregational preachers—were
Connecticut's lords spiritual and temporal. Their church drew support from
the public taxes—a favour denied to the Episcopalians, Methodists, and
Baptists—and they themselves named Governors and magistrates, usually

out of the ranks of the lawyers. It may be added that Judge Tapping Reeve heartily approved of the system.

This was the Standing Order, as it was and always would be—unless those fellows in the pantaloons, with their unkempt shocks of hair and their absurd practice of wearing shoes laced with leather thongs, worked some mischief with this nonsense they were beginning to talk about Toleration.

It was inconceivable that the Standing Order could fall. God would not fail his servants; and it was with confidence that Lyman Beecher had dedicated his life to one of its major objects—the rearing of sons for the ministry.

Roxana seemed to be defeating this holy purpose. Since her last lying-in there had been a hiatus of three years in the rhythm of her productivity. On that occasion, one has reason to believe, her husband had also expected a son, to the point of choosing a name for him—Henry Ward, in part after General Ward of Guilford, Roxana's grandfather. When the babe, as Lyman and Roxana usually called the current infant, proved to be a girl, they feminized Henry into Harriet and complimented Roxana's spinster sister, Harriet Foote.

The 1808 Harriet Beecher lived but one month. In the swarming pioneer families, parents were apt to waste no effort in naming children. The 1811 Harriet inherited not only the deceased one's crib and swaddlings but her name as well. The parents added Elizabeth, but she dropped her middle name in later life.

The impatient Litchfield divine had to wait two more years for a Henry Ward Beecher to bless his house, but in this second Harriet fate was having its benign joke with him. What price a woman-child in 1811? This one would outpreach her father and all her gifted brothers combined. Lyman Beecher would live to see her take Parnassus for a pulpit and count into her flock the peoples of the earth. The "great gun of Calvinism" had begotten a major prophetess.

Her New England blood, though plain, was impeccable. The great man of her immediate ancestry was General Andrew Ward, of Guilford. He was a Revolutionary commander who took part in the surprise of Trenton and afterwards kept the camp-fires burning, while Washington drew off his army. His father was Colonel Andrew Ward, who participated in the sack of Louisburg, on Cape Breton Island. The officers of that expedition were paid off in rum. Colonel Ward was a teetotaler but also a Connecticut

Yankee. He sold his rum and invested the proceeds in silver spoons. The "Louisburg spoons" remained in the family as a symbol of sobriety. In Harriet Beecher's generation it was a boast that no descendant of Colonel Ward had ever taken to strong drink.

But Harriet's character was to unfold much more in the Beecher pattern than in that of her mother's line. The original American Beechers came to New Haven with the pioneer Davenport party in 1638, eighteen years after the *Mayflower* rode off Plymouth Rock. The founder was Hannah Beecher, a widow whose husband died in England just before the colonists sailed. She was a midwife, and the leaders granted her her husband's share in the enterprise, if she would come with them to the New World. She consented and brought with her John Beecher, her adult son.

Lyman's father was David Beecher, a learned blacksmith of New Haven, who made the best hoes in New England, could carry a barrel of cider into his cellar and quote Scripture, Astronomy, Geography and History with the best of them. He boarded Yale students, largely to gain access to their books and notes evenings. Squire Roger Sherman, the Signer who had gone to Congress after the War, always consulted with David Beecher when he came home from Washington.

The 1811 fusion of these strains opened bluish-grey Beecher eyes upon a household in which the festive celebration of Christmas and Easter was regarded as sinful, upon a village to which the farmers brought their wives and daughters on pillions, upon a county in which the brandy bottle passed at the Congregational synod and the parsons grew merry, puffed long pipes, and told stories scarcely to be associated with the winning of souls; upon a State in which slavery was legal (though there were not many slaves), upon a Nation in which Mr. Adams and Mr. Jefferson still lived, upon a world in which George III still sat on the English throne.

It was hard to see much change since the Revolution. Litchfield had its earnest of the permanence of the known and familiar in the courtly form of Colonel Benjamin Tallmadge. On a June afternoon one might look across the shrubs and see the snowy queue and cocked hat of the Colonel as he took the air on his grounds on North Street above the bank, noting how his Virgaloo pears had set and observing the ripening of the sweet cherries in his front garden. A little stiff in manner, the veteran was kind at heart and was a pious Congregationalist and an effective supporter of the Rev. Lyman Beecher. Yet even the Beechers were awed by the man who had commanded

Major André's guard and who had felt so close to utter distraction when the gallant spy was led to the scaffold.

It was not to last long. The great era had come to its final twilight, and the infant prophetess absorbed none of it. In another year war intervened, and everything was thereafter changed. Pantaloons vanquished knee-buckles, the Standing Order fell, Lyman Beecher preached his Five Sermons on Temperance, and America moved on into the Nineteenth Century.

Truly, as Henry Ward Beecher wrote, Litchfield was a blessed place for birth and childhood. Was it not the most beautiful village in New England? Many said so. Upon the broad Litchfield Hill—which was a full mountain, reckoned by sea-level—the founders laid out two immense avenues at right angles in the form of a Greek cross. Along these they planted rows of elms and buttonball trees. By 1811 the elms had grown to such size that they would have arched ordinary streets. The buttonball trees were then growing decrepit, and they had all disappeared by the middle of the century.

Some configuration of the land seemed to keep a perpetual summer breeze blowing above the village. On the calmest days the top branches of the elms would sway mysteriously. A small Beecher could lie on the turf when the hoary head of the tallest dandelion was motionless, see and hear the soft commotion so far above, and wonder what made it.

At the intersection of the cross the pioneers set apart their Green, also shading it heavily with elms. The ends of the avenues thus divided became simply the North, East, South, and West streets. Along these and around the Green were the mansions of the aristocracy. Humbler folk built their cottages on the side streets.

Sunrise and sunset painted themselves above flanking hills—Chestnut to the east, a wild terminus for rides or walks, a hunting ground for Parson Beecher and his sons; to the west the smooth height of Prospect Hill. Far in the southwest rose the cone of Mount Tom, blue in summer, amethystine in March dusks. In November one could catch a glimpse of steely Lake Bantam, feeding its noisy river. Nearer was Little Pond, on which Pa Beecher kept his fishing skiff, *The Yellow Perch*. All seasons were ultra, to use a word soon to come in vogue—springs late but singularly exquisite, autumns of a glory that later made a famous authoress think of rainbows, winters that smoothed the roads with hard snow and froze the lakes to granite.

But it was not appearance or setting that made Litchfield famous. This isolated village—a week's journey from New York, and farther from Boston —rivaled both as a centre of culture. The two Litchfield schools, each preëminent of its kind, contributed to the village's lustre, but in national repute they were matched by the resident society—the Wolcotts, the Tallmadges, the Seymours, the Buells, the Tracys, the Daggetts, and other celebrated Connecticut families. Ethan Allen was born in Litchfield, Aaron Burr, Judge Reeve's brother-in-law, had lived there. John C. Calhoun had attended the law school. The poet John Pierpont was a Litchfield native and still brought his family back from Boston summers, when perhaps he worked on his *Airs of Palestine*.

Litchfield was proud of its brilliancy, and some of its sons bragged unmercifully. One was Senator Uriah Tracy, noted for his wit and his mordant friendship with Randolph of Roanoke. Once he and the Virginia Representative were standing on Pennsylvania Avenue in Washington, when a drove of mules passed, raising a cloud of dust as they headed for the Potomac bridge.

"Ah, Tracy," observed Randolph, "some of your constituents, I see."

"Yes, Sir. On their way to Virginia, to teach school."

At a Presidential ball a beautiful Litchfield woman, Mrs. Goodrich, a member of the Wolcott family, was enjoying a social triumph. The British Minister could not restrain his admiration.

"By Jove, Senator," he said to Tracy, "that lady would ornament the Court of England."

"Yes, Sir," was the unblinking response. "She is distinguished even on Litchfield Hill."

The Wolcott living in Litchfield in 1811 was Oliver Wolcott, third of that name, who enjoyed the prestige of having succeeded Hamilton as Secretary of the Treasury in Washington's cabinet. His father and grandfather had been Governors of Connecticut. Secretary Wolcott, though a Congregationalist, had adopted the new Toleration heresy and to underscore his opinions would attend only one of Mr. Beecher's services on the Sabbath. A little later he led the tippling folk and ruff-scuff to political victory and became the third Governor Oliver Wolcott of Connecticut.

But no resident of Litchfield was more celebrated than Judge Tapping Reeve. By 1811 Reeve had begun to decline. He had taken in the polished and polite Judge Gould and thrown upon the younger shoulders of his partner most of the burden of conducting the law school. The common classroom was a white, one-story building in Judge Gould's yard next to Colonel Tallmadge's on North Street. Of the two partners, Judge Gould was the better lawyer. Legal minds admired Reeve's *Treatise on Domestic Relations* but said it leaned too much to women's rights, whereas as late as the 1880's the American bar considered *Gould on Pleading* the ablest law book ever written.

The reputation of Litchfield as an urbane, Christian community contributed almost as much to the prosperity of the Female Academy as the genius of Miss Pierce herself for teaching. There were no dormitories. The young ladies of the school boarded with Litchfield families, as did also the law students. Parents of girls, from Portland, Maine to Charleston, South Carolina and even from the new settlements of Ohio, sent their daughters to Miss Pierce as much to give them the social advantages of Litchfield as the schooling.

Then, too, more than one mother must have considered the chances of their daughters' finding desirable husbands while at Miss Pierce's. The law students, equally diverse in origin, were the flower of American young manhood. Sally Pierce was indulgent with her pupils, insisting only that they obey the house rules of the various families with whom they boarded. A few domiciles were monastic, like that of the Misses Edwards, whose house the law students dubbed the Nunnery; but most Litchfield families, though often deeply religious, were lenient about hours and chaperonage.

As a result, the young beneficiaries of this precursor of coeducation enjoyed almost the freedom of college students today. They took straw rides to Goshen for roast turkey and oysters, with black Caesar along to play jigs on his fiddle. There were merry skating, coasting, and sleighing parties. Boys and girls strolled through the summer fields, rode horses over the stony roads, went together on October nutting expeditions, and occasionally dressed in their best elegance for a grand ball at Grove Catlin's tavern, on the Green.

Such proximity was fertile in romance. When the law school closed after Judge Gould's death, Litchfield could list some fifty weddings that had resulted from it.

The animation lent by these young sojourners to the native enlightenment and polish of the community made Litchfield in the zenith of her glory a village unique in New England, if not in American, annals.

The Beecher residence stood at the far upper end of North Street on the west side, next door to Mrs. Lord, widow of High Sheriff Lynde Lord and mother of Mrs. John Pierpont. It could not be called the parsonage in the sense that it was church property. Lyman Beecher owned it himself, having bought it with the first substantial sum of money that ever came into his possession.

In his first parish, the dour fishing village of East Hampton, out on the seaward end of Long Island, he bought a cottage for $800. When he left East Hampton, in 1810, he had the good luck to sell this property for $1,800.

"Only speculation I ever made." It was a speculation with him because he turned a profit.

When he rode from New Haven to Litchfield, he carried the whole sum in cash in his pocket. He was so afraid of being robbed that, when dusk overtook him only a few miles from his goal, he stopped overnight with a brother minister rather than risk riding in the dark. As soon as he reached Litchfield next day, he deposited his treasure with Judge Reeve, who helped him finance the purchase of the North Street house.

It was a ramshackle box with a hipped roof, side chimneys, and an L for kitchen, well room, woodshed, and carriage house. The two front rooms of the ground floor were bedrooms, separated by the entry and stairs, and another bedroom and the dining-room divided the rear. Upstairs there were four more bedrooms. The garret was a mere windowless loft under the pyramid roof.

This was the house in which Harriet was born. The Litchfield salary, though larger than the one that had failed to support them in East Hampton, soon proved inadequate for the family. Roxana, with her love of beautiful things and now enjoying friends like the Reeves and Goulds, could no longer be contented with the starved existence that satisfied East Hampton. Even to keep modest pace with the new life around her cost more than Lyman received, and presently she was taking into the cramped quarters one or two of Miss Pierce's girls as boarders.

Then, Roxana's Uncle Justin Foote, a wealthy trader of New York, died and left her a life annuity of $200. On the promise of this the Beechers built a gabled wing on the south side of the square house, providing a parlour, several bedrooms to let to students, and, in the garret space, a study for the young preacher, the first he ever had. Since the joiners had finished their work before Harriet's third birthday, this was the house as she remembered it.

The old dining-room was now renamed the drawing-room, though the family table was still set up in it. It contained a built-in heating device known as a Russian stove, which was a marvel in its day. It warmed six rooms at once, three below and three above, and kept them warm even during the night.

Less agreeable was the fact that the old hipped-roof house was overrun with rats. Try as he might with trap, gun, and mousing cats, Lyman Beecher was never able to get rid of them.

And the wind in the chimneys! Each room had its corner fireplace. When Litchfield's great winter winds blew across the housetops, these flues emitted hollow, huffing roars, each of its own diapason. One learned to identify the different rooms by their wind-sounds. Rats and the vocal gales remained in the Beecher memories to give this Litchfield home its particular stamp.

When Harriet arrived, the house was already overcrowded. Five surviving sisters and brothers had preceded her. Catharine Esther, the oldest of the children, was now nearly ten. This first-born—"thou little immortal!"— bore the names of Lyman's "Aunt Benton" and his mother, respectively. After Catharine came William, then Edward, then Mary, then George, who was now about four years old.

Six children, with their parents, would seem to have filled the house sufficiently, but they constituted little more than half its human population. In 1811 Roxana's sister, Mary Hubbard, lived with them most of the time. There was also an orphaned ward of the pastor's, Betsy Burr, who lived with the Beecher family as a member up to the time of her marriage. There were usually two of Miss Pierce's girls as boarders. Finally there were the sisters Zillah and Rachel, the two Negro bondservants who had been brought from Long Island. They were but children, Zillah, the older being fifteen in 1811, but they had complete charge of the kitchen.

Add to this human life the family horse, the cow, the chickens, perhaps the pigs—Lyman Beecher kept pigs at the parsonage in East Hampton— add also the pets, the families of cats, the dogs—as a hunting man the parson was never without his dog. The corner acre was a swarming lot.

But there was more to the family in Litchfield. The first house down the side street, next to the Beechers' back fence, was owned by Mrs. Bull, and she rented half of it to Grandma and Aunt Esther Beecher. For the parson and his family, Grandma's half-house was merely an annex to their establishment, connected by a garden path and a gate.

Grandma was Lyman Beecher's stepmother—David Beecher's fifth wife—and Aunt Esther was her daughter. Lyman was the only child of his mother, who was Esther Lyman of New Haven, and David's third and (according to Lyman) best-beloved wife. The much-married fathers of this nation did not hesitate to rank their various wives in their affections.

Aunt Esther was a spinster who, though not yet thirty, was already regarded as an old maid. She was prim, methodical, and a little cranky, with a horror of dirt, disorder, and waste. Her brass andirons showed no fingerprints, her red and green parlour carpet was fleckless, the fragile cups and saucers in her cupboard were always stacked in precisely the same way. One need look no farther for the prototype of Miss Ophelia in *Uncle Tom's Cabin*.

Although Lyman never met Esther until he was a lad of nine or ten, she became his dearest sister. He himself was a seven months' baby, his mother dying of tuberculosis two days after he was born. His Aunt and Uncle Lot Benton at once took him to raise on their farm near Guilford, Uncle Lot eventually changing his will and making Lyman his heir.

When Uncle Lot saw that the boy would never make a good farmer but wanted to go to college, he partially restored him to his father. The two men undertook together to put Lyman through Yale. In his senior year the money ran low. Lyman had a chance to buy the college butler's concession. He borrowed $300 to buy the buttery stock and worked hard, trundling his barrow loads of melons across the green unabashed before the eyes of the college. With the ministry already in sight, this future founder of the Temperance movement in America sent a connoisseur to New York to bring back a hogshead of porter for sale. At the end he took up his note, paid his graduation expenses, bought a new suit of clothes, had $100 in cash, and still could fret about the $100 due him in bad debts. This experience convinced him that he would have been a good business man.

David Beecher was gathered to his fathers. The year Harriet was born, his widow and her daughter closed the New Haven homestead and moved to Litchfield to be near Lyman, already the great man of the family. After Grandma Beecher died, Aunt Esther joined the preacher's establishment, and she remained with her half-brother to the end of her days.

Despite her prickly nature Aunt Esther had a talent most interesting to childhood. She was an amateur naturalist and knew dozens of stories about the small beasts with which Connecticut children were familiar. This equipment was doubly valuable during tedious convalescences; and one small invalid could say, after her aunt's visit, "Only think! Aunt Esther has told me nineteen rat stories!"

But Aunt Esther, who was "forever reading," was equally versed in Chemistry and Philosophy. And it was she who introduced to Harriet the poetry of Lord Byron.

In such an environment any childhood must have been full of event. With Pa as the dominating element, that of the young Beechers was a long, boisterous adventure. The dynamic parent, who could pursue a sinner or a cottontail rabbit with equal relish—indeed, who confessed that the sensations were about the same—was unpredictable. Although he was a strict disciplinarian, a believer in the rod, the typical glimpse of him in his home is that of playfellow. He required instant and complete obedience, but his commands were few, since he was much too careless and disorderly himself to impose any burdensome code upon his household. When for a twelve-month a strict domestic regime later took hold of his house, none was more galled by it than the mercurial parson himself.

He soared and drowned in emotion; and, since he naively took his family into his full confidence, his fits of despair and his extravagant exaltations became his children's own. Hypochondria was such a familiar devil in the family that they called it "the hypo." Lyman was afflicted with digestive acidity, but his fears made it anything else—consumption, cancer—at any rate, fatal.

In his more uncomfortable attacks he would collapse, gather his dear ones about him, and inform them blackly that the end was at hand. Their outcries were grateful in his ears, since it was meet that children should mourn the death of a father. Yet on the dread morrow, likely as not he would be routing out the children at dawn to go on a chestnutting expedition, or throwing the household into turmoil by announcing the annual apple-butter frolic.

On their honeymoon he warned Roxana he was a passionate man—"quick, and quick over." If she were quick too, they must clash. The tears sprang to her eyes as she realized that this meant the surrender of her will to his. Yet she made it. Once she nearly violated his commandment. He tried hard to control his temper, but in East Hampton "the fire hadn't got out." His pigs enraged him, and he went after them with a club. Roxana interposed. He spoke sharply to her. A retort was on her lips, but she repressed it, turned, and started for the house. He came leaping after her, caught her and embraced her, weeping as he begged forgiveness. Their tears mingled. Never again did they come so close to a quarrel.

The fiddle on which he scraped so raspingly became the outlet for his violent feelings. The beggarly salary at East Hampton forced Roxana to keep a small school for girls, turning an upper chamber of the parsonage into a classroom. Lyman loathed teaching as much as he hated farming. His dull pupils exasperated him.

In Litchfield he had his temper in hand but was still capable of playing the most outrageous pranks. Once he sat in the kitchen thinking about his sermon, in his abstraction just aware that the two black girls, Zillah and Rachel, were filling the tub on the wash-bench, when little Catharine, primped for some errand, marched through. With a bound he pounced upon her, and before the startled child knew what was happening, he had ducked her under—"to see what she would do." Any little girl, concerned for her dignity and physical well-being, would keep an alert watch upon such a father.

Of course, his children adored him. Their various family bees became crusades into which the parson urged his growing clan by exhortation, precept and artifice. Was the slicing of apples and quinces for the annual manufacture of apple butter (which they called cider-applesauce) a drudgery? Who could repeat most of Walter Scott's *Tales of My Landlord?* They were all proficient, and the knives flew. Or Pa would raise some elusive theological point, and debate ensued—give and take and no quarter shown. "The argument lies so, my son; do that, and you'll trip me up." Thus he trained preachers, but a little girl could listen and profit.

A great event was the minister's wood-spell, a Connecticut institution at that time. The wood-spell provided the parson's house with its annual supply of fuel. It occurred usually in February, when the farmers had finished their winter cutting in the woods, and the roads were at their best for the bobsleds.

What a preparation it meant in the Beecher household! First, the trying of the pork fat for the lard in which to boil and brown incredible numbers of doughnuts. Then the making of pies, to be baked, frozen, and stacked in the shed against the coming festival. The boys collected the materials and brewed gallons of beer, for even the founder of the Temperance Movement could hardly refuse the traditional "flip" at his wood-spell.

On some clear and frosty day word would arrive that the sleds were approaching. As each hooded and mittened parishioner threw off his load and tethered his smoking team, the parson welcomed him into the kitchen, where a great fire blazed. Soon the place would be crowded and around would circulate the doughnuts, cakes, cider and beer, the smaller boys bringing the hot flip-irons from the coals to sweeten the brew. In the window stood the preacher publicly admiring the merits of the logs and privately counting them. "Only twelve loads!" He was within his rights. Although the wood-spell took the form of a pious charity, and contributions were voluntary, it was none the less the legal obligation of the church society. The minister's contract called for "salary and wood."

With characteristic shiftlessness the parson left the wood where its donors had thrown it, through snow, sleet and rain, until a warming of April sunshine told him that the brooks were full and the suckers and bullheads biting. It reminded him also of his cucumbers. Each spring he vied with his friend Dr. Taylor, the New Haven heretic, to produce the earlier ones. Brother Beecher usually won, for he started his cucumbers in cold-frames, whereas Brother Taylor, on the more genial coast, relied for victory on a providential withholding of May frosts.

At each break of spring Mr. Beecher discovered that the logs were piled in the very corner he needed for his frames. Once more with shout and command he rallied his clan for concerted effort. Saws sang, axes rang, chips and the parson's jokes and stories flew. Splitting was boys' work, but the girls could help pile the billets in the shed and rake up the litter afterwards. Sometimes for reward they, too, could go on the fishing trip which followed.

In the midst of such household and neighborhood diversions the family head remained always the leading clergyman of Connecticut, a volcano of militant energy. He preached almost daily—thrice on Sundays—worked on future sermons that were to become historic, promoted a reform society, took the initiative in founding a Congregational magazine and keeping its columns filled, wrote tracts, corresponded widely on questions of doctrine and policy, laboured for missions, kept a suspicious watch of the Toleration horde, served as counsel in church trials—having already gained repute as a wily ecclesiastical lawyer—and conducted revivals.

In fact, the early years of his ministry were a perpetual revival which, when it did not frankly break out into "protracted meetings," persisted in the evangelical note he brought into his sermons. If he were not on the trail of at least one unregenerate, the pastor was always downcast. He watched the faces of his congregation for signs of "anxiety." If he detected an emotional disturbance, he marked his man down and thenceforth with prayer and holy threat kept after the quarry until he either had him safe within the circle of "hope" or had sorrowfully bid him farewell for eternity.

The Beecher children followed these evangelical man-hunts with pious attention, sharing the devout Nimrod's discouragements and jubilations and perhaps something of his excitement of the chase.

Another influence in that household, strongly and permanently impressing itself upon the young lives unfolding there, is less explicable from this distance of years. To the end of their days the two most gifted Beechers— Harriet and Henry Ward—testified that their mother presided over their lives as guardian angel; yet Henry could not remember her at all and her image in Harriet's memory must have been shadowy in the extreme.

With the years Roxana Beecher grew into the mythos of the Beecher clan. Henry Ward Beecher could say, "My mother is to me what the Virgin Mary is to a devout Catholic." He could move his vast Plymouth congregation to tears by his references to her. At the age of sixty-nine he said to an informal gathering, "I do not see your faces more clearly than I see those of my father and my mother." He was barely two years old when Roxana died. He had to take thought to remember that he did not actually remember her. Nearly all her children gave descriptions of her at later periods, but she scarcely attains flesh and blood in the sum of their efforts. Harriet attempted a literary portrait in a sketch entitled *Aunt Mary,* but produced only a generalization that could apply to almost any good woman of a century ago.

Roxana became pure spirit with them all, an ideal, the family's Virgin Mary, the symbol of all that was most perfect in womanhood. Was not this worship really the tribute these men and women of God unconsciously paid to as tender a love story as there is in our pioneer annals? Lyman Beecher kept it alive. He saw the youngest of her children into middle age, yet Roxana always remained vivid to him. She was the last clear memory to remain when age extinguished his mind.

She was one of the brilliant Foote girls, whose fame in the 1790's had spread far from their home at Nutplains, two miles outside of Guilford, Connecticut. There were four of them—Harriet, Roxana, Mary, and Catharine—who, with several brothers, were the orphaned children of Eli Foote, an Episcopalian lawyer of Guilford, who had remained a Tory during the

Revolution but had managed to make his peace with his Patriot neighbours afterwards. The Footes were also a pioneer Connecticut family.

Eli Foote abandoned the law for business after the War, trading with the West Indies. In 1792, while visiting his factory on the North Carolina coast, Foote died of yellow fever, leaving his widow and ten children penniless in Guilford. Roxana Foote, the widow, was old General Ward's only living child. The general at once took her and her brood into his home at Nutplains and adopted all the children except John, who had been taken for adoption by his uncle, Justin Foote, the New York merchant and shipper.

The orphans found themselves in as liberal and as enlightened a home as there was in southern New England. Though born a Calvinist, General Ward in his old age inclined to the Episcopalian Church—or, as the orthodox put it, to Arminian views. He was a religious free-thinker. There were no literary taboos in his house; fiction and poetry held the lead in his library. When Lyman Beecher first came a-courting, young Roxana tossed her head and vowed she would never marry until she found the like of Sir Charles Grandison. "I presume she thought she had," chuckled Lyman afterwards.

General Ward was a State legislator, and, for the benefit of his new family, he fell into the habit of investing his legislative pay in books. What an orgy there was every time Grandpa returned from Hartford, as they pounced upon the new publications! In the evenings he read aloud to them all. Books were the great excitement of their circle. When an American printing of Fanny Burney's *Evalina* appeared, pretty Sally Hill jumped on a horse in Guilford and galloped all the way out to Nutplains to show it to Roxana.

Guilford was an advanced community, with a public library. Roxana read all the classics on its shelves. Her interest turned to scientific subjects, especially chemistry. In a chatty letter to another girl she could write: "Mary has, I suppose, told you of the discovery that the fixed alkalies are metallic oxides." Monsieur Gomarre, an elderly fugitive from the slave insurrection in Haiti, who had settled in Guilford, taught Roxana to read and speak French fluently. But her best talent was for handicraft. She could draw, paint, spin, embroider, and make cobweb and other varieties of lace, all beautifully.

As she and her sisters came to maturity, the young sprigs of the law and pulpit in southern Connecticut hovered around the old spinning-mill at Nutplains, where the young people gathered. Though a Guilford boy,

Lyman Beecher did not meet the Foote girls until he was a Sophomore at Yale. His classmate Ben Baldwin took him to Nutplains. Ben was engaged to the Foote girls' cousin, Betsy Chittenden.

It was a lively circle—one to put a New Haven blacksmith's son on his mettle. The oldest Foote sister was the smart, witty Harriet—"a little too keen," Lyman thought her. There was Sally Hill, "pretty beyond measure" and "full of witchery," out from Guilford as usual; also the black-eyed, black-haired Betsy Chittenden. Mary Foote was there, the prettiest sister of them all but still a child of 13 in 1797. "Roxana was queen among those girls . . . She shone preëminent."

After that introduction, the dozen miles between New Haven and Guilford often heard the click of Lyman's horse's hoofs. The learned blacksmith's son, with his magnetic presence, the odd attraction of his rustic speech, his spiritual intensity, and the romantic appeal of a young life already vowed to poverty, bore off the Nutplains prize.

Their engagement was tentative. "Quite bravely" each agreed to inform the other of any repentance. He had two years of study ahead of him, and the question of their religious differences must be resolved—resolved his way, since she was Episcopalian, accepting such fatal heresies as freedom of the will and salvation without conviction of sin. Lyman's love letters became doctrinal expoundings, hortatory, evangelical, and at length they brought her into submissive acceptance of Calvin's most savage dogmas, which the young zealot then believed to the letter.

They were married on September 18, 1799. The night before, the bridegroom wrote in his journal: "Oh, that my heart might be impressed with gratitude to God for his favours, and especially for providing for me a loving and beloved friend."

She always remained that. His wisdom and mandates became to her like those of God. That he rose swiftly to fame could not have surprised her. His domestic failings paled to insignificance before the majesty of his earthly mission. It might have been vexing to have him leave on a winter journey, with insufficient wood split for the fires, but "he is everybody's man . . . preached seven or eight times a week the whole winter . . . meetings afternoons and evenings, and sometimes in the forenoon. I have not in the least exaggerated . . ."

Queen it as she did over her Nutplains circle, in a general company Roxana was shy, blushing to meet strangers, too retiring to take up the duties of a clergyman's wife, which meant leading the women in parish activities, visiting the sick, serving in fact as assistant pastor. Yet there was never a whisper of complaint. It testifies to Lyman Beecher's love that that furious worker in the vineyard never tried to exact such service from her. He was contented with Roxana as she was.

Litchfield saw her always in her place, an aloof Madonna, faithful and devout but too self-conscious ever to take the slightest part in the services. When she died suddenly, the village mourned her but discovered it did not know her. Nobody knew her except her family and a few chosen friends.

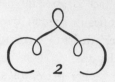

Entry into Israel

IN ENGLAND Miss Austen brought out the first of her realistic novels of
domestic life in 1811 without a reference to Napoleon, who had not yet
reached the Kremlin and might be supposed to have been filling Europe
with terror.

People seem to have taken the incessant wars with indifference, but in the
sensitive Beecher household there was no apathy toward the one which
broke out in 1812. Both the parson and his retiring wife opposed it, Lyman
smelling conspiracy in Washington to wipe out American liberties. God
intervened for the Republic, and the Litchfield preacher could shout, "The
snare of the fowler is broken, and we are escaped."

Roxana took the occasion to turn pacifist. This was too much for her
husband, who, though adoring her, gently insisted upon dictating the
family opinions. He thought he convinced her; but at the end, when Mr.
Madison was proposing to tax the post for revenue, Roxana was urging a
New York brother to reply quickly, since "we don't intend to do anything
to support this war, not even to write letters."

Her instinct was sound. The war, with its embargoes, cost her the annuity
on the promise of which they had already built the expensive wing to the
house. Uncle Justin Foote's company failed. Lyman bleakly contemplated
bankruptcy; but the congregation, in alarm lest they lose their engaging
minister, took up a collection and paid the parsonage debt.

This disaster and rescue came too early to influence the childhood of
Harriet, though in subsequent years such appearances of God's ravens were
not to be infrequent on her bank of the brook Cherith. Too fluid still was
the infant mind to retain the memory of a day in June, 1813, when they lifted
up a baby brother for her to see—the Brother Henry, who was to be closest
to her through life in sympathy and thought.

Before this her uncomprehending eyes must have watched her father about the strange business of screwing heavy iron staples into the kitchen walls. Presently from these hooks depended a West Indian hammock on which reclined a fragile, beautiful lady who smiled at the dancing flames in the fireplace and occasionally coughed, leaving a pink stain on her handkerchief.

This was Mary Hubbard, Roxana's pretty sister, who, though evanescent, fills a niche in the corridor of Harriet's life.

Years later, Mrs. Stowe, explaining the genesis of *Uncle Tom's Cabin,* wrote that her first horror of African slavery was imparted to her by this aunt, who had married an English settler in Jamaica, only to be crushed by the scenes of degradation and cruelty she witnessed on his plantation.

"I often heard her say that she frequently sat by her window in the tropical night, when all was still, and wished that the island might sink in the ocean with all its sin and misery, and that she might sink with it."

Here the authoress's memory outran the fact. Aunt Mary Hubbard died a few weeks after Harriet's second birthday. However, poor Mary's story was often retold in the house after Harriet reached impressionable years, and told in full detail, since the Beecher family, though puritan, was never prudish. Of the essential truth that Mary Hubbard was one influence that led to the writing of the most memorable American novel, there can be no doubt.

Gentle Aunt Mary, whom Catharine Beecher called "the poetry of my childhood," was the most literary of the Foote sisters—the family poetess, in fact. When her younger brother Samuel first went to sea, she dedicated a tender ode *To a Brother:*

> A sister anxious for thy fate,
> With feelings most affectionate,
>   Presents her parting prayer;
> And—venturing forth life's dangerous road—
> Weeping, commends thee to her God
>   And asks His guardian care.

Subsequent stanzas follow Brother Sam—possibly to the dismay of the homesick apprentice—through perils and temptations until finally, stricken with fever in "a fervid clime," he sinks to death, supported by the "everlasting arm" of "that Better Friend."

John James Hubbard, a Jamaica merchant, possibly introduced into the Nutplains circle by Uncle Justin Foote, the Caribbean trader, wooed, won, and wed the romantic Mary in 1803, when she was eighteen. In his new happiness, Hubbard engaged young Sam Foote as clerk in his mercantile establishment, and all three sailed together on the wedding voyage.

Disillusionment awaited Mary in Jamaica. In her new home she found a family of mulatto children fathered by her bridegroom with one of his slave women. It was a dreadful shock for a New England bride, whose horror was not mitigated by Hubbard's bewilderment at her attitude. By law and custom he had the right to propagate his own human livestock, if he chose.

Mary stood it about a year. Then, herself now sinking in a fervid clime and abetted by her loyal brother Samuel, she packed herself aboard one of Uncle Justin's schooners and left her husband forever.

Such was the story (adorned with Aunt Mary's apocryphal death of a broken heart) that went into Harriet's literary stores—perhaps as first told her, with awful emphasis, by her older sister Catharine, Aunt Mary's favourite. The effect was permanent. Harriet was to encounter at first hand other instances of miscegenation in slavery, but none left the impression of this wrong done to one of her own kindred.

Harriet could not remember the sad event of her Aunt Mary's death in September, 1813, nor the visit to Nutplains that followed. She may have been there the entire winter, for at the break of spring Roxana was writing to her sister Harriet Foote that she had delayed sending for "little Harriet" because the builders were about to start putting up the new wing. Little Harriet was to be a good girl and not forget her mamma and brothers and sisters. Except for her birth, this is the first reference to the future authoress in the Beecher records.

In July her mother brought her home and by November the slow craftsmen had the parsonage addition completed. That month there is another reference to Harriet, her mother writing, "Henry is hanging round my neck and climbing on my back, and Harriet is begging me to please to make her a baby." The year 1815 was blank for her, unless she remembered an October day when they showed her her new brother Charles—the gentle Charles Beecher, last of Roxana's children, whose passion in life was to be music.

It must have been about that time that Harriet ate her mother's Dutch tulip bulbs, one of the first definite memories of her life. Uncle John Foote had sent them from New York. Harriet found the sack in a closet and persuaded chubby little Henry Ward that they were onions, a vegetable denied to the younger children. They had sampled and ruined all of them (finding them of an odd, sweetish flavour), when Roxana discovered the catastrophe. She was too philosophic to scold. The damage was done, and there would be no more Dutch tulips for her.

In the spring of 1816 there was a memory of Ma reading to them Maria Edgeworth's juvenile story *Frank,* which had just appeared. In June, as they noted Harriet's fifth birthday and Henry's third, Roxana counted Baby Charlie's fourth tooth, and Mary, having attained twelve years, began to attend the Female Academy, to become Miss Pierce's star pupil. Then came the family's supreme tragedy.

About the middle of August Lyman and Roxana drove to Bradleysville, two miles outside of Litchfield, to visit some parishioners and take tea with one of them. It had been sultry, moist weather, but during tea the sky cleared, and, as they started home at twilight, a high, cold northwest wind had sprung up. Roxana shivered, pressed against her husband, and told him she was not long for this earth. She had had a vision of the blessed hereafter.

Strangely enough, he did not contradict her or laugh at her morbid fears, though less than a month before she had been writing to Nutplains about her good health. He saw that she was "ripe for heaven." Next morning he was off before breakfast for New Haven, where he remained a week. He stopped with the Taylors, repeating to them his belief that Roxana's days were numbered.

How briefly numbered he could not realize. As he drove through the Green on his return, Grove Catlin ran out of the tavern to ask him if he had yet seen Mrs. Beecher. She was badly taken and on Sunday had sent a note, asking the prayers of the congregation. Lyman whipped up North Street to find out. The older members of the family were weeping in Roxana's bed-chamber, and his tears joined theirs, as he looked at her. She had galloping consumption.

The days that followed remained a confusion to Harriet. Aunt Harriet Foote came up from Guilford, there was a hushed stir day and night in the house, grown-up people whispered together in the hall, and little children were kept out from under foot. One day Harriet was taken to see her dying mother, bringing out an imperishable recollection of a fair face with bright red spots on the cheeks. She was asleep in the early morning of September 25 and did not hear the murmur of her father's voice, as in an ecstasy of grief and religious exaltation he heralded the wife of his youth up to the jasper gates.

"Roxana, you are now come unto Mount Zion, unto the city of the living God, the heavenly Jerusalem, and to an innumerable company of angels; to the general assembly and church of the first-born which are written in heaven, and to God the Judge of all, and to the spirit of just men made perfect, and to Jesus the Mediator of the New Covenant, and to the blood of sprinkling that speaketh better things than the blood of Abel."

Henry, with his golden curls and dressed in his best black frock, was, Harriet remembered, accounted too little to go to the funeral; but she remembered the slow walk to the cemetery, the gathering at the grave, the circle of solemn farmers and village people, her mourning dress, the sobs of her older brothers and sisters, the graven face of her father, the voice of some speaker, the final closing. Within a few days into the family legends went that of little Henry Ward Beecher digging industriously in the yard to find heaven and Ma.

Lyman Beecher was the tragic figure. To a hundred death-beds and funerals he had brought the consolation of his Israel. If the chief end of man was to attain heaven, then those of the elect who went earlier were the more blessed. Those left should not mourn but rejoice. Resolutely he repeated this to himself and his children and wrote it to intimates in reply to their letters of condolence. It was all play-acting; the physician could not heal himself. He went around in a daze. A time would come when he would kick contemptuously a box of dusty manuscripts—the sermons he wrote during the year after Roxana's death. They were good for nothing. He had never used one a second time nor attempted to work one over. In vain he wrote his pious platitudes—the sweet and gentle spirit doubtless would not wish to return—but his cry burst out, *"I am alone; Roxana is not here!"*

His children felt his heartbreak at Thanksgiving, a celebration which in that Calvinist household combined the gift-giving of Christmas with the traditional feast in gratitude for the year's bounty. It was the happiest day since the funeral. A closet was full of presents, ready for distribution. Sympathetic parishioners had brought in many toothsome dishes to support the parson's turkey. The long board was spread, and the family, now augmented by Grandma and Aunt Esther Beecher, took their places. Father Beecher arose as usual to ask the blessing, but no words would come. He stood there, looking straight ahead, the tears trickling from his eyes. There was no sound, except the sniffling of the younger children. Then, recovering his poise, with no reference to Roxana the clergyman quietly repeated his usual formula of benediction.

This scene was not in Harriet's experience, for she spent the Thanksgiving at Nutplains. Aunt Harriet Foote took her godchild back to Guilford after the funeral, and little Harriet remained there nearly a year. It was her first impression of the genial household which was to be a second home to her, even supplanting Litchfield in her affections.

Its head in years, if not authority, was Grandma Foote, who wept silently over little Harriet at first and who, in 1816, read the prayer for the King and the Royal Family in the privacy of her own devotions—gentle, sympathetic Grandma, who could secretly take a little granddaughter's part against the severities of her efficient aunt. Roxana took her lenient nature from her mother, who believed that the best way to raise children was to let them do about as they pleased. Harriet remembered the silvery-haired old lady seated beside the great round table on which were her work-basket and books—Bible and Prayerbook, of course, Lowth's *Isaiah*, Bishop Heber's *Life*, Shakespeare, and the works of Dr. Johnson, whom she considered the greatest of Christian souls, yielding before the dissenting Beechers not an inch to President Edwards. With the personages of the Bible she lived as among acquaintances and friends. Did the disciple Peter make an awkward remark? "Now that's just like Peter—always so ready to put in!"

Another member of the household was Uncle George Foote, whose hands were horny from farm-work but who played chess in the evenings, recited Scott's ballads, and answered a little girl's interminable questions by reading aloud from Rees's *Cyclopaedia*.

About the house were mementos of another uncle, Samuel Foote, the sea-captain, now away on one of his long voyages. The canopy over little Harriet's bed was of East India stuff brought home by the mariner from one of the seven seas. She never tired of studying the pagodas, mandarins, and mammoth trees and birds printed on the linen. In various drawers were other rare objects—Mogadore mats and baskets, frankincense from Spain. The exotic collection formed a romantic prelude to the subsequent entry of this fascinating uncle into Harriet's consciousness.

But the head of the Nutplains household was Aunt Harriet, unmarried and approaching the age of forty. The wit of her girlhood was becoming sarcasm; her keenness, to which Lyman Beecher objected, now savoured of asperity. She called Harriet "niece" and required the two Negro servants

to address the child as "Miss Harriet." Harriet must always say, "Yes,
ma'am," and "No, ma'am," never romp and shout about the house in the
boisterous Litchfield manner, never tear her dresses, and have her regular
hours for sewing, knitting, and Catechism.

Only on the subject of Harriet's religious education was Aunt Harriet
in doubt. She herself was such a convinced Episcopalian that, admire Lyman
Beecher as she did, when visiting in Litchfield she could on Sunday mornings walk firmly past his "meeting house" to the Church for her worship.
There was only one Church for Aunt Harriet, who declared that while it
was possible that persons outside the Episcopal Church might be saved at
last, they were relying entirely on "uncovenanted mercy."

Should she abandon her own godchild to such a precarious spiritual state?
Hardly. But would not Lyman think it a breach of trust, if she educated
his daughter outside of Congregationalism? Her solution dismayed a five-
year-old. Little Harriet must learn *both* Catechisms.

There was no comparing their relative attractiveness. The Episcopal
Catechism's first question, "What is your name?" any child could answer
with fine authority; but the answer to that of the Primer—"What is the
chief end of man?"—defied young memory. Calvinistic instruction, therefore, so lagged behind Episcopalian that after a few days Aunt Harriet, her
conscience cleared, told Grandma that the Presbyterian Catechism might
wait until Niece got home.

But Aunt Harriet had her more comfortable side. She could soften at a
table surrounded by youngsters and keep them gasping with her comedy
until they begged for time to drink their tea. She knew all the lore of family
and neighbourhood, implanting in Harriet's memory fragments she was to
use in her many sketches and tales of New England life.

Niece was missing less pleasant experiences at home, where Lyman
Beecher had persuaded his sister Esther, much against her will, to take charge
of the motherless household. Aunt Esther, of the troubled soul, had been
reared to have so little confidence in herself that she ordered all existence by
the infallible rules. One of them was, "a place for everything and everything
in its place." This brought revolution into the parsonage.

Aunt Esther began with a general housecleaning and inventory. Discarded
garments brought to light had to be patched for further use, while everything beyond redemption was nevertheless sorted and packed neatly away.

GRANDMOTHER FOOTE

"Gentle, sympathetic Grandma, who could secretly take a little granddaughter's part against
the severities of her efficient aunt." (Page 41.)

From a miniature painted on ivory by Roxana Beecher

Waste not, want not. Pegs and hooks went up everywhere, as disorder retreated with Mr. Beecher to the sanctuary of the barn.

Debt was Esther Beecher's nightmare, and her indwelling fear was that under her administration expenses might outrun income. She became parsimonious, and the family might have suffered except that at this time the sympathy of the village for its bereaved pastor was at its quickest, taking the form of clothes for the children and victuals for the table. No day passed but that some beaming neighbor-woman brought in a masterpiece of cookery or an embarrassed farmer drove up with a freshly smoked ham or flitch of bacon. The healthy Beechers fared abundantly, and Aunt Esther ran the house on nothing at all.

They all loved Aunt Esther, and so, paced by Pa's pious mendacity, the family assured her that innately it preferred such a precise existence and that it had only taken her genius to bring out the trait. Yet there is no doubt that her advent was a visitation nor any doubt of the general relief when her reign ended.

Catharine Beecher, now seventeen, became the family secretary. In February, 1817, she reported (to Aunt Harriet in Guilford) the family in good health, three boarders in the house, Edward away at school, William employed in Mr. Collins's store, Mary attending Miss Pierce's school and George Miss Collins's, Henry turning into "a remarkably interesting child"; and, "he often speaks of his sister Harriet and wishes spring would come, so that she might come home and go to school with him." Baby Charles, fat as ever, could speak a few words. . . .

In June, Grandma Beecher was unwell—her lungs affected. Everybody else well. Charles, still "fat as ever," had fallen into the fire twice and been burned. Henry was still impatient for sister Harriet to come. She must have returned soon after that—returned in time to witness something of a public event which rescued her father from his spiritual paralysis and in its consequences was to have an effect on the lives of all of them.

At last Lyman Beecher's "tippling folk and ruff-scuff" had joined with the "minor sects" to threaten the Connecticut Federalists and the Standing Order, nominating Oliver Wolcott for Governor on a platform of Toleration. Ordinarily the coalition would not have been dangerous; but the Episcopalians, who had always supported the Calvinists in politics, were now disgruntled because the State Legislature had failed to grant them an appropriation for their bishops' fund, and had joined the Methodists and Baptists and the infidels. Furthermore, there was a quarrel in the Federalist Party.

Beecher was quick to see the oncoming disaster, and in letters to his brother clergymen he sounded the tocsin. But the crowds at the hustings were already cheering every attack on the Connecticut lords spiritual, who clamped on every neck the iron enforcement of their puritan morality. Lyman Beecher himself, now the recognized leader of entrenched privilege, bore the brunt of the vilification. He charged snorting to the counter-attack, but too late. The tally, after a brief campaign, swept Wolcott into office; and the last established church in the North had gone down.

John P. Brace, Miss Pierce's nephew, who was already teaching in his aunt's school, announced it to the parsonage: "Oh, the Democrats have beaten us all to pieces!" and the wails of the family rose. More picturesque was Pa's "They slung us out like a stone from a sling." He slumped into a rush-bottomed chair in the kitchen, arms dangling, his chin sagging to his breast. The cause of Christ itself seemed irreparably damaged. The children were too frightened to cry. Catharine dared ask, "Father, what are you thinking of?" "The CHURCH OF GOD," he replied in a hollow voice. Yet in a few months he could jubilate, "Best thing that ever happened to the State of Connecticut."

After this débâcle, the disfranchised clergy, their prestige shattered, determined to lie low until some of the odium vanished with time. Such cautious counsel was not to the stomach of the Litchfield divine, who as a Yale student had pursued an intruder through his window one night, caught him on the street, and then, since the watch and the gaoler were asleep, took the thief back and by sheer force of character held him prisoner beside his bed until morning. He pulled strings and had himself invited to deliver a secular address in that hotbed of Toleration and Beecher-haters, New Haven, his native town.

The meeting was packed against him; but, as he faced the jeering and hissing, the old eloquence at last flowed back into his tongue, and he soon conquered by the magic of his speech. The success emboldened him to accept an invitation to deliver an ordination sermon at the Park Street Church in Boston—Boston, where Unitarianism, that fire in Lyman Beecher's bones, was swollen with insolence, having usurped the Harvard Chair of Theology, which existed on the income from orthodox funds. His sermon, *The Bible a Code of Laws,* was the belated challenge of Israel to the Philistines and their Agag, Channing. The Connecticut preacher "took sight and struck on all the points" and, in his own estimation at least, scored a perfect victory.

This sermon, though a landmark in the ecclesiastical career of Dr. Beecher, held a different but not less important implication for his famous daughter and her brothers and sisters. It took their father to Boston for the first time in his life. A decent interval had elapsed since Roxana's death; and to a Congregational preacher a wife was as essential a piece of professional equipment as his Cruden or Bible. He knew exactly what he wanted. As a stripling, before he met Roxana, he had coolly laid down his specifications. He needed a woman of sense; she must possess strength to lean upon. Where was a likelier place than Boston to find such a woman? Can we doubt that as he rode across the "elegant Connecticut" at Hartford and struck the turnpike for Worcester, he was promising himself to keep his eyes open?

At any rate, he met in Boston one who seemed to fill his requirements. She was Miss Harriet Porter, of Portland, visiting her sister, Mrs. Homes, wife of a prosperous hardware merchant on Boston's Dock. She was young— certainly not past her twenties—she was beautiful, she was a converted and intense Christian by the Assembly's definition, there was no doubt of her good sense and still less of her strength to lean upon. Her family was eminent. Her father was one of the best-known physicians in the Down East country. One uncle was at different times Senator from New York and Minister to England, another was Governor of Maine, a third was a Member of Congress.

Lyman wasted no time in courtship. He left Boston at the end of his stated week, bearing the acclaim of the downtrodden Presbyterians and the promise of Harriet Porter to marry him in the near future.

There followed a quaint interchange of letters. As the oldest child, Catharine Beecher wrote first, formally welcoming Miss Porter into the prospective "tender alliance," asking rhetorically, "Who can fill a *mother's* place but a *mother?*"

No less correct was Miss Porter's answer. Oh, no, she was not to take the place of that mother. "To succeed such a woman is, indeed, a momentous concern." Lyman Beecher had left her under no misapprehensions. His consort, yes, but never his queen. The deceased mother must live in the children's memory and affections; "but have you not room for me also?"

Is it only imagination reading into these words a certain confidence that Roxana's memory, though always hallowed, would not be forever supreme? If it is not, then Harriet Porter was moving into a most wretched personal tragedy. Certainly, something poisoned her life. Less than twenty years later she was to die in agony of spirit, though why it was never revealed. Prone as they were to exploit their intimate and tender domestic scenes, the Beechers were not fond of opening closet doors on their skeletons. One can only surmise, remembering that when the fissure at last opened in the clan, it divided Harriet Porter's children from those of Roxana. Surely, to spend one's entire youth in vain and unfair rivalry with a departed saint, whose perfection gained splendour with the years, might have curdled the nature of the most godly and submissive of women.

They were married in Portland in October, or early November, 1817, and the wedding trip was a round of visits to "her" relatives and then the journey from Boston to Litchfield, all in the parson's old family chaise. It had no luggage compartment, so "her things," in an immense yellow leather trunk, went around to New Haven by water. Cold weather froze the harbour ahead of the slow bow of the packet schooner, and the second Mrs. Beecher did not get her trunk until spring. "She had to patch up for the winter."

Little Harriet remembered her coming. Harriet slept in a room with her younger brothers, Henry Ward and Baby Charles. A night commotion in the house awoke them, and they heard their father's voice. "We . . . started up in our little beds, crying out as he entered our room, 'Why, here's Pa!' A cheerful voice called out from behind him, 'And here's Ma!' " They were abashed by her unexpected beauty. Her eyes were blue, her hair was a soft auburn bound with a black velvet bandeau, her delicate cheeks were cool from the frosty night as she kissed them all, but it was her hands that fascinated the tiny children—her white beautiful hands. They had never seen such rings. In her presence they felt like rough little country louts indeed; yet in a few days Harriet had gained courage to express her childish resentment to her new stepmother. "Because you have come and married my pa, when I am big enough I mean to go and marry your pa!"

The new Mrs. Beecher's letters that winter give a revealing picture of the parsonage in its neighborhood. Appraising, though well-disposed, eyes took in the stepchildren. A more agreeable family she had never seen. Edward, probably, would be a great scholar. He and William were soon to go away to school. Catharine was a fine-looking girl—"not handsome, yet there is hardly anyone who appears better." Mary, she thought, would make a fine woman—rather handsome than otherwise—and was already, at twelve, "almost the most useful member of the family." George, the next, "quite a large boy, takes care of the cow, &c., goes to school . . . learns well." How accurate the years proved her predictions to be!

But, perhaps because of some reserve that still existed between her and these adolescents, the smaller children interested Mrs. Beecher most, and especially Harriet—Harriet who at six and one-half years could already read fluently and had committed to memory twenty-seven hymns and two long chapters in the Bible. She was as lovely a child as ever Harriet Porter Beecher had seen, "amiable, affectionate, and very bright." She and her little brother Henry were always hand-in-hand. Since all the children now stayed all day in school, except the baby, who was usually with his grandma, "we have not much noise."

An acute critic of Mrs. Stowe was to remark sapiently that she was incapable of understanding Southern aristocratic character because she was of the "professing Christians" of the North who "form an Israel of their own, carefully distinguished from the rest of the world in the midst of which they live by manners, by habits, and even by a certain shibboleth of speech."

About the time of the advent of her stepmother, Harriet became aware of the frontier of her Israel. For instance, she made the discovery that year that the Episcopalians celebrated a day called Christmas, a name not in Zion's shibboleth. On Christmas Eve the scanty Episcopal parish dressed its church with boughs and tallow dips for an "Illumination," to which as much of Litchfield flocked as could pack into the small wooden Gothic edifice on the Green. That was all of it—no presents, no feast. On December 25 school kept as usual, and the bank and Buell's store were open, as redeemed and unredeemed went about their accustomed daily chores.

Sometimes (if Pa had a neighborhood prayer-meeting on Christmas Eve) even the Beecher children might flit down North Street over the spectral snow and crowd in with the others to marvel at the lights and the home-made gilt star hanging over the Episcopal altar. If Parson Beecher discovered the small treason, he was not too severe about it, secretly gratified, perhaps, that it supplied him with an easy theme for a sermon next Sabbath, convicting the Episcopalians of their error. He could prove beyond dispute that the primitive Christians never celebrated Christmas and, secondly, that Christ was not born anywhere near the twenty-fifth day of December.

Harriet attended Ma'am Kilbourne's school that winter, towing little Henry Ward. Miss Pierce did not take girls until they were twelve years old, though she admitted a few boys (of selected Litchfield families only) of younger age. Lyman Beecher had made a reciprocal arrangement with Miss

Pierce, teaching the Saturday Bible class in return for free tuition for his children; and that winter George Beecher, now ten or eleven, joined his sisters Catharine and Mary in the famous Female Academy.

In May, 1818, occurred a great event in the family. A Vermont college gave the parson his Doctorate. "Oh dear! what if there should be a word spelt wrong in this epistle! I think it is likely to be so; and now, being a D.D., how it must look!" Yet he was proud of the new title, for all his banter, and to the end of his long life bore it as emphatically as had Samuel Johnson himself.

In a Puritan village the great holiday of the year was the Fourth of July. Harriet remembered that of 1818. Early in the morning the Meeting House bell began pealing its cocky gratulation (to use a favorite Beecher word), while the parsonage was hasty with morning prayers and breakfast in order to pack the impatient boys off with six pennies apiece for spending money and warnings not to get burned by powder. At nine o'clock came the muster of the militia (some of the train-bands from distant settlements had marched since midnight) followed by the formal exercises, the picnic dinner on the Green (not too far from Grove Catlin's taproom), the afternoon review of the troops by Colonel Tallmadge, erect on his white horse, and finally the sham battle, in which the Americans completely routed the British and Indians. (The ranks of the Redcoats had to be filled by lot, though there were plenty of volunteers for Indian rôles.)

But for Harriet this intoxicating day pivoted on the exercises in the Meeting House, for there Pa, more and more resembling another Father of hers, took his appointed place. Politics were suspended for the day, Governor Wolcott sitting on the platform beside the Federalist ex-governor, and, it had been hoped, religious differences also. The humourless young Episcopalian rector, however, nearly spoiled the symphony by declining to deliver the closing prayer, lest he should be giving an official recognition of the ordination of the unauthorized sectarian Dr. Beecher. Only the willingness of a Minor Sect clergyman to substitute saved the day's neutrality.

A Democrat, a Methodist, or even an infidel could join as earnestly as the Beecher children in one of Harriet's "twenty-seven hymns."

> Let children hear the mighty deeds
> Which God performed of old;
> Which in our younger years we saw,
> And which our fathers told.

It was New England's national anthem. Not for fourteen years would an
Andover student scribble inspired words to an English tune already in
several national repertories—"My country, 'tis of thee." A silver-tongued
student of the Litchfield law school gave the oration, but the supreme
moment came when Harriet saw the Revolutionary figure of Colonel
Tallmadge, in military blue and gold, rise to read the Declaration of that
Independence which he had helped so signally to win. If the words fell
with solemnity and power upon her comprehension, if the seven-year-old
sibyl longed "to do something, she scarce knew what; to fight for her
country or to make some declaration on her own account," we may
remember that nearly every old and middle-aged man listening there—a
prideful local historian says *every* one—had served as a soldier to support
that document.

In January of that year Julia Anna Shepard, riding on a pillion behind
her father, had come from the Susquehanna to enter Miss Pierce's school
and find board with Mrs. Bull on Prospect Street, where the mother and
sister of Parson Beecher lived. On July 25 she wrote to her parents in
Pennsylvania: "I must hasten to tell you that a few days since I saw a
Christian die. It was Mrs. Beecher, mother of the minister. She met death
as a welcome guest."

For the third time in Litchfield the Beecher children put on their mourning to weep at a family funeral—and another was soon to come. Dr. Beecher
began impelling his older sons and daughters toward that miraculous conversion without which none could hope to enter the Kingdom of Heaven.
A family such as his presented "a broad mark for the arrows of Death."
Time was flying, sin hardening. "Oh, my son . . . let me not, if you should
be prematurely cut down, be called to stand in despair by your dying bed,
to weep without hope over your untimely grave." This to William; but "I
shall attend to Catharine, and Mary, and George, and Harriet, with the
hope that God will bless them with salvation." If they balked at the
Calvinistic enormities, he grew impatient with them. They were careless,
unawakened, even stupid.

In October Harriet Porter Beecher gave birth to the first of her children,
a son whom they named Frederick, but the population balance in the
"nest of genius" was maintained, as Edward went away to Yale College.
Almost immediately the Freshman got into a scrape, the report to Dr.
Beecher picturing his scholarly son as taking a riotous lead with club and

stones. "Ned's" own story put a different face on the affair, and the preacher withdrew his chiding.

Two other fledglings left the nest in 1819. William secured mercantile employment outside of Litchfield, possibly in Hartford, and Catharine went to Boston to study music and drawing. It made room for *five* boarders in the parsonage. A family letter gives a glimpse of Harriet at eight, wrinkling her nose and making faces, loving to be laughed at—she was "just as odd" as ever. Was it the perusal of this letter years later, when she was helping to arrange and write her father's "autobiography," which gave her the idea for a book of her own under the title, *Early Days of An Odd Little Girl?* At all events, it resulted in one of the most successful of her New England stories, *Poganuc People.*

But there were glances at her brothers and sisters. The merry, light-hearted Catharine, who was to become the pioneer woman educator of America, was the life of the household. (She studied not at all and confessed in subsequent writing that she made good marks with Miss Pierce by taking part in a cheating system at examination time.) Quiet, studious George, now a lad of thirteen, was "as usual." Little Charles was the mischief—always being switched or spanked and always in new trouble. But he was an honest little boy, and they all loved him dearly. Henry Ward was the disconcerting one. He, as surely pledged to the ministry as the other sons of Roxana, had developed an impediment in his speech which did not improve. He was thick of tongue, unable to pronounce correctly such sibilant words as *justice.*

For the ease of the happy-go-lucky family, the stepmother was no great improvement over Aunt Esther. There was no relaxation in the rules of order and conduct (though Mrs. Beecher governed without any "vulgar scolding"), and, besides, Roxana's successor, in spite of her beauty, lacked Aunt Esther's charm in the latter's moments of relaxation and good-humour.

All the first brood of Beecher children professed the highest love and veneration for their stepmother, but there is evidence that at least two of them were not too fond of her. Harriet could look at her critically in retrospect. Harriet Porter was "naturally hard, correct, exact, and exacting"; and Henry Ward Beecher's "she . . . was a woman of profound veneration, rather than of a warm and loving nature" may not have referred entirely to his stepmother's attitude in prayer.

When Dr. Beecher took his wife with him in July on a preaching foray to Boston and Salem, the suppressed spirits of the children erupted. Aunt

Esther, as mother-in-charge, wanted to "hang half a score of them." The worried relative even looked sourly on tongue-tied Henry, who was "not fond of his books." As if mutiny were not enough, a new series of misfortunes overtook the hapless Charles. Scarcely recovered from a facial powder-burn, he fell and cut one eye so badly as to need medical attention, then, once more convalescent, fell again and did the same thing to the other.

But it was a wounding summer at the parsonage. Before he left for Massachusetts, Dr. Beecher, energetically sawing off an end of the barn, collapsed it on the head of old Mr. Culver, who sometimes helped as handyman. When the neighborhood dug him out, old Mr. Culver had a three-inch cut in his scalp that exposed his skull. A morning or so later the unmoored barn started to back down hill and after two hours of cracking and racking wound up in a corner of the yard six rods away, where an exasperated Doctor of Divinity proposed to leave it until it tumbled down from old age.

Then when Dr. and Mrs. Beecher returned from Boston in August, they found poor Charlie once more bed-ridden, this time with a broken leg sustained in a fall. Such events made it a season of interest for eight-year-old Harriet, but the brightest spot of that summer was the fact that, with her age disqualification waived, she began to attend Miss Pierce's school.

It was not a children's world in which her childhood was unfolding. Nothing was planned commercially for the amusement of children. There was no public entertainment, except for school Exhibitions and the Fourth-of-July battle. Except for one or two of Miss Edgeworth's stories, there were no "juvenile" books. There were no toy shops or toy counters, at least in Litchfield no manufactured toys at all. The only boughten toy Harriet could remember having owned was a wooden doll, carved and painted no doubt by some village puppeteer.

Yet what little girl needed store toys when she had a brother who could slobber over a segment of willow or elder, pound it with the handle of his jack-knife, slip off the neat tube of bark, and, by hollowing the exposed wood, produce a whistle that could charm back Arcady? A little girl herself could cut a prickly squash frond, sever leaf from stem, slit the closed end, and have a horn with a soft, deep note remindful of Triton. Then, the pets— Trip, the dog; the fat horse in the stable, "waiting for his journey"; the many cats, including the fecund tabby who, having appropriated the Doctor's manuscript closet, bedded in discarded sermons and from time to time, as a humorous novelist remembered in her old age, "led forth coveys of well-educated, theological kittens." If one of these Calvinistic felines met an untimely end, "our Harriet is chief mourner always" at the funeral. She asked sister Catharine for an "epithet" for one Tom, Jr. Catharine complied with:

> Here lies our kit,
> Who had a fit
>   And acted queer.
> Shot with a gun,
> Her race is run,
>   And she lies here.

Who needed toys, when she had a vasty cellar to explore, its apple-bins filled in autumn with Pearmains, Bristers, Golden Sweets, and Seek-no-furthers—when she had a wood shed and a carriage shed to serve as *mise-en-scène* for many an imaginative invention; when she had not one but *two* attics to enjoy?

Every night on her way to bed she had to pass through the small garret above the kitchen. Its most interesting fixture was an iron door in the chimney concealing a chamber in which the Doctor cured his hams and sides of bacon. If a little girl tugged open the warm metal and looked inside, the hurrying smoke and the glow coming up from the depths reminded her of Christian, as he opened the hillside door and found himself staring down the lurid byway to Hell. In the other attic, where lay on sheets the flinty ears of seed corn which the rats gnawed and rolled, she was more likely to have company. There on inclement Saturday afternoons the boys gathered to whittle out wind and water mills, rabbit traps, and sticks for kites. In a proscribed corner hung the family medicine, the dried bundles of catnip, boneset, elder-blow, hardhack, tansy, and pennyroyal. She always helped to gather these simples, and in winter their dusty smells made her think of explorations along lush ditches and of summer afternoons when she bent down the elderberry stalks to reach their floral galaxies.

In both garrets were barrels of old sermons and tracts which she sometimes examined. A sermon on the death of George II opened with words that stuck in her memory like burrs—"George! George! George is no more!" There seemed to her to be exasperating thousands of a tract with the title, *An Appeal on The Unlawfulness of a Man's Marrying His Wife's Sister.* But in one of the barrels she found the first book that ever addressed itself directly to her childish taste—*Arabian Nights.*

How she treasured that volume, hiding it and hugging it to herself, to produce it whenever she was left alone, as she often was. She read it again and again, until she knew it almost as well as young vision-seeing Calvin Stowe, now tending the fires of a paper mill in Natick, Massachusetts, knew his one book, *Pilgrim's Progress,* which is to say, by heart.

When Dr. Beecher brought home a new two-volume edition of Cotton Mather's *Magnalia,* still another world opened for Harriet and one at least as interesting as that of *Arabian Nights.* For these wonderful stories of witches, of Indian raids, and of awful punishments that had overtaken sinners, were about America and were, moreover, true. No book was ever better devised to impress upon a young mind the consecrated rightness of her own country and of her own Israel. God even visited a plague upon the Massachusetts-Bay Indians to clean up the country and make it ready for the Pilgrims. "He drave out the heathen and planted them."

Sabbaths loomed large in that childhood, though for one as young as Harriet they meant only the morning and afternoon services at church. The afternoon meeting was the ordeal, for then she and the rest of the congregation had eaten dinner, and it was hard to stay awake.

Yet the long discourses drilled the generation in close listening and logical thinking, and the man who could be so interminably dull in the pulpit was chief magician in the enchantment which all the Beechers felt lay over their childhood in Litchfield. In Harriet her father was now building up that "perfectly triumphant faith" in himself which was not to be shaken throughout her life. He was at his best after the evening meeting, when he came home with nerves so taut he had to let himself "run down" before he could attempt to sleep. Then the children were allowed to stay up, and Pa spent a riotous hour with them, joking, laughing, and capering. He dragged down his violin and his old yellow music-book and played *Auld Lang Syne* to them, and *Bonnie Doon* and *Mary's Dream.* (He never mastered *Money Musk* and *College Hornpipe,* because they were in unfavourable keys.) And if Mamma had retired early with a headache brought from the stuffy church, he could be prevailed upon to scrape off an unholy jig-tune entitled *Go to The Devil and Shake Yourself* or even to execute a still less sanctified double-shuffle he had learned in wild youth.

And what fun it was to be delegated to wake Pa up in the morning! Invariably he would throw a little daughter into a delicious panic by professing fear that there was a lion under his bed, ready to nip his foot, if he stuck it out. Not until she, braver of the two, made an exploration and found the coast clear would he consent to budge, and even then the breakfast bell must sound several times before he gathered courage to launch forth into a new day.

Poverty was always with them, but its pinch was seldom bitter. However, the ravens could not be expected to provide luxuries; and when Edward in Yale, elected to Phi Beta Kappa in the autumn of 1819, wanted a watch and chain on which to hang his Key, Dr. Beecher's chagrin at being unable to buy one took the form of a scolding for his collegiate son. His own watch he had bought with money earned by himself after he was out of college. He had no objection to watches, but the wearing of one by Edward would be indicative of more foppery than Dr. Beecher had yet observed in his son. Poor Edward! Two years later the Doctor was still grumbling over his inability to buy Ned his watch.

With sixty other pupils, including various Wolcotts, Seymours, Buells, and Goulds from Litchfield, Harriet was that winter attending Miss Pierce's school, where John P. Brace had begun his distinguished career as a teacher. Though Mary Beecher was now consistently "Head of Papers" in the school, term after term, and George Beecher that year won the prize in Drawing, Harriet did not get on the honor roll. By some error, she was entered as Harriet F. Beecher, and as Harriet F. she remained to the end in the school's records. That she never noticed the mistake or never bothered to correct it was an early indication of that carelessness in spelling and in other technical details of writing which was to characterize her entire career.

In 1820 Dr. and Mrs. Beecher attended the "May Anniversaries" in New York, returning to Litchfield just in time to confront another family tragedy. In mid-June the black canker, as scarlet fever was then usually called, struck into the parsonage, attacking Harriet and the baby, Frederick. Little Freddy died, and Harriet had the closest brush with death she was ever to know until her final summons. For two days she hovered on the margin, remembering later a lucid moment when she became aware of low western sunshine slanting across the room and her father at her bedside invoking "her blessed mother, who is a saint in heaven."

Harriet's destiny moved a stride nearer in 1821, when her sister Catharine, having finished her training in Boston, secured a post as teacher of art and music in a girl's school in New London, Connecticut. Out of this obscure event sprang consequences radically affecting the lives of Catharine and Harriet and casting a profound influence over the distinguished career of Edward Beecher.

Otherwise it was another year of calamity for the parsonage. Poor Charlie's annual accident that summer was a fall which drove a rusty nail into his knee. The wound did not heal, affected the whole joint, crooked the boy's leg, and threatened for months to make him a permanent cripple. Then in July Dr. Beecher broke down. His speaking voice failed to a whisper. Stomach pains racked him, he grew thin, fell into black despondency, and his hand shook with fear as he contemplated imminent death from consumption. If not that, then "cancer internal."

He gave up clerical duties and tried hunting and fishing. Charity sent him on a journey for health, and he rode as far as Niagara Falls but was back in a month unimproved, though in Geneva, New York, he underwent a tonsillectomy—without anaesthetics, needless to say. The demon in his vitals drove him East with Mrs. Beecher in September, his wife's first visit to her family in Maine since her marriage. Aunt Harriet took charge of the parsonage, and we have another report on the children: Edward at home on vacation, Mary qualifying herself to teach in the New London school, George preparing for Yale, Henry in school, and Charles, "clumsy as ever," recovered enough to limp along with his brother. "Harriet reads everything she can lay hands on, and sews and knits diligently."

In October the parents came down to Boston, and there at last Dr. Beecher fell under the care of a physician to whom a modern practitioner could bow with respect. Dr. Jackson diagnosed the complaint as nervous dyspepsia brought on by overwork, prescribed a diet and exercise; and the neurasthenic minister, his darkest fears dissipated, began to get better.

He returned to Litchfield in November to find more trouble. The wound in Charlie's knee had broken out again. The joint was badly swollen, the leg crooked, and Dr. Sheldon had called in a consultant to determine whether to try blistering or an operation. Aunt Esther Beecher was in feeble health, worn out by the management of such an unpredictable family. Catharine returned from New London and found her father, too, down with one of his relapses. However, blistering repaired the knee, the various invalids improved, and they had a happy Thanksgiving after all.

Catharine shone with happiness. Her year as a teacher had profited her $100 in savings, but she brought other news, more portentous. At New London she had met and fallen in love with one of the most brilliant young men in New England, Alexander Metcalf Fisher, and had given her tentative promise to marry him.

Fisher, the son of Deacon Caleb Fisher, a substantial citizen of Franklin, Massachusetts, had been a prodigy whom Yale graduated at the age of nineteen, and who as a Sophomore was correcting errors in the textbooks of higher mathematics. Now, at twenty-five, he was Professor of Mathematics and Natural Philosophy at his Alma Mater. His portrait still hangs on a collegiate wall at Yale.

Her ideas enlarged by travel, and already seeing herself as matron of a professor's house, Catharine found the Litchfield parsonage overcrowded. Aunt Esther had become a permanent member of the household. Catharine herself had resigned her position in New London and was planning an extended visit at home. To make ends meet Mrs. Beecher had to keep four boarders. A new baby was expected, and Catharine wrote to Grandma Foote that they could spare a child for a few months—Harriet or Henry. Grandma Foote chose Harriet, who went to Nutplains in January, 1822.

Harriet was now in her eleventh year, an awkward age in which much of the charm she bore in early childhood seems to have left her. She was turning into a solitary bookworm, shy and peculiar. The suddenly matured Catharine scolded her—she must learn to stand and sit straight at Nutplains and hear what people said to her. Already she had begun to fall into those profound fits of reverie that were to become almost pathological with her— a trait she took from her Beecher blood, her grandfather, David Beecher, having been notorious for his absent-mindedness. Her shyness, too, grew and almost equally distinguished her young womanhood.

It may have been on this visit to Nutplains that she first met her sailor uncle, Samuel E. Foote. He was no ordinary Connecticut sea captain but a master of sail whose ability was respected from the Hellespont to Callao. Harriet's subsequent books contain more than a few romantic allusions which trace to this sailor's stories. In common with his sisters, he admired Lyman Beecher but was free-thinker and Episcopalian enough to enjoy twitting the Calvinists' stalwart on his New England provincialism. He loved to push over the Litchfield family's icons. He considered the Turks an upright and agreeable people. He had carried as sea passengers Catholic prelates who were Christians every bit as holy and sincere as any Protestants he knew. Who could question the judgment or veracity of erudite Uncle Samuel, who knew the world so well? Thus was planted a bit of the leaven of tolerance in the Beecher loaf—did not Harriet almost turn Catholic in Rome?—which may help explain the Doctor's own complacency in his old age at the warm heterodoxy of Henry Ward Beecher or the sight of his own children leaving the Church of his Fathers.

Harriet returned to Litchfield in the spring to find a new half-sister—Isabella, born in February—and the parsonage glebe increased by eight adjoining acres which Papa, as they must now call a D.D., had bought to farm as a therapy.

She was just in time to receive the full force of the year's disaster, which was a heavy one. In January Alexander Metcalf Fisher had come to Litchfield to seal his engagement to Catharine. Yale was sending him abroad to buy apparatus for his laboratory. The young mathematician had method and must have informed Dr. Beecher that he had drawn his will, making Catharine his heir. He sailed at the break of spring. On April 22 the *Albion* was wrecked on the Irish coast, and "the hope of Yale, our country, and Europe" was one of the lost.

The belated news crushed Catharine, though (always the poet-laureate of the family) her first impulse was to expose her broken heart in an introspective dirge. Her grief was not mundane. The earthly loss of her lover she could have sustained. So far as anyone knew, the otherwise exemplary Professor Fisher had never been "converted." Catharine had lost him for eternity.

Bleeding for her almost literally, Dr. Beecher could hold out to his daughter but scant hope. It was possible—such things had happened—that Fisher had seen the true light in the presence of Death. Frantic with uncertainty, Catharine fled to her fiancé's parents in Franklin, remaining with them a year as she searched the life of her beloved. She found his private journal and knew the worst. For years he had struggled for that conviction of depravity and broken-hearted penitence which alone were the passport to heaven. He had never been able to experience them.

From that moment Catharine began to doubt the validity of a God who could grant His supreme grace to thieves and murderers and withhold it from an upright man like Professor Fisher. She laid bare the struggle of her soul in letters to her father and to her brother Edward, that spring valedictorian of his class at Yale. Lyman Beecher's replies were afterwards published as the clearest exposition of the Presbyterian doctrine yet penned. Edward's, though equally orthodox, were less pontifical and perhaps conveyed the greater solace.

In the Beecher family the consequences of this tragedy were tremendous. It started the drift toward apostasy. It changed Catharine Beecher from a careless, rather lazy girl into a poised woman, firm, self-opinionated, even domineering, devoted to a life of spinsterhood, goaded by an eternal unrest into vast and noble, though scattered, purposes. From it resulted, long subsequently, three family books which would have been burned in public by the Connecticut theocrats who ordained Lyman Beecher. Catharine's was a refutation of Edwards's philosophy of determinism, a refutation which more than one savant thought unanswerable. Edward Beecher's was his masterpiece, *The Conflict of Ages,* which put him in the foremost rank of theologians. Harriet's was *The Minister's Wooing,* one of her more important novels. In the work that passes for her autobiography Mrs. Stowe authorized the statement that the story derived from this same unhappy event of her childhood.

She might have gone further. Idle as it is to ask what might have been in the history of nations or of men, it is perfectly clear that the accidental drowning of a young man she never saw altered the whole course of Harriet Beecher's life. It launched Catharine upon an unexpected career. Circumstances threw Harriet's lot in with her sister's, setting her feet upon a path whereon she encountered those scenes and experiences out of which she built the story of *Uncle Tom's Cabin,* the novel which shook the world.

But there were more immediate consequences. As part of her legacy, Catharine received Professor Fisher's library, which she shipped to the Litchfield parsonage. One day Dr. Beecher came skipping down from his study, a volume of *Ivanhoe* closed on his thumb. He had forbidden novels to his children, but "they must read these"—memorable release for Harriet, who began at once to annex to her Araby and bewitched New England the realms opened by Walter Scott.

Previously she had become acquainted with Byron's poetry, in which she had her father's blessing. The Doctor did not condone Byron's defiant profligacy but unclerically chose to keep apart the works of genius from its depravities. The ministerial surcingle often galled him. He admired Napoleon. When a brother of the cloth rebuked him, pointing to the Emperor's evil life, "Pshaw!" the hero-worshipper retorted, "the Bourbons were not a whit better morally, and imbecile to boot."

Dr. Beecher loved poetry. Milton was impeccable, almost a second Bible. Many a parsonage evening was beguiled by Papa's readings from *Paradise Lost.* The lofty words led him into that unique eloquence of his which could hold even a hostile audience rapt. Sometimes it was too much for the reader's own emotions. Harriet remembered how he broke down over the fallen Lucifer's attempt to address his banished cohorts.

Thrice he essayed, and thrice, in spite of scorn,
Tears, such as angels weep, burst forth—

Thrice the Doctor tried to go on but could not, his voice choked, the ready tears in his eyes.

Aunt Esther Beecher, who retreated from life's perplexities into her own world of books, introduced Harriet to Byron, handing her a copy of *The Corsair* one day when the child was teasing for something to read. The beauty of the lines soon had Harriet "astonished and electrified" and exclaiming over the wonderful things she found.

"Aunt Esther, what does it mean—'One I never loved enough to hate'?"

"Oh, child, it's one of Byron's strong expressions."

After that she read every line of Byron she could find and opened her mind to every word she could hear about him, and she heard many at Dr. Beecher's table. She knew about the poet's separation from his wife and his subsequent crucifixion at the hands of the British public—which may have echoed reminiscently when, years afterwards and because of this same Byron, she found herself harried by the rabble's hue and cry. How could one write such divine words as Byron's and not be pious? To this early infatuation of her soul may be traced Harriet's lifelong obsession that genius should devote itself primarily to the work of Christ.

For it was at the height of the Byron fever in America, and rare was the instructed youth not caught up by it. The new century having swept away the last traces of the old, the young men of Judge Reeve's law school were affecting Byronic collars and cravats. The tender bosoms of Miss Pierce's young ladies were sighing over *Childe Harold* and *Manfred,* and not one more deeply than that of Harriet Beecher, on the threshold of adolescence, as she fell in love with an angelic face linked to a heavenly talent, linked also—and the more fascinating for it—to sins beyond the ken of a Congregationalist child in Litchfield, Connecticut. It was no accident that as a novelist she dwelt fondly on beautiful, brilliant and cynical heroes who, if not downright wicked, were at any rate not "pious."

In the autumn of 1822 the fortunes of the family began to rise. Edward could now buy his own watch for his Phi Beta Kappa Key, his reward for standing first at Yale being the Head Mastership of the Hartford Grammar School. The appointment enabled Dr. Beecher to place his son George in a first-class preparatory academy without payment of tuition. The "nest of genius" was clearing out. With William studying in Boston and Catharine still in Franklin, Harriet was next to the oldest of Roxana's children left at home.

She was still attending Miss Pierce's school, now accompanied by Henry Ward and little Charles, whose chain of accidents had come to an end. She was too young to fall directly under the stimulating instruction of John Brace, but she could surreptitiously listen when the older classes recited in the common schoolroom. Brace's discourses, she testified afterwards, first excited in her a desire to write good school compositions.

Catharine's principal inheritance from Professor Fisher was the cash sum of $2,000, which must have seemed a glittering fortune to the Litchfield household. With such capital, her soul having at length found repose, she planned a career for herself. What career offered itself then to a woman? Only one, and not much of one at that—teaching a female school.

Her equipment for teaching was sketchy, her only professional experience having been instruction in art and music. How she regretted now the wasted hours with Miss Pierce! Such knowledge as she had had *walked into her head*. The year in Franklin had shown her her deficiencies, for she had served as private tutor to her late fiancé's two young sisters. She had had to review her entire Arithmetic ahead of them and had mastered Algebra in six weeks. She had dabbled enough in Geometry to believe that she could acquire that subject "without more labour than I would willingly give."

Thus was she writing to her father in February, 1823. Where should she open her academy? Hartford needed a good "female school," and besides, her highly educated brother Edward was in Hartford, and he could help her. In fact, Catharine, as the one supplying the capital, foresaw herself as taking the "general superintendence" only, which would leave her "considerable time for improvement." The whole evidence is that Catharine Beecher liked the actual drudgery of teaching not one whit better than had Mr. Beecher in East Hampton. Although she was to become one of the most eminent figures in the history of American education, her preferred place was always in the "general superintendence."

Dr. Beecher went to Hartford and reported that such a school was greatly needed and that there would be no difficulty in obtaining scholars enough to justify opening. But the Doctor knew his own daughter.

It will not, however, answer for you to engage in it listlessly, expecting yourself to superintend and do a little, and have the weight of the school come on others. I should be ashamed to have you open and keep only a commonplace, middling sort of school.

In April Dr. Beecher rode to Boston to take part in the great revival there. He must have returned through Hartford just in time to see Catharine's school—the Hartford Female Academy—open with fifteen pupils, each paying a tuition of six dollars a quarter. Mary Beecher, who had not wasted her schooldays, had come on to be Catharine's principal teacher, and another fledgling was out of the Litchfield nest, never to return.

In late life Harriet remembered herself as "one of the brightest scholars in Litchfield Academy," though Miss Pierce's records do not strongly support the fond boast. She took no prizes, but in the school-year of 1823-1824 —her last in the academy—she received mention for excellence in Music and English. At the school Exhibition which ended the year, Harriet's was a genuine distinction when her essay was one of three selected to be read by Mr. Brace to the élite of the village who had gathered for the occasion.

This extraordinary composition bore the formidable title, *Can The Immortality of The Soul Be Proved by The Light of Nature?*, the tenor of which may perhaps be indicated in the opening paragraph:

It has justly been concluded by the philosophers of every age that "The proper study of mankind is man," and his nature and composition, both physical and mental, have been subjects of the most critical examination. In the course of these researches many have been at a loss to account for the change that takes place in the body at the time of death. By some it has been attributed to the flight of its tenant, and by others to its final annihilation.

All of Mrs. Stowe's biographers have repeated the story of the composition —Dr. Beecher, on the platform as the school's guest of honour, pricking up his ears at these unexpected words of profundity and inquiring the name of the author, to be told that it was his own daughter. At least one critic of a modern school which has coined the name Bible Belt for the Evangelical Israel, recites the episode with rather more than a broad wink, pointing out how easily a word-slinging parson like Lyman Beecher might have written the essay for his daughter and pretended to know nothing about it.

But there is not the slightest reason for disbelieving the story. E. D. Mansfield, one of the most conscientious annalists of his times, and one of the most engaging, was then a Litchfield law student in love with a young lady of Miss Pierce's school. He attended the Exhibition and remembered the incident perfectly, mentioning it in his memoirs, which appeared a full decade before the source biography of Mrs. Stowe resurrected the story from her memory.

Even without Mansfield's testimony, the story bears the stamp of authenticity. A casual reading of the composition itself shows it to be a juvenile treatment of the subject, something that might well have been written by a precocious thirteen-year-old nurtured in the most theological family circle in Connecticut. As for the clerical jargon of the essay, it will not do to forget those accessible barrels of sermons in the attics nor the fact that the conversation at Dr. Beecher's dinner table had steeped the mind of an odd little girl, who listened more than she spoke, in the idiom of evangelism.

Besides, Harriet was thinking that spring about the immortality of the soul—her own, and Lord Byron's. For Byron was dead. Although the rheumatic fever had taken him off at Missolonghi in April, it was not until June that the news reached Litchfield. Harriet remembered her father's announcement so well: "Byron is dead—*gone!*" His voice was like a tolling bell. "Oh, I'm sorry. I did hope he would live to do something for Christ. What a harp he might have swept!" Then, speaking from his Israel: "Oh, if Byron could only have talked with Taylor and me, it might have got him out of his troubles!"

Wild strawberries were ripe in the meadows. That afternoon Harriet took her basket and went to gather them but was too dispirited to do anything but lie in the daisies and look up at the blue sky and the full-bosomed clouds which Henry Ward Beecher said always seemed to float above Litchfield. Beyond them was that great eternity into which Byron had entered. What was his soul doing there? Now she could never hope to be able to meet him.

On the following Sunday Dr. Beecher struck the psychological note. All the law students who went to church at all, attended the Congregational services to hear him. Miss Pierce's pupils went in a body. Among such young people the cult of Byron was something almost incredible. It was a hot, somnolent afternoon, and the preacher was at his dullest, when suddenly he swept his spectacles up on his head and took off on one of those extemporaneous flights which so galvanized his audiences. E. D. Mansfield remembered it.

> He . . . began with an account of Byron, his genius, wonderful gifts, and then went on to his want of virtue, and his want of true religion, and finally described a lost soul, and the spirit of Byron going off, wandering in the blackness of darkness forever! It struck me as with an electric shock and left an imperishable memory.

But what of Harriet's own soul? Catharine's frantic rebellion at the eternal fate of Fisher must have apprised the younger sister of the disconcerting truth that one might be born and dwell in Israel and yet not be of the blessed community. First it was necessary to go through a mystic experience called conversion. Yet conversion came only as God's free gift. One had not the ability to attain it himself as a conscious act of will, yet at the same time it was one's duty to seek it. Small wonder that the contradiction was unfathomable by a child's mind, when it was the rock on which Presbyterianism was to break apart. Lyman Beecher was already splitting a theological hair into natural and moral ability, while the watchdogs of President Edwards's dogmas snuffed the wind for heresy.

Harriet's conversion was a simple experience after all. The King of Heaven had spread His table that Sunday, and the snowy cloth covering the bread and wine accented her alienage. Only the initiated could partake of the sacred feast. Her father preached from the text, "I call you not servants, but friends." "Come, then, and trust your soul to this faithful friend." Wishfully, she felt a conviction of her sins, and tears gathered in her blue eyes as her heart throbbed, "I will." That evening she told her father, who pressed her to his breast. She felt tears fall on her head. "Is it so?" he said. "Then has a new flower blossomed in the Kingdom this day."

It may not have been the blinding light that struck down Saul of Tarsus, but it would serve one of the most consistently Christ-minded women America ever produced.

Catharine came home for the summer vacation full of enthusiasm for her new venture. She and Mary had come successfully through the first term, and there was a promise of a much greater enrollment of pupils for the coming year. Harriet, too, must join the school as a pupil, Catharine having made the arrangements. It was customary then for families to trade children, when sending them away to school. Mrs. Isaac Bull, wife of a wholesale druggist in Hartford, would take Harriet to board. Mrs. Bull's daughter would board at the Beechers' in Litchfield and attend Miss Pierce's school.

In the autumn of 1824, Harriet, then aged thirteen, her small possessions packed in a carpet-bag, was driven over to Hartford, thirty miles away. Never again was she to live under her father's roof, except as a visitor.

II

◎ HARTFORD ◎

1824-1832

The Dream House at Hartford

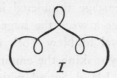

I

A Boyless Girlhood

Mrs. Bull's arrangements for the daughter of the famous Lyman Beecher were such as to mitigate the first possible homesickness of a country mouse alone in the city. Harriet found herself in a room all her own! It was a small hall-bedroom, but she was a small child, and the room was a sweet setting for the single bed made up with cold, creased sheets and an immaculate counterpane. Every morning the impressed little boarder readied it neatly and smoothed the bed "with awful satisfaction." Good Mrs. Bull's motherly nature could comfort a forlorn thirteen-year-old in the dreary experience of falling ill in a strange place.

Mr. Bull's wholesale drug house was on Front Street, where two of his three sons, Albert and James, worked as clerks. The Bull family was fashionably religious. The sons played flutes, and the morning and evening prayers were enlivened by rousing hymns to which a great deal of what would now be professionally called the "lick" was contributed by the rich voice of Miss Mary Anne Bull, who on Sabbaths was soprano soloist in the Centre Church choir. Like everybody else, Harriet loved hymns, and these fireside services helped make her feel at home from the start.

There was another attraction for Harriet in this friendly household—a courtship going on. Mary Anne Bull was one of the beauties of Hartford. Harriet remembered "her long raven curls falling from the comb on the top of her head." A worthy young man of the neighborhood, Samuel Collins, was formally wooing her. Except for Professor Fisher, whom Harriet did not see, there had never been any beaux in the Litchfield parsonage. Small wonder that her perhaps none too sly appraisal took in with interest the phenomenon of the inarticulate Samuel sitting in the parlour "most impressively and solemnly" with the glamorous choir singer.

Hartford, with its five or six thousand people, was to Harriet a booming metropolis, her only previous acquaintance with cities having been the

fleeting one of driving through New Haven. Hartford's Main Street was
cobbled. Thrice a week the stage thundered in from Boston, halting at
Ripley's Coffee House. Thrice a week the stages left for New Haven, five
hours away. One could travel to New York more comfortably than by
stagecoach, if less securely, by making the empirical voyage down the Connecticut and through Long Island Sound with the "Steam Boat *Experiment"*; fare, $5.00.

Hartford's shops were a marvel, after the cluttered shelves of Buell's General Store in Litchfield. A child who had always fallen heir to the cast-off
dresses of two older sisters could scarcely dream of making purchases for
herself in these specialized places; but it was a treat to be taken along when
Mary bought a new "Gipsey bonnet" from Sarah Weeks, "a few rods north
of the State House," or when Catharine went to a drygoods store for three
yards of tartan-plaid bombazette with which to fashion a spencer cape.
Hartford had daily newspapers. A bookworm who pounced on every
printed word she could find was bound to be transfixed by such headlines
as HORRID TRANSACTION, REMARKABLE OCCURRENCE, or
MELANCHOLY SHIPWRECK.

Harriet found friends in the school from the first moment, Catharine
having persuaded two of her older pupils, Miss Cogswell and Miss May, to
write advance letters of welcome to the odd little sister coming from Litchfield. Catherine Cogswell, daughter of the leading physician of Hartford,
was quite the star of the new academy. She was amiable, sprightly, and
sunny-tempered, and most of the girls had crushes on her. Harriet was much
too shy to force herself upon this sought-after divinity, but still Catherine
Cogswell "did keep a little place here and there for me."

Georgiana May was different. She was one of a brood whose mother was
a well-to-do widow of Hartford. She was older and less lively than Miss
Cogswell and less in demand, and Harriet could have more of a monopoly
of her. In gratitude she lavished upon Georgiana a homesick affection that
solidified into one of the few real intimacies she ever made in the course
of a long life. It was upon Georgiana May that she cast the burdens of
her spinsterhood and early married life and after Georgiana that she
named her prettiest daughter. Harriet's letters to this close friend are curi-
ously unrevealing of Miss May's personality. The inference is that Georgiana
was more mother to her than sister. It was the Hartford girl's reward to live
to see the country waif she befriended become the most famous woman in
America.

Catharine Beecher did not coddle Harriet as a pupil. The older sister had discovered for herself that one did not need much time in which to master an elementary school subject. The female academy needed teachers; but, with twenty-five scholars paying six dollars apiece for a quarter's tuition, the Principal could afford to hire none. Edward had taken his savings from a year as Head of the Hartford Grammar School and departed for the Andover Theological Seminary to prepare himself for the ministry. Thirteen-year-old Harriet Beecher was indicated as the next addition to the family.

Latin was an example. There being no other beginners, she applied herself alone that fall to the grammar. The following June she contributed to the final Exhibition a metrical translation of some of Ovid's elegiacs. She kept up her regular subjects, and Catharine, with an eye to the future curriculum, procured an outside tutor for her in French and Italian. Still she had plenty of time to live in those enervating, self-indulgent imaginings that were already a fixed part of her nature. It was never claimed for her that she was a child prodigy. Only her memory, fed from infancy on Catechisms, hymns, and Biblical chapters, was prodigious. Henry Ward Beecher was to say that if he had had Harriet's memory, he could have doubled his effectiveness in the pulpit. Harriet's mind was a trap that caught every attractive scrap entering its field and held it forever. Her memory indeed led her to an impatience with records which filled her books with inaccuracies.

Satan found work for her idle hands. This mite of a sybil, in maturity only five feet tall and thin and small-boned besides and at thirteen thoroughly repressed by an aggressive crew of older brothers and sisters, was more and more retreating into reverie for the happiness more normal children found in play. Her life has left no record of a chum or playmate outside her family. How should she justify the heady rôles she assigned to herself in these ecstatic excursions? "It was my dream to be a poet." In the solitude of the hall-bedroom she began a tragedy in blank verse.

The unfinished, unacted, and unpublished *Cleon* bears the distinction of having anticipated by some decades a plot-idea made famous by such divergent novelists as Lew Wallace and Henryk Sienkiewicz—the plight of the noble Christian at the court of Nero. It was not banal in 1825. In this blighted masterpiece Harriet also drew the first of her Byronic heroes. Who was Cleon, the luxurious, cynical young Athenian, beautiful as a Parthenon sculpture, gay, wicked, if not Augustine St. Clare in sandals, toga, and bay wreath? This play-boy of the corrupt court was

> . . . a perfect prince in entertainments—
>
> *   *   *
>
> Such show of plates and cups, both gold and silver,
> Such flaming rainbows of all coloured stones,
> Such wine, such music . . .

And also—

> Diversion is his labour, and he works
> With hand and foot and soul both night and day;
> He throws out money with so flush a hand
> As makes e'en Nero's waste seem parsimony.

Naturally, the pathetic elf in her Hartford bedchamber set forth to "convert" this demigod, whom, in addition to his other gifts, she made an Olympic champion.

Cleon is "convicted utterly" and turns to Christianity. The fiendish Nero sends his former favourite to the torture chamber, then relents and tries persuasion upon the "weak and faint" martyr. But the Emperor makes the mistake of calling Christ "a crazy Jew," and Cleon becomes what Byron ought to have been.

> Cleon [*starting up*].
>
> *   *   *
>
> I could sit still and hear myself reviled,
> But not my Sovereign!

Baffled, Nero permits Cleon his new faith, if he will but dissemble before the court.

> Nero.   Art thou so versed in smooth, decoying phrase
> And cannot turn off blank enquiry?
>
> *   *   *
>
> But we can put you in a post of honour,
> So that all men shall wink upon thy will.
> Cleon.   My lord, I scarce can trust myself to answer,
> Since I have heard such degradation named.
> In place of open, bold apostasy
> Thou dost propose an hourly, daily lie.
> &c.   &c.

At about this point sister Catharine made an unexpected call at the hall-bedroom, discovered blank book after blank book filled with the *Cleon* pentameters, and, perhaps a little jealous of her own place as family poetess, clamped down on such an occupation. If Harriet had so much leisure, let her begin the study of Joseph Butler's *The Analogy of Religion, Natural and Revealed, to the Constitution and Course of Nature*. Accustomed to unprotesting obedience, the child filled the rest of her blank pages with abstracts of the *Analogy*. Perhaps it was just as well. The most indulgent reader of Harriet's later poems, widely popular as they were, can assign them no high place in our literature; whereas by digesting the arid chapters of Butler's *Analogy* she was training a mind that one day was to lecture, and with effect, an empire greater than Nero's on its shortcomings.

The following autumn Harriet began to teach the *Analogy* to a class of girls as old as herself, "being compelled to master each chapter just ahead of the class I was teaching." That year—1824-1825—they saw a good deal of Father Beecher in Hartford. He had taken the initiative in proposing a religious newspaper for Connecticut, the Hartford *Observer*. Having founded it, he discovered that the only way he could keep its columns filled was to do the writing himself—without pay, of course—while at the same time keeping up his pastoral duties in Litchfield. He urged Edward at Andover to read the new journal, which began, with 1,400 subscribers, in January, 1825. "There is so much of your father in the paper after the first No., and will be for some time, that I have directed the paper to be sent on."

Had they let Harriet alone, her transition from a conviction of her depravity into a state of "hope" might have been the gentle experience its beginning promised. But, as the aged authoress was to say humorously (and at second hand), this lamb could not come into the fold "without being first chased all over the lot by the shepherd." Especially the realistic Catharine, who had never been honestly able to accept "conviction" for herself, doubted the validity of small Harriet's conversion.

Harriet took communion in her father's church during the summer vacation, still in serene security. Her separation from home now evidently permanent, she took her father's advice in the autumn of 1825 and joined the First Congregational Church in Hartford. Its pastor, when she presented her timid application, was as sceptical as Catharine.

"Harriet," he spoke awfully to the shrinking young one, "do you feel that if the universe should be destroyed, you could be happy with God alone?"

The heaven of her dreams vanishing, she could only gasp a frightened "Yes, sir."

"You realize, I trust, in some measure at least, the deceitfulness of your heart, and that in punishment for your sins God might justly leave you to make yourself as miserable as you have made yourself sinful?"

"Yes, sir."

Thus having, as he hoped, turned her attention inward upon her own wickedness, the good Doctor of Divinity welcomed her into his church.

He was highly successful. Soon the fourteen-year-old girl was writing to Edward, the family confessor, "My whole life is one continued struggle. I do nothing right. I yield to temptation almost as soon as it assails me. My deepest feelings are very evanescent. I am beset behind and before, and my sins take away all my happiness." Thoughts straight from the old Adam sprang unwelcome into her adolescent consciousness. She knew her soul was black with evil. For years this struggle kept up. Without Catharine's bereavement, she went through all of Catharine's tortures. Not until she was in her twenties did Harriet emerge from this morass of doubts and morbid speculations. The modern psychologist must marvel that the sensitive children of the Puritans ever came through adolescence with their sanity.

It was, after all, no commonplace, middling sort of school that Catharine Beecher was keeping in Hartford but an institution of such rising fame that the fall term of 1825 brought an auspicious influx of new scholars. Perhaps the young academy left its hall above the harness-shop that autumn. At any rate, it outgrew its quarters twice in its first three years, ending this phase of its history in the basement of a Hartford church, with eighty girls enrolled as pupils.

A salaried faculty being a near prospect, it was no longer necessary to cram Harriet through the curriculum. She kept up her class in the *Analogy* (a subject in which she grew "very much interested") but otherwise attended her sister's academy as a pupil. "I devote most of my attention to Latin and to arithmetic," she wrote Grandma Foote, in Guilford.

Lyman Beecher had vowed that he would never leave Litchfield while Judge Tapping Reeve was alive. But now Judge Reeve was dead; and October, 1825, brought the Doctor's fiftieth birthday and the realization that he had reached life's descent on a salary that had never risen above $800 a year—he the most celebrated preacher in America! He looked around for something better, and the new Hanover Street Church in Boston providentially sent him a call. Henry Ward Beecher embalmed the legend. "Having written a letter to Dr. Taylor, of New Haven, informing him of his purpose and asking his help in procuring some proper place, he carried it to the postoffice. But before depositing it in the mail, he looked over the letters received and found one from Boston inviting him to this new church. He always regarded this as a remarkable providence."

It was as authentic as any of the family miracles—except one. Actually, Dr. Beecher had an inkling that the Hanover Street congregation was looking toward Litchfield. On December 30 he wrote Edward of "rumours floating here from Boston." He had been sounded on his possible availability. If he was reading the signs right, his own people in Litchfield would "unship" him, if they could. The rumours were confirmed a week later, when already he could see in the episode the hand of God.

In March, 1826, Dr. Beecher removed himself and the remnant of his clan to Boston, setting up his parsonage at No. 18 Sheaf Street, near Copp's Hill. The news came as a shock to Aunt Esther, the transition seeming such a formidable undertaking. As it turned out, Aunt Esther made the passage to Boston by degrees, stopping for a year in Hartford to make a home for the three Beecher girls there.

Harriet's life-record for the next year or so is scanty and uncertain. In middle-age she wrote to her brother Charles that at this period of her life she saw a great deal of her father in Boston. Even the attractions of Beacon Street, however, could not take the diminutive, wool-gathering schoolgirl out of her painful introspection. "I wish I could die young and let the remembrance of me and my faults perish in the grave, rather than live, a trouble to everyone. How perfectly wretched I often feel—so useless, so weak, so destitute of all energy!" Thus the fifteen-year-old child of destiny to her sister. She tried to *appear* cheerful, but her laughter was so shrill it made a dyspeptic father catch her up for it sharply. Thus was she misunderstood.

Meanwhile, events were happening in the family. Edward finished at Andover that spring, the great Park Street Church sent the brilliant stripling a call to its pastorate, on his father's advice Edward accepted it, and Boston saw two Beechers in its pulpits challenging the Unitarian devil. In the fall term of 1826, the Hartford school took such a spurt in prosperity that Catharine Beecher, her ambition always out ahead of present realities, proposed a specialized schoolhouse of its own. She incorporated the Hartford Female Seminary and by February 16, 1827, could report to her father that the stock was all subscribed.

But Catharine was worried about Harriet and her hint of suicide. The child must come back to Hartford, where she would have the cheerful society of young people like Catherine Cogswell and Georgiana May. "I can do better in preparing her to teach drawing than any one else, for I best know what is needed." Catharine's classroom manner was growing on her. More and more this elder sister was assuming the authority of mother over Roxana Beecher's children.

At any rate, Harriet came back to Hartford; and at the spring vacation Catharine packed her and Georgiana aboard the New Haven stage, bound for the diverting scenes of Harriet's beloved Nutplains. Georgiana, at least, to judge by her bread-and-butter letter to Grandma Foote, enjoyed the visit; and even Harriet must have been lifted temporarily out of her melancholia as she listened to the further adventures of Uncle Sam Foote, the mariner.

Home was this sailor at last. Samuel Foote had married Miss Elizabeth Elliott, of Guilford, who must now be called Aunt Elizabeth. Before she consented, Miss Elliott exacted from Samuel his promise never to go to sea again. Methodically, Captain Foote kept his promise by combining his wedding trip with a personal survey of the residential possibilities of the United States, fixing upon Cincinnati, where his hard-headed brother, John P. Foote, had settled some years previously and was said to be prospering.

Cincinnati—already calling itself the "Queen City of the West"—was another spelling of romance to rustic New England homebodies. How like Sam Foote, who had contended with bandits in Morocco and mutineers under the Line, to choose the frontier with its perils for his landlubber's habitation! (That Cincinnati was the one place in the Republic most remote from the temptations of the seaboard where a reformed and sophisticated sailor might also enjoy urban comforts may have been incidental.) But the West was sounding its first call, and even so sleepy a village as Guilford felt a certain disquiet. Ploughs were breaking the gumbo of the Mississippi bottoms, the Conestoga wagons were creaking along Indiana's corduroy trails, every keelboat drifting down the Ohio, with its deckload of children, chickens, and family wash, was to be broken up and rebuilt into a settler's cabin, while out through Virginia crept a turnpike surfaced by the new bound-stone method invented in England by John McAdam.

There were signs that next summer that morbid Harriet was recovering from her depression. She seemed (in her very protests against baring her thoughts—"we never wish to have our feelings analyzed down") to be even enjoying her distinction as the family's spiritual problem-child. She had a satisfactory talk with Edward and afterwards felt, if not happy, "not as unhappy as I had been." But she would forget, write Grandma Foote of her new happiness, then a dozen lines later fall into her tragic pose and exclaim dolefully that, if her mother had lived, "I might have been both better and happier than I now am."

But there was family happiness for her to share that summer of 1827. Hammers were racketing through the halls of Catharine's new seminary building, and the gentle, studious, efficient Mary Beecher became betrothed to Thomas Clapp Perkins, a well-to-do young attorney of Hartford. The wedding took place on November 7. Two weeks later Catharine dedicated the new schoolhouse, which had cost five thousand dollars, all subscribed by Hartford people. With more than one hundred pupils enrolled, the Hartford Female Seminary was being mentioned on an equality with such institutions as Miss Willard's school at Watertown, New York, and that of Miss Lyons and Miss Grant at Ipswich.

Harriet joined the teaching staff that autumn, though her contribution for the first year was a single course in Virgil. Otherwise, she kept up with her study of French, but gave most of her time "from nine in the morning till after dark at night" to the practice of painting and drawing, developing considerable skill as an artist. Her roommate was now her former French tutor, Miss Degan, "a very interesting and agreeable Italian lady" who had taken the Seminary's classes in French and Italian. Including Catharine, there were three other teachers. The "gentle, affectionate, modest, and retiring" Miss Hawks roomed with Catharine; Miss Clarissa Brown was Assistant Principal.

During the following spring Harriet was still trying to make her social adjustment. The more she looked at human companionships, the better she loved Christ. "I have had more reason to be grateful to that friend than ever before. He has not left me in all my weakness. He will never be irritated or impatient." Was she glancing now at Catharine? "He will never show me my faults in such a manner as to irritate without helping me. . . . All through the day in my intercourse with others, everything has a tendency to destroy the calmness of mind gained by communion with Him. One flatters me, another is angry with me, another is unjust to me."

But her thoughts that spring were notable for something else. The diminutive prophetess, still twenty-five years from Sinai, caught a half-glimpse of her future power. She agreed with her brother Edward that a predilection for literature was a snare, lamenting "with tears and indignation" that everything beautiful and lovely and poetical had been laid on profane altars. (By Byron, for example?) But, "I do not mean to live in vain. He has given me talents, and I will lay them at His feet, well satisfied, if He will accept them. All my powers He can enlarge. He made my mind, and He can teach me to cultivate and exert its faculties."

This prediction, made when she was still only sixteen, could with changed tenses stand as the pattern of her long, tumultuous career.

It is probable that Harriet spent the summer of 1828 in Boston, getting better acquainted with the fascinating father she had been too young to study and understand in Litchfield. No doubt she accompanied him on a favourite walk from Sheaf Street to the cemetery on Copp's Hill, young Henry Ward Beecher choosing the tops of the more difficult fences for his footpath. In the burying ground they searched out the places of the old Puritan worthies, while Henry Ward leaped from tombstone to tombstone or slid down the precipice into the causeway.

Such contacts with the historic dead had a profound effect on the patriarch. Henry Ward likened him to a shore on which rolled great waves from storms far out at sea. After one such communion he said to his congregation, "I stood today by the grave of the Mathers. I looked back to the early days of New England. I called the God of our fathers to witness that I would never give up this battle until the faith of the Puritans was vindicated and accepted among their posterity."

For Dr. Beecher's feet were now on congenial terrain—a battlefield, and on it against him arrayed the scornful hosts of Unitarianism and Harvard College. (No Beecher son was ever to attend that faithless institution.) The new stone church in Hanover Street, so soon to be given to the flames, carried out the military impression. Squat, mullioned, crenellated, it was as forbidding as a Norman stronghold.

Harriet grew familiar with this ugly edifice; and also, with her brother Henry, she visited the hardware store kept by their stepmother's brother, Mr. Homes, in Dock Square. Uncle Homes was proud of his Beecher connection and was usually good for a jack-knife or a key ring when one of the younger boys visited his establishment. Later his financial aid helped

Henry Ward to go through Amherst and Charles to matriculate at Bowdoin.

Lyman Beecher's leadership was gathering a small but noble army of potential martyrs, young men mostly, and among them that summer one whom Harriet would have done well to observe closely. This was Calvin Ellis Stowe, who had come through poverty and a worldly college into a Calvinism as staunch as Dr. Beecher's own. At twenty-six, he held a new diploma from Andover Theological Seminary, and was doing some editorial work on the Boston *Recorder* before taking up the duties of an assistant professor at Bowdoin, his alma mater. Young Mr. Stowe was no ordinary candidate for the ministry. As a Bowdoin undergraduate he had distinguished himself by publishing, with learned notes, his own translation of Jahn's *History of The Hebrew Commonwealth;* and he was on his way to be the leading Orientalist of his generation.

This impressive young man, with his stocky build, vast head, and bushy brows, may never have noticed such a shrimp of a schoolgirl as Harriet Beecher, even though she was his great leader's daughter. But if Harriet talked with him for as long as a minute, her sensitive ear surely caught his Massachusetts-village dialect, and her quick perception of the ludicrous appreciated the glint of humour that ran through his conversation like a metallic vein—humour as homespun as her father's own, and as droll.

In the autumn Harriet Porter Beecher bore her final child, James, and the Doctor's procreative days were over. There were now eleven brothers and sisters, all of whom were to survive at least to adulthood. All became extraordinary men and women. More than half grew famous. Two became preëminent. To these eleven soldiers of the cross add Lyman Beecher himself, in his later years as much brother as sire, and you have, as an observer was to point out, twelve. Twelve, the apostolic number!

Eighteen, and no beau yet—and in an age when, if a girl reached her twentieth or twenty-first year unmarried, she could begin to look forward to a life spent as an old maid. Nor was Harriet ever to have a beau, even as that term was understood in the 1820's—no youth of her age to flirt with her and take her for walks or sleigh-rides, or even, like bashful Sam Collins in the presence of Mary Anne Bull, to sit with her in a prim parlour on stated evenings. In all of Harriet's letters written during her spinsterhood, there is only one reference to a young man, and he seems to have been only a casual acquaintance.

How she must have sought the answer in her mirror! If she animated her look, as she could, she did not need to be Narcissus to find beauty there. If she were low in spirit, she saw first her Beecher nose, too prominent for the rest of her features, aquiline, and rather sharply ridged. Her chin was perhaps a little heavy. She saw a head and throat somewhat large for the small, frail body supporting them.

But these were her worst points. Her brow was broad and smooth. Her cheeks, delicately hollowed below strong bones at the eyes, were only prevented by the blunt chin from giving her an oval countenance. Her hair was brown, fine, and luxuriant in growth. Harriet wore it in long curls dropping on each side from a middle part, a style becoming to her. Her eyes, unusually wide apart, could be wells of violet light. Her mouth, which kept gaining a professional petulance, was generous in size, passionate, even sensual.

It is a curious fact that the many observers of Harriet over the entire span of her life, Elizabeth Barrett Browning among them, have independently but unanimously called attention to her dual physical personality. In her most famous years she bore the reputation of being plain, ugly—"homely" was the contemporary word for it—yet people were constantly being astonished to find her beautiful. "Why did you never tell me that she was beautiful?" a Boston society woman exclaimed to Annie Fields.

It depended upon whether Harriet were awake and interested. Those spells of abstraction which were her worst infirmity, which caused her to commit outrageous breaches of courteous deportment, and which so exasperated her neurasthenic husband, transformed her physically. Her features became leaden, her eyes dull. Despite all Catharine's injunctions, she then forgot good posture and stooped; and a certain relative heaviness about her shoulders gave her a dwarflike appearance. At such times, as Henry Ward Beecher said of his sister, she went "owling about."

Then would come one of her awakenings which gave such pleasure to those who, like Mrs. Fields, loved her. She straightened up and bubbled with animation, her eyes gathered depth and light and her cheeks colour, and the owlet had become, if not a peacock, a trim and alert wren. Not one of the Beecher children, her brother testified, was then better company.

In her early life, before fame set its mysterious cachet upon her, Harriet lacked that equally mysterious quality called personality. In any considerable gathering she became invisible. She listened much and spoke seldom; but if she did venture some shy remark, it was likely to contain wisdom so sharp and unexpected as to make an intelligent observer like E. D. Mansfield, the Cincinnati law professor, stare at her with sudden astonishment. If Harriet had this habit when she was eighteen years old, it was well designed to scare off any eligible young men she might have met in Hartford.

But she had little time that spring to brood over her social woes. Beginning in January, 1829, she had become a full-time teacher at the Hartford Seminary, taking the classes in rhetoric and composition, subjects which she proved to be best fitted to teach. During Harriet's absence Catharine had made a considerable change in the teaching staff. Miss Hawks and Miss Clarissa Brown were gone. New faces were those of Miss Fisher, Miss Mary Dutton, Miss Brigham, and Mrs. Gamage. Harriet went in to room with the Misses Fisher, Dutton, and Brigham; and Mary Dutton became her best friend, the second great intimacy of her life.

Miss Dutton was a New Haven girl, the daughter of a Congregational preacher. She was two years older than Harriet but no larger in stature, for which reason, perhaps, Harriet promptly fell in love with her. Mary taught mathematics. Harriet thought her as proficient in that subject as most male college graduates, in a day when there was no college open to women. The lives of these two girls were to fall together for several years, and Harriet still wrote to Mary when both were middle-aged women. Her girlhood letters gushed affection.

But Mary seems to have attracted masculine notice, emphasizing to Harriet her own forlorn existence. "The desire to be loved forms, I fear, the great motive for all my actions." It was making her hypersensitive. "I wish I could bring myself to feel perfectly indifferent to the opinions of others. I believe that there never was a person more dependent on the good and evil opinions of those around than I am." The least thing that crossed her feelings rendered her unhappy for days and weeks.

Such introspection brought her to the worn subject of sin. Her pastor prayed every Sunday, "We have nothing to offer in extenuation of any of our sins," whereas Harriet thought that we had everything to offer. "It seems to me we all come into the world in such a way that it would be miraculous if we did not sin." Renewed examination of her depraved nature plunged her into another depression from which she did not emerge until summer, when she could report to Brother Edward that she had never been so happy, although "I began it in more suffering than I ever before have felt." At last her mind was able to put aside the brutal *impasse* of her father's metaphysics and retreat upon Christ-worship, which she was never to leave. Her spiritual turmoil had ended.

Mary Dutton did not return to Hartford in the autumn of 1829 but took a position with Miss Peters's school in New Haven, where she could live at home. Harriet missed her sorely, as did Catharine, for that matter, though for different reasons. More and more the oldest Beecher child was showing herself to be the possessor of the strongest Beecher mind. Her study of education had led her to take a revolutionary step. She proposed to turn the Hartford Seminary into an institution for the training not only of the minds of young females but of their characters as well, and she needed Miss Dutton's help in this project.

Today Catharine's ambition for her school seems innocent and laudable, but in 1830, in Calvinistic Connecticut, it rather more than smelt of heresy. How could you train character, when everyone's character had been fore-ordained since the beginning of time? For Lyman Beecher's daughter to be so presumptuous was a church scandal. There were signs of a growing liberality in the laity, however, since the attendance at the Seminary passed one hundred and twenty students that spring, with "new ones coming in—some very handsome ones." But Mary Dutton was not to be coaxed from the safe protection of her reverend father's wing to engage in any such dubious undertaking.

Harriet wrote to Mary in the tone of gay affection, a letter full of the news and gossip of a girls' school.

> I am quite busy preparing for my composition class. Have been reading Rasselas and writing a letter in imitation of Dr. Johnson's style—think it is improving me by giving a command of language. The man writes as if some fairy had spellbound him and given him the task of putting every word in his great dictionary in his book, as a means of release. I have been spouting at Catharine respecting "general and transcendental truth" and "errors of exaggeration and declamation" ever since.

After a few items about new members of the faculty, the letter speaks about some of the "young ladies" whom Mary knew.

> S. Willis is as well and lively as ever. She is a lovely girl, but a proud one. I want to be acquainted with her but dare not. She is sometimes a sort of *Noli me tangere*. J. Strong is well [and] is much improved—the finest girl

that I know. S. Ladd's character rises daily in my estimation; she has many agreeable and some noble traits. . . .

* * *

Catharine and myself are riding on horseback every morning before breakfast. . . . I must tell you that I have had quite a John Gilpin adventure. The first time we went to ride was in the evening, and they mounted me on a perfect Bucephalus, and the consequence was that before Catharine was mounted I was half-way out to Lord's Hill, and for the best of reasons— because my horse *would* go. I turned him and rode back to meet her, and no sooner had we got riding together than my courser set off again on a canter—and such a canter! I went up and down like an apple. From that he proceeded to a run, and I went up Lord's Hill like a streak. My gentleman did not stop till he had taken me through the asylum yard to the fence on the other side, and I got down quite crestfallen. (I must not omit to say that for the greater part of the way I wore my bonnet on my shoulders behind.) All that night I was meditating how it was that people found such pleasure in riding.

At present I ride a beautiful young white horse and Catharine a ditto black one. All the difficulty is that my horse has so much of the evil spirit of emulation in him that he won't suffer Catharine's to come near him. The moment he hears the hoofs of "Tinker" behind him, he goes like all possessed, and I am forcibly reminded of that line in Horace which begins, "Jounce, jounce, jounce." Nevertheless, we have pleasant times of it.

(The reference to "the evil spirit of emulation" is pointless today but was not in 1830 when pedagogy was debating as its heaviest problem whether children should be inspired to study in school by the offer of prizes and the publication of class standings or by the abstract appeal to their innate desire for learning. Catharine Beecher was an anti-emulationist.)

When Harriet reached the conclusion of the letter, something of her envy of more fortunate girls than herself made a shadowy appearance behind the lines. Her lofty air of patronage hardly hid the sour mouth she was making at grapes she could not reach. She began with a tiny sarcasm.

Your daughter Ann [Ann Fisher, one of the pupils who was Mary Dutton's special protégée] wears an open-work cottage hat, lined and trimmed with blue, and a blue scarf. She looks very sweet and pretty. If you see A. Baldwin, tell him that I shall write him a series of "Sketches of Female Character" as soon as I get a letter from him to make it excusable for me to write to him. Miss Fisher says, "Tell her I hope she'll enjoy herself and get a husband into the bargain." If such an acquisition would be to you the *summum bonum* of earthly felicity, I heartily join in the request. I think you spoke to tolerable purpose on the felicity of the wedded state, Mary;

suppose you try. Miss Degan is launching out into the praise of the Eighth Wonder of the World, her brother Charles, and the Ninth, the angelic Miss Cheeseborough, his beloved. By her description it is *death* for a female eye to rest on one so fascinating. I love to hear sisters speak of their brothers. There is no pride I can so readily tolerate as pride of relationship.

During all her life Harriet scarcely ever closed an informal letter without a postscript. This one was no exception.

This letter is for news and the lighter particles of thought. In the next you shall have wise saws and grave reflections, profound speculations, and all that might become the female *Savante*. I do not think this specimen of my epistolary powers will so far frighten you as to deter you from writing me. Do, my dear Mary, write me soon. You were wont to be a punctual correspondent. *Write me soon*. I am head over heels in debt. I have five correspondents now to whom I ought *vides meliora prologue sed deteriora sequor*. I am sometimes lazy, sometimes inclined to procrastinate. Catharine is just dying to put in a *postscriptum,* but I am determined she shall not put you off without a whole letter—so I diligently abstain from giving her any opportunity—

Here Harriet's postscript, which she was trying to string out to the bottom of her sheet, ended abruptly, as Catharine, possibly in a mirthful scuffle, snatched the pen from her sister and found room for this final sentence of her own:

That is possible, for she is only conterary [sic] as the mule she rides.

This is the most revealing letter of Harriet Beecher's girlhood. Her other communications which have been so reverently preserved have mainly to do with the welfare of her immortal soul, and in them she adopted a style which seemed to her fitted to such a solemn subject. Then, too, in them she was a child raised by her spiritual problem to an adult's importance, and she spoke accordingly. Her letter to Mary Dutton is quite another thing—the schoolgirl talking to her chum—and in it we see the real Harriet. As to the mordant touches, the young cynicism, the frequent use of sarcasm, the play of humour of a robust and even masculine type, the schoolgirlish but rather pleasant affectation of Latin phrases, her sound observation that the schoolmen of her day were not teaching composition thoroughly, the ability to read human character and express it in a few words, the letter speaks for itself. Most of these implied qualities were to characterize her writings throughout life.

One point needs to be emphasized to the reader, who has not yet the advantage of a full view of her life. The clue lies in the reference to "S. Willis," the girl with whom Harriet wanted to be acquainted but dared not. Harriet Beecher was what would be known today as a "difficult" person. Richly as her nature was endowed, it lacked the gift of friendship. Respect, even veneration, came to her in full but never personal popularity. She could live for years in a community, as we shall see, and leave behind not one friendship which she continued by correspondence.

In her early life, at least, she was critical of people. She did her best to correct her social attitude and at any rate succeeded in veneering it over. But behind the affectionate terms which she could eventually address even to strangers, one feels her blue eyes weighing and appraising. Her bitterest critics were to attack her knowledge of character, especially Southern character. They could not have assailed her at a stronger point. Character was what she *did* know, for she spent her life reading character.

As Harriet was writing this letter to her friend, an epoch in her life was nearing its close, though the end of it was to be postponed for more than a year by the burning of Dr. Beecher's Norman stronghold in Hanover Street, Boston, in February, 1830.

The circumstances of that fire were curious. The Doctor had recently delivered from this pulpit his famous *Six Sermons on Temperance,* which he had first preached in Litchfield a few years previously. He thundered against alcoholic drink quite unconcerned with the fact that the basement of the church itself was full of ardent spirits belonging to a merchant to whom the church society rented the space for a warehouse. The Prohibition movement was then so new its adherents had not yet worked out their subsequent consistencies; and besides, the rental collected from the liquor dealer did much to pay Dr. Beecher's Boston salary of $2,000 a year "and $500 settlement."

Moreover, the press of Boston was holding up Lyman Beecher to the populace as the arch-Puritan who was fighting to end personal liberty and restore the enforced morality of the Mathers. As a result, when the firemen saw the blue flames of rum pouring from the basement windows, they treated the conflagration as a joke, refusing to pump, and singing, "Satan's kingdom's tumbling down, glory, hallelujah!" They shouted jokes about "Beecher's oil jug."

The Boston Tract Society occupied quarters in the church. The casks in the basement began to blow up, each explosion whitening Hanover Street with pious literature, as the mob chanted:

> While Beecher's church holds out to burn,
> The vilest sinner may return.

Calvin Stowe was in Boston that day, and he remembered the aftermath. Next morning a committee of the congregation assembled gloomily in Pierce's bookstore, wondering what to do. Dr. Beecher skipped in, gay as a lark.

"Well, my jug's broke," he announced cheerfully, picking up the jibe of the firemen. "Just been to see it."

Such optimism carried everything before it. In a short time the congregation had acquired a new site in Bowdoin Street and had let contracts for another church edifice.

In May Dr. Beecher attended the General Church Assembly in Philadelphia, and there something happened of immense importance to his daughter Harriet. Of what happened there is no existing record; but we can guess that it was a meeting between Lyman Beecher and one F. Y. Vail, a Presbyterian clergyman from Cincinnati, Ohio. Whatever it was, it caused Dr. Beecher to forget his vow at the grave of the Mathers (was not the Boston struggle looking hopeless?) and to fill his greying head with the vastest ambitions of his career. No mere Kingdom on earth now did he envisage himself as conquering for God, but an Empire—the West.

In July he was writing about it to Catharine.

". . . While at Philadelphia and since, my interest in the majestic West has been greatly excited and increased, and my efforts have not been without effect to create a love and a waking up both there and here. The moral destiny of our nation, and all its institutions and hopes, and the world's hopes, turns on the character of the West, and the competition now is for that of preoccupancy in the education of the rising generation, in which Catholics and infidels have got the start of us."

That the Doctor had something more definite in mind than a general foray into the wilderness at the head of his filial cohort, it seems reasonable to suppose; yet in July, 1830, his name had not yet appeared in the minutes of the Trustees of the Lane Theological Seminary, of Cincinnati, with which much of his future was to be identified. At that time Lane consisted of an idea, a charter, an endowment of some $5,000, sixty acres of piously donated woodland in Walnut Hills, near Cincinnati, the foundation masonry of a building, three students, and one professor. The idea was to rear in this upland grove another and greater Andover for the ebullient West, a broader Princeton, a more influential Yale.

In the Chair at the Board meeting of September 30 of the same year sat the Rev. Dr. Joshua Lacy Wilson, pastor of Cincinnati's First Presbyterian Church and the leading clergyman of the West. Since he played a certain part in the story of Harriet Beecher, we are justified in pausing for a moment's look at him. Harriet described him as tall, grave, having strong and rather harsh features, very pale, with a severe seriousness of face and great formality and precision in every turn and motion. He was an appalling Calvinist. It was said he would not tolerate a portrait or picture in his house, because it smacked of the graven image forbidden by Holy Writ. Dr. Wilson was rigidly honest, devoid of all sense of humour, rather slow of wit, and as strait and stubborn a Puritan as ever hanged a witch.

To this meeting the Seminary's collector reported the complete failure of the financial campaign, whereupon the single professor resigned. It was then that the Rev. Mr. Vail rose to express his belief that if they could secure for the presidency of Lane such a man as Dr. McAuley or Dr. Beecher, "the most prominent, popular, and powerful preacher in our nation," adequate endowment money would be forthcoming in the East. The Board authorized this optimist to make the attempt, to which resolution Dr. Wilson was quoted as saying, "Amen!," a benediction he was soon to rescind.

In New York Brother Vail secured from Arthur Tappan, the wealthy merchant, the promise of $20,000 to endow a professorship of theology, provided Lyman Beecher could be induced to fill it. In October Vail was talking to Dr. Beecher, who was strongly moved to accept. The Doctor's congregation, however, told him he was in honour bound to remain in Boston at least until he had built and dedicated the new church, and he was forced to decline the Cincinnati offer. Meanwhile, the Lane Trustees had elected him president of the Seminary and let this appointment stand on the books, until such time as Dr. Beecher's duty might be made clear to him.

Lyman Beecher himself might go to his grave claiming victory in his war against the Boston Unitarians, but he could hint at defeat for his son Edward, who, as pastor of the Park Street Church, had been one of his chief lieutenants. In September, 1830, Edward received a call to the presidency of Illinois College at Jacksonville, then a remote outpost in the western wilderness, and was glad enough to accept it. Dr. Beecher expressed his attitude: "There are

many and great things in favour of his going, and nothing very inviting in
his remaining where he is."

Early in November Edward left for his new charge, thus actually leading
the Beecher invasion of the West.

The two years following Edward's departure for the West—Harriet's
twentieth and twenty-first, marking her transition into adult womanhood—
were singularly uneventful for her. No similar segment of her life anterior
to her extreme old age has left so faint a trace of itself.

We must think of her in this period as devoting most of her energies to
her classes in the Hartford Female Academy, sitting elfinlike and often
dreamily above groups of inattentive girls, most of them larger and some of
them little younger than herself. There are indications that she liked to teach
school no better than did her sister Catharine; and if she was anything ex
ceptional as a teacher, not one of her pupils ever testified to it.

The problem of her human adjustments still vexed her, if anything more
painfully than ever. The odd little girl had grown up to be an odd young
woman. She looked back upon these years as a period of disillusionment
While more normal girls accepted their social vicissitudes as unquestioningly
as flowers accept sunshine and rain, Harriet became calculating, weighing
the value of a possible friendship before attempting to cultivate it.

Mary Dutton still resisted Catharine Beecher's appeal during the school
year of 1830-31, and it is not clear whether she ever returned to Hartford
In January, 1831, an angry, uncompromising man of Boston, William Lloyd
Garrison, brought out the first number of an anti-slavery journal he called
The Liberator—"I am in earnest—I will not equivocate—I will not excuse—
will not retreat a single inch—and *I will be heard."* Harriet would have done
well to note this portentous event, but probably did not.

In June, 1831, Lyman Beecher dedicated the new Bowdoin Street Church
The release, however, had no immediate effect. His dearest friend, Dr
Taylor, of the Yale Divinity School, was trying to induce him to join the
faculty of that institution. That Dr. Beecher was never diverted from his
plan to win the West from the infidels and Catholics is shown by a letter
which Catharine wrote in September, in which she again urged Miss Dutton
to return to the Hartford Academy.

"I may immigrate with father to the West," she confided to Mary. "I wish
you would not speak of any probabilities of my leaving, except to your
father."

In spite of his daughter's assurance, Dr. Beecher, at least publicly, still maintained an attitude of indecision. But in Cincinnati that fall something occurred that crystallized his resolution and made his early departure inevitable. From across the Alleghenies his ear caught the faint trumpet-call of a personal challenge.

The Rev. Dr. Joshua Lacy Wilson had never been quite easy in his conscience about the sudden election of Dr. Lyman Beecher to the presidency of Lane Theological Seminary. Even the leading preacher of the West, with its four million inhabitants, could be momentarily dazzled by the prospect of securing so eminent a man. But on second thought (and following some suggestion from Princeton College) Dr. Wilson was disturbed. To accept, without question or the slightest examination, even a Lyman Beecher to head the institution that was to turn the Mississippi Basin into a Calvinist empire, seemed to his slow, methodical mind the height of folly. He decided to make an investigation of his own.

What he discovered filled him with disquiet. In the first place, Dr. Beecher was openly the friend of Dr. Taylor, of Yale; and the word heresy was being widely applied by the Old School Presbyterians to Taylor's softening of the Edwardsian edicts. Dr. Wilson then turned to Dr. Beecher's published sermons and knew the worst. He found them, or so he thought, shot through with heresy.

Dr. Wilson's belated opposition to the man whose election he had supported brought no responsive chord in Cincinnati. Although the vigorous Queen City had not yet organized a Chamber of Commerce it was already imbued with the booster spirit that was later to sweep the West. In the 1830's the churches were so important in the national life and thought that the best publicity asset a city could have was a famous preacher. For Dr. Wilson to attempt to bar from Cincinnati the most celebrated divine of all, was something close to downright disloyalty.

Undeterred by the municipal frown, Dr. Wilson nevertheless carried his fight into the Board of Trustees of Lane Seminary. Already Old and New Schools of Calvinistic thought were aligning for the split not far ahead. At the meeting of the Trustees in January, 1832, the New School men (with perhaps some moral support from Cincinnati business interests) held a majority. They voted down Dr. Wilson and his followers and renewed the invitation to Dr. Beecher to come to Cincinnati.

Dr. Beecher did not accept with any unseemly haste, agreeing only to visit Cincinnati and look over the prospect. Nor may this have been entirely the politic gesture of a man with his mind made up. Before committing himself irrevocably to the great evangelistic adventure, he may have wished to size up Dr. Wilson's strength in the Cincinnati Synod. The Ohio man had made an ugly accusation, and such an old head in church counsels as Lyman Beecher could not underestimate the danger. Going West might mean for him facing an ecclesiastical court on a charge of heresy.

Taking Catharine with him, he left Boston late in March and reached his destination about the middle of April. The details of the difficult journey have dropped from the record; but a letter from Catharine to Harriet gives us our first picture, through Beecher eyes, of the city which was to supply an unseen prophetess with her materials for the most devastating novel of all time.

The letter reached Harriet in Hartford less than a month before her twenty-first birthday. As she read Catharine's ecstatic description of the fateful stage which for the next two decades she was to watch from an obscure seat, could she for a moment have had a presentiment of destiny. In her enthusiasm Catharine painted with Turner's colours. Cincinnati' amphitheatre of hills was an Elysium, every vista was a Paradise. Uncle Sam's house, where she and her father were stopping, was in the upper town, and from its windows there was a noble view of the lower city, the river, and the hills and settlements on the Kentucky side. As for Walnut Hills, the region was so salubrious that people actually had to move away in order to fall sick and die—or so it was said.

In short, "I know of no place in the world where there is so fair a prospect of finding everything that makes social and domestic life pleasant."

Dr. Beecher remained about a month in Cincinnati, at the end of which time he accepted the presidency of Lane Seminary. The unanimous proffer also of the pastorate of the Second Presbyterian Church, perhaps unexpected, may have helped his decision. The congregation was willing to share him with the Seminary and be content with what time he could spare from his professorial duties. It had now become actually to his financial advantage to leave Bowdoin Street for Cincinnati, though it must be stated that considerations of salary, provided only he could support his family, could not influence Lyman Beecher.

While Dr. Beecher was securing his dismissal from the Bowdoin Street Society and wrestling with God for His blessing on the great western campaign, and while Catharine was settling her affairs in Hartford, Harriet was

spending her summer vacation in Nutplains. (Catharine's plan to entrust her
school to Miss Reed and Miss Dutton never materialized, but she made a
better arrangement, turning over the school to her old teacher, John Pierce
Brace of Litchfield, "a man who branched outside of actual subjects being
taught." It was as Principal of the Hartford Female Seminary that Brace
made a national reputation as a teacher.)

At Nutplains Harriet found her Uncle Samuel Foote, back East on a visit,
and from him could learn at first hand something more about her future
home.

Uncle Samuel was comforting to Harriet that visit. With his wide
knowledge of the world, he never allowed himself to fret over personalities
or go into a fit of the blues over a fancied slight or disloyalty. *"Horas non
numero nisi serenas,"* he quoted to her—an inscription he had copied from
a Venetian sundial—and Harriet adopted it for her motto. "I have come to
a firm resolution to count no hours but unclouded ones and to let all others
slip out of my memory and reckoning as quickly as possible."

Her friends had been chiding her for her unsocial attitudes; and she had
decided, she wrote to Georgiana May, "to give up the pernicious habit of
meditation . . . and try to mix in society somewhat as another person would."

> I am trying to cultivate a general spirit of kindliness towards everybody.
> Instead of shrinking into a corner to notice how other people behave, I am
> holding out my hand to the right and to the left and forming casual or inci-
> dental acquaintances with all who will be acquainted with me. In this way I
> find society full of interest and pleasure—a pleasure which pleaseth me more
> because it is not old and worn out. From these friendships I expect little,
> therefore generally receive more than I expect. From past friendships I have
> expected everything and must of necessity have been disappointed. The
> kind words and looks and smiles I call forth by looking and smiling are not
> much by themselves, but they form a very pretty flower border to the way
> of life.

It is a lonely and pathetic little figure she presents as she stands at the
threshold of her adult years, a misfit, but aware of it as she valiantly seeks a
formula for popularity and happiness. She was never to find popularity, but
her self-discipline taught her to love and understand humanity itself as few
have ever loved and understood it. The acquired faculty was better than
instinct.

To her few real friends she clung passionately. Georgiana May was one of
them, and now she had said good-bye to Georgiana. Her modest possessions

were in her trunk, and Nutplains that summer was but a stop on Harriet's way to the portentous West. A letter came from Georgiana, and how she fell upon it! She skimmed through it hastily, then laid it aside for a feast at bedtime. Harriet went to a party that evening, and when she finally returned to her room, there it was, still, on the dressing table. She read it through once more, then answered it before she said her prayers and blew out her candle.

It seems to me uncertain, improbable, that I shall ever return and find you as I have found your letter. Oh, my dear Georgiana, it is scarcely well to love friends thus! The greater part that I see cannot move me deeply. They are present, and I enjoy them; they pass, and I forget them. But those that I love differently—those that I *love*—and oh how much the word means!—I feel sadly about them. They may change; they must die; they are separated from me, and I ask myself, why should I wish to love with all the pains and penalties of such condition? I check myself when expressing feelings like this, so much has been said of it by the sentimental, who talk what they could not have felt. But it is so deeply, sincerely so in me, that sometimes it will overflow. Well, there is a heaven, a world of love; and love, after all, is the life-blood, the existence, the all-in-all of mind.

But it was a different Harriet who three months later (October 6, 1832) was beginning a letter to her stepgrandmother: "Well, the great sheet is out." The hegira of the Beechers had begun, they were in New York, and Harriet had constituted herself clerk of the expedition for the benefit of the folks left behind in Boston and Portland. There are no enervating soul-analyses now, no "pernicious habit of meditation" in evidence. Harriet, never before farther from her birthplace than Boston, is amid the fabled splendours of New York, and still only at the start of the romantic, unprecedented journey. She bubbles with excitement, floats on the sense of high destiny; her words take on a travelled, metropolitan air. "Father is to perform tonight in the Chatham Theatre, 'positively for the *last* time this season.'"

Be the adversary a Litchfield woodpile or Belial in his western wilderness, Lyman Beecher had only to sound a crusade to rouse his clan to the same enthusiasm. When he expressed the hope to consecrate all his children to God in the West, he spoke not idly. Nearly half of them were now self-supporting adults; but, except for the comfortably married and settled Mary in Hartford, he carried them all with him on his holy enterprise. One strain of his pibroch transplanted a family that had had its roots in New England soil since the earliest settlement.

They did not all go with the main party. Edward was already their John the Baptist in Illinois. William was a preaching licentiate in Newport, Rhode Island, though prepared to relinquish his charge as soon as some post could be found for him on the main battleground. Henry Ward was in Amherst, Charles was in Bowdoin.

But the rest were an army with banners—the Doctor himself, his wife, Aunt Esther Beecher, of course, Catharine (now generally called Kate), George, Harriet herself, Isabella (with Harriet variously Sister Belle, Bell, or Bella), Thomas, and James, a toddler of four years. George Beecher, who was promising to have one of the most brilliant minds in the family, was leaving Dr. Taylor and the Yale Divinity School (in which his father had placed him as a rebuke to the conservatism of Andover) to be the first Beecher student at Lane in Cincinnati. At Yale George had become a jubilant Taylor heretic, something that the Doctor, who preached the Taylor theology, would never call himself.

As a proper ministerial family, the Beechers eschewed hotels and bivouacked with the laity, which rejoiced to open its doors to such celebrated company. (It was a habit Harriet found hard to break, even after she became rich and famous.) In New York one of their hosts was Henry Tallmadge, son of Litchfield's Revolutionary hero. The other was possibly the philanthropic Arthur Tappan.

The stop in New York was protracted. A condition which Arthur Tappan attached to his endowment was that Lane Seminary must itself raise the endowments—$20,000 each—for two other professorships. The collectors for the institution had succeeded in one of these tasks and made some progress with the second. Dr. Beecher did not wish to cut loose from the moneyed East until this professorship (Biblical Literature) was assured. As Harriet wrote, "the incumbent is to be C. Stowe."

(Having completed his year as an instructor at Bowdoin and another as associate editor of the Boston *Recorder,* C. Stowe had accepted the Chair of Languages at Dartmouth, where he was perhaps at the moment courting Eliza, daughter of Dr. Tyler, president of Dartmouth College and, later, Lyman Beecher's theological arch-enemy.)

Dr. Beecher was a new hand at raising money but found himself extraordinarily effective as a beggar in a good cause. A brief interview with S. Van Rensselaer brought a thousand dollars. The Doctor's account of this success must have been a rousing one. Harriet forbore to pass it along to Mrs. Porter, since "I can not tell you as father told us." Next day's hunting bagged $2,000 more. The Doctor was in a transport of excitement, shaking from his shoulders the burden of his years (he celebrated his fifty-seventh birthday during this visit) and of his Boston rebuff and becoming again the joking, stimulating, soul- and perch-fishing parent of the old Litchfield days.

"He is all in his own element—dipping into books—consulting authorities for his oration—going around here, there, and everywhere—begging, borrowing, and spoiling the Egyptians—delighted with past success, and confident for the future."

Harriet was keyed equally high. "I believe it would kill me dead to live long in the way I have been doing since I have been here. It is a sort of agreeable delirium. There's only one thing about it, it is too *scattering*. I begin to be athirst for the waters of quietness."

Dr. Beecher's enthusiasm might thus communicate itself to an adoring daughter but it scarcely reached to the two older ladies of the party. When Dr. Beecher broke the news to Aunt Esther that he was about to carry her with him to Cincinnati, that lady, who had taken two years to transplant herself from Litchfield to Boston, was, as the doctor reported, "frightened," a statement we can readily believe. But Mrs. Beecher herself was far from being delighted with the prospect of leaving her New England for the howling Ohio Valley. In New York these two ladies confronted the unknown future with dismay.

They arrived in Philadelphia late on a Saturday evening in dull, drizzling weather—"poor Aunt Esther in dismay—not a clean cap to put on—mother in like state—all of us destitute. We went half to Dr. Skinner's and half to Mrs. Elmes's—mother, Aunt Esther, father, and James [Harriet forgot Thomas] to the former; Kate, Bella, and myself to Mr. Elmes's. They are rich, hospitable folks, and act the part of Gaius in apostolic times."

They moved on next day, though not before Harriet found time to comment on a Philadelphia journal, which likened the exodus of Dr. Beecher and his family to the migration of Jacob and his sons. Harriet thought this was, "as Paul says, speaking 'as a fool.'" She herself, frequently a little inept in her figures of speech, preferred the analogy of Noah, though they travelled on land and took no animals with them. Evening of the first day's journey brought them to Downingtown, thirty miles west of Philadelphia, where Harriet wrote: "Here we all are—Noah, and his wife, and his sons, and his daughters, with the cattle and creeping things, all dropped down in the front parlour of this tavern."

From Philadelphia onward the Beecher caravan became in fact a crusade, moving with song and prayer and souls blessed by the wayside. And never did crusade of the Middle Ages set forth with more joyous hearts or holier hopes, nor more surely foredoomed to heartbreak and defeat. It was the effervescent George who turned a stage ride into an evangelistic road show—though one seems to hear, too, the rasp of Lyman Beecher's fiddle. But let Harriet tell it:

If today is a fair specimen of our journey, it will be a very pleasant one—obliging driver, good roads, good spirits, good dinner, fine scenery, and now and then some "psalms and hymns and spiritual songs"; for with George on board, you may be sure of music of some kind. Moreover, George has provided himself with a quantity of tracts, and he and the children have kept up a regular discharge at all the wayfaring people we encountered. I tell him he is *peppering* the land with moral influence.

Thus, no doubt leaving behind a topic to keep an astonished Pennsylvania countryside in conversation for many a day, the Beecher coach made its pious, vocal progress to Harrisburg, arriving there on a Saturday evening, or just in time for a delighted clergy to offer the famous Dr. Beecher their pulpits for the following day. On Sunday evening Harriet infringed the rules of perfect Sabbath observance enough to enter a brief note in her log.

Mother, Aunt Esther, George, and the little folks have just gathered into Kate's room, and we have just been singing. Father has gone to preach for Mr. De Witt. Tomorrow we expect to travel sixty-two miles, and in two more days shall reach Wheeling; there we shall take the steam-boat to Cincinnati.

It was not to be so easy. At Harrisburg they entered the mountains; and to gain speed, or, more likely, to save expense, they abandoned the stage-coach for private hired conveyances. But they found only poor horses and so took eight days for a journey the regular mail-stages accomplished in forty-eight hours.

A modern critic complains that Harriet made no mention on this classic journey of the sublimities of the Alleghenics, though she was seeing mountain gorges, peaks, and precipices for the first time in her life. Therefore, the critic argues, she was blind to the more dramatic effects of nature. But did Peter the Hermit pause to note the grandeur of the Balkans, did Tancred drop his gaze from Jerusalem to admire the dyed profundities of the Bosporus? Harriet would not have been the daughter of Lyman Beecher, if the religious mission of their caravan had not captured her chief attention. Later in life she was to admire and praise sublime scenery—even to overpraise Niagara Falls, after the fashion of the time.

At Wheeling (then a town in western Virginia) they were met with dismaying intelligence. Asiatic cholera was raging in Cincinnati—the city Lyman Beecher had chosen because its situation was so salubrious. Now it was a charnel-house. Scared passengers on the up-bound steamboats on the Ohio spoke of coffins stacked in doorways, death hanging like a pall above the stricken town. A real pall of smoke was arising from open street fires of bituminous coal, called prophylactic against the plague. A boat was ready to take them down-river, but they decided to remain in an uncontaminated place until the epidemic should subside.

It was not time wasted. Wheeling rejoiced at the opportunity to hear the celebrated pulpit orator, and (wrote George Beecher) "father preached eleven times—nearly every evening—and gave them the Taylorite heresy on sin and decrees to the highest notch; and what amused me most was to hear him establish it from the Confession of Faith. It went high and dry, however, above all objections, and they were delighted with it, even the strong Old School men, since it had not been christened heresy in their hearing."

In the fullness of time the family chartered a stagecoach and resumed their journey, though rather uncertainly, crossing the river at Wheeling and proceeding down on the Ohio side as far as Granville.

Expounding, exhorting, labouring with the unconvicted, singing hymns, and passing out tracts, the crusaders turned inland at Granville to avoid the great bend of the Ohio, making for their first time the acquaintance of some of Ohio's corduroy roads, paved with logs laid crosswise. George, no doubt taking his father's word for it, wrote that such roads were good for dyspeptics. They travelled via Columbus and on the 14th day of November, 1832, reached their destination. The dreadful epidemic had passed, but they saw the blackened façades of the buildings, the hasty foundations of Cincinnati's first orphanage, and in the cemeteries hundreds and hundreds of new furrows that would grow no grass until spring.

Uncle John and Uncle Samuel Foote, who put them up temporarily, would have on their tables copies of the daily *Gazette,* and the *Chronicle,* for which Harriet, with the inquisitiveness of the small, would make a dive. A curious and observant mind could get a quick impression of the flavour of a new place from an examination of its newspapers.

So, among smudgy, one-column advertisements for India-rubber shoes, ink powder, chariottees, Jane Austen's works, whale-oil lamps, and the extension of the engagement of Mr. Fletcher, the celebrated delineator of Roman and Grecian statuary, her quick eye would catch the imprint of a stock woodcut of a stooping Negro with stick and bundle over his shoulder and under it some such display as this:

100 DOLLARS REWARD!

The above reward will be paid by the subscriber for the apprehension and delivery of Humphrey, a slave, who is about 17 years of age, and who made his escape from the undersigned in Boone County, Ky., on the 22nd ult.

A. W. Gaines,
Boone Co., Ky.

God had at length set down his anointed handmaiden at the fiery contact-point of Freedom with Slavery.

III
◉ CINCINNATI ◉
1832-1850

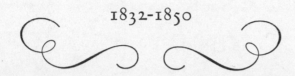

The Beecher Home at Walnut Hills, Cincinnati

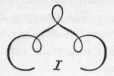

London of the West

IT WAS a thrilling city that welcomed the crusaders. Lyman Beecher was still in his prime, but he had been a fourteen-year-old boy trying to learn farming in Guilford before the first settler built his hut on the Ohio bank across from the mouth of the Licking, which came up from Kentucky's dark and bloody ground. At the turn of the century the village numbered only 750 souls. By that time a Commander at Fort Washington had renamed it Cincinnati from the order of Revolutionary War officers to which he belonged.

At the date of Harriet Beecher's birth the village had become a town of 2,500 inhabitants. During the next decade its growth, though swift as reckoned by percentages, was too steady to attract outside attention. About the middle of the 1820's, or shortly before Dr. Beecher felt the call of the West, rumour crept through the East that something like a miracle was happening on the Ohio's north bank. America had its first boom town, as Cincinnati's population began to shoot upward to metropolitan numbers. By the end of 1832, when the Beechers arrived, it was already a city of 30,000.

What made the development seem so miraculous was that it was entirely unpremeditated and unfostered by conscious promotion. There was no inducement of free sites with tax exemption, no Chamber of Commerce to conduct the municipal diplomacy and fill the eastern newspapers with advertisements. German immigrants gave the growth its first great impetus. In the noble banks of the Ohio River, retreating in sylvan terraces to heights five and six hundred feet above low water, they saw a resemblance to their own Rhineland. Many in the broadening tide of population that was following down the river highway, chose to drop out here and adopt urban life in the New World.

Cincinnati had work for all who would stay. The South had entered the golden era of cotton-growing prosperity that was whitening Mississippi,

Alabama, Georgia and the Carolinas with the columned châteaux of the great slave-owning proprietors. The one-crop South imported nearly all its supplies. Cincinnati, at a watery crossroads when waterways bore the bulk of all traffic, became the first important supply city for the open-handed kingdom of slave-grown cotton.

In 1832 some two hundred steamboats were plying the Western Waters, as the Mississippi system was called—and blowing up on them, too. Since 1815, when steam navigation began, about 350 steamboats had been built, largely on the Ohio River and sixty-eight of them in Cincinnati, which at the beginning of the 1830's was launching new ones at the rate of eight or ten a year. Seven boiler plants on Cincinnati's river-front clamoured the advertisement of her shipbuilding.

Gentlefolk like Mrs. Lyman Beecher, in safe and Christian New England, still thought of the West as a wilderness traversed by Indian warpaths. Actually settlement had reached the Mississippi, and Ohio had a population of more than one million, most of them farmers. Those in the southern part of the State raised hogs; and the South and the East could use salt-pork, bacon, and lard. Cincinnati's first pork-packing establishment began slaughtering in 1827. Five years later meat-packing houses were scattered through the city, the Germans had usurped the business, and Cincinnati was nicknaming itself Porkopolis. Seven breweries and distilleries were adding a lucrative export, and pork had brought in the by-product industries of button-making and soap manufacture.

But it was not all stink of slaughter-pen, hide warehouse, and fermentation vat for Cincinnati, not all whine of saws from her five steam sawmills, not all smoke from the rolling mill, not all steam jets from the two flour mills, the two paper mills, and the two cotton mills. Cincinnati had its aesthetic side, self-conscious and aggressive. Catharine Beecher had caught it in her first pioneering glance. "A great number of the houses are of brick and very handsomely built. The streets run at right angles to each other and are quite wide and well paved."

No, the keelboats were no longer stopping at Cincinnati. Cincinnati was building of brick and stone, solidly for the future. This community was the flower of the new civilization that had occupied the wilderness. It was the "Queen City of the West"; and its best citizens—Catharine's New England sort of folks—proposed that it should be queen of culture as well as of commerce.

Education came first. In 1832 Cincinnati had been pioneering for two

years in free public schools for boys—"a mortgage on all property, irre-
deemably and forever," the die-hards had called it—and three years later
Harriet Martineau, the English traveller, was to view the annual school
parade and write that she had never seen such graceful children. A settler
with the good fortune to stake out his homestead between the future routes
of Cincinnati's Main Street and Broadway, had endowed the Woodward
High School, of which in 1832 Harriet's Uncle John P. Foote was a trustee.
It supplied free instruction to poor boys but charged tuition from those who
could pay. What Middle Western schoolchild, even as late as 1890, did not
know Ray's Arithmetic or McGuffey's Readers? Both Dr. Joseph Ray and
Dr. William Holmes McGuffey were in the 1830's on the faculty of Woodward High School, which still exists in Cincinnati's public school system.

The town had made a start with Cincinnati College, having obtained a
charter and put up a building. The college was soon to start functioning. Its
medical and law schools it bequeathed without a break to the present University of Cincinnati, the only American university maintained by one
municipality's funds.

In its issue of Saturday, November 17, 1832, the Cincinnati *Chronicle*
printed the following notice:

Mechanics' Institute

The lecture for this evening is unavoidably postponed. It will be given on
next Saturday evening by the Rev. Lyman Beecher.

Ready as he was to extemporize sermon or evangelistic exhortation, two
days had probably been too short for the Doctor to prepare a learned lecture.
But the item serves to introduce an institution of which Cincinnati was
already proud. In 1828 a group of forward-looking citizens, John P. Foote
among them, had endowed the Mechanics' Institute to offer free instruction
to poor young men and a meeting-place to keep idlers off the street corners.
Soon, however, the whole town, rich and poor alike, was attending the
weekly lectures. Today, as the Ohio Mechanics' Institute, it continues to give
practical courses to several thousand students annually, besides affording
them the use of a splendid library.

"Our family physician is one Dr. Drake," Harriet wrote in her first letter
to her sister, Mary Perkins, in Hartford, "a man of a good deal of science,
theory, and reputed skill, but a sort of general mark for the opposition of all
the medical cloth of the city. He is a tall, rectangular, perpendicular sort of

body, as stiff as a poker, and enunciates his prescriptions very much as though he were delivering a discourse on the doctrine of election."

Harriet could have said much more about Dr. Daniel Drake, who was Cincinnati's first citizen, if not first citizen of the West. The physician, who was to have a definite influence on her career, was one of those versatile men whom pioneer conditions bred in this country. There was no brew for Cincinnati's civic improvement, from local sanitation to railroad promotion, in which he did not have a hand, often the leading hand. He edited the first medical journal to be published in the West. He was the author of several standard medical textbooks and also of a now-forgotten classic of pioneer literature, his *Letters* to his children, in which he described his life as a boy in Kentucky during the Indian wars. He gave Ohio its nickname, the Buckeye State. He was one of the founders of the Semi-Colon Club and the sole sponsor of the Buckeye Club, in the meetings of both of which Harriet Beecher first felt her power as a writer.

Adult citizens of this sudden metropolis of a West still building its worm fences, were forming mutual cultural societies. One was the Cincinnati Lyceum, the secretary and moving spirit of which was young Salmon P. Chase, who had recently hung out his law shingle. The Lyceum promoted lectures, but its chief ambition was to found a public library. Only recently by ordinance had Catholics been permitted to build churches within the city limits of Cincinnati, and we may easily suppose they were excluded from membership in the Lyceum. At any rate, the able and tolerant Bishop Purcell, who was to become Harriet's friend, started a rival Catholic Atheneum, planting a seed which eventually grew into St. Xavier College.

Besides these public and semi-public enterprises, various commercial undertakings promoted the Queen City's culture. Patriotic local criticism ranked Judge James Hall's *Western Monthly Magazine* on a literary parity with *Graham's* or the *National,* of Philadelphia. The semi-monthly *Ladies' Museum* was to rival *Godey's Lady's Book.* There were two agricultural journals published in the city, one by John P. Foote, whose finger was in many a commercial pie. There were three daily, two semi-weekly, and three weekly newspapers, to say nothing of two or three book publishers. There were two theatres in Cincinnati, together offering more than two thousand seats in view of boards trodden that year by Edwin Forrest. There were two natural-history museums, privately owned and charging admission. One of them, Dorfeuille's, for its Chamber of Horrors displayed a mechanical representation of Hell, designed and executed by the celebrated Cincinnati sculptor Hiram Powers. And finally there was Mrs. Trollope's Bazaar.

Mrs. Frances Trollope was Cincinnati's obsession in 1832. In the spring she had brought out her *Domestic Manners of The Americans,* a successful work that started her on a career as a voluminous travel-writer but which cut an innocent Queen City to the unsophisticated quick. Having failed in a fantastic business in Cincinnati, Mrs. Trollope in this volume paid off her grudge by making uncomplimentary remarks about the personal habits of the pioneers, especially those inhabiting the city that had swallowed her fortune.

Cincinnati people believed that the steamboats bumping each other for wharf room at the Public Landing were floating palaces, the last word in travel luxury. Mrs. Trollope said she preferred a pig pen *with its occupants* to the cabin of one of these packets when filled with American citizens. She said that at table the Americans rammed their knives half-way down their throats and afterwards picked their teeth with jack-knives.

She said of Cincinnati, "I think Main Street is the only one entirely paved. The *trottoir* is of brick, tolerably well laid, but it is inundated by every shower, as Cincinnati has no drains whatever."

Mrs. Trollope also said some nice things about Cincinnati, but the city rallied only weakly. One or two commentators made bold to assert that Mrs. T. had never really met the best people of the Queen City, which was probably true. She had come to Cincinnati in 1828 when she was neither a celebrated authoress nor the mother of two even more celebrated author-sons, but only an English widow seeking to set up her son Henry in business in the New World.

She took the Gano place in the suburban village of Mohawk, which is now the squalid down-town district known in Cincinnati as Over The Rhine. It was a roomy, white house with green Venetian blinds, but it stood in a weedy field which the neighbourhood was surreptitiously using for a dump; and the Ganos, though they became a leading Cincinnati family, had never yet gathered energy enough to finish the driveway up to the front door.

But Mrs. Trollope did not seem to mind such surroundings. Her head was buzzing with schemes for Henry; and when she evolved her final one, it out-Barnumed a contemporary Connecticut youth who was still fourteen years away from his Broadway Museum and General Tom Thumb. Was there something in early Cincinnati air that inspired absurdities? In her Bazaar Mrs. Trollope proposed to house 'under one roof the following entertainments and enterprises: a Stock Exchange, a department store, an art gallery, a dance hall, a banquet hall, an ice-cream parlour, a saloon, and a cyclorama exhibit. Mrs. Trollope's idea of 'Change was, however, feminine. In her Bazaar the brokers would sit sipping cocktails, juleps, toddies and punches while arranging their tiresome quotations and transfers.

The exterior of this remarkable edifice, as it materialized in brownstone from the plans of a Mr. Palmer, was an architectural promise of the manifold activities enclosed.

Alas, this Greco-Arabic-Gothic-Egyptian masterpiece was never finished. In 1830 Mrs. Trollope's money gave out, mechanics' liens snowed upon the Bazaar, and she retreated to England, light in purse but heavy with saleable reminiscences. The fate of her Cincinnati memorial was melancholy. The Mechanics' Institute took up the liens but could not meet subsequent obligations and abandoned it to litigation. Now and then the Bazaar cropped out in Cincinnati's history. Miss Martineau, who thought Cincinnati so beautiful that the Capitol should be moved there from Washington, saw her countrywoman's building in 1835 and called it "the great deformity of the city." A subsequent owner whitewashed and papered over the Hervieu murals, moving Harriet's Uncle Sam Foote to write to the *Gazette,* condemning such "vandalism." The paintings may not have been great art, he said, but they were too good to be obliterated. Mrs. Trollope's famous son Anthony came in 1861 and found the building occupied by a catch-penny medical school run by a quack doctor. The Bazaar existed until 1881, when it was torn down.

Despite its public schools, its college, its divinity school, its hospitals and medical schools, despite its coterie of gifted citizens, despite Lyceum, Atheneum, and Institute of this "Athens of America," despite its forty churches, its fifty-six lawyers and forty-seven doctors, its paid night watch, its volunteer fire department with fifteen hand-pump engines and ten brick fire cisterns (kept filled by the wooden mains of John P. and Samuel E. Foote's water company), its ten hotels, its sixty-four weekly mails (thirty-six by stage, seventeen by steamboat, eleven by post riders)—despite these and other attributes of the settled civilization so many of the citizens had left behind in the East, at heart and in spirit Cincinnati was still a frontier town, and a rough one.

THE CINCINNATI HARRIET KNEW

Charles Dickens: "I have not often seen a place that commends itself so favourably and pleasantly to the stranger at first glance."

(Page 210.)

The pork-packers set up their plants about as they pleased, with small regard for the sensibilities of the community. Mrs. Trollope complained that when she tried to take a country walk, she found a certain brook had become a stew from the discharge of the abattoirs. Harriet Beecher was not long in discovering Porkopolis. In her first letter to sister Mary Perkins, written a few days after the arrival in Cincinnati, she told of seeing her four-year-old brother Jamie parading in the street with his arm over the neck of a fat hog. More magnanimous than Mrs. Trollope, Harriet added: "So much for allowing these animals to promenade the streets, a particular in which Mrs. Cincinnati has imitated the domestic arrangements of some of her elder sisters, and a very disgusting one it is."

Judged by modern standards, the human population of Cincinnati in the 1830's lived much like the pigs in the streets. Dickens admired the city's "clean houses of red and white, its well-paved roads, and footways of bright tile." But those red and white façades were placarded with ineffectual no-nuisance signs, the bright tile footways were foul with tobacco juice, and as late as the year 1845 a Cincinnati editor was urging his fellow citizens to bathe themselves more frequently. "We have not *time* to bathe. . . . The man who goes without bathing from week to week during any period of the year, is injuring his health. During the heats of summer he is absolutely committing suicide."

But it was worse than that. Cincinnati was a river town, always harbouring a floating population of roustabouts, gamblers, sharpers, and other questionable characters. Moreover, the slaughter-houses attracted a violent type of men, with stomachs for blood and guts. As a result, in the coffee-houses, as the barrooms then glorified themselves in title (though the righteous called them "doggeries"), lurked a mob never out of earshot of any incendiary call, a mob, moreover, the more dreadful because it was often silently supported by the business and political powers. In the two decades between 1830 and 1850 the Cincinnati mob wrote a disgraceful history and one interwoven with the life of Harriet Beecher Stowe.

Such in some of its highlights was the Cincinnati that received the Beechers. The year 1832 was auspicious, for it was near the beginning of a new era. Each generation must, for its content, sweep aside the past and recreate the world. That of the 1830's was no exception. One heard and read everywhere the phrase, "The March of Intellect." It was as though a young, confident world was for the first time applying intellect to humanity's progress.

Yet the era really was new. Mankind was turning toward the scientific approach to many ancient problems. (That very year the young Charles Darwin was serving as field naturalist with the *Beagle* expedition, cruising along the coasts of South America.) Dress fashions showed the change. The 1830's swept away the last traces of court influence in style, as the high-waisted Empire fashion for women vanished and gave way to full, rather short skirts, tightly corseted but naturally-placed waists, and elaborately puffed and tucked sleeves, imparting to the wearer a broad-shouldered effect. Poke bonnets increased in size and took on ornamentation. Male fashion, too, differed. The close-fitting trousers, strapped under the boots, lingered; but now the long, tight-waisted frock coat with broad lapels, the wide cravat wound around a flaring collar and knotted either in front or back, and the fuzzy, bell-shaped beaver top-hat in some light hue characterized the typical costume.

However, Cincinnati's frontier spirit manifested itself in a certain contempt for the dictates of fashion. The heart of gold in a rough exterior was still the local ideal. It extended to the ladies, who ignored seasonal trends and dressed in a manner that even Hartford would have considered frumpy. (But in Philadelphia young Mr. Louis Antoine Godey, whose *Lady's Book* was ending its third year, was soon to see about this attitude.) A Cincinnati gentleman left to the steamboat gamblers the last word in fancy waistcoats, or the *dernier cri* in otter hats to the young agents of New York houses come to inspect their western investments.

But if Cincinnati did not dazzle sartorially, its hospitality was abundant. The evening party filled an important place in the community life, and a Cincinnati party was unique. The back rooms of the entertaining mansion were reserved exclusively for gentlemen. Ladies remained in the front parlours, attended by such men (usually the young ones) as preferred their society to that of the stag quarters. As E. D. Mansfield wrote: "But with the old, sedate, and unfashionable gentlemen the back room was the charm. There stood the tables, with ham and beef, and venison, turkey, and quails, with bottles of brandy and wine, and there were cards for those who wanted to kill time." From these groaning boards hired waiters and volunteer swains carried out to the ladies "the best of cakes and confections."

To these comfortable functions—and to the lectures, sermons, prayer-meetings, and theatrical performances that gave the Queen City the rest of its night life—Cincinnati walked through a Main Street, at least, lighted by sperm-oil lanterns hung at the corners on wooden posts carved by the energetic Hiram Powers, who was still five years away from Italy and an international reputation. Sperm-oil lamps brightened the better residences. The frugal used tallow dips for illumination.

The moral tone of Cincinnati, as expressed by its press, was formidable; for here Puritanism, which had already lost its grip on New England, was still entrenched. Religion divided most of the public attention with business. Infidels felt an uneasy sense of the reality of Powers' Inferno at Dorfeuille's dime museum and could jump and yell as sincerely as any Christian when they touched the electrified hand rail. Collected sermons made profitable books. Current novels, unless from local pens, lay under suspicion. Reviewers denounced the fashionable English novel dealing with erring girls and profligate rakes, with nothing said about literary worth. One editorial mentor urged the boycott of a French journal then widely sold in America. "I ask and will accept nothing further as evidence of its character than that the infamous Madame George Sand is announced as one of the contributors."

It is a strange fact in the life of Harriet Beecher Stowe that this exhilarating town, with its broad contrasts of good and evil, of culture and hoodlumism, and for all its premonition of the coming greatness of the Middle West, made but the faintest of impressions upon her as a literary woman. Here she was to live for the next eighteen years—for the remainder of her youth—longer than she ever dwelt in any other place, except Hartford. Here she experienced some of her greatest joys, one of her sharpest griefs, and the worst of her tribulations. Here she married, bore her children, buried one of them. Here she began her professional career. And one can read through from beginning to end the score and more of her principal works and never find a reference to Cincinnati or any use of the city as a background.

Such neglect was not characteristic of her. She was to live less than two years in Brunswick, Maine, yet draw from it the scene and theme of one of her best novels. She wrote about Florida, where later she had a winter home. She staged stories in Hartford, in Litchfield, in Italy, through which she toured, even in Newport, which she knew only as a visitor. The period between adolescence and the gateway to middle age is for most novelists a season for harvesting grain their mature powers are to winnow and mill. Most novelists, living Harriet's life, would have found the brawling, pretentious capital of the West the most suggestive of all the environments they knew. Yet nothing in it seemed to hold any appeal to her literary cupidity.

There is no evidence that she hated Cincinnati, as did her stepmother. Her apparent attitude was one of indifference. Western enthusiasm could catch up her sister Catharine completely and for a while her father and brothers. Harriet was impervious to it. How should she sing the Lord's song in a strange land? Catharine had grandly celebrated the exodus with an ode, *The Emigrant's Farewell*. Harriet's quiet comment was clairvoyant: "My symptoms have been of a less acute kind, but, I fear, more enduring."

They were to endure to the end, buttressing the disturbing thought that she was here for one purpose and one only. She was fasting in the wilderness, being about her Father's business. What did the immediate environment matter? Wheeling, Marietta, any Ohio River town might have given her an equally useful picture of African slavery. Cincinnati's gift of it was incidental. Harriet pitched none of the story of *Uncle Tom's Cabin* in the city where she gathered it.

While her young years slipped away, she remained in Cincinnati the perennial exile, aloof, unassimilable, and deep. The Queen City was entertaining its prophetess unawares. When Harriet's sudden fame came, Cincinnati discovered it had little recollection of her. So obscure was her trace that in the present day there is a movement in Cincinnati to make a Harriet Beecher Stowe shrine of a house in which she never lived. And when at last Harriet brushed from her worn shoes the final clay of the Ohio bank and faced toward home and high destiny, she was leaving behind not one friend with whom she ever kept up any correspondence.

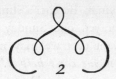

2

First Adjustments

THE house into which Dr. Beecher moved was a curiosity to his family. Harriet called it "the most inconvenient, ill-arranged, good-for-nothing, and altogether to be execrated affair that ever was put together. It was evidently built without a thought of a winter season. The kitchen is so disposed that it cannot be reached from any part of the house without going out into the air. Mother is actually obliged to put on a bonnet and cloak every time she goes into it. In the house are two parlors with folding doors between them. The back parlor has but one window, which opens on a veranda and has its lower half painted to keep out what little light there is. I need scarcely add that our landlord is an old bachelor and of course acted up to the light he had, though he left little enough of it for his tenants."

They could all joke about this curious dwelling, since it was to be merely a temporary camp for them. Catharine was already planning her school in town, while out in Walnut Hills, a two-mile climb up the stony and rutted Montgomery road, were rising the brick walls of the president's house, which Dr. Beecher and his dependents would occupy when it was ready.

Besides, the Doctor, during these first days, was too busy receiving his welcome to pay much attention to home comfort. Cincinnati had pounced upon "the most quoted American, except Benjamin Franklin." One day it was a sermon, the next a lecture, the third a council or public meeting. We may be sure his audiences were large. The prideful city felt that the capture of New England's leading clergyman was its greatest achievement. With this Boanerges thundering from the Second Presbyterian pulpit, Cincinnati, still a little uncertain of itself, could look New York or Philadelphia in the eyes, or even Boston. The London of the West, the Paris? Nay, the Athens of America!

Soon the town was building up its own Beecheriana. As a good Whig, the Doctor detested President Jackson, whose triumphant reëlection in November had added nothing to Lyman Beecher's slim store of good-will toward Democrats. "O Lord," he prayed one Sunday morning before a packed Cincinnati congregation, "grant that we may not despise our rulers—and grant that they may not act *so we can't help it.*" The town was convulsed. What made it the funnier was that the Doctor had been perfectly sincere in his unconventional petition.

The devout of Cincinnati at once deified him. The threadbare, middle-height figure held some mysterious "hiding of power." A platform is filled with dignitaries. Beecher enters, and the throng gets "a new sensation." "There is mystery and majesty about that plain, ruddy, nervous old man which begets awe and reverence." Yet he was most democratic, conducting himself on all occasions with "a familiarity that flattered us all." A clerical idolator saw him standing among his brethren "like Daniel Webster in the Senate—alone!"

A small group was failing to join this chorus. "Dr. Wilson's folks" were still finding it "wisest and best to be still." Their silence was ominous. Already they had rammed the charges into their muskets and pushed on the caps. They were waiting to see the whites of Dr. Beecher's eyes.

Dr. Wilson was biding his time, eating meat fed him by the crafty theologians holding the inner stronghold of Calvinism at Princeton. The Princeton doctors nursed a double grievance against Lyman Beecher. His Yale origin and his friendship with Yale's Dr. Taylor would have been enough; but Princeton, too, had planned to sponsor "the great Presbyterian divinity school of the West" and had made a start with one at Pittsburgh. Lane Seminary, under Lyman Beecher's presidency, was threatening to throw this feeble institution into an eclipse. The Princeton sages, therefore, were treating with Dr. Wilson in Cincinnati, who took their advice to read Beecher's sermons carefully. He found them veined with heresy.

On New Year's Day, 1833, Judge Hall brought out in Cincinnati the first number of his *Western Monthly Magazine.* It was an event of some significance for Harriet Beecher, since this publication was to buy her first contribution and thus launch her, at any rate in her family's eyes, on a writer's career. James Hall, pioneer lawyer, jurist, and author, still remembered for his *Legends of The West* and other vivid annals of early days in the Mississippi Basin, had started his magazine three years before in Vandalia, Illinois, calling it the *Illinois Monthly,* but could not resist the drift of culture into Cincinnati. Harriet must have met this gentleman soon after her arrival, for Judge Hall, who was still in his late thirties, had at once joined the enlightened circle of which Captain Samuel Foote was a member.

The novelties of the bustling new city—the press of steamboat bows on the paved slope of the quay, the cluster of public hacks at the top, each mounting a tobacco-spitting Jehu and towing behind a two-wheeled baggage cart, the unwonted appearance of many Negroes in the streets, the towering hills that walled the amphitheatre to the northward, in places already hatched with Nicholas Longworth's vineyards and pierced by his wine-caves—mitigated the nostalgia of the small, quiet, observant girl who had left her heart in New England and postponed for her the boredom she was to find in this scene. Many things reminded her that this was no provincial town like Hartford, but a metropolis like New York or Boston. The shops were alluring—too alluring for Harriet, they proved—the entertainments metropolitan. Whatever New York enjoyed, so later did Cincinnati. In January the bills went up announcing the Siamese Twins to be at the Pearl Street House on February 1 "for a few days' stay. Admission, 25 cents." Besides, Harriet was busy that winter, writing her first book.

Catharine was planning a girls' school for Cincinnati, and this time Mary Dutton *must* come from New Haven and join the teaching corps. At last Catharine felt in a position to realize an ideal which her father had vetoed in Hartford ten years earlier. No more drudgery of teaching for her! She would own the school and give it the Beecher name; but Mary Dutton must be Principal, and Mary must stop in Hartford and secure either Georgiana May or Miss Leyman, of the Female Seminary, for her assistant.

My former nervous liabilities are so hanging about me, that *I* can assume no responsibilities of any kind in regard to a school. Harriet also feels that she has had so much wear and tear of feeling and nerves that she ought to have at least a year to recruit. She has employed herself this winter in writing some books for children, and as she finds this will be a means both of usefulness and of money, she has concluded to defer taking any responsible part in a school for the coming year and to continue her present employment.

There was more than a little pretense in this lofty explanation. "Feeble health" was, of course, a fashionable pose for a lady in that day. Perhaps Catharine's health was somewhat reduced after the business of winding up her affairs in Hartford; but if Harriet had suffered any wear and tear of her nervous system, her sprightly letters at the time do not indicate it. Both these Beecher daughters were to go through life complaining of "nerves" —no surprising fact, perhaps, in view of the psychological atrocities of their upbringing—but both reached great age, Catharine always in great physical vigour.

Also, for "some books for children" in Catharine's letter, read "a book" for exact truth. It was a geography, written down for young minds. Harriet, no doubt on her sister's suggestion and perhaps with her help, had started to write it the previous summer, when she was visiting in Guilford and in Newport, where her brother William had his pastoral charge. The letter implies that by February 3 the sisters had found a publisher for this work. Though she did none of the writing, Catharine signed the geography as co-author and shared equally in the "avails." It took the sanguine Beecher temperament to regard this success as a warrant for Harriet to quit salaried employment for the hazards of writing as a professional career. The Cincinnati publishers, Corey & Fairbank, bought the manuscript of the geography outright. Harriet's share was $187.

That same temperament, however, had in less than two weeks expanded a simple girls' school in Cincinnati into a project of national scope. Some local business men had offered Catharine financial assistance, on the mere word-of-mouth rumour that the Beecher daughters were to open a school, forty pupils had already signed for the spring term, and Catharine was writing to Mary Dutton:

> The plan is to start a school of the first-rate order, which shall serve as a model to the West, and which shall gradually grow into a large institution as its conductors gain experience and public confidence.
> . . . Harriet, I expect, will devote herself to the moral and religious improvement of the pupils, but neither of us will be pledged to the public as the *teachers* of the school.
>
> * * *
>
> I intend to have a school room handsomely furnished, with a carpet, curtains, and each pupil to have a desk and chair of her own. Also a piano to render Calisthenics interesting. Also recitation rooms, as many as necessary, furnished with black boards. The gentlemen interested are going to put 3 or 400 dollars into my hands for this purpose—for which I choose to pay interest.

How different was Catharine's version of her motives in Cincinnati, when, a few years later, her school had failed, the academies deficient "in all the most essential interests of education" were casting lots for its garments, and Catharine herself was engaged in the dismal business of liquidating its pitiful affairs! Then she could fling out querulously at Mary: "I began this school as a matter of self-denial, giving up ease and literary pursuits and the ability to make more money by my pen for the responsibilities, care, and vexation of a school that has been more plague to me than all I suffered in Hartford for ten years. I did it because father wished it, because Harriet needed some means of immediate support, because I was urged by various friends, and from the hope of doing good by starting such a school."

Something that lies between the two explanations is probably the truth. No doubt her father and her Cincinnati friends urged her to start the school; no doubt Harriet needed a position on its teaching staff; but there was no self-denial on Catharine's part. She thought the school would make money for her. As for giving up literary pursuits, her claim is nonsense, for she had none to give up. Not until after the school opened did the unexpected success of the geography show Catharine the money that might lie in her pen.

This *volte face* of Catharine's, this propensity to dress statements to fit a purpose, was characteristic of the Beechers, or of four of them—Lyman himself, Catharine, Henry Ward and Harriet. Especially characteristic of Harriet. Well might Mrs. Browning have wondered later if her mouth were quite frank. In any public display of her personal affairs, Harriet was seldom frank. Like her father, the crafty polemist, politician, and church lawyer, whose very homespun speech and appearance were calculated, she modified dull truth to make "a good story." These Beechers, who then would not travel on a public conveyance on Sunday, were half-blind to another commandment. They had, and Harriet not least of them, the Jesuitical mind, with its faint contempt of the public. They fed the public what they thought the public should have. But this trait was the worst of Harriet's flaws.

For the first quarter Catharine offered Mary Dutton her travelling expenses to Cincinnati—"mine were $53"—her board, and $50 for salary; after that, $500 per annum flat." The letter ended with the postscript, "Harriet sends love." Miss Dutton capitulated. In May she came to Cincinnati, and Harriet was reunited with one of her two closest friends.

In the Cincinnati newspapers of March 8, 1833, appeared an advertisement, of which the following is the text:

A NEW GEOGRAPHY
FOR CHILDREN

Corey & Fairbank have in the press,
and will publish in a few days, a

Geography for Children

with numerous maps and engravings,
upon an improved plan.

By CATHARINE E. BEECHER.

Poor, eager, little authoress—her first book, and its announcement did not carry her name! How disappointed Harriet must have been with this notice! She had written the geography, from beginning to end—she, who was to stand at the top of American authorship. Yet now she was so obscure, so small and childlike in appearance, so negligible in personality, that an impatient publisher could drop her off altogether and attribute her book to the emphatic Beecher daughter, who had made a reputation for herself as an educator. Not until the geography began to shoot upward in sales did Harriet's name appear in the advertising.

Slavery at once began to show her its ugly side. The best citizens of Cincinnati, like those of New York and Boston and Hartford, were, if not pro-slavery, at any rate anti-Abolitionist. Many of them, like the Beechers, while disapproving of slavery, adhered to a visionary scheme of gradual emancipation called Colonization. Actually, the slaves were breeding faster than Philanthropy could buy them out of bondage and send them to Liberia; but in the early 1830's the Colonization Society was a stronger organization than the Abolitionists' Anti-Slavery Society, if not so noisy.

It was one thing to observe slavery abstractly from an ivory tower in New England, another to encounter it in the black flesh on the Ohio. (Harriet made powerful use of this essential point in *Uncle Tom's Cabin*—in the dilemma of Senator Bird, the pro-slavery legislator, who, when confronted with the desperate Eliza and her baby, assisted the fugitives in their escape.) A Rev. Mr. Thomas Brainerd, of Cincinnati, discovered the same truth one March day in 1833 on a stroll along the city's river-front. Brainerd, a kind, just, moderate, and able young man was a fair representative of Northern Christian opinion of slavery. In theory he believed it to be an evil; in practice he thought it was impossible to get rid of it. The country could not then think in the billions it would take to end slavery by governmental purchase of the slaves, and anything else meant confiscation of property, which was as abhorrent to good people then as a century later. Nor was Mr. Brainerd blind to the good points of slavery, especially the one most often raised by the South, namely, that slavery was Christianizing a heathen race. This was no feeble argument for a generation that thought it almost better to save a soul than a life.

But Mr. Brainerd was editor of the Cincinnati *Journal;* and after he left the landing that day, he went to his office and penned the following editorial:

UNRIGHTEOUS TRAFFIC

Passing along the wharf Tuesday morning last, our attention was attracted to an unusual number of colored persons on board the steam boat *Emigrant*. Making enquiry, we found they were a cargo of negroes, of all ages and both sexes, amounting to 150 in number, bought in Virginia and Kentucky and intended to be landed and sold at Vicksburg, Mi. They were under the care of two beings in human shape, named Dorsey and Miller, who it seems make the purchase, transporting, and sale of slaves a gainful business. This internal negro traffic appears to be managed in this manner. The traders pass through the northern slave-holding States, and whenever they find (which is a rare case) a master willing to sell his slaves to he knows not whom, to be carried he knows not where, a bargain is struck. Husbands and wives are torn asunder—parents and children are forcibly separated— all the tender sympathies of kindred are recklessly broken up, and all the pleasant associations which cluster around the home of childhood are dissolved. While the process of buying is going on, the victims are collected at certain points and lodged for safe keeping in jails, etc. When enough have been purchased for a *drove,* all are brought together, chained two and two, and in this manner, well guarded, they are driven to the place of embarkation. There they are crowded into the upper deck of a steam boat, confined in irons if necessary for safe keeping, and after a short passage are landed, sold, and distributed in the lower countries. The trader often gains a hundred per cent on the entire lot, making by every drove thousands of dollars.

Of those fellow citizens in adjoining States who have inherited slaves from their ancestors, and who are compelled by a proper regard to their own personal safety, and by a reference to the welfare of the slaves themselves, to hold them in subjection, we have never been disposed to complain. Many masters and mistresses in these circumstances, by giving their slaves proper instruction and uniform kind treatment, make the best of an evil which they have inherited from other generations and which they have a disposition, but not the power, to remedy.

But no apology can be offered for the master who raises *human beings to sell,* and no character on earth is more intrinsically hateful or more universally despised, than that of a slave jockey. We could wish such persons no heavier punishment than to have the natural sympathies of humanity for one day restored to their hearts, and then to let them listen to the thousand sighs which they have wrung from the bosoms of their victims—to have them gaze upon that ocean of tears which they have caused to flow—to have them see in one deep, broad stream the blood which their merciless thongs have drawn from human flesh—and to have their consciences tell in accents of dreadful truth the guilt which those incur who make their wealth by adding mountain weights to the already grievous load of human misery.

The reading of this article probably gave Harriet her first harsh impression of slavery. That she read it there can be little doubt. Besides being, though a weekly, one of Cincinnati's best newspapers, the *Journal* was the leading Presbyterian newspaper of the West. The Rev. Mr. Brainerd, its editor, was an intense admirer of Lyman Beecher and was a little later to become Dr. Beecher's pastoral assistant in the Second Presbyterian Church. Harriet, who read everything, could scarcely have missed the leading editorial in what had already become virtually the family organ of the Beechers.

In April occurred two civic events more or less connected with Harriet's story. Colonel Davies was elected Mayor, Editor Brainerd hailing him as a "capable, firm, and patriotic" man for that place. Cincinnati celebrated its forty-fifth birthday, on which occasion Dr. Daniel Drake made his famous "buckeye" speech, extolling the horse-chestnut tree as one of the chief aids to the settlement of the valley. From this widely circulated address Ohio took its nickname.

During that month, too, the "Misses Beecher" announced the opening (on May 1) of their Western Female Institute. Catharine had incorporated the school, having persuaded thirteen of the town's leading citizens, John J. Foote among them, to serve as the Board of Trustees.

The Misses Beecher were to be in general charge, assisted by several former Hartford teachers—"a Miss Dutton of New England" and "a Miss Baldwin," whom the Misses Beecher had sent three years earlier to found a school in Alabama. There were to be three terms a year of fourteen weeks each; tuition, $18 a term, books furnished free.

In the issue of the Cincinnati *Journal* in which this announcement appeared Harriet may have read about the loss of the steamboat *Reaper,* which struck a snag in the Mississippi and went down in seventy feet of water with the pilot, mate, engineer, "and eight slaves chained together." This ordinary disaster struck Editor Brainerd with peculiar force, because Mate Sells was his next-door neighbor. Still indignant over the slave cargo at the Cincinnati wharf, to his account of the accident Mr. Brainerd added this comment:

"The fate of the slaves is hardly to be deplored. In their watery grave they no longer feel the 'galling chain.' They are free."

The Geography, "by C. and H. Beecher," came out early in May. The novelty of the Geography was that Harriet wrote it as a continuous narrative, instead of a series of facts, names, and figures to be memorized. She had the knack of writing for children, and it never left her. She kept children in mind as readers when she worked on her most serious novels. Perhaps she always considered herself a children's writer.

Once more she was back in the routine of the schoolroom. She wrote to her Hartford friend, "My whole time has been taken up with the labor of our new school, or wasted in the fatigue and lassitude following such labor. . . . Now, Georgiana, let me copy for your delectation a list of matters that I have jotted down for consideration at a teachers' meeting to be held tomorrow night. It runneth as follows. Just hear! 'About quills and paper on the floor; forming classes; drinking in the entry (cold water, mind you); giving leave to speak; recess-bell, etc., etc.' 'You are tired, I see,' says Gilpin, 'so am I,' and I spare you."

Cincinnati was beginning to pall on her already. She could write to Georgiana about the beauty of the road to Walnut Hills—she thought the boles of the beech trees were like columns of a Druid temple—but the town was losing its interest for her. Each day was humdrum and drab— to school each morning, back to her room at night, worn out. Harriet had Mary Dutton, her "Duck," with her now but was otherwise friendless. Life ahead must have looked bleak to her. She was nearly twenty-two, and she was evidently going to be an old maid. There was no suitor yet. As the new western environment lost its tang, she began to fall back again into her morbid state, exclaiming, "Thought, intense emotional thought, has been my disease." She longed to be in some place where she could not help being "thoughtless."

Recently I have been reading the life of Madame de Stael and *Corinne.* I have felt an intense sympathy with many parts of that book, with many parts of her character. But in America feelings vehement and absorbing like hers become still more deep, morbid, and impassioned by the constant habits of self-government which the rigid forms of our society demand. They are repressed, and they burn inward till they burn the very soul, leaving only dust and ashes.

In the spring the divinity students at Lane Seminary had humbly petitioned the new faculty for hot coffee with their meals. The faculty and trustees considered the request, and refused it, unable to supply such a luxury for the pittance they charged for board (menu: "change in bread, vegetables, meats, and soups"). Lodging alone, for example, cost the student $4.50 a month.

Instead of the coveted accompaniment of the "change of bread," the faculty gave the young gentlemen, it is tempting to say, a stone. At any rate, a cemetery. "Inasmuch as those who are studying for the ministry need time and opportunity for meditation and self-examination, a cemetery in proximity to the institution will afford a favorable retreat for that purpose." Accordingly a consecrated acre of the campus was fenced off, though until it should receive tenants it was no more stimulating to meditation than any cow-pasture.

The tenantry were soon to arrive. Asiatic cholera had been smoldering all winter and spring in Cincinnati, with a few deaths every month but one. Because of its late start under the new direction, Lane held a summer term that year. In July there was a sudden outburst of cholera in the Seminary. Lyman Beecher might have quarantined himself safely in his city home but chose to go out to the dormitory, where he suspended classes, appointed a student Board of Health, and put the institution on a hospital basis. In two weeks he stamped out the epidemic, though not before four of his boys had laid down their lives to aid the cause of meditation in the new graveyard.

Though it meant nothing to her materially, Harriet must have been pleased to read in late July the jubilant advertisement of Corey & Fairbank (who owned the book outright) that "Miss Beecher's geography" had gone into its third edition. "Two editions and a large part of the third of this very popular little work have been sold within the last two months." Harriet's first book was a best-seller!

She must have noticed only casually in the August number of the *Western Monthly Magazine* the announcement of a Prize Contest—fifty dollars "for

LYMAN BEECHER

"There is mystery and majesty about that plain, ruddy, nervous old
man which begets awe and reverence." (Page 110.)

the best TALE that shall be presented for publication previous to the tenth day of November, 1833; and Fifty Dollars for the best ESSAY on a literary or scientific subject." A board of "five literary gentlemen" was to award the premiums.

Who was Harriet to imagine she might enter and win this competition, when Judge Hall had such talent as Caroline Lee Hentz's at his disposal?. Mrs. Hentz's new novel, *Lovell's Folly,* was just out and beginning its successful career. Judge Hall called it "the best novel yet published in the West." Besides, Harriet was just then held by a new interest. To the end of her life she loved to "take trips," and now a most delightful one was in prospect—a journey into Kentucky. It was on this famous visit that she got her only first-hand impression of the patriarchal side of slavery and secured the scene of the Shelbys' plantation in which she opened the story of *Uncle Tom's Cabin.*

It is necessary to reconstruct this visit from probabilities, since the accepted biographical account is inaccurate. It seems to have been Mary Dutton's trip primarily, and not Harriet's. Harriet made no friends among her Cincinnati pupils of whom she left any mention. The lively and loveable Mary Dutton inspired schoolgirl crushes. One of her Cincinnati adorers, we can guess, was a child from Washington, Kentucky; and during the summer vacation this young lady's parents invited Mary down for a visit. Mary took Harriet with her.

It was an easy and pleasant journey—by steamboat from Cincinnati sixty miles to Maysville, Kentucky, then back into the country a dozen miles to Washington, climbing the river-canyon wall by a road so steep an extra team had to be hitched to the stage. Though a small village, Washington was important as the western terminus of the post road from the great Washington, the capital. From here the mails were sent down to Maysville and the steamboats.

The accepted account that Harriet stopped here at the plantation which served as the original for the fictional one in her novel cannot be true, if we trust the civic research that has placed a marker on the premises. It was a village home that received Harriet as a guest, a comfortable house, neither large nor especially magnificent, on Washington's principal street nearly opposite the bank. Its half-acre of yard could not have accommodated such slave quarters as Mr. Shelby's, and indeed there is no trace of any having been there, no outline in the deep grass to mark the site of an Uncle Tom's cabin. The most interesting object on the place was and is an ancient brick blockhouse in the rear, with loopholes for the rifles of beleaguered settlers.

But Washington stands on a fertile plateau. Within a radius of a few miles were a number of large plantations, with manor houses and slave quarters like those of the fictional Shelbys. Harriet's village host was a well-to-do man whose womenfolks must have been acquainted with the households of the neighbouring squires. What is more likely than that the three girls—the two little Yankee schoolma'ams and their younger hostess— went cantering out through the August heat on visits? In that open-handed time and place, a visit may have lasted more than a day—though one day would have been ample to give Harriet an indelible memory of a slave-holding Kentucky farm.

She seemed, however, to be retaining nothing, for Harriet took that social occasion to go into one of her long fits of wool-gathering. Mary Dutton years later remembered the future authoress's behaviour. "Harriet did not seem to notice anything that happened, but sat much of the time as though abstracted in thought. When the negroes did funny things and cut up capers, she did not seem to pay the slightest attention to them. After-wards, however, in reading 'Uncle Tom,' I recognized scene after scene of that visit portrayed with the most minute fidelity, and knew at once where the material for that portion of the story had been gathered."

The two teachers returned to Cincinnati in time for Harriet to meet an old acquaintance and a new friend. During the final week in August the stubby, square Calvin Ellis Stowe arrived to take up his duties on the Lane faculty. He brought with him his bride, the former Miss Eliza Tyler. Harriet wrote, "I fell in love with her directly."

Eliza Stowe must have been similarly attracted to Harriet, for the com-radeship of the pair began immediately. Within a week they were attending together the September 3 meeting of the Cincinnati Presbytery which received Professor Stowe's papers and admitted him to membership.

"Let me introduce you to Mrs. Stowe," wrote Harriet, "—a delicate, pretty little woman, with hazel eyes, auburn hair, fair complexion, fine color, a pretty little mouth, fine teeth, and a most interesting simplicity and timidity of manner."

But this Presbytery was important on another score. Dr. Wilson and his adherents chose it as the occasion for their first test of strength with the forces of Lyman Beecher. The strategy was good. Having completed his studies at Yale and Lane Seminary, George Beecher was applying for a licence to preach, which meant that he must undergo that Presbyterian ordeal, a public examination into his beliefs by questioners seeking to upset him. Although the accused invariably denied it, it was always the assumption that as one Beecher thought, so thought all. Unquestionably George was coming up for his test bearing his father's blessing. It would be much easier for the inquisitors to confound a stripling than a seasoned wrangler like his father. If George Beecher could be cast out as a heretic, the inference would follow that Dr. Beecher was also heretical; and Dr. Wilson would have occupied an important outpost in readiness for the major engagement to come.

Harriet described the proceedings in a letter to someone back home— probably Mary Perkins in Hartford—and no more vivid writing had come from her swift pen up to this time. The letter, springing from joy and triumph, is more than a mere account of a clerical meeting. Besides exposing the tight clannishness of the Beecher family, it gives us a clear glance at some of Harriet's own characteristics at twenty-two—the sharpness of her observation, her ability to etch pictures in words (all her life she was to believe in the efficacy of "pictures"), her loyalty to the clan, her scarcely concealed venom for its enemies.

"Mr. Beecher, do you believe in the doctrine of election? Will you please to state your views on that subject?" "Mr. Beecher, do you believe in the imputation of Adam's sin?" "Mr. Beecher, do you believe infants are sinners as soon as they are born?" "Do you believe that infants have unholy natures?" "Do you believe that men are *able* of themselves to obey the commandments of God?" "Mr. Beecher, do you believe that men are active or passive in regeneration?" "Mr. Beecher, do you make any distinction between regeneration and conversion?" "Mr. Beecher, do you think that men are punished for the guilt of Adam's first sin?" "Do you believe in imputed righteousness?"

There was George—eyes flashing and hands going, turning first to right and then to left—"If I understand your question, sir—" "I do not understand your terms, sir." "Do you mean by *nature* thus and so? or so?" "In what sense do you use the word imputation?" "I don't exactly understand you, sir." "Yes, sir" (to right). "No, sir" (to left). "I should think so, sir" (in front).

*   *   *

The following Sunday George Beecher preached his trial sermon. The Presbytery accepted it, ordered him ordained, and assigned him as a probationer to the church at Batavia, located in the adjoining county of Clermont.

Professor Calvin Stowe plunged immediately into Cincinnati's cultural life, for on September 11 he was lecturing before the College of Professional Teachers. He later became so strongly identified with this organization that more than one historian has named him as one of its founders. Actually, the "College" was organized in 1829; but after the advent of Stowe and, a little later, McGuffey, it took on new life.

Inasmuch as the College of Teachers figured influentially in Harriet's life, we must look at it for a moment. It was not a college in the modern sense of that name but an association of teachers somewhat like the present National Education Association. It took in members from all States west of the Alleghenies, met in convention once a year (usually in October), and published its proceedings. Until 1843 it met always in Cincinnati, but after that in Louisville and other western centres of population. The annual session of the College was one of the great events in Cincinnati. The meetings were open, and so great was the popular interest in education that only the city's largest churches and halls could hold the crowds that flocked to hear the various debates, lectures, and papers.

Edward Beecher addressed the College that year. He appeared in Cincinnati unexpectedly, throwing Harriet into a sudden fit of homesickness.

"Edward is with us—poked in like a ghost upon us one day just after George's examination," she wrote in a family letter. "The first that father knew of the matter was seeing him go by the window, and exclaiming, 'There's a man looks like Edward!' and the next minute we were all electrified by seeing him standing among us. To-night Edward and Professor Sturtevant, father, and George have been holding a long chat. At last father and Edward went down cellar to saw wood. Don't that seem natural? I have come up and left them. . . . Oh, it seems like old times, and I am really happy—only a little tired. But, oh dear! he is going away. I wish he could stay a month."

It was a solace, though, to show Edward the Cincinnati newspapers current during his visit. The Geography had now gone into its *fifth edition*, and the advertising was now calling it "The Miss Beechers' Geography."

In October the Miss Beechers, with this success to their credit, were invited to join with the cultural élite of Cincinnati in forming the literary coterie or salon that was for a number of years to flourish as the Semi-Colon Club.

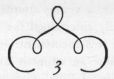

3

The Literary Clubs

THE name of the original proponent of Cincinnati's Semi-Colon Club of the 1830's has been lost in antiquity. It may have been Samuel E. Foote, in whose commodious residence the weekly reunions were most often held. It may have been Dr. Daniel Drake, who was most active in the Club and whose home on Vine Street at the corner of Baker Street (which he loved to call Buckeye Hall) sometimes served as the meeting-place. It may have been any of several others, for Harriet in her old age indicated that there were a number of promoters.

We may be sure, however, that Uncle Samuel Foote had no greater part than that of acquiescence in naming the club. The name was not Mogadore or Cadiz or even Guilford; it was pure pioneer-Cincinnati, cut from the same piece of goods that had already produced Mrs. Trollope's deplorable Bazaar. Even as an old lady Harriet was rather shamefaced about it.

"You know that in Spanish Columbus is called 'Colon,'" she quoted the originator as explaining. "Now he who discovers a new pleasure is certainly half as great as he who discovers a new continent. Therefore, if Colon discovered a new continent, we who have discovered in this club a new pleasure should at least be entitled to the name of 'Semi-Colons.'"

However ridiculous the name, the Semi-Colon Club itself was not ridiculous. It took in as a member nearly everyone in Cincinnati with any pretensions to literary ability—the suburban children, Alice and Phoebe Cary, were too young to have known about it—and a dozen or more of the "Semi-Colons" left their names permanently in the American collections of biography.

For instance, there was young Ormsby M. Mitchel, two years older than Harriet and destined to become a leading astronomer of the United States and discoverer of the period of rotation of the planet Mars, and to die of yellow fever in the South in 1862 as a Major General in the Union Army.

There was William Greene, a young attorney, who lived next door to Samuel Foote and occasionally entertained the Club. He later returned to his native Rhode Island and was Lieutenant Governor of his State during the Civil War. Greene became an eminent constitutional lawyer. Rhode Island called him "Constitutional Billy" Greene.

Charles W. Elliott became well-known later as a historian of New England. James W. Ward made more than a local reputation as a poet and naturalist. General King, the Beecher children's distant relative, was a "witty and entertaining" man with "manners of the old school and the spirit of the new." His wife became such a great social leader in Cincinnati that she inspired a biography of herself which saw publication. Nathan Guilford was the father of Cincinnati's public school system.

Besides these, among the charter members were Judge Hall, Caroline Lee Hentz and her husband ("so sensitive and retiring, he hid away"), Salmon P. Chase, Professor Stowe and his wife, Dr. Drake, Capt. Samuel Foote, and his wife, Elizabeth Foote, and Catharine and Harriet Beecher. Mrs. Foote's sister, Sarah Elliott, of Guilford, who lived with her in Cincinnati, was also a member.

The proceedings of the Club followed a set programme. The circle met Monday evenings at 7:30 o'clock, elected a reader for the evening, then listened to the contributions, which could be submitted signed or anonymous. Following a discussion, the Club relaxed for refreshments, "topped off with a gay Virginia reel led by the reader of the evening and a merry-hearted girl." When Capt. Samuel Foote gave the *soirée,* the guest could rely on a glass of that connoisseur's fine old sherry or Madeira with the sandwiches and coffee.

E. D. Mansfield, another of the Club's founders, remembered the behaviours of the Beecher sisters on these engaging evenings. "Miss Harriet Beecher was not distinguished for conversation, but when she did speak, she showed something of the peculiar strength and humor of her mind. Her sister, Miss Catharine Beecher, was a far more easy and fluent conversationalist. Indeed, few people had more talent to entertain a company or keep the ball of conversation going than Miss Beecher, and she was as willing as able for the task."

The activities of the Semi-Colon Club suited Harriet Beecher, as she would have expressed it, to a T. She had begun to take delight in exercising her literary powers. Her family and other intimates were already treasuring her letters as works of genius. The Club's tolerance of, indeed its preference for, anonymity was precisely to her young liking. She was still too shy, too sensitive to criticism, to send her own identity uncloaked out upon such a stage. In fact, she was never quite to lose this juvenile shrinking from public responsibility. The plaudits and flattery of the world could not build in her a complete self-confidence. The afternoon of her career found her writing under a pseudonym. The name Harriet Beecher Stowe was familiar from St. Petersburg to San Francisco, but until senility came upon her she invariably signed her letters with a simple "H. B. Stowe."

Anonymity released Harriet's fancy, and from the start she devoted much of her leisure to writing for the Semi-Colon Club. She was soon at work upon a character sketch of her father's foster-father, his Uncle Lot Benton, of Guilford. Lyman Beecher had, in his inimitable way, told his children so many stories of this crusty type that Harriet knew the dead-and-gone Uncle Lot almost as well as if she and not her father had been his foster-child.

The story of this sketch, which was to win Judge Hall's fifty-dollar prize, to convince Harriet that authorship was her true *métier,* and to fill for the student a niche in the history of American fiction, offers some perplexities.

It does not seem to have been so simple as the accepted biographical statement, to wit, that Harriet wrote *Uncle Lot* for the *Western Monthly Magazine's* contest, submitted it, and "easily took the prize." That she took it easily there is no reason to doubt—more easily, perhaps, than Annie Fields, who wrote Mrs. Stowe's standard biography, may have supposed. There are grounds for thinking that Harriet had the assurance of winning the prize before she ever consented to enter the competition.

When he announced the contest in August, Judge Hall set November 10 as the date on which all competing manuscripts must be in his hands, promising to publish the winning story in the December number of his magazine. Instead, in December he announced that because of the disappointing quality of the entries, he was extending the contest to February 1, 1834, "in order that all who are competent may have the opportunity of entering into the competition." Harriet Beecher, therefore, did not submit her winning entry within the original limits of the contest.

How, then, did she happen to compete, when her own timidity would have told her that she had no chance to win? She could not bear criticism, she thought; but what implied criticism would be harder to bear than to have her contribution rejected in a contest? It is unnecessary to repeat here the argument supporting the belief that she wrote *Uncle Lot* that fall only as an anonymous offering to the programme of the Semi-Colon Club. Judge Hall heard it read, discovered the name of the writer (and how diligent must have been the enquiry to reveal an authoress so uncertain of her powers that she shrank from stepping out alone even upon the title-page of a prosy school-textbook!), and persuaded her to submit her composition in the prize contest, extending the time to allow Harriet to expand into a rounded fiction-tale what was still only an indeterminate sketch.

We can well believe that the judge-editor pricked up his ears at the unfolding of this sketch and that his fellow-members of the Club were hushed and fascinated as they listened. Whether they knew it or not, they were hearing a new note struck in American literature, a note still sounding in Twentieth-Century ears. We of today find the character of Uncle Lot commonplace, for we have met him and his kind in dozens of stories, plays, and novels dating from Sarah Orne Jewett to the present. It was not commonplace on a Monday evening in November, 1833. Harriet was then introducing her New England to the American audience for the first time— the shrewd, pious, capable, humorous New England that has gone into our tradition rather than the tragic New England portrayed by her contemporary, Nathaniel Hawthorne. It was one of the two great pictures she painted that proved imperishable. The other was that of African slavery.

She took unusual care in the composition of *Uncle Lot*. With fame and professional assurance was to come a carelessness of technique comfortable to her impatient nature but which marred some of her most important work. As a tyro athirst for local applause, she ran no risks. Immature and undistinguished as *Uncle Lot* is as a story, it nevertheless contains some of Harriet's most deft writing. E. D. Mansfield always insisted that her earlier stories and sketches, which few read even during her years of supremacy, exhibited all the genius of her later masterpieces. As for *Uncle Lot,* Harriet's first published story, if indeed it is not the first fiction story she ever wrote, John Erskine, the modern critic who has made the closest study of Mrs. Stowe's works, remarks that "the heroic flame already burns in it."

It has been a convenience here to refer to the story by the title of *Uncle Lot.* Harriet called it that in her authorized biography, and subsequent writers followed the precedent, though actually the story never appeared under that name. Judge Hall published it in the April, 1834, number of his magazine as "*A New England Sketch,* by Miss Harriet E. Beecher." It spread over the front half of the issue and was followed immediately by *The Lost Pilot,* a poem by Hannah F. Gould, the Massachusetts poetess. Harriet was making her professional bow in good company, for Miss Gould, though an exceedingly minor poet, held a respectable place in periodical literature.

Though negligible as a literary product, *Uncle Lot* has deserved this more than sidelong glance, and not only because of its historical place in the forefront of American realism. Harriet looked back on the story as the work that "gave her an insight into her own ability." It gave the same insight to some others who formed a group perhaps more influential in Harriet's early career than the little authoress herself—the members of her family. Slender as was to be her literary output during the eighteen years to come, the Beechers never flagged in their belief that Harriet was a genius and never allowed her to forget it. Spiritually and mentally they pointed her for her destiny. From this time forth she was the family prophetess.

An interesting coda attaches to the story of *Uncle Lot.* In 1843 Harriet collected fifteen of her published sketches and short stories (which may have been all of them) and brought them out as a book, entitled *The Mayflower; or, Sketches of Scenes and Characters among The Descendants of The Pilgrims.* The well-known educator, Catharine E. Beecher, whose influence probably induced Harper's to undertake the volume, introduced it to the public with a preface in which she justified the writing and reading of fiction of the "safe and valuable" sort. Some such apology was needed by a daughter of Lyman Beecher and sister of Dr. Edward Beecher.

By that time Harriet had gained a certain professional poise. It struck her then that her first story was entirely too personal for presentation upon a national stage. In it she had used outright the name of her father's foster-father and had put forth as fiction an episode soon to appear in Lyman Beecher's autobiography as fact. Accordingly, she changed the name of Uncle Lot in the story, and it appeared in the *Mayflower* as *Uncle Tim.*

This was not to be the only instance of Harriet's changing her mind about the title of a published work. Her novel *Dred* was out ten or a dozen years when on a new edition she rechristened it *Nina Gordon.* Then, before the end of her life, she repented of this alteration and once more restored the original name. To add a touch to the comedy, it may be remarked that neither title was adequate for the novel.

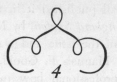

4

End of Spinsterhood

HARRIET's letter about the stormy Presbytery had grazed two men who were soon to step with effect into her life-story. Theodore Dwight Weld had entered Lane Theological Seminary that fall as a divinity student, arriving in Cincinnati as a deck-passenger on a steamboat from Pittsburgh. Deck-passengers paid no fare, "found" themselves, enjoyed no cabin privileges, and were expected to help fuel the boat at the wood-landings.

To a daughter in Israel like Harriet, Weld was a romantic and even glamorous figure. He was a well-recognized type of the neo-pioneer times, the itinerant zealot—a knight-errant of God's kingdom on earth, a sort of evangelical Johnny Appleseed scattering seeds of salvation, "manual-labour" colleges, Temperance, and, of late, Abolition of American slavery. The last-named variety shot up and bore fruit poisonous to Lyman Beecher and his talented daughter.

In 1833 Weld was thirty years of age. His personality was fascinating, especially to the young; his oratory and eloquence no less so. Indeed, he towered so high above the crest of Walnut Hills that even contemporary Cincinnati historians supposed him to be a member of the Seminary's faculty. He was never that, though he had the confidential promise of a professorship and may have nursed a secret ambition to supplant Lyman Beecher himself. Already he had a national reputation as a lecturer. He came to Cincinnati no stranger to Dr. Beecher, having some years previously been one of the youths who attached themselves to the Doctor in Hanover Street, when he was battling the Unitarian Satan. At that time Weld was a member of the pious troupe travelling with the celebrated revivalist, Charles Grandison Finney.

Prophecy came to pass in the autumn of 1833. Dr. Beecher's presidency of Lane Seminary brought an enrollment of more than one hundred earnest young men. At one bound the institution had become the second strongest

school in Ohio. No inconsiderable part of the sudden increment was a
response to the volunteer missionary work of Theodore D. Weld.

He was that *beau ideal* of evangelical Protestantism, the sinner reclaimed.
Threatened with blindness when a schoolboy in Phillips (Andover)
Academy, he mastered a practical subject for himself—the scientific cultivation of memory—so well that at seventeen he began to lecture on it. Fringe
sciences, such as mnemonics and phrenology, were then gaining a wide
credence and vogue. (Harriet and Henry Ward Beecher both became converts to phrenology later.) Weld expounded mnemonics to paying
audiences for three years, travelling as far south as North Carolina; and
then, replenished in purse and somewhat restored in vision, at twenty-one
he entered Hamilton College, at Clinton, New York.

Evangelist Finney came to near-by Utica to conduct a protracted meeting,
reaching out for the Hamilton students. Weld opposed the revival in the
college, where his influence was strong. Finney tricked him into a service
and preached a sermon straight at him, by name and in the second person.
Weld was furious. Next day he met Finney and publicly reviled him; but
the evangelist took the tirade with such Christlike humility that Weld's
heart was broken. He flung himself into Finney's arms, and the two
emotionalists sobbed and prayed together. Weld abandoned Hamilton
College and attached himself to Finney's train as implicitly as the Galilean
fishermen obeyed the Master's "Come ye after me!"

Thereafter Weld became an adventurer for the Lord, travelling from
Labrador to Alabama, lecturing and exhorting, serving as fiscal agent for
and part-time student in the new and radical Oneida Institute, and finally,
in 1831, as general agent for the National Manual Labour Society.

Weld came to Lane Seminary in 1833 a recent convert to the cause of
Abolition. As a youthful lecturer, observing slavery in North Carolina and
Virginia, he had turned against the "peculiar institution"; but, like the
average opponent of slavery, North or South, he had adopted the palliative
of Colonization. In the summer of 1832 William Lloyd Garrison brought
out his crushing *Thoughts on African Colonization,* in which he branded
the scheme as "the scurvy device of the men-stealers." The book convinced
Weld, who, on his tour of the South that year talked immediate Abolition
everywhere he went and even debated it with the Rev. Dr. Allen, the leading
Presbyterian clergyman of Huntsville, Alabama, if not of his State. It throws
a significant light on the state of feeling toward the fatal question that a

Yankee could crusade for Abolition in the deep South as late as the year 1832.

And not only crusade but make converts, though it has to be admitted that Theodore Weld was no ordinary Yankee. An Oberlin professor later testified of him that he had seen "crowds of bearded men held spellbound by his power for hours together, and for twenty evenings in succession." On this trip, partly no doubt because of his former brief friendship with Lyman Beecher, partly perhaps for private and personal reasons, he had begun to plump for Lane Seminary. As a result of his debate, several young men of Huntsville resolved to attend Lane the following year, including Dr. Allen's son.

Weld made an even more important convert to Abolition in Huntsville. A well-to-do lawyer and cotton planter named James G. Birney was an elder of Dr. Allen's church. He was a pious, conscientious man, already an adherent to Colonization. Young Weld's arguments convinced him so thoroughly of the error of Colonization that he liberated his slaves and moved back to his birthplace, Danville, Kentucky, to devote the rest of his life to the Abolition cause. Birney, whose influence, direct and indirect, was to be a power in Harriet's career, became the Anti-Slavery party's candidate for President in 1840 and 1844.

On his way south in 1832, Weld had stopped in Cincinnati, where he lectured for a week on Manual Labour. The Beechers had not yet arrived. While there Weld met the Rev. Mr. F. Y. Vail, the Lane agent whose initiative was bringing Lyman Beecher to Cincinnati. The two had been in correspondence before, and Vail had become privy to an ambitious educational scheme incubating in the East. Some wealthy gentlemen in Rochester, New York, had offered to back young Weld in setting up "a great model Manual-Labour institution for the nation."

The prospect of educational funds far greater than any Lyman Beecher could attract, excited the eleemosynary greed of the Rev. Mr. Vail. Why, he argued with Weld (and, it appears, with Weld's backers), waste such an institution on the East, when there was a chance to do something for "the rising millions of the West"? Why spade new ground at Rochester, when at Cincinnati there was already a nucleus to build around? Vail hinted at even greater endowments, if Weld would adopt Lane Seminary for his project: "We only need to have your plan and efforts identified with our own . . . to make it strictly a national, model institution. We want now, dear brother, just such a man as you are (I do not flatter you) to be the mainspring in the whole concern."

Mainspring does not necessarily mean *President,* though an ambitious young man could interpret it so. In the summer of 1832 Vail was equally cautious, whispering to Weld, "And remember that, by God's blessing, you are yet perhaps to bear one of the four corners of our institution by occupying the chair of Sacred Rhetoric and Oratory." He was speaking to a man without formal education adequate to a professorship, without even a college degree—to a man whom Lyman later could call "uneducated."

Weld listened, inhaled the exhilaration of the West, went over the prospects at Walnut Hills, and "was satisfied that was the place for us." He crossed the Ohio already an impromptu missionary for Lane Seminary. Did Lyman Beecher know of this private understanding when Theodore Weld arrived in Cincinnati as a student? Probably not, though he was to be apprized of another connection of this extraordinary Freshman equally embarrassing.

Weld had not been the only Colonizationist converted to Abolition by Garrison's *Thoughts.* In New York the philanthropic merchant, Arthur Tappan, had been equally brought around by that book—and Tappan's unsecured note-of-hand was the "endowment" which paid Lyman Beecher's salary. Upon his return from the South, Weld called on Tappan, and it did not take the two reformers long to discover that they saw eye to eye on slavery. After telling the financier something about his work and ambitions for Lane, Weld spoke of his intention "to introduce anti-slavery sentiments" into the Seminary, receiving Tappan's full support. It is an illuminating footnote to history. A body of serious-minded divinity students may be presumed to have been as well abreast of the times and of issues as any special group to be found, and yet in 1833 it was necessary to *introduce* the question of slavery to the students of Lane Seminary as a conscious effort. Slavery as an issue virtually did not yet exist in the North. It was not in the range of familiar thought.

Weld went on to Oneida, where he ruthlessly raided the Institute which had once employed him, his influence persuading some twenty-six of the Institute's students to transfer to Lane Seminary. With three comrades from Oneida, Weld made his way to western New York, where, at the headwaters of French Creek, the godly quartette bought a boat for six dollars and drifted down to the Allegheny River and thence to Pittsburgh and the economical deck of the steamboat. It was a typical voyage, for the drifters stopped at every opportunity to talk Abolition and hold prayer-meetings. One such halting-place must have been Meadville, Pennsylvania, a centre of piety and the seat of Allegheny College, which the Methodists had just taken over from the Presbyterians.

Armed with his secret understanding with Vail, standing closer in the confidence of the Seminary's principal "angel" than did Dr. Beecher himself, this disconcerting undergraduate at once began to assume authority. Did the students object to the professor of Ecclesiastical History as a dull bore? Weld led a committee to inform President Beecher that the class would attend the despised lectures no longer. A bewildered president could only compromise. His "boys" must make a show of obedience, attend Professor ——'s class once a week, "and behave," but—"Stowe and I will take care of you the rest of the time."

Small wonder Lyman Beecher thought his charges "a little uncivilized"! This understated his real opinion, for Weld was a hair shirt for president and faculty. "In the estimation of the class," complained an old, old man, "he was president." But bitterness now lay in ashes, and the octogenarian consoled himself with an afterthought—"We never quarrelled, however."

If they had quarrelled, had Beecher pitched out the autocrat of the dormitory or gone down himself to dignified defeat, his daughter Harriet might never have made history. A sheltered, contented prophetess could not have acquired that complete kinship with the lowly necessary to make her the first proletarian novelist. Weld bore her no ill will; but his subsequent deed, besides blighting her father's career, cast over the remainder of Harriet's youth the shadow of poverty and despair.

By the end of 1833 the new President's House at Walnut Hills (on the Montgomery turnpike, adjoining the Seminary yard on the north) was ready for occupancy, and Dr. Beecher moved out there with all his dependents and retainers, except Catharine and Harriet. Those two went to board with a Mrs. S. Wright to be near their school, which spread through a series of rooms at the corner of Fourth and Sycamore Streets.

Catharine Beecher that term attained her ambition to direct a school from without but appears to have forgotten her promise to let her sister retreat with pay into the comfortable position of spiritual adviser to the pupils. Harriet continued to teach her regular classes. The teachers all had stated salaries, but Harriet chose to dip into the school treasury only as she needed money. She kept no accounts, was thoughtless about her expenditures, and thus progressed toward one of the unhappier experiences of her life.

Indeed, the little spinster seems to have resigned herself that year to a life spent in the halls of pedagogy. Despite Catharine's grand prospectus of Harriet living by her pen, the future author's entire literary output of the winter was the brief and ineffective sketch of her mother, Roxana Beecher, which appeared (under the title, *Aunt Mary*) in the *Western Monthly Magazine* three months after the publication of the Prize Tale. For the rest, Harriet threw herself into church work, being elected secretary of the Home Missionary Society of the Second Presbyterian Church (Catharine was secretary of the Female Tract Society), amused herself with anonymous contributions to the Semi-Colon Club, and contemplated the teaching profession which seemed to be her fate.

Being a Beecher, she contemplated it with an eye to reform, and the reform she and her sister proposed was a daring one. To understand how radical was their position, we have to realize that in the 1830's the only teaching opportunity for women—in fact, the only profession open to them, except for the talented few who could earn a living as writers—lay in the female dovecotes, where they instructed young ladies in deportment and a few elegant accomplishments. Boys received male instruction. The "deestrict schoolmaster," with his cane and dog-eared primer, was the universal type of elementary educator.

The two Beecher girls proposed to open this vast field of public education to women as teachers. Catharine Beecher stands today as the pioneer in this eventually successful movement, though we can not doubt that Harriet contributed to the inception of the splendid project. Her mind was never one to accept leadership blindly. She always listened to reason but chose in the end to form her own decisions. As she grew older this characteristic stiffened. Her whole life for the next twenty years was to be a hard training in independence of thought and action.

Dr. Beecher's house at Walnut Hills was a substantial brick structure with a rear wing supporting a balcony at the second story. It stood in a grove of oak trees on an eminence above the road, which it fronted. At the end of the wing in back was a barn for the horse, cow, and family carryall. Beyond the stable flowed a small brook, and the brook hemmed the virgin forest.

(The house still stands in Cincinnati, at the corner of what are now called Gilbert Avenue and Foraker Street. Around this cradle of a race's emancipation has gathered an extensive coloured population, and the historic Beecher residence, no longer in a grove or near a stream, is a Negro boarding house. Diagonally across Gilbert Avenue abuts one end of a short thoroughfare called Beecher Street. It is Cincinnati's civic tribute to the most famous family it ever entertained as citizens.)

The Doctor's study was a ground-floor room, this time, at the end of the house facing Lane Seminary. It had its own outside door, making it a professional office. Even the newness and convenience of this room could not make Dr. Beecher orderly. He covered the floor at once with a vast accumulation of sermons and other papers, which he meant to sort and discard or file neatly away but somehow never got around to doing.

At fifty-eight, the sporting blood still coursed in the Doctor's arteries. One of his sons has left an unforgettable picture of the clergyman at work in his sanctum, bending in absorption over his manuscript, his dusty authorities piled high on the desk before him. Beside the outer door stood his fowling-piece, loaded and primed. At the migrating seasons the flights of passenger pigeons were darkening the sky above suburban Cincinnati. Now and then some weary flock descended to the tulip and beech trees across the brook, weighting the boughs sometimes to the breaking-point. The whistling thunder of wings could always take Dr. Beecher's attention from his sermon. He dashed out, seizing his gun as he ran. Presently the son heard shots, and then back in popped the Doctor with a basket of dripping game for supper.

Commodious though the house was, it was none too large for the new ménage, since it now took four white servants—two hired women inside and two hired men outside—to maintain Dr. Beecher's position. The carryall which the Doctor bought was put to such constant use that soon it was the "old carryall." Everything had to be bought in town. It was a day when the family marketing was done by the heads of households. If you wanted to meet the élite of Cincinnati—its lawyers, judges, doctors, bankers, and leading merchants—you visited one of the fine markets early in the morning. They were all there, with their baskets on their arms.

Dr. Beecher's clerical duties at the Second Presbyterian Church often took him into town in the evening. Thus, what with shopping tours and social calls added, the carryall was constantly on the road, Old Charlie, the spotted white horse, making half a dozen trips every day. On Saturdays the carryall brought out Catharine and Harriet, the latter to renew and cement her friendship with pretty Mrs. Stowe. Professor Stowe, we have to assume, had rented a house near the Seminary, though houses in Walnut Hills were then few.

From Dr. Beecher's study door a path led across his driveway to a gate in the Seminary fence. Over this path he could skip quickly to chapel or his lectures, but the path was equally convenient for Theodore Weld and his grievance committees, when they wanted to gain the ear of titular authority. Weld was not scrupling to go over the head of the Seminary president and report on conditions at Lane directly to the institution's financial supporter, Arthur Tappan; and so, that spring, we have the painful spectacle of Lyman Beecher making explanations to his financial support.

Primed by someone whose identity we can guess, Tappan had wanted to know if Lane Seminary were inhospitable to Negro students. On the contrary, Beecher replied, there was at the moment a Negro student enrolled in the new class—James Bradley, who had been a slave. True, Bradley had been too timid to attend the students' levee with which the Doctor had "warmed" his new house; but, as Beecher had said to Weld at the time, "if I had thought of his feeling so, I would have gone to him personally and told him he *must* come." Having disposed of this question—and Dr. Beecher did not need to tell Tappan specifically that Lane was then the *only* theological school in America that would admit a Negro—the beset president went on to state his own attitude toward slavery.

> Were it in my power to put an end to slavery immediately, I would do it; but it is not. . . . I would press the consciences, so far as they have any, of the Southerners, and shake their fears, and press their interests, as the Abolitionists are doing; but then, that the pressure might avail, I would not hermetically seal their hearts by cutting off the facilities of emancipation, and tempt them to delay it till insurrection might do the work, but offer them an easy, practicable way of doing their duty, as the Colonizationists are doing.

We may imagine that this plea met a cold reception in New York. Colonization had become the *bête noire* of the Abolitionists, and Tappan was a new convert to Abolition.

Weld's letter of complaint to Arthur Tappan had been mere sniping on his part. During the winter he canvassed thoroughly the student-body of Lane Seminary and by April was ready to go ahead with his plan to turn the school into an Abolition centre. "We . . . knew pretty well where we stood." He therefore proposed a Seminary debate on the slavery question and went through the formality of asking faculty consent.

Dr. Beecher, while expressing entire sympathy with the sentiment behind the project, deferred decision, consulted with the trustees, and then "advised postponement." He was too cautious to forbid the debate. Weld brushed aside the semi-disapproval, and the discussion began. For eighteen evenings it continued, as Cincinnati took cognizance of the disturbance in the hills and grew uneasy. Dr. Beecher could not ignore the conflagration under his official roof. When had that enchanting eloquence ever failed— the magic that had won over the hostile Toleration audience in New Haven, that in Unitarian Boston had restored the prestige of the Puritan? It failed now. The Doctor took the floor to uphold the negative.

"Boys, you are right in your views but impracticable in your measures. Mining and quiet strategy are better as well as safer methods of taking a city than to do it by storm. You are right, but in your way you can't succeed."

Thus he pitted his influence against Weld's with "his boys," and the result was humiliating. Even with the advantage of speaking to many who were Southerners—slave-owners themselves, and the sons of slave-owners— Dr. Beecher could swing only one vote to the support of Colonization. The resolution advocating immediate emancipation carried unanimously.

The students at once formed themselves into the Lane Seminary Anti-Slavery Society and began to take practical measures.

"We have formed a large and efficient organization for elevating the colored people in Cincinnati," Weld wrote to Arthur Tappan; "have established a Lyceum among them, and lecture three or four evenings a week on Grammar, Geography, Arithmetic, Natural Philosophy, etc. Besides this, an evening free school, for teaching them to read, is in operation every week-day evening, and we are about establishing one or two more. . . . I visited this week about thirty families, and found some members of more than half . . . were in bondage."

This was painting the picture prettily. The students had caused to be published in the Cincinnati papers their declaration of principles, one article of which proclaimed their belief in "social intercourse according to character, irrespective of color"; and a scandalized city saw white divinity students walking its streets with groups of Negroes, male and female, in perfect fraternity. The town's anger began to rise, nor was it confined to the Main Street bars and the dives of the river-front. Dr. Beecher warned the mutineers—"If you will visit in colored families, and walk with them in the streets, you will be overwhelmed."

They would not listen. One zealot moved down into the city to board with a Negro family. The volunteer teachers, when belated, passed the nights in coloured households. They freely accepted the hospitality of Negro tables and continued to flaunt their defiant democracy before the town, rejoicing in the insults flung at them. A group of young Negresses hired a carriage and drove out to the Seminary, where the students received them "with marked attention." The Cincinnati mob was growling now, and the newspapers in alarm ceased to publish any more developments of the scandal.

Dr. Beecher's implied reproof for the students and assurance for the city was a sermon in advocacy of Colonization preached from his Second Presbyterian pulpit. The hard-hitting logician, Professor Stowe, delivered a public lecture in Cincinnati, proving beyond peradventure that Colonization was the only practicable method of ending slavery yet advanced. Officially, at least, Lane Seminary still stood for the rights of property and reform by orderly processes.

Dr. Beecher himself believed that it would all blow over. Admitting that "his boys" were an undisciplined lot, he calmly "waited for the teachings of wisdom and experience from above. If we and our friends do not amplify the evil by too much alarm, impatience, and attempt at regulation, the evil will subside and pass away."

Was Harriet's faith in her father so "perfectly triumphant" now? Probably so, though her own belief in Colonization, if she held it, was to be shaken by events before much more time passed. But that spring a new anticipation diverted her attention from the excitement at Walnut Hills. Henry Ward Beecher was to be graduated from Amherst in June, and she made up her mind to attend the Commencement.

The journey, to be taken with Mary Dutton, was not daunting to even a frail young woman who possessed the Beecher courage and had already made the trip into the West—stagecoaches to Toledo, Lake Erie steamboat to Buffalo, thence by stage via Albany into Massachusetts. Henry would come back with her, for he intended to enter Lane as a student in the autumn. He was her nearest brother and her favourite one, and she wanted to see him receive his diploma. She had never witnessed the graduation of any other brothers. The cost of the trip was no obstacle, since she could draw all the money required from the treasury of the Western Female Academy.

Was there not the thought in her mind, too, that this might be her last chance? The masculine West, where New England spinsters went to find husbands, had not produced one for Harriet, nor even a lover. It would take an extraordinary set of coincidences to generate a mate for this sphinxlike maiden—a mind capable of understanding the depth of her own and thrown by some chance into intimacy with her. She was too singular for casual appreciation. But during an idyllic June week on an eastern campus she might well meet her mate. How comfortable would be the prospect of a life spent in her own New England as a clergyman's wife, far from this frontier and its great Trouble!

On her journey she played the family genius for those left behind in Cincinnati, practising her trade in her letters. She described the passengers in the Ohio stagecoach:

> There was a portly, rosy, clever Mr. Smith, or Jones, or something the like; and a New Orleans girl looking like distraction, as far as dress in concerned, but with the prettiest language and softest intonations in the world, and one of those faces which, while you say it isn't handsome, keeps you looking all the time to see what it can be that is so pretty about it. Then there was Miss B., an independent, good-natured, do-as-I-please sort of a body, who seemed of perpetual motion from morning till night. Poor Miss D. said, when we stopped at night, "Oh, dear! I suppose Lydia will be fiddling about our room till morning, and we shall not one of us sleep."
>
> Then, by way of contrast, there was a Mr. Mitchell, the most gentlemanly, obliging man that ever changed his seat forty times a day to please a lady. Oh, yes, he could ride outside,—or, oh, certainly, he could ride inside,—he had no objection to this, or that, or the other. Indeed, it was difficult to say what could come amiss to him. He speaks in a soft, quiet manner, with something of a drawl, using very correct, well-chosen language, and pronouncing all his words with carefulness; has everything in his dress and travelling appointments *comme il faut;* and seems to think there is abundant time for everything that is to be done in this world, without, as he says, "any unnecessary excitement." Before the party had fully discovered his name he was usually designated as "the obliging gentleman," or "that gentleman who is so accommodating."

But in that day and place there was no escaping the problem on which a sensitive and well-brought-up young lady tried in vain to close eyes and ears.

Yet our friend, withal, is of Irish extraction, and I have seen him roused to talk with both hands and a dozen words in a breath. He fell into a little talk about abolition and slavery with our good Mr. Jones, a man whose mode of reasoning consists in repeating the same sentence at regular intervals as long as you choose to answer it. This man, who was finally convinced that Negroes were black, used it as an irrefragable argument to all that could be said, and at last began to deduce from it that they might just as well be slaves as anything else, and so he proceeded until all the philanthropy of our friend was roused, and he sprung up all lively and oratorical and gesticulatory and indignant to my heart's content. I like to see a quiet man that can be roused.

The week at Amherst was, at any rate, idyllic. Henry was popular with his classmates. He was gay, full of the Beecher humour, devoted to the girlish-looking older sister over whom he towered, though he was not a tall man. A latter-day Demosthenes, he had practised remedies for his thickness of tongue, and with effect. He who had been so dull with his books as a child surprised Harriet with his statement that he had stood "next to the head of the class" in mathematics, a weak subject with him. He added hastily, "We were standing in a circle."

Lamentably the record gives few other details of this first visit of Harriet to the East after her western migration. The first bit of steam railway built west of the Hudson River was in operation in 1834 between Schenectady and Albany, New York, but we do not know if Harriet availed herself of the novel transportation and became the first Beecher to ride on "the train of cars." Undoubtedly she visited old friends in Hartford and Guilford. We know that she and her brother went to New York and travelled from there to Cincinnati. They "thought themselves fortunate" that the trip took only ten days.

Before she left the East, however, a letter brought Harriet a severe shock. Her dearest Cincinnati friend, Mrs. Eliza Stowe, was dead.

It was a dismal summer for the Queen City. For the third successive year the cholera appeared. The outbreak was not so acute as that of 1832, but it was persistent and steady. An atmosphere of hopelessness and despair fell over the sun-baked town. As the well-to-do fled to healthier regions, many shops put up their shutters indefinitely, and business went into a deep but local depression. Numerous citizens, convinced that Cincinnati would always be a plague-spot, threw their properties on the market at distress prices. Real-estate values slumped to a panic level.

On July 18 a relieved president saw Lane Seminary close for the summer. The little anti-slavery flurry would die out before the resumption of the school in October, and Dr. Beecher departed on a money-raising tour of the East, accompanied by his daughter Catharine, whose mission it was to secure more teachers for her Western Female Academy. Professor Stowe probably intended to be one of the party, but his young, pretty wife was ailing, and he remained at Walnut Hills with her. It was a fatal time in Cincinnati for anyone to be ailing.

Dr. Beecher's departure was succeeded by a heat-spell of an intensity unusual even for Cincinnati. In it Mrs. Stowe wilted, until before they knew it she was at death's door. The conscientious and efficient Aunt Esther Beecher moved over and took charge for the helpless Professor. Mrs. Lyman Beecher, herself in a decline, called as often as she could, morbidly fascinated by death. Mrs. Stowe died on August 6 and was buried in the Seminary graveyard.

Her obituary notice in the *Journal* was an extraordinary composition even for a time in which the clergy were apt to welter publicly in their personal bereavements. The death notices of ordinary folk were much as they are today; but a preacher was derelict who did not use the last moments of some dear one to point a moral for sinners, afford forensic material for his brethren of the cloth, or adduce an implied proof of the existence of that hereafter which the dying are supposed to see in their transitional gaze. Calvin Stowe—we can assume that he wrote his wife's obituary, since it was of a piece with other examples of naive exhibitionism on his part which will punctuate this history—went further. Besides bringing in the glimpse of Paradise, he supplied clinical information.

After reciting Eliza's name, age, parentage, domestic status, and education, and summarizing her as "a lovely woman and a sweet singer," the notice stated that "she became pious in the year 1825 during the revival in Dartmouth College, her father being the president of that institution. . . . She was beloved with an ardor and devotedness of affection not often awarded to an imperfect mortal." About six months before she came to the West "she was attacked by scrofulous disease" which "laid her loveliness in ruins. . . . Everything taken upon the stomach occasioned distress." When her husband saw the end was near, he "wept aloud. She sweetly said, 'Weep not for me,' and asked him to repeat the 14th and 15th chapters of John." In her final moments she exclaimed, " 'Oh, joy—joy unspeakable and full of glory—full of glory!' Her last words were, 'I am a lamb'—evidently thinking of her favorite 23rd Psalm."

It is a shame to smile. Calvin Stowe worshipped his lost bride. If he chose to expose his domestic intimacies, it was just his innocent way.

The little flurry at Lane did not die out in Dr. Beecher's absence but became a tempest that set a date in the history of the Abolition movement. Like many college students in those days of tedious and costly travel, some fifty or sixty of the undergraduates elected to pass the long vacation in the dormitory, paying the nominal board charged them. There was a new mass interest to make time pass quickly—the elevation of the black people of Cincinnati. With no lectures or examinations to compete for their attention, the students threw themselves recklessly into their missionary work.

(In 1834 the coloured community of Cincinnati numbered less than a thousand individuals. In 1829 there had been nearly four times that many in the city, each claiming to possess legal freedom. Following a bloody disturbance in 1830, the authorities, as a good-neighbour gesture toward the South, began to enforce a registration law designed to establish the civil status of Ohio's Negro residents, and the Cincinnati colony melted away. The vanishing members presumably made their way to Canada or to free States less inquisitive than Ohio.)

There was no canny president now to caution his boys against giving offense, but one pair of vengeful eyes watched Theodore Weld. The flouted Professor of Ecclesiastical History knew that he or Weld must leave Lane Seminary, and he intended to force out Weld, if possible. His chance came in mid-August, when the white theologians entertained another picnic-party of Negresses on the Seminary grounds. Cincinnati's wrath erupted in an editorial denunciation of the Lane Anti-Slavery Society as a disgrace to the institution and a threat to the noble cause of education. "The indignation of the public will put it down."

This and the perhaps feigned alarm of the outraged professor convinced what trustees remained in the pestilential city that the mob was about to start out the Montgomery Pike for Walnut Hills. The executive committee could speak with authority if not with legal force for the full Board, and it adopted a resolution announcing the intention to abolish the Lane Anti-

Slavery Society at the beginning of the full term and to prohibit the discussion of the slavery issue "in any public room of the Seminary."

The committee not only adopted this resolution but—over the protest of Professor Stowe, who roused from his grief to see the danger—*published it*. Thus, what might have been hidden as a private difficulty became a national scandal, as newspaper after newspaper scissored the Cincinnati exchanges brought by the slow mails, and in New York an aghast *Evangelist* wanted to know in what age and country we were living, "and with whose endowments was the Seminary founded? and who is its president?" The promised prohibition appeased the Cincinnati hotheads, but Theodore Weld was only waiting in the dormitory to see what President Beecher would do about it.

Letters apprized President Beecher of the disturbance, but he was now galloping on a new witch-hunt and discounted the danger. In September the swelling racket brought him to his senses. Sending an express to the Cincinnati papers to announce his arrival, he hurried home, only to find that events had not waited for him. The full Board had confirmed the action of its executive committee, and Weld had led out the entire student-body and was encamped in the suburb of Cummingsville while he reconnoitred for "an institution where free discussion would be tolerated." With him was Professor John Morgan, head of the Lane preparatory department, an Abolitionist whom the irate trustees had kicked out for good measure. The rebels were also receiving comfort from Asa Mahan, a trustee who resigned from the Board in protest.

Resign is what Lyman Beecher should have done, as he knew only too well later. In a vital question of college discipline, solely the faculty's business, the trustees had disregarded his injunction not to interfere and without even showing him the courtesy of waiting for his return. But the Doctor had no heart for giving up a good fight once started. He had been stirring the rapt congregations of New England and New York with his *Plea for The West,* assuming leadership of the campaign to wrest an empire from the infidel and the Pope. Could he allow an extraneous incident, however provoking, to defeat his great ambition—permit a wound to his pride to make him cry defeat before the real battle began? At the worst, the walk-out meant only a lean scholastic term. Otherwise the Seminary's prospects were never rosier; for Dr. Beecher had brought back from the East in his beaver hat a new chapel, the nucleus of a library, and the nest-egg for an endowment of another professorship.

He swallowed his mortification and carried on, dedicating to a fore-

doomed failure the sunset of an eminent career—by his influence dedicating
also to that same failure the rising career of Calvin E. Stowe, who was
soon to marry Dr. Beecher's most gifted daughter.

Beecher's indignation won concessions from the trustees. One was the
head of the Professor of Ecclesiastical History. Another was a modification
of the law against the Anti-Slavery Society, putting its enforcement in the
discretion of the faculty. But Weld was not to be coaxed back by these sops.
He was no longer to be persuaded by anything, even the surrender of the
trustees; for there had come to him the prospectus of a new school opening
at Oberlin, Ohio, on principles so radical that it admitted *females* as students, becoming, in the more modern coinage, the first co-educational college
in America. This time Weld dictated his terms in advance, the Cummingsville seceders meanwhile organizing classes among themselves and conducting a sort of coöperative divinity school of their own.

To anticipate, the fell news of Weld's negotiations came to Walnut
Hills in the spring of 1835. A reorganized Oberlin was opening with two
hundred students. The presidency had gone to Lane's dissenting trustee,
Asa Mahan. John Morgan, the late seditious member of Lane's faculty, had
accepted a professorship. The professorship of Law had been offered to
Weld's Alabama convert, James G. Birney. As a final rebuke to Lane Seminary, the "princely liberality" of Arthur Tappan had endowed at Oberlin a
theological department open to students "irrespective of color"; and at its
head was none other than Weld's earliest idol, Evangelist Charles G. Finney.

The student-dictator's triumph was complete. He marched away with his
seceders, followed by Cincinnati's relieved sigh—and the last hopes of Lane
Seminary. Most of his band he delivered to Oberlin, though a few dropped
off at Western Reserve College, the "Western Yale" at Hudson, Ohio. To
finish with Weld, he became editor of publications of the American Anti-
Slavery Society and married Angelina Grimke, one of the two celebrated
Grimke sisters of Charleston, South Carolina, who adopted the Quaker
faith, freed their slaves, and came north to devote their lives to Abolition and
women's rights. After the War, Weld conducted a private school at Boston
along advanced lines. He lived to a great age, passing away only a year
before the celebrated Hartford authoress whose young life he had unwittingly saddened but enriched.

The revolt at Lane Seminary marked the first real gathering of that
emotional cyclone which expended itself only in civil war. It threw a sudden
beam upon slavery as an issue and not as an irremediable fact of human

existence. In Ohio, for instance, a State that had been less than lukewarm toward Garrison and his cause, the immediate effect was the formation of a State Anti-Slavery Society, and elsewhere in the North Abolition gained strength from it.

Lane Seminary did not recover for decades. In the years following, as the pulpits of Ohio and Indiana filled with Oberlin graduates, the old man who was to have built at Walnut Hills the great theological school of the West could imagine his deserted classrooms to mourn: "Who hath begotten me these, seeing I have lost my children and been desolate?"

The Rev. John Rankin—whom Harriet had called a "handsome, modest, amiable-looking young man" when he served the Presbytery as moderator—was pastor of the Presbyterian Church at Ripley, a settlement on the Ohio bank of the river a few miles below Maysville, and every night he hung in his window a lantern which he left to burn there until morning. He had been doing this since 1825.

Not all the Abolitionists were as vocal as Garrison and Weld, or even as the boastful Cincinnati Quaker, Levi Coffin, who served Harriet for the model of Simeon Halliday in *Uncle Tom's Cabin*. Here and there along the free frontier were secretive men whose hatred of slavery was so intense that they could gain satisfaction only by breaking the law and helping slaves to escape.

Rankin was one of these. The hills rose abruptly behind Ripley's narrow shelf. On the crest of the plateau stood the preacher's cottage, fronting only clear space and the Kentucky hills three miles to the south. Nobody in the village could look up and see the house or its light. Whether the slaveholders across the Ohio observed the faint twinkle, its significance was known in the slave quarters and coffles of that part of Kentucky. If a bondsman could reach the beacon, he was well on his way to Canada and liberty, for Rankin's light marked a railhead of what was soon to become known as the Underground Railroad. Many did reach it. Rankin kept his light kindled as long as bondage existed, and afterwards one of his sons estimated that more than two thousand slaves passed to freedom through the Ripley parsonage. Their property value, at an average price, was well over a million dollars.

In October, 1834, the Cincinnati Synod met at Ripley, and Harriet Beecher went with her father to attend it. The Rev. Mr. Rankin entertained them as his house guests, and also Professor Stowe, with the band of mourning around his hat. It did not need a mind as retentive as Harriet's to remember that house forever. Few American residences were so dramatically placed.

The house itself was a small, story-and-a-half brick affair with so few rooms that one wonders how the preacher could have sheltered guests in addition to his growing family of sons. A narrow porch ran along the southern face of the house, and from this porch one could see for miles up and down the bending river. Large trees shaded the shallow lawn. At the front fence of pickets, one looked almost straight down through the crowns of mighty trees to the steeples and roofs of the village, several hundred feet below. Clinging to the precipitous slope was a goat-path up and down which the agile Rankin scrambled on his pastoral duties, being by this route only a minute or so away from his church. The carriage road had to seek a ravine and wind for a mile or more before reaching the level of the plateau behind Rankin's barn.

From the picket fence the prospect of the river was a majestic one. So harmonious were the proportions of the valley that one on this height, lacking objects of comparison, would never suppose the Ohio to be one of the great rivers of the earth. It was only the speck that was a skiff riding the strong current, the dot that was a dray on the Kentucky landing, the ant making imperceptible progress that was the ferry, that brought out the immensity of valley and stream. Those hills opposite that rose to the level of the eye were six hundred feet high, the waterway below was half a mile wide.

On an October evening, when a star or two glistened through the leaves, when a high moon had turned to silver the distant bend of the river, and the last katydids before frost were chirping their hoarse triolets, a clerical party, returning weary from the Synod, might sit down on the dark verandah for a few minutes of rest and meditation. It was an hour that invited confidences—an hour when, as the voices of dimly seen speakers discussed grave topics, an owlish mite of young womanhood, who always came awake at sundown, might expose something of the richness of her bemused nature. Calvin Stowe had the perception to receive a sudden revelation of the charm of this insignificant girl, whom he had scarcely noticed in Boston but who had become his wife's close friend. It is as easy as tempting to believe that Calvin and Harriet's love story began on this romantic spot during that autumn week in Ripley.

The hour invited Brother Rankin's confidences also. He must have made sure of the sympathy and discretion of his guests before saying anything about the business that occupied the secret half of his double life. Perhaps the lantern in the window wanted explaining. At any rate, during that week he told them a curious story of an escape from slavery in which he had taken part—the story of Eliza Harris.

Eliza was a young Negress who belonged to a woman living in the back country of Kentucky across the river from Ripley. Her mistress treated her cruelly, and she made up her mind to escape. One March afternoon she bundled up her infant and fled, making her way safely to the settlement at the ferry. It was after dark when she reached the river, but she had the good luck to fall in with a Scotch riverman who was drunk enough to be willing to assist her. He showed her the distant light up on the Ohio side and told her she could find safe refuge there.

It had been a severe winter, and the Ohio was still frozen across, though a spring thaw had set in some days before, and water was running over the ice. Nevertheless, the desperate woman started out. The running water made the surface so slippery that a cat would have lost its footing. Again and again during the long passage Eliza slipped and fell, soaking herself to the skin with icy water but always managing to keep her baby dry. A man on the Ripley side directed her to the path up the hill to Rankin's house. The preacher and his family received her, gave her food and dry clothing, and that same night drove her to the home of confederates who lived in Greenfield, some miles back in Brown County.

The curious part of the story followed. Even as the benevolent preacher was ministering to Eliza Harris, he heard the distant thunder that told of the spring break-up of the Ohio. By morning the river was running full of grinding ice floes. When the pursuers reached the river and had interviewed the befogged Scot, they gave Eliza up for lost, assuming that she had attempted to cross on the drifting floes and had been drowned. Nevertheless, they secured a boat and went across themselves. On the Ripley bank they found a shawl or other garment which was identified as one Eliza had wrapped around her infant. They therefore assumed that the slave-woman had accomplished the feat of crossing on the floes.

Eliza's husband, George Harris, escaped some weeks later and by Rankin's aid was reunited with his wife and child at Greenfield, whence they were forwarded by the "Underground" to Canada.

Such is the authentic origin of the fictional episode with which Harriet has been most closely identified by posterity. In southern Ohio there exist

THE RANKIN HOUSE AT RIPLEY, OHIO

(To Reach Which Eliza Crossed the Ice)

"During that week he [Rev. John Rankin] told them a curious story of an escape from slavery in which he had taken part." (Page 146.)

other versions of the Eliza story put forward by reputable and sincere people. One Margaret Garner, an ex-slave-woman who lived in Cincinnati after the Civil War, escaped over the frozen Ohio River and thought she inspired Mrs. Stowe's story. The wealthy and philanthropic Mrs. Lars Anderson, of Cincinnati, who died in 1934, wrote positively that as a child she knew Eliza well as a servant in the home of her father, Dr. George Mendenhall, a leading Cincinnati physician. A coloured man of Oberlin, Ohio, who lived into the 1890's, claimed to be the original George Harris, Eliza's husband. Levi Coffin declared that he met both Eliza and George in Chatham, Ontario, after the War. To complicate a confused history, Harriet herself told an attentive world that she got the Eliza episode from a news item in the *National Era*. Her most devout biographers questioned that misstatement.

Rankin's account of the most celebrated escape from American Slavery is the only one that stands the tests of circumstance and probability. Before she left the Ripley minister's eyrie, Harriet must more than once have stood at the picket fence and looked down on the river and thought of the March night and the hunted slave-woman floundering across on her wild passage. Stories Rankin could tell of the poor fugitives, hunted with dog and gun for the crime of sharing the primitive human affections, weighed on a heart that had no business to concern itself with a political question. Behind that distant bastion, painted now with autumn colours, were rising the laughter and songs, the cries and groans of three million such victims. How a crusader's daughter wanted to *do* something about it—and a small hand gripped the picket, as though it already held the thunderbolt.

Cincinnati was made more bearable for Harriet that fall by the presence of both Henry Ward Beecher and her youngest full brother, Charles, who, though still an undergraduate at Bowdoin, had come out with his father to enter Lane Seminary as Henry's classmate. Charles could not bear to be left in the East alone. His sister Mary, in Hartford, being so much older than he, did not count, and William was leaving Newport, having through his father's influence received a call to the church at Putnam, Ohio, across the Muskingum River from Zanesville. By Christmas the exodus of the family was complete. They were all in the West except Mary Perkins.

Except Catharine Beecher, too, for at last Catharine was embarked on the career that suited her best and which was to engage the rest of her life, that of travelling missionary for the cause of women's higher education.

Her paper, *The Education of Female Teachers,* which she read before the American Lyceum in New York the following spring, was historic in pedagogical annals. She does not seem to have returned at all to open her Western Female Institute in September. Mary Dutton and Harriet could take care of everything now, and Catharine flitted importantly from town to town, stopping wherever she could with friends and acquaintances.

(There is evidence that her visits were not always welcomed. The children of Dr. Taylor, in whose New Haven home she would stop "for weeks at a time," did not like Miss Beecher. Catharine was growing more and more self-opinionated and dictatorial. At table she monopolized the conversation and was capable of frowning down an inwardly seething child who had ventured to interrupt.)

Catharine's new peripatetic existence made a change in Harriet's life, for the older sister now planned to stay with her father at Walnut Hills, whenever she was in Cincinnati. They therefore broke up their joint quarters, and Harriet went to board with E. F. Tucker on Plum Street, between Third and Fourth Streets. This was then in the western outskirts of the town and almost next door to the school, which had moved to the corner of Plum and Third Streets.

Charles Beecher, whose infancy had been so fraught with woe, had grown up to be the gentlest and most sensitive of the Beecher sons. Harriet grew to love him as much as she did Henry and perhaps even more, since there was an element of the maternal in her affection. Though in physical size he dwarfed her, she became his protector in life, often his benefactor, always his fierce champion, though she failed to carry him with her, later, into the Episcopalian faith. Practical men might call Charles's character weak, but his mental honesty was rugged and not to be influenced by family ties.

Charles's passion was music. In the East he had been studying theory, and he was becoming a competent performer on the violin. He was a true Beecher in that he related music almost exclusively to religious worship. In the 1830's congregational singing was not the commonplace it is today. Lyman Beecher pioneered with it in the Second Church of Cincinnati, especially after Charles arrived to help him. But the great promoter of church singing was to be Henry Ward Beecher, whose enormously successful *Plymouth Hymnal* of which he was compiler and chief royalty-collector (though Charles collaborated and may have done most of the work) almost monopolized the pew-racks at the middle of the last century.

When he yielded to Charles's homesick pleas in Boston, Lyman Beecher could scarcely have dreamed that the presence of his two sons—free scholars both—would actually be needed that year to help fill up the depleted classes of Lane Seminary. Still, though the campus was half-deserted, the institution presented the look of prosperity. The new seminary building was 100 feet long and four stories high, a substantial brick structure. There was the dormitory building, a steward's house, and two faculty residences, also of brick. Besides these, the money was in hand for a new chapel and a large addition to the library, which already had three thousand volumes. The Doctor was far from downcast.

Then, in the January number of the *Liberator,* William Lloyd Garrison took revenge for the slight he had received when, in 1830, he solicited Dr. Beecher's support for his projected anti-slavery journal. The great Bowdoin Street pastor was evasive—he had too many irons in the fire, as it was.

"Then," cried Garrison, "you had better let all your irons burn than neglect your duty to the slave."

Secure in his superiority of years and position, Dr. Beecher was patronizing.

"Your zeal," he told the pale, young man, "is commendable, but you are misguided. If you will give up your fanatical notions and be guided by us, we will make you the Wilberforce of America."

In January, 1835, the *Liberator* published the statements of both the seceding students and the faculty, with Garrison's comment: "Lane Seminary is now to be regarded as strictly a Bastille of oppression—a spiritual Inquisition." All this was reprinted in a pamphlet, 18,000 copies of which were circulated by Arthur Tappan and other New York Abolitionists, reaching the very class of people that sent its sons to divinity schools.

It was terribly effective, heaping upon the Seminary "a load of prejudice as a pro-slavery institution." In February Dr. Beecher might have observed a straw to show the wind's direction. Dr. John C. Young, president of Centre College at Danville, Kentucky, who had been offered the Chair of Sacred Rhetoric at Lane, unexpectedly declined it. Though not an Abolitionist of the Garrison stamp, Young was an opponent of slavery, a believer in *gradual* emancipation. The eastern Abolitionists crowed that Lane's "bad reputation" had turned aside this able educator.

Another straw was the attitude of John Rankin, their recent host at Ripley. Having read all the evidence, Brother Rankin wrote a letter to the Cincinnati *Journal* taking the Lane faculty to task for its attitude in the students' strike. Professor Stowe replied, and for some months the debate of the two gentlemen continued at long intervals in the columns of the *Journal*. At times the language grew clerically acrimonious, though each letter ended, "Affectionately yours."

Whatever Harriet thought of the revolt, her interest in Calvin Stowe was heightened that winter by a remarkable autobiographical paper which the widowed professor wrote (and signed) for the Semi-Colon Club.

All his life this square-visaged and semi-bald young man (he was now aged thirty-two) had been subject to visions which were so real to him, so detailed and clear and logically progressive in action, that he was a half-grown lad before he discovered the phenomenon to be unique in himself and not a universal human experience. The blunt, tactless Calvin Stowe was the last man on earth to be suspected of being imaginative or hysterical in temperament. He may almost be said to have possessed no imagination, except a strong morbid bent that plunged him continually into melancholy and hypochondria.

Stowe's mind was eminently that of a scientist. He was the leading Hebrew scholar of his day and the leading authority on the origins and histories of the books of the Bible and of sacred writings associated with them. Add to these traits an utter and sometimes even embarrassing honesty, and you get a mind that could not possibly have invented the visions or even imagined them, in the ordinary sense of that term.

In his Semi-Colon paper the professor examined the nightmarish side of his life with the detachment of a psychiatrist setting down the case-history of an interesting patient. The result was an exhibit perhaps unmatched for authenticity in the literature of psychical research. A good scientist, Professor Stowe expressed no opinion on the nature of his visions, whether supernatural or illusory. He merely gave in plain language a history of his uncanny esoteric life, related a few unearthly episodes he had observed, and described the weird personages that moved most habitually in the occult region into which he almost daily peered—personages whose names and characteristics he knew as well as those of his material friends.

We can imagine the impression this creepy narrative made in the club-meeting; and to the timid Semi-Colon, hurrying home through the dark streets that night, it must have been reassuring to remember the appearance of the seer himself, whose frank, open countenance (framed between un-spectral sideburns), whose turnover collar flaring away from a doubling chin, frock coat, wrinkled waistcoat, and baggy trousers proclaimed him so unequivocally of the earth, earthy. With no question at all about Professor Stowe's good faith, the sceptics could explain the apparitions as figments arising from some mental slip that brought his dream-world before his waking eyes. A mystic like Harriet Beecher would be prone to regard the visions as genuine manifestations of the other world.

She lived ever on the border of that world herself. God was a person only less tangible than her own father. Beyond the clouds she could almost see the battlements of heaven. She could feel the presence of departed spirits hovering about her. Why should there not be here and there a mortal able to pierce the thin veil? The prophets had seen the angels clearly, and so had the Apostles. Calvin Stowe stood revealed to Harriet as a living witness to the truth of the miracles in her Bible, and the fact drew her to the stocky professor, who seems to us to have been such a humdrum antithesis of the haloed John of Patmos.

Besides, that winter she was investing the Walnut Hills widower with a special glamour. Always magnificent in his professional sweep, Calvin projected a ponderous series of Sunday-evening sermons—or "exegetical lectures"—to be delivered from the pulpit of the Second Church. The very titles of these discourses would have daunted a brain less well stocked— *Proofs that Moses is The Writer of The Five Books which Bear his Name; Hypothesis of Those who Dispute the Genuineness of the Pentateuch; Vicissitudes and Present Condition of the Hebrew Text;* etc. No particular limit was set to the series, which extended through twelve Sunday evenings and then ended apparently because the sage was tired out. He is not to be blamed for any lack of persistency, having already uttered the equivalent of a fat book. However, he did not rest, but went on to give, with Dr. Beecher, a series of alternating Sunday-evening discourses on *Inspiration, Miracles, and Prophecy.*

All of these lectures were voluminously reported for the *Journal* by a correspondent who signed each of the nineteen instalments with the initial H. Have we to speculate on "H's" identity? By this time Editor Brainerd was virtually a member of the Beecher household, drawing heavily upon the literary talents of that "genus in themselves," as a contemporary called the family. The Doctor's sermons took care of many a column in the *Journal.* Catharine contributed verse and an occasional provocative Letter to the Editor. Charles was projecting a series of technical articles on church music—articles that make uncommonly dull reading today. The gifts of the schoolmarm Beecher were not to be wasted. "H" was Harriet.

The assignment gave "H" a view of Professor Stowe in his most attractive rôle—as "a man mighty in the Scriptures and powerful in the pulpit." "If ever a woman feels proud of her lover," wrote Lyman Beecher's daughter in her novel *Dred,* "it is when she sees him as a successful public speaker." With this professional family, eloquence in a man was as beauty in a woman. Calvin Stowe cast no Beecherian spells, but contemporary testimony agrees that his solid rhetoric was clear and entertaining. Of course such sacred discourse had to be reported "just right." It meant weekly conferences for the pair, a constant association that lasted nearly five months.

Harriet, to judge by love scenes in her novels, could regard the association alone as courtship. Love was tongue-tied in her Israel. In lieu of the clichés of passion, her heroes and heroines exchanged thoughts on ethical themes. A sigh, a meaning look, an attitude of tenderness, a pretty *gaffe* with its attendant blush, an unusual air of deference, a suddenly averted glance, an indulgent smile, could speak worlds even when the two were only editing newspaper "copy"—and all in a suggestive atmosphere raised by the nods and innuendos of various matchmakers. In the intervals there were other subjects to touch upon, especially an uppermost one, the deceased Mrs. Stowe. Tears sprang easily into the wide, prominent eyes of the professor, moving Harriet to moisten a sympathetic handkerchief.

In a Plum Street boarding-house a calm little spinster told herself that at last she had a lover, who needed only to come to the point to be her promised bridegroom. She was not yet twenty-four years old. Come to the point, though, was something Calvin Stowe could not do, correctly and delicately, until Eliza had been dead one year.

Two other enemies snapped at the heels of the beset Dr. Beecher that spring. Harriet's erstwhile benefactor, Judge James Hall, had taken umbrage at sentiments expressed by the Doctor in his *Plea for The West,* his New England address of the previous summer. In his zeal to drum up subscriptions to the Seminary endowments, Beecher had painted a gloomy picture of the Christian and cultural state of the Mississippi Valley. What the new country most sorely needed was "New England principles, the matchless bounty of a bountiful Providence." He called upon New England's sons to go among the Westerners, though "not in a mass, to excite an envious feeling, but to mix with them as leaven in a loaf, and thus produce a saving and enduring influence."

As he read this complacent utterance, the spiritual ancestor of all the thin-skinned regional boosters who have followed foamed over. He penned an attack on Dr. Beecher under the satirical headline, *The March of Intellect*. Doubtless to his surprise, the slandered pioneers failed to share Judge Hall's wrath. On the contrary, one secular editor in Cincinnati reproved the judge for using sarcasm "against a grave doctor of divinity."

Committed now to a crusade against Lyman Beecher, Judge Hall turned to the really vulnerable part of the *Plea for The West*. Arriving in Boston, Dr. Beecher had found a new grouping in the religious wars. The Irish were coming in, and Puritans, Unitarians, and even infidels had forgotten their quarrels to unite against the Catholics. Beecher made the swift discovery that what the West really needed to be saved from were the machinations of "Popery," extemporizing a violent onslaught on Catholicism and one so effective that the Bowdoin Street congregation tossed $4,000 for Lane Seminary into the collection baskets. Excitement ran high in Boston. A mob sacked an Ursuline convent in the suburb of Charlestown, as the militia pitched camp on the Common.

It was upon this portion of the address that Judge Hall delivered his major attack, denouncing Dr. Beecher for bigotry and intolerance and accusing him of having incited the Charlestown mob. (This charge could not be sustained, since the mob was in the nunnery at the very moment Dr. Beecher was speaking in Bowdoin Street.) Though publicly silent under the cudgeling, Dr. Beecher sought legal advice on the possibility of a libel action against Judge Hall, while a private letter of 1835 shows that the attack got under the grave D.D.'s skin.

However, he did not need to take personal reprisals. Though there were then only five thousand Catholics west of the Alleghenies, the Doctor was seated in a firm saddle—a saddle that seats the political adventurer firmly to this day. It was a fatal blunder for Judge Hall to commit. A dozen publications of the West at once denounced the *Western Monthly Magazine* as a Catholic organ. The worried jurist penned a scathing justification of his position, left instructions with his printer for the make-up of his next number, and departed on a vacation to recuperate.

Judge Hall's printer, Eli Taylor, was his partner in the ownership of the *Western Monthly,* and Taylor also owned and published the *Journal*, Dr. Beecher's principal champion. When Hall returned to Cincinnati he

found his diatribe suppressed, his partnership dissolved, and half his subscription list locked up in Eli Taylor's safe. For his long effort to raise the
literary taste of the West, the jurist could show only the title and empty
shell of his magazine and a lawsuit against Taylor. He tried feebly to
carry on for a few months with another publisher, then quit journalism
in disgust and took a clerkship in a bank. He lived, however, to become
a solid figure in Cincinnati's financial world.

A more formidable foe was the Rev. Dr. Joshua Lacy Wilson, who took
advantage of Dr. Beecher's tarnished prestige to file formal charges with
the Presbytery.

"1. Heresy on the subject of ability, original sin, and Christian perfection;

"2. Hypocrisy in claiming belief in the Confession of Faith;

"3. Slander in claiming his opinions are those of the evangelical Church
in all ages."

A stout indictment even for an epoch when heretics squirmed at every
church conference. The trial came along in June, 1835. Dr. Wilson opened it,
basing his charges upon statements in the sermon, *The Native Character
of Man,* which Dr. Beecher had preached and published some ten years
previously. If the old Confession meant what it said, Dr. Wilson made a
complete case.

The culprit sat on his own pulpit-steps amid mountains of authorities.
When he rose in his own defense, he talked an entire afternoon, quoting
Luther, Calvin, Howe, Twisse, Henry, Edwards, and the whole company
of the Fathers, splitting a score of hairs and proving black white. Then,
when he had the opposition thoroughly "foggified," he put down the
final "Authority" and pulled out the *vox humana.*

He read into the record Dr. Wilson's letter to the Hanover Street Society,
which urged that congregation to allow Dr. Beecher to come to Lane
Seminary, and went on in heart-broken tones: "How could Dr. Wilson
send such a letter, to tear me away from a confiding people, when for
seventeen years he had known my sentiments on natural ability, which
is the main heresy charged? Was it right thus to reach out a hand to
beckon and even draw me away from Boston and then meet me with a
club as soon as I reached the West?"

Dr. Wilson was right, of course—as right, for instance, as Judge Hall
had been in accusing Lyman Beecher of fomenting religious hatred—but

no more successful than the battered editor. The vote for acquittal was twenty-three to twelve, and another victim lay bleeding under the wheels of the Doctor's chariot. The numbed Dr. Wilson picked himself up and appealed to the Synod.

Worried as he was by the condition of the Seminary and his duties as pastor of the Second Church, Dr. Beecher's victory was the more notable in that even as he pelted down to Cincinnati to face his accuser, his second wife, Harriet Porter Beecher, lay dying in the Walnut Hills house. She passed away on July 7 and joined Eliza Stowe in the campus graveyard.

Dr. Beecher mourned her sincerely, though with a reservation or two. Her absent stepchildren wrote letters of condolence and eulogy; but, a few days after her death, there appeared in the Cincinnati newspapers a most curious and cryptic obituary of the poor lady. This contribution, which seemed to carry a defensive attitude, as though replying to gossip, was signed "C." Only two members of the Beecher family bore that initial. Charles can be passed over. It leaves the harsh and headstrong Catharine, who had her own way about everything and never shrank from coming to grips with unpleasant truth.

Mrs. Beecher's virtues, recited in the obituary, "baffled the keen scrutiny of the gossip and the tattler." Regarding her residence in the West as "a trial and privation," she was depressed at the end of her life. "When approaching the presence of a perfect and holy Being, the retrospection of the deficiencies of the past brought such anxiety and dismay that her spirit died within her, and it was not until after the most contrite acknowledgment of all she deemed her failings in duty to others . . . that her spirit found peace."

Perhaps the gossips and tattlers understood these obscure references. A century later we can only guess at their meaning, but the cruel obituary could apply to a woman whose complaints had made her husband's life a burden and who had treated *his* children shabbily.

"Intellect" strode forward that spring when one Clayton, a young mechanic, inflated a silk balloon with gas and floated off into the east one calm evening, as half of Cincinnati watched. Days passed without news of him, while the town talked of little else, and then he returned with his balloon and the astonishing story that he had landed on a Virginia mountain, having travelled *350 miles in nine hours!* Truly the new age had begun.

Henry Beecher, as the reporters called him, was emerging in the Cincinnati scene, and first as a founder (with Salmon P. Chase and others) of the Young Men's Temperance Society. In March Catharine Beecher alighted in town long enough to contribute an "ode" to the programme of Henry's Temperance Society and to introduce the Rev. T. H. Gallaudet, of Hartford, to the teachers and pupils of the Western Female Institute. She was trying to enlist the support of the pioneer of deaf-mute education for her western schemes.

The new age moved toward its pattern with a sudden upsurge of anger on both sides of the slavery issue. In Circleville, in mid-Ohio, a mob set upon Theodore Weld when he tried to preach Abolition, giving the anti-slavery movement its third historic date, as in Cincinnati the Rev. Lyman Beecher, who had reason to know, defined an Abolitionist as a mixture of "vinegar, aqua fortis, and oil of vitriol, with brimstone, saltpetre, and charcoal to explode and scatter the corrosive matter." A few weeks later another Lane secessionist, Amos Dresser, peddling books in the South, was caught distributing Abolition literature and flogged by a Tennessee mob. It was in the same South that only two years before had tolerated Weld and his Abolition debate. The flames were beginning to roar, and the Nashville *Banner,* an early prophet, warned the North to curb its Abolitionists or risk civil war and a severance of the Union.

Sentiment stiffened in Kentucky, home of Clay and formerly the most liberal of the slave States, and in his native town of Danville James G. Birney found himself unable to continue publication of his anti-slavery journal, *The Philanthropist.* In July the "free" Negroes of Cincinnati dared to hold a demonstration, hauling floats showing Liberty striking the shackles from the black man and bearing banners which proclaimed, "WE BY STEAMBOATS LIVE AND OUR FAMILIES MAINTAIN," the odd phrasing suggesting German sponsorship in the background. The procession was witnessed by a travelling English Baptist, the Rev. J. Hoby, who remarked that "many were offended and scandalized; but the parties were so truly respectable, and those who employed some of them so in-fluential and determined, that it was deemed expedient to let all pass."

Meanwhile the Cincinnati *Gazette* was publishing the proceedings of the lawsuit of Meek vs. Phillips in the Circuit Court of Davidson County, Tennessee. Phillips was the overseer on Meek's plantation. For a misdemeanour he whipped one of Meek's slave boys to death. Meek sued to recover the slave's value and won the verdict. No criminal charge was brought against the brutal overseer.

"These things sink into my heart," Harriet had Eva say in *Uncle Tom's Cabin,* when the angelic child heard the story of the drunken old slave-woman Prue and her desire to be in eternal torment and out of her earthly miseries, "—they sink into my heart." Such things as the trial of Meek vs. Phillips were sinking into Harriet's heart, and some day it was going to be useless to tell her that the flogging of slaves to death did not occur in the "peculiar institution." It was going to be useless to tell her, too, that the breaking up of slave-families by sale was so rare as to be exceptional. Her *Journal* reported that summer the address of the Rev. Dr. Graham before the Colonization Society of Fayetteville, North Carolina, in which the clergyman made the statement that 7,000 slaves had been sold on the New Orleans market "last winter," that Virginia was annually selling 6,000 blacks to the deep South, and that in twenty years 300,000 slaves had been sold south out of Virginia and North Carolina alone.

Violence spread like an epidemic, as the South conceived the notion that the Abolitionists were secretly plotting a slave rebellion and held up the dread picture of Haiti and Toussaint l'Ouverture. A race war broke out in Washington, D. C. In Mobile, Alabama, a clergyman found circulating Abolition pamphlets, was hanged by a mob. A Mississippi mob caught an anti-slavery agitator, stripped him and flayed him by dragging a cat by the tail across his naked body. He was flung into a cell, where he hanged himself.

It was the real beginning of the struggle that at last would appeal to the "arbitrament of arms." From this time forth there would be no peace between the sections. In the North the moderates—and that means the overwhelming masses of the people—were dismayed. In Cincinnati the respectable liberal opinion found expression in the *Journal,* whose editor had by this time become the outsider closest within the confidence of Lyman Beecher. We may take his editorial of September 25 for the 1835 attitude toward slavery of the Beecher family, Harriet and Henry Ward included.

Editor Brainerd denounced *immediate abolition* and its agitators on eight counts. 1. Though slavery is sinful, not all slaveholders are sinful, many of them believing that instant emancipation would be a curse to the Negro. 2. Immediate emancipation would turn loose a horde of ignorant, vicious idlers and thus perpetuate slavery by the bad example they would afford.

3. The Abolitionists are not sincere, since for all their incendiary utterances the most they expect to win is gradual emancipation. 4. It is politically unwise to urge immediate emancipation. 5. The method of the Abolitionists in denouncing slavery in the territory where it doesn't exist, is wrong. 6. The Abolitionists take no pains to conciliate Southern Christians. 7. Their campaign tends to promote the spirit of violence and civil war. 8. Their method is the slowest way to emancipation; Delaware, Maryland, Virginia, Kentucky, Tennessee, and Missouri were all moving toward emancipation when the Abolition movement arose.

"In the frenzied excitement now abroad," went on the *Journal,* "no editor can be calm and candid without incurring censure from violent partisans. If the Abolitionists go on in this same spirit, no Southern philanthropist will long dare to advocate even gradual emancipation or colonization. All that has been gained by years of labor and watching and prayer will be swept away, and starless midnight will brood over the hope of the slaves until the progress of time shall bring the day of retribution."

More constructive events of that memorable year could distract a brooding nature from dwelling too long on the cruelty and injustice of men. In August the railroad excitement reached Cincinnati. Dr. Daniel Drake was first to realize what was coming. The steam cars were already moving over a segment of the future Baltimore & Ohio, and New York had begun construction of a line to Lake Erie. Drake called a railroad mass-meeting in the Commercial Exchange. It is a footnote on the attitude of the 1830's that Cincinnati did not think first of a rail connection with New York. The Queen City was nobody's tributary, and the meeting passed a resolution to agitate for a line to the Carolina tidewater, cutting through the heart of the southern market. The town foresaw itself as the metropolis of America, with the federal Capitol in Covington, across on the Kentucky side.

In September a great domestic happiness absorbed the attention of the Beechers to the exclusion of all else. After making his annual tour of the East that summer, Edward brought back his sister Mary Perkins with him. Catharine was at home that fall. William came down from Putnam and George from Batavia. So it happened that the old Doctor, after a late Saturday-night return from Dayton, stood with streaming eyes one Sunday morning and surveyed the faces of all his children.

Catharine, Edward, William, Mary, George, Harriet, Henry, Charles,

Isabella, Thomas, James—eleven of them! It was the first time their twice-widowed father had ever seen them together. It was the first time they had ever seen each other in a single group. Mary had never seen James before, and had seen Thomas only once as a baby. Edward scarcely knew the three youngest children.

Such an occasion, occurring in such a family, whose daily acts were historic, called for no ordinary domestic jollification. The weeping Lyman Beecher made a ritual of it, a three-day programme. A worshipful eye-witness reported it for the press.

There were more tears than words. The doctor attempted to pray but could scarcely speak. His full heart poured itself out in a flood of weeping. He couldn't go on. Edward continued, and each one, in his turn, uttered some sentences of thanksgiving. They then began at the head and related their fortunes. After special prayer, all joined hands and sang *Old Hundred* in these words:

"From all who dwell below the skies."

Edward preached in his father's pulpit in the morning, William in the after-noon, and George in the evening. The family occupied the three front rows on the broad aisle. Monday morning they assembled, and, after reading and prayers, in which all joined, they formed a circle. The doctor stood in the middle and gave them a thrilling speech. He then went round and gave them each a kiss. They had a happy dinner.

Presents flowed in from all quarters. During the afternoon the house was filled with company, each bringing an offering. When left alone at evening they had a general examination of all their characters. The shafts of wit flew amain, the doctor being struck in several places; he was, however, expert enough to hit most of them in turn. From the uproar of the general battle, all must have been wounded. Tuesday morning saw them together again, drawn up in a straight line for the inspection of the king of happy men. After receiving particular instructions, they formed into a circle. The doctor made a long and affecting speech. He felt that he stood for the last time in the midst of all his children, and each word fell with the weight of a patriarch's. He embraced them once more in all the tenderness of his big heart. Each took of all a farewell kiss. With joined hands, they sang a hymn. A prayer was offered, and, finally, a parting blessing was spoken. Thus ended a meeting which can only be rivaled in that blessed home where the ransomed of the Lord, after weary pilgrimage, shall join in the praise of the Lamb. May they all be there!

Cholera failed to reappear in Cincinnati that year, and the result was a bound in prosperity and optimism of which the railroad excitement was only one manifestation. It was therefore ominous that the October matriculation at Lane Seminary produced so few new students that the classes, including the holdovers, averaged only five members each. Dr. Beecher knew now that the wounds inflicted by Weld and Garrison were grievous ones.

His trial before Synod, which met that year in Dayton, came up in October. Since the delegates from the Cincinnati Presbytery, from which the appeal was taken, could not vote under the rules, it amounted to a packed jury for Dr. Wilson. Even with the Cincinnati men voting, Dr. Wilson and the Old School faction controlled the Synod, "constituting" it and electing their own moderator by a majority of seven.

Nevertheless, it was the story of the Presbytery trial repeated. Dr. Wilson spoke, Dr. Beecher replied at length, and the stampeded delegates voted ten to one to sustain the verdict of the Presbytery. Dr. Wilson took long thought and, "pale as a ghost," appealed to the General Assembly of the Presbyterian Church. He was pale because, under the Book of Discipline, if he failed to prove his charges, he would himself be subject to censure as a slanderer of the Gospel ministry.

Calvin Stowe had gathered his "exegetical lectures" together, and that autumn Corey, Fairbank & Webster (simultaneously announcing that the sale of the Miss Beechers' Geography had reached 100,000 copies) published them between covers as an *Introduction to The Criticism and Interpretation of The Bible.* Judge Hall, to whom anything connected with Lane Seminary was now anathema, gave the work a chilly notice in his faltering magazine. A loyal daughter and indignant fiancée could perhaps find satisfaction in the failure of the judge's second prize contest for want of meritorious entries.

For fiancée she was, now. Judge Hall's slighting review caught the professor-lover on his knees. The Cincinnati *Journal,* in its issue of November 19, 1835, published as a paid advertisement the following notice:

WESTERN FEMALE INSTITUTE

The public are informed that this institution was commenced with the understanding that the Miss Beechers were to be responsible only for securing experienced teachers competent to carry forward their peculiar views of education and methods of instruction. As soon as an adequate supply of such teachers was obtained, the Miss Beechers relinquished the duties of principals to Miss Dutton and Miss Tappan and the past year have acted as assistants only. During this time the school has prospered and has gained public confidence, and the Miss Beechers now wish to withdraw from further responsibility to the public. Whatever the school has been the past year it will continue to be, as the same ladies who have managed its concerns the past year will continue to do so, and the places of assistants now vacated by the Miss Beechers will be filled by other ladies who are engaged and are well qualified to perform the duties thus relinquished.

This notice could mean only one thing. It was no longer necessary to maintain the school to give Harriet "some means of immediate support." Harriet was engaged to be married to Calvin Ellis Stowe.

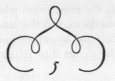

Suitor and Husband

CALVIN STOWE as a romantic figure is a tough morsel for our cultivated taste in heroes. That the thick-shouldered, baldish, bearded scholar, gluttonous, neurasthenic, timid and lazy, a scatter-brain in emergencies, and quite devoid of that talent for getting things done which Harriet called "faculty," could have inspired any strong passion in a deep nature, taxes the modern credulity. Indeed, there has been critical attempt to show that Harriet's career represented a love-frustration turning to literary work for solace.

The facts, however, do not support such a contention. During the first fifteen years of her married life Harriet wrote little for publication but did bring forth to Calvin's fatherhood seven children. Then, as if her debt to the race were paid, she turned to her writing-desk and in the next quarter of a century produced some thirty volumes of novels, stories, sketches, and poems, a masterpiece among them here and there, to say nothing of a steady stream of prefaces, introductions, open letters, journalistic pieces, and (perhaps not least of her labours) autographs for collectors.

There is no reason to believe that her marriage was infelicitous. She had been married several years when she wrote to Calvin, "If you were not already my dearly beloved husband, I should certainly fall in love with you," which was language more vigorous than she permitted her heroines to employ. Calvin's very weaknesses seemed to endear him to Harriet. Upon his worst failing, his cowardice, she closed her eyes. He had an indolent man's craving for peace—peace even at the price of knuckling down when in the right. Harriet's most censorious attitude toward him was a sort of indulgent disdain for his fears, as if he were a child.

They got on each other's nerves—he with his perpetual "blues," she with her exasperating fits of abstraction—but, as she wrote in one novel, "anger is the near neighbor of love." With the years their mutual affection strengthened. When Calvin grew too old to travel, Harriet willingly gave up her winter home in Florida, the greatest pleasure her money ever bought for her. She remained steadfastly at his side during the long months of his dying, and when he was gone she mourned him as a bride.

Their relationship, after Harriet became famous, was the usual one imagined by the humourists, though it may not be common in actual existence. The early years of adversity, which only wove sinews into Harriet's character, crushed Calvin's weaker morale, and, when plenty came at last, he slipped comfortably into the rôle of a celebrity's husband. Now and then he rebelled, but his roaring assertions of headship fooled nobody, unless it were Harriet. That bantam wife, who gloried in battle and gave small heed to enemies, added to the comedy by never seeming to picture herself as other than the weak vessel leaning on the strong support of a dominant male. Unconsciously she flattered her husband's dignity by looking to him always for guidance in her affairs; but when the hour came for action, she followed her own valiant path, often to the trembling Calvin's complete dismay.

How could Harriet so well love this fat and palpitating professor, nine years her senior, who seems so unattractive to us now? Leaving aside the fact that Harriet's ideal was the man of God (and Calvin *looked* the preacher so satisfactorily!), it is easy for a modern sceptic to miss the fact that Calvin Stowe had a most engaging personality. Men universally liked him, and so did women, and children, too. In fact, children preferred him to Harriet, whom they also liked, however, as there are old people still alive to testify.

His personal popularity is first to be noted when he was in college. After a harsh boyhood he went up to Bowdoin to find himself almost the only practising Christian in a godless company of students. His piety alone would have been a handicap with such a crew, but Calvin added to it a propensity to grind that made him valedictorian at his graduation. Nevertheless, there is no contemporary dissent to the statement that he was a popular man in his class. One who assented was Calvin's classmate, Franklin Pierce, another man of charm, who as President admitted brazenly that he got good marks in college because at the examinations he "sat next to Stowe." Longfellow and Hawthorne were a class behind. The fastidious poet seems not to have been drawn into Calvin's train (though both were to become Germanophiles), but Hawthorne remembered him pleasantly, the Stowes and Hawthornes becoming family friends in later life.

Had Calvin lived a century later, his acquaintances would have called him a wisecracker. He sprinkled his conversation and even his formal oratory with sharp, humorous remarks, often in the bucolic idiom of his native Natick, a town of eastern Massachusetts, near Boston. When the beetle-browed savant wanted to be arch in pulpit or parlour, he was wont to introduce his *mot* with an incongruous "*'spect.*" He 'spected this or that, couching his expectation in what he put forward as the Natick dialect. Topsy's famous " 'Spect I grow'd" came straight out of Calvin's repertory. Even from the platform in England Calvin threw out his quaint solecisms; and British audiences, to whom the speaker must have been as refreshing as a Hottentot, seemed to enjoy his Yankee expressions as much as audiences at home.

But this seasoning of the scholar's speech was only a sort of by-product of a great stock of stories which Calvin told, and told uncommonly well, about various village types in Natick and its vicinity. Despite his immersion in the dead languages, the man was, and had always been, as acute an observer and appreciator of human idiosyncrasy as Harriet herself. Especially New England idiosyncrasy, so that marriage to him confirmed Harriet in her literary preoccupation with the New England scene. In Cincinnati Calvin was as much an exile as Harriet.

In his own circles Calvin was famous for his Natick stories, and he had no readier listener than Harriet. In that household it was never a case of the bored wife yawning as papa started to tell another of his old chestnuts. Harriet paraded Calvin as *raconteur* before company and finally took his best stories, which ranged from the uncanny to the extravagantly humorous, and gathered them, largely in her husband's own language, into a novel, *Oldtown Folks,* which ranks next to *Uncle Tom's Cabin* as her master-piece. There could be no better proof of her affection for Calvin Stowe. Had she resented him at first, when she needed his support, and despised him later when she had attained security and independence, she would most certainly have extended her contempt to his background.

Calvin was born in Natick in April, 1802. The family was poor and its poverty became desperate when the father died of one of the usual "wasting diseases" of that early day. Calvin was then six years old. He could not remember how he learned to read, or when, but it was "at an early age." The first book he ever saw was the Bible, and he always remembered how fascinated he was with the weirder parts—the first chapters of *Job, Revelation,* and chapters of *Ezekiel* and *Daniel.* Somebody lent him Jedidiah Morse's *History of New England,* which introduced the visionary boy to witchcraft and Indian legend. He came upon an old schoolbook, *The Art of Speaking,* and learned by heart its numerous quotations from Milton and Shakespeare. For a while he lived with his grandmother, who told him tales out of Mather's *Magnalia,* which she called the "Magnilly."

"But," Calvin wrote reminiscently, "of all the books that I read at this period, there was none that went to my heart like Bunyan's *Pilgrim's Progress.* I read it and reread it night and day; I took it to bed with me and hugged it to my bosom while I slept; every different edition that I could find I seized upon and read with as eager a curiosity as if it had been a new story throughout; and I read with the unspeakable satisfaction of most devoutly believing that everything which 'Honest John' related was a real verity, an actual occurrence."

At the age of fourteen Calvin was apprenticed to a paper-maker. It was his duty to arise at three in the morning and go to the mill to start the fires under the boiler that there might be steam up when the men came to work at six. In some way he managed to get a preparatory education at Bradford Academy. Perhaps the Natick parson secured some sort of scholarship for the precocious boy. Perhaps Calvin's relatives contributed to help the family prodigy along on his obvious way to the pulpit.

At this time Calvin's surname was Stow, and as Stow he was graduated from Bowdoin in 1824. In 1826 Bowdoin College conferred the degree of Master of Arts upon Calvin Ellis Stowe, the recipient having picked up the terminal *e* in the interval. For this rotund and sometimes comical man, so profound in his subjects, so rustic in speech and appearance, so coarse-fibred by nature, so devoid of and blind to the urbanity of the sophisticated world to which he aspired and into which circumstances at length lifted him, was at heart vain. Names and their public impact were a sort of hobby with him, and he pondered long upon them, considering himself something of an authority in nomenclature.

His vanity also took the form of various dramatizations of himself in his appearance at different periods of his life. The man Harriet married was Calvin the Orator. The soft sideburns, the receding brow, the hair bushing over temples and around the nape of the neck, the wide mouth firmed with ecclesiastical authority, all expressed the little giant of the pulpit.

Fame came to Harriet, and in the cultured circles of the East the celebrity's husband found his chief social asset to be his store of New England tales. We now have Calvin, the Down-East Yankee. The sideburns have been encouraged to cascade over the angles of the jaw and join in a long neck fringe at the junction of the collar-bone, so that the shaven countenance seems to emerge from an Eskimo parka.

But George Eliot tickled him immensely by thinking he looked rabbinical. The Orientalist put away his razor, and the eloquent mouth disappeared behind an orthodox mask of whiskers. Behind, a silvery mane fell below his coat-collar, and a skull-cap covered his bald dome. This was Calvin the Rabbi. Harriet gave him the fond nickname of Rab and to their friends referred to him as "my old Rab."

Then, at the end of his life, he produced his masterpiece, the fruit of a lifetime of research, his *Origin and History of The Books of The Bible*. The success of this work was as great as it was welcomed in the Stowe household. It brought the author into his final phase—Calvin the Patriarch and Sage. The razor has come out again, and a space has been cleared to expose the profound mouth, but the mane is thick as ever, and the full, snowy beard falls to the top button of his waistcoat.

That there might be no mistake, the Sage sat for his photograph holding in one hand a sheet of parchment manuscript, while from a coat pocket protruded a bundle of the same. On these exhibits he caused the retoucher to letter a number of Greek words in characters so relatively vast that his public could read them even in a small reproduction. On the parchment held in his hand appeared the Greek title of the *New Testament*—'Η καινή διαθήκη—while other Greek words of Scriptural connotation appeared on the pocket MS. These linguistic displays linked Calvin's scholarship both to Attic learning and to the Bible, and thus were perfect.

But what set Calvin Stowe apart from all other men of note and stability was his familiarity with the occult. Had he been less of the logician and scholar or more of the dreamer and mystic, we could pass over his visions as wishful exaggerations of what were perhaps only natural and explainable phenomena. But there was no trace of the charlatan in his make-up, he never exploited his psychic peculiarity, and so far as we know never wrote about it, except on the one occasion when he entertained the Semi-Colon Club in Cincinnati. Even then he held no brief for the validity of his uncanny experiences but stood off and examined himself with all the curiosity of an outsider.

"The facts," he wrote soberly in the club paper, "appear to me to be curious and well worth the attention of the psychologist. I regard the occurrences in question as the more remarkable because I cannot discover that I possess either taste or talent for fiction or poetry. I have barely imagination enough to enjoy, with a high degree of relish, the works of others in this department of literature, but have never felt able or disposed to engage in that sort of writing myself. . . . The only talent of a higher kind that I am conscious of possessing is a turn for accurate observation of men and things, and a certain broad humor and drollery."

Calvin spoke of his "feeble constitution" and his easily excited nervous system, then went on:

"As early as I can remember anything, I can remember observing a multitude of animated and active objects, which I could see with perfect distinctness, moving about me, and could sometimes, though seldom, hear them make a rustling noise, or other articulate sounds; but I could never touch them. They were in all respects independent of my sense of touch, and incapable of being obstructed in any way by the intervention of material objects; I could see them at any distance, and through any intervening object, with as much ease and distinctness as if they were in the room with me, and directly before my eyes. I could see them passing through the floors, and the ceilings, and the walls of the house, from one apartment to another, in all directions, without a door, or a keyhole, or crevice being open to admit them. . . . These appearances occasioned neither surprise nor alarm, except when they assumed some hideous and frightful form, or exhibited some menacing gesture, for I became acquainted with them as soon as with any of the objects of sense."

In his paper Calvin spoke as if his weird psychic experience lay in the distant past and was a phenomenon of his childhood. Perhaps because he did not care to be considered a monstrosity by his friends, he did not mention that the visions were continuing. Perhaps Harriet herself did not learn of this fact until later. As late as 1860, at least, Calvin was still seeing visions and hearing voices and music which by that time he had more or less convinced himself came from the spirit world.

Before the Semi-Colon Club he also called them a delusion, without qualification; but a young professor could not be expected to risk blighting a promising career by permitting himself to be thought abnormal. What gave, and still gives, peculiar weight to his testimony was the fact that his apparitions had little in common with the banal "materializations" of the professional medium. Some of the wraithlike "objects" he saw, and some of the attributes of all of them, seem to be figments of disordered dreams, transcending conscious human imagination.

"They exhibited all possible combinations of size, shape, proportion, and color, but their most usual appearance was with the human form and proportion, but under a shadowy outline that seemed just ready to melt into the invisible air, and sometimes liable to the most sudden and grotesque changes, and with a uniform darkly bluish color spotted with brown, or brownish white."

Having made these and other general remarks on the nature of the phenomena, including a statement that the apparitions, while they preferred darkness or even candlelight to daylight, nevertheless often appeared in daylight, sometimes when the seer was in the midst of company—with the curious notation, too, that the forms gained neatness of outline and motion according to the degree of neatness of the room in which they appeared— the extraordinary professor, to the eye as plain and wholesome as a plate of New England boiled dinner, went on to clinch his case by relating some of his adventures with his ghostly familiars. Poe and Coleridge and Washington Irving and all the Gothic novelists combined, let alone Calvin Stowe, could not have imagined the details of these fearsome episodes. Their vague familiarity comes from their association with our worst nightmares.

Two years before the father's death, when Calvin was four, the Stow family moved into another house, not far from the one in which the vision-seer was born. The club-paper continued: "Our new dwelling was a low-studded house of only one story; and, instead of an upper chamber, I now occupied a bedroom that opened into the kitchen. Within this bedroom, directly on the left hand of the door as you entered from the kitchen, was the staircase which led to the garret; and, as the room was unfinished, some of the boards which inclosed the staircase were too short and left a considerable space between them and the ceiling. One of these open spaces was directly in front of my bed, so that when I lay upon my pillow my face was opposite to it.

"Every night, after I had gone to bed and the candle was removed, a very pleasant-looking human face would peer at me over the top of that board, and gradually press forward his head, neck, shoulders, and finally his whole body as far as the waist, through the opening, and then, smiling upon me with great good-nature, would withdraw in the same manner in which he had entered. He was a great favorite of mine; for, though we neither of us spoke, we perfectly understood, and were entirely devoted to, each other. It is a singular fact that the features of this favorite phantom bore a very close resemblance to those of a boy older than myself whom I feared

CALVIN ELLIS STOWE

"The soft sideburns, the hair bushing over
temples, the wide mouth firmed with ecclesiastical authority, all expressed the little giant of the
pulpit." (Page 165.)

and hated: still, the resemblance was so strong that I called him by the same name, Harvey.

"Harvey's visits were always expected and always pleasant; but sometimes there were visitations of another sort, odious and frightful. One of these I will relate as a specimen of the rest.

"One night, after I had retired to bed and was looking for Harvey, I observed an unusual number of the tunnel-shaped, tremulous clouds already described, and they seemed intensely black and strongly agitated. This alarmed me exceedingly, and I had a terrible feeling that something awful was going to happen. It was not long before I saw Harvey at his accustomed place, cautiously peeping at me through the aperture, with an expression of pain and terror on his countenance. He seemed to warn me to be on my guard, but was afraid to put his head into the room lest he should be touched by one of the clouds, which were every moment growing thicker and more numerous. Harvey soon withdrew and left me alone.

"On turning my eyes toward the left-hand wall of the room, I thought I saw at an immense distance below me the regions of the damned, as I had heard them pictured in sermons. From this awful world of horror the tunnel-shaped clouds were ascending, and I perceived that they were the principal instruments of torture in these gloomy abodes. These regions were at such an immense distance below me that I could obtain but a very indistinct view of the inhabitants, who were very numerous and exceedingly active. Near the surface of the earth, and, as it seemed to me, but a little distance from my bed, I saw four or five sturdy, resolute devils endeavoring to carry off an unprincipled and dissipated man of the neighborhood, by the name of Brown, of whom I had stood in terror for years. These devils, I saw, were very different from the common representations. They had neither red faces, nor horns, nor hoofs, nor tails. They were in all respects stoutly built and well-dressed gentlemen. The only peculiarity that I noted in their appearance was as to their heads. Their faces and necks were perfectly bare, without hair or flesh, and of a uniform sky-blue color, like the ashes of burnt paper before it falls to pieces, and of a certain glossy smoothness.

"As I looked on, full of eagerness, the devils struggled to force Brown down with them, and Brown struggled with the energy of desperation to save himself from their grip, and it seemed that the human was likely to prove too strong for the infernal. In this emergency one of the devils, panting for breath and covered with perspiration, beckoned to a strong, thick cloud that seemed to understand him perfectly and, whirling up to Brown, touched his hand. Brown resisted stoutly, and struck out right and left at the cloud most furiously, but the usual effect was produced,—the hand grew black, quivered, and seemed to be melting into the cloud; then the arm, by slow degrees, and then the head and shoulders.

"At this instant Brown, collecting all his energies for one desperate effort, sprang at once into the centre of the cloud, tore it asunder, and descended to the ground, exclaiming, with a hoarse, furious voice that grated on my ear, 'There, I've got out! dam'me if I haven't!'

"This was the first word that had been spoken through the whole horrible scene. It was the first time I had ever seen a cloud fail to produce its appropriate result, and it terrified me so that I trembled from head to foot. The devils, however, did not seem to be in the least discouraged. One of them, who seemed to be the leader, went away and quickly returned, bringing with him an enormous pair of rollers fixed in an iron frame, such as are used in iron-mills for the purpose of rolling out and slitting bars of iron, except, instead of being turned by machinery, each roller was turned by an immense crank.

"Three of the devils now seized Brown and put his feet to the rollers, while two others stood one at each crank and began to roll him in with a steady strain that was entirely irresistible. Not a word was spoken, not a sound was heard; but the fearful struggles and terrified, agonizing looks of Brown were more than I could endure. I sprang from my bed and ran through the kitchen into the room where my parents slept, and entreated them that they would permit me to spend the remainder of the night with them. After considerable parleying, they assured me that nothing could hurt me, and advised me to go back to bed. I replied that I was not afraid of their hurting me, but I couldn't bear to see them acting so with C. Brown.

"'Poh! poh! you foolish boy!' replied my father, sternly. 'You've only been dreaming; go right back to bed, or I shall have to whip you.'

"Knowing that there was no other alternative, I trudged back through the kitchen with all the courage I could muster, cautiously entered my room, where I found everything quiet, there being neither cloud, nor devil, nor anything of the kind to be seen; and, getting into bed, I slept quietly till morning. The next day I was rather sad and melancholy, but kept all my troubles to myself, through fear of Brown."

The clairvoyant boy could also see fairies. "I awoke one bright, moonlight night and found a large, full-length human skeleton of an ashy blue color in bed with me! I screamed out with fright and soon summoned the family around me. I refused to tell the cause of my alarm but begged permission to occupy another bed, which was granted.

"For the remainder of the night I slept but little; but I saw upon the window-stools companies of little fairies, about six inches high, in white robes, gamboling and dancing with incessant merriment. Two of them, a male and female, rather taller than the rest, were dignified with a crown and sceptre. They took the kindest notice of me, smiled upon me with great benignity, and seemed to assure me of their protection. I was soothed and cheered by their presence, though after all there was a sort of sinister and selfish expression in their countenances that prevented my placing implicit confidence in them."

Such was the character of the paper that sent a subdued company of "Semi-Colons" home through the dark Cincinnati streets one night; and such was the view Harriet had of the inner life of the substantial Professor of Biblical Literature who was to propose to her a year later. Their engagement was short, and they were married on January 6, 1836.

Both engagement and wedding they kept as a secret to which they admitted only their families and most intimate friends. Harriet could not quite invite the smirks of the matchmakers. Of the wedding itself we know about only a few of the arrangements, but presumably it took place in the President's House at Walnut Hills, and presumably Dr. Beecher conducted the ceremony. The only outsider present was Mary Dutton, who served as maid-of-honour—the charming Mary of the many beaux, whose contemplation of the married state had brought the simulated scorn of a homely virgin in a Hartford boarding-house. In 1836 there was no husband for Mary yet in sight. Was Harriet's satisfaction a little wicked?

There was another friend whom Harriet was preceding to the altar—Georgiana May—though Georgiana was now affianced. At the last moment Harriet could not resist speaking out of experience to her older chum, who had once held the monopoly of wise counsel. Gowned for the ceremony and awaiting only the bridegroom, Harriet sat at a desk and dashed off a note to Georgie.

Well, my dear G., about half an hour more and your old friend, companion, schoolmate, sister, etc., will cease to be Hatty Beecher and change to nobody knows who. My dear, you are engaged, and pledged in a year or two to encounter a similar fate, and do you wish to know how you shall feel? Well, my dear, I have been dreading and dreading the time, and lying awake all last week wondering how I should live through this overwhelming crisis, and lo! it has come, and I feel *nothing at all*.

The wedding is to be altogether domestic; nobody present but my own brothers and sisters, and my old colleague, Mary Dutton; and as there is a sufficiency of the ministry in our family we have not even to call in the foreign aid of a minister. Sister Katy is not here, so she will not witness my departure from her care and guidance to that of another. None of my numerous friends and acquaintances who have taken such a deep interest in making the connection for me, even know the day, and it will be all done and over before they know anything about it.

Well, it is really a mercy to have this entire stupidity come over one at such a time. I should be crazy to feel as I did yesterday, or indeed to feel anything at all. But I inwardly vowed that my last feelings and reflections on this subject should be yours, and as I have not got any, it is just as well to tell you *that*. Well, here comes Mr. S., so farewell, and for the last time I subscribe,

Your own
H. E. B.

Had Harriet grown calm enough on her wedding-day to glance over the Cincinnati newspapers? If so, she may have noticed an advertisement that appeared in the *Republican*—

$1000 REWARD

RAN AWAY from the Subscriber, on Saturday the 12th instant [December, 1835]

ELEVEN SLAVES

First, DANIEL, aged about 55; ABBE, his wife, about 50; and their children: Daniel, about 25; Adam, about 22; Jonathan, about 21; Anthony, about 20; Judy, about 19; William, about 16; James, about 11; Reuben, about 10; Moses, about 9.

The above Slaves are all remarkably likely Negroes—light complexion, tall, and of fine appearance, and no doubt well-dressed and independent in their appearance, having been much indulged by me.

I will give the above reward of One
Thousand Dollars for the delivery of
the above family of Slaves to me, or
the securing of them in any jail, either
in or out of this State, so that I can
get them. Or, I will give One Hundred Dollars for the securing and delivery of each one of them, and pay all
reasonable expenses incurred in the delivery of them, or any one of them.

JAMES TAYLOR

Newport, Ky.

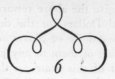

6

Brush with Slavery

HARRIET did not at once despatch her nuptial letter after all. The wedding trip intervened. Towards the end of January, 1836, when she had settled herself in her new Walnut Hills home—presumably the same rented house in which Eliza Stowe had died—she found the unsent letter in her portfolio and added to it from later experience.

> Three weeks have passed since writing the above, and my husband and self are now quietly seated by our own fireside, as domestic as any pair of tame fowl you ever saw; he writing to his mother, and I to you. Two days after our marriage we took a wedding excursion, so called, though we would most gladly have been excused this conformity to ordinary custom, had not necessity required Mr. Stowe to visit Columbus, and I had too much adhesiveness not to go too. Ohio roads at this season are no joke, I can tell you, though we were, on the whole, wonderfully taken care of, and our expedition included as many pleasures as an expedition at this time of the year *ever* could.
>
> And now, my dear, perhaps the wonder to you, as to me, is how this momentous crisis in the life of such a wisp of nerve as myself has been transacted so quietly. My dear, it is a wonder to myself. I am tranquil, quiet, and happy. I look *only* on the present, and leave the future with Him who has hitherto been so kind to me. "Take no thought for the morrow," is my motto, and my comfort is to rest on Him in whose house are many mansions provided, when these fleeting earthly ones pass away.

Once more she laid the letter aside, this time perhaps not entirely through carelessness. Hartford was in the most distant postal zone, and it cost twenty-five cents to send a single-sheet letter to Georgy. Two-sheet letters cost fifty cents, and so on, and a quarter of the 1836 dollar bought as much food and shelter as three or four quarters will today. As a result, people in the circumstances of the Stowes did not waste quarters on personal greetings. Indeed, the high postal rates must have done much to form the characteristic handwriting of that period—the finely etched script that Harriet used to the end of her life.

When the "wisp of nerve" did resume the Hartford letter, she had arresting news to tell.

Dear Georgy, naughty girl that I am, it is a month that I have let the above lie by, because I got into a strain of emotion in it that I dreaded to return to. Well, so it shall be no longer. In about five weeks Mr. Stowe and myself start for New England. He sails the first of May. I am going with him to Boston, New York, and other places, and shall stop finally at Hartford, whence, as soon as he is gone, it is my intention to return westward.

He sails the first of May! Calvin's professional business in Columbus was to address the Western College of Teachers on *Prussian Education,* meaning education in Prussia. His address commanded attention in the capital of a young State whose chief problem was the public education of its youth. There was an element of prearrangement in it. William Henry Harrison privately intervened, and the State Legislature passed a resolution requesting C. E. Stowe to collect, "during the progress of his contemplated tour in Europe," information on public instruction abroad that might be of value to Ohio in setting up a public-school system.

So the tour had been contemplated, perhaps for a good many months. Europe was obviously the place to buy books for the Lane library, but the thousands Dr. Beecher had collected for that purpose were, after all, limited. To send Stowe to Europe would cut heavily into them. General Harrison may have suggested the solution. The small, sallow County Clerk, none too popular personally in Cincinnati but a national power politically (the Whigs were to nominate him for President that year), seems to have taken a strong interest in the profound and amusing young professor at Lane Seminary. Perhaps Harrison was of the scant audience that sat through those lectures the oratorical beauties of which "could be had only by attendance." At any rate, he spoke a word in Columbus where it would do good, and the thing was settled—the former paper-mill boy was on his way to hobnob with the lords and kings of Europe. To be sure, the Columbus resolution said nothing about expense money, but the Seminary could rely on the good faith of General Harrison, Governor Lucas, and other friends at the State Capital.

Harriet, no doubt, would have given her eyes to go with Calvin, but it was out of the question. His journey meant snapping off her honeymoon, but that was the penalty one paid for belonging to a public family. Her reward was to be another trip to New England.

That was probably the winter when Harriet and Calvin were guests of General Harrison for a few days at North Bend, his imposing mansion on a river bluff sixteen miles down from Cincinnati. The hero of Tippecanoe had been territorial governor, member of Congress, and United States Senator, but perhaps preferred the obscure Clerkship of Hamilton County to any other office except the Presidency. The fees paid by a truculent population enabled him to maintain the hospitality of North Bend on a baronial scale. Four years later, during Harrison's triumphant "Log Cabin and Hard Cider campaign," the imagination of Whig orators converted the mansion into a log hut covered with coonskins. The diminutive Indian fighter did drink hard cider, but it took searching to find traces of the log walls of the original cabin around which the great house had risen.

A Cincinnati impression that Benjamin Harrison was born at North Bend during the Stowes' visit is erroneous. Ben was born in 1833. Nevertheless, the rest of the civic boast was true enough—that the North Bend "roof of brooding import" did shelter at once two future Presidents of the United States and the future great propaganda-novelist of the mid-century.

The "wisp of nerve," however, was not to enjoy the sight of New England that spring. By the middle of April, when Calvin had to leave, Harriet had discovered that she was on the path to motherhood and must not risk the hardships of pre-railroad travel. To her sorrow but everlasting professional gain, she remained in Cincinnati, which almost at once exhibited to her the ugliest side of the slavery issue she was ever to observe at first hand. No future twelvemonth did so much as that summer to fix her attitude toward the Peculiar Institution.

Full of regret, full also of a sense of importance and various last-minute instructions, the bridegroom therefore departed alone, to be gone almost a year, as the *Journal* (which by absorbing a Kentucky religious weekly had become the *Journal & Western Luminary*) announced with satisfaction that its columns were to be honoured by the great man's travel-letters.

Before sailing, Calvin had undertaken to carry out two important missions in the East. One exhibited him in a faintly comic rôle. It was this earnest young religionist's fate to have two fathers-in-law who had risen to become the leaders respectively of the two factions which were soon to split the

Presbyterian Church. Actually, they were figureheads, or champions, the war really being between the Princeton and Yale theologies. In Dr. Bennett Tyler, who had become president of the Theological Institute of Connecticut, at East Windsor, the conservative Princeton doctors had found a Joshua. Though Dr. Beecher did not completely subscribe to the Yale interpretations, because of his loyal personal attachment to Dr. Taylor and because of his great fame and influence in the church, he stood as the David of the Yale liberalism. As long as Beecher flourished the Taylor heresies would spread. Dr. Tyler was, therefore, in the spring of 1836, gunning for the head of Dr. Beecher.

Perhaps on his own suggestion, for he was a man of peace, Calvin Stowe undertook to bring about a reconciliation between Father Tyler and Father Beecher. Calling at East Windsor on his duty to describe the last days of Eliza to her bereaved parents, he took the occasion to spread forth Dr. Beecher's position. This he did by *reading aloud* to Dr. Tyler a letter which Dr. Beecher had addressed to an enemy of his in Richmond, Virginia—Dr. Plummer—answering at length certain questions propounded by Dr. Plummer with the design of searching out Dr. Beecher's orthodoxy.

Dr. Tyler was unimpressed. While protesting his love for Brother Beecher personally, he regarded his doctrinal answers as slippery. The war went on, as in Cincinnati Dr. Beecher packed up and set forth to its first major engagement in Pittsburgh, where Dr. Wilson intended to present his heresy charges to the General Assembly. With him travelled a fellow delegate, Mr. Brainerd, who had turned over direction of the *Journal & Western Luminary* to an editor-pro-tem, unnamed until at the end of his service but who all religious Cincinnati knew was Henry Ward Beecher, the Lane divinity student.

For this record it is only necessary to observe that at Pittsburgh the Old School faction, finding itself outnumbered, persuaded Dr. Wilson to withdraw his charges. This the wronged prosecutor did with reluctance, informing the Assembly that he was yielding only to his friends' importunities. There was a ticklish moment as Dr. Beecher pretended to debate whether to accept the withdrawal. It was his right to insist that the trial go on, in which event his enemies foresaw their western leader disciplined for slander. But Dr. Beecher was only playing with Dr. Wilson. He consented to the *nolle prosequi,* and both sides girded their loins for the next Assembly. Beecher and the faithful Brainerd went on to tour the East, leaving the *Journal's* editor-pro-tem to serve until the next snow flew.

Handsomely in funds, booked as transatlantic passenger along with an Ambassador—and was he not a sort of diplomat himself, representing the sovereign State of Ohio?—Calvin stopped in only the best places. In New York it was the new Astor House, just opened at Broadway and Vesey Street. In all his thirty-four years Calvin Stowe had entered few hotels as guest, and never one so splendid as this. He was so impressed he made the "superb mansion" the subject of his first travel-letter to the *Journal*.

After reciting (to the inch) the staggering dimensions of the edifice, he dwelt on its "308 rooms for boarders," its "80 servants," its "400 locks, all different." The "furniture alone cost $90,000!" It was "entirely lighted with gas," and, "Every room has a water-closet attached to it." In sum, the seasoned traveller pronounced the Astor House to be "an honor to New York."

The young editor-pro-tem of the *Journal* must have deemed such details, though fascinating in themselves, somewhat out of character for an admired Professor of Biblical Literature. He used the letter as a filler for his local column, crediting it merely to "a correspondent."

Panoplied with credentials and letters of introduction, Calvin embarked on June 8 on the sailing-vessel *Montreal,* Captain Champlin. Among his documents was a letter which bore in fine script the positive instruction that it was not to be opened until he was at sea. A lover and somewhat apprehensive cabin-passenger might interpret "at sea" to mean the tedious but smooth passage down New York Bay. The little bride in Cincinnati could already pamper her husband's pet affliction, his "blues," with affectionate admonition.

Now, my dear, that you are gone where you are out of the reach of my care, advice, and good management, it is fitting that you should have something under my hand and seal for your comfort and furtherance in the new world you are going to. Firstly, I must caution you to set your face as a flint against the "cultivation of indigo," as Elizabeth calls it, in any way or shape. Keep yourself from it most scrupulously, and though you are unprovided with that precious and savory treatise entitled "Kemper's Consolations," yet you can exercise yourself to recall and set in order such parts thereof as would more particularly suit your case, particularly those portions wherewith you so consoled Kate, Aunt Esther, and your unworthy handmaid, while you yet tarried at Walnut Hills. [A footnote in Harriet's supervised biography describes *Kemper's Consolations* as "a ridiculous book from which Mr. Stowe derived endless amusement."] But seriously, dear one, you must give more way to hope than to memory. You are going to a new scene now, and

HARRIET BEECHER STOWE

"Slim, sun-complexioned, active, intelligent, simply dressed, and perfectly self-
possessed." (Page 370.)

From a daguerreotype by Southworth and Hawes
(This recently discovered Hawes daguerreotype is pronounced by experts to be a portrait of Mrs. Stowe and is so identified by her grandson, Lyman Beecher Stowe.)

one that I hope will be full of enjoyment to you. I want you to take the good of it.

Only think of all you expect to see: the great libraries and beautiful paintings, fine churches, and, above all, think of seeing Tholuck, your great Apollo! [Frederich Tholuck, professor of theology at the University of Halle.] My dear, I wish I were a man in your place; if I wouldn't have a grand time!

The year 1836 was critical in the antebellum struggle over slavery, for that year the first resentments on both sides set into the permanent mutual hatred that eventually brought on the war. To gain a true picture of the great contention, it is necessary to bear in mind the not always appreciated fact that abolitionism began as a Southern and not a Northern movement and remained almost entirely Southern until about the year 1830. In 1829 four-fifths of the nation's anti-slavery societies existed in the South, and an even greater proportion of members. New York and New England together, for example, could count only three hundred enrolled Abolitionists. In North Carolina alone there were ten times as many.

Ten years later not one anti-slavery society was to be found in the South and scarcely one professed Abolitionist. Something had caused a revolution in sentiment. The theory that it was owing to cotton prosperity will scarcely bear examination. In the decade 1831-41 American cotton production increased only 50 per cent. It had doubled from 1821 to 1831 and tripled between 1811 and 1821.

Not cotton but Northern agitation killed the abolition movement in the South. When Garrison brought out the *Liberator* in 1831, he fired the first gun of the Civil War. A few months later a Virginia slave of remarkable personality, Nat Turner, gathered a band of black conspirators, massacred several white families in Southampton County one terrible night, and gave the South an attack of nerves from which it was not to recover while slavery existed. (Harriet later used the "Nat Turner Rebellion" as a principal theme in her novel *Dred*.) Out of the Virginia tragedy raced the dreadful suspicion that the Yankee fanatics were inciting a servile revolt, and the anger of the South became deadly.

The Lane student-strike brought the gathering tension into focus, as the membership of Southern anti-slavery societies melted away. "I detest it [slavery] as the political and domestic curse of our Southern country," wrote the Rev. Dr. Witherspoon, of Charleston, South Carolina, that summer to Lyman Beecher, "and *yet I would contend to the death* against Northern interference with Southern rights." If that was the attitude of a gentle man of God, what thought the planters and mill-owners whose livelihood and solvency were bound up in slavery and whose families lay under the menace of a hundred thousand Nat Turners? They did not lack Northern sympathizers. In his magazine Judge Hall was referring to abolitionist Oberlin as the "one school in which murder and robbery are openly inculcated as Christian virtues."

It made 1836 a riotous year everywhere, but nowhere were the flames hotter than at the Cincinnati spearhead. That winter James G. Birney, balked a second time by public opinion in the suburban river village of New Richmond, Ohio, moved his weekly anti-slavery *Philanthropist* into the Queen City for the greater security offered by a metropolis. Cincinnati replied with a mass-meeting that condemned Abolition and all its adherents. The postmaster at the landing of Augusta, Ky., announced that thenceforth he would refuse to forward newspapers addressed to subscribers in Ripley, across the Ohio River.

Birney could not have picked a moment less opportune for his invasion of Cincinnati. The railroad excitement stirred up by Dr. Drake had risen to a fever as construction gangs went to work on half a dozen routes in the East. Kentucky enthusiasts had already slapped down twenty-five miles of rails between Lexington and Frankfort. Then the Kentucky Legislature voted a right-of-way to the Louisville, Cincinnati & Charleston R. R., and Cincinnati went mad with joy, celebrating on the evening of February 25 with a grand "illumination." A heavy snow was falling, but it did not stop the entire town from turning out with torches to sing and shout through the muffled streets as bonfires blazed on the landing and street corners, churchbells rang, cannon thundered, and in his tailor-shop window Platt Evens put lamps behind a transparency reading:

CINCINNATI & CHARLESTON RAIL ROAD OFFICE
Seats May Be Taken Within
Through in 48 Hours

In the excitement the city paid scant notice to the action of the Ohio Legislature in chartering at about the same time both the Little Miami and the Cincinnati, Columbus & Cleveland railroads—the Queen City's first actual links with the transcontinental lines creeping westward from New York. But Cincinnati was obsessed with its dream road to the Carolina tidewater—

and here in its bosom it must nurture an estimable but wrong-headed man bent on advertising the city as a foe to the institution on which the prosperity of the great market was founded. The business community turned the face of stony hostility upon Mr. Birney and his Abolitionist rag.

At Calvin Stowe's departure Harriet closed her new home and went to live in the bereaved household of her father—the first time his roof had sheltered her, except as a visitor, since she left it at the age of twelve. It was like old times to be there in daily association with her dearest brothers, Henry and Charles, and with Aunt Esther Beecher, still worrying, in charge. Charles's preoccupation was the series of weekly letters on music he was contributing to the *Journal*. He signed these with the initials S. H. C., which may have been the inversion of an abbreviation of his name.

Harriet could regard life happily that spring. Her Geography had reached a sale of 100,000 copies and was, according to the advertisement, "generally introduced into the schools in the West." Less pleasant was it to drive into town, with its atmosphere of tension and danger. Indeed, there was a week in April when the danger was more than atmospheric. A street fight between two boys, one white and the other coloured, developed into a race war that burned a street of Negro houses in the "Swamp" district, shot or clubbed to death an untold number of the dispossessed, and brought out the militia, with Governor Lucas himself in command. That same week the *Journal* reprinted an offer of the city of Savannah to pay $10,000 for the person of A. A. Phelps, "a leading Tappanite." It was the first of many such "rewards" posted by Southern fire-eaters for the heads of Abolitionists.

It was a little depressing for Harriet to call on Mary Dutton, who since the break-up had gone to board with Uncle John Foote, in town. Mary was in the dumps, for the Western Female Institute, shorn of the magic name of Beecher, was not flourishing. But Catharine was writing Mary cheerily from the East, where she was raising a general education fund, part of which was promised to Mary's school. If Mary and Miss Tappan would hold on, they could depend on owning their own building within eighteen months. And Mary was to remember how much better off she was than had been Catharine during those first years in Hartford. Why, "in Cincinnati you have our house, and Uncle John's, and Uncle Sam's, and Mr. Wright's, and Mrs. Perry's as *homes*."

In May Mr. Brainerd departed with the Doctor for Pittsburgh and the East, leaving as an unnamed editor-pro-tem "a gentleman of piety, talents, and scholarship, and a thorough Presbyterian by birth, education, and choice." What fun it was going to be for Harriet to help Henry edit a real newspaper! Henry's first *Journal* was the issue of May 26th. Against Brainerd's usual half-column, he contributed three columns of editorial thunder, among other things extolling "temperance" and excoriating the theatre, as Harriet, in the diary she was keeping for Calvin (forwarding it to the traveller once a month), wrote, "I am quite proud of his editorials; they are well studied, earnest, and dignified. I think he will make a first-rate writer." Even a religious editor had to quarrel, or the readers would think him a man of mean spirit. Henry found a *casus belli* in a published prediction of Mr. Birney that Lyman Beecher was moving toward Abolitionism and would carry over his sons with him.

"Do young men never presume to think differently from their parents?" demanded the exponent of the 1836 youth-movement.

Henry commented frequently on the Peculiar Institution in a vein which, if not Abolitionist, was strongly opposed to slavery. A retort came from the postmaster at Pontotoc, Miss., who ordered the publishers not to send any more copies of the *Journal* through his postoffice, because of that paper's sentiments "on a certain subject." Henry answered with a fiery editorial so particular to his heart that he signed it at the bottom, "Editor-pro-tem." Then, asserting his independence of mind, he penned for another column an attack on Garrison, contrasting that violent Abolitionist with the "courteous, calm, and able" Birney. "We," added the editor-pro-tem, "are partizans with neither side."

July brought trouble to Cincinnati. In that city James G. Birney had found an able coadjutor in a young surgeon at the Cincinnati Hospital, Gamaliel Bailey. Dr. Bailey, a Methodist and deeply religious, and still in his twenties in 1836, was, like Samuel Foote, a Cincinnati citizen with deep-sea experience. Upon his graduation from medical college seven or eight years earlier, he had made a voyage to China as a ship's doctor. His first-hand observation of slavery on the free frontier had made him an Abolitionist. He was one of the few who gave comfort to the Lane secessionists, when they were encamped in Cummingsville. Soon after Birney brought his *Philanthropist* to Cincinnati, Bailey joined him as assistant editor. The surgeon had had previous journalistic experience as editor of the *Methodist Protestant,* of Baltimore.

Disapproving resolutions, almost universal hostility, and even the action of the Jackson Administration in forbidding the mails to "incendiary publications" (a regulation, incidentally, which Washington could never successfully enforce against the Abolition journals), failed to discourage Birney and Bailey. Week after week their *Philanthropist* appeared. July brought the semiannual influx of Southern "buyers" into Cincinnati. At the same time the great "Southwestern Railroad Convention," in which the nine States of Ohio, Indiana, Kentucky, Tennessee, Virginia, North and South Carolina, Georgia, and Alabama were participating, met in Knoxville, Tennessee. The Ohio delegation included Dr. Drake and E. D. Mansfield, of Cincinnati, and was headed by the Governor.

On the evening of July 12 the tension broke into violence as a well-organized mob, "composed in the main of young men of the better class," broke into the printing establishment of Achilles Pugh, a Quaker who published the *Philanthropist* for Birney, wrecked the forms, and to some extent damaged the press, as leading citizens of Cincinnati looked on complacently. Here was an earnest of the Queen City's true spirit enacted for the buyers and rich Southern planters occupying the most expensive suites in Cincinnati's hotels.

To the anger of the town, Birney refused to be awed by the display of force. Next day he and his people reset the edition and brought it out nevertheless. It was evident that the trouble was not over. Mayor Samuel W. Davies, whose election the previous autumn Editor Brainerd had hailed as a guarantee of good government, issued a proclamation against the rioters, offering $100 as a reward for the conviction of any member of the mob, then vitiated the edict by including a warning to the Abolitionists. The answer was an overnight blossoming of Cincinnati's bulletin-boards with handbills offering $100 for the arrest of Birney as a fugitive from Kentucky justice. Merchants, opening their shops, found under their doors notes signed "Anti-Abolition" ordering them to post their slavery sentiments in their windows or suffer the consequences. Seventeen "boarders" at the Franklin House, where Birney lived, told their landlord, William Johnson, to kick out the Abolitionist or they would leave. Johnson refused, and a dozen of them carried out their threat. Henry Ward Beecher wrote in the *Journal:* "One may doubt after all whether these men are not friendly to Abolitionists. They are laboring more busily than anybody else to make them."

It was a time when any lady might be justified in retiring to her chamber out of sight and hearing of such violence, not to say an expectant mother, now nearing her confinement. But when the Beecher blood boiled, it could overcome physical handicaps. One evening Harriet and Henry sat across a table and cooked up one of those disingenuous little by-plays of which both were always to be so fond when they gave the public what they thought the public ought to want. Henry needed a letter-to-the-editor on which to hang his remarks upon the current disorders. Harriet wrote the letter, signing it, "Franklin." All her writing days she was to show a liking for the shelter of pseudonyms, and it is a curious fact for the psychologically-minded that on such occasions she invariably masqueraded as a man. Harriet began her first published utterance on the slavery question:

MR. EDITOR:—A few days ago at the dinner table of a friend, a man of sense and intelligence, the following conversation took place:

"So," said Mr. L., flourishing his carver, "I hear Birney's press is broken open at last. I knew it must be so. Well, I can't say that I'm sorry. It will teach him better than to be setting these ultra measures on foot in our city."

"You are glad of it!" said I. "You, a Christian man and a lover of good order, not sorry that the laws of the city have been violated and the rights of private property invaded? My good sir, I am astonished at you!"

"Why, no," said my friend, looking somewhat puzzled, "I disapprove of mobs and unlawful proceedings of every kind—no man more—but then Birney and these fellows are so ultra and immoderate, and their measures are so calculated to throw community into a ferment!"

By adroit questions "Franklin" slowly backs his host into a corner.

"But you must allow [says the host] that it is undesirable to have that Birney here sending out these inflammatory things."

"Why? What harm do they do?"

"Why? They inflame community."

"Well, and what harm is there in inflaming community?"

"Why, it makes men furious, gives rise to popular commotions and disturbances, and *mobs,* and so forth," he said hastily, beginning to see where his own logic was taking him.

". . . Now, my friend, do you think the liberty of the press is a good thing?"

"Certainly—to be sure."

"And you think it a good article in our Constitution that allows every man to speak, write, and publish his own opinions, without any other responsibility than that of the laws of his country?"

"Certainly, I do."

"Well, then, as Mr. Birney is a man, I suppose you think it's right to allow *him* to do it in particular?"

"But Mr. Birney's opinions are so dangerous!"

"That is to say, so *you* think them. There are a large class of people in the nation who are just as sure that they are not. Now, how is the Constitution to be worded: 'Every man in the State may speak, write, print, and publish his own sentiments on any subject, provided that nobody in the nation thinks they are dangerous?'"

"Pshaw!" said my friend. "Of course, no law could run that way; but there is a point, you know, where all men of sense are pretty much agreed."

"Then," said I, "perhaps you would recommend that the Constitution should provide that every man may print and publish his sentiments, except in cases where all men of sense are *pretty much agreed* that they are dangerous?"

"Why," said my friend, after an uneasy silence of a few moments, "really you are getting to be quite a warm Abolitionist. I had no idea that you were so much inclined to favor Birney."

"Franklin" denies the impeachment and, after some more conversation of the sort, preaches his sermon.

"Just suppose that there was a train of gunpowder extending under every house in the city and the incendiaries had begun to explode it under some unsightly old buildings which specially disfigure the place. You stand on a hilltop and look down with great complacency—'That's right—can't say I'm sorry—glad to see those ugly old things blown sky-high.' 'You fool,' says a man, running up out of breath, 'don't you know that the same train of powder runs under your house and mine and every house in the city? Let it go twenty minutes longer, and they will all go together!' Now, this is precisely the case with these mobs. Every man is glad of a mob that happens to fall in with his views, without considering that if the mob system gets once thoroughly running, it may go *against* as well as *for* them.

*   *   *   *

"Now, the only way to prevent all this is for every man to stand sternly up for the principles of law and frown with indignation on every violation of them, even though they may accidentally accomplish something that he thinks desirable. The minister and Christian must treat with as much severity a mob against gambling as a mob against ministers and churches, the patriot statesman frown alike on the mob that advances as on that which retards his plans; and all lovers of good order must declare with one voice that they will regard nothing with approbation, compromise with nothing, and accept of nothing as a good deed that is purchased by outrages endangering those rights of property and of free opinion which are the pride and treasure of every American citizen."

Thus a feminine "Franklin," as across the table Henry Ward Beecher was writing, "This communication gives us an opportunity to express some views on this subject which we have felt until they have wrought in us an abiding hatred of the least approach to the violation of our Laws." Henry's editorial, *The Spirit of Our Times,* likened the riotous events to "flame jets which never come unpursued by the earthquake."

Other Cincinnatians concurred. E. D. Mansfield, returning from the Knoxville railroad convention, was appalled by what he found at home. He joined with Charles Hammond, the conservative editor of the daily *Gazette,* and Attorney Salmon P. Chase in calling a meeting to reprove the city. A blood-scenting opposition packed the meeting against them and howled down Chase's resolutions, whereupon a more popular convocation crowded the Lower Market and elected a committee to warn Birney out of town. Some of Cincinnati's leading citizens accepted membership on the committee, including, to Harriet's deep disgust, her Uncle John P. Foote. "I wish father were at home to preach a sermon," was her entry in her diary for that day.

Birney faced the law-abiding vigilantes stubbornly. They could only publish an account of their failure in the newspapers and pharisaically wash their soft, counting-room hands of the consequences. "They [the committee] owe it to themselves and those whom they represent to express their uttermost abhorrence of everything like violence, and earnestly implore their fellow citizens to abstain therefrom." The Cincinnati mob scarcely needed such sanction from on high. Everybody expected the violence to break out the coming Saturday night, when the town would be having its week-end spree and the riffraff of the wharves and packing-houses would throng the streets and bars. Only a week earlier Harriet, as "Franklin," was smugly declaring herself outside of Birney's slender band. Now she forgot even impending maternity, as she wrote in her journal for Calvin:

For my part, I can easily see how such proceedings may make converts to abolitionism, for already my sympathies are strongly enlisted for Mr. Birney, and I hope he will stand his ground and assert his rights. The office is fireproof and inclosed by high walls. I wish he would man it with armed men and see what can be done. If I were a man, I would go, for one, and take good care of at least one window.

On Saturday evening (July 30) the mob, still led by the city's "young men of the better class," gathered indeed at the intersection of Seventh and

Main Streets, watched from an upper window by Mayor, but did nothing more than yell threats against the damned Abolitionists. Sunday was a hot day and full of foreboding, as rough men loafed on the corners and the Negroes, vanishing from the streets, cowered in their houses and loaded such pistols as they owned. Cincinnati was then an "open" town on Sundays. That night the mob again assembled, this time for business.

It went first to Pugh's printing office on lower Main Street, wrecked it, tossed the type out of the windows, smashed the press, and carried the debris down to the river and dumped it in. The necessary job having been done, Mayor Davies appeared. "Well, lads," he dismissed the rioters, "you have done well, so far. Go home now, before you disgrace yourselves."

But the lads refused to be dismissed. The better-class young men could organize a mob but could not control it afterwards. This one had only begun its work. The next job was to harry the Abolitionists themselves. Birney lived in the Franklin House, but the rioters had not yet worked themselves to the pitch of storming a hotel. A private residence was more attractive, and the lawless throng rumbled over the warm cobbles to the home of Achilles Pugh, on Walnut Street. The Quaker printer was not there. Other Abolitionists dwelt in the vicinity, but in their houses the mob found only frightened women and children, whom it left unmolested. The anti-slavery men had taken warning and secreted themselves.

But Birney was supposed to be at large, and the murderous rabble started back for the Franklin House. One young man, who had been following events anxiously and indignantly, sped ahead. Of Cincinnati's 35,000 people, he was one of the last to be suspected of friendliness to Birney, let alone of willingness to defend the Abolitionist in person. Salmon Portland Chase was, in the first place, a social ornament in a frontier town largely populated by immigrants and the children of pioneer adventurers and ne'er-do-wells. He had background—an eminent New Hampshire family, one uncle who was the Episcopal Bishop of Ohio and the founder of Kenyon College, another who was a United States Senator. Young Chase himself was a connoisseur of art and music. As a law student in Washington, he had been in Daniel Webster's circle of friends. He already had fame of his own. Hanging out his shingle in Cincinnati, he used his fee-less years to collect and annotate the Ohio statutes. The published work, which remained standard for years, brought him instant reputation and important clients. In 1836 he was, at the age of twenty-eight, counsel for two of Cincinnati's leading banks.

Every professional interest of this young corporation lawyer lay on the pro-slavery side. At this date he had never met Birney. President Lawrence, of the Lafayette Bank, Chase's principal client, had served on the committee that notified Birney to leave Cincinnati. Nevertheless, when the mob reached the Franklin House, it found the door barred by the young patrician lawyer.

"No one can pass here," Chase said.

"Who are you?" demanded one of the mob.

Chase spoke his name.

"You will answer for this, Mr. Chase," said the ringleader.

"I can be found at any time."

They confronted each other, and for a few moments Ohio stood in danger of losing a future Governor and Senator, Lincoln a Secretary of the Treasury, and the nation a Chief Justice. Then, to Chase's relief, as he afterwards confessed, a thoroughly alarmed Mayor Davies appeared in the doorway to assure the rioters that Birney was not in the hotel and plead with them to go home. Instead, they returned to Pugh's printing office.

This time they carried out all the furniture and threw it into the Ohio, then invaded Church Alley to hunt the Negroes living in that slum. Two pistol shots sent them stampeding to the Exchange Hotel bar, where they excitedly told each other that one of their number had been killed by the shots, though no witness had actually seen the supposed victim fall. It was enough, after a round or two of drinks, to send them back to the alley for revenge. The Negroes had fled, and the mob contented itself with sacking and wrecking the miserable alley shacks.

With such alarms and excursions the night passed. Next day, Monday, the disorders continued, and another night of ferment was in prospect. Cincinnati was then unpoliced during daylight, maintaining only a Night Watch of a Captain and half a dozen patrolmen. Mayor Davies therefore swore in a corps of volunteers, with authority to bear arms and shoot to kill. Among those who enlisted were some of the chastened "young men of the better class" who had started the trouble. Among them, too, was Henry Ward Beecher. Harriet found him in the kitchen, pouring melted lead into a mold.

"What on earth are you doing, Henry?" she asked.

"Making bullets, to kill men with," was the sepulchral reply of the future Plymouth Church pastor.

"For a day or two," wrote Harriet in her journal, "we did not know but there would actually be war to the knife, as was threatened by the mob, and we really saw Henry depart with his pistols with daily alarm, only we were all too full of patriotism not to have sent every brother we had, rather than not have had the principles of freedom and order defended."

Her journal tells how it turned out.

> The mob, unsupported by a now frightened community, slunk into their dens and were still; and then Hammond, who, during the few days of its prevalence, had made no comments, but published simply the Sermon on the Mount, the Constitution of Ohio, and the Declaration of Independence, without any comment, now came out and gave a simple, concise history of the mob, tracing it to the Market-House meeting, telling the whole history of the meeting, with the names of those who got it up, throwing on them and on those who had acted on the committee the whole responsibility of the following mob. It makes a terrible sensation, but it "cuts its way," and all who took other stand than that of steady opposition from the first are beginning to feel the reaction of public sentiment, while newspapers from abroad are pouring in their reprehensions of the disgraceful conduct of Cincinnati. Another time, I suspect, such men as Judge Burnet, Mr. Greene, and Uncle John will keep their fingers out of such a trap, and people will all learn better than to wink at a mob that happens to please them at the outset, or in any way to give it their countenance. Mr. Greene and Uncle John were full of wrath against mobs, and would not go to the meeting, and yet were cajoled into acting on that committee in the vain hope of getting Birney to go away and thus preventing the outrage.
>
> They are justly punished, I think, for what was very irresolute and foolish conduct, to say the least.

Though Cincinnati was to see other slavery riots far more sanguinary than this one, no other so impressed itself on the city's memory and history. One immediate result of it was to rid Cincinnati of the presence of James G. Birney, after all. With no question of personal courage in it, Birney was not made of the stuff of martyrs. He had no taste for physical conflict and soon turned over the *Philanthropist* to Dr. Gamaliel Bailey, to devote the rest of his career to the Abolition stump and lecture platform. He did not live to see the slaves freed, but five of his six sons laid down their lives in that cause as Union soldiers. The temperate and level-headed Dr. Bailey ran the *Philanthropist* until 1847, when he became editor of the new *National Era* anti-slavery weekly in Washington, D. C.

More important was the effect of the Birney Riots in another direction. Well might the South have prayed to be delivered from its Cincinnati friends! The benevolent intentions of the city's business men converted to Abolition a young lawyer of some local reputation, an unknown divinity student, and the bride of a poorly paid college professor. Chase wrote long afterwards, "If any chose to call me an Abolitionist on that account, I was at no trouble to disclaim the name." Though neither Harriet Stowe nor Henry Ward Beecher became acknowledged Abolitionists until the 1850's, there is no doubt that the dark, last week in July, 1836, made them Abolitionists, too, at heart.

Chase as the lawyer carrying his anti-slavery causes to the Supreme Court, Chase in the Senate driving the North into frenzy by his denunciation of the Kansas-Nebraska betrayal; Henry Ward Beecher, with his maddening "slave-auctions" from the Plymouth pulpit; Harriet with her devastating novel—no other trio was so fatal to the Slave Power as this one. No other trio—not even one that included John Brown and Abraham Lincoln. With no *Uncle Tom's Cabin* to prepare the public mind, John Brown would have been a dangerous criminal at Harpers Ferry and not a nation's martyr. Without *Uncle Tom's Cabin,* or so William H. Seward said, there would have been no President Lincoln.

In August Dr. Beecher returned from the Boston marriage mart, bringing with him his third wife, who had been Mrs. Lydia Jackson, a widow with several children of her own, two of them married. There is a published statement that Catharine Beecher and this stepmother were never congenial; and, if we judge by the almost complete silence about the lady on the part of the other writing Beechers, they shared Catharine's opinion of the third marriage. Mrs. Lydia Beecher brought her two youngest children, Joseph and Margaret, to dwell in the Walnut Hills homestead; but the children of Roxana and Harriet Porter never admitted the Jackson children to their tight clan.

In August Professor William Holmes McGuffey, of Miami University, came down from Oxford, Ohio, to become president of Cincinnati College. In the issue of the *Journal* that noted this arrival, the editor-pro-tem announced that "next week we shall begin a series of letters, or rather, familiar notes of travel, from a gentleman in Europe distinguished for *accurate statement,* extensive learning, and refined taste." This gentleman proved (in the September 1 issue) to be none other than Calvin Stowe, who began his first travel letter at sea "between the Gulf Stream and the Bank of Newfoundland."

The Professor continued to send on his letters both to the *Journal* and to his wife. In Stuttgart he achieved a masterpiece, inditing a paper which should serve jointly as a letter for Harriet and a contribution for the programme of the Semi-Colon Club. It was an account of the private domestic life of Frederick William III, King of Prussia, gathered by Calvin from the gossip of the Lutheran coteries in Berlin. Calvin wrote this on September 29, 1836, a more important day in his life than he then knew, for, in far-away Cincinnati, his wife was that day (a little earlier than she expected) brought to bed of twin daughters. She named them Eliza Tyler and Isabella Beecher.

Even Cincinnati's young enthusiasm could not dispel the gloom settling over business that autumn. State and private banks, which Jackson encouraged, were extended with loans. The credit expansion sent prices upward and created feverish markets. The public was not deceived by the specious prosperity and began to hoard and save at every turn. Lane Seminary, already under the blight of adverse reputation, opened its new scholastic year with only thirty students. The enrollment at the Western Female Institute was also off sadly. Lane's new Gothic chapel, however, opened for services.

Truman & Smith, Cincinnati publishers, issued Professor McGuffey's *First* and *Second Readers,* with an advance sale of 10,000 copies. The *Third Reader* was in the press. In November Henry Ward Beecher reviewed in the *Journal* two new books that still live—Irving's *Astoria* and Captain Marryat's *Midshipman Easy*—shortly before the *Journal* announced that "the name of Mr. Brainerd, as editor, has been continued until this time, although he has been absent since the early part of May, and in the meantime Mr. Henry Beecher has occupied the post of editor," which was all the public thanks Henry got. The paper had changed hands, Brainerd and Henry were out, and the Beecher family promptly transferred its allegiance to the rejuvenated *Chronicle,* of which their old Litchfield friend, E. D. Mansfield, had become editor. Charles resumed in the *Chronicle* his articles on music. Harriet, before the winter ended, contributed her third piece of professional writing, another New England story called *Cousin William,* ingenious in plot and a creditable work for its day.

Calvin Stowe, the Germanophile, had naturally taken Germany first in his travels, reaching England in October. There he found an order for $3,500, which Dr. Beecher had raised in Boston and elsewhere the preceding summer. The globe-trotter had now become so cosmopolitan that in his letter of acknowledgment he referred to the sum as £700. For Ohio he visited the principal universities of England and Scotland and for Lane the principal booksellers, and by November 19, when he sailed for home in the good ship *Gladiator,* he could regard his trip as a complete success. Letters perhaps had gone astray, for he does not seem to have heard before sailing of the surprise awaiting him in a pair of Walnut Hills cradles.

The voyage was unusually tempestuous and long, even for the days of sailing-vessels. Calvin spent Thanksgiving, Christmas, New Year's, and his wedding anniversary on the tossing *Gladiator,* disembarking at New York on January 20, 1837, after two months and one day at sea. There, according to the record, he first learned about the twins. He saw his cargo of books through the customs, attended to some other necessary errands, and hurried west. The *Chronicle* of February 11 noted his safe return to Cincinnati— and also his intention to deliver immediately a series of Sunday-evening lectures in the Second Presbyterian Church on "conditions in England, France, and Germany."

The rose-petal twins, already old enough to smile and expose toothless gums when a delighted father waved a finger before their noses, were, of course, lovely; but their names—*mmh!* Eliza, yes, since Hattie wanted it that way; but Isabella—no. Hattie was being too modest. Calvin's twin daughters must bear the names of *both* his wives. So, after five months of existence, the twins were rechristened Harriet Beecher and Eliza Tyler Stowe, and Harriet Beecher and Eliza Tyler Stowe they remained to the end of their long, gentle, virgin lives.

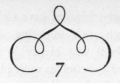

Hard Times

CATHARINE BEECHER, too, had felt the pinch of tight money in the East. She returned to Walnut Hills that winter with her grand general fund for education still a dream of the future. Nevertheless, she was able to contribute $900 to Mary Dutton and the shadowy Miss Tappan to help keep the Western Female Institute afloat. It was evident, however, that the school must fail unless accorded more generous support by Cincinnati; and in February one "Charitus" wrote an ill-tempered letter about it to Mr. Hammond's *Gazette*. Charitus was Catharine Beecher.

But the irritable Catharine was merely intervening for the female institute out of a sense of duty to her successors. She had a more immediate interest in Cincinnati that winter. McGuffey's *Third Reader* was out, and the "Eclectic Series" was already a great success. Truman & Smith wanted a *Fourth Reader*, but Dr. McGuffey was too busy with his new duties at Cincinnati College to prepare the text. He engaged Catharine Beecher to do it for him—to "ghost" it, as we say today.

In March 1837 the economic structure of the country trembled as a number of New Orleans banks and business houses failed for a total of $1,500,000. The repercussion brought failures elsewhere—more than two hundred important ones before the end of April. In May the New York banks suspended specie payments, the banks of Cincinnati and other large cities did the same as the news reached them, and the country was in the grip of one of the three worst panics it ever knew.

Slavery continued to obtrude itself into the troubled attention of people who wanted only to forget its existence. Upon reopening their Walnut Hills house, Harriet and Calvin had engaged in Cincinnati as a servant a coloured girl who claimed to be legally free. One day the girl returned from a visit in town and confessed the truth—she was a fugitive slave from a Kentucky plantation, and she had learned that her master was in Cincinnati hunting for her. She begged Harriet to save her.

In her authorized biography, Harriet gave Calvin the credit for engineering the girl's escape, though such initiative was scarcely typical of that "handless" man. More likely it was Henry Ward Beecher who went into action. He and Calvin armed themselves with pistols and took the slave girl on a night drive over rough back roads to the farm of John Van Zandt, a dozen miles north on the Montgomery turnpike. There the fugitive remained in safety until the pursuit gave up. Harriet worked this personal experience into her account of the night drive of Senator Bird with the fleeing Eliza Harris. Van Zandt, who inspired Harriet's character of "Old John Van Trompe" in *Uncle Tom's Cabin,* was a rough Kentucky farmer who had freed his slaves and moved to Ohio to battle slavery with his own hands. We are soon going to encounter him again in this story.

An octoroon slave girl named Matilda gave Cincinnati its annual slavery excitement that spring. Matilda, who was employed in James G. Birney's household as a servant, had been the property of a Missouri planter travelling down the Ohio with his family. When the steamboat touched at Cincinnati, Matilda vanished into the city and was hidden by the Birneys. The girl was light enough in complexion to pass for white.

A year later a professional hunter from Missouri found Matilda and dragged her into court under the fugitive-slave laws. Cincinnati rejoiced at the opportunity to dispose of Birney himself. A Grand Jury indicted him for harbouring a slave, and it seemed likely that the leading Abolitionist of the West would go to prison.

Salmon P. Chase, now out in the open as an Abolitionist, took both cases. There was on the Ohio statute books a dead-letter law providing that if a master voluntarily brought a slave into the free State, the slave was automatically free. Chase applied under this law for a writ of *habeas corpus* for Matilda, but the court denied his plea. Before he could perfect an appeal, Matilda was spirited to Kentucky and sold down the river.

Using the same law, Chase attempted the defense of Birney on the criminal charge, but with no better chance of success. A hostile Cincinnati jury brought in a verdict of guilty. Chase carried his appeal to the Ohio Supreme Court before he could win, and there only on a technicality of law.

In April the Cincinnati Presbytery licensed Henry Ward Beecher to preach, and the senior divinity student was keeping his ears open for a "call." Charles's theological education, however, had only made him an agnostic, or, as he termed it, a fatalist. George Beecher was married—perhaps that spring—to Miss Sarah Buckingham, of Batavia, New York, where the young preacher had his parish. The Beecher records are silent about this wedding, making it seem unlikely that any of the Cincinnati family went east to attend it. It was a good match for George, the Buckingham family being well-to-do. Harriet later maintained a warm friendship with Sarah, who accompanied the authoress on her first trip abroad.

For its Fourth of July celebration Lane Seminary held a picnic in its campus grove and a public exhibition of the library brought back from Europe by Professor Stowe. The Professor wrote a letter to the *Journal* describing its glories—5,000 new volumes, including the Greek and Latin Church Fathers, from Justin Martyr to Bernard and Hildebert; proceedings of all the Church Councils from 324 A.D. to 1664; the works of Huss, Wickliffe, Luther, Calvin, and Melanchthon, the Catholic historians and theologians, 200 Greek and Roman classics, works on ancient and modern history, various encyclopaedias, 50 quarto volumes of *Memoirs of the French Academy,* 160 volumes of proceedings of the Royal Society, 70 volumes of British poets, 56 volumes of French and German poets, and many standard German works.

A few days later a bank messenger drove out to Walnut Hills with appalling news. The draft for Dr. Beecher's salary had come back from New York *dishonoured.* The House of Tappan had failed, and the "endowment" of Dr. Beecher's professorial chair, represented only by a note, had gone into the schedule of liabilities, like any other debt. The Doctor was left with only the inadequate salary paid him by the Second Presbyterian Church, which, however, promptly raised his stipend $200 a year. George and Sarah Beecher responded with a cash advance of $200, while hard-pressed but pious people in Cincinnati made other scattering donations.

Still at the height of his influence, the most celebrated preacher in America approached his middle sixties as an object of charity, writing in his "commonplace book" out of a broken heart, "Thus has the ground of my support failed, and the considerations which brought on me a sense of duty to leave Boston and my people have, in a degree, failed also." The entry betrays the secret abode of Lyman Beecher's heart. Cincinnati and the Second Church congregation were never to be "my people."

It was all too much for Harriet, who was pregnant again that summer and feeling wretched. She needed a change of air, but the precarious family finances precluded any long journey. The home of Brother William Beecher, at Putnam, Ohio, offered itself. Catharine, having finished her work for

Dr. McGuffey, went along with Harriet and the babies. At Putnam we catch a glimpse of Harriet's attitude toward slavery. She wrote Calvin:

> The good people here, you know, are about half Abolitionists. A lady who takes a leading part in the female society in this place, yesterday called and brought Catharine the proceedings of the Female Anti-Slavery Convention.
>
> I should think them about as ultra as to measures as anything that had been attempted, though I am glad to see a better spirit than marks such proceedings generally.
>
> Today I read some in Mr. Birney's *Philanthropist*. Abolitionism being the fashion here, it is natural to look at its papers.
>
> It does seem to me that there needs to be an *intermediate* society. If not, as light increases, all the excesses of the abolition party will not prevent humane and conscientious men from joining it.
>
> Pray, what is there in Cincinnati to satisfy one whose mind is awakened on this subject? No one can have the system of slavery brought before him without an irrepressible desire to *do* something, and what is there to be done?

This letter must be read with remembrance of Harriet's characteristics. She was never one to ally herself uncompromisingly even in private communications with causes that were unpopular or dubious, however much she might secretly believe in them. As Mrs. Browning observed, her mouth was not quite frank. Her attitude toward spiritualism was an example. Her public utterances seemed to exhibit her as a disbeliever (though actually they pledged her to nothing); yet for thirty years at the end of her life Harriet Beecher Stowe consulted "mediums," operated the ouija board, subscribed to spiritualist publications, befriended professional spiritualists and promoted their works, injected spiritualism into one of her novels, and argued cautiously for spiritualism with her friend George Eliot.

So with Abolition in 1837. Abolition was unpopular with the kind of people Harriet knew, and therefore she could not espouse it, even in a letter to her husband. However, her mind was "awakened," "light" was increasing, she longed to *do* something about it; she felt the lack of an "intermediate society"—one, shall we say, untainted by the past violences of the ultras. Harriet asked for the game without the name. She was an Abolitionist. And the atmosphere of Brother William's household could not have been exactly hostile to the cause of Garrison and Birney.

While the sisters were in Putnam, the Cincinnati publishers issued McGuffey's *Fourth Reader*, as the news reached the West that King William IV was dead and the young Victoria had ascended the British throne. Another calamity met Harriet and Catharine upon their return. Uncle Sam Foote went bankrupt. The generous sailor had gone on a good deal of his friends' "paper." They defaulted in the panic, and Uncle Sam was ruined. Trained to accept vicissitudes, Uncle Sam accepted the disaster philosophically, turned over his beautiful home to the creditors, remodeled his sidewalk "row" of one-story offices as living quarters for himself and family, and began life anew in the insurance business.

(Since we may not meet Samuel E. Foote again in this narrative, it is well to finish with him now. He built up another fortune in Cincinnati, becoming secretary of the Ohio Life Insurance & Trust Company. Along in the 1840's he moved back to Connecticut, for no other reason than that he was annoyed by "the superiority of the rights of children in the West generally to those of parents." In the hope that they would pick up some good breeding, he put his own saucy sons into a New Haven military school and on Whitney Avenue in that city bought for himself an estate of twenty acres known as Windy Knowe, which had once belonged to General David Humphreys, the Hartford Wit. This tract Uncle Sam, at his own expense, turned into an experimental farm—"as an example to New England farmers." By applying scientific methods Foote was able to produce such crops as 253 bushels of potatoes from five-sixths of an acre, 80 bushels of corn from one acre, and 800 bushels of carrots from three-fifths of an acre.)

Uncle Sam Foote's failure carried down the Semi-Colon Club also. It had lost the spacious Foote residence for its meeting-place, and its prime movers were too discouraged that fall to organize the club for its winter season. Nor did it ever reassemble.

The nebulous Miss Tappan vanished in the financial storm, but Mary Dutton tried to carry on with the Western Female Academy, now "with the assistance of two young ladies highly qualified as teachers." The Tappan failure did not affect Calvin Stowe's salary; but other so-called endowments were faltering, and the welfare of the Lane faculty depended much upon student-attendance. When only fifteen boys reported in October for the beginners' (or Junior) class, Calvin was for giving up. His faint-heartedness spoke a language foreign in Dr. Beecher's ears. The Doctor was writing begging letters to men in Boston and New York and actually bringing in enough money to keep the Seminary going from month to month. "The failure of my support," he commented years later, "would have disheartened the trustees, disbanded the faculty, and for a long time paralyzed, if not finally suspended, the institution."

Would troubles never end? In November came the word of Lovejoy's assassination at Alton, Illinois, accompanied by the rumour that Edward Beecher had perished with his friend. A year earlier the Rev. Elijah Lovejoy had found St. Louis too hot for his Abolition paper, the *Observer,* and, encouraged by Edward Beecher and others, moved it to Alton. In November, 1837, a new printing press arrived for the *Observer* by Mississippi steamboat and was stored in a warehouse on the quay. The pro-slavery mob stormed the warehouse to destroy the press, but Lovejoy and his people were there to defend it. A shot from the warehouse window killed one of the rioters, whereupon the mob set fire to the storage shed. Lovejoy went up to the roof to extinguish the blaze and was shot dead. The murder made an immense sensation in the country, North and South, and gave the Abolition orators another date for their speeches. Edward Beecher, who had been helping Lovejoy establish his paper in Illinois, was not, however, present at the riot and so escaped.

On January 14, 1838, Harriet gave birth to a son, whom they named Henry Ellis Stowe. To help Harriet with her housekeeping burden, Calvin brought on his mother from Massachusetts that spring, and fat Aunt Nabby, in Natick, had a little peace with her meals. Henry Ward Beecher was lingering in Walnut Hills, waiting for a call; but Charles Beecher had definitely given up the ministry and had taken a place as clerk in a New Orleans brokerage house. Of all the Beecher sons, the musician seemed the least well adapted to a business career. Harriet was to mine for rich ore Charles's experiences with slavery in the deep South, for Charles told her about Simon Legree.

One mild April afternoon in 1838 the most shocking disaster in the history of Cincinnati brought the inhabitants of the city and its suburbs to the river. The Cincinnati-built steamboat *Moselle,* only a month in commission but already a record-holder and the pride of the river, blew up as she was backing away from the landing, with the loss of 136 lives. Bodies of victims were found on roofs more than a block away from the river. An investigating committee found that navigation companies paid little attention to the professional qualifications of engineers and called on Congress to set up an inspection service. Pioneering in a technique familiar today in boom communities, the Cincinnati business interests suppressed the report as harmful to the city's welfare. It took the efforts of Dr. Drake, Salmon

Chase, Dr. McGuffey, and a host of petitioners to force the report into print.

Strangely enough, the bad times were resulting in a boom for Cincinnati, as the unemployed in eastern centres drifted west by the thousands. The immigration created an acute housing shortage and a consequent appearance of roaring prosperity, as hundreds of new houses went up. The banks resumed specie payments that spring, but there was little specie in Cincinnati. The great building boom of the late 1830's subsisted almost entirely on barter, as site-owners, lumber dealers, supply men, and mechanics intertraded with each other.

In May the Presbyterian Church split permanently at Philadelphia, but that city scarcely noticed the historic fact in the face of a greater excitement. Even as New School and Old School were organizing their separate Assemblies, the sky was red with the flames of the new Pennsylvania Hall, in which the American Anti-Slavery Society was simultaneously holding its annual convention, burning at the hands of a mob. When, next day, the Abolitionists met in another hall, the rabble set fire to it, too. The Philadelphia Fire Department, which had merely let Pennsylvania Hall burn, tried to extinguish the second blaze, but the mob cut the hoses. In Cincinnati the life of the Western Female Institute flickered out, and Mary Dutton went home to Connecticut, the poorer for her Western experience by some hundreds of dollars.

But times so stirring and events so momentous or immediately sad seemed remote to Harriet that spring and summer. She was preoccupied with her babies. Love for the helpless—for children, for dogs and other pets, for the oppressed—was always to be a dominant characteristic of her nature; and her own children possessed her heart as not even her husband or her father or brothers and sisters could do. On June 21 she wrote about them to Georgiana May.

My dear, dear Georgiana:—Only think how long it is since I have written to you, and how changed I am since then—the mother of three children! Well, if I have not kept the reckoning of old times, let this last circumstance prove my apology, for I have been hand, heart, and head-full since I saw you.

Now, today, for example, I'll tell you what I had on my mind from dawn to dewy eve. In the first place, I waked about half-after-four and thought, "Bless me, how light it is! I must get out of bed and rap to wake up Mina, for breakfast must be had at six o'clock this morning." So out of bed I jump and seize the tongs and pound, pound, pound over poor Mina's sleepy head, charitably allowing her about half an hour to get waked up in,—that being the quantum of time it takes me,—or used to. Well, then,

baby wakes—*quâ, quâ, quâ*—so I give him his breakfast, dozing meanwhile
and soliloquizing as follows: "Now I must not forget to tell Mr. Stowe about
the starch and dried apples"—doze—"ah, um, dear me! why doesn't Mina
get up? I don't hear her"—doze—"ah, um—I wonder if Mina has soap
enough! I think there were two bars left on Saturday"—doze again—I wake
again. "Dear me, broad daylight! I must get up and go down and see if Mina
is getting breakfast." Up I jump, and up wakes baby. "Now, little boy, be
good and let mother dress, because she is in a hurry." I get my frock half on,
and baby by that time has kicked himself down off his pillow, and is crying
and fisting the bed-clothes in great order. I stop with one sleeve off and one
on to settle matters with him. Having planted him bolt upright and gone
all up and down the chamber barefoot to get pillows and blankets to prop
him up, I finish putting my frock on and hurry down to satisfy myself by
actual observation that the breakfast is in progress. Then back I come into
the nursery, where, remembering that it is washing-day and that there is a
great deal of work to be done, I apply myself vigorously to sweeping, dust-
ing, and the setting-to-rights so necessary where there are three little mischiefs
always pulling down as fast as one can put up.

Then there are Miss H—— and Miss E——, concerning whom Mary will
furnish you with all suitable particulars, who are chattering, hallooing, or
singing at the top of their voices, as may suit their various states of mind,
while the nurse is getting their breakfast ready. This meal being cleared
away, Mr. Stowe dispatched to market with various memoranda of provi-
sions, etc., and baby being washed and dressed, I begin to think what next
must be done. I start to cut out some little dresses, have just calculated the
length and got one breadth torn off, when Master Henry makes a doleful lip
and falls to crying with might and main. I catch him up and, turning round,
see one of his sisters flourishing the things out of my workbox in fine style.
Moving it away and looking the other side, I see the second little mischief
seated by the hearth chewing coals and scraping up ashes with great apparent
relish. Grandmother lays hold upon her and charitably offers to endeavor to
quiet baby while I go on with my work. I set at it again, pick up a dozen
pieces, measure them once more to see which is the right one, and proceed
to cut out some others, when I see the twins on the point of quarreling with
each other. Number one pushes number two over. Number two screams:
that frightens baby, and he joins in. I call number one a naughty girl, take
the persecuted one in my arms, and endeavor to comfort her by trotting to
the old lyric:—

> So ride the gentlefolk,
> And so do we, so do we.

Meanwhile number one makes her way to the slop-jar and forthwith proceeds
to wash her apron in it. Grandmother catches her by one shoulder, drags her
away, and sets the jar up out of her reach. By and by the nurse comes up

from her sweeping. I commit the children to her, and finish cutting out the frocks.

But let this suffice, for of such details as these are all my days made up. Indeed, my dear, I am but a mere drudge with few ideas beyond babies and housekeeping. As for thoughts, reflections, and sentiments, good lack! good lack!

I suppose I am a dolefully uninteresting person at present, but I hope I shall grow young again one of these days, for it seems to me that matters cannot always stand exactly as they do now.

Well, Georgy, this marriage is—yes, I will speak well of it, after all; for when I can stop and think long enough to discriminate my head from my heels, I must say that I think myself a fortunate woman both in husband and children. My children I would not change for all the ease, leisure, and pleasure that I could have without them. They are money on interest whose value will be constantly increasing.

By the terms of his employment, Calvin was entitled to the use of a faculty house, rent free. It came as a disappointment to the professor and his wife that spring when the Seminary found itself financially unable to build one for him, as promised. And another trouble was beginning to weight Harriet's heart. Mary Dutton, having had time to think things over at home, had written to Catharine suggesting that she be reimbursed for the $500 she had lost by coming to Cincinnati. Catharine was gradually liquidating the affairs of the defunct school. Mary's letter had been humble and conciliatory, but Catharine replied to it rather sharply from Detroit, where at the moment she was stopping with friends. Lost $500, had Mary? What about Catharine herself, who had drawn only $200 a year from the school against Mary's $500? Nevertheless, Catharine was willing to divide the "avails" of the liquidation equally with Mary. Mary bristled at the implication that she was asking for more than her due, and a rift opened between her and Catharine.

Worse, when Catharine returned to Cincinnati, she showed Mary's letter to Harriet, insisting that Harriet must have taken from the till more money than she was entitled to have. Otherwise, where had it gone? It was dismaying to Harriet, who had only a nebulous idea of how her old account stood with the school. She and Calvin had managed to save a little money against the purchase of furniture for the new house, when it was built—and Harriet knew that in a dispute over finances she would be no match for Catharine.

The masterful older sister was leaving unturned no stone under which she might find money for herself. That summer she revised and induced Truman & Smith to publish as one of the popular Eclectic Series of schoolbooks, an obscure textbook she had written in Hartford, entitled *Miss Beecher's Moral Instructor*. It appeared in its new reprint on August 9, 1838. Within a week thereafter its author, who was rapidly becoming known as the leading educator of the West, suffered the worst blow to her prestige she was ever to know.

In the August number of the *American Annals of Education* "Mr." Alcott (probably William and not his cousin Bronson) reviewed McGuffey's *Fourth Reader* and denounced it as a plagiarism—"compiled on the most flagrant and impudent system of literary piracy that has ever come to our knowledge." Specifically, Alcott charged that McGuffey had stolen the whole plan and many of the rules of his book from Worcester's reader and had also lifted from Pierpont, "including," as the reviewer jeered, "errors." Alcott cited a specimen rule from Worcester—

When you do not know how to pronounce a word, or are obliged for any other reason to hesitate while reading, do not cough or say *hem* or *eh,* but stop silently till you are ready to proceed.

—which appeared also in McGuffey, word for word.

The vexed Dr. McGuffey, who, having sold the book outright to Truman & Smith, had nothing to lose by the injunction suit promptly brought by Worcester's publishers, stepped from under by casting the blame, if blame there were, upon Miss Catharine Beecher, who, he acknowledged, had written "the rules, questions, and spelling lists" for the *Fourth Reader*.

Thus flushed from cover, Catharine defended herself both in a letter to Alcott and in a long, signed communication to the Cincinnati *Gazette*. Admitting that eight pages of the *Fourth Reader* came from Worcester, she denied the indictment of the plagiarized rules, except for the one cited. The injunction petition claimed that McGuffey had stolen thirty-three of Worcester's rules for his *Fourth Reader*. Catharine insisted that she had written all these from memory, and that they were, in fact, rules she had worked out for herself in her years of teaching before any Worcester readers had been published. She left the implication that Worcester had taken his rules from *her*. Besides, she argued, any school reader was but a compilation of other men's work. By any strict definition Worcester himself was a plagiarist. The dispute was too technical to excite much public interest; and in a day when even magazine editors snipped freely from other publications, authors' rights in their published material were vague. The warring book-merchants settled their differences, and the *McGuffey's Fourth Reader* marched in triumph through the mid-West schools until the century waned.

That summer the Presbyterian churches of the district divided between two Synods; the Old School Synod, now dominated by Dr. Wilson, made the gesture of reading Lyman Beecher and Professor Stowe out of the church. Henry Ward Beecher underwent examination by the New School Presbytery of Cincinnati, to which authority his new congregation at Lawrenceburg, Indiana, had elected to adhere, and was ordained as a preacher. His formal installation in November was a family affair, Dr. Beecher presiding, and Brother-in-law Calvin "charging" the people. Harriet must have been present on that great occasion, for Lawrenceburg was but a short distance down the Ohio River.

But it was a disconsolate brother-in-law who fulfilled that affectionate duty. When the new chapel bell rang in October to proclaim another scholastic year at Lane Seminary not one candidate appeared for matriculation. Defections caused by the hard times and the church schism had reduced the membership of the two upper classes combined to ten or a dozen students. The Seminary was virtually dead.

Calvin Stowe wanted to give up then and there and let the institution go, but he was talking to a man who was indomitable. Lyman Beecher took to the road, and we have the spectacle, as dreary as it is admirable, of the famous president of the "School of The Prophets," beating the hedges for students to give his courses and classes the appearance of existing. At Marietta College he secured four or five. Going into a Louisville store, he recognized the proprietor as a former parishioner at Bowdoin Street. In an afternoon he persuaded this man to sell out and take up the ministry of God, preparing at Lane Seminary. Edward Beecher, out of his abundance at Illinois College, let his father have six more students; and the Doctor returned to Walnut Hills in triumph at the head of a dozen prospective Isaiahs. In his melancholia Calvin had retreated to his bed.

"Wake up, Stowe!" cried the Doctor. "I've brought ye twelve students. Get up and wash, and eat bread, and prepare to have a good class."

His cheer brought only a half-hearted response. Calvin Stowe was already, in the privacy of his four walls, railing against Lane Seminary and shouting his intention to resign. Too late, he saw a dreadful prospect—he, the prodigy who had risen from a paper mill to international fame while an under-

graduate, who spoke German in a time when Theodore Parker walked from
Watertown to Boston to find a German dictionary, who preferred his New
Testament in the original Greek, whose career had promised such riches,
entangled by wife and children at the age of thirty-six with the fortunes
of a fading old man in a bankrupt and shunned college in the God-
forsaken West. His roars, as he knew and confessed, were as the crackling
of thorns under a pot. Not until Lyman Beecher was ready to retire and
the Seminary had been more or less reëstablished did Calvin muster the
resolution at last to break away.

The calamity that prostrated her husband only spurred Harriet's ambition. She had, she wrote to Mary Dutton, made a new arrangement.

> I have realized enough by writing, one way and another, to enable me to
> add to my establishment a stout German girl who does my housework, leav-
> ing to Anna full time to attend to the children, so that by method in dispos-
> ing of time I have about three hours per day in writing; and if you see my
> name coming out everywhere, you may be sure of one thing—that I do it for
> *the pay.* I have determined not to be a mere domestic slave, without even the
> leisure to excel in my duties. I mean to have money enough to have my
> house kept in the best manner and yet to have time for reflection and that
> preparation for the education of my children which every mother needs. I
> have every prospect of succeeding in this plan, and I am certain as yet that
> I am not only more comfortable but my house affairs and my children are
> in better keeping than when I was pressed and worried and teased in trying
> to do more than I could. I have now leisure to think—to plan—contrive—
> see my friends, make visits, etc., besides superintending all that is done in my
> house even more minutely than when I was shut up in my nursery.

A stout German girl in the kitchen and a governess in the nursery do not
sound exactly like poverty; but, if an extravagance, they were not a great
one. The day-to-day cost of living was at a low level. The best meat cost five
cents a pound, and Calvin could take a market-basket, or a wheelbarrow, if
he chose, to any Cincinnati packing-house, and the butchers would load it
gratis with spareribs and other unwanted cuts of pork. Anna was an English
girl who seems to have joined the household soon after the birth of the
twins. She remained with the Stowes for several years, and we can be sure
that for her services she received little more than the shelter of a Christian
home. Harriet spoke of her as her "faithful Anna." At a time when factory
hands got $4.20 a week the wages of house-servants were microscopic. If the
Token, Keepsake, Affection's Gift, Lily, or any of the sentimentally named

"annuals" that seasoned the bookstore counters at the New Year, paid Harriet E. Beecher Stowe, as she then signed her offerings, $25 for a sermonette or bit of moralizing, the sum would keep a Mina at the dishpan and washtub for several months.

After she became a famous woman, Harriet disseminated a heroic picture of herself at this period of her life as the professional woman of letters driving ahead on her career in the midst of a clamour of household and maternal cares. The picture rests largely on a sketch of Mrs. Stowe written (years later) by a neighbour, possibly the wife of another Lane professor, which showed the little genius, a tot or two clinging to her skirt and a baby in her arms, seated at the kitchen table as on one hand she dictates a story to an amanuensis and on the other directs Mina with the baking. The humour of the contribution lies in the comic pertinency of Mina's questions to the story in hand. Harriet is dictating to her friend, who tells the story in the first person:

" 'I know my duty to my children. I see the hour must come. You must take them, Henry; they are my last earthly comfort.'

" 'Ma'am, what shall I do with these egg-shells and all this truck here?' interrupted Mina.

" 'Put them in the pail by you,' answered Harriet.

" ' "They are my last earthly comfort," ' said I. 'What next?'

"She continued to dictate:—

" ' "You must take them away. It may be—perhaps it *must* be—that I shall soon follow; but the breaking heart of a wife still pleads, 'a little longer, a little longer.' " '

" 'How much longer must the gingerbread stay in?' inquired Mina.

" 'Five minutes,' said Harriet.

" ' "A little longer, a little longer," ' I repeated in a dolorous tone, and we burst into a laugh."

If this pictured, as she intimated, a typical day in Harriet's early married life, the work she produced was exceedingly fugitive, since she never collected any of it into books—and Harriet did not often miss an opportunity to re-exploit her published writings. After she had won an idolatrous following, she even republished her antiquated *Geography,* which had long since vanished from the schoolrooms.

Catharine appeared in January, full of determination to clear up the mess left by the failure of the Female Institute. She tackled the books and presently confronted Harriet with some disagreeable figures. Harriet stood overdrawn on the school's books to the amount of $114. She could scarcely believe it, but Catharine had the items.

Bowled over by the brutal figures, and having no defensive memoranda of her own, Harriet, in lieu of a cash restitution, meekly surrendered her share in the school's remaining assets, which the poor little housekeeper had depended on to add something to her furniture fund. With equal directness Catharine apologized to Mary Dutton. Had she accused Mary of carelessness with the school finances? It was all explained now.

Mary forgave all, and in a final letter Catharine relaxed into gossip.

"Harriet is not very well as to *nerves,* but no discouraging prospects as yet in the maternal line. I hope she is to have an interval of rest from further services at present in that line."

In the spring of 1839 the Cincinnati business men organized the first Chamber of Commerce of the West. Henry Ward Beecher, thanks to the Fourth of July oration he had delivered the previous summer, received and accepted a call to the new New School Presbyterian Church in Indianapolis. The salary was $800 a year; and, except for Edward, who was now thirty-six, no other Beecher son held so good a post. The family's ugly duckling was rapidly becoming its swan.

Harriet got her "interval of rest," as Catharine hoped, and also her trip to New England in the summer, when Calvin went to Dartmouth to deliver the Phi Beta Kappa address. One result of the family reunion of 1835 had been an agreement of the Beecher children and their father to keep in touch with each other by "circular letters." That is, a letter that made the circle of the family, each recipient adding news and observations of his own, and forwarding the letter on to the next address in the chain. On April 27, 1839, Harriet had one of the letters before her and contributed the following:

> I am going to Hartford myself, and therefore shall not write but hurry along the preparations for my forward journey. Belle, father says you may go to the White Mountains with Mr. Stowe and me this summer. George, we may look in on you coming back. Good-by.

Harriet took only one twin, her namesake, with her when she departed with Calvin, leaving Eliza and Baby Henry at Walnut Hills with Anna. She stopped in Hartford, while Calvin went on to Natick to see his relatives and prepare his address. Harriet heard from him in the interval—a letter in which Calvin characterized several of the amusing New England village types of which his wife was so fond.

"I have had some rare talks with old uncle 'Jaw' Bacon, and other old characters, which you ought to have heard. The Curtises have been flooding Uncle 'Jaw's' meadows, and he is in a great stew about it. He says: 'I took and tell'd your Uncle Izic to tell them 'ere Curtises that if the Devil didn't git 'em for flowin' my medder arter that sort, I didn't see no use o' havin' any Devil.' 'Have you talked with the Curtises yourself?' 'Yes, hang the sarcy dogs! and they took and tell'd me that they'd take and flow clean up to my front door, and make me go out and in in a boat.' 'Why don't you go to law?' 'Oh, they keep alterin' and er tinkerin'-up the laws so here in Massachusetts that a body can't git no damage fur flowin'; they think cold water can't hurt nobody.' "

Harriet joined Calvin, and they went up together to Hanover and thence into the White Mountains, where Harriet discovered a summer playground which she was to make her own, year after year, when she came to affluence. They got back to Walnut Hills in August to find the new house ready for occupancy. The fresh environment stimulated Harriet to write another New England story for Mr. Mansfield's *Chronicle*. She called it, embracingly, *Isabelle and Her Sister Kate and Their Cousin,* but held it in such light esteem that she omitted it from her *Mayflower* collection in 1843.

Harriet did not think much of the new house, to judge by her complete silence regarding its features in such letters of hers as remain. It stood on the east roadside of the Montgomery pike (Gilbert Avenue) not far above a crossroads centre now known to Cincinnati as Peeble's Corner. Even in 1839 there were stores there, and the Walnut Hills postoffice. Between the house and Dr. Beecher's residence to the north lay the expanse of the Seminary campus. We can guess that the Stowe house, where Harriet lived for nearly eleven years, was of frame construction, for it has disappeared, whereas the Seminary's brick buildings, including the President's House, still stand. A Catholic church and parish house now occupy the site from which Harriet watched for eleven years the farm wagons, the stages, the chaises and carryalls, and, occasionally, the fugitive slaves pass along this main highway to the north.

They moved in with their new furniture and, as they "settled," talked of their bleak prospects at Lane, and how much better they liked the East, and Harriet's plan to write a story about Uncle Jaw Bacon of Natick (it turned out to be *Love versus Law,* with which she led off her *Mayflower* collection), and Henry Ward's cabbages in Indianapolis (he had just become editor, as a side issue to his preaching, of the *Western Farmer and Gardener*), and Calvin's king in Prussia (whom by now they familiarly called "Old Fritz"), and the nuisance of having another baby.

For Harriet's "interval of rest from further services" was over, and once more her "prospects in the maternal line" were "discouraging." This time pregnancy and confinement cost her a year of active life. It began with a "neuralgic complaint" in her eyes (iritis?) that put her into a dark room for two months, and afterwards there was a long convalescence when she could not focus on print. The baby came in May, 1840—another son—and the birth was hard for her. For weeks afterwards she lay bedridden; and only the ministrations of Anna, "kindest of nurses," and the fact that the children had "'come to more' than the care of them" enabled her to bear up under her tribulations. It was not until December that she found strength to write to Georgiana May and tell her about a year that had been blank both in literary production and in letters.

By the spring of 1840 Calvin Stowe had persuaded himself that he was acquainted personally, if not intimately, with King Frederick William III, of Prussia. In Berlin he had met the Koenig's chaplain, who had told him some harmless and unremarkable things about his royal patron's private life. Another Berlin clergyman, whose name the Semi-Colon members must never reveal (an injunction sedulously obeyed, since Calvin neglected to identify his informant), told him some less pleasant facts about King Frederick. The gossip of the Berlin drawing-rooms about the mistress and morganatic wife (the relationship, of course, was "pure" to an Ohio preacher) gave Calvin a fine feeling of cosmopolitan sophistication. Once Calvin peered through the fence and saw the stout monarch taking the air in the royal garden, and no doubt more than once he saw the king driven through the Berlin streets.

This "inside" information about a royal figure was the chief trophy Calvin Stowe brought back from Europe. In his home he talked constantly about the *koenig,* whose heavy features gradually took on the lineaments of a close acquaintance. Calvin and Harriet began calling King Frederick William III a familiar "Fritz" or "Old Fritz" to each other, and not in jest, either. Calvin *knew* Fritz. As the intervening time lengthened, his admiration for the monarch grew. That Frederick William III was as stupid, pusillanimous, and callous an autocrat as 19th-Century Germany knew, made no difference—the king was pious, at least in outward form, and kept his deceased queen's New Testament on his desk. Calvin even regarded as firmness the dull despot's slaughter of the flower of his kingdom for adherence to a patriotic movement which the Crown Prince (whom Calvin thought less talented than his father) at once adopted as royal policy after his accession to the throne.

When, therefore, in May Harriet gave birth to a manchild, a name for him was at hand. (Did Calvin write to the royal godfather and tell him of the homage paid him in Cincinnati? It was quite in the innocent Germanophile's character.) The second son and fourth child of the arch-priestess of human liberty in America took the name of its arch-enemy in Middle Europe—Frederick William Stowe. They omitted the III.

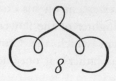

The Drab Years

DESPITE its dearth of ready cash, it was a booming Cincinnati that entered the century's fifth decade, with 46,000 inhabitants and almost as many more in the surrounding Hamilton County. Dickens, a year later, found the city "cheerful, thriving, and animated. I have not often seen a place that commends itself so favourably and pleasantly to the stranger at first glance."

But Harriet, who was not seeing it at first glance, did not like it. She reached her thirtieth birthday in June, 1841, and could regard the "godless West" as having swallowed her youth. Ahead of her stretched endless years of exile; but her brother George had partially repatriated himself by securing a church in Rochester, and George had passed along to William his vacated pulpit in Batavia, New York. The Beecher crusade had begun its retreat.

Harriet's birthday coincided with the start of the bloodiest riot in the dark history of Cincinnati mob rule. An English immigrant named Burnett hid a fugitive slave and assaulted the Kentucky owner when he came with a constable to search the premises. A mob howled at Burnett's door, but the Abolitionist and his three sons were safe in the city gaol. The murder of a German farmer by Negro berry-thieves and the raping of a white woman on Cincinnati's Broadway in August so increased the tension that in September a street brawl turned into a race war that terrorized the city for a week and was only put down by the militia commanded in person by Governor Corwin. Both sides used firearms, the mob loading cannon with boiler punchings and raking the streets of the Negro quarter. The toll of dead and injured was not counted. The feeling persisted into October, when the Methodist Anti-Slavery Convention found every Methodist door in Cincinnati closed to it.

It was not so pretty, as Harriet's "Franklin" had predicted, when in

January, 1842, the mob turned in another direction. The failure of the Bank of Cincinnati brought out a mob that wrecked the banking rooms, while Mayor Davies again looked on. An aroused Cincinnati's wrath this time took the form of a resolution of the City Council, censuring Davies for his inactivity. The mayor died a few days later; some said, of chagrin.

In April of that year Harriet may quite probably have seen the start of what became the *cause célèbre* of the whole slavery contention in Cincinnati. John Van Zandt, driving into town from his farm, met on the Montgomery road in Walnut Hills a parcel of nine slaves, who were escaping from a Kentucky owner. Van Zandt turned his covered wagon around and stowed the fugitives inside. But even that doughty Abolitionist did not quite dare take a more direct part in the escape. He placed one of the slaves, a boy named Andrew, on the driver's seat and went on into Cincinnati on foot.

Fifteen miles out two white men stopped the wagon to ask a question and became interested in its lading when Andrew took to his heels and vanished into the woods. They found the rest of the slaves inside and, scenting a reward, drove them in Van Zandt's wagon back to Kentucky. Salmon P. Chase procured the indictment of the two "bold villains" on a charge of kidnapping, but a Cincinnati jury acquitted them. The exposure was disastrous to Van Zandt, for the Kentucky owner sued him for the value of the lost Andrew, with such penalties for harbouring as the Ohio law allowed. Chase defended Van Zandt but lost the decisions all the way to the Supreme Court, as finally the nation looked on. Though Chase served without fee, the fines, damages, and court costs ruined his client.

Van Zandt was a familiar figure to Harriet, as for ten years he passed back and forth before her front door. It was probably this episode as much as his reception of the servant girl he sheltered for the Stowes that caused Harriet to use him for her Old John Van Trompe in *Uncle Tom's Cabin.*

In the three and one-half years that had elapsed since Harriet imparted her mighty vow to Mary Dutton, if she had not exactly qualified as a professional writer, or if Mary had not seen her name "coming out everywhere," at any rate she had been industrious enough by spurts to make it come out somewhere. Often enough to confirm her family in the belief that she was a genius and a celebrity—though as late as 1850 one of those ponderous combination anthologies and dictionaries of literary biography which the book agents carried around, spared to Harriet's career half a dozen lines while granting a page to her much more famous sister Cath-

arine. Often enough to enable her to keep in her kitchen a string of successors of Mina to save her from the housework she detested, the current
one being a Mrs. Whipple. (One of the sketches Harriet sold in this period
was a humorous and elegant discussion of the ages-old servant problem,
as illustrated by her own experiences.) Often enough so that in the spring
of 1842 she could contemplate another trip to the East.

She had an excuse for the journey. Catharine, who got around and knew
everybody, had been talking her up with the Harpers, in New York, and
the publishers had expressed interest in a volume of Harriet E. Beecher
Stowe's stories. Harriet found a dozen or more things of hers she thought
might do. Most of them had been published locally, one or two under
Catharine's signature, and several in a forgotten Cincinnati magazine then
faltering through a brief life, the *Souvenir*. The Stowes were acquainted
with the editor, Mr. Fisher, personally. Calvin, who knew more about
European kings than American magazines, predicted a great future for the
Souvenir.

It was so important Harriet thought it best to approach the New York
editors in person, and Calvin concurred. Harriet again took little Hattie,
now aged six, with her, leaving the other three children in charge of Anna
and Mrs. Whipple. Aunt Esther Beecher, along in her sixties and feeling
rather dispossessed anyhow by the third Mrs. Lyman Beecher, moved over
to watch after Calvin's comfort. Harriet made Mary Perkins's home in
Hartford her headquarters, attending to her business in New York on the
way up. Harper's accepted the book, which Harriet named *The Mayflower*.
The title had nothing to do with any of the stories but was apt historically.
This *Mayflower* was landing the New England village character on the
Plymouth Rock of American realism.

The ease of the transaction, the suavity of the editors, their subtle flatteries
for the daughter of Lyman Beecher (to be sure, they drove a hard bargain
with the tyro), and Harriet's renewed contact with all the poise and urbane
bustle of the dominating East, gave her a splendid sense of her individuality.
She was something more than the daughter, sister, and wife of celebrated
men. She stood above these hurrying thousands, one of the elect. This great,
teeming America was hers to help direct, if she chose. She had the power in
her. Ambition once more filled her to bursting, and she wrote to Calvin in
professional phrases that lifted her high above the humdrum sphere of a
poor Walnut Hills housewife.

I have seen Johnson of the *Evangelist*. He is very liberally disposed, and I may safely reckon on being paid for all I do there. Who is that Hale, Jr., that sent me the *Boston Miscellany,* and will he keep his word with me? His offers are very liberal—twenty dollars for three pages, not very close print. Is he to be depended on? If so, it is the best offer I have received yet. I shall get something from the Harpers some time this winter or spring. Robertson, the publisher here [Hartford], says the book will sell, and, though the terms they offer me are very low, that I shall make something on it. For a second volume I shall be able to make better terms. On the whole, my dear, if I choose to be a literary lady, I have, I think, as good a chance of making profit by it as any one I know of.

Calvin was tremendously impressed and made it a partnership on this upper plane by offering her some sage technical advice.

My dear, you must be a literary woman. It is so written in the book of fate. Make all your calculations accordingly. Get a good stock of health and brush up your mind. Drop the *E* out of your name. It only encumbers it and interferes with the flow of euphony. Write yourself fully and always Harriet Beecher Stowe, which is a name euphonious, flowing, and full of meaning. Then, my word for it, your husband will lift up his head in the gate, and your children will rise up and call you blessed.

Warmed by the affectionate praise, Harriet became nobly for a few moments the devoted mother. Could she "lawfully" divide her attention from her children by literary efforts? Evidently she intended to, for she went on:

There is one thing I must suggest. If I am to write, I must have a room to myself, which shall be *my* room. I have in my own mind pitched on Mrs. Whipple's room. I can put a stove in it. I have bought a cheap carpet for it, and I have furniture enough at home to furnish it comfortably, and I only beg in addition that you will let me change the glass door from the nursery into that room and keep my plants there, and then I shall be quite happy.

Calvin heartily approved, and spurred her new ambition by mentioning possibilities at home.

The little magazine [*The Souvenir*] goes ahead finely. Fisher sent down to Fulton the other day and got sixty subscribers. He will make the June number as handsome as possible, as a specimen number for the students, several of whom will take agencies for it during the coming vacation. You have it in your power by means of this little magazine to form the mind of the West for the coming generation. It is just as I told you in my last letter. God has written it in His book that you must be a literary woman, and who are we that we should contend against God? You must therefore make all your calculations to spend the rest of your life with your pen.

If you only could come home today, how happy should I be! I am daily finding out more and more (what I knew very well before) that you are the most intelligent and agreeable woman in the whole circle of my acquaintance.

It was becoming almost a second courtship, as Harriet wrote in answer to his letter:

I was telling Belle yesterday [Isabella was now attending school in Hartford] that I did not know till I came away how much I depended upon you for information. There are a thousand favorite subjects on which I could talk with you better than with any one else. If you were not already my dearly loved husband, I should certainly fall in love with you.

Since they were being so frank with each other—and it is the most intimate exchange of letters they left to their posterity—Harriet made it a general housecleaning.

One more thing in regard to myself. The absence and wandering of mind and forgetfulness that so often vexes you is a physical infirmity with me. It is the failing of a mind not calculated to endure a great pressure of care, and so much do I feel the pressure I am under, so much is my mind often darkened and troubled by care, that life seriously considered holds out few allurements—only my children.

In returning to my family, from whom I have been so long separated, I am impressed with a new and solemn feeling of responsibility. It appears to me that I am not probably destined for long life; at all events, the feeling is strongly impressed upon my mind that a work is put into my hands which I must be earnest to finish shortly. [Harriet lived to be 85.] It is nothing great or brilliant in the world's eye; it lies in one small family circle, of which I am called to be the central point.

For all they were "so prodigious poor," Calvin came East for her in the summer. Late in August they went home together by easy stages, stopping with relatives, the Beecher family being now so disposed that a member could journey from Boston to the Mississippi and reach a fraternal roof almost every night. The pair, with little Hattie, travelled from Albany to

Batavia, New York, by the new railroads, the first time any of them had ridden on the cars.

But the grand dreams inspired by the tingling air of the East never came to reality. The drudgery of keeping house on an inadequate income, another long period of ill health and lassitude preceding the birth of Harriet's fifth baby, whole years when the Seminary was unable to pay more than part of Calvin's meagre salary, years when an anonymous ten-dollar bill sent by sympathetic charity was welcomed with tearful thanks to God, Calvin's heartbreak and her own at the career he was wasting on the forlorn Walnut Hills enterprise, were too much for a frail woman unequal to any great pressure of cares. Whether Harriet realized her pathetic wish for a room of her own, she never wrote anything in it worth preserving. It was all hack-work turned out in desperate need as occasional opportunities arose. In fact, from this time she wrote nothing that found its way between covers until from her instrumentality issued the miracle of *Uncle Tom's Cabin*.

The years began to swing past her now, the drab, blank years in which the prophetess seemed to have lost her mission. One or two sharp misfortunes left their marks on her, but, except that her character was firming into a mould that could carry her unchanged through intoxicating experiences that turned so steady a head as Calvin Stowe's, no other period of her earlier life had so little effect upon Harriet's writing as the years between 1842 and 1851. She did not even improve them by polishing a style that was always slipshod and often deplorable. They seem to have been almost a sheer waste. The one thing Harriet's character gained from the poverty and sorrow of the 1840's was a humility that endured through the giddiest and most fantastic success any American woman ever knew.

The year 1843 saw the beginning of the Millerite excitement which gripped Cincinnati for nearly two years. Miller was one of the prophets of the Millennium, in a succession which has not yet ended. He gained such a following that he was able to conduct a journal, *The Midnight Cry*, within his cult and to build on Seventh Street a square tabernacle in which two thousand of his believers were to assemble to hear the last trump on December 31, 1843.

It grew serious for Cincinnati as solid business men closed out their interests, trusted employees resigned their jobs, workmen sold or gave away their tools, and servants became of little use to their employers as the hour drew near. One of Miller's converts was cashier of a leading Cincinnati bank; another was a successor of William Henry Harrison in the County Clerk's office. All the Millerites who could paid off their debts, which was one benefit the city gained. Those who faced eternity insolvent ran notices in the press asking the forgiveness of their creditors.

Upon the solicitation of his fellow citizens, and particularly that of Dr. R. D. Mussey, who was attending Harriet through another adventure in maternity that year, Professor Stowe took a hand in the disturbing affair. He was the leading Biblical authority in Cincinnati, or anywhere else, for that matter. Miller took his prophecy from the twelfth chapter of *The Revelation,* the allegory of the woman with child and the seven-headed dragon waiting to devour her offspring when delivered, and particularly from the sixth verse:

And the woman fled into the wilderness, where she hath a place prepared of God, that they should feed her there a thousand two hundred and three-score days.

Miller interpreted *days* to mean *years* and counted down 1,260 years from the date of the Great Apostasy. It brought him to the year 1843.

Calvin's refutation of Miller, addressed as a letter to Dr. Mussey, was published in pamphlet form and distributed in Cincinnati to check the spread of the superstition. In the first place, stated the Lane authority, nobody knew the date of the Great Apostasy within even a hundred years of accuracy. Secondly, there was no authority for the use of the number 1,260 any more than for any other mystic number in the Bible. Finally, it disgusted Calvin that all the latter-day prophets, when it served their purposes, assumed that *day* means *year* in the Bible. Did it rain forty days or forty years to make the Deluge? asked the Professor. Did Christ fast forty days or forty years in the wilderness? Calvin's argument was sustained at midnight of December 31, when the assembled Millerites heard only the trumps of New Year revellers.

Harper's brought out *The Mayflower* early in 1843. That year produced the usual riots in Cincinnati, occasioned by the action of a group of Abolitionists in spiriting away a slave girl belonging to a New Orleans traveller named Scanlon. Already the system of escape was being called the Underground Railroad. During the disorders the Scanlon mob again attacked the house of Abolitionist Burnett and threw so many stones through the windows that Burnett collected a barrelful of them. For years he kept the barrel of stones on his front porch, labelling it, "PRO-SLAVERY ARGUMENTS."

The insecurity of the Seminary's endowments, which produced income one year and nothing the next, had at length grown intolerable to Dr. Beecher and the faculty. Inspired perhaps by Edward Beecher's suggestion, the Doctor had in 1842 broached to certain key persons in the East the idea of a general philanthropic society for the support of Western Protestant institutions of higher education. Getting a favourable response, Dr. Beecher went East in May, 1843, and remained there several months, crusading for the society with his sons Edward and William. They met with good success.

Ironically, however, it was not Dr. Beecher nor the eastern philanthropists who became the salvation of Lane Theological Seminary, but a horned and forked-tailed gentleman who might be supposed to bear no love for the School of the Prophets. That same year—1843—Nicholas Longworth was planting the hillsides to grapes, digging caverns, and producing an excellent Catawba wine. Within ten years his example had turned the valley into the chief wine-producing region of the United States and sent the price of grape-lands up to $1,000 an acre. Lane Seminary found itself solidly endowed by its original farm.

In July, when Harriet was on the verge of confinement, her brother, George Beecher, accidentally shot and killed himself in the garden of his new home in Rochester. The tragedy shook Harriet's whole soul, she wrote, "like an earthquake." It shook the whole family, for George was the pride of them all. He was shooting robins out of his sweet-cherry tree with a double-barrelled, muzzle-loading shotgun. Nobody saw the accident, but Henry Ward Beecher remembered his brother's dangerous habit of blowing into the muzzle of his gun to expel the smoke.

After that the calamities piled upon Harriet. Her baby, a girl born in August and named Georgiana May, had only a precarious hold on life. The birth made an invalid of Harriet for months. Then Anna, who does not seem always to have been so gentle a soul as her mistress's letters had indicated, became difficult to manage; and the Professor dropped into the direst poverty that winter he was ever to experience.

Harriet did not know "where the ground might open next." She "felt an indistinct terror, as if father, brothers, husband, any or all, might be just about to sink." The new Eastern endowment had not yet filtered down to Calvin Stowe. "Our straits for money this year are unparalleled, even in our annals," Harriet wrote to Georgiana in Hartford. "Even our bright and cheery neighbor Allen [Professor D. H. Allen, of the Lane faculty] begins to look blue, and says $600 is the very most we can hope to collect of our salary, once $1,200." A year or two later she looked back on that winter of misery and remembered how day and night she was "haunted and pursued by care that seemed to drink my life-blood. A feeble, sickly child—a passionate, irritable nurse with whom I feared to leave it, from whom I feared to withdraw it—slowly withering in my arms, and yet I exerting my utmost care for it in vain—harassed, anxious, I often wondered why God would press my soul with a weight of cares that seemed to hold it prostrate on the earth."

Yet they survived. And little Georgie lived, too—to become the cleverest, gayest, and most tempestuous of the Stowe children.

When the sun rose as usual on January 1, 1844, Millennial Prophet Miller was ready with a new date in March. March ended safely for sinners and brought a final, positive prediction—the world would end on October 22. Nonbelievers planned on a longer future, as that spring they opened with ceremonies the Little Miami Rail Road as far north as Xenia. The retreat of the clan continued that summer, Edward Beecher resigning as president of Illinois College to accept the pastorate of Salem Church, in Boston; while to Calvin Stowe came the windfall of an invitation to address the American Institute of Instruction at Portland, Maine, for a fee and expenses paid. He went in August, leaving behind him a wife still "half-sick with confinement to the house and overwork," as she wrote to him. "If I should sew every day for a month to come, I should not be able to accomplish a half of what is to be done, and should be only more unfit for my other duties."

But in the midst of such tribulations there was solace for Harriet in Walnut Hills that year. Her brother Charles, having rid himself of theological doubts, had given up his clerkship in New Orleans and was back in his father's house brushing up for his examination before Presbytery. He had much to tell his sister about life in the deep South. He told her about Louisiana plantations so insalubrious in climate but rich in fertility that it was cheaper for the planters to work their slaves to death and buy new than to doctor them when they fell sick. On the boat Charles met an overseer from one of these places. He had a fist like an oak burl and made Charles feel of it. "I got that from knockin' down niggers," the man boasted. Harriet had her Simon Legree.

It took slight provocation to incite the Cincinnati mob, and the Millerites' Doomsday brought it out on October 22. It took the whole Cincinnati police force to protect Miller's two thousand purged believers, singing hymns in the square tabernacle as they awaited their haloes. Here and there on Main Street a closed shop displayed on its locked door the notice—

THE LANE FACULTY IN THE 1840'S

C. E. Stowe   Lyman Beecher   D. H. Allen

"Even our bright and cheery neighbor Allen begins to look blue, and says $600 is the very most we can hope to collect of our salary, once $1,200." (Page 217.)

From a portrait hitherto unpublished

"Gone to meet the Lord!" The ransomed remained in faithful prayer until the evening of the twenty-third, then gave up and went sadly back to their abandoned occupations.

In November Charles was installed as pastor of a New School church in Fort Wayne, Indiana, and Dr. Beecher, in his seventieth year, saw his great ambition attained. All of Roxana's surviving sons were in the ministry. There was more doubt about Harriet Porter's. James was away at school, and Thomas, twenty years old now and feeling himself a man grown, had a bent for chemistry. Tom was the only child left at home and hypersensitively suspected that people were calling him a sponger on his aged father. But the Doctor was detaining him. "They're all gone, Tom. Jim's at college. You musn't go 'way and leave me. I want one chicken under my wing."

The winter of 1844-45 was somewhat brighter financially for the Stowes, as the Seminary met Calvin's salary on time, and Harriet sold an occasional contribution to the New York *Evangelist*. But Harriet had never recovered strength and spirits after Georgiana's birth and that winter fell into another long spell of illness. By the next summer her condition alarmed her husband. It was as much soul-sickness with Harriet as bodily ailment. Poverty and its dull grind had at length worn her down. Life was a meaningless feat of endurance, and it had lost its zest. Furthermore, in their hopelessness she and Calvin had fallen out of the habit of frank, personal expression with each other. It was only during their rare separations that they could take the domestic inventory by correspondence. And so, when in June Calvin was sent as a delegate to a church convention in Detroit, his first act was to write her a letter which Harriet said was as agreeable as it was unexpected.

In this he told her of his fears for her. After Detroit the Seminary was sending him East on business. If Harriet could only come with him! The trip might do her good. But there was the old question of expense—the money.

"As to a journey," Harriet replied, "I need not ask a physician to see that it is needful to me, as far as health is concerned, . . . but I feel no particular choice about it. If God wills, I go. He can easily find means. Money, I suppose, is as plenty with Him now as it has always been, and if He sees it is really best, He will doubtless help me."

Of the many letters Harriet left to her posterity, this is her most despondent one. It was a wet, sticky June in Cincinnati, and Harriet was "sick of the smell of sour milk, and sour meat, and sour everything, and then the clothes *will* not dry, and no wet thing does, and everything smells mouldy; and altogether I feel as if I never wanted to eat again."

The Lord did provide the means, and Harriet went East with her husband later in the summer, not returning to Walnut Hills until the end of October; but she was so dispirited that when in her old age she was trying to reconstruct her life, she could remember little about this journey. They visited the Perkinses in Hartford, Edward Beecher in Boston, and Calvin's people in Natick. In Hartford, though confessing herself "an *invalid,* and very much of one," she had strength enough to intercede with Mrs. T. P. G. Bannister, a leading Eastern educator, in behalf of Catharine's scheme to import New England women into the West as schoolteachers.

How long it had been since Harriet left this home-land of hers! Thirteen years! "I am in New England, comparatively a stranger," she wrote Mrs. Bannister. She adopted her Uncle Samuel Foote's pet indictment of the Western country in urging tact as the first requisite in any teachers sent— "because at the West the children govern more than their parents, and a teacher can succeed only as she wins their hearts."

But the most important thing about her visit this time was Harriet's discovery of a new institution in the East—a "water-cure" sanitarium run by a Dr. Wesselhoeft at Brattleboro, Vermont.

They got back to Cincinnati, with Harriet little the better for her travel. All during the winter she drooped in health and spirits, paying now in neurasthenia for the scarring spiritual experiences of her adolescence, until it seemed to her that her only hope of life was to get to the Brattleboro water-cure. She had heard such wonderful stories about this institution back in New England—miraculous cures, and almost invariably in patients whom "the doctors had given up." It was just the sort of place for one whose maladies were none the less real because they eluded physical diagnosis. Besides, it was fashionable to visit a hydro; and, while Harriet, even when able to indulge all her impulses, was never overly fond of fashionable people, she liked to affect a fashionable attitude and do fashionable things.

But Brattleboro was out of the question for even such a managing family as the Stowes, who were always hard up and always doing about what they pleased. The sanitarium was as expensive as a mountain or seaside hotel, and, to get the full benefit of the cure, one must remain there weeks and months. Still, if God willed Harriet to go and be cured, go she would. He would find the means. Meekly and with more than a mustard-seed of faith, the prophetess took up her abode beside Cherith; and, as the ravens had fed her father in a similar crisis, so they sustained Harriet now. Charity gave her a year of the water-cure.

Harriet, who found it so hard to resist the dramatic when relating her experiences, left it obscure how total strangers in distant cities could hear of her need and contribute to her. If one wanted to call this intervention a miracle, one was at liberty to do so. Perhaps, though, the miraculous could be resolved into material letters sent out from Walnut Hills, it might even be on some chain system. The neighbourhood felt sorry for the shabby little wife of good Professor Stowe, sticking so heroically to his poorly paid place in God's service, and no doubt brought the pious family's plight to the attention of the philanthropic.

"The money for my journey has been sent in from an unknown hand in a wonderful manner," Harriet wrote to Hartford on the eve of her departure; but Calvin, in his first letter to her, was less mysterious. "When I returned from the steamer the morning you left, I found in the post office a letter from Mrs. G. W. Bull, of New York, inclosing $50 on account of the sickness in my family. There was another, inclosing $50 more, from a Mrs. Devereaux, of Raleigh, N. C., besides some smaller sums from others. My heart went out to God in aspiration and gratitude. None of the donors, so far as I know, have I ever seen or heard of before."

Just the prospect of respite from her domestic cares raised Harriet's spirits, and once more the humour began to bubble up in her letters. With the little mother about to be gone on such a long visit, the Professor must assume some of the maternal duties, and he started to practise under his wife's approving eye. "My husband has developed wonderfully as house-father and nurse," Harriet wrote to her friend Georgiana. "You would laugh to see him in his spectacles gravely marching the little troop in their nightgowns up to bed, tagging after them, as he says, like an old hen after a flock of ducks."

Harriet left Cincinnati late in March. Travel had become easier in the fourteen years since 1832. It now took less than six days to go to Boston—steamboat to Wheeling, stage and railroad to Philadelphia, railroad to New York, steamer to Boston; total fares, $25.50. Add five dollars more for meals and porterage. She made her usual family visits in the East and entered Dr. Wesselhoeft's establishment in May. She remained there until March of the following year.

Hydrotherapy, with its full schedule of sweats and icy baths, needle showers and strong jets of hot and cold water played upon the shrinking spine, is rigorous treatment even for the hale and athletic. With the fragile, bird-like Harriet, it must have been little short of kill-or-cure. Months after she began to take the baths she was still crying out against "that terrible douche." Once that summer she wrote to Calvin, "I go through these tedious and wearisome baths . . . thinking of my children," and she added feelingly: "They will never know how I love them."

With each other Calvin and Harriet had resumed their familiar occupation, *in absentia,* of taking stock of each other and their mutual relationship. Calvin had complained that one of the faults of their household was its lack of order. The letter depressed Harriet. "I really pity you in having such a wife. I feel as if I had been only a hindrance to you instead of a help." But she acknowledged the truth and good sense in his analysis.

"We have now come to a sort of crisis. If you and I do as we should for *five years* to come, the character of our three oldest children will be established. [Harriet wrote this almost on the twins' tenth birthday.] This is why I am willing to spend so much time and make such efforts to have health. Oh, that God would give me these five years in full possession of mind and body, that I may train my children as they should be trained! I am fully aware of the importance of system and order in a family. I know that nothing can be done without it; it is the keystone, the *sine qua non,* and in regard to my children I place it next to piety."

Dr. Wesselhoeft and the invalids she observed on his broad verandahs were making Harriet an apostle of health. "I think," she wrote to Calvin, "you might make an excellent sermon to Christians on the care of health, in consideration of the various infirmities and impediments to the developing the results of religion, that result from bodily ill health, and I wish you would make one, that your own mind may be more vividly impressed with it. The world is too much in a hurry. Ministers think there is no way to serve Christ but to overdraw on their physical capital for four or five years for Christ, and then have nothing to give but become a mere burden on His hands for the next five."

That summer also the family was astonished and diverted when Dr. Beecher, perhaps encouraged by the response of Providence to Harriet in her need, suddenly announced that he was going to take a trip to Europe. He had no money and no particular reason for going, except that he had never been abroad and wanted to add that experience to his life before it ended. Through prayer, he put himself into a receptive attitude, and Providence, as usual, obliged. The money came to hand, and the Doctor spent a month in England, preaching and exhorting for Temperance.

Life at the sanitarium, with its mixed crowd of idle, well-to-do health-seekers, was giving Harriet her first intimate association with people who dwelt outside her own Israel. The experience was broadening. At a time when her brother, Henry Ward Beecher, was beginning to thunder against the dance-hall and the theatre as the ante-chambers of sexual vice, Harriet was prodding her Professor with a shocking worldliness.

I am anxious for your health, do be persuaded to try a long walk before breakfast. You don't know how much good it will do you. Don't sit in your hot study without any ventilation, a stove burning up all the vitality of the air and weakening your nerves; and, above all, do *amuse* yourself. Go to Dr. Mussey's and spend an evening, and to father's and Professor Allen's. When you feel worried, go off somewhere and forget and throw it off. I should really rejoice to hear that you and father and mother, with Professor and Mrs. Allen, Mrs. K., and a few others of the same calibre, would agree to meet together for dancing cotillons. It would do you all good; and if you took Mr. K.'s wife and poor Miss Much-Afraid, her daughter, into the alliance, it would do them good. Bless me! what a profane set everybody would think you were, and yet you are the people of all the world most solemnly in need of it. I wish you could be with me in Brattleboro and coast down hill on a sled, go sliding and snowballing by moonlight! I would snowball every bit of the *hypo* out of you! Now, my dear, if you are going to get sick, I am going to come home. There is no use in my trying to get well, if you in the mean time are going to run yourself down.

As Harriet blossomed, Calvin faded, until he had dropped into one of his blackest fits of melancholy, nor did he scruple to ask for his wife's sympathy. She answered his letter during the first week in January, 1847— and a significant week it was for her, since her friend Dr. Gamaliel Bailey was that week bringing out in Washington his first number of the *National Era*. Harriet's spirits were now so exuberant that she could only laugh at Calvin's gloomy vapourings.

My dear soul, I received your most melancholy effusion, and I am sorry to find it's just so. I entirely agree and sympathize. Why didn't you engage the two tombstones—one for you and one for me?

But, seriously, my dear husband, you must try and be patient, for this cannot last forever. Be patient and bear it like the toothache, or a driving rain, or anything else that you cannot escape. To see things as through a glass darkly is your infirmity, you know; but the Lord will yet deliver you from this trial. I know how to pity you, for the last three weeks I have suffered from an overwhelming mental depression, a perfect heartsickness. All I wanted was to get home and die. Die I was very sure I should, at any rate, but I suppose I was never less prepared to do so.

Harriet left the sanitarium in March, but again visited in the East, and did not reach her home until May, fourteen months after she left it—to be welcomed, her son wrote, "with sincere demonstrations of joy by her husband and children." To be welcomed also with another sort of prospect, for almost immediately she conceived her sixth child.

This pregnancy and subsequent confinement were a severe test of the new health she had built up in Brattleboro, for her condition brought on another attack of the "neuralgic affection" of the eyes that all but blinded her for months. It made 1847 another blank year in which she scarcely wrote even a letter.

Calvin contributed little cheer during the difficult period, for he felt his health declining to an ebb from which only the miracles of the Brattleboro spa could restore it. There was greater optimism the other side of the Lane campus. The rising real-estate values had reached Walnut Hills, and there was a good prospect that the Seminary might pay off to Lyman Beecher the years of back salary it owed him. "I have become quite unexpectedly rich in my old age," the Doctor wrote to Aunt Esther Beecher, now helping Charles and his young wife bring up their first babies in Fort Wayne.

Whether Lane Seminary owed Professor Stowe any back salary, it did owe him a sabbatical year. The poor man was tired out. In fifteen years he had enjoyed no real vacation, and at forty-five he knew he had so far wasted his life on a futility. After nearly twenty years of existence the School of the Prophets could count only a hundred or so Western pulpits filled by its graduates. Calvin's struggles against the net were feebler now. He wanted only to rest.

As Harriet groped about her house that fall, Henry Ward Beecher returned from a brief vacation in the East bringing a call (which he had accepted) to the pulpit of Plymouth Church in Brooklyn, a new institution promoted as a business enterprise by an ecclesiastical impresario named Henry C. Bowen. With the exception of Charles (Thomas and James were in Yale) and the flitting Catharine, Harriet was the last of the Beecher children left in exile.

Harriet's third son and sixth child, Samuel Charles Stowe, was born in January, 1848; and already it had been decided that Calvin was to have a year of absence and was to spend it at Brattleboro. The fat Professor, growing more and more rotund in his middle age, merely dragged through his academic routine that spring; but the birth of her baby, whom they called Charley, restored Harriet to good health. Dr. Wesselhoeft had built solidly for her. Calvin left in June, to be gone fifteen months in his turn. By being away during much of 1849, he missed sharing with his wife the most frightful experience she was ever to know.

It was a big, tough, river city that went into the fatal year of 1849. More than a hundred thousand people swarmed in its dirty, noisome streets. Pickpockets worked the steamboat landing and the crowd in the depot at the daily departure of the cars for Sandusky, the morning list of holdups and burglaries was formidable, counterfeiters in slum dens struck off spurious coins, while carelessness and worse burned down buildings at a reckless rate. Prostitutes elbowed gamblers and confidence-men on the Main Street sidewalks. The year 1849 was remembered as the Murder Year, as Mrs. Howard was acquitted of murder (to the satisfaction of the just) after shooting her rival, Burglar Jones shot Policeman Brasher and got life, while a degenerate youth administered poison to his entire family. The mob still growled—a more vicious mob than ever. It stormed the Sycamore Street gaol to lynch two returning German veterans of the Mexican War accused of raping a child, later proved to be a liar and a tool in the hands of her parents who were plotting to rob the soldiers of their land warrants. A volley from the Greys killed eleven of the rioters and dispersed the mob.

Before the year was out gold was discovered in California, and the windows of Broadway and along the Public Landing blossomed with advertisements of routes and fares to Sacramento. Gas lights illumined the streets but did not make them safe at night. Several horse-drawn omnibus lines connected Cincinnati with the booming suburb of Walnut Hills, so that Harriet no longer had to depend upon her father's carriage.

"Georgy, I am thirty-seven years old!" she was writing her Hartford friend one January evening, when, if she had looked from her south window, she could have seen the Cincinnati sky lighted by the burning Shires' Garden at Vine and Third Streets, the most popular amusement resort of the Ohio Valley. Harriet was nearer thirty-eight, but she did not mind it. "I like to grow old and have six children and cares endless. I wish you could see me with my flock all around me. They sum up my cares; and, were they gone, I should ask myself, What now remains to be done? They are my work, over which I fear and tremble."

When Calvin left for the water-cure, Harriet had resolutely taken hold at Walnut Hills to maintain the household until his return. There were no ravens to feed Calvin, and she knew from experience that the expenses at the sanitarium would consume the greater part of his salary. To eke out what she had left of it, she filled her spare rooms with boarders and even conducted a small home school that next winter. She does not seem to have made any attempt to earn money by writing.

It was the small, busy housewife now who boarded the omnibus before daylight and took the basket down to the Cincinnati markets. She saw a town not what it had been in days which she herself could now regard as early. The old figures who had given the place its savour for her had dropped out of sight or been submerged in the rising population. New ones were coming in, like young Rutherford B. Hayes, who opened his law office in Cincinnati that year. But Salmon Chase was prominent and was just then successfully defending Dr. Beecher in ouster proceedings brought against him by the Old School crowd, to whom the enriched Lane Seminary had become a prize worth taking.

And still in Cincinnati, a city saint now, was Dr. Daniel Drake, who on May 10 notified his fellow-townsmen of the presence of epidemic Asiatic cholera. This time no jealous rival practitioners scoffed at his announcement.

But at first nobody paid much attention to it. The cholera had been more or less endemic in Cincinnati since the original outbreak in 1832. One grew to expect a few sporadic cases every summer. Even the spectacle of eight funerals wending through the campus drive to the seminary graveyard between May 1 and May 16 did not fill Harriet with any undue alarm.

By mid-June, however, it became evident to the population that this was no ordinary epidemic. Funerals were becoming so numerous that the supply of hearses was inadequate, and people uneasily watched coffins being carried to the cemeteries in open carts. On June 14 the Health Office reported a daily average of thirty new cases and seven deaths. This was not too severe; but the very moderateness of the report sent Cincinnati into a panic, as the rumour spread that the true figures were being suppressed. Actually the authorities were not suppressing anything; but before they could allay the hysteria, the epidemic suddenly jumped to the proportions feared.

Up, up, up went the fatality list, rising in a week from seven daily deaths to fifty and sixty. On June 25 eighty-four persons died in their homes or on the sidewalks, and Cincinnati, suddenly hushed, lay a city of the damned in the festering valley heat. Traffic, except for the incessant funerals, diminished to a trickle. The clusters of hacks at the upper corners of the Public Landing disappeared, some pressed into the mortuary service, others driven by their Jehus to the safer air of the country. Few steamboats were stopping at the Landing, anyhow, as passengers shunned the pesthole and crews grew mutinous at the order to land or receive freight.

But the bars of Cincinnati were doing a roaring business. Half the town, it seemed, was trying to drink immunity into itself or to drown out the universal terror. No one knew if he would see the morrow's sun, and the streets were full of drunken parties of men and women carousing past doorways in which the loaded coffins were stacked five and six deep, awaiting transport.

"The demand for coffins and hearses is so great that it is with difficulty the former can be supplied," wrote the *Gazette* man, "and for the latter every kind of vehicle is used. In conveying to places of burial, two or three coffins are seen in one vehicle alone, and the only accompanying friend sitting on the coffins in it. Drivers are becoming reckless, and race their hearse teams; and more than once, on the river road, the coffin has been pitched out in the race and the dead uncovered."

But the worst discomfort for the living was the coal smoke. On every street corner smouldered a heap of Pomeroy soft-coal, while Pro Bono Publico wrote to the papers demanding to know why the authorities did not import Youghiogheny coal, which was softer and greasier and smokier. Bituminous-coal smoke neutralized the fatal miasma in the air, and to double its effectiveness sanitary squads went about the city throwing sulphur into the coal fires—and also liming the places where the public committed its "nuisances." Soot festooned shutters and sills, it penetrated sealed doors and windows and settled on drygoods and hardware and books and stationery and meats and vegetables; office men who stuck to their desks were black with it before they left for their noon dinners.

The Fourth of July was a ghastly day in Cincinnati. The plague reached its peak that week, with 1,081 cholera interments in the cemeteries. In the face of death and mourning, terror, drunken orgies, and the perpetual pall of smoke, the young celebrated as usual. The authorities, fearing conflagration, had taken the precaution to dampen the smudge-heaps that day, and on July 5 the *Gazette* noted: "The coal fires burned dimly in the streets yesterday, much to the chagrin of the boys, who depended on them as *conveniences* during the Fourth of July fire-cracker jollification."

The papers were full of grisly instances—seven dead in one house on Race Street, eight deaths in one Jackson Street family, five members of one family on Sycamore Street dying on Sunday morning between dawn and eleven o'clock. "We heard of a mother visiting a sick friend, accompanied by her child; whilst on the visit the child was violently seized. The mother started with it for her home, a short distance off, but before reaching it the child died."

Even in its desperation Cincinnati could pause to be amused by the innocent proclamation of an old darky root-and-herb doctor, who allowed that if people would boil all the water they used, they would be safe from the cholera. Even the worried Dr. Drake could smile at this bit of superstition, since he firmly believed the accepted theory that the plague spread through an influence in the air.

During the final days of July the epidemic abruptly died out in Cincinnati, though now it was spreading elsewhere, as President Zachary Taylor in Washington proclaimed the first Friday in August as a day of National Fasting, Humiliation, and Prayer "that the Supreme Ruler may stretch forth His hand and stay the career of the dread pestilence which is now desolating our homes." By that day, however, Cincinnati had extinguished its coal fires and counted its toll of 4,488 cholera deaths. A city that had been overcrowded eight weeks before now sought tenants for 2,500 vacant houses.

Harriet Beecher Stowe lived through this dreadful time and lived valiantly. We know how she felt from day to day, because she kept a journal for her absent husband. Indeed, Calvin seems to have expressed the wish, though perhaps not too insistently, to come home and be with her through the ordeal. Harriet earnestly forbade it. "To exchange the salubrious air of Brattleboro for the pestilent atmosphere of this place, with your system rendered sensitive by water-cure treatment, would be extremely dangerous."

She did not need Calvin in this crisis. She was capable of managing alone. She was a lioness protecting her young, and she wanted near her no trembling hypochondriac ready to faint at first contact with the pestilence. No explorer lost in jungle or Arctic waste ever faced desperate uncertainties with a finer fortitude than Harriet's. What raw courage there was in her entry of June 29! No one had yet fallen a victim; but "if we were sick, there are so many of us that it is not likely we shall all be taken at once."

On July 1 she wrote, "A universal panic seems to be drawing nearer than ever before." July 3: "We are all in good health and try to maintain a calm and cheerful frame of mind. The doctors are nearly used up. Our own Dr. Brown is . . . prostrated, but we are all resolute to stand by each other." On July 4 she reported "all well" and no very dangerous cases near them. But in the town—"one hundred and twenty burials from cholera alone yesterday, yet today we see parties bent on pleasure or senseless carousing, while tomorrow and next day will witness a fresh harvest of death among them. How we can become accustomed to anything! Awhile ago ten a day dying of cholera struck terror to all hearts; but now the tide has surged up gradually until the deaths average over a hundred daily, and everybody is getting accustomed to it. Gentlemen make themselves agreeable to ladies by reciting the number of deaths in this house or that."

One or two groundless alarms froze her blood. On July 9, at a time when "a slight illness seems a death sentence," the baby, Charley, fell ill. With little hope, she carried him to Dr. Pulte, but it proved to be only one of the summer complaints so common in prerefrigeration times. But Calvin was not to come home. "It is decidedly not your duty to do so."

At one o'clock in the morning of July 12, Miss Stewart, one of the boarders, opened Harriet's door and cried, "Mrs. Stowe, Henry is vomiting!" Henry—her oldest boy—eleven years old now! With an unphrased prayer in her terrified heart, she hurried to him; but it was just an ordinary upset for him. How wonderful it was next day in the sunshine to find Henry well again and Baby Charles getting better and "auspiciously cross"! "Never was crossness in a baby more admired. Anna and I have said to each other exultingly a score of times, 'How cross the little fellow is! How he does scold!'"

And between Charley's indignant yells Harriet could hear the clatter of hoofs, as another "sable train" made its way back to the burying-ground that was part of the Seminary's academic equipment.

It kept striking nearer and nearer to them, as they all felt prostrated by the air, which was "of that peculiarly oppressive, deathly kind that seems to lie like lead on the brain and soul." On the morning of July 16 their little dog, Daisy, who had been ailing, suddenly ran out into the yard and died in a spasm. The children were mourning their pet, when news came that Aunt Frankie, an old coloured woman who had done their washing only yesterday, had died of cholera that morning. The twins helped Anna and Harriet make the shroud, and Harriet sewed a burial cap for poor old Aunt Frankie.

And then it came. On the nineteenth Charley went into convulsions. Dr. Pulte came and shook his head. This time the baby had Asiatic cholera, and there was no hope for him. Four days later Harriet was writing to Calvin: "We have been watching all day by the dying bed of little Charley, who is gradually sinking. There is now no hope of his surviving the night. Every kindness is shown us by the neighbors. Do not return. All will be over before you could possibly get here, and the epidemic is now said by the physicians to prove fatal to every new case. Bear up. . . . I do not trust myself to say more but shall write again soon."

Dr. Beecher was in the East, attending the Yale commencement; but Harriet attended to everything herself. She buried her baby in the Seminary graveyard and then wrote to Calvin:

At last it is over, and our dear little one is gone from us. He is now among the blessed. My Charley—my beautiful, loving, gladsome baby, so loving, so sweet, so full of life and hope and strength—never was he anything to me but a comfort. He has been my pride and joy. Many a heartache has he cured for me. Many an anxious night have I held him to my bosom and felt the sorrow and loneliness pass out of me with the touch of his little warm hands. Yet I have just seen him in his death agony, looked on his imploring face when I could not help nor soothe nor do one thing, not one, to mitigate his cruel suffering—do nothing but pray in my anguish that he might die soon. I write as though there were no sorrow like my sorrow, yet there has been in this city, as in the land of Egypt, scarce a house without its dead. This heartbreak, this anguish, has been everywhere, and when it will end God alone knows.

No mother who ever lived loved her children with more passionate affection than Harriet Beecher Stowe. No one was ever readier to rejoice in their virtues and triumphs or to condone their faults and sins. And it was to be the lot of this mother that fate should strike her oftenest and most tragically through her children. Charley's death in the cholera epidemic was but the first of the disasters that overtook them.

Within a few months Harriet would be sorting over the dead Charley's baby things as she prepared to leave Cincinnati forever. Within two years she would be writing of another mother doing the same thing—the wife of Senator Bird selecting from her dead baby's wardrobe an outfit for the baby of the escaping Eliza—and the autobiographical words came straight out of her heart.

Mrs. Bird slowly opened the drawer. There were little coats of many a form and pattern, piles of aprons, and rows of small stockings; and even a pair of little shoes, worn and rubbed at the toes, and peeping from the folds of a paper. There was a toy horse and wagon, a top, a ball,—memorials gathered with many a tear and many a heart-break! She sat down by the drawer, and, leaning her head on her hands over it, wept till the tears fell through her fingers into the drawer; then, suddenly raising her head, she began, with nervous haste, selecting the plainest and most substantial articles, and gathering them into a bundle.

They were going back East to live! When he returned in September, Calvin brought with him a medicine better than wavebaths and douches— the offer of a post on the Bowdoin College faculty, at Brunswick, Maine. Not much of a post, either—the poorest at Bowdoin in point of salary. Even for Calvin it meant a cut in income. Two rather obscure clergymen of the East had already declined the Bowdoin job. Eastern parishes of importance were by now paying their incumbents more than the thousand-a-year that went with the new Collins Professorship of Natural and Revealed Religion.

Still, to the blighted Professor Stowe just then, $1,000 a year in New England seemed better than twice that in Cincinnati. There was never much doubt about what Calvin would do; but, before he could accept, he must secure his release from Lane. To his astonishment, the Lane trustees at once offered him $1,500 a year to remain.

How he and Harriet must have raged to each other about that! An institution which in the name of the Lord had devoured the career of one of the most promising men of his generation and kept him in obscurity, had been willing also to let him and his family starve, though able to pay him adequately! That year when Calvin was fighting for health at Brattleboro and Harriet slaved with boarders and school classes—that year need not have been such a struggle. The effect on Calvin was to make him hard. In his house there was no longer any pious talk of loyalty to old Dr. Beecher, still clinging to his presidency. Calvin used the Lane offer to exact more money from Bowdoin,—a bonus of $500, out of which, he wrote his mother, "I must hire my own house, at an expense of $75 to $100 a year."

In this same letter Calvin told his mother he was turning down a New York offer of $2,300 a year in order to serve with his alma mater, but we can take the filial boast with a grain of salt. Perhaps the New York "offer" was only the possibility of one. At any rate, before he was seated in the Collins Professorship Calvin did receive a *bona fide* offer of a position much more attractive; and his wriggling to squirm out of the Bowdoin contract—he had already taken and *spent* the bonus—was a sad sight indeed.

For Harriet it meant putting her shoulder to the wheel, but the East was worth every effort, and that fall she turned to her long-neglected writing. The only thing she had produced in a year was an introduction for her brother Charles's first book, *The Incarnation; or, Pictures of The Virgin and Her Son,* brought out by Harper's. The new New York *Independent* had had some pleasant things to say about the book and the "introductory essay," too. No longer did Harriet think of "sketches," as she called her short fiction stories, when she wanted to help boil the family pot. She now wrote the easier journalistic pieces, speaking of "my engagements with newspaper editors,"—moral parables and sermonettes—"Mrs. Stowe's heavy Scripture lessons," a woman who did not like Harriet called them. They were heavy, but Harriet loved them. All her life she wrote sermons—for the newspapers, in her books, and in letters to her friends. She turned to them for relief from the more arduous work of writing fiction, for she could reel off her Scripture lessons by the yard. One "newspaper editor" with whom she probably made contact at this time was Dr. Gamaliel Bailey, of the *National Era,* in Washington. When little more than a year later she broached to Dr. Bailey the idea of *Uncle Tom's Cabin* as a serial, she spoke as an established contributor.

But the whole Beecher family was heading into journalism. In Boston Edward had just been appointed editor of the new *Congregationalist;* while on October 11, 1849, the *Independent* published a first contribution signed with an asterisk, while an editorial note elsewhere in the paper announced that the new correspondent who was to sign with a Star was Henry Ward Beecher, whose two years at Plymouth Church had already made him a figure in New York life. The first of the famous Star Papers was an attack on erotic magazines, or, as the writer called them, journals like the *Police Gazette* and *Scorpion,* which pandered to "the warm-blooded and licentious vices."

In April, 1850, Bowdoin College elected Calvin Ellis Stowe to the Collins Professorship; and, although he was not to be inducted until autumn, the Stowe family could wait no longer. Indeed, Harriet would have to go at once, if she were not to spend another summer in Cincinnati—with the poison of the cholera perhaps again creeping up the Ohio on the west winds. She was expecting a new baby in July. Calvin would have to serve out his time until the end of the scholastic year in June, and even that prospect appalled him.

In April, therefore, Harriet packed what she could, took three of the children, left the other two for Calvin to bring on, and departed for Brunswick, where they seem to have engaged a house already. She was to buy furniture for this house and settle it ready for the second contingent. She was also to see Eastern editors, for after this it was going to be imperative that she earn something with her pen. And she was to do all this during the final three months of a pregnancy. But she preferred even this prospect to another summer in the West.

She went by way of Pittsburgh, and there could have been few tears shed at the parting on Cincinnati's Public Landing. A few for Anna Smith, the English nurse, who was staying behind and thus passing out of Harriet's life; but none from Calvin, who would be following in a few weeks, and probably none from the lachrymose Dr. Beecher, who, his final prop gone and a substantial sum voted him for arrears of salary, was retiring—"not with the regrets of mortified ambition"—to devote the rest of his life (in the East, of course) to revising and publishing his sermons. Except for Charles, still at Fort Wayne, the retreat of the family was accomplished.

Harriet was too busy for tears, since Calvin was never of much use on such occasions, and Father Beecher was growing senile. She herself had to assemble the baggage at the bulletin board, buy the tickets, and see to it that Freddie didn't fall into the river when the packet came churning in to the landing stage. While they waited, she could glance idly at a hand-bill posted here at the gateway to Kentucky—

$1200 TO 1250 DOLLARS FOR NEGROES!!

The undersigned wishes to purchase a large lot of NEGROES for the New Orleans market. I will pay $1200 to $1250 for No. 1 young men and $850 to $1000 for No. 1 young women. In fact, I will pay more for likely

NEGROES

than any other trader in Kentucky. My office is adjoining the Broadway Hotel, on Broadway, Lexington, Ky., where I or my agent can always be found.

WM. F. TALBOTT.

How familiar this sort of thing was to her now—the stock figure of the darky with stick and bundle, the inky type! She had seen dozens of such bills. Human beings, with souls Christ came to save, graded like livestock—No. 1 young men, No. 1 young women! It was this she was going to forget in the Maine forest, breathing a balsam that was like the odour of freedom. There slavery would be a far-off, unreal thing, and she could close her eyes upon it at last.

After nearly eighteen years she was leaving Cincinnati without a regret or a friendship she would continue. Nor would she ever return, except as, many years later, Cincinnati was a stop on one of her lecture tours. She thought she had received nothing from Cincinnati. True, it had given her a husband, but it had swallowed the best years of his life to no avail, and hers with it. It had taken her baby from her, and she was leaving it without a backward glance.

But Cincinnati had, nevertheless, given her gifts more precious than friendships and pleasant memories. It had given her courage and self-reliance, humility and wisdom. And it had filled her quiver with sharp arrows.

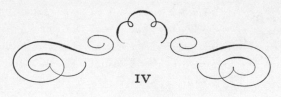

IV

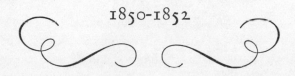

◉ BRUNSWICK ◉

1850-1852

The Home in Brunswick, Maine

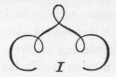

I

Immigrant Woman

IT WAS a forlorn little family group that faced the east on the deck of the Ohio River steamboat after the last handkerchief had been waved and the smoke of the big town closed in the river behind. The diminutive mother, shabby, life-worn, looking older than her thirty-nine years, her shawl scarcely hiding her condition of maternity, clutched with one hand a frayed and darned little boy, Freddie, now aged ten, and a patched and made-over little girl, Georgie, aged seven, while beside them, equally threadbare, stood Hattie, the twin, who in her fourteenth year was as tall as her mother.

They were so painfully the poor family looking its best for a grand occasion! At Brunswick a few weeks later the good ladies of the Bowdoin faculty were shocked by Harriet's appearance. Could this be the daughter of Lyman Beecher, the wife of the legendary Professor Stowe, herself a writer whose fame had reached academic circles of the East? The universal compassion she inspired took the form of charitable acts which Harriet remembered forever with gratitude. Indeed, the poverty of the erstwhile college genius as he returned to the scene of his early triumphs, made the Bowdoin authorities deal leniently with Calvin in their financial transactions a little later on.

There is a story that on this journey, while Harriet was making one of those atrocious after-midnight train connections with which early railroading inconvenienced the public, an ignorant station-agent in Pennsylvania evicted them from his waiting-room in the belief that they were an immigrant family. Harriet did not disillusion him. She had the sense of humour that could laugh at her own discomfitures, and often told this story later. In few famous women has the sense of inferiority been less complex. Harriet was genuinely humble.

She was humble now, standing with her brood, as Cincinnati dropped back behind her—past Point Pleasant, past Ripley, where she could point

237

out Parson Rankin's brick cottage high on the hill and tell the children again about the poor slave woman who crossed here on the ice; past Maysville, where she had visited in that distant girlhood of hers.

She faced the east; and despite her poverty, despite the uncertainties of the future and the new life moving within her, her heart was high. Nay, because of that new life. One of her children, at least, would be New England-born.

At Pittsburgh they transferred to the canal-boat. The canal crossed the main ridge of the Alleghenies near Hollidaysburg in a series of locks known as The Slides. It was five o'clock in the morning when they reached The Slides, but they got up to watch, "amid exclamations of unbounded delight from all the children, to whom the mountain scenery was a new and amazing thing." As she drew nearer the East, health and strength were flowing into Harriet. "I was able to walk a good deal between the locks on the canal." The railhead was at a place called Jacktown, where they got on the cars "at two o'clock in the night." This was probably the place where the depot man was so disagreeable. The jerkwater train did not deposit them in Philadelphia until three o'clock that afternoon.

Then it was "boat and railroad line for New York." At Lancaster Harriet had used the new telegraph to let her brother Henry in Brooklyn know when she would arrive. It was nearly eleven o'clock that night when they stepped off the ferry in New York, tired out—"we had ridden three hundred miles since two o'clock that morning." Cousin Augustus (one of the Footes) met them and took them over to Brooklyn.

After a good night's sleep Harriet began to bubble. And first, how wonderful it was, the way her closest brother, Henry Ward Beecher, was getting along! "Henry's people are more than ever in love with him, and have raised his salary to $3,300, and given him a beautiful horse and carriage, worth $600." Such figures were fabulous to Calvin Stowe, who must have writhed as he read his wife's letter. Calvin loved Henry Ward Beecher, but he knew him well. He had been Henry's teacher and for a year his roommate; and he knew that he knew more in a minute about the Bible and the basic theology of the preaching business than Henry Ward ever would know. Yet here was young Henry rolling in success and wealth—for he was selling his Star articles and beginning to lecture besides—while Calvin, two years away from his fiftieth milestone, was snatching at an Eastern berth with a salary on which he knew he could not exist. No wonder Calvin replied in a depressed mood.

There was a week in Hartford, where she saw Mary Perkins and her friend Georgiana, who was married at last and was now Mrs. Sykes. It was the first time Georgiana had seen her namesake, little Georgie, or Freddie either; and the two younger children were also meeting their Aunt Mary for the first time. Then Boston, where Harriet found everybody in Edward Beecher's circle talking about the debate in Congress over Mr. Clay's compromise proposals and particularly about Senator Daniel Webster's speech defending the compromise and reproving the North for having flouted the fugitive slave laws of 1793. Senator Clay was proposing a much more stringent law which inflicted federal penalties for harbouring escaped slaves and removed from State courts the power of recovering fugitives in federal custody through writs of *habeas corpus*.

Since the murder of his friend Lovejoy, Edward Beecher had been an avowed Abolitionist, and so had Mrs. Beecher. Edward and his friends regarded Webster's speech as a betrayal of freedom, if not of Jesus Christ himself. They were reciting Abolitionist John G. Whittier's *Ichabod—*

> So fallen! so lost! the light withdrawn
> Which once he wore!
> The glory from his gray hairs gone
> For evermore!

(To be sure, many good people in the North, if not the majority, were receiving the compromise with feelings of relief. It admitted California as a free state, thus throwing the South into a minority in the Senate; it abolished the slave trade in the District of Columbia; it left open the question of slavery in the new territories of New Mexico and Utah until they should apply for statehood. If it strengthened the fugitive-slave laws, it was but implementing the Constitution itself, which guaranteed the slave property. For ten years two great sections of this country had been existing side by side in a state of dangerous tension, though a static tension which had moved little or no nearer to a fatal disruption. The Northern moderates hoped that the compromise, while pleasing neither side, would eventually appease both and lead to a permanent, peaceful settlement of the great problem.)

But Edward Beecher and his friends were not moderates, and it was into an atmosphere of anger and apprehension that Harriet dropped when she reached Boston. How she reacted to it, we do not know. Late in life she permitted her son to say that "when she arrived in Brunswick her soul was all on fire with indignation at this new indignity and wrong about to be inflicted by the slave-power on the innocent and defenseless." No doubt she was indignant—she had seen slavery at first hand for many years, and she detested it—but her letters from Boston show no agitation of the spirit. If in Edward's house she acted in character, she listened in that owlish, inscrutable way of hers to the denunciations of the compromise, and held her peace. Slavery was politics and therefore none of a woman's business. So Harriet could listen, and be silent, and she could have her own opinion, and in the far northern air of Maine she could find relief from that frantic feeling which her contacts with slavery had always given her.

Even Brunswick and journey's end meant no rest for her, but only the beginning of toil, for there would be a house there to be cleaned and painted and warmed and settled, with all that implied in unpacking and lifting and arranging and stowing away, and all the while working against time, for the new baby was coming soon now.

Out of the tribulations of this journey (later, during an enforced leisure) Harriet wrote a little masterpiece of a sermonette, entitled *Earthly Care a Heavenly Discipline*. Reprinted as a tract, for the next half-century it was to comfort Christians borne down by troubles.

> Why should these cares my heart divide,
> If Thou, indeed, hast set me free?
> Why am I thus, if Thou has died—
> If Thou hast died to ransom me?

She answered these lines:

"To the Christian who really believes in the agency of God in the smallest events of life, that confides in His love and makes His sympathy his refuge, the thousand minute cares and perplexities of life become each one a fine affiliating bond between the soul and its God. . . . We learn to know God as the infant child learns to know its mother and its father, by all the helplessness and all the dependence which are incident to this commencement of our moral existence; and as we go on thus year by year and find in every changing situation, in every reverse, in every trouble from the lightest sorrow to those which wring our soul from its depths, that He is equally present, and that His gracious aid is equally adequate, our faith seems gradually almost to change to sight; and God's existence, His love and care, seem to us more real than any other source of reliance, and multiplied cares and trials are only new avenues of acquaintance between us and heaven."

This was Harriet's philosophy, and it sustained her now and throughout life.

On May 22 she and the children reached Rives Landing at Maquoit (which local speech pronounced McQuate), Brunswick's river port, three miles from town. As they descended to the wharf, a lashing rain drove into their faces from the northeast. One of the faculty ladies, Mrs. Upham, met them and took them and their baggage temporarily into her home in Brunswick.

For a week the nor'easter persisted, to the disgust of their hosts and the discontent of the Stowe children, who had heard so much from their father about this fairest of New England spots and who wanted to be out seeing it. But it was not an ill wind for Harriet Beecher Stowe. It was holding back the schooner bringing her household goods, thus giving her a week of perfect rest in as calm, comfortable, and well-ordered a household as there was in the State of Maine, the home of the Uphams.

The Uphams were a childless couple who loved children and who had adopted several for their own. Professor Thomas Upham, who left his mark in the annals of Bowdoin College, was tall, spare, and stoop-shouldered, and he was perhaps the shyest college professor who ever undertook to address a class. He could barely bring himself to speak aloud in the presence of strangers. His motherly, efficient wife after one look at Harriet devoted the rest of a rainy week to the business of getting a house ready for the Stowes to move into when their effects came—"taking charge of my affairs," as Harriet wrote, "in a way without which we could not have got along at all in a strange place and in my present helpless condition." There would be plenty of preliminary things to do—pay the rent, have the lease signed, see that locks worked and that broken windows were reglazed, and get in scrub-women for a general cleaning.

Good Mrs. Upham's heart bled for poor little Mrs. Stowe, so sweet and quiet, so cultured—and the children were so bright and well-mannered, though Georgie was a bit of a hoyden. But they were so poverty-stricken! Harriet never forgot Mrs. Upham's kindness to her that week and subsequently. The peace of the Uphams' home fell on her taut soul like a balm, and she wrote to Calvin: "This family is delightful, there is such a perfect sweetness and quietude in all its movements. Not a harsh word or hasty expression is ever heard. It is a beautiful pattern of a Christian family, a beautiful exemplification of religion . . ."

It was all of that.

The house Harriet had taken was on Federal Street. Federal Street and Maine Street were two of the best residential streets in Brunswick. They were parallel and adjacent and ran north and south between the business district and the north line of the Bowdoin campus. Federal Street was the easternmore of the two. The Stowes had engaged the old Parson Titcomb house, built in 1806, which seems to have been in some disrepair. Harriet's subsequent account of her tribulations in getting settled in this place, conveying the impression that she was a pioneer battling with primitive conditions of living, makes such an ardent State of Maine man as Robert P. Tristram Coffin, the poet and professor at Bowdoin, hot under the collar in this day, nearly a century later. Mr. Coffin admires Harriet but thinks that in playing up Brunswick in 1850 as a backwoods community she was drawing a mighty long bow.

Primitive conditions indeed! In 1850 Brunswick was as urbane, cultured, and cosmopolitan as Boston itself, even though, unlike Cincinnati, it did not then enjoy a municipal water system. Otherwise, Cincinnati was a frontier town by comparison. As for the Titcomb house, whatever its interior condition, it had been good enough a quarter of a century earlier for Henry Wadsworth Longfellow to live in it as a Bowdoin sophomore, and also for his brother, Stephen Longfellow. It was one of those spacious frame mansions of bland and hospitable mien which the New England joiners knew so well how to build. Harriet never again lived in a house so distinguished architecturally. Beside it, the jigsaw palace she built for herself later in Hartford—at such disastrous expense—was a rank absurdity.

However, Harriet was merely being dramatic about herself—and no great harm done, either. Of course, she was enjoying it, really. With a Boston letter inclosing the bill of lading had come one from Calvin filled with complaints. "He is sick abed, and all but dead; don't ever expect to see his family again; wants to know how I shall manage, in case I am left a widow; knows we shall get in debt and never get out; wonders at my courage; thinks I am very sanguine; warns me to be prudent, as there won't be much to live on in case of his death, etc., etc." And what did Harriet, in the ninth month of her pregnancy and busy with a thousand tasks and problems in house-settlement, do about this lugubrious epistle? In her own words, "I read the letter and poke it into the stove, and proceed . . ."

Calvin, with twin Eliza and young Henry Stowe, now in his thirteenth year, just did beat the stork to the house in Federal Street. They arrived during the first week in July, the baby on July 8. Following a family precedent, he became their Charley, too, but with a slight difference. The lost Charley had been Samuel Charles. This one they named Charles Edward. With his birth ended Harriet's child-bearing. Charles Edward Stowe lived to become his mother's biographer.

While Harriet reposed in blessed peace after Charley's coming, a real nurse to look after her and a stack of Walter Scott's novels on her bedside table, Calvin was less comfortable. His predicament was complicated. He had driven a hard bargain with Bowdoin, yet was immediately forced to demand a further concession. Despite Harriet's economy and budgetting and despite the sum lent her by her sister-in-law Sarah, George Beecher's widow—it seems to have come without solicitation—the money had run out. On the plea that a new baby, unexpected when he made his original dicker, had added to his expenses, Calvin asked for, and received from an indulgent Board of Trustees, an additional one hundred dollars. This was not a loan. It was an increment to his bonus.

But Calvin was holding something back. Lane Seminary had as yet failed to secure a worthy successor to Professor Stowe, and probably always would fail, at the salary offered. At any rate, the Lane trustees had cajoled or brow-beaten the pliant Calvin into an agreement to return and give his regular course of lectures during the coming winter term—with pay, of course. No doubt Lane wanted him back for the entire academic year, but it took more than a firm-chinned trustee to get Calvin Stowe back to Cincinnati during the cholera season.

Having secured his hundred dollars, therefore, Calvin, who had not yet taken his professorial seat at Bowdoin, asked for a leave of absence of three months during the winter of 1850-51 in order to fulfill his Lane engagement. He pleaded his poverty, his need for the extra income, and it was an effective plea. The Visiting Committee investigated and "reported the request reasonable," which was its 1850 way of saying that the star of the Class of 1824 had never had the breaks. No doubt Mrs. Upham's missionary work had something to do with the decision. Something simply had to be done for those poor Stowes.

Calvin might have breathed easier now, except for a new complication that had arisen. After the long winter of neglect, good fortune had begun to pour her gifts on him. He received the offer of the Professorship of Sacred Literature at the Theological Seminary of Andover, Massachusetts. What the offer was, we do not know; but Andover was the leading divinity school of the East, well endowed, and notoriously generous in the treatment of its faculty. Its professorships were better than those in the secular colleges. It is safe to assume that Andover offered at least twice the salary attached to the Collins Professorship, and Andover supplied houses to its professors.

Calvin Stowe was soon to turn fifty. He had seen contemporaries without half his ability win competences for themselves, while he remained a pauper. The man was desperate for the rewards he had thought would be so easily his, when as an undergraduate he had done work that had brought him international reputation. His children should have a decent education, too; his brilliant wife would not have to drudge through life like a servant girl. Whatever his obligations to Bowdoin College, or to Lane Seminary, he had no intention of letting this chance slip through his fingers; and Harriet agreed with him. How little did Calvin realize that within a few months the Andover chair, which seemed to him now as the great and worthy prize in any scholar's life, would by comparison become something trivial and embarrassing, a burden to be sloughed off his indolent shoulders at the first convenient opportunity!

The offer came informally through Professor E. A. Park, of Andover, who approached Professor Stowe to inquire about his availability for the appointment. Calvin's reply was too enthusiastic. There were some details that would have to be settled, but Calvin minimized them too much. Andover Seminary announced his election to the Chair of Sacred Literature. Lane Seminary had already announced that Professor Stowe was remaining on its faculty for another year. Bowdoin had announced his election to the Collins Professorship, and the invitations for his induction were out. A correspondent of the New York *Independent* commented sarcastically: "How far Dr. Stowe approximates to the faculty of omnipresence, we are not informed; but if, as the papers have stated, he is to have an actual and effectual connection with one college and two theological seminaries at the same time, he must stand in need of something like it."

That is what Calvin thought, too. Especially when a predisposed Board of

Trustees at Bowdoin took amiss his request to resign at once—perhaps accompanied with the promise to repay the bonus in some indefinite future. There was a limit to which Christian sympathy could go. The Collins endowment had provided for no bonus; it had come from Bowdoin College funds. Besides that, the trustees had granted him leave of absence for almost half of his first year in the Collins Professorship. They would do no more and informed Professor Stowe that they intended to hold him to his contract.

Calvin rushed to Andover to see if the Seminary would bear with him until he extricated himself. The Seminary would. It wanted Stowe now on any terms within reason. Calvin assured the Andover authorities that his difficulties could last only one year. At the end of a year he would feel himself morally free to leave Bowdoin. Meanwhile, there was a possibility that Lane might let him out of his winter engagement, in which event as an earnest he would come to Andover and conduct his course during those three months.

The Bowdoin trustees had had time to think it over. After all, Stowe had had plenty of provocation for his greedy attitude—and Bowdoin would not want a disgruntled professor on its faculty. Such men as Professor Upham may have interceded for the worried Calvin. At any rate, when he returned he found a better feeling and could write on September 18, 1850, to Professor Park:

> "My dear Sir, I find on my return home the troubled waters all calm, and a very pleasant state of feeling existing. It is getting to be the very general impression that *in due time and in a proper manner* they must give me up and let me go to Andover. I have written to Cincinnati, making a strong statement of my circumstances and desires, and requesting them to release me from my engagement to lecture there this winter. If they will do that (and perhaps they may), then the whole question is amicably and at once settled, for the Bowdoin folks will make no objection to my being at Andover instead of Cincinnati; and after this year I consider myself free."

Then a thought struck Calvin. Knowing the Lane folks, he doubted in his heart if they would let him off. Why couldn't a member of the Andover faculty—Dr. Edwards, for example—go out to Cincinnati as his substitute? Such an arrangement would solve everything. As an inducement to Professor Edwards, Calvin commented drily, "He would have a very mild climate and few students."

But Bowdoin College did not consider Professor Stowe free "after this year." The authorities insisted on a full year of work from him, after which they would tear up his contract. Even this was generosity, partially induced perhaps by a compliment Calvin paid to the Bowdoin boys. The 1850 brood at Bowdoin may not have been as brilliant as the 1824 student-body, which produced a major poet, a major novelist, and a President of the United States, to say nothing of a Calvin Ellis Stowe; but it was greatly improved in morals. In fact, Calvin thought, if the advance continued, Bowdoin might expect the millennium in twenty-five more years.

As Calvin suspected, Lane Seminary would not release him, nor was Professor Edwards tempted by the mild climate and intimate classes at Walnut Hills. Calvin had to go back to Cincinnati and pay his own pound of flesh. Then Bowdoin relented and during his second year permitted him to go to Andover during the winter for a three months' preview of his course of lectures. He appeared permanently in Andover in the summer of 1852. By that time great things had happened. He could consider himself a rich man.

Meanwhile, though his prospects were so bright in the summer of 1850, his family faced the brutal fact that for a long time it would have to get along on $1,000 a year. After two weeks of luxury for Harriet, they dismissed the trained nurse, and a governess came in to help. The identity of this lady is not given, except that she was "a relative." There were no Beechers in these parts, and the Porters of Maine could scarcely be classed as poor relations. The following summer we find old Dr. Beecher in the Federal Street house editing his sermons with the help of one of his Jackson stepdaughters, Mrs. Laura Dickinson. Since the married Jackson children all lived in or near Boston, Mrs. Dickinson may have been the Stowes' governess.

At any rate, Harriet cashed in on her relative in the autumn of 1850 by starting a small private school in her home, with the governess as principal teacher. Harriet herself gave an hour a day to the pupils, teaching them English history.

And Harriet wrote. "I have written more than anybody, or I myself, would have thought," she told Sarah Beecher in her Christmas letter. The generous life in Brunswick spurred her pen. Beside these urbane, wantless, academic homes, Faculty Row at Walnut Hills had been little better than a slum. Merely to begin to hold up the Stowes' end and escape from pity, Harriet had to earn money. Necessity drove her to her desk. At this time she cemented her relations with the *National Era,* becoming a regular contributor. The paper's star was Grace Greenwood, a much younger woman whom nevertheless Harriet admired humbly and sincerely. Harriet wrote everything but letters. Her December letter to Sarah Beecher, in Rochester, was her first acknowledgment of her sister-in-law's gift of money, which Harriet had received in Cincinnati before starting East.

The minute cheques from the newspapers were trickling in, the home school was adding its bit of income, and the Stowes began to look more prosperous.

Harriet became a dynamo of energy. In her summer convalescence she had rediscovered Walter Scott and now undertook to read all his historical novels aloud to her older children, giving up two hours to them every evening after tea. On a December Saturday she could write, "Tonight I finish *The Abbot;* shall begin *Kenilworth* next week." To this preliminary refreshment John Erskine attributes the Scott influence in *Uncle Tom's Cabin.*

Harriet resumed her drawing and painted pictures for her Brunswick friends. To save money, she dispensed with a cook and did all the housework herself. "Since I began this note," she told Sarah Beecher, "I have been called off at least a dozen times; once for the fish man to buy a codfish; once to see a man who had brought me some barrels of apples; once to see a book man; then, to Mrs. Upham to see about a drawing I promised to make for her; then to nurse the baby [she fed all seven of her infants at the breast]; then into the kitchen to make a chowder for dinner; and now I am at it again, for nothing but deadly determination enables me ever to write. It is rowing against wind and tide."

Harriet was growing nautical in her expressions, for Brunswick was a nautical town. It was the heyday of Maine shipbuilding—the same shipbuilding that had inspired Longfellow—and Casco Bay bottoms were fretting the waters of the Seven Seas. There were shipyards everywhere along the complicated shores of the Bay and its rivers—in Brunswick itself, at Maquoit, at Harpswell and Middle Bays, close at hand. The launching ways themselves were shaded early mornings and late afternoons by the clean-boled white pines that worked into such excellent planking and ship timbers. Indeed, shipbuilding was so profitable that inland carpenters built ships in their back yards and hauled them with oxen overland to salt water. Brunswick had seen ships on rollers moving right down the middle of Main Street.

The same families that built the ships also sailed them. Brunswick ship-captains knew Havana and Leghorn and Falmouth almost as well as they

did Portland. Their spacious white houses, in Brunswick and on the head-
lands and islands of the Bay, were full of Turkey carpets and Chinese inlays
and vases, of Hindoo tapestries, Ceylon silks, and all the rare and precious
things Harriet meant when she said frankincense and myrrh. Primitive conditions at Brunswick? Really, the academic households, for all their culture,
formed the provincial element in this community.

Here Harriet was meeting the sea for the first time in her life. Previously
she had known only such warmed-over and littered backwaters of it as
Long Island Sound and Massachusetts and New York Bays, but this was
the clean, blue water, spreading without a break to Africa and the Brazils.
As soon as Harriet was able to get around after Charley's birth, the Uphams,
or some other neighbour, hitched up and took the Stowe family down to
Harpswell. Here Harriet found a most romantic mixture of bays, islands,
promontories, ridges, unexpected coves still as landlocked tarns, rocks, reefs,
farms, beaches, capes, all embraced by the jagged evergreen forest. All her
life she preserved a youthful relish and enthusiasm for scenery exotic to
her native Litchfield—though the majesty of the Ohio River failed to impress her—and this fairyland enchanted her.

A trip to Harpswell became her favourite excursion while she remained
in Brunswick. It was not far—five miles or so south of the Bowdoin campus;
if they started early and took a day to it, they could even walk and return at
night not too tired. One of the spiny fingers of land that dug down into
Casco Bay broke at the end into segments connected with each other by
causeways and bridges. One of the segements was Orr's Island, which
Harriet loved so much she wrote a novel about it later. It was good to go
down there on a family picnic, bathe in the cold salt water, and afterwards,
while Calvin and the boys fished for cunners and flounders, to sit in the
warm sunshine on the rocks of the causeway and gaze across a flashing bay
at distant islands, capes, and coves.

So Harriet gloried in the exotic sea and learned to make chowders and to
boil lobsters—and use nautical terms in her letters. The very multiplicity
of her home duties gave her unexpected leisure, for they forced her to adopt
system and dispatch. She found time on her hands. The railroad was new
then. The steam cars began to run that year. Harriet's home on Federal
Street was only a couple of doors away from the track. There was no "wrong
side of the track" in Brunswick. The right-of-way cut through the heart of
the good residential district. The Uphams' "wide, cool, and hospitable"
house adjoined the track on Main Street. The home of Professor Cleave-

land, of the Bowdoin faculty, was on Federal Street next to the railroad on the south. A mile or so east of Federal Street the railroad split into a Y, one branch going to Bath and Rockland, the other to Bangor. One train a day came in from Rockland and one from Bangor to join forces at Brunswick for the rest of the trip to Portland and Boston, and the dispatcher's schedule brought both in at precisely the same moment. Consequently it was a race between the engineers to reach the junction first and capture the main track. Little Horace Chandler, Professor Cleaveland's grandson, always went out in his yard to see who won, and he usually saw little Mrs. Stowe, no larger than himself, out in her yard to watch the same contest.

On Sundays the Stowes attended the First Parish Church, across the street from the northwest corner of the Bowdoin campus. It was a tall Gothic edifice of frame construction, but its wooden sides were weathered to the hue of Notre Dame. Most of the pious students and professors of the college were communicants here, and it was the church of the leading seafaring families of Brunswick. They were as clannish as the Beechers and sat as groups. The stalwart Pennells usually rode up on Sundays from Middle Bays. The Pennell men had robust voices, and they were musical. From the Pennell section came the lead in the congregational singing. But there were various groups of Skolfields, Merrymans, Dunnings, Otises, and Minots, all of whom Harriet came to know well. Some of them suggested characters for her *Pearl of Orr's Island*. Harriet's pew in the First Parish Church now bears a historical marker, for it was there that she had her vision.

About once a week that autumn the Stowes and Uphams used to go to the home of Professor Smyth, the mathematics teacher, for an evening visit. Most of the talk was about slavery and the new fugitive law, which was already stirring up trouble. Professor Upham, who had no difficulty in speaking before friends, predicted more than once in these sessions that the slavery issue would not be settled without bloodshed. Little Newman Smyth sometimes listened to the grown folks' talk, and he remembered how "Mrs. Stowe used to sit silently with her face supported by her hand, as one dreaming of the future."

Harriet probably found time that fall to make a short trip to Boston. At any rate, at some time before she wrote *Uncle Tom's Cabin* she talked with the Rev. Josiah Henson at her brother Edward's home, and there is no record of her having met the coloured preacher and social worker during her spring visit to the Edward Beechers. Henson was in Boston that year, having brought out a schooner-load of black walnut lumber, *via* the St. Lawrence, from his African Utopia at Dawn, Ontario, now the town of Camden. The Canadian Government was encouraging the Dawn co-operative experiment, since it offered a chance for self-support to the fugitive slaves trickling across the United States border.

"Father" Henson was as saintly a man as Harriet ever knew, black or white. When he was a youth a brutal master in Maryland had broken both his shoulders in a flogging, and he remained crippled in his arms throughout life. Yet, when he "got religion," Josiah forgave his assailant and prayed for his soul. Another master treated Josiah scurvily. Although illiterate until nearly thirty years of age, Josiah had a better mind than his owner, who entrusted him with missions into the free States. While travelling in Ohio on parole, Henson learned to preach in the Methodist church.

His comparative liberty enabled him to earn a little money for himself, and he bargained with his master to buy his freedom. They agreed on a price of $600, and by slow degrees Henson had nearly paid this sum, when he discovered that his cheating owner had written into the sales agreement a price of $1,200. Learning that his owner was going to sell him down the river to get rid of him, Henson walked off into free territory and made his way to Canada, where he educated himself. By 1850 he was a well-known lecturer and exhorter in our northern cities. A little later he was to take an exhibit of Dawn products to the Crystal Palace Exhibition in London, and there meet Queen Victoria and all the great people of England.

At Edward's house in Boston this able black man told Harriet something of his story—and it was a story to make her Beecher blood boil. Her character of Uncle Tom was a composite of Henson and several other Christian slaves she had known personally or by reputation, plus her own imagination, but Father Henson was the dominant element in the creation. Later, when Henson wrote his autobiography, Harriet furnished an introduction for it.

In December Calvin Stowe left for Cincinnati, but already the deep, white winter had gripped Maine. It had taken Brattleboro to remind Harriet how much she had missed in Cincinnati the snows and zero temperatures of her native country. Here at Brunswick the drifts were deeper, the ice on the ponds thicker, the cold more profound even than on high Litchfield Hill, and in this latitude on a crystal January night the aurora borealis might paint tenuous bars and banners and fans of light in the north. Revelling in the climate, Harriet resumed her snowball therapy.

The gentle slope of Federal Street from the railroad track north might offer no attraction to an Olympic team, but, when the runners of bobs and sleighs had packed down a new powdering, it afforded satisfactory coasting to a determined little mother bent on snowballing health into herself and progeny. She bought sleds for the children, and Horace Chandler remembered how she joined them in their coasting parties, as red-cheeked and merry as any. There were no motor-driven wheels then to worry the most cautious of parents. At the foot of the long, leisurely run, there would be an up-bound bobsled to tow them all back again—with brave Henry and Freddie riding the runners and hanging to the batter-boards, and that little monkey of a Georgie wishing she might, too.

The problem of existence was almost as acute as ever; but there was hope ahead. She was in her New England to stay, and Harriet was probably never happier in her life than she was that first year in Brunswick.

Before 1850 ended Congress passed the Fugitive Slave Act, and the trouble began. Contemporary Abolition literature, including some of Harriet's, gives the impression that the North at once turned into a Saturnalia of fleeing blacks pursued by armed slave-snatchers. Actually, arrests of fugitives under the Act were few, but the excited press made a *cause célèbre* of every one.

In Syracuse a party of righteous townsmen stormed the gaol and rescued a respectable local coloured cooper named Jerry, who had been taken as a fugitive slave, and the whole country rocked with the news. In New York one Henry Long, fugitive, was taken, a federal judge signed the warrant delivering him over to the claimant, for which, as a newspaper jeered, "he doubtless received the extra five dollars generously awarded by Congress to every magistrate in a free State who can bring himself to consign a fellow man to slavery."

Boston, where there was a considerable colony of fugitives who had escaped on coastwise vessels sailing from Southern ports, painted itself as a pandemonium of "men-stealers" and their hapless black victims, though the lens of after-examination reveals only four or five incidents arising under the enforcement of the Act. The hubbub raised over these, however, was enough to make a worried Administration threaten to send troops to Boston to enforce the law, and—with such a conservative journal as the New York *Independent* advocating resistance to the Act—enough to make an Abolitionist family like the Rev. Edward Beecher's sick with indignation and shame. In the opinion of Abolitionists like Edward Beecher, the law by its terms made every Christian in the North, whatever his views, share the guilt of the darkest national crime to curse the earth since Nero fed the martyrs to the lions.

To whom, therefore, should a militant Mrs. Edward Beecher turn in her woman's helplessness but to her gifted sister-in-law, Harriet Stowe, the family's genius? "Hattie," she wrote to Brunswick, "if I could use a pen as you can, I would write something that will make this whole nation feel what an accursed thing slavery is." The story, as it goes on from here, is not apocryphal. Harriet's children remembered it well. She read their aunt's letter to them, then rose to her feet, as if in an act of solemn consecration, the crumpled letter in one small, clenched hand. "I *will* write something," she said. "I will if I live."

In her biographies it is made to appear that Harriet was thus dedicating herself to an *Uncle Tom's Cabin,* to a thundering novel that should blast through slavery like bolts from the Almighty. It was nothing of the sort. At that time she had no idea that any contribution she might make to the anti-slavery cause would be other than a humble one. It was self-renunciation enough that she had determined to write anything at all on the subject of slavery. To write on a political question went against forty years of her training. Woman's place, her world believed, was at the hearth and not the plough, as Mr. Tennyson, in England, had just written. Harriet would risk being classified with such strident females as Mrs. Weld and her Grimke sister, who were shaming their sex by shouting from platforms. She would risk the disapproval of people she esteemed most in life. Nevertheless, she who knew slavery was so moved by the Fugitive Act that she was ready to make the sacrifice.

Perhaps it was just as well that the timid Calvin was in Cincinnati. Calvin might not have approved.

It was one thing to determine to write something to make the nation feel what an accursed thing slavery was and quite another to find a theme. All she could think of now was the ability of liberated slaves to take care of themselves. There was Willie Watson in Cincinnati, who not only got along but bought several friends out of bondage—and Father Henson may have given her some suggestions, too. But obviously this was no world-shaking subject. She began to think about pictures.

Harriet had not taught school ten years for nothing. She had learned something about the psychology of influence. She knew that one concrete instance cut more swiftly and deeply into the ordinary mind than any amount of abstractions. Mr. Garrison and the other orators could shout themselves black in the face with their abstract truths, to move the great, inert public you needed pictures. Harriet had never heard of a propaganda novel, for there had never been any. She called propaganda pictures—word-pictures, fiction. Show people slavery in pictures, in the human terms of ravished girls, mothers bereaved by the auctioneer's hammer, families broken and desolated, saints brutalized by devils, masters debauched by arbitrary power—show them the pictures, and they would know slavery for what it was and tolerate it no longer.

The trouble was, she had not as yet thought of any pictures to give them. She had other things to engage her attention, among them a nursing baby that disturbed her rest. As long as he slept with her, she wrote her sister-in-law in Boston, she could not write "that thing" she had promised; but she would, if she lived. Strange how during her early and middle life she always thought herself to be dwelling in the Valley of the Shadow— she who was to live so long and never know a serious illness until the final one! A neighbor gave them a clumsy Newfoundland puppy. They named him Rover, and "a jollier, livelier, more loving creature never wore dog skin." Harriet felt lost without a pet or two around. She played with Rover, and stepped out to see whether Bangor or Rockland won the train-race, and coasted with the children, and wrote pieces for her newspaper editors.

She wrote about their Christmas holidays in Brunswick and sent it to the editor of the New York *Evangelist* under the title, *A New Year's Story*. She wrote about Calvin's unskillful attempt to keep a vegetable garden in Walnut Hills and sent it to Dr. Bailey of the *National Era,* calling it *A Scholar's Adventures in the Country*. She wrote the one about the liberated blacks and their economic problems and sent that to Dr. Bailey, too, then opened her new copy of the *Era* and went into a fit of the blues. It was the end of the year, and Dr. Bailey would be making up his schedules for 1851. With such names as J. G. Whittier, Grace Greenwood, and Mrs. E. D. E. N. Southworth on his list, she felt sure he must be "overstocked with contributors" and would not want in the new year the services of a domestic little housewife in Brunswick, Me., who needed the money ever so badly.

But Dr. Bailey did want more of her services. He accepted both articles, with encouraging words, the three most encouraging being *One Hundred Dollars* written on a cheque. Harriet's spirits took a bound. A fortnight earlier she had been telling Calvin that she did not see how she could possibly bring the expenses within "our salary." Now she exulted, "Our income this year will be seventeen hundred dollars in all, and I hope to bring our expenses within thirteen hundred."

On January 8, 1851, New York, and Boston, too, were seething over the decision in the Henry Long fugitive case, and that evening the Rev. Henry Ward Beecher, of Brooklyn, lectured in the Tremont Temple in Boston for the Mercantile Library Association, his subject being, *Character*. A Boston journalist wrote: "The lecture was brilliant with those unreportable pyrotechnic splendors which fascinate an audience."

An evening or so later another blizzard was whipping up Federal Street in Brunswick, tearing at the branches of the elms, roaring about the eaves and down the parlour chimney of Harriet's house and packing drifts over her front walk, as the old building shuddered under the assault. Harriet was awake, though not from the storm-noises. Her brother Henry was coming to see her, and she was waiting up for him.

The Boston train was hours late, and it was midnight before he stamped on her front sill after his three blocks' struggle from the depot. He came in, shaking the snow from the felt hat and the romantic cape he now affected. How distinguished he looked to an adoring sister, how noble and godlike! At thirty-seven Henry had reached the prime of his physical attractiveness. His voice had the thrilling hoarseness of the professional orator. His dark hair fell to his shoulders in back, on his countenance sat a high, proud look—though a critical observer might have seen in the face something a little loose not usually associated with the ascetic saints. Harriet's face was lean and tense; it had what we call character. That was what the strait years had done for her, the years of living valiantly in the face of death at the head of a singularly helpless family.

She crammed the air-tight stove with wood, and she and Henry talked. They talked about slavery and the Fugitive Law, and they talked until morning. When Henry went to bed, Harriet went to the kitchen to prepare breakfast for her early-rising brood. In those hours of storm the brother and the sister, one already famous, the other still obscure, brewed, as nearly as any two persons then living could brew it, the bloodiest war in our history.

They planned their propaganda against slavery, though they did not call it that; and these two were to be the leading war-propagandists of the antebellum doubling of fists. Henry was determined to fight slavery from

HENRY WARD BEECHER

(In His Thirties)

"How distinguished he looked to an adoring sister, how noble and
godlike!" (Page 254.)

he pulpit of Plymouth Church. He now held his congregation in the palm
of his hand—the annual sale of pews that week brought in $12,000—and
could say and do what he chose. He had just opened Plymouth Church to
Wendell Phillips, when every other auditorium in New York shut the
Abolitionist out.

Harriet confided to her dearest brother the risky promise she had made to
Edward's wife to step forth as a female agitator and write against slavery.
"Do it, Hattie," he exclaimed heartily. "Finish it, and I will scatter it
thick as the leaves of Vallombrosa."

That took a weight off her heart. If Henry approved of her radical step,
she could face any disapproval. But Henry Ward Beecher never kept his
promise to Harriet. He was an egoist and now the Great Man of the family
giving careless encouragement to his poor, threadbare sister. His head was
full of his own importance and his own purposes. It could scarcely have
occurred to him that violent night in Maine that what Harriet should write
would put him, the Great Preacher, back into the ranks of the family crusade.

Next to *Uncle Tom's Cabin,* Henry's auctions were the most cutting lash
produced by anybody to whip up sectional hatred—until John Brown
appeared at Harpers Ferry. But as propaganda, *Uncle Tom* was worth a
hundred seductive slave girls standing emancipated beside Henry on the
Plymouth stage, and worth at least two Harpers Ferries. Henry Ward
Beecher did not read his sister's epic novel until it was out a year, and
then everybody had read it. Not a few were saying that Henry Ward
must have written it and given it to his sister to sign.

Harriet scattered her own leaves of Vallombrosa.

Henry had gone, leaving no pictures behind him. Harriet had to have
pictures for what she planned to do, and God gave her one to start with.
You couldn't escape slavery in Maine, after all. The accursed Fugitive
Act brought it all back before one's eyes. The newspapers were full of it—
coloured citizen's wife and child kidnapped by a slave-hunter in Philadelphia, a recaptured slave rescued from a deputy by a Boston mob. Then
Norfolk deputy found a fugitive named Shadrach working as a waiter
in a Boston restaurant and rushed him, apron, napkin and all, through the
streets to the United States Commissioner, clamouring for an instant decision. But new Paul Reveres were riding, and half a dozen leading Boston
attorneys, among them Richard H. Dana, author of *Two Years Before The
Mast,* raced to the Commissioner's court to defend Shadrach. Their tactics

delayed the case, and Shadrach was lodged in gaol, whence he was rescue
by a coloured mob.

In the midst of the Shadrach excitement in February, 1851, Communio
Sunday came to the First Parish Church in Brunswick, and Harriet attended
There, during the service, she fell into a spiritual state "not perhaps unlik
the sudden visions of the old prophets," as a modern commentator ha
said. The sermon ended, the communion ritual began, but she was onl
distantly aware of it. The choir was singing softly—

> The King of Heaven His table spreads,
> And blessings crown the board.

Harriet went forward mechanically with her group, ate the bit of bread tha
represented the body of her Lord Jesus Christ which was given for he
sipped of the wine that was His blood, returned to her pew, all in a daz
fighting back her tears.

For she was seeing a vision—seeing it as plain as if she were ther
present, in the flesh, and the actors, too. There was an old slave, with whi
wool, clothed in rags—a gentle, Christian man, like Father Henson—bein
flogged to death by the white ruffian who owned him—such a man as th
overseer Charles met on the New Orleans boat, the man with the fi
hardened by knocking down niggers. This brute was too cowardly to do th
murderous work himself but ordered two degraded slaves, ragged an
dirty as their victim, to lay on the whips. The lashes fell, the ebony ski
broke, and blood as red as any white man's flowed from the stripes. An
as he died, the black saint prayed the Lord's forgiveness for his torturer

From far away Harriet heard the benediction pronounced and walke
home in a trance, down Federal Street and across the track. At the dinne
table she was still deep in reverie, but the children were used to the
mother's spiritual absences and chattered about their own concerns. The
Harriet went to her bedroom and wrote out the picture given her in th
vision. She, who never held back in realism, made it almost unbearab
Even the names of the actors were coming to her now. The negro saint w
Uncle Tom. The two slave executioners were Sambo and Quimbo. Th
name of the hairy, ape-like master was a sheer inspiration—Simon Legre
Few fictional names hold such sinister suggestion. Harriet elaborated t
picture. The example of Christian steadfastness set by Uncle Tom in h

agony touched even the savage hearts of the "imbruted blacks," Sambo and Quimbo. They saw the light and were brought to God.

When Harriet recovered her normal senses, she read to the children what she had written. They wept convulsively, and Henry cried out, "Oh, mamma! slavery is the most cruel thing in the world!"

She had a picture, and a powerful one, but when she read it in cool blood, she could only regard it helplessly. As it stood, it was nothing to offer for sale even to Dr. Bailey. It was too horrible to use unsupported, an apparently needless harrowing of a reader's feelings. To give it meaning and effect, it must be fitted into a frame with other details, and Harriet had never dealt with frames larger than those which held single sketches. She needed more pictures.

It sent her into a chronic condition of day-dreaming, from which she emerged at intervals to find a world still in ferment over the Fugitive Act. The pictures were coming more easily now, but each new set crowded out the series she had contrived before, until her shuttling imagination departed entirely from the original vision. She lost herself in a maze of fantasy, the sketch of Uncle Tom's death forgotten on her desk.

Then, early in March, Calvin returned, his term in Lane Seminary served out. Harriet even forgot to tell him what she had done. He was putting away his own papers and came from the bedroom one day with some sheets of her manuscript in his hand. His broad cheeks glistened with tear-runnels. He asked what it meant, and she told him about her vision.

"Hattie, you must go on with it," he said. "You must make up a story with this for the climax. The Lord intends it so."

Calvin's ever-imminent tears did not matter. What mattered was his endorsement. With this final support, she could face any censure. Harriet turned back to her problem with new determination. It seemed to arrange itself for her as a few sketches—three or four—a fortnight's work perhaps.

But the way to begin was to begin. Trying to plan it out in advance had only led her into confusion. She must start with something, and what was better to start with than her own introduction to slavery, when she visited with Mary Dutton in Kentucky? Uncle Tom would have to be a slave there; but since the only people she met in Kentucky were nice people, she could not make villains of them. To bring in Simon Legree, she must have Uncle Tom sold by his kindly Kentucky master. She would want to show that anyhow in a picture—the sale of a slave and the result in his family.

She might do something, too, with the slave woman who carried her baby across the frozen Ohio to Brother Rankin's house.

So one day she sat down at her desk and began to write in that fine cobweb script which expensive postage had formed for her: "Late in the afternoon of a chilly day in February, two gentlemen were sitting alone over their wine in a well-furnished dining parlor in the town of P——, in Kentucky."

The hair-line of ink was starting out on a long journey. Harriet did not know where it would end, but it ended at Gettysburg and Appomattox.

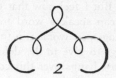

2

Woman of Carthage

I N THE very first words the magic appeared. The great wings of divine inspiration—which she was never to feel again—lifted her from the start, and at once she began to write in the universal language of the human heart. Moujiks on Siberian steppes, ship-workers on the Clyde, merchants in Siam, Hottentots at African missions, peasants tending Alpine herds, millers beside Dutch canals, a queen in a London palace, an archbishop in another, a great poet in Germany, an epic novelist in Russia, carters on the Paris boulevards, and millions of Harriet's fellow-countrymen, old and young, male and female, North and South, would read these words and all, even those who hated and feared them most, would find in them the same enchantment.

That was the great miracle. With a skill that was uncanny (if you call it skill) she chose just the right pictures and on a vast canvas portrayed the institution of American Slavery. Ninety years of counter-propaganda have failed to disfigure her portrait.

But, having made her start, Harriet must prepare the medium for its publication, and she wrote to Dr. Bailey, on the *National Era,* in Washington. The inspiration was fully upon her as she dipped her pen to begin this letter. Though as yet she had no idea of the scope of her appointed enterprise, the finger was touching her shoulder, and she spake not as the Scribes:

Brunswick, March 9.

Mr. Bailey, Dear Sir: I am at present occupied upon a story which will be a much longer one than any I have ever written, embracing a series of sketches which give the lights and shadows of the "patriarchal institution," written either from observation, incidents which have occurred in the sphere of my personal knowledge, or in the knowledge of my friends. I shall show the *best side* of the thing, and something *faintly approaching the worst.*

Up to this year I have always felt that I had no particular call to meddle with this subject, and I dreaded to expose even my own mind to the full force of its exciting power. But I feel now that the time is come when even a woman or a child who can speak a word for freedom and humanity is bound to speak. The Carthagenian women in the last peril of their state cut off their hair for bow-strings to give to the defenders of their country; and such peril and shame as now hangs over this country is worse than Roman slavery, and I hope every woman who can write will not be silent. . . .

My vocation is simply that of *painter,* and my object will be to hold up in the most lifelike and graphic manner possible Slavery, its reverses, changes, and the negro character, which I have had ample opportunities for studying. There is no arguing with *pictures,* and everybody is impressed by them, whether they mean to be or not.

I wrote beforehand, because I know that you have much matter to arrange, and thought it might not be amiss to give you a hint. The thing may extend through three or four numbers. It will be ready in two or three weeks.

* * *

Yours with sincere esteem,
H. Stowe.

Good Dr. Bailey must have caught something of her excitement from her letter, for in the casual manner of early periodical journalism he offered her a handsome price for her serial of three or four installments—$300, sight-unseen. She accepted gratefully. Poor Harriet! Her "three or four numbers" became forty, and almost a whole year had elapsed before she finally gathered together all the threads of her great tapestry and tied all the knots. God, with an eye single to the stern purpose of the work, was not too considerate of the material welfare of His chosen handmaid. Harriet actually wrote *Uncle Tom's Cabin* at a financial sacrifice and in a year when she could ill afford to lose any income. Dr. Bailey did not raise the price, as the story went on and on. Harriet worked until the following March for the original $300.

It was early in March, 1851, when Harriet began to cut off her hair of mid-century female delicacy and twist it into bow-strings to vibrate at Antietam and in the Wilderness and flail the ground with Minié balls, grapeshot, and cannister. If her frenzy cooled for want of fuel, she had only to look up from her desk (which, much of the time, was the kitchen table) to receive more.

In April one Tom Sims, a fugitive slave from Savannah, was apprehended in Boston by a Southern deputy. The news raced through town, and Tom was tried in a roped-off court house defended by two companies of militia. It took three hundred policemen in a hollow square to escort the slave safely to the Savannah steamer, while bells tolled in Plymouth, Lynn, and Waltham, as they had in 1776. Dr. Edward Beecher preached against the deportation but was the only Boston clergyman to open his mouth on the subject.

The *Independent* of May 15 again set Beecher blood boiling in Brunswick. The British, having abolished *their* slavery some eighteen years earlier, were feeling highly virtuous toward the sinful States; and the Congregational Union of Gloucestershire questioned the propriety of admitting to English pulpits that year, because of their expressed pro-slavery opinions, certain American clergymen planning to attend the London "May Anniversaries" as delegates. The May Anniversaries, it was unnecessary to explain to any Protestant in 1851, were the simultaneous conventions of the principal church and philanthropic societies held in May each year in the leading cities of America and Europe.

To justify the pious British concern for the purity of its pulpits, the Bristol (England) *Mercury* published a list of slavery utterances attributed to a number of American clergymen; and this list, reprinted in the *Independent,* sent into white incandescence a little woman writing away in a Maine kitchen. Among the pulpiteers quoted was the Rev. Joel Parker, D.D. Dr. Parker was a personal friend of Harriet's husband and of her father and brothers, and he was an eminent man, having been president of the Union Theological Seminary. In 1851 he was pastor of the Clinton Street Presbyterian Church, in Philadelphia. The utterance attributed to him was this: "There are no evils in slavery but such as are inseparable from any other relation in civil and social life."

These slippery words, if they meant anything, meant that slavery as an institution was not guilty of its crimes, the blame for which lay at the door of human depravity. It was therefore as illogical to abolish slavery for its abuses as to abolish marriage, business, or any other civil or social institution for theirs. Such statements made Harriet seethe; the complacent attitude of the Northern clergy toward slavery became her obsession. "What," she asked her Boston sister-in-law, "are folks in general saying about . . . the stand taken by Boston ministers universally, except Edward? To me it is incredible, amazing, mournful! !" She appropriated from the legend of her Aunt Mary Hubbard: "I feel as if I should be willing to sink with it, were all this sin and misery to sink in the sea." In this mood she brought several preachers into *Uncle Tom's Cabin* as characters, but only one in a favourable light.

She and Calvin exclaimed indignantly over the suave apologies in the *Independent,* and then Harriet filed the paper away and went on with her work. But she did not forget the Rev. Dr. Joel Parker.

Despite all her resolution and the clear light flooding in to her, the work at first went slowly. Having started it, Harriet was organizing her story. She was daydreaming now to some purpose, and in her mind the story grew in sweep and intricacy. As the "three or four numbers" became five or six and the fortnight it was going to take to turn them out was already a month and she was still only on the threshold of the story, Harriet became aware that she was setting forth to write a novel. In 1851 a novel had to have an *or* and a subtitle. Harriet's supertitle seems to have come to her solidly at the start. To the subtitle she had to give some thought.

The name *Uncle Tom's Cabin* appeared in print for the first time on May 8, when the *National Era* displayed a modest notice:

A NEW STORY
BY MRS. STOWE

Week after next we propose to commence in the *Era* the publication of a new story by Mrs. H. B. Stowe, the title of which will be "Uncle Tom's Cabin; or, The Man That Was A Thing." It will probably be the length of the Tale by Mrs. Southworth, entitled "Retribution."

On May 15th the subtitle was still *The Man That Was A Thing,* and also on the 22nd, the promised date of the first installment. Dr. Bailey, however, at that time merely informed his readers that "the first two chapters have been received, but we shall not be able to begin their publication till week after next." Perhaps Editor Bailey hoped to get the whole manuscript in hand before starting publication and not risk an uncertain lady author's missing an edition.

Although literary in its contents and ranked as a magazine, the *Era* was in form an 8-page newspaper of standard size. In the issue of June 5, at the top of the first column of Page One appeared the following heading:

For The National Era.
UNCLE TOM'S CABIN:
or
LIFE AMONG THE LOWLY
By Mrs. H. B. Stowe.

Then followed three and one-half columns of the opening paragraphs of the novel. One suspects the hand of Calvin Stowe in the new subtitle. Why neither title nor subtitle referred to slavery remains an enigma, though the subtitle shared in the story's strange universality. The downtrodden classes of Europe, and especially of England, took the book to their hearts and read their own miseries therein, with scarcely a thought for the shackled Negroes of the United States about whom Harriet wrote.

The second installment, in the *Era* of June 12, shrank to a column in length, as the popular Grace Greenwood resumed her accustomed place in the first column with a short story. But from the start Harriet's story began to bite. Readers were writing to the paper about it in such swelling numbers that Editor Bailey in July did an unusual thing in that period of journalism: he printed one of the "fan letters," as we call them now.

Sir: "Uncle Tom's Cabin" increases in interest and pathos with each successive number. None of thy various contributions, rich and varied as they have been, have so deeply interested thy female readers of this vicinity as this story of Mrs. Stowe has so far done and promises to do.

The letter, which was dated New York, July 1, 1851, Dr. Bailey published unsigned.

Early in July Harriet had the fleeing Eliza Harris at the home of Senator Bird, whom in the serial version she called Senator Burr, but she was already seeing far ahead in her story. She foresaw Uncle Tom sold down the river to a cotton plantation. She knew nothing about cotton plantations; and the reader-response to the five installments of the novel (she was still calling them "articles") emboldened her to write to so busy and important a man as Frederick Douglass, the Negro Abolitionist, for information.

In the course of my story the scene will fall upon a cotton plantation. I am very desirous, therefore, to gain information from one who has been an actual laborer on one, and it occurred to me that in the circle of your acquaintance there might be one who would be able to communicate to

me some such information as I desire. I have before me an able paper
written by a Southern planter, in which the details and *modus operandi*
are given from his point of sight. I am anxious to have something more
from another standpoint. I wish to be able to make a picture that shall be
graphic and true to nature in its details. Such a person as Henry Bibb, if
in the country, might give me just the kind of information I desire. You
may possibly know of some other person. I will subjoin to this letter a list of
questions, which in that case you will do me a favor by inclosing to the
individual, with the request that he will at earliest convenience answer them.

Whether Douglass obliged we do not know. Possibly not. Harriet's imagination was quite good enough to furnish a convincing picture of any cotton
plantation, and the major part of her long letter to the African leader is
given over to a defense of the church against the allegations of the
Abolitionists, Douglass among them, that it was pro-slavery. It was not the
last glimpse she would give of a curious mental attitude she maintained
during these antebellum years. She wrote to other Abolition leaders in
defense of the church, while reserving to herself the right to castigate the
clergy in her books.

Late in June *Uncle Tom's Cabin* had reoccupied the first column of the
National Era, and from that time until the serial ended months later the
weekly instalment seldom failed to have the foremost position. It was not
easy to write in the Federal Street house that summer. Old Dr. Beecher
was there with his stepdaughter, fussing with his precious sermons, quite
unaware that his respectful daughter was turning out a masterpiece to
upset the world. The sermons were the important thing; and when the
Doctor and his secretary occupied the kitchen table, the neighbours saw
little Mrs. Stowe sitting on the back steps, her writing portfolio on her
many-petticoated knees.

For all her industry, the printing-press in Washington caught up with
her in July, as sympathetic Boston juries began acquitting Shadrach's res-
cuers, one by one. In the *National Era* of July 24, Dr. Bailey had to inform
the subscribers that "the instalment of Mrs. Stowe's story, 'Uncle Tom's
Cabin,' for this week, reached us at so late an hour that we were compelled
to divide it. It increases in interest as it progresses. We trust no one will
omit to read it." The division drew such a remonstrance from Brunswick
that Editor Bailey never risked doing it again.

On August 21 occurred a calamity which Dr. Bailey must have been dreading. Harriet missed the edition. The editor forestalled the readers' protest by inserting a note, which read: "Chapter XII of 'Uncle Tom's Cabin' reached us at too late an hour for insertion this week. Mrs. Stowe having requested that it should not be divided, our readers may look for the entire chapter in the next *Era*."

But Harriet had a good excuse for being late with her twelfth instalment. Chapter XII of *Uncle Tom's Cabin* was a famous one, entitled *Select Incident of Lawful Trade,* and there is no more powerful a piece of writing in the entire novel. In it Uncle Tom, having been sold by his master, embarks with Trader Haley's coffle of slaves on the Ohio steamboat *La Belle Rivière;* and the chapter deals with Haley's various transactions in human flesh at the Kentucky landings where the boat stops.

And particularly it tells the brief, tragic story of the slave-woman Lucy. Having been secretly sold, with her infant, to Haley, Lucy was tricked aboard the *La Belle Rivière* by the assurance that she was merely being sent to join her husband, who had been hired out by her master as a cook in a Louisville restaurant. It was only after the boat had left her landing that Haley told Lucy the truth. She was on her way to the deep South.

Haley, who had an uneasy feeling that this whole business was wrong, and who aimed to get out of it and repent in time to reach heaven, was glad to see that Lucy had grit and took it easy. After her first passionate disbelief that her "Mas'r" could cheat her that way, she subsided and only said dully, when the bill of sale had been read to her as proof, "Then it's no account talking." But she clasped tightly to her bosom a slave-mother's solace, her baby.

The baby was not to rest there long. A gentleman from a plantation near Louisville bought him from Haley for forty-five dollars. At the Louisville landing Lucy went to the rail to see if her husband might not have heard she was on the boat, and she could have her last look at him. When she returned to her place, her baby was gone. The boat had started, and Haley told her what had happened—told her warily, for Haley disliked scenes, and he was afraid Lucy might scream and raise a commotion. She didn't. As Harriet wrote: "The shot had passed too straight and direct through the heart for cry or tear."

Haley attempted to comfort her—she was a "likely gal"; he would sell her to a nice place "down river" and she'd soon find a new husband. The woman could only get out the words, "Oh, don't, Mas'r, don't!"

At this point Harriet remembered the Rev. Dr. Joel Parker and his comfortable sophistry, and she used it in a piece of blazing sarcasm:

Tom had watched the whole transaction from first to last, and had a perfect understanding of its results. To him, it looked like something unutterably horrible and cruel, because, poor ignorant black soul! he had not learned to generalize, and to take enlarged views. If he had only been instructed by certain ministers of Christianity, he might have thought better of it, and seen in it an every-day incident of a lawful trade; a trade which is the vital support of an institution which an American divine tells us has *"no evils but such as are inseparable from any other relations in social and domestic life."* But Tom, as we see, being a poor ignorant fellow, whose reading had been confined entirely to the New Testament, could not comfort and solace himself with views like these. His very soul bled within him for what seemed to him the *wrongs* of the poor suffering thing that lay like a crushed reed on the boxes; the feeling, living, bleeding, yet immortal *thing,* which American state law coolly classes with the bundles, and bales, and boxes, among which she is lying.

In the middle of the night Uncle Tom, sleeping with the rest of Haley's gang on the floor of the lower deck of the steamboat, felt something brush by him and heard a splash in the water. The chapter ends with Haley next morning dejectedly entering the Lucy item in his pocket account-book under the head of *Losses.*

When Harriet read over the completed Chapter XII, she paused at Dr. Parker's quotation. Why should that suave apologist escape responsibility for his own words, even though he had not foreseen them cast into obloquy by association with such a scene of human agony? With a sudden impulse Harriet marked an asterisk after the words, *an American divine,* and at the bottom of the page wrote, "Dr. Joel Parker, of Philadelphia." The instalment, with its perilous footnote, ran in the August 28 number of the *National Era.*

She found time that summer for other things besides her weekly instalments of the story. She found time to enjoy Brunswick. The family went on picnics down to Harpswell and Orr's Island, where Calvin and the children would catch flounders and wade at the beaches while Harriet sat on the rocks and received new visions to picture on her canvas. There was a safe, shallow pond near their house, and she encouraged the boys to build a raft on it and take the twins on voyages of exploration. With other townsfolk they now and then attended a launching, for 1851 was at the peak of the Maine shipbuilding fever. In fact, the whole writing of *Uncle Tom's Cabin* went on under the singing of saws in the Brunswick mills cutting timbers for new ships.

It went on under a more sinister racket in the nation that summer, as federal prosecutors tried to indict for *treason* persons who flouted the Fugitive Slave Law, and the discredited Webster was thundering, "This agitation must cease!" And there were family events to claim a share of Harriet's attention. Calvin had received an honour. The town of Natick, Massachusetts, was to celebrate the two hundredth anniversary of its settlement in October and had invited its former mill-boy to deliver the principal discourse. In September the delighted Calvin was devoting himself *"unquibus et rostro"* to the preparation of the great address.

Calvin had by this time secured a second leave of absence from Bowdoin and was to give his course at Andover during the winter term. It meant more money for them; with Harriet writing week after week for the original $300 from the *Era,* they needed it sorely, and Calvin wrote to Professor Park to make an economical arrangement for him in Andover—"to occupy a room in the [main] building as a study and board and lodge at Mrs. Johnson's. I am to be on the ground the 1st of Dec. and stay to the 1st of April, or longer."

During the summer Catharine Beecher published the most important book she had yet written, her *True Remedy for The Wrongs of Women.* Elizabeth Cady Stanton and others had recently begun to agitate for woman-suffrage; and Catharine, a firm "Anti" from the start, brought out her timely volume to spike Mrs. Stanton's guns.

As she neared her fiftieth birthday, Catharine was more contentious and dictatorial than ever. That summer she broke with the Board of National Popular Education, of which she was a founder, and was once more battling alone for her cause, now represented by an embryo high school for girls in Milwaukee. Somehow Catharine had managed to contribute $1,000 of her own money to this institution.

But a tiny crack had appeared in the family solidarity. Henry Ward Beecher, young, ambitious, successful, and forever alert to the main chance, was on the point of adopting the woman-suffrage cause for his own and even of assuming leadership in it. He grew impatient with the restless, domineering Catharine and her eternal schemes; and, what was worse, was influencing his old father, who was growing childish, against Catharine.

This was a great pity. Proud as he was of his preacher-sons, Dr. Beecher had always felt closest in spirit to his eldest daughter, his first-born.

The most loyal member of the clan lived in Brunswick; and in September she could pause long enough in her fiction-writing to intercede for Catharine. Harriet granted to Henry that she thought Catharine "strange, nervous, visionary, and to a certain extent unstable"—but Catharine was nevertheless their sister. Harriet pleaded with Henry at least to read the *True Remedy* and also to try to influence men of means to support the Milwaukee school. "Do what you can to help."

Harriet repeated this letter in substance to Dr. Beecher, now, his sermons polished, occupying his "own hired house" in Hayward Place, Boston, near Edward. One wonders if the unstudious Henry Ward ever even glanced at Catharine's *True Remedy,* with which he thoroughly disagreed, when it took him a year to get around to *Uncle Tom's Cabin,* the most vivid piece of realism yet produced by an American.

The *Lawful Trade* instalment of the serial brought another flurry of reader-letters, and once more Editor Bailey did the unusual thing and noticed them in his issue of September 4:

> UNCLE TOM'S CABIN.—We receive letters by every mail inquiring whether "Uncle Tom's Cabin" will be published in book form after its completion in the *Era.* Mrs. Stowe, having taken out a copyright, of course intends to publish it in a separate form. When it will be so published and what will be the price of it, we do not know. A note from the author touching these points might be of service.

Harriet's note of that date could have informed the *Era* that negotiations for the book were in progress. Catharine Beecher was a clanswoman, too. When she descended unexpectedly into Brunswick at the end of August to tell Harriet about the trouble with Henry, she read the instalments of *Uncle Tom's Cabin* her sister had thus far written. Catharine knew powerful writing when she read it—and Harriet told her about the stir it was making among the *Era's* readers. Catharine decided it was time somebody took charge who knew more about the exploitation of literary work than a pair of country innocents like Harriet and Calvin. A few days later she stalked into the offices of her new publishers, Phillips, Sampson & Co., of Boston, who had just brought out her *True Remedy,* and offered them a fortune. She told them she was empowered to negotiate for book-publication of her sister's story, which was attracting a great deal of attention as a serial.

Two of the partners, Phillips and Sampson, both Democrats and anti-Abolitionists, rather favoured the idea. The third partner was William Lee (later of Lee & Shepard), a Whig and an opponent of slavery. He vetoed it.

Mr. Lee was all business. An antislavery novel from an antislavery newspaper? They could never sell a thousand copies of it, Lee predicted; while a success with it (as publishers then regarded success) would be worse than failure. Phillips, Sampson & Co. did a large business in the South. An antislavery novel on their list might ruin that trade. The firm declined *Uncle Tom's Cabin.*

It was no set-back for Harriet—not with Mrs. Jewett in Boston following the serial in the *National Era,* overcome, like tens of thousands of other women at the time, by its terrible power. Her husband was John P. Jewett, who ran a small publishing house specializing in "practical" books. Mrs. Jewett's enthusiasm induced him to read the back instalments. Though fiction was out of his line, this novel seemed an attractive gamble to him. He wrote to Harriet, and on September 18 the *Era* could announce:

> MRS. STOWE'S STORY.—We learn through a private source that Mrs. H. B. Stowe has just completed an engagement with Messrs. Jewett & Co., of Boston, for the publication of her story, now appearing in our columns. The stereotyping commences this week; and it will be corrected [sic], complete, from the press immediately after its close in the *Era.*

The notice indicates how little Harriet as yet understood the scope of her masterpiece. At the middle of September she thought the end of the work so near that she could tell Jewett to begin setting it up in type. Actually, on that date she had written only one-third of it.

But the story was pouring molten from her now. The instalments in the *Era* began to run through four, five, and even six long columns every week. The wings of inspiration bore her high, with might and sureness. "The Lord Himself wrote it," she said afterwards many times. "I was but an instrument in His hand." She had but to spread out her paper and dip her pen, and the story gushed forth.

Scene after scene, dramatic, humorous, tragic, pathetic, ironic, sentimental, glorious, and every one damning, marshalled itself into the effective sequence. The steel of her passion struck the flint of life, as a recent critic said of Harriet in this work. Her imagination embraced reality to the point of pain. A cosmic procession of characters crossed her fine-spun pages, all pulsing and breathing with life, a few immortal. The poet Vachel Lindsay used Legree as a figure of mythology.

And it all came out of her own life-experience. Did she need comedy as relief from the tragedies that occurred in St. Clare's house? There had been Celeste, a small, black limb of Satan she had vainly tried to Christianize in her Cincinnati Sunday School class. Celeste became Topsy. Must she contrive a novel means of escape for Cassy and Emmeline? She remembered Jackson, the Cincinnati barber, whose white Creole wife had dressed him in female attire and boldly brought him north in a cabin of a Mississippi steamboat as her personal maid. Sam, a coloured boy employed by Dr. Beecher at Walnut Hills, disappeared for two years, then showed up again, saying he had been working for the Government up at Columbus. They found out afterwards that Sam had been in the State's prison. He became the comical Sam who so adroitly hindered Haley's pursuit of Eliza. As a passenger on an Ohio steamboat, Harriet had seen a newly sold slave tricked into the manacles of a dealer's gang.

A year later Harriet, following the mistaken notion that she had to defend the veracity of *Uncle Tom Cabin,* assembled a mass of supporting data—court decisions, newspaper clippings, church proceedings, and the like—and published it in a volume entitled *The Key to Uncle Tom's Cabin.* As if her novel required any proof! Thomas Carlyle, who had never seen American slavery, wrote Harriet that he knew her story represented the facts truthfully. *Uncle Tom* carried its own conviction of truth; and only a great book, as John Erskine has remarked of this novel, can impart that confidence to a reader.

Those who share Harriet's view of its inspiration must agree that her Lord in His revelation was limited by the technical deficiencies of his

A MANUSCRIPT PAGE OF UNCLE TOM'S CABIN

"The hair-line of ink was starting out on a long journey. . . . It ended at Gettysburg and Appomattox." (Page 258.)

Uncle Tom

The cabin of Uncle Tom was a small log building close
adjoining to "the house" — as the negro always par excellence
designates the master's dwelling   In front it had a neat
garden patch where strawberries, raspberries & a variety of
fruits & vegetables made careful tending — &c   The whole
front of the dwelling was covered with a large scarlet
Bignonia & a native multiflora rose which entwisting
& interlacing left scarce a vestige of the building
to be seen & to the offering rose reclimbed with

instrument. The fastidious reader, even in the 1850's, found *Uncle Tom's Cabin* superficially far from being a great work of art. It followed two distinct stories, only vaguely connected with each other; it contained no love story at all, it swooned in sentimentality, it was coarse in imagination, often affected in style, sometimes choked with morality and preaching. It was great because it had the essential simplicity of naive art and because in its passions it was as fundamental and universal as an epic.

Harriet herself apologized later for the novel's technical deficiencies. She "no more thought of style or literary excellence than the mother who rushes into the street and cries for help to save her children from a burning house, thinks of the teachings of the rhetorician or the elocutionist." As the spider-web pen-line raced ahead in the autumn of 1851, such a detail as punctuation almost ceased to exist for her. An easy dash, a comma here and there, were enough for her. She let Dr. Bailey's proofreader wrestle with problems of quotation marks, interrogation points, colons, and full-stops. As she filled each sheet, she pushed it aside, never to look at it again with any revisionary eye.

But she looked at the sheets again to read them aloud. As awed and amazed and excited by the development of the story as any listener in her circle, she became the ruthless author, ready to read her pages to any who would consent to hear, and sometimes even to the helpless. The serial was keeping her poor, and she convened her little private school in September as usual. Just at that time she was introducing Little Eva into the story, and to her class of school-children she read her first description of the most saintly child in American literature. Newman Smyth remembered that day. Sometimes Harriet read her instalments to the evening gathering of neighbours at Professor Smyth's house. Professor Smyth and tall, shy Professor Upham must have realized that they were seeing a miracle unfold before their eyes.

What was going on at the Smyths was also occurring in thousands of other homes in towns and villages of the United States. Somebody was reading aloud the current instalment of *Uncle Tom's Cabin,* and an audience was laughing and crying and clenching its fists. One of the miracles wrought by the story was the national furore it created as a serial in an obscure paper—and there is no evidence that *Uncle Tom's Cabin* increased the circulation of the *Era* to any great extent. The New York *Independent* was a broad-minded, liberal journal, opposed to slavery, yet in its monthly reviews of the magazines in 1851 it never once noticed the *National Era.*

When, later, Dr. Joel Parker was asked why he did not register an objection to Mrs. Stowe's unauthorized use of his name in the *Era,* he replied that he thought nobody read that paper.

A great many were reading it, however. It is doubtful if any magazine since has had so many readers in proportion to its circulation. In every community there was likely to be one Abolitionist, at least, who subscribed to the *National Era.* As the fame of the serial spread, his copy was passed from family to family, until often it was quite worn out. A contemporary biographer of Mrs. Stowe remembered his own experience as a boy in a remote and puritanical New England village—remembered "how *Uncle Tom's Cabin* was the theme of universal discussion, and how those in his home and all through the village, too, who had never before bowed down to any idols of fiction nor served them, were so completely demoralized by this novel, that they not only read it but read it to their children; and how the papers which contained it, after being nearly worn out in going through so many hands and in so many different homes, were as carefully folded up and laid away as if the tear-stains on them were sacred, as indeed they were."

But Harriet's best audience was her family—Calvin and the children. The characters of the story seemed to form a neighbourhood on whose fascinating activities they were permitted daily to spy. And Harriet shared this feeling with them. Every night there was a clamour to hear what she had written.

For the entranced Freddie his mother's words were spelling death—as they were spelling it for many another Freddie and Johnny and Charley and Willie alive that day, North and South.

As it stretched out, the end ever eluding her, the story more and more became Harriet's tyrant. Whatever she did, wherever she went, the spectre of next week's instalment stood forever at her elbow. It rode like an incubus on her frail shoulders. It followed her to Boston on a trip she could not avoid, and she wrote in her brother Edward's study. She had to keep up her cooking and housework, and her boisterous family drove her frantic.

As one of his perquisites, Calvin had a professor's room assigned to him in Appleton Hall. Harriet occupied it, and the college gasped. No female had ever taken quarters before in the scholastic quiet of old Appleton. Harriet had her way, however, and that fall and winter the Bowdoin boys got used to seeing Professor Stowe's funny little wife trudging along their campus walks, after blizzards her head no higher than the flanking furrows of snow. In December Calvin went to his other job at Andover, and Harriet had his office alone.

She had not the physical strength to endure such a strain. Her copy missed the October 30 issue of the *Era* completely. It seems to have been a momentary failure of the inspiration. She had just finished the pathetic scene in which Eva writes Uncle Tom's letter for him to his home folks in Kentucky and was introducing Topsy—the famous 'spect-I-growed chapter. Dr. Bailey must have waited to the last moment for the manuscript, for he was unable to print a note of explanation. His omission brought down on himself a storm of letters.

Another was regarding the ever-increasing length of the novel with dismay. John P. Jewett, the Boston publisher, had bargained for no such monument. The most he foresaw when he engaged the book was a slender volume which could sell at a low price. If it failed, his loss would be small, and he could regard it as a contribution to the Abolition cause. By the end of October *Uncle Tom's Cabin* was beginning to look like a two-volume novel; and Jewett, whose resources were not great, was alarmed. He wrote to Harriet, begging her to terminate the story. She was writing on an unpopular subject; two volumes might be a fatal obstacle to the work's success.

Jewett could not have addressed then a more receptive listener. A weary Harriet was ready to cry for mercy. But God was a taskmaster as relentless as her own Legree. He answered in the voice of the people. The *Era* published the suggestion that since the story had already run to great length, Mrs. Stowe could finish it quickly in a few matter-of-fact paragraphs telling how everything turned out. *Vox populi* answered a thundering No! One reader wrote:

> Please signify to Mrs. Stowe that it will be quite agreeable to the wishes of very many of the readers of the *Era* for her *not to hurry through* "Uncle Tom." We don't get sleepy reading it. Having resided many years among slaves and being familiar with their habits, thoughts, feelings, and language, I have not been able to detect a single mistake in·her story in any of these respects—'tis perfect in its way—will do great good.
>
> Yours,
> J.D.L.

(On the point of the story's "language," Harriet was writing for the first time the American Negro dialect substantially as we know it today. She had no models to guide her in 1851 but depended solely on her own ear for speech. If her ear in imagination failed to catch a needed expression, she could substitute one of Calvin's Natick solecisms, and the uncritical reader of her day was satisfied. British reviewers especially praised the dialect of *Uncle Tom's Cabin*. Before that book's advent the darky dialect of fiction and the stage was a sort of heathen Choctaw never spoken by man.)

Editor Bailey hastened to reassure his subscribers. "When Mrs. Stowe commenced her admirable story, we did not suppose, nor did she, that it would run through so many numbers as it has already done. She will take good care not 'to hurry through it,' but will *complete* what has been so well begun."

Harriet wrote on.

In November the fame of the *National Era's* serial had penetrated into an elegant sanctum in Philadelphia. Harriet received a letter from Sarah J. Hale, asking for her daguerreotype and biographical facts about herself which Mrs. Hale could use in writing a compendious book about distinguished women writers of the earth. Mrs. Hale was editor of *Godey's Lady's Book*.

Harriet was immensely flattered and pleased, and also dismayed. Her daguerreotype? Daguerreotypes were such a new thing that they were still being called "chemical pictures." They cost from $15 to $25 apiece, depending on the size. In 1851 Harriet did not even own a silk dress. She had no money to spend on such a vanity as a daguerreotype. She answered Mrs. Hale as follows:

> Dear Madam:—I was quite amused, I must say, at your letter to me, wholly innocent as I am of any pretensions to rank among "distinguished women." However, I read it to my tribe of little folks assembled around the evening centre table to let them know what an unexpected honour had befallen their mamma.
>
> The idea of the daguerreotype especially was quite droll, and I diverted myself somewhat with figuring the astonishment of the children, should the well known visage of their mother loom out of the pages of a book before their astonished eyes.
>
> But in sober sadness, having reflected duly and truly on my past life, it is so thoroughly uneventful and uninteresting that I do not see how anything can be done for me in the way of a sketch. My sister Catharine has lived much more of a life and done more than can be told of, than I whose course and employments have always been retired and domestic.
>
> The most I can think of is that I was born in Litchfield, Conn., and was

a teacher from my fifteenth year till my marriage, that I have been mother to seven children, six of whom are now living, and that the greater portion of my time and strength has been spent in the necessary but unpoetic duties of the family. These details you can throw into two or three lines—as great a space as I should have any claim to occupy in such a company.

I am well pleased with the selection you have made as any, and shall be very curious to see the book, when it appears. From the multitude of fine female writers who have appeared in our country of late years, I should think that America might show no inconsiderable share in the list. Wishing you all success, I remain,

Brunswick, Nov. 10.   Truly Yours, H. B. Stowe.

P.S.—In answer to one of your enquiries, I would say that I have never published but one book, "The Mayflower," by the Harpers.

Harriet's modesty in this letter was no pose. This was always her attitude, even in the moments of her greatest triumphs.

On November 6 the Cleveland, Ohio, house of Proctor & Worthington (138 Superior Street) announced in the *Era* that they were going to handle Harriet's novel, when published, in the West. It was the first public advertisement for *Uncle Tom's Cabin.*

"Now is the time to subscribe," the *Era* was chanting at the end of November, when the serial seemed established for the winter—

BILLS

This is the time for renewing subscriptions. Look out for Bills! A large number of subscribers will receive bills in their papers this week. In their hurry to read Mrs. Stowe's story, they must not let them slip out and be lost.

The *Era* for December 18 appeared without any instalment of *Uncle Tom's Cabin;* but at the top of Column One, its familiar place, appeared a profuse apology by the Editor—"so profound is the interest taken in her story by nearly all our readers." The Editor feared Mrs. Stowe was sick.

And about that moment she was. Harriet had cause to be late with her twenty-sixth instalment. To write it, she had had to dip her pen into her own maternal heart. The instalment appeared in the Christmas-Day issue of the *National Era.* It portrayed the death of Little Eva. Harriet needed the week's respite. Having translated Evangeline to heaven, almost in a veritable ascension, Harriet took to her bed for forty-eight hours, exhausted. It had been almost a personal bereavement.

After the turn of 1852 Harriet gathered strength and for the first time since she started to write began to move ahead of the printing-press in Washington. Dr. Bailey found himself with his current issue provided for and an instalment in hand! Then there were two instalments in hand, then three. Having disposed of Little Eva—and what agonized letters she received about *that,* reproaching her for heartlessness!—Harriet was in the end-action of her story, though she was still to conceive the whole Gothic episode of Cassy and Legree, a memorable corner of the great canvas. She had only to write to the death of Uncle Tom, tie a few knots, and be done. The way ahead lay clear.

If the Inspiration suffered from the instrument's defective technique, it gained by the fact that Harriet was a born advocate. Instinctively she addressed *Uncle Tom's Cabin* to the people of the South and honestly thought it a hand held out for peace. Indeed, she had a tiny worry that she might be driving away Dr. Bailey's subscribers. The kindest, most philanthropic, and most upright characters in the novel were, with some minor exceptions, all Southerners and slave-holders—excepting, too, St. Clare's New England cousin, Aunt Ophelia—and there were rabid Abolitionists in the North who refused to concede to a slave-owner a single Christian virtue. Harriet did not overlook the pleasant, patriarchal side of slavery, which was one thing that made her book so hard to answer. And when she drew Simon Legree, the arch-villain of American literature, she made him a Vermonter. It is not often noted that she brought into the story, momentarily and at second-hand, another brutal overseer and assigned him also to Vermont. Harriet must have met some cruel people that year she spent in Brattleboro—or perhaps it was only the memory of the dreadful douche.

In 1851 she was not so presumptuous as to think that her story was inaugurating an epoch; but she did believe that if the South once saw slavery in its stark reality, it would voluntarily manumit its slaves. Sitting in her own Israel, she believed this as sincerely as she believed that her father might have converted Byron, if he had met him in time. Harriet did not know she was weaving bow-strings to destroy the children of America, one of her own among them. She regarded *Uncle Tom* as a messenger of peace. Her belief was naive and visionary, but it did credit to her heart.

And the Inspiration benefited also by Harriet's amazing powers of correct observation. It is often brought forth as a modern discovery that the Southerner understands the Negro better than the Northerner, likes him much better, and knows better how to manage him and get along with him. Harriet was writing this very thing in 1851 and 1852. Aunt Ophelia could not bear to touch Topsy, but Eva's favourite perch was Uncle Tom's knee. It took a shrewd eye to note that point a century ago.

The fine pen hurried on. The chapter on the death of Uncle Tom—the sketch she had written a year before—dovetailed into its place, and Harriet had gained another instalment in the race with the press.

In February the unsung hero of the novel's book-publication made a final attempt to save some of his slender capital. John P. Jewett's agreement to issue the book was as yet only informal. With the end of the writing in sight, it was time to arrange the terms of the contract. Calvin Stowe went into Boston from Andover to attend to that business. Jewett proposed that the Stowes put up half the cost of publishing the two-deck book and share equally with him the profits from its sale, if any. Calvin declined in favour of a royalty of ten per centum on all sales. Another story is that Calvin before deciding sought the advice of his friend Philip Greeley, then a Congressman from Boston, who strongly urged the Professor to take the alternative of royalty, since there was little likelihood that the novel would enjoy a large sale.

Some of Calvin's descendents have been disposed, humorously, to criticize their grandfather's business acumen in this transaction. It is true that if Harriet had owned a half-interest in *Uncle Tom's Cabin,* the first year's sales in this country alone would have made her independently rich, whereas actually she got less out of the book in that time than many a second-rate novel today brings for its subsidiary rights. But Calvin scarcely needed Congressman Greeley's advice to act as he did. He had no money at all and could certainly not have borrowed any to risk in a speculation in which even the publisher had little faith.

Harriet was well pleased with the contract. "I hope," she said, "it will make enough so I may have a silk dress." Mrs. Upham and Mrs. Smyth had silk dresses to wear to church Sundays.

Early in March there appeared in the Boston and New York newspapers the first publisher's advertisement for "THE STORY OF THE AGE." Jewett announced March 20 as the publication date. It meant that Harriet had finished the work at last.

Harriet ended it on an abrupt and startling note: "Farewell, dear children, till we meet again." It was her first mention of children as her readers in the course of the entire epic. Had she actually, all the time, been in her own mind writing for children this violent and tragic tale, spattered with murder, lust, illicit love, suicide, sadistic torture, profanity, drunkenness, barroom brawls, and other things her world considered unfit for young ears to hear?

She had been doing precisely that—she, the great propagandist of her time—and moreover attracting thousands of children as readers. And her novel would go on to condition a whole generation of children to march in the spirit of crusaders ten years later up to the cannon's mouth.

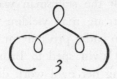

Success Story

3

ON SATURDAY, March 13, 1852, Calvin Stowe signed Jewett's contract in Harriet's behalf. By that date *Uncle Tom's Cabin* was in page-plates, and Jewett was running off a first edition of five thousand copies. Having finished his stint at Andover, Calvin was on his way to Brunswick and his final term at Bowdoin. While waiting for the first books from the bindery, he stopped with his father-in-law in Hayward Place. Old Dr. Beecher was in an after-sunset glow over the reception of his second volume of *Sermons,* as the religious press paid homage to the last great voice of the Puritans. Eighteenth-Century ears in Hayward Place could scarcely catch the rumble of power-presses in Jewett's printing plant at work on another kind of sermon.

Before the rumble began, Harriet had sent down a list of corrections. One changed the name of the Ohio Senator from Burr to Bird. She forgot about the Joel Parker footnote. She hoped the book might bring her a silk dress, but Calvin was indulging in a brighter dream. If Jewett sold the entire edition, Harriet would receive for her exhausting year of work more than the equivalent of her husband's salary for the same period. It would make 1852 a red-letter year for the Stowes.

John P. Jewett was not so confident, yet there were harbingers of something unusual about to occur in the book trade. Retail bookshops were announcing their prospective stocks of *Uncle Tom,* and that had never happened in advance of the publication of any other American novel. In Boston, Bookseller Light, No. 3 Cornhill, advertised "copies sent by mail under 500 miles free of postage," and a "discount for purchase in quantity."

In the week of March 14, Jewett opened his account with Mrs. Stowe with a debit item: "1 copy U.T.C., cloth, $.56." It was the first copy sold. Calvin presented it to his friend and adviser, Congressman Greeley, who boarded the night train for New York and Washington. Once settled in the coach, Greeley opened Volume I. At Springfield he decided to make a stopover. Against his will the statesman was affording his fellow-passengers the spectacle of a strong man yielding to emotion. In Springfield he retired to a hotel room to bathe privately in his tears.

With other early copies Calvin sped to Brunswick to give Harriet the sweet satisfaction of handling her own work done up at last in new, stiff covers. Jewett was describing the book as "published in 2 vols., 12mo., 312 pp. in each vol., with six elegant designs by Billings, engraved by Baker; in three styles of bindings: paper cover for $1, cloth $1.50, cloth full gilt $2, with discount to the trade." A bibliophile adds these details: "*Uncle Tom's Cabin* made its bow in a black cloth binding, blind stamped, with the title-page vignette, wherein 'the young folks roll on the little cabin floor' (or one of them rolls on the ground just outside it, at any rate), reproduced in gold on the front cover."

The "cloth full gilt" style is described by this authority as "a veritable orgy of gold." These de-luxe copies "were bound in lavender cloth, with four heavy gold rules enclosing not only the vignette but corner and top and bottom ornaments, in gold as well. This design was duplicated, gold and all, on the back cover, and the back-strip bore four groupings of gilt floral ornaments. All the edges, too, were gilt."

March 20 was publication day. The book business of 1852 was innocent of today's promotion methods. There were no advance review-copies. As a result, *Uncle Tom's Cabin* was born in a complete editorial silence that continued unbroken for nearly a month, as the reviewers digested the extraordinary work and probed for new adjectives to express their enthusiasm or wrath. In New York City the first notice of the novel's existence came from the laity. To the April 1 issue of the *Independent* one "Mather" contributed a sonnet that was lamer in technical form than in spirit—

TO THE AUTHOR OF 'UNCLE TOM'S CABIN'

Some the magician play for paltry hire,
And some God's gift of genius dedicate
To thrilling tales that melt and enervate,—
And some will picture, with pen of fire,
Passion, and pleasure, and unblest desire,
And mighty be to blast, and not to bless,
To weave the witchery of wickedness.
HAIL! FICTION'S BETTER MISTRESS! skilled to trace
The piteous woes that o'er "The Lowly" roll,

Oppression's murderous work upon the soul,
The good that can in misery deathless be,
Truth, natural wit, and love, and piety,—
Most skilled to hold, with equal nerve and grace,
The damning mirror up to SLAVERY'S Ethiop face.

Before Mather composed these lines, Calvin Stowe in Brunswick had made an unpleasant discovery. At the bottom of page 191, Volume I, of *Uncle Tom's Cabin* he found the *Era's* footnote attributing to Dr. Joel Parker the pro-slavery sentiment which Harriet had used with such devastating effect. Calvin was perturbed. He had never approved of the reference in the serial, but here it was worse, perpetuated in a book. Here it might make trouble. To Harriet, Calvin pleaded that a factual footnote in a novel violated the artistic canon of fiction-writing—and besides, why single out Dr. Parker for censure, when a hundred other clergymen had expressed similar opinions?

Harriet admitted the mistake. She had, in fact, intended to omit the footnote from the book; but now the fat was in the fire. The book was printed, nothing could be done about it. Yet, since there *might* be another printing, Harriet wrote to Jewett instructing him to chip Dr. Parker's name from the stereotype-plate of page 191.

Her letter reached her publisher on a morning of excitement. The first edition on *Uncle Tom* was out, and the market had devoured it in two gulps—three thousand copies sold the day of publication, the balance next day, with unfilled orders piling up by night. Jewett threw a second printing into the presses, and so hurriedly that to the eternal annoyance of book-collectors he forgot to "slug" it as a second edition. He also forgot to excise the footnote.

Before the interested parties in Brunswick could realize it, before any reviews appeared, Jewett had printed and sold two more editions of equal size. Twenty thousand copies in three weeks! It made Calvin's head swim to calculate Harriet's "avails." In the newspapers were appearing evidences of the stir. The editor of the Portland (Maine) *Inquirer* apologized: "Our readers will please excuse any omissions this week, for we are reading *Uncle Tom*." The Boston *Traveller* took cognizance of the phenomenon to be observed in Jewett's publishing house—three power-presses running twenty-four hours a day, "Sundays only excepted"; one hundred book-binders at work, three mills running to supply the paper, and "the publisher is still thousands of copies behind orders."

A young man in the employ of Putnam, the New York publisher, also took cognizance of what was going on in the book business, thoughtfully wrapped up a two-volume set of *Uncle Tom's Cabin,* and mailed it to a publishing contact of his own in the British Isles, together with a letter saying he would appreciate a trifle for his pains. This act of treachery to a countrywoman was costing Harriet her English copyright and her English royalties, but it occurred in a day when even the most reputable publishing houses brazenly pirated any literary work whose author was careless about its protection. The vicissitudes of this copy we shall follow later. In due time "Putnam's young man" received his thirty pieces of silver—in English money, £5. It is conservative to estimate that the piracy deprived Harriet of four thousand times that amount in royalties.

On April 15 the first great gun spoke as the New York *Independent* devoted a column and a half of its space to an editorial review of *Uncle Tom's Cabin,* taking for its text, "Spread it around the world!" By 1852 the *Independent* had attained a position in national influence second only to Horace Greeley's *Weekly Tribune.* Its hosannah for the novel was signed with an *S,* which was the signature of its "stated contributor," the Rev. Richard Salter Storrs, Jr., a founder and editor of the *Independent* and pastor of the great Church of The Pilgrims in Brooklyn. Dr. Storrs regarded *Uncle Tom* as a mighty and moving sermon on Slavery and wound up his praises with the exhortation, "Let ALL MEN read it!"

The book was scarcely out when its author for some reason thought of England. Twenty-five years later Harriet wrote that she was afraid that the Slave Power might extend the operation of the Fugitive Law to Canada, though, with Great Britain just then wrapped in the mantle of self-righteousness over the liberation of its own slaves, there seems at this distance to have been little danger of such a thing's happening. But England was the home of all that was perfect in literature, and Harriet may have sought some authoritative confirmation of the nice things the *Era's* readers were saying about *Uncle Tom's Cabin.* Or, it may have been just the splendour of that auriferous lavender binding.

At any rate, she sent presentation copies of the novel and wrote letters to some of the leading men of the British Isles. She wrote to the Duke of Argyle and to the Earls of Carlisle and Shaftesbury, philanthropists interested in the cause of human liberty everywhere. She wrote to Dickens, Macaulay, and Charles Kingsley, liberals whose sympathies were with the underprivileged. She even wrote to the Prince Consort. Doubtless it was Calvin who reminded her not to overlook royalty.

Having despatched her letters to the great, Harriet, her son-biographer was to write under her eye, "committed the result to God and calmly turned her attention to other affairs."

Perhaps not so calmly. The copies of the novel which Jewett was sending to various influential figures began to fill the Federal Street house with daily gratifications. How could a plain Brunswick housewife, dicing potatoes and onions in her kitchen for a chowder, remain precisely calm when her husband brought from the postoffice such a letter as this:

> I congratulate you most cordially upon the immense success and influence of *Uncle Tom's Cabin*. It is one of the greatest triumphs recorded in literary history, to say nothing of the higher triumph of its moral effect.
> With great regard, and friendly remembrance to Mr. Stowe, I remain,
> > Yours most truly,
> > HENRY W. LONGFELLOW.

Whittier wrote her a Quaker letter.

> Ten thousand thanks for thy immortal book. My young friend Mary Irving [of the *National Era*] writes me that she has been reading it to some twenty young ladies, daughters of Louisiana slaveholders, near New Orleans, and that they, with one accord, pronounce it true.
> > Truly thy friend,
> > JOHN G. WHITTIER.

Thus the great welcomed Harriet to their number, and not only the poets but the statesmen and agitators and politicians. Charles Sumner of Massachusetts, whose speeches against slavery in the Senate were called half-battles, wrote her his congratulations. Senator Seward of New York called *Uncle Tom's Cabin* "the greatest book of the times" and recommended it to his Southern colleagues to show them the error of their ways. The angry Garrison made his peace with the daughter of the man he had regarded as an enemy. The propagandists were not over-estimating the political power of the novel; it was worth all their speeches and tracts and poems and editorials. Harriet's shrewd faith in her "pictures" was justified.

Nor did the reviews, which began to appear thickly by the end of April, conduce to calm in Federal Street. They carried on the tone of Dr. Storrs's shout, swelling into a chorus of extravagant praise. Jewett printed columns of excerpts from them, running into bold type to advertise "The Greatest Book of Its Kind Ever Issued from The American Press."

By May 15 Jewett & Co. could announce the sale of the fifty thousandth set of the two-volume novel—100,000 volumes printed and bound in eight weeks—something "without a precedent in the history of book publishing in this country." With sales booming at such a rate, Harriet early in May could regard herself as rolling in wealth. For the first time in her life she could indulge any whim without first stopping to count the pennies. She felt that she owed herself some little reward for going through the long ordeal of writing *Uncle Tom's Cabin,* so she took a trip.

It was the first of many trips she was to take from this time on. Her whole life since childhood had taught her to enjoy faring abroad on visits; yet, except for the excursion she and Mary Dutton made from Cincinnati into Kentucky so many years before, she had really never in her life gone anywhere just for the fun of going. Now she decided to go to New York.

She could plead a business reason, for the editors of the *Independent* had expressed a desire for a conference with her. In some elegant Broadway establishment, too, she could buy that silk dress she had promised herself. Yet primarily it was a pleasure-trip for her, and she journeyed to New York by easy stages, "touching," as Henry Ward Beecher wrote a little later, at Boston, Hartford, and New Haven on the way.

From Boston she reported to Calvin that business in the sale of the novel was brisk and herself "in such a whirl" the whole time. "Jewett animated." He had been down to Washington, promoting *Uncle Tom* among the legislators. In Hartford Harriet stopped with the Perkinses. What a delight it was to revisit these familiar and well-loved homes as a celebrity! Everybody wanted to meet the author of *Uncle Tom's Cabin.* Harriet came to Hartford this time as a woman of means, and her brother-in-law, Thomas C. Perkins, was a well-to-do, conservative lawyer and financier. On this visit Harriet gained his ready consent to act as her business adviser, and he served her in that capacity until his death, nearly twenty years later. Once she had money, Harriet never looked to Calvin for financial guidance; and she did not always heed the counsel of Perkins, to her subsequent regret. In New Haven the authoress stopped at the home of the Rev. Dr. Dutton, Mary's father.

Harriet had scarcely left Brunswick on her tour when Calvin received a letter that gave him a fright. The footnote, as he had apprehended, had made trouble. Dr. Joel Parker had recently removed from Philadelphia to

Eng'd by A. H. Ritchie.

Harriet Beecher Stowe

"Harriet's face was lean and tense; it had what we call character."
(Page 254.)

New York to become pastor of the Bleecker Street Church, in the section now known as Greenwich Village, and his attention had been called to the footnote on page 191, Vol. I, of *Uncle Tom's Cabin*. It had also been called to the same footnote in the *National Era* the preceding August; but it was one thing to be quoted, not too disagreeably, in a miserable little Abolitionist sheet that nobody read, and quite another to be dragged behind the car of the most triumphant novel of the century, branded as a frocked Beelzebub and exposed to the reprobation of the world. Especially when one had not used the words attributed to him. Or not exactly those words.

Prodded by certain individuals who held no love for Beechers, the put-upon and somewhat reluctant clergyman took action, and in his procedure he was nothing if not chaste. In this day, if a man felt himself injured by a woman's novel, he or his attorneys would write to her direct and think nothing of it. It was not so in the etiquette of 1852. One had to approach a lady indirectly or be suspected of holding her virtue in light esteem. The Rev. Dr. Parker wrote his letter of protest to Harriet, but he enclosed it in a covering note addressed to his dear friend and brother, Professor Stowe. This missive, with its smug assumption that a husband held dominion over his wife and all her works, even her works of art, was enough to make such new feminists as Elizabeth Cady Stanton and Lucy Stone gnash their teeth when they read it, as they did a few weeks later.

May 8, 1852.

REV. CALVIN E. STOWE, D.D.

Dear Sir:—It is with extreme regret that I have yielded to the necessity of addressing to Mrs. Stowe the communication transmitted under cover of this note to yourself.

I have long regarded you as being at least so far my friend, that you could not be suspected of cherishing anything like personal hostility to me.

Hence I was filled alike with sorrow and surprise to find my Christian character and professional reputation assailed so injuriously from a source which your counsels might fairly be supposed to govern.

My friends concur with me in the belief that a proper self-respect does not allow me to make a less serious matter of it, or to demand a less reparation.

I remain faithfully and truly yours,
JOEL PARKER.

New York, No. 2 Leroy Place.

The letter to Harriet, which was left unsealed so that Calvin might see it contained no improper proposals, read as follows:

New York, May 8, 1852.

MRS. HARRIET BEECHER STOWE.

Madam:—My attention has been called to an allusion you was [sic] pleased to make to myself *by name* in your widely-extended book entitled "Uncle Tom's Cabin."

I am sorry to say that I feel myself compelled to take some notice of what you have judged proper to send forth to the public as *my words* and *my sentiments* regarding the institution of Slavery.

It is to me a matter of profound regret, that before you made this assault upon my Christian and ministerial character, you had not conferred with me or sought information from some reliable source, so that I might have been spared an aspersion so widespread and so injurious to my professional reputation and usefulness.

Under these circumstances I feel myself compelled to demand a full and public retraction of the calumny referred to.

Respectfully your friend,
JOEL PARKER.

Calvin forwarded this letter to Harriet in Brooklyn and answered Dr. Parker himself in haste and in kind. He was not going to let a grave brother of the cloth suspect that Harriet might have had a mind and will of her own in writing her famous novel.

Brunswick, Me.,
Bowdoin College,
May 11, 1852.

REV. JOEL PARKER, D.D.

My Dear Sir:—Your name was used in Mrs. Stowe's work without my knowledge and, of course, without my consent. As soon as I discovered it, I told her it was wrong, and she must have it erased. She agreed with me and wrote to her publisher to have the name erased and some other corrections made. As I have not read the late issues, I had hoped the corrections were made; and am very sorry to find by your note of the 8th instant, just received, that they have not been made. Mrs. S. is now on a visit to her brother, Rev. H. W. Beecher, in Brooklyn, where she will be happy to see you and put all things on an amicable footing. I regret the occurrence and am glad to find that you consider the statement a "calumny" and a "serious matter."

Very truly, yours,
C. E. STOWE.

Calvin could not help that final flick at Dr. Parker. After all, he had read the clerical pro-slavery quotations in the *Independent,* too, and had been just as indignant as Harriet over them. Besides, he knew the bantam spirit of his wife, and he was sending her a copy of his letter to Dr. Parker. He must not make it too abject.

Harriet touched leisurely at Hartford and New Haven and found Dr. Parker's and her husband's letters waiting for her when she reached Brooklyn. She was not perturbed. In fact, she did not answer Dr. Parker for several days. She had arrived in the midst of the May Anniversaries, and New York was rocking with acclaim for *Uncle Tom's Cabin*. The fact that Mrs. Stowe was visiting the city was news. To whatever crowded meeting she went, she was always the centre of an admiring throng. Everybody was trying to meet her. She was being lionized. About one thing, though, she was certain. She was not going to retract what she had written about the Rev. Dr. Joel Parker. She knew what she had read in the *Independent*. If Dr. Parker wanted to be put right before the public, let him do his own retracting and confess his sin. Calvin's letter made her think the injured divine would be calling on her one of those days. She forgot about Dr. Parker and his grievance.

Dr. Parker waited until May 19 and then wrote Harriet—directly this time—a second letter. Though composed in a spirit of injured innocence, it was much stiffer than the first. It threatened a libel suit. Still, Harriet was not alarmed. She replied stoutly, taking the former president of Union Theological Seminary to task for his sins and refusing to retract anything. But she was careless with this letter. She addressed it merely to Dr. Joel Parker, New York. She gave it to Henry's friend, John T. Howard, to mail for her. Howard passed it along to John Keeler, one of his employees. Keeler gave it to the company's mailing clerk. The mail clerk took it to the postoffice. It was delayed a week in transit. Before Dr. Parker received it he had placed his case in the hands of Benjamin F. Butler, the eminent attorney, and had despatched to Harriet a third letter.

It all led to a comedy of errors and a tangle of cross-purposes so intricate that for clarity's sake the entire episode must be treated separately, in a subsequent chapter. Here it is enough to note that on June 24 the public was privileged to read in the New York *Tribune* the following "card":

UNCLE TOM'S CABIN.—Mrs. H. E. B. Stowe has requested us to publish the following correspondence:
"MRS. H. B. STOWE: Dear Madam: I write to ask an interview with you, at such time as may be convenient, for the purpose of laying before

you such evidence as will, I think, satisfy you that you have been misled in quoting, in your recent work, 'Uncle Tom's Cabin,' certain language as mine.

"I feel deeply aggrieved by the use made of that paragraph, and I am sure that you will not refuse to right me before the public, when I shall have laid the whole matter before you.

"I am, with great respect,

"Yours, JOEL PARKER."

"DR. JOEL PARKER: Dear Sir: I have attentively considered the papers which you left for my examination. I am quite satisfied that the language quoted (page 191, vol. i, of 'Uncle Tom's Cabin') conveys a meaning widely different from that which you intended to express in the articles which I have read; and you will allow me to say that my mind is greatly relieved from a painful conviction which I innocently, but, so far as you were concerned, unjustly entertained in regard to your real views.

"It is due to myself, however, to state that I did not carelessly employ the language attributed to you. It was published first in American newspapers, requoted in English journals (the *British Banner* being one). It was understood to have been employed in a large meeting of Congregational clergymen in England as one of the evidences of complicity of American ministers with Slavery. It appeared next in the letter of the English correspondent of the *Independent,* and finally was embodied in the annual report of the American Anti-Slavery Society for 1851. During all this time you had never publicly contradicted the truth of this representation, and I understood your silence to be an admission of its correctness.

"While, therefore, I do not see how I *could* have acted with more caution in employing an allegation which had become historical, I am yet heartily glad to find that a sentiment so shocking to every Christian mind is not yours.

"I shall order the immediate alteration of the paragraph in question, and shall be glad in any other way which shall appear proper, to set you right before the public.

"I am, dear sir, respectfully yours,

"H. B. STOWE."

"MRS. H. B. STOWE: My Dear Madam: I thank you for your prompt kindness in examining the documents which I submitted to you, and for the favorable opinions which you express. If you will allow me to publish your letter, I think that *that* will be all that is needed to place me right in regard to this unpleasant affair.

"I am, with unabated esteem,

"Yours, JOEL PARKER."

How tongues must have clacked in church circles over these letters—and nearly everybody belonged to some church circle or other. The public saw in them the end of a hidden dispute. Actually, they were but the beginning of one.

Harriet's visit to New York provided another subject for the country to talk about. Those conferences in the *Independent* office had been fruitful; and on May 22, when Harriet was still neglecting to answer Dr. Parker's letter, that journal led off its editorial page with an important announcement:

NEW CONTRIBUTOR
MRS. HARRIET BEECHER STOWE.

The proprietors of *The Independent* have effected an arrangement with Mrs. Harriet Beecher Stowe by which the columns of this journal will receive from her pen frequent and perhaps weekly contributions. These contributions will be of a miscellaneous description, embracing every variety of incident, of subject, and of character, from the "Mayflower" to "Uncle Tom's Cabin:" sometimes an essay, sometimes a story, sometimes a graphic picture of home life or a sketch of the olden time—in short, whatever the cultivated taste, the well-stored memory, the fertile imagination, the dramatic and descriptive talent, and the experienced pen of such a writer can produce, to instruct or to entertain. Mrs. Stowe's articles will be known by the initials of her name, H.E.B.S. The article in this week's paper shows that Mrs. S. will not want for topics even outside the pale of lighter literature.

Harriet had become a newspaper's "stated contributor," America's first female journalist, or, as we would call her today, its first woman-columnist— Harriet, who scarcely a year earlier had shrunk from any exhibition of herself on a public rostrum. And her column in the *Independent,* when she bestirred herself to fill it, was the first column on Page One, which had previously been occupied most often by the Star contributions of her brother, Henry Ward Beecher.

Her first excursion into journalism took her indeed well outside the pale of light literature. Penned in Henry's house amid the excitements of Anniversary Week and in minutes snatched from business and social interviews, dinners, and receptions in her honour, while Dr. Parker's letter lay unanswered on her bureau, it was an attack on the conservative old religious weekly newspaper of New York, the *Observer*.

In this initial effort of his sister, Henry's influence shows clearly. Even a Star Reporter on a religious paper in 1852 needed a personal enemy to abuse in print, and Henry's *bête noire* was the *Observer*. The *Observer* was the *Independent's* traditional rival, insofar as the *Independent* had built up a tradition in the half-dozen years of its existence. The *Observer* was "Old School," pro-slavery, anti-feminist, anti-liberal, anti-almost-everything that Henry Ward Beecher believed in and was an obvious target for the Star Reporter's invectives.

It was on this visit to Brooklyn that Harriet cemented an important friendship in her life, with Mr. and Mrs. John T. Howard and their children. The Howards were wealthy Wall Street operators, devout church-goers, and almost idolatrous followers of Henry Ward Beecher. (However, they kept their business and their religion severely apart.) John T. Howard had been one of the founders of Plymouth Church and one of the men who persuaded Henry to come to Brooklyn from Indianapolis.

On Harriet's previous visit to Brooklyn, in the spring of 1850, the Howards do not seem to have paid much attention to the almost destitute little woman from Cincinnati; but Harriet in 1852 was different. The wealthy Howards took the celebrity to their bosoms so warmly that when Harriet left for home in June, Mrs. Howard went with her, at least as far as Hartford.

Thereafter Mrs. Howard was Harriet's most dependable source of information about Henry and his activities. Henry himself was always too busy to dash off more than a few lines to Harriet, and Eunice Beecher was unsympathetic with the clan's interest in its most magnetic member. Eunice was not fond of the Beecher tribe and made it plain (except to Harriet) that her house was not a stop on the family caravan route. Some of the Beechers, in fact, charged that Eunice was trying to alienate Henry from the clan. Harriet, however, kept on friendly terms with her sister-in-law; but when she wanted news of her brother it was to Mrs. Howard that she applied.

Besides the lionizing she received, Harriet was tasting other unfamiliar sweets of fame on this visit. Her sister Catharine was in New York at the time, though presumably not stopping with Henry Ward and Eunice Beecher. Catharine was organizing her new American Women's Educational Association to raise endowments for girls' schools in the West and particularly for Catharine's pet high school for girls in the little city of

Milwaukee, Wisconsin. When Catharine announced her Board of Managers, Mrs. Stowe's name stood at the top of it. It was a pleasure for Harriet to do this for the sister who had been foster-mother to her. Whether Harriet's prestige carried the campaign to success, the American Women's Educational Association raised $20,000 for the school, which became known as the Milwaukee Normal Institute and was to be a lasting monument to Catharine Beecher.

Jenny Lind was completing her conquest of musical America and was booked for her final New York concert during Anniversary Week. Of course, Harriet, the famous, must attend—the Howards insisted on *that,* though Harriet had never heard a first-class musician in her life. The trouble was, Castle Garden had been sold out for months; but Broker Howard knew that money talked. He went straight to Otto Goldschmidt, the Nightingale's pianist and recent bridegroom, to receive only polite regrets. There were no seats to be had.

"Pshaw, that's too bad," said Howard. "Mrs. Stowe will be greatly disappointed."

"Mrs. Stowe!" exclaimed Goldschmidt. "The author of *Uncle Tom's Cabin?*"

"Yes," Mr. Howard said. "She is very desirous of hearing Jenny Lind."

"Mrs. Stowe shall have seats. Wait."

Goldschmidt went to his suite in the hotel and in a few minutes returned with two choice tickets enclosed in a long-treasured envelope addressed to Harriet in Jenny Lind's own hand. Howard was immensely impressed. He showed the tickets to everyone that day and at night told Harriet and his family that he could have sold them at any time for ten dollars apiece!

Harriet attended the concert, which she found "a bewildering dream of sweetness and beauty." She wrote a note of thanks to Jenny Lind, and the songstress replied with a letter of praise for *Uncle Tom's Cabin.* "Certainly God's hand will remain with a blessing over your head."

And there was poor old Milly Edmondson, of Washington, at hand to give the flushed authoress more gratification and publicity. Four years earlier Henry Ward Beecher had ransomed two of Milly's daughters, who were in Bruin & Hill's slave warehouse in Alexandria, Virginia, waiting to be sold down the river to the brothels of New Orleans. At that time Henry had made such a moving plea to his congregation that it returned the whole upset price of $2,250 on the girls at a single passing of the plates.

Now Milly was back on Henry's doorstep again, with a tale of her two remaining slave children about to go under the hammer. By this time the Edmondson family was cold potatoes to the pastor of Plymouth Church; but Sister Hattie was providentially in his house, and he passed old Milly along to give Hattie a turn.

Harriet jumped at the chance to play the rôle expected of the author of the great Abolition novel. She received Milly and promised her not only the liberty of the two children, on whom there was a price of $1,200, but Milly's own freedom as well. "If I can't raise the money otherwise, I will pay it myself." Harriet thought first of Jenny Lind and wrote to her about the slave children, suggesting an interview. The Swedish Nightingale was packing up and doing a thousand things preparatory to her final departure from the United States. She sent her subscription for $100 and her regrets, probably sincere, that she could not meet Mrs. Stowe.

"The time is short. I am very, very sorry that I shall not be able to *see* you. I must say farewell to you in this way." She sent Harriet her best wishes, and she was "Yours in friendship, Jenny Goldschmidt."

Harriet, who during the next two decades was certainly as great a name in the world as Jenny Lind, set almost pathetic store upon the songstress's letters to her. Another great woman might have regarded the incident as trivial; but Harriet, when in her late seventies she was selecting from her papers material for her son Charles's biography of herself, produced her Jenny Lind correspondence with emphasis. She told Charles to call it "an epistolary interview."

In her later life Harriet was sometimes accused of being snobbish. One virulent critic declared that she grovelled before foreign titles. It was a false accusation. Once she was established as a luminary in the world of the great, titles meant little to her. But, though she could move comfortably enough in that realm as a peer, she was never part of it. She remained the small-town wife and housekeeper, and the glamorous friendships she made in the arts and letters she sometimes could not resist parading before her army of followers, who were themselves small-town people at heart. Jenny Lind was the first of such trophies for Harriet, though only an "epistolary" one.

Having adopted the Edmondsons, Harriet showed what a good committee-worker she was. She organized a meeting of the ladies of Plymouth Church and had Milly there as the speaker. She did the same in Dr. Cox's church in Brooklyn. She wrote to Mrs. Edward Beecher in Boston and secured her support and also communicated with church friends in Portland. She lugged Milly up to New Haven and had her speak to the ladies of Dr. Dutton's church and also to those of the congregation of Dr. Leonard Bacon, whom Harriet had recently met in the *Independent* office. The eminent Dr. Bacon was one of the editors of that journal and a stated contributor. He became Harriet's fast friend, a wise man to whom she could turn when she needed a father-confessor.

As a result of these efforts the emancipation fund swiftly grew. Jenny Lind's $100 headed the subscription list. Mr. Bowen added $100 to it; and what a warm feeling it gave Harriet to be able to write to Calvin, "I have put my own name down for an equal amount." The Brooklyn collection brought in $600, and the other campaigns progressed so well that before Harriet left Brooklyn she gave Milly a cheque for the entire cost of her freedom and that of her children.

Such draughts from the cup of success (in spite of the fuss Dr. Parker was beginning to kick up) made the Brooklyn visit the most ecstatic interval Harriet had ever known. New friends, new and important engagements, new opportunities begging at her door, the homage of the city— their effect on Harriet was to increase her self-confidence and strengthen her resolute nature. She became executive, made decisions, including one to remove from Brunswick to Andover immediately and not wait for fall, when Calvin's new professorship should begin.

"For my part," she wrote to Calvin, "if I *must* leave Brunswick, I would rather leave at once. I can tear away with a sudden pull more easily than to linger there, knowing that I am to leave at last. I shall never find people whom I shall like better than those of Brunswick."

She never did—nor people who liked *her* better than had the Uphams and Smyths.

But in making this sudden decision Harriet probably had something else in mind. Her triumphal days in New York were showing her that henceforth she was going to be a famous woman. She would receive visits from the great, and she must have a home in keeping with her position. She doubted if any faculty house at Andover would suit her, at least without drastic renovation. She had the money now, or soon would have it, to provide herself with what she needed, and she was impatient to start preparing her future and, as she thought, permanent home.

Thus Harriet put on the trousers of the Stowe family, and she was going to wear them thenceforth. A few months later an Andover drayman would be bellowing to an acquaintance that he was taking his load of lumber "up to the Widder Stowe's." He had never heard of Professor Stowe nor observed any husband in the management of the Stowe job.

But in the midst of her resolutions to conduct her own life, Harriet could think with heightened tenderness of Calvin—her helpless old professor, so afraid of his own round shadow that even then he was hurrying down to Boston for the moral support of old Dr. Beecher in the crisis which Joel Parker had raised. Perhaps, too, Harriet thought of the vanity of fame and the fickleness of the crowd. Calvin was steadfast. Like Father Beecher's Roxana, he was just there, trembling perhaps, but loyal.

"It is not fame nor praise that contents me," the new celebrity wrote him from Brooklyn. "I seem never to have needed love so much as now. I long to hear you say how much you love me."

Harriet ended her New York visit about the middle of June. She travelled homeward by easy stages, stopping first at the Duttons' in New Haven, whence she sent to the New York papers her "retraction" of the accusation against Dr. Parker in her novel. Mrs. Howard seems to have been travelling with her, for Harriet's next stop was Hartford, and the well-to-do Brooklyn lady accompanied her there. They stayed over night with the Perkinses, occupying the same bedroom "at Mrs. Stowe's request."

Mrs. Howard remembered the scene, after they retired. The prosaic Brooklyn lady undressed and got into bed, but Harriet was slower about it, having fallen into one of her fits of abstraction. She took off her uncomfortable load of petticoats, loosened her stays, let down her hair, and then, in dishabille, dropped cross-legged to the floor and sat there in a profound reverie, brushing her abundant curls. Mrs. Howard looked in silence at "her little girlish figure gathered in a heap." By now the Brooklyn idolator was in such awe of the small prophetess that she would not have dreamed of interrupting the precious flow of thought by uttering a word.

But the genius on the floor was not then plotting a second world-shaking fiction. She was appraising the miracle of the first and appraising it sapiently. It was Harriet who broke the long silence. She remarked that she had just received a letter from Edward Beecher. Brother Edward had been reading the New York papers, and he was afraid all the praise and publicity Harriet was receiving might turn her head—"induce pride and vanity," as Harriet said, "and work harm to my Christian character." Mrs. Howard reported the rest of it:

"She dropped her brush from her hand and exclaimed with earnestness,

'Dear soul, he need not be troubled. He doesn't know that I did not write that book.'

" 'What!' said I. 'You did not write "Uncle Tom"?'

" 'No,' she said, 'I only put down what I saw.'

" 'But you have never been at the South, have you?' I asked.

" 'No,' she said, 'but it all came before me in visions, one after another, and I put them down in words.' "

This is the earliest recorded instance of Harriet's claim of divine inspiration for *Uncle Tom's Cabin*. Forty years later she was repeating the same claim, and in the interval she had never deviated from the attitude that the novel was God's and not her own.

Uncle Tom's Cabin was thundering on. Before Harriet left New York the *Independent* announced that the volume of sales had grown to ten thousand copies a week. The Mercantile Library had had to buy forty-six copies of the novel to meet the demands of its card-holders. Eastern papers were already advertising "A BOOK FOR THE TIMES!," entitled *Life at The South; or, Uncle Tom's Cabin as It Is*, by W. L. G. Smith, to be published by a Buffalo house. It was the first of a flood of books and pamphlets that attempted to climb on *Uncle Tom's* bandwagon—publications became so numerous by the end of the year 1852 that Norton's *Literary Gazette* coined for them the comprehensive name of "Uncle Tom Literature."

Whittier, who took a good deal of his inspiration from the daily headlines, had already been inspired by *Uncle Tom's Cabin* to produce *Little Eva*, the quality of which may be judged by the first stanza—

> Dry the tears for holy Eva,
> With the blessed angels leave her;
> Of the form so sweet and fair
> Give to earth the tender care.
> For the golden locks of Eva
> Let the sunny Southland give her
> Flower-pillow of repose—
> Orange bloom and budding rose.

The Quaker poet achieved such phonetic similarities to Eva as "never," "grieve her," "believer," and "river," but it took a Down-East Yankee to recite the poem in rhyme. In Boston Professor Manuel Emilio set this pious doggerel to music, and by the end of June agents were hawking the song on Broadway surrounded by knots of bearded and beaver-hatted gentlemen eagerly buying the sheets to take home to their loved ones. By this time half a nation was weeping over the untimely death of that angelic child, wantonly slain by her maker for a literary effect.

There was much home distraction, too, for Harriet. Success had transformed the humble routine of poverty in the Federal Street house. There was a cook in the kitchen now, a housekeeper in the front rooms, and a governess to look after the children. Upon her return after her long visit to Brooklyn Harriet found an accumulation of mail so formidable that she brought up her half-sister Isabella to help her with it as secretary. Isabella, a lush brunette, aged thirty, was married to John Hooker, who had been a law clerk in Thomas Perkins's office in Hartford. Hooker was now practising law independently in Farmington, Connecticut, near Hartford.

The mail which Harriet took up with the help of Sister Belle brushed her against a world she had not known before. The reception accorded *Uncle Tom's Cabin* by the two sections was not at first what might have been expected. The attack on the veracity of the novel began in the North. The earliest reviews from the South showed no hatred of either the book or its author but did display, and convincingly, too, an air of shocked and injured innocence. To the Southerner the exasperating quality of *Uncle Tom* was that while the truth of none of its details could be successfully challenged, Harriet's complete picture of slavery was not the slavery the average Southerner knew or recognized.

The typical attitude was expressed by the editor of the *Alabama Planter,* who wrote: "The plan for assaulting the best institutions in the world may be made just as rational as it is by the wicked (perhaps unconsciously so) authoress of this book. The woman who wrote it must be either a very bad or a very fanatical person. For her own domestic peace we trust no enemy will ever penetrate into her household to pervert the scenes he may find there with as little logic or kindness as she has used in her 'Uncle Tom's Cabin'."

Harriet felt herself particularly abused by this comment, singling it out for inclusion in her biography. She called it "a most solemnly savage attack upon me"; though, read today, it seems, considering the provocation, temperate and even "Christian" in tone.

The financial nerve was first to react to the danger inherent in *Uncle Tom's Cabin*. Harriet herself was aware that she could not pin the sin of

ORIGINAL ILLUSTRATION FROM "UNCLE TOM'S CABIN"

"Little Eva Reading the Bible to Uncle Tom"

"To her class of school-children she [Mrs. Stowe] read her first description of the most saintly child in American literature." (Page 271.)

slavery exclusively upon the South. There was plenty of Northern money invested in the cotton business, which lived by slavery. *"All the wealth of America* may be said to be interested in it,"* Harriet wrote to the Earl of Shaftesbury. The spokesman for that wealth was the New York *Journal of Commerce,* which at the end of May fired the first big gun against *Uncle Tom's Cabin,* attacking its essential truth. Editors throughout the United States at once picked up the gage, for and against Harriet, and a great newspaper debate began.

This was an abrupt development, and it was followed at once by another, equally sudden. Up to this time *Uncle Tom's Cabin* had been merely a controversial novel, circulating as freely in the South as in the North, and, there is evidence to indicate, making its converts in the South, too. As Harriet wrote, "At first the book seemed to go by acclamation." Then all at once—approximately in June, 1852—both sides perceived how powerfully it affected every mind it touched, and both sides saw the truth. This was not just a novel, but a mine planted at the foundations of the republic, and the fuse was hissing.

"It penetrated the walls of Congress," wrote a contemporary, "and made the politicians tremble. It startled statesmen, who scented danger near." The little Maine housewife had become a dangerous figure whom state-craft and diplomacy must defeat, if possible. From that moment the Civil War became inevitable. Harriet's deadly propaganda suddenly fired sectional hatreds that were not to subside until the hearts that beat so hotly with them had gone back to the dust.

In the South the immediate effect was the spontaneous suppression of the book. It became dangerous to own or display a copy of *Uncle Tom's Cabin.* Jewett still claimed to be shipping thousands south of the Mason and Dixon Line, but if so, their circulation must have been surreptitious. Southern mothers began to hold Harriet up before their children as a wicked ogress. A distant relative with whom Harriet sometimes corresponded spent her winters in Georgia. The following December she besought Harriet not to write her name and return address on the envelopes of her letters. "Amiable and excellent people" in Georgia were asking the cousin if such a person as Mrs. Stowe "could be received into reputable society at the North."

Henry Pellew, heir to the Earldom of Exmouth and fresh out of Cambridge, was touring America that summer. In Boston he read *Uncle Tom's Cabin* and was deeply moved by it. In Charleston, South Carolina, he met a young lady of family who expressed a desire to see the book. With some difficulty H. Pellew procured a copy and sent it to her. A few days later some friends came to him quietly and advised him to leave town immediately. The countryside was up in arms against him, and he was going to be challenged for the insult he had offered to a Southern lady. The future Earl of Exmouth stayed not on the order of his going, not wishing to fight any duels or confront any aristocratic mobs in defense of one side of an American political question.

Harriet herself felt the first sickening breath of this new hatred during those final June days in Brunswick. She began to receive anonymous letters from the South, threatening, scurrilous, and obscene, many of them, and once Calvin unwrapped a small parcel out of which fell a black human ear, sliced from the head of some recalcitrant slave and sent to the woman now being widely branded as a fomenter of servile rebellion, that nightmare which had troubled the Southern pillow since Nat Turner had massacred the half-hundred Virginians in 1831.

Harriet's retort to this attack was a subterfuge which she was to adopt again when under fire. She pretended not to have read the anonymous letters. Nevertheless, she could characterize them. "Their like could only be expressed by John Bunyan's account of the speech of Apollyon: 'He spake as a dragon.'"

Meanwhile something else of moment to Harriet was occurring in a distant part of the world, though she was unaware of it. Her novel went on the presses in London during the final week of June, 1852. The copy sent abroad by "Putnam's young man" went to one Mr. Bogue, a publisher, who after a contemptuous glance at the novel decided he did not care to embark in cheap reprints of American authors. However, he passed the book along to his friend Henry Vizetelly, who read it and thought there might be something in it.

Vizetelly did not wish to undertake the entire speculation alone. He proposed a triple partnership with two other free-lances in the English publishing field, Messrs. Salisbury and Clarke. Vizetelly retained his one-third interest in the enterprise, but Salisbury and Clarke took unto themselves another partner, Mr. S. O. Beeton. The piratical quartette took the firm name of Clarke & Co. To anticipate and thus have done with Messrs. Vizetelly *et alii,* Clarke & Co. brought out the first British edition of *Uncle Tom's Cabin* on July 8 in a cloth binding, crown octavo size, selling for half-a-crown. It fell flat. Not until others had pirated the novel and *Uncle Tom* had begun to sweep England did Clarke & Co. cut down their unsold pages to foolscap-octavo size and issue the book anew at a shilling; and in that form it shared the sudden prosperity which Harriet's pen brought that year to British publishing.

In the early part of July Harriet removed permanently to Andover, making occasional trips to Brunswick during the summer to see Calvin and the children and arrange for the moving. She had made two previous visits to Andover that spring—one to take over various items of personal baggage, including her private papers, and a second, overnight, trip to get her copy of a letter needed by Henry Ward Beecher, who was conducting Harriet's side of the quarrel with Dr. Joel Parker in New York. Her family did not come down to Andover until September. It is likely that Harriet stopped at first with the family of Professor Edward A. Park, of the Seminary faculty. If so, this in itself was a treat for her. Dr. Park, a tall, gaunt, emotional and eloquent preacher, celebrated for his sermons— his "Judas Sermon" and "Peter Sermon" were well-known in New England —was also a witty and polished man of the world. He was noted as "a brilliant converser." The Parks became the Stowes' closest friends in Andover.

As Harriet apprehended, the free house available for the Professor of Sacred Literature would not suit, nor would other prospects which she examined. Her eye fell speculatively upon an ugly, rectangular, old stone edifice that stood at one end of the great common that then separated Andover Theological Seminary from Phillips Andover Academy. This structure had for many years been the carpenter shop for the "manual-labour" theological students, but had lately been converted into a gymnasium. In the East the Manual Labour Plan was giving way to organized athletics.

The principal product of the Seminary's factory enterprise had been coffins. Coffins, besides offering a means of self-support, served the Andover theologians as the campus cemetery did those of Lane Seminary—as a reminder of the brevity of life and the imminence of heaven and hell. If an Andover boy were too squeamish to line coffin-lids with satin, he could build wheelbarrows, which had a cultural background, having been invented by Leonardo da Vinci. The Andover wheelbarrows enjoyed almost as good a reputation as Andover coffins.

Harriet was undaunted by the rather gruesome past of the stone structure. She had long wanted to build something for herself, ever since she wrote critically of the inconvenient house the Beechers had first occupied in Cincinnati. This was her chance. She proposed to the authorities that the Seminary remodel, under her supervision, the former coffin-shop into a residence for Professor and Mrs. Stowe.

The trustees, however, had no money to devote to such an extravagance. Then, at the end of July, Harriet received from John P. Jewett her first cheque for royalties. It amounted to $10,300. With this in hand she proposed to the trustees that she advance the money for the alterations, superintend the work herself, and at the end take the Seminary's note for what the renovation cost. This proposal, too, probably met with a mixed reception. But Harriet was now mounted in a triumphal car, riding down all opposition. The trustees gave in, and Harriet had her way.

Harriet was perfectly happy that summer. Fame, money, and a dazzling future were securely hers. She was building her own house, each day delighted to see the charm her imagination was bringing into the ugly stone shop. Much as she loved her husband and children, after the years of worry and drudgery it must have added something to her peace to be alone for a few weeks—with evenings to spend in the delightful company of Dr. and Mrs. Park. At the Parks' she met those who were to be her neighbours—the Emersons, the Jacksons, the Dexters, Professor Phelps and Mrs. Elizabeth Stuart Phelps, the elder, who was to die that autumn in childbirth. Harriet's letters were rapturous with a bliss not even the annoyance of a Dr. Parker could disturb. Wasn't it, her Puritan conscience asked her, even a little wicked to embrace such undeserved blessings?

Success proved Harriet to be no dilettante in authorship. Freed at last from household cares, instead of basking in her new fame and wealth she at once turned professionally to the planning of another novel—to "composing" it, as she said, though by composing she always meant daydreaming scenes and characters. But our first realist had to have models in her work; she knew no other way of writing.

"I greatly need living studies for the filling in of my sketches," she informed Calvin from Andover. "There is 'old Jonas,' my 'fish father,' a sturdy, independent fisherman-farmer, who in his youth sailed all over the world and made up his mind about everything. In his old age he attends prayer-meetings and reads the 'Missionary Herald.' He also has plenty of money in an old brown sea-chest. He is a great heart with an inflexible will and iron muscles. I must go to Orr's Island and see him again."

Well, this country is still familiar with Old Jonas, though in 1852 Harriet was "composing" him for the first time. We have met him in *Way Down East* and *Shore Acres* and *Captain January* and even in radio's Uncle Seth Parker. Harriet began to compose him for a novel she was to call *The Pearl of Orr's Island,* one of her better efforts which still stands conspicuously in every well-selected Maine library and is still read by summer visitors to the Maine coast and reread by the natives. But Harriet was not to write her Maine story immediately, as she thought. Eight crowded and eventful years for her intervened before she started to write it, and the guns of Fort Sumter interrupted the half-finished work.

In her own felicity Harriet stepped forth in the rôle of Andover's Lady Bountiful. There was poor Mrs. Edwards, struggling to get along. Her late husband, the scholarly Professor B. B. Edwards of the Seminary faculty, editor of the profound *Bibliotheca Sacra,* who had accomplished the feat of securing the indolent Calvin Stowe as a contributor, had died in April while on a tour of the South, leaving his widow penniless, of course. Mrs. Edwards turned to the universal recourse of cultured gentlewomen thrown on their own resources in that day. She opened a "select boarding-school for young ladies."

With her new power as a journalist, Harriet inserted a free puff for Mrs. Edwards's school in the *Independent.* It appeared anonymously, but Harriet's touch was unmistakable. "We speak as a parent, having daughters of our own," she wrote—words which certainly left the impression that she was sending her daughters to Mrs. Edwards. But when school opened that fall, Harriet sent the twins and Georgie to Abbot Academy, an already famous girls' school which helped make Andover attractive to the theological students.

An artist named Stevens had opened a studio in Andover for taking daguerreotype likenesses, and Harriet sat for her first portrait. In the opinion of many of her contemporaries, it was also her best portrait. It does not make her as physically beautiful as some others taken a little later, but it displays to advantage her dark, abundant hair, the intense spiritual quality of her thin face, the high intelligence of her brow and eyes, and great character in the nose, mouth, and chin. In that repository of civic memories, the Andover Historical Society, it remains the favourite portrait of Harriet Beecher Stowe.

Thus passed that blissful interlude which was Harriet's first summer of success. On August 15 Jewett announced the sale of the hundred-thousandth copy of *Uncle Tom's Cabin,* "with hardly an abatement of the demand." Gold-miners on the Sacramento were reading their few copies in turn, paying twenty-five cents apiece for the privilege. A San Francisco printer brought out a pirated pamphlet edition, but he was too far away for Harriet to do anything about it.

In England *Uncle Tom* was causing one of those sudden, vast emotional upheavals which make a modern sceptic wonder if there were not, after all, something supernatural in the book, as its author claimed. After lying dormant on the bookstalls for several weeks, the novel all at once exploded into popular favour, as half a dozen London publishers, discovering that the text was unprotected, brought out their editions simultaneously.

In Paris, where President Louis Napoleon was openly and cynically plotting to become Emperor of the French, alert editors were importing British copies of *Uncle Tom's Cabin* and giving them to translators. In America, amid the din of the editorial debate on the point of the novel's truth, *Bleak House* was running almost unnoticed as a serial in *Harper's New Monthly Magazine.* New "Uncle Tom" songs were appearing every week, and new "replies" to Harriet's indictment of slavery. The South increased its vituperation of her and her novel, as on Richmond's streets children were beginning to chant:

> Go, go, go,
> Ol' Harriet Beecher Stowe!
> We don't want you here in Virginny—
> Go, go, go!

Meanwhile, the diminutive cause of the uproar was perched on the head of an Andover barrel, her crinolines draped over its sides, quarrelling humorously but firmly with a boss carpenter, sketching elms, and sometimes writing gentle and undistinguished hymn-verses.

The family came on at the end of August; and all of them—Harriet, Calvin, the children, the servants, and Rover—went to live at the "Samaritan" house, a boarding-house which had once been the Seminary's hospital. The remodelling of the stone coffin-shop would not be finished before snow flew. The removal of Rover from Brunswick to Andover must have offered quite a problem in that day of primitive railroad transportation. However, the dog, now a sedate and bulky Newfoundland, came—perhaps with the wagons that brought down the heavier household goods over the dusty roads.

The Seminary inaugurated Calvin Stowe in his professorship during the first week in September. In the joy of the reunion Harriet penned for her column a hymn, entitled, *When I Awake I Am Still with Thee*. The children, except Baby Charley, began treading new paths to school. That month *Uncle Tom's Cabin* attained the classic company of the Tauchnitz titles. Harriet was beginning to pay attention to the reiterated charges that her book exaggerated the evils of slavery. She wrote an introduction to the Tauchnitz edition, citing the Louisiana slave laws, known as the *Code Noir,* as justification of everything in *Uncle Tom's Cabin*.

And then, at the end of September, 1852, Harriet was rudely yanked from her Elysium. The New York *Observer,* whose position as the leading religious journal of the United States was challenged only by the *Independent,* came out with the sensational charge that Mrs. Stowe's retraction of her libellous statement about the Rev. Joel Parker, published the preceding June, was a forgery perpetrated by Henry Ward Beecher. And Harriet read herself branded as coarse and unladylike, a mercenary coward, and a liar. No reputable paper had ever applied such language to an American woman before.

Harriet knew now what it meant to twist her hair into bow-strings.

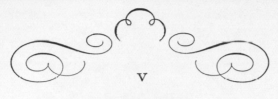

V

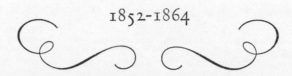

ANDOVER

1852-1864

The "Stone Cabin" at Andover

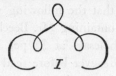

Harriet in Battle

HARRIET was in Brunswick when the *Observer's* blast of September 23, 1852 came out against her. She was there to close the Federal Street house and say farewell to her friends. To make a convincing defense of himself and his sister, Henry needed Harriet's file of the Parker correspondence. He telegraphed to her at Andover. Two days, including Sunday, intervened before the message reached Harriet in Brunswick, and then too late for her to catch the train south that day. She went to Boston Tuesday morning and reached Andover at half-past one that afternoon, with only thirty minutes at her disposal, if the "papers" were to go off to Henry that day.

Engaging the depot hack, Harriet galloped to the Samaritan House, breathlessly explained her appearance to a startled family, bundled up the letters, and dashed back to the depot, just in time for the two-o'clock cars. Later that afternoon she mailed the package in Boston. Henry received them next morning, but it was too late now for the September 30 number of the *Independent,* which went to press that night. Henry, therefore, merely inserted a "card," denouncing "the untruth and wickedness of the *Observer's* editorial" and promising a waiting world "a full history of this affair in the next *Independent* [Oct. 7]."

Such advance notice gave the Rev. S. Irenaeus Prime, editor of the *Observer,* who had access to Brother Parker's file, time to prepare his own bill of particulars. On October 7 both papers, the *Observer* and the *Independent,* came out with the Stowe-Beecher-Parker correspondence, with "intervening remarks." So much depends on point of view! By these "genuine letters" the *Observer* could show Henry and Harriet to be a pair of elusive, unfeeling villains; with the identical documents Henry demonstrated that he and his sister had acted as high-minded Christians interested only in the cause of justice and truth.

The affair was an immense sensation. The edition of the *Independent* was snapped up so quickly that the following week the paper announced its publication of an Extra containing Mr. Beecher's deply to the *Observer* in full, which it would wholesale at $2 per hundred—"orders by mail attended to." The public had never before read an attack of such violence upon a woman, unless she were such a creature as George Sand or one of those British lady novelists who wrote erotic fiction and could be supposed to have no morals. But Harriet was one of the Beechers and the present darling of a large portion of the reading public.

From this distance in time the Stowe-Parker imbroglio bears a good deal of resemblance to an extravaganza. About the whole attack of Dr. Parker and Mr. Prime upon Harriet and her brother floats an aroma of hypocrisy and exaggeration. The worthy Doctor could not possibly have felt so damaged by *Uncle Tom's Cabin* as Attorney Ben Butler assured him he was. His tears of injured innocence have today a cold, saurian feel. Harriet had indeed misquoted him but had not ascribed to him any opinion that was far divergent from his real sentiments toward slavery. In fact, the whole behaviour of Prime and Parker in the affair gives colour to Henry's charge that it was all a conspiracy to impair the influence of *Uncle Tom's Cabin*.

On the other hand, the tragic attitude struck by Henry Ward Beecher under the *Observer's* fire was equally exaggerated. In his autobiography he maintained that the accusation of forgery was the severest challenge he ever had to face until his private morals were questioned in the famous Beecher-Tilton scandal. Perhaps so; but it seems incredible that the public of 1852 could regard even the unauthorized use of Dr. Parker's signature at the bottom of an open letter published in the New York press as a forgery. The reasonable inference would be that there had been some sort of misunderstanding. Yet Henry chose to take the impeachment at its face value, and so under a national spotlight the extravaganza acted itself out, both sides striking magnificent poses.

On their face the Stowe-Parker letters were undoubtedly open to some such interpretation as Mr. Prime gave them, leaving out that gentleman's malice; and if so, Harriet and Henry had only themselves to thank for the fact—Harriet because of the casual way in which she received Dr. Parker's first complaints, Henry because of his carelessness in dealing with a man who hated him and would have been glad to destroy him, and Henry again because he could not resist the temptation to give the public one of those exhibitions of play-acting to which he, and Harriet too, were so addicted. In this instance Harriet preferred to make a simple, straightforward statement, but anything so naive would not do for Henry's showmanship. He must cook up a supposed correspondence between his sister and Dr. Parker—letters never written by either nor exchanged by them but merely adopted by the signatories as their own. That was what made the trouble.

To get at the truth in this comedy of errors and cross-purposes, it is necessary to go back to that enchanted May evening when Harriet received Dr. Parker's second letter and realized that the Bleecker Street divine was not coming to negotiate with her but was expecting a public withdrawal of the "libel" in *Uncle Tom's Cabin* upon his peremptory demand.

> You have made this assault [Harriet read] upon a minister of the Gospel, upon one whose professional reputation, like the reputation of your sex for chastity, is blasted by mere suspicion. You have done this, too, without the least provocation, public or private. . . . I have never used such words. I have never maintained such views. Why I am singled out and held up to such scorn, I do not understand. What your motives may be I will not attempt to say. But I do say, with indignant remonstrance against the injustice of this libel, that your language is untrue and slanderous, and I again demand a full and public retraction. If such retraction is not made in a prompt and satisfactory manner, I shall feel obliged to take the best means that I can to throw off from myself the odium which you have sought to heap upon me.

Far from being alarmed by this threat or moved by Dr. Parker's plea of his own innocence, Harriet tore herself away from the distractions of Anniversary Week long enough to answer him in detail, and her letter entirely lacked that mollifying touch which Calvin had already been able to put into his. She recited the names of various newspapers and publications in which the Doctor's pro-slavery utterance had been quoted and told of having for more than a year "searched the papers week after week with the eye of a friend" for Dr. Parker's denial of the cruel words. When no such denial appeared, "I therefore with great regret set you down in my mind as a leader on that side of the question, and quoted you as such— and I think I had reason to do so." Harriet then went on maddeningly:

> Under this attitude you must perceive that it's not in *my* power to set you right before a Christian public, who probably have formed their opinion from the same sources from which I formed mine. It is to the Christian

public generally, as I apprehend, that *your* denial of such sentiments and expressions should be addressed; and to them you should explain why you have allowed yourself to be so publicly and frequently and notoriously ranged on that side of the question, and why you have taken no notice of what you say you consider a "libel," when it has been so very publicly and for such a long time proclaimed in the ordinary channels of intelligence. . . . When you shall have satisfactorily explained the subject, I will with pleasure do anything that may lie within my power to obviate the misconceptions that have arisen from your long silence.

This was the letter which Harriet's carelessness delayed for a week in the mails. Meanwhile Henry Ward Beecher had run down the original source of Dr. Parker's remark, which that clergyman had uttered in the course of a "debate" on slavery with a Rev. Mr. A. Rood. The discussion had run through fourteen issues of the Philadelphia *Christian Observer* in 1848. Several of Henry's ministerial brethren, speaking from memory, assured him that Harriet had not misquoted Dr. Parker, and Mr. Rood himself wrote, "If Dr. P. denies the statement made by Mrs. Stowe, it will be strange."

Such assurances stiffened Harriet in her resolution not to yield an inch to Joel Parker. Still, Henry thought it best to find the Doctor's exact words and sent to Philadelphia for the file of the debate numbers of the *Christian Observer*. Meanwhile, not having had any reply from his two letters to Harriet, Dr. Parker fondly believed that he had frightened the lady speechless. He whipped his dudgeon higher and crashed down upon the authoress with a third note, rankling with menace:

New York, 2 Leroy Place,
May 25, 1852.

MRS. H. B. STOWE.

Madam:—I have addressed to you two communications respecting your holding me up to public odium. In each I have demanded an open and full retraction. You have not proposed any reparation of the wrong, nor even deigned a reply. My letters were under date of the 8th and 19th instants. Sufficient time has elapsed. The calumny is still spreading. I am not bound in justice to wait longer.

Yet it is my desire to exercise a spirit of Christian forbearance. I sincerely deprecate the necessity of placing you in an embarrassing position. I beg of you, do not compel me to do so. I have no resentments to gratify. I do not wish, because you have injured me, to injure you. On the contrary, it will afford me great pleasure to be spared the necessity of a public conflict with a lady, a professed Christian, and the wife of a clergyman.

Though you can never repair the wrong you have done, you can make such amends as will, if made now, satisfy me. Should you find yourself in difficulty hereafter, therefore, be pleased to remember that it is not of my seeking. I greatly prefer that you should not compel me to appear before the public in a conflict with you respecting a matter which you can so easily bring to an amicable adjustment, and that too without doing anything which one who has inflicted a wrong ought not to regard as a pleasure to perform.

Respectfully,
JOEL PARKER.

This letter went over to Brooklyn by messenger. Harriet answered it immediately; and her reply, also sent by hand to Leroy Place, gave the Rev. Dr. Parker his first inkling of her attitude toward his claim. The threat of adverse publicity might well have daunted Harriet in a day when a lady regarded any kind of publicity for herself with distaste. Only a few unpleasant females like Mrs. Stanton and Mrs. Weld deliberately courted notoriety. But Harriet's courage remained high. She had made her choice.

After apologizing for the delay in the transmission of her former letter (and, incidentally, both Dr. Parker and Mr. Prime chose to disbelieve her statement that she wrote and sent that communication when she said) Harriet came at once to the point: "In regard to the threats implied in your letter, give me leave to say that though for many reasons I should regret a public encounter on this subject, yet my conviction, derived from facts, documents, and the testimony of *living* witnesses, is that such an issue would be far more unfortunate for you than for me." She repeated her injunction to Dr. Parker to make his own peace with an outraged Christian public and ended her letter: "Any further communications must be addressed to my brother, H. W. Beecher, who is in full possession of the subject."

In his "intervening remarks" Irenaeus Prime called this letter "the coolest epistle we ever read." Cool it may have been, but it threw the Parker camp into confusion. Dr. Parker at once bore Harriet's unexpected defiance to his attorney, Benjamin F. Butler, who took the case under advisement over night. That eminent lawyer, who had been Andrew Jackson's Attorney General, may not have approved of the political sweep of *Uncle Tom's Cabin,* but he was better aware than his client of the weight of the personal popularity which Dr. Parker proposed to challenge. The best advice he could offer next day, which was Saturday, May 26, 1852, was for Dr. Parker to avoid a libel suit if possible but try still to secure from Harriet a public retraction. To that end Mr. Butler suggested that a mediary be sent to Mrs. Stowe to coax the lady into a more reasonable attitude.

Thus it was the lines of the adversary that gave way first. The diplomat selected for the delicate mission of interviewing Mrs. Stowe was Hiram Barney, an able lawyer of the courteous, persuasive type who had formerly been Ben Butler's law partner. But Barney was also a member of the Plymouth Church congregation and an admirer and warm friend of Henry Ward Beecher. He was an ideal choice.

It was Saturday evening after tea when Mr. Barney called at 126 Columbia Street in Brooklyn. Harriet would not receive him. Was not Henry "in full possession of the subject"? Harriet retreated behind her usual screen of "feeble health"—poor fragile thing, just then conducting her campaign for the Edmondsons, attending crowded meetings and concerts, and about to turn into a dynamo of energy on an Andover house-remodelling job. Henry received Barney alone, explaining that "Mrs. S. would lose a night's sleep, if the subject were then introduced to her." Mr. Barney therefore stated his case to Henry, to be relayed to Harriet in the morning.

He explained to Henry that he had that day examined the original documents and could state at first hand that Mrs. Stowe had not only not quoted the exact language of Dr. Parker but had been still more unfortunate in representing the sentiment of what he did utter on the supposed occasion. Henry, of course, could not doubt Brother Barney's veracity or even his interpretation of Parker's language, still—and he was speaking for his sister—he preferred to wait until he had examined the original statement. He had sent to Philadelphia for the papers, which were expected at any moment.

Furthermore, Henry went on, his sister was of the opinion that "this talk about a suit was a mere matter of intimidation." "I do not believe," Henry said for himself, "that he would dare bring a suit; and if he should bring one, he could not recover more than sixpence damages, if he could maintain it at all." Besides, said Henry suspiciously, how did he and Harriet know but what Dr. Parker had used the very language quoted on some occasion other than in the debate? The sentence had been widely published, and such an unusual and ambiguous arrangement of words could hardly have sprung into existence without authorship. They sounded like Parker's.

But after Barney had left that evening, a messenger brought from the postoffice the bundle of *Christian Observers,* and Henry knew the worst. Harriet, he realized, or thought he realized, was on untenable ground. Dr. Parker's exact words had been:

> What then are the evils inseparable from slavery? There is not one that is not equally inseparable from depraved human nature in other lawful relations.

At first glance these words seemed to be not much different from the ones Harriet had quoted. Both utterances contained a quick silver quality that eluded the finger trying to pin them down to a definite meaning; but if there was any meaning in them, it was substantially the same in both. But when read in their context, Dr. Parker's authentic sentences magically reversed themselves.

Mr. Rood had been arguing that the flagrant evils of slavery—the disruption of families, the holding of human beings for mere purposes of gain, the forbidding of education, and the physical sufferings of the slaves— were inherent in the system and could not be separated from it. Dr. Parker replied not so. "There is not one [evil] that is not equally inseparable from depraved human nature in other lawful relations." In different words, there was no evil that could *not* be separated from slavery, except the evils that attend every lawful relation. That was the new meaning which Henry saw in the words. Or thought he did.

Next morning he explained it to Harriet, and she thought she saw, too. At any rate, she trusted Henry's judgment and that same morning— Sunday, too!—she wrote to Dr. Parker what was for her a contrite and conciliatory note, conceding that his words were open to an opposite construction from that which she had given them and expressed her willingness to make amends, adding, however, what was for an innocent person a curious proviso:

> I would like to see *you* without lawyers or witnesses, and I think you will find that whatever my sense of duty may have led me to say, my *feelings* have always been kind, and that I am fully disposed to do all I can in consistency with truth and sincerity.

Dr. Parker snorted at this wary invitation and dashed off an answer refusing it. "The whole matter on my part has been confided to able counsel, and any proposition or overtures which you may have to make, you will please make to him." To keep Harriet on tenterhooks (she had written that she would be disengaged only until 10 o'clock Monday morning), Dr. Parker dropped this letter into the post. That afternoon he regretted it, "thinking it more kind to grant her request for a personal interview," as he wrote Calvin a few days later. More likely he had heard some plain advice from Attorney Ben Butler. He tried to withdraw his offensive letter from the mail, but it was Sunday and he was blocked there. Next morning he called at 126 Columbia Street and met Harriet on her own terms—without witnesses.

Another interview followed. They could not agree. Dr. Parker wanted "a simple retraction of the wrong." Harriet "insisted on connecting with it a representation of what she deemed my actual position in relation to slavery." Harriet pleaded a headache, the need of retiring from this hurly-burly to think it over. She would send the Doctor a form of retraction from New Haven for his approval.

Meanwhile Calvin Stowe was doing his best to call off the vengeful Parker. Even while Harriet that Sunday morning was citing to Dr. Parker Scriptural sanction for unwitnessed interviews between adversaries—"If thy brother trespass against thee, go and tell him his fault between thee and him alone"—Calvin was in Father Beecher's house in Hayward Place, Boston, writing to placate the Bleecker Street pastor. The day before, Calvin had stopped into Jewett's publishing office.

> I have acted on my own responsibility, and in accordance with my request the publishers have now obliterated your name from the stereotype plate.

Just the presence of Lyman Beecher, however, stiffened Calvin's morale.

> Dr. Lyman Beecher tells me that gentlemen in Philadelphia are ready to make oath that you did utter the words and the sentiments ascribed to you in the obnoxious paragraph; but neither he nor I desire to make any use of their testimony, unless it should be absolutely necessary.

The old Doctor still enjoyed a good fight, but he was wily as ever, addressing soft words to his dear New York brother while industriously gathering evidence to prove him a liar. He wrote to Dr. Parker:

Your rights and character are as dear to us as our own, and our friendships are of too long standing and too pleasant to be wrecked by misunderstandings that can easily be rectified. Wait a little, and you will hear from us satisfactorily, I have no doubt, and then we will love one another so much better as to compensate for our trials and our pains.

In New Haven Harriet's confusion grew worse confounded. She was no longer so firmly convinced that she ought to make any retraction at all. What did Dr. Parker's words mean, really? Henry had seemed to make them clear to her; but she showed them to Dr. Leonard Bacon, who was a scholarly man, and he could see no difference in meaning between what Dr. Parker had said and what Harriet had quoted him as saying. Dr. Dutton thought the same.

"Not one that is not equally inseparable"—the double-double negative danced through her brain. It grew maddening. The crafty sentence purged slavery of its evils and it justified slavery with all its horrors. The unstable words were like those optical blocks that one moment stood in a neat pyramid and suddenly, under one's gaze, turned inside out and formed a tophcavy heap. Nevertheless, having given her word, Harriet managed to compose a card of retraction that suited her.

It was a very feminine card and characteristic of a lady who had taught school before she turned authoress. Harriet barely conceded herself any fault at all. "The language of the quotation in the book is not the precise language of Dr. Parker." No. She wrote the two quotations in parallel columns to show the difference and remembered Henry's explanation lucidly enough to show readers by the context what Dr. Parker had really meant—"although the author does not agree with this statement of Dr. Parker's in itself." She found it, however, "far more favorable to his character as a man and a Christian than the other." But mainly the "retraction" laid the blame on Dr. Parker's shoulders for what had occurred. Harriet sent the draught to Henry in Brooklyn with a covering letter.

I told him I would not publish anything without his seeing it, and therefore I send you the card inclosed to show to him. If he likes it, publish; if he wants the phraseology altered in any wise, you have *carte blanche* to act in the matter. Of course, you will have equal respect to my honor and his.

Now I am under this misfortune: I cannot say that *I* am satisfied he never used the words in my book, for the simple reason that I *am* not. I should not be the least surprised if it should appear that in the course of some of the multifarious things he has said and written, this very form of expression should turn up. It does seem to me that *in its present form* it must have had an origin.

Now, he evidently shrinks from my publishing in this form: that "Mr. Parker authorizes me to deny," &c.—and wants me to substitute the form, "I am satisfied that he has never," &c. That is, *I* take the responsibility. I inclose my ultimatum. *I* am well pleased with it. It is all I will do, and if he won't have this, *I* will publish it, and he may do "wot he likes."

Henry Ward Beecher's monumental reply to the *Observer's* charges in October appeared first in the New York *Evening Post* and next day in the *Independent*. By some mischance Harriet's final clause in this letter slipped into the *Independent's* version, though Henry had been at pains to strike it from the *Evening Post's* copy. Beaten down by the evidence, Irenaeus Prime could only pick flaws in the argument. He pounced upon Harriet's "wot he likes."

In passing, we remark that the slang phrase, *he may do "wot he likes,"* is omitted in the copy published in the Evening Post. The suppression of the vulgarism was creditable to the taste of the one who struck it out.

The self-centred Henry was again occupied with his own affairs when he received his sister's letter. With Harriet in New Haven, her controversy with Brother Parker retreated to a back apartment of his mind. He was getting ready to go on a lecture tour into Indiana; his "flock of three thousand souls" demanded his final attentions. He put Harriet's "card" into his pocket and forgot it.

Dr. Parker grew impatient with Harriet's long silence and wrote to his friend Calvin Stowe a letter that was something less than admirable for a former president of Union Theological Seminary. It was a whining, tattle-tale letter, penned under the feudal impression that Calvin remained the lord and master of his brilliant wife. There were no omissions of the word *obey* in Dr. Parker's wedding services. And no doubt the Doctor knew Calvin's pliant nature and his preference for the paths of peace. Dr. Parker wrote a full account of Harriet's contumacious behaviour to the man who could be expected to correct it and found space to retort to Calvin's threat from Boston:

You are mistaken about the testimony which you fancy may be found to substantiate Mrs. Stowe's allegation. Any attempt to prove it will only aggravate the libel.

The letter threw Calvin, alone in Brunswick now, into a panic. He replied to Dr. Parker instantly:

Bowdoin College, June 7, 1852.

REV. JOEL PARKER, D.D.

Dear Sir:—Yours of the 5th instant I have just taken from the office. I am disappointed by it, for I supposed from Mrs. Stowe's last note to me the business was adjusted. I am sure she thought so. I shall immediately consult her father, and I hope very soon to see her. I will write you again in a few days the result of these consultations, and if need be will come on and see you. I know she is a Christian woman and desires only to do right—and I trust you are a Christian man and have only the same desire. It would be an everlasting disgrace to all parties concerned, and to the church of Christ a grievous scandal, to have any public quarrel on this subject. *It can and it must be settled privately.* Dr. Beecher and myself are good friends to you, and of course we both love Mrs. Stowe as our own hearts' blood. Be patient then till you hear from me again.

Truly, yours,

C. E. STOWE.

At length Henry Ward Beecher remembered Harriet's card in his pocket. He was then on the point of departing for the West and, to despatch the business quickly, took the document in person to Dr. Parker. Dr. Parker wrote that the interview was "friendly." It was during this hour that Henry threw away Harriet's card and substituted the supposed correspondence that appeared later as the public retraction. Henry described the scene in a letter to Harriet that gives us an insight into the irreverent attitude of this fun-loving brother and sister as they worried an eminent D.D. Henry had considered Harriet's card too involved, but, he wrote,

nevertheless, I took it to Joel. He made wry faces. We tinkered a little, as you will see, and in this shape he agreed to let it go. But I felt bad about it. I said to him, "Mr. Parker, I don't like the whole thing. If you will give me pen and ink and leave me alone, I will write one to my mind." So I wrote the enclosed: i.e., two letters as from him and one as from you. I am satisfied that these will make a good impression.

And if Harriet approved the substitution, she was to send a copy in her own handwriting to William Harned, Anti-Slavery Society Rooms, 48 Beekman Street, New York, who would insert it in the *Tribune, Era,* and *Independent.*

Years later there was read in a New York court a paper signed by Henry
Ward Beecher in which by implication the famous Brooklyn pastor confessed to having had adulterous relations with the wife of his former friend
and protege, Theodore Tilton. On the witness stand Mr. Beecher repudiated
this "confession," saying he had signed it without reading it, having supposed it to be something entirely different. A majority of the jury believed
him; but Beecher's enemies, whose name was legion, laughed at his
explanation. They could scarcely conceive of the man who in a few years
had run a backwoods Indiana parish into one of the highest-salaried positions in America being so childish as to sign, at a great crisis in his life,
any document without reading it.

But Henry's negotiations with Joel Parker in 1852 certainly show that
he was capable of doing just such a thing. There was a largeness in Henry's
nature that made him impatient with the petty hesitations of more suspicious minds. In Dr. Parker he was treating with a leading Northern
apologist for slavery, a man with many friends in the South (he had held
an important pastorate in New Orleans), who did not want Harriet's
money, but who did want the strongest confession of error he could get to
harm the influence of *Uncle Tom's Cabin*. Had the issue been graver,
Henry's carelessness in dealing with this man would have been criminal.

Dr. Parker testified later, and probably with truth, that he never dreamed
that the "letters" which Henry dashed off in twenty minutes—"I was a
little anxious to know how it would strike his mind to see himself in
letters which had sprung from my mind"—were anything more than a
rough draught of a retraction with which he and his attorney could
"tinker" until they had it to their liking. Muttering that the letters "might
lead to the settlement of the difficulty," the clergyman stipulated that
Henry must show them to his counsel, Mr. Butler.

In the grand assumption that he had Dr. Parker's consent, if Butler
concurred, Henry went to see the old lawyer that same evening. Butler
read the "correspondence," shrugged his shoulders, and said that if Parker
was satisfied, he had no particular objection to offer. Later, however,
Butler testified that he supposed of course he would have opportunity to
discuss the retraction in private with his client. Henry plunged to the
conclusion that it was all settled, so far as the New York end was concerned, sent the letters and her rejected card back to Harriet, and left next
morning for Indiana. In New Haven Harriet made wry faces over the new

retraction. She liked her own composition much better. Still, since she had entrusted the "subject" to Henry, she yielded.

During the final week of June, when Harriet was, with Sister Belle's help, catching up with her correspondence in Brunswick, a bolt fell from the blue upon the Federal Street household. It took the form of a letter to Calvin from Dr. Parker—a letter beginning with these words: "Are you aware of the fact that the letters published in the Tribune and Independent as purporting to have been written by myself, were *not written nor signed nor sanctioned* by me?" The Rev. H. W. Beecher had written them and then walked away with them, presumably to leave them with Mr. Butler, and the next thing Dr. Parker knew, "to my astonishment I learned that these letters had been published without modification, *without my knowledge or consent.*" Dr. Parker could not yet believe that Mrs. Stowe would intentionally authorize their publication—some third person must have made the mistake. As yet the Doctor was refraining from any public repudiation of the correspondence, preferring "that Mrs. Stowe should have the privilege of explaining the mistake."

But Dr. Parker was still labouring under the delusion that Professor Stowe exerted the will of his domestic establishment, or else he was simply showing wisdom. At any rate, he wanted no more traffic with the difficult authoress.

It has seemed to me all along, that it would have been better for *you* to have come and seen me about this business. I cannot consent to stand before the public as one soliciting it as a favor from Mrs. Stowe to set me right before the public. I wish her to set herself right in respect to what she has done in relation to me. I am not impatient. I allow time. But it is not a matter for compromise, as if there were wrong on both sides. I do not wish to afflict Mrs. Stowe and would not knowingly consent to her doing anything on my account that would not be, under the circumstances, the very best thing for her character and her reputation as a Christian woman. Had you not better come on and see me? I have had my full share of trouble about the business, and in my earnestness to settle the matter amicably, I have borne much more than my friends think I ought to have done. I have no doubt that you and I could settle the whole affair by a conference of an hour or two, and I quite agree with you that it would be a great shame that we should have any sort of public conflict in relation to it.

To bolster this plea, Dr. Parker appealed simultaneously to Lyman Beecher in Boston. "You could not, of course, have known that they [the published letters] were drawn up by your son, H. W. Beecher, and that they were without my signature, as a mere form of negociation, to be revised. . . . How they came to be published I do not know. I hope and trust that it was not intentional." And Dr. Parker had no doubt "that a full conference either with yourself or Professor Stowe would set everything right."

Harriet at once took charge of the letter to her husband. She struck off a copy and sent it to Henry Ward Beecher, who found it in Brooklyn upon his return from Indiana, and who, when reading it, could not tell "whether amazement or indignation was the strongest." In ordinary courtesy Calvin replied to Dr. Parker's letter, but, although four weeks earlier he had been suggesting a personal interview with the Bleecker Street sophist, he now discovered his health to be too feeble for such an undertaking. "I am suffering from Neuralgia, and a journey to New York would be inconvenient and painful to me."

Calvin suggested arbitration of the dispute. "You take Mr. B. F. Butler for your friend, I take Mr. T. C. Perkins, of Hartford, for mine; they two agree on a third." Calvin was no longer available. "My health is so frail this summer that I must avoid all excitement so far as possible." And Calvin saved his face with a postscript: "Mrs. Stowe, at my request, has written her account of the matter, which I inclose."

Irenaeus Prime later jeered at the innocent Professor Stowe. "We are certain that any reader of Prof. Stowe's letters will be satisfied that Mrs. Stowe is accustomed to take care of herself." Harriet's first words to Dr. Parker left no doubt about the location of headquarters in the *Uncle Tom* camp. "As your letter addressed to my husband is one that I can answer better than he, I shall now reply to it by stating to you, briefly, all I know of the matter under consideration."

In her statement she was provoking as ever, easily slipping from the trap Dr. Parker thought he had set for her. "You will perceive at once that the case lies between you and my brother Henry, who, judging from the tone of his letter to me, considered himself to be acting with all kindness, fairness, and good faith, *as he always does act.*"

Harriet's letter, shifting her quarrel to Henry's shoulders, stopped Dr. Parker. He did not write to her again nor she to him. Henry did nothing about the published retraction, and Dr. Parker did not repudiate it. His libel suit died of inanition. At best, having allowed the misquotation to pass unchallenged for so long, he had only technical grounds for a com-

THE BRUNSWICK HOUSE WHERE "UNCLE TOM'S CABIN" WAS WRITTEN

"One of those spacious frame mansions' of bland and hospitable mien which the New England joiners knew so well how to build." (Page 242.)

plaint; and he wanted no further contention with a nimble-witted woman who always managed to weave ahead of him a maze of irrelevant issues and counter-charges. The Doctor loved to tell tales, and he took his revenge by permitting the *Observer* to publish the whole story, with the worst interpretation Editor Prime could put upon it.

Henry rose magnificently to the defense after the *Observer* published its sensational charges of forgery and venality, occupying twelve of the *Independent's* Theban columns with his reply.

> For myself I profess that no event of my life, not the loss of my own children, nor bereavement of friends most dear, nor sickness, nor all of them, have ever filled me with so deep a sorrow as that which I have in being made a party to a public dispute, where three of the persons concerned are ministers of the Gospel, and where the fourth is a woman and the wife of a clergyman. At the very best it is a shame and disgrace. To avert it I labored most earnestly and with all my might. And now, nothing but the alternative of personal disgrace, and the yet greater shame to the cause of Christ, should I be proved as bad a man as the *Observer* has depicted me, induces me to enter this arena. Yet there is a reason even stronger than all these:—God has put into my hands the defense of the honor of a sister, next born to me, and dearer than I am to my own self, and whom the *Observer* has treated so contemptuously as no man could treat a woman—unless his passions had, for a moment, led him to forget God's greatest gift, besides Himself, to man —a mother; and the next, the true and right noble hearts of wife and sister!

In his conclusion Henry called the *Observer* and Dr. Parker every liar he could and keep within the bounds of ministerial language.

> When the *New York Observer* represents Dr. Parker as offering evidence to Mrs. Stowe, in the first instance, to satisfy her that she was in error, it is shown that it stated an untruth; when it declares that Mrs. S. "took no notice of his letter," it is proven to have stated an untruth; &c.

He went on point by point, ending with a glorious burst:

> It was my prayer to God when I began this narrative that my brain might not reel nor be left to error; and it was my promise, if He would give me grace and wisdom to strike a true blow for a sister that should set her free from the accursed enchantment in which her reputation stood spellbound before the public, that I would hardly ask a thing for myself. But God has

given me all and more, and the work is done, and eternity will not untwine the cords with which this monstrous iniquity is bound for the sacrifice!

I commit this narrative to the sober judgment of all good men; and myself I commit to the charge of Almighty God!

When selecting the material for her official biography, Harriet suppressed the story of her encounter with Dr. Parker. In the calm evening of her life, old rancours forgotten, perhaps she felt a little ashamed of the harsh manner in which she had treated a clergyman and, according to his lights, a servant of God.

But she withheld from him another reparation. The comedy, as our modern taste relishes, ended on a note of comic surprise. Despite her assurances, and Henry's and Calvin's, Harriet never deleted the offending footnote from *Uncle Tom's Cabin*. The research behind this study has not attempted the formidable task of running down Jewett's many printings of the novel to ascertain if that publisher carried out Calvin's instructions to excise Dr. Parker's name, but the footnote was appearing in copies as late as the tenth edition.

It still appears in *Uncle Tom's Cabin,* for the novel has never been "out of print." Subsequent publishers, and particularly after the expiration of the copyright, have gone for their text back to Jewett's original edition and have used it, footnote and all. Joel Parker continues his ride down the ages, exhibited as a pious monster condoning the abduction of a poor slave-woman and the theft of her baby, the last solace of her humble life. Truly for him Harriet builded a monument more enduring than bronze—a monument of infamy.

And she was not yet through with Irenaeus Prime.

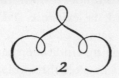

First Woman of America

WHEN he read the *Observer's* scandalous attack upon his wife and found his worst fears of the preceding spring justified, Calvin Stowe was like a young father at the birth of his first child. He did most of the suffering. He wrote at once to Harriet in Brunswick a piteous letter, and she paused in her work long enough to comfort him.

> For myself I have not an anxiety, but am only *vulnerable* through you. That you should be exposed to this annoyance on my account is the real and only trouble I have had. For me, what harm can Mr. Prime or anyone else do to me?

Indeed, though she was living through the then unique experience of being a woman under public attack, an experience supposed to crush a lady of the 1850's with its utter shame, Harriet could even find humour in it. She wrote to Mrs. Howard:

> I am reminded of one of Aunt Esther's stories: A man, when very drunk, had the habit of using very abusive language to his wife, to which she paid no attention, but went about her affairs as usual. At last he fell to praying about her, saying all manner of horrid things against her in his prayers. Still she gave no heed.
> "Why, do you hear," said a neighbor, "how that man goes on?"
> "Oh, poh!" said his wife, "he'll get over it by and by."
> "But do just hear him praying!"
> "Let him pray. Nobody minds his prayers."
> So it has struck me that both the secular and the pious abuse of the *Observer* are equally unworthy of attention. All we have to do is to *live on*.

Harriet went back to Andover and lived on, as the Stowe-Parker controversy racketed through the press. The *Independent,* which on its editorial page maintained an aloof attitude toward the acts and opinions of its "stated contributors," studied the evidence and "after mature deliberation" decided the case entirely in favour of Harriet. This verdict bore a taint of prejudice; but Harriet's complete vindication came in the New York *Times* in which a legal correspondent took three columns to review the evidence and give the opinion that Dr. Parker should have approved and accepted Harriet's original retraction but was talked into "a false position" by scheming friends who used him in an attempt to undermine Henry Ward Beecher's reputation and the authority of *Uncle Tom's Cabin.*

There had never been any doubt of the popular verdict.

In the midst of the uproar Harriet wrote a poem that reflected her state of mind. She called it *Hymn,* and its first lines ran:

> When winds are raging o'er the upper ocean,
> And billows wild contend with angry roar,
> 'Tis said, far down beneath the wild commotion,
> That peaceful stillness reigneth, evermore.

It remains one of her more famous poetical efforts. Perhaps the tumult was hurting her ears. But the news came of the death of the great Duke in England, and simultaneously Daniel Webster lay in his last sleep at Marshfield, and the passing of these two great men drew public attention from the nine-day sensation. It never came up again in the national memory.

Uncle Tom steadily gathered momentum. By autumn it was a firm classic, its author apotheosized upon Olympus. A reader of the *National Era* besought Editor Bailey to defend the novel against "the tide of vituperation." He replied in print: "We should as soon think of coming out in defense of Shakespeare." No one jeered, for a dozen European countries were now translating the novel; and Paris was falling upon the daily issues of *La Presse,* which was running a pirated serial version of *La Cabine de l'Oncle Tom.* American literature had produced a universal masterpiece.

By the end of September Americans were playing, singing, and shedding tears over eight Uncle Tom songs. Besides Whittier's *Little Eva,* they were H. Swift's *Uncle Tom,* J. S. Adams's *I Am Going There,* F. Howard's *Uncle Tom's Glimpse of Glory,* Woodbury's *Uncle Tom's Lament,* and an industrious Miss Collier's *Death of St. Clare, Eva's Parting,* and *Eliza's Flight.* Sales of the book had passed 150,000. A Providence, Rhode Island, manufacturer of home-amusement devices was advertising a card game called "Uncle Tom and Little Eva," the play consisting of "the continual separation and reunion of families." A dramatization of *Uncle Tom's Cabin* had begun in August to be played in the Museum Theatre in Boston and another at the National Theatre in New York—separate versions in neither of which did Harriet have any financial interest, as she did not in any of the myriad dramatizations which followed. An author's copyright did not protect dramatic rights until 1870. From the autumn of 1852 until 1931, at least, *Uncle Tom's Cabin* was never "off the boards" in America.

"Anti-Tom," the counter-propaganda, swelled in volume, with such titles in the book-stores as *Uncle Tom's Cabin As It Is; or, Incidents in The Real Life Among The Lowly; Life in The South, a Companion to Uncle Tom's Cabin; How Do You Like Uncle Tom?, Uncle Tom in England; or, Proof That Black's White, Recollections of A Southern Matron.* Philadelphia was a publishing centre for the Anti-Tom books. Peterson, of Philadelphia, brought out *Life in The South.* Harriet's old Cincinnati acquaintance of the Semi-Colon Club, Caroline Lee Hentz, now conducting a girls' school in the deep South, was writing a "reply" novel for Hart, of Philadelphia. In Philadelphia Sarah J. Hale, editor of *Godey's Lady's Book,* was bringing out two works which, if not replies to *Uncle Tom's Cabin,* were intended to be antidotes for its political venom. Of her *Life, North and South* the *Independent* said that it was "designed to weaken the force of Uncle Tom's pictures without offending 'northern prejudices,'" and Mrs. Hale was at work on a similar book—*Cabin and Parlor; or, Slaves and Masters Northward.*

Another Philadelphia concern, Lippincott, Grambo & Co., lineal ancestors of the publishers of the present biography, brought out that fall the chief and best of all the replies to *Uncle Tom's Cabin—Aunt Phillis's Cabin; or, Southern Life As It Is,* by Mary H. Eastman. Harriet's own *Independent* called this story "insipid" and in its review resorted to sarcasm: "The pictures of the intense happiness of the slaves are so very charming one wonders why the inventors do not make haste to sell their children to the slave-traders."

From abroad the news of *Uncle Tom's* triumph was even more exciting. Suddenly—so suddenly that the exact date of August 20 could be named for the phenomenon—the novel turned from a moderate success into a national sensation, with sales "perfectly overwhelming." One piratical publisher, putting it out in penny parts, was disposing of *Uncle Tom's Cabin* at the rate of 30,000 a week. A shilling "railway edition" had sold 95,000 by the middle of September.

There was something about this book that precluded temperate statement. It created blind enthusiasts and only less blind enemies. By the autumn of 1852 the faintest criticism of *Uncle Tom's Cabin* was regarded by the book's followers as might be an attack on the Bible itself. In September the London *Times* dared to disapprove in a review filling three and one-half of its columns—"of itself," commented Agricola, London correspondent of the *Independent,* "unwonted homage to genius." Agricola dismissed the Thunderer's appraisal with the sentence: "The *Times* calls it 'absolute and audacious trash'." The scholarly "T" wrote that the *Times* had tried "to write it down, artistically and morally."

But the *Times'* review was perhaps the sanest analysis of *Uncle Tom's Cabin* made on either side of the ocean. The review that was said to "write down" the novel, "artistically and morally," had this to say of "Mrs. Stowe's striking production":

> . . . for striking and meritorious it undoubtedly is. The lady has great skill in the delineation of character; her hand is vigorous and firm, her mastery over human feeling is unquestionable, and her humorous effects are unimpeachable. We know of no book in which the Negro character finds such successful interpretation and appears so lifelike and so fresh.

Regarding the novel as a work of art, the *Times* found fault only with its construction. The narrative was only "a succession of detached scenes," and "the reader is interested in the fate of two heroes, but their streams of adventure never blend."

What the Catholic control of the *Times* found to be "absolute and audacious trash" were the miraculous conversions of those who came in contact with the saintly Uncle Tom—St. Clare, Cassy, and the brutal Sambo and Quimbo. If trash means improbability, modern opinion can scarcely disagree with this judgment. For Harriet's powers as a propagandist the *Times* had only a wry admiration, conceding that "unscrupulous fighting is the rightful warfare of the crusader."

But in its aloof tower in London, the *Times* could see the dreadful implications of Harriet's propaganda more clearly than contemporaries nearer the scene. Through the storm of passions which *Uncle Tom's Cabin* had aroused, the reviewer caught a glimpse of cannon-clouds and embattled lines in uniform.

Let us have no more *Uncle Tom's Cabins,* engendering ill-will, keeping up bad blood, and rendering well-disposed, humane, but critically placed men their own enemies and the stumbling-blocks to civilization and to the spread of glad tidings from Heaven.

But the *Times'* thunder was, for once, only a whisper in the general hub-bub raised in England by Harriet's novel. Two Royal Academicians were at work upon pictures to be exhibited at the next "Academy" (where Harriet would see and pass upon them). G. P. Manley was painting "Uncle Tom and Cassy." J. S. Alpenny, R.A., was putting his best talent into a drawing of "Eva's Farewell." The story was inspiring British song-writers, too, and Londoners were buying such titles as *The Little Evangelist, Poor Uncle Tom, The Slave Wife, Eva, The Fugitive Slave, Emmeline,* and *A Tear for Uncle Tom.* Cassell was bringing out *The Uncle Tom's Cabin Almanac* for 1853. One of the piratical publishers had a twinge of conscience and sent Harriet his cheque for £500. A British Lazarus doing nicely on the crumbs dropped from our Lady Dives' generous English table was entitled *Uncle Tom's Companions; or, Stories of Fugitive Slaves.* Queues were long at the Adelphi Theatre, where a dramatic version "of considerable constructive merit" was playing to hysterical audiences. The *Spectator* was calling it "Tom-mania."

By November a score of British publishers were issuing rival editions of the novel. The London press rejoiced in the wholesale piracy, when for once John Bull evened scores with Uncle Sam. Usually the shoe had been on the other foot. The great George Cruikshank himself was drawing twenty-seven illustrations for a new edition which John Cassell would begin to publish at Christmas in thirteen weekly numbers at two-pence each, with a binding case at six-pence. Gilbert, Leech, Nicholson, Sears, and Thomas had already illustrated other London editions. The lucky publisher of the one-shilling "railway edition" could in November count a sale of 150,000 copies. *Uncle Tom* thus inaugurated in England "a new era in cheap literature," which, in fact, has never ended.

Fraser's Magazine printed *Some Account of Mrs. Beecher-Stowe and Her Family,* by "An Alabama Man," which, though fair and friendly in tone, was also shrewdly critical, and Harriet ranked it as an attempt "to pervert the public mind of England and do away with the impression left by *Uncle Tom's Cabin."* The authoress was becoming hypersensitive. Cassell, however, used the article as the Introduction to his Cruikshank edition. In the British Museum Curator Thomas Watts, recognizing the importance of the phenomenon to the history of printing, began what has become the greatest collection of Uncle-Tomiana extant.

Dickens reviewed *Uncle Tom's Cabin* in *Household Words,* calling it "noble but defective." The Congregational Union of England and Wales adopted a resolution extending its "congratulations to Mrs. Harriet Beecher Stowe on the unexampled degree to which public attention on both sides of the Atlantic has been concentrated on this subject by her recent publication designed to portray the evils of slavery, and cordially thank her for the distinguished service she has thus rendered to the cause of humanity and Christian truth." In London a great mass-meeting of labourers at Hawkstone Hall took up a collection and sent Harriet "a magnificent Bible."

But the army of her novel's disciples took in those of high degree as well as the lowly. Old Lord Palmerston, who had not read a novel for thirty years, read *Uncle Tom's Cabin* through from cover to cover *three times*— "not only for the story but for the statesmanship of it." Lord Cockburn, on the Queen's Privy Council, declared that *Uncle Tom* had "done more for humanity than was ever before accomplished by any single book of fiction." Lord Denman, the former Lord Chief Justice, published an elaborate analysis of *Uncle Tom's Cabin,* answering the *Times'* strictures and even reproving Charles Dickens for suggesting that the Stowe kettle was black. Uncle Tom's disciples conceded him *no* faults.

It was not enough for the British nation to adore an American saint *in absentia.* The British public must see her in the holy flesh, must touch the hem of her garment. Accordingly on the 10th December, 1852, the "venerable and eminent pastor of Glasgow, Scotland," Dr. Ralph Wardlaw, was writing to Harriet from Easter House, extending in the name of the Committee of the New Ladies' Anti-Slavery Society in Glasgow and that of the Committee of the Glasgow New Association for the Abolition of Slavery an invitation to "Mrs. and Professor Stowe" to visit the British Isles at the expense of the said Committees. Arrangements to the season of paying the desired visit, and whatever else it might be necessary to fix, in conformity to Harriet's and Dr. Stowe's convenience, could be subsequently made.

Tom-mania had leaped the Channel. From Paris "Franc Parleur" was writing to the *Independent:*

When in your far-off land you turn your eyes toward the East and think of our ever-changing France, what do you suppose is occupying chiefly now the light-hearted French people? Your answer is, of course, the coming Empire, or something of the sort. Mistake, gentlemen, mistake; that which fills the larger part of the newspapers, that which causes the greater emotion and is the topic of most of the public talk—would you ever guess?—it is "Uncle Tom's Cabin."

Six pirated translations were on sale in the *librairies*. *La Presse, Le Siècle,* and *Le Pays* were serializing *Uncle Tom's Cabin* simultaneously, each with its own version. Readers eagerly bought all three papers to discover if one might not have included parts omitted by the other two. Bewildered boulevard book-sellers found themselves the beneficiaries of a run on Bibles; but before the valets in their baize aprons and the *porteurs* in their stocking-caps would lay down their francs, they demanded to know if *"c'est bien la Bible véritable de l'Oncle Tom?"* "Franc Parleur," a Protestant minister of Paris, declared that the novel was making in France "a kind of epoch in the literary as well as in the moral history of the time."

George Sand dissipated a great deal of her bad notoriety in America by eulogizing *Uncle Tom's Cabin* for two columns in *La Presse,* loving the novel's very faults. It was not a review of the book, Chopin's mistress wrote, but an "homage" to it—"and never did a generous and pure work merit one more tender and spontaneous."

> I can not say she [Mrs. Stowe] has talent as one understands it in the world of letters, but she has genius, as humanity feels the need of genius,—the genius of goodness, not that of the man of letters, but of the saint. Yes—a saint!

Harriet thoroughly, and, at least once, vigorously disapproved of Madame Sand, but she preserved the eulogy conspicuously in her biographical remains.

The mania swept southward and northward and eastward—eastward even to Muscovy where Nicholas I, Tsar of all the Russias, was permitting the translation of *Uncle Tom's Cabin* into Russian, and where a few months later Tolstoy would be ranking Harriet's novel among the great achievements of the human mind. Before 1852 ended it achieved a translation into Finnish.

Il Mediterraneo was serializing *Uncle Tom* in Genoa and *Risorgimento* in Turin. In Brussels *l'Emancipation* was stealing its serial from *La Presse* of Paris, but *l'Echo de Bruxelles* was making its own translation. A Swedish edition brought to Harriet a letter of congratulation from the great Fredrika

Bremer. A Portuguese edition circulating in Rio de Janeiro was spading the ground for the emancipation of Brazil's slaves. The walls of Vienna blossomed with daily announcements of "some new and cheaper form of the work to suit the pockets of the less wealthy."

In Germany, too, it was the same story—Germany, where one reviewer could find in "the whole modern romance literature of Germany, England, and France . . . no novel to be called equal to this."

And in Paris, chained to his "mattress grave," Heinrich Heine read the novel in German and, after a lifetime tortured with religious doubts, turned again to his Bible. "With all my sense I have come no farther than the poor ignorant Negro who has just learned to spell. Poor Tom indeed seems to have seen deeper things in the Holy Book than I."

As Uncle Tom conquered Europe, nation by nation, the engravers of each country produced portraits of Harriet for popular sale, copying from portraits that had gone before. But the French made her a Frenchwoman, the Italians a *signora,* the Dutch a Dutch *vrou,* and at each remove from the original the likeness grew more lamentable.

At Andover the cause of this upheaval of humanity's emotions was rising in October dawns to write a poem continuing her theme of Christ's peace in a tumultuous world. She was superintending painters and paper-hangers in the "Stone Cabin," as she had named the remodeled coffin-shop. (But Andover called it "Uncle Tom's Cabin.") She was commiserating with her husband, who was having trouble with the new-fangled railroad that ran from Boston up to Brunswick.

The plaguey railroad had been careless with the Professor's papers he had shipped down to his new home; and while Queen Victoria wept in unison with Albert over the death of Eva (had not the Prince Consort's secretary written a kind note to Harriet, acknowledging receipt of the lavender gift copy of *Uncle Tom's Cabin?*), Calvin was writing wrathily to his friend, Professor Cleaveland, of Bowdoin:

My dear sir, When my goods arrived here about the middle of Sept. last, displaced, injured, and destroyed to the amount of 30 or 40 dollars, that box for Prof. Newton was missing. I immediately wrote to the Superintendent in Portland, described the box minutely, & directed him to send it on. No notice whatever was taken of my letter. I wrote him a second time. No notice whatever was taken of my letter; and now the fellow writes to Brunswick to know about that box! The box has not come to me. I shall have nothing more to do with that Portland fellow but shall write to the President of the R.R. Co. to ascertain if I am to have any redress for the destruction of my goods.

Truly yours,
C. E. STOWE.

P.S. I have waited till Saturday hoping to hear from the box.

The last of the clan left in the West, the Rev. Charles Beecher, secured a charge in Newark that fall and came East. It was nice to have Brother Charles near once more. Harriet always felt a great tenderness for him, as her musician-brother was gentle and always a little helpless in the world.

At the end of November Andover was plunged into mourning by the unexpected death of Elizabeth Stuart Phelps, wife of Professor Austin Phelps, of the Seminary. As author of the immensely popular *Sunny-Side,* Mrs. Phelps had been the literary lionness of Andover, until Harriet's advent. Perhaps this fact made Mrs. Phelps's daughter, Elizabeth Stuart Phelps (Ward) a little critical of Harriet in her autobiography, *Chapters from A Life.*

In New York Jenny Lind's successor in Barnum's establishment was General Tom Thumb. Jewett was advertising that more than a million copies of *Uncle Tom's Cabin* had been sold, but he was counting the European piracies. The holiday gift-edition of *Uncle Tom* was to contain "one hundred superb engravings from designs by Billings" and "an elegant steel-plate portrait of Mrs. Stowe" which friends pronounced "an exact likeness." "We intend to make it one of the most splendid books ever published in America."

Jewett was getting out an edition in German for immigrants. Robert Everett, editor of *Cenhadwr,* was publishing it ("with the consent of Mrs. Stowe") in Welsh "for 100,000 Welsh emigrants in this country." (Even Dickens never attained a Welsh translation.) A pirated German translation appeared in Pennsylvania. Through Attorney T. C. Perkins, of Hartford, Calvin and Harriet sued for an injunction, but lost their case two years later in the United States Court of Appeals, which rendered the astonishing decision that a translation embodies so much original thought as to take legal rank as an original work, eligible for its own copyright.

In December the Stone Cabin was ready, and the Stowes moved in. Elizabeth Stuart Phelps (Ward) remembered the long parlour with its deep, brightly cushioned window-seats. Harriet kept flowers everywhere and

framed the deep windows in ivy growing from pots. She had a knack with
flowers. Another little girl who grew up remembered that the "goddess
from Olympus," as the awe-struck Andover children regarded the Seminary's new "eidolon," would when arranging her flowers step across the
room to study the effects. The gossips thought this just silly, but admitted
that Mrs. Stowe "could make any room a bower of beauty." She had "the
home-touch." Mrs. Ward's memory populated the house with children,
Harriet's and their friends; and clumsy Rover was but the forerunner of a
succession of dogs, big and little. It was "an open, hospitable home, human
and hearty and happy." Years later Phillips Academy converted the Stone
Cabin into a campus inn for the entertainment of visiting parents.

Here Harriet was at once moved to write her *Key to Uncle Tom's Cabin,*
a documented indictment of the abuses of slavery. She said she did this in
the apprehension that the attacks on her great novel were impairing its
influence. If she held any such fear, it was unwarranted. Uncle Tom needed
no battalions behind *him,* as the "Alabama man" had said the Beechers did.
It will not do to forget that Jewett needed another book by Mrs. Stowe to
rivet to herself as authoress the vast following raised by *Uncle Tom's Cabin,*
and the mass of evidence in support of the novel's allegations sent to Harriet
by readers anxious to help her refute the "vituperation," clamoured for easy
publication. And Harriet's new study in the Stone Cabin, an inviolable
retreat for her now, invited to fresh work. She must have been crowded in
the Samaritan boarding-house.

At any rate, she began her *Key* the week she occupied the Stone Cabin,
and on December 16 "D. Y. N.," the *Independent's* Andover correspondent
announced that the author of "the Book of the Age" was "completing 'A
Key to Uncle Tom's Cabin,'" which was to be "a triumphant reply to the
many denials and contradictions of Mrs. Stowe's statements which have
been thrown out less by Southerners than by 'compromise' men and papers
at the North. . . . An interesting feature of the new work is to be a narrative of the historical facts which suggested the plot and characters of 'Uncle
Tom's Cabin.'"

This impression—that the *Key* was made up of the materials Harriet had
before her when she wrote *Uncle Tom's Cabin*—has persisted and deceived
even so discerning a man as Dr. Erskine, who marvelled at "Mrs. Stowe's
skillful or fortunate restraint" in selecting the incidents for the novel. But
God had done the selecting for her in arranging her experiences with
slavery. She wrote her pictures out of her memory, and she wrote all of them.

It was not only the mail that brought supporting testimony to Harriet; individuals sought her out with evidence. A dramatic picture in *Uncle Tom's Cabin* is that of the escaping George Harris, masquerading as a gentleman, entering a crowded Kentucky tavern and coolly reading his own description, posted by his master—coolly reading it, though he is aware that one white man in the room has recognized him.

RAN AWAY

From the subscriber, my mulatto boy, George. Said George six feet in height, a very light mulatto, brown curly hair; is very intelligent, speaks handsomely, can read and write; will probably try to pass for a white man; is deeply scarred on his back and shoulders; has been branded in his right hand with a letter H.

I will give four hundred dollars for him alive, and the same sum for satisfactory proof that he has been killed.

Harriet invented the text of this bill, but she had seen similar ones in Cincinnati. The dead-or-alive offer, however, was widely attacked as a pure falsehood. In Jewett's office Harriet met a young Mr. Underwood who had done newspaper work in Kentucky and assured her he had seen such advertisements in the country exchanges.

One of those who denounced the George Harris reward as "an absurdity and an impossibility" was Governor Jones, of Tennessee. This he did in a letter to Senator Charles Sumner, of Massachusetts, who had been using *Uncle Tom's Cabin* as his oratorical textbook, and who therefore wrote to Jewett in Boston to enquire what proof Mrs. Stowe had of the essential veracity of her fictional advertisement. Calvin saw the letter in Jewett's office, and it made too good an opportunity to miss for Harriet to become acquainted with the champion of Abolition in Congress.

Calvin wrote to Senator Sumner, giving the substance of what Mr. Underwood had told Mrs. Stowe, ending his letter:

I see that yourself, Hale, and Chase have the honor of being excluded from all Committees. A distinguished honor it is, worth more to your fame than the most conspicuous niche in the Parthenon. Please present my hearty congratulations to my personal friends, Messrs. Hale and Chase; and assure Mr. H. that I feel more honored in having been his college cotemporary [sic] than in having been General Pierce's mess-mate. . . . Wait a little, trust in the good God (*Der lieber Gott,* as the Germans so beautifully say) & your helpers will increase day by day.

On the excuse that she needed to clarify her husband's statement, which she did by repeating Mr. Underwood's exact words, to the best of her memory, Harriet added to this letter, as a postscript, a flight of her own rhetoric for the statesman whose words were half-battles:

Can it be that no man of honor, no man thirsting for immortal fame, will yet rise *from the South* and win himself eternal glory by being the leader of a movement for *universal* freedom? Can such a man as Soulé—I know not if I have rightly conceived of him, but I think of him as an impersonation of nobility and chivalry—can he be willing to be the tool of tyranny and the leader of despotism, when Freedom is holding up an unfading crown to be worn by some deliverer? What a glory would be that Southern man's who should liberate his country and the world from this shame!

It was the beginning of a long friendship between Charles Sumner and Mrs. Stowe. The Mr. Underwood of the letters was probably Francis H. Underwood, who, a little later, was to found the *Atlantic Monthly* and secure Harriet as that magazine's first contributor.

"D. Y. N." had also apprized the readers of the *Independent* of the invitation to the Stowes from Glasgow, where they were assured of "a reception as enthusiastic as that of Jenny Lind." On December 14 Harriet had written to Dr. Wardlaw that "should God spare my life till April, I trust to mingle prayers and Christian affections with the Christians of Scotland." She signed it, "Yours, in the Gospel of Jesus." As the second person addressed, Calvin waited the decent interval of five days and then sent his acceptance. "We will, therefore, with pleasure accept the kind invitation extended to us and, if God permit, will be in Glasgow early enough to make a visit there and then attend the May anniversaries in London."

Senator Sumner replied immediately to Harriet's note, sending her the text of an alive-or-dead slave bill that had come into his hands. Harriet answered with a letter rationalizing her coming journey across the sea (which was thrilling her in prospect); and as she implicitly accepted a place in the leadership for Freedom, her voice took on a Delphian tone that sounds today a good deal like smugness.

I have a hope of doing good by going to Europe. I shall decidedly reject empty parade and useless flattery. I have a purpose there. I think I am not mistaken in thinking I can do some good. In the access of private connection I can make leading and judicious minds there understand points where they may essentially serve us. I can influence and shape the *tone* of articles and journals. I can enlist those to speak who *must* be heard. So I hope. *The public opinion of the world* is our last hope. The public sentiment of our country is corrupted—the salt has lost its savor. There must come from universal Christianity and humanity an appeal.

By the end of the year, with the clamour of praise, abuse, and contention over *Uncle Tom's Cabin* still in crescendo, Harriet had become an American minor deity. "She herself never doubted that she was a priestess," wrote one historian. Her own *Independent* threw up its hands.

Should we publish all that comes to us about *Uncle Tom's Cabin,* the tributary verses to its author, the proposals to have it published for Sunday School libraries by the American Sunday School Union, the critical judgments of the most competent literary men setting forth its merits—or should we publish all that comes to us in the form of approbation from different points in the wide field of our circulation or in the form of censure on the course of some of our contemporaries,—much more, should we publish all that comes to aid the discussion of questions connected with slavery—our ample sheet would have little room for anything else.

Harriet misjudged the time it would take her to compile her *Key*. At first she expected to do the work in three weeks. At the end of that time she was writing to Sumner, "The Key will be out in a month," adding, "It is a terrible Key—the Key to a land of 'darkness as darkness itself, when the light is as darkness'." Actually she spent a nerve-racking winter at the task. That sailing-date, which had seemed so comfortably far in the future when she set it in December, rose higher and higher as an inexorable deadline. She finished the *Key* on the eve of her departure for England—exhausted, pleading martyrdom:

Worn as I was with the subject, with every nerve sensitive and sore, I was obliged to spend three months in what were to me the most agonizing researches. The remembrance of that winter is to me one of horror. I could not sleep at night, and I had no comfort in the daytime. All that consoled me was that I was bearing the same kind of suffering which Christ bore, and still bears, in view of the agonies and distresses of sin in this world.

As a relief, she turned once or twice to her correspondence. Lord Chief Justice Denman had written her a flattering note. Replying on January 20, she had dropped the grand manner which had temporarily characterized her communications with the mighty in 1852. This was the real Harriet in the time of her greatest success—humble, earnest, and awe-struck by what she had done in the world:

> I am utterly incredulous of all that is said; it passes by me like a dream. I can only see that when a Higher Being has purposes to be accomplished, he can make even "a grain of mustard seed" the means.

Keeping her promise to Senator Sumner, she urged Lord Denman and other "great minds of England" to continue their pressure upon America for the liberation of the slaves.

> Anyone here can be hushed down, for all the capital, all the political power, and much of the ecclesiastical, is against the agitation of this subject. But you can force them to agitate. In your reviews, in your literature, you can notice and hold up before the world those awful facts which but for you they would scornfully go on denying, as they have done.

On February 9 Harriet addressed to Daniel Reeves Goodloe, a well-known Abolitionist of North Carolina, a statement of her personal attitude toward the South at the moment when the Southern attack on her was most bitter—a sort of *apologia pro vita sua* which, a post-bellum Southern historian predicted, "will cause them [the Southern people] to entertain more kindly feelings towards the author of the great anti-slavery novel." Harriet wrote:

> It has seemed to me that many who have attacked the system have not understood the Southern character, nor appreciated what is really good in it. I think *I* have; at least I have tried, during this whole investigation, to balance my mind by keeping before it the most agreeable patterns of Southern life and character. While at the South I am regarded with so much bitterness as their accuser at the bar of the world, I am sure I have every disposition in my heart to be their advocate, that is, in all things which are defensible. . . .
>
> I respect and admire the true, chivalric, noble ideal of the Southern man, and therefore more indignantly reprobate all that which is no part of him, being the result of an unnatural institution, and which is unworthy of him, and therein, I think, show myself more fully a friend than those who undertake to defend faults and all. . . .
>
> I cannot hope to be regarded as a friend and must comfort myself with the simple pleasure of feeling friendly.

It warmed Harriet's heart in February to receive a letter from the famous Mrs. Eliza Lee Cabot Follen, of Boston, who, since resigning as editor of *Child's Friend* in 1850, had been making an extended visit to London. As an adolescent schoolgirl Harriet had read Eliza Lee Cabot's *The Well-Spent Hour* and later on had read it to her own children, for by the 1840's that book was a juvenile classic. Harriet had often thought of writing to Mrs. Follen to thank her for the pleasure that lady's poems had brought into the Stowe household.

Mrs. Follen—James Russell Lowell's

> . . . Eliza Follen,
> Who scatters fruit-creating pollen
> Where'er a blossom she can find
> Hardy enough for Truth's north wind

—was one of a group of aristocratic and wealthy Boston women who had espoused Garrison's cause at a time when Harriet would scarcely have permitted herself to be identified with it. Her sensational marriage to the much younger Charles Follen, German political refugee who had become the first Professor of German Literature at Harvard, and Follen's tragic death in the burning of the S. S. *Lexington* on Long Island Sound in 1840 were still fresh in the public's memory.

Now in her sixties, Mrs. Follen had retired from active literary work to devote the rest of her life to Sunday Schools and Abolition after a "recruiting" season abroad. In Boston, a city which reverenced her, she was best-known as the sponsor of the Anti-Slavery Bazaars, held annually in Faneuil Hall during the holidays, to attract the Christmas shoppers. In London Mrs. Follen was curious about the new Joan of Arc of Abolition who had risen so meteorically in America during her absence; and, being an outspoken person, she wrote boldly to the Beecher prophetess, inquiring about her with pointed questions. Harriet answered with a famous and much-quoted letter.

> So you want to know something about what sort of a woman I am! Well, if this is any object, you shall have statistics free of charge. To begin, then, I am a little bit of a woman,—somewhat more than forty, about as thin and dry as a pinch of snuff; never very much to look at in my best days, and looking like a used-up article now.

This seems to be the whimsical severity of a lady who is, say, dissatisfied with her nose as she looks into her mirror. It is interesting to compare it with other descriptions of her looks at this period of her life made by persons more disinterested.

An American journalist who interviewed Harriet within two years of the date of the Follen letter, wrote of her:

> We think no one could mistake her for an ordinary woman. There is a look of conscious power in her face. There is strength of character expressed in it. She is not a beautiful woman, and yet her eyes are not often surpassed in beauty. They are dark and dreamy and look as if some sorrowful scene ever haunted her brain. In dress she is very plain and homely; in manners gentle, without a particle of false gentility.

Agnes Park, one of Professor Park's children, years later remembered Harriet as the "pinch of snuff" of her own description; "but," she added, "when she talked to me with such animation and vivacity, such sympathy and drollery, such kindness and desire to please, I thought her the most delightful lady I had even known."

Harriet went on to Mrs. Follen with another much-quoted sentence.

> I was married when I was twenty-five years old to a man rich in Greek and Hebrew, Latin and Arabic, and, alas! rich in nothing else. When I went to housekeeping, my entire stock of china for parlor and kitchen was bought for eleven dollars. This lasted very well for two years, till my brother was married and brought his bride to visit me. I then found, on review, that I had neither plates nor teacups to set a table for my father's family; wherefore I thought it best to reinforce the establishment by getting me a tea-set that cost ten dollars more, and this, I believe, formed my whole stock in trade for some years.

But she was "abundantly enriched with wealth of another sort" and told Mrs. Follen about her seven children and the death of one in the great cholera epidemic.

> I allude to this here, because I have often felt that much that is in that book [Uncle Tom's Cabin] had its root in the awful scenes and bitter sorrows of that summer.

She told how she began to write and sell sketches to "certain liberally paying 'Annuals'."

With the first money that I earned in this way I bought a feather-bed! for as I had married into poverty and [was] without a dowry, and as my husband had only a large library of books and a great deal of learning, the bed and pillows were thought the most profitable investment.

She had not wanted to sign these sketches, but her family had insisted that she do so in order to build a reputation. So she became an author;

and if you ever see a woodcut of me, with an immoderately long nose, on the cover of all the *U. S. Almanacs,* I wish you to take notice that I have been forced into it contrary to my natural modesty by the imperative solicitations of my dear five thousand friends and the public generally.

She told of her numerous contacts with slaves and ex-slaves in Cincinnati, several of whom had worked for her as servants. Mrs. Follen had not hesitated to inquire how much money Harriet had made by her pen. Harriet told of her first royalty-payment of ten thousand dollars. "I presume as much more is now due."

I have very much at heart a design to erect in some of the Northern States a normal school for the education of colored teachers in the United States and in Canada. I have very much wished that some permanent memorial of good to the colored race might be created out of the proceeds of a work which promises to have so unprecedented a sale.

She was willing to "give largely" to such an institution, but she thought that the publishers, especially those of England, ought to make a handsome contribution to it.

She told Mrs. Follen of her work with the *Key* and the pain of it.

I suffer exquisitely in writing these things. It may be truly said that I write with my heart's blood. Many times in writing "Uncle Tom's Cabin" I thought my health would fail utterly; but I prayed earnestly that God would help me till I got through, and still I am pressed beyond measure and above strength.

This horror, this nightmare abomination! can it be in my country? It lies like lead on my heart, it shadows my life with sorrow; the more so that I feel, as for my own brothers, for the South and am pained by every horror I am obliged to write, as one who is forced by some awful oath to disclose in court some family disgrace. Many times I have thought that I must die, and yet I pray God that I may live to see something done.

Among those to whom Mrs. Follen showed this engaging letter in England was George Eliot, who found it "delightful," writing to a friend the same day, "The whole letter is most fascinating and makes one love her." Out of this incident grew, years later, one of the most prized intimacies of Harriet's life.

Even under the pressure of finishing her *Key* in time, Harriet had to attend to certain other affairs. She decided to close the Stone Cabin during her coming absence, and it was necessary to dispose of the children. The twins, Harriet and Eliza, were to leave Abbot Academy for the spring term and go down to New Haven and stay with the Duttons, attending boarding-school there. Georgiana and Baby Charley—just then convulsing an admiring family by trying to scratch his ears with his pink toes, "like Rover"— were to be placed "with relatives." Campus friends would take care of Henry and Freddie and, no doubt, of Rover, too, who was going to miss his little mistress as much as her children would. That sedate animal now attended the family prayers and at night slept under the conjugal bed.

There were family letters for her to write, to tell everyone about the journey. Harriet would need a private secretary on her tour, and she hit upon exactly the right person for that post—her brother Charles. His Newark congregation would give him leave to go on such an important journey, and of all the Beecher family Charles would appreciate most the music and art and culture of Europe. A secretary was a legitimate expense to be paid for by her Glasgow hosts, and Charles, moreover, physically the handsomest of the Beechers, would add impressiveness to Harriet's *entourage*. His six feet of stature dwarfed Calvin and Harriet, and he looked like a poet.

It had been a pleasure for Harriet that winter to do her share in guaranteeing to old Dr. Beecher an annuity that would keep him in comfort for the rest of his days. Her letter to her sister-in-law Sarah, in Rochester, brought an unexpected reply. The widowed and wealthy Mrs. George Beecher announced her intention of joining the Stowe party on the journey abroad, bringing with her her son George and her brother, William Buckingham, a Rochester businessman. Harriet's nephew George had the ambition to become a painter.

How exhilarating it was, after so many grinding, humdrum years, to be the cause of so much joy and excitement in the Beecher family! The post brought Harriet an engrossed resolution of a Dublin mass-meeting, signed by the Lord Mayor, thanking her for having "done much to hasten the day of universal emancipation." The London correspondent of the New York *Observer* wrote that "Mrs. Stowe's book is stirring up the old animosity of England toward the U.S.A." The *Southern Baptist* wishfully predicted that "Mrs. Stowe has a bubble reputation which will burst when her *Key* gets under the critics' fire."

On March 20, 1853, the nation's press observed the first anniversary of the publication of *Uncle Tom's Cabin*—observed it with exclamation points. John P. Jewett announced that the year's sales had been 305,000 copies, "with demand heavy as ever." In proportion to population, a novel today, to do as well, would have to reach a sale of 1,500,000 in a year. The Boston *Congregationalist* estimated that in all countries the sale of "poor, grand, old, world-wept, polyglotted *Uncle Tom*" had reached a total of 2,500,000 copies.

Meanwhile a certain English enterprise had been causing agitation all that winter on both sides of the ocean. Like many American women who read *Uncle Tom's Cabin,* thousands of the book's British women-readers also wanted "to *do* something." Unlike their American sisters, who merely wrote impotent letters to the *Era* and *Independent,* the British converts *did* something. A group of them, including Queen Victoria's friend, the Duchess of Sutherland, the Duchess of Bedford, the Duchess of Argyll, the Countess of Shaftesbury, the Lord Mayor's lady, Viscountess Palmerston, Mrs. Milman, Mrs. Tennyson, Mrs. Dickens and a score of other ladies as conspicuous in the social, philanthropic, and literary worlds of England, met at Stafford House, the Duke of Sutherland's palatial London residence, and drew up "An Affectionate and Christian Address of Many Thousands of Women of Great Britain and Ireland to Their Sisters, the Women of The United States of America." The text of this remarkable document was as follows:

SISTERS,—A common origin, a common faith, and, we sincerely believe, a common cause, urge us, at the present moment, to address you on the subject of that system of negro slavery which still prevails so extensively, and, even under kindly disposed masters, with such frightful results, in many of the vast regions of the Western world.

We will not dwell on the ordinary topics,—on the progress of civilization, on the advance of freedom everywhere, on the rights and requirements of the Nineteenth Century; but we appeal to you very seriously to reflect, and to ask counsel of God, how far such a state of things is in accordance with His Holy Word, the inalienable rights of immortal souls, and the pure and merciful spirit of the Christian religion. We do not shut our eyes to the difficulties, nay, the dangers that might beset the immediate abolition of that long-established system. We see and admit the necessity of preparation for so great an event; but, in speaking of indispensable preliminaries, we cannot be silent on those laws of your country which, in direct contravention of God's own law, "instituted in the time of man's innocency," deny in effect to the slave the sanctity of marriage, with all its joys, rights, and obligations; which separate, at the will of the master, the wife from the husband, and the children from the parents. Nor can we be silent on that awful system which, either by statute or by custom, interdicts to any race of men, or any portion of the human family, education in the truths of the Gospel and the ordinances of Christianity. A remedy applied to these two evils alone would commence the amelioration of their sad condition. We appeal to you, then, as sisters, as wives, and as mothers, to raise your voices to your fellow-citizens, and your prayers to God, for the removal of this affliction and disgrace from the Christian world.

We do not say these things in a spirit of self-complacency, as though our nation were free from the guilt it perceives in others.

We acknowledge with grief and shame our heavy share in this great sin. We acknowledge that our forefathers introduced, nay, compelled the adoption of, slavery in those mighty colonies. We humbly confess it before Almighty God; and it is because we so deeply feel and unfeignedly avow our own complicity, that we now venture to implore your aid to wipe away our common crime and our common dishonour.

Having composed this indictment, the sponsors sent out cohorts of canvassers to secure to it the signatures of the "Many Thousands of Women of Great Britain and Ireland." They were successful beyond belief, as the vast feminine army of *Uncle Tom's* English readers, "from the very steps of the throne down to the very humblest conditions in life," and even abroad "from Paris to Jerusalem" indulged their indignation that they had brought from the pages of Harriet's novel.

In vain the London *Times* thundered against this unblushing piece of international busybodying. Unable to check the ladies, it resorted to a sarcastic acceptance of an unpalatable fact, entreating "the indulgence of the American people to a proceeding calculated to wound their *amour propre.*" Even anti-slavery newspapers in the United States resented the interference. The Duchess of Sutherland was widely denounced for having "the audacity to set herself up as the chief censor of our institutions."

By the end of the winter more than 500,000 British women had signed the "Affectionate and Christian Address." Gathered together, the page of vellum and its signatures filled twenty-six massive folio volumes bound in black leather, "each bearing on its back the imprint of the American eagle."

Who should be nominated to receive this impressive exhibit in the name of the American sisterhood? Whom would the women of the United States accept by acclamation as their surrogate and embodiment? There was only one who measured to such a specification—Harriet Beecher Stowe.

One tumultuous year after the publication of *Uncle Tom's Cabin*, Harriet was the foremost woman of America.

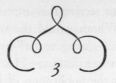

3

Queen of Scots

THE Stowe party sailed from Boston for Liverpool Wednesday, March 30, 1853, on the steamer *Niagara*. Harriet had imagined the voyage as something like a trip to New Orleans "on one of our floating river palaces," and so had put aboard the *Niagara* "a magnificent provision in the way of literature and divers matters of fancy work, with which to while away the time."

But not a book did she open the whole eleven days at sea, not a crochet needle did she pick up. At once she made the discovery that "ship life is not at all fragrant. . . ." She was seasick.

They had been eight days at sea when the S.S. *Devonshire* sailed from New York for London. One of the *Devonshire's* passengers was the Rev. Samuel Irenaeus Prime.

The first landfall made by the *Niagara* was the coast of Ireland, early on Sunday morning, April 10. Presently the ship was running within a mile of Kinsale Head, but Harriet did not observe that her life had completed one of its great circles. On that headland the *Albion* was wrecked so many years earlier, carrying to death Catharine Beecher's betrothed, Professor Fisher—the first link in the chain of circumstances that produced *Uncle Tom's Cabin*. For her father Harriet made a sketch of the cape from the east, noting that "the *Albion* struck just round the left of the point, where the rock rises perpendicularly out of the sea."

It was nearly noon when they neared Liverpool—"a real New Yorkish place" as viewed from the Mersey, which Harriet found to be "dingy and muddy." The *Niagara* dropped anchor, and a steam tender puffed alongside, bringing the customs officers. As Harriet's baggage was passed, the officer pasted on each article a sticker "with the royal arms of England and the magical letters V.R., to remind all men that they have come into a country where a lady reigns, and of course must behave themselves as prettily as they can."

344

During this formality it suddenly struck the Stowes that they had no idea of what to do when they reached shore. They were inquiring for a convenient hotel, when a young man who had come out on the tender found them and told them that he was taking them as guests to the home of his uncle, John Cropper, at Dingle Bank. This name meant little to them then; but the Croppers were one of the wealthiest and most philanthropic families of Liverpool. Their young guide's mother, Mrs. Edward Cropper, was the daughter of Lord Chief Justice Denman. His wife was Matthew Arnold's sister.

They bade good-bye to the "old ship," which Harriet could now regard with some affection, and boarded the tender to be taken up to the city, exclaiming at the greenness of the lawns and the prettiness of the cottages. The ringing of church bells reminded them it was Sunday. But it was all so unreal! Yet Harriet felt "the thrill and pulsation of kindred." After the wastes of ocean the transition to another hemisphere struck her as "something like what we should suppose might be the thrill of awakening from life to immortality, and all the wonders of the world unknown." It gave her "a strange, throbbing feeling."

Not all the dispatches from abroad nor even Charles Kingsley's friendly warning had prepared Harriet for what was to come. The author of *Alton Locke* had written her about "the foolish yet honest and heartfelt lionizing which you must go through." But that, of course, meant lionizing by people she would meet—in the homes of friends where she would be the guest. She was a little surprised to find so many at the wharf to meet the passengers of the *Niagara*—on Sunday morning, just at church time. Young Mr. Cropper had to clear a lane for his charges to get them to the carriage.

Then all at once Harriet realized that these people had come to see *her*. As she passed through them, the men took off their hats, and everybody bowed and smiled at her. All in a decent Sabbath silence. She reached the carriage and got in, and the crowd surrounded it, and the horses could not move. For some time they confronted each other—the American prophetess and this fringe of her British army of worshippers. She was a little frightened, the people were so "evidently very much determined to look." They all seemed to be such vigorous, healthy, rosy people. They made her feel "more withered and forlorn than ever," after her seasickness. But the carriage shook loose and clattered through the Liverpool streets, and all along the way on the pavements were knots of people standing, the men lifting their hats respectfully, the women bowing and smiling and waving.

Dingle Bank proved to be a small private residential park on the Mersey about two miles above Liverpool. In it were the homes of three families of Croppers, who were wealthy merchants. Harriet called them cottages, the contemporary English press accounts as firmly insisted that they were mansions. Harriet, already beginning to preach home beautification, had never seen anything in America like the Croppers' "Dingle." The green of the turf on April 10 dazzled her, and the lawns were enclosed by banks of Portugal-laurel. They rolled in over a long, winding drive of washed gravel to an ivied porch, where deft servants took charge of the visitors, leading Harriet to the most delightful bed-chamber she had ever seen. A fire of coals blazed in the grate, a bright little tea-kettle steamed on the hearth. Before the fire was a comfortable chair and beside it a low table on which were a vase of flowers, books, writing materials.

Weary and dizzy, Harriet would gladly have disrobed and remained in this nest for the next twenty-four hours; but it was well past noon and there was only time for a short rest before she must change to the first of the new gowns in her travelling trousseau and be ready for dinner. John Cropper was too considerate a host to worry his lioness with presentations the day of her arrival. Dinner was strictly a family affair, but in the course of it Mrs. Edward Cropper came in from her near-by "cottage" to meet the celebrity and invite her to breakfast next morning. Harriet was a little surprised by this invitation, but, since everybody seemed to expect it, she accepted graciously.

Harriet retired early that evening, but she had brought her sea-legs ashore with her. The bedroom rolled and pitched all night with the ship's motion, and she did not sleep a wink until a new dawn was graying. Even then her nap was a short one. She awoke to realize that it was broad day. Stepping to her window, she drew back the curtains and found herself looking right out into a little copse of holly trees. The sight of these exotics so entranced her that then and there she sketched a spray for the edification of her father. She also observed her first "robin redbreast," who was "not at all the fellow we in America take him to be." She concluded that the English robin could rightfully claim the "family estate and title," our own robin being "probably some fourth cousin who, like others, has struck out a new course for himself in America."

It would have been nice just to have had breakfast with the John Croppers, or even a tray in the delicious bed-chamber; but Harriet had accepted an invitation, and in due time she and Calvin presented themselves at the home of Mr. and Mrs. E. Cropper, Harriet "in all innocence" supposing only that they were going to share a platter of bacon and a tray of toasted scones with the family of their temporary neighbors. To her astonishment she found thirty or forty guests assembled and waiting for her—the leading citizens of Liverpool and their wives and daughters. The ladies were in *demi-toilette* and kept their bonnets on.

It was all quite formal. When breakfast was announced, each gentleman offered his arm to the lady assigned to him, and the company walked to the dining-room, where they found place-cards on the tables, which were bright with flowers from the conservatory and agleam with plate and glass. Harriet described it all minutely in a letter to old Dr. Beecher in Boston. She herself was taken out by the Rev. Dr. McNeile, the leading Church of England clergyman of Liverpool. The breakfast was "an abundant cold collation," the servants passing tea and coffee.

When the collation had been consumed, Dr. McNeile rose to extend Liverpool's welcome to Harriet:

> Mrs. Stowe: I have been requested by those kind friends under whose hospitable roof we are assembled to give some expression to the sincere and cordial welcome with which we greet your arrival in this country. I find real difficulty in making this attempt, not from want of matter, nor from want of feeling, but because it is not in the power of any language I can command to give adequate expression to the affectionate enthusiasm which pervades all ranks of our community.

He was not exaggerating, though the Stowes may have thought so then. As a lady, in 1853, Harriet, of course, could not reply. Calvin, no doubt according to previous arrangement, replied for her, in a speech equally brief. This ended the ceremony, but there was another surprise in store for Harriet. John Cropper and his brother maintained as their own philanthropy a school for the education of poor children of Liverpool, free education for the underprivileged of England being still a private charity. Such schools as the Croppers', of which there were many in England, were known as "ragged schools." A guest at the breakfast, Sir George Stephen, also maintained a ragged school in Liverpool.

At the conclusion of the breakfast, it was announced that the pupils of Croppers' School were out on the lawn waiting to greet Mrs. Stowe. Harriet went out, accompanied by all the guests; and as the gentry arranged themselves in a *tableau* facing the pathetic wards of charity, our authoress had time to note that the ragged-school children were not themselves ragged. On the contrary, they were all neat, starched, brushed, red-cheeked, soaped, and shiny. When all was quiet, Mrs. E. Cropper raised a baton, and the urchins sang a song they had been practising ever since it was known that the great Mrs. Beecher-Stowe would land in Liverpool and be the guest of the Croppers—

> I thank the goodness and the grace
>   Which on my birth have smiled,
> And made me in these Christian days
>   A happy English child.
>
> I was not born a little slave,
>   To labour in the sun
> And wish I were but in my grave
>   And all my labour done.

This ditty, as events proved, might be called the theme-song of Harriet's tour of the British Isles. As enthusiasm for her and for purging the United States of their crime became a national hysteria, the entire English population, it seemed, grew more and more glad it did not live in sinful America. At the conclusion of the song, one of the philanthropic gentlemen congratulated the "ragged" children upon being born in a land where not one of them could ever be bought or sold. For this blessing the urchins (most of them destined to labour not in the sun but in the mills, mines, and sweatshops of England) gave three cheers. It made Harriet "feel rather sad; but still," she philosophized, "I could not quarrel with English people for taking all the pride and all the comfort which this inspiriting truth can convey."

Next day was given to sight-seeing, the principal excursion taking Harriet to Speke Hall, a moated grange some eight miles out in the country. This was the first "really old thing" she had seen, and she revelled in poetic thoughts. The housekeeper brought out her copy of *Uncle Tom's Cabin* for Harriet's autograph. On the way home they visited some village cottagers. Everybody had read *Uncle Tom's Cabin,* and when the villages discovered the visitor's identity, the people gathered to look at her. In the evening the Edward Croppers drove the Stowes to a private party of anti-slavery people.

Calvin made a speech. As they were leaving, the hostess begged Harriet to meet the servants, who were assembled in the dressing-room. Harriet graciously consented. She noticed how much more deferential English servants were than our own and made the shrewd observation that this difference appeared to arise "quite as much from self-respect and a sense of propriety as from servility."

All that winter the ladies of the Liverpool Negroes' Friend Society had been taking a "penny subscription" for presentation to Mrs. Beecher-Stowe (as the English instantly began to call her, with or without the hyphen) "as a token of admiration for the genius and of high esteem for the philanthropy and Christian feeling which animate her great work, *Uncle Tom's Cabin.*" The pence were now converted into one hundred and thirty gold sovereigns tucked into a handsome, if somewhat weighty, purse.

At the presentation next morning (Wednesday, April 13), in the hall of the Charitable-Institution House, Harriet made her only public appearance in Liverpool. Adam Hodgson, Esq., made the presentation with appropriate remarks, one being that the Liverpool signatures to the "Affectionate and Christian Address" had numbered 21,953. Mrs. Beecher-Stowe received the purse with a bow and movement of the lips. Replying for her, Professor C. E. Stowe, D.D., read "from her own pen" Mrs. Stowe's response, conveying her thanks for the offering and her rather cryptic "trust it may be so employed that the blessing of many 'who are ready to perish' will return upon your heads."

Then it was back to Dingle Bank for a hasty bite of dinner and to pack up; and early in the afternoon all the Croppers accompanied the Uncle Tom Deputation to the station to see their visitors off for Glasgow. There was a crowd outside the station house and on the train platform "a great number of friends." A first-class compartment was reserved for the authoress and her party. In it Harriet found a gorgeous bouquet and an affecting note from the wealthy but bed-ridden gentleman who sent it. The guard locked their door, little Harriet waved from the window, and with the huzzas and God-speeds of the hospitable Liverpool folk in her ears was safely dispatched on the most astonishing reception ever accorded an American by the British public until Charles Augustus Lindbergh flew across the Atlantic.

Conceding the superior comfort and good keeping of their present accommodation, right away the Yankee travellers voted in favour of the democracy of the American cars. There were just six seats in the first-class compartment and there were just six members of the Deputation, therefore no informed native traveller was with them to tell them about the sights. Calvin thought they were "just like the six old ladies that made their living by taking tea at each others' houses." Harriet observed that an English family numbering six could travel from one end of the country to the other and, by engaging hotel suites, never meet an outside soul.

They had no guide, but they had the guide-book, and Calvin kept his stubby finger in it. On this journey he shows us some of the engaging qualities that endeared him to Harriet and his children and to many another who knew him. The fat little professor was like a schoolboy on an exciting lark. Harriet and Sarah might nod, Brother Charles dream of London concerts, and even little George Beecher grow somnolent in the monotony of the wheels, but Calvin skipped back and forth across the compartment so as to miss nothing on either side of the track. Harriet wrote to Aunt Esther Beecher:

> If he had been appointed on a mission of inquiry he could not have been more zealous and faithful. I began to think that our desire for an English cicerone was quite superfluous.

"There's something! What's that?" was the cry.

"Carlisle," came Calvin's ready answer.

"What!" said Harriet. "The Carlisle of Scott's ballad?"

"What ballad?" inquired Charles.

"In *The Lay of The Last Minstrel*—the song of Albert Graeme."

Henry Ward Beecher testified to Harriet's amazing memory of things she had read. Her descendents claim that she could recite the whole of *The Lay of The Last Minstrel*. At any rate, she was never at a loss for a quotation from that poem and gave them one now—

> It was an English laydie bright,
> When sun shines fair on Carlisle wall,
> And she would marry a Scottish knight,
> For love will still be lord of all.

"I always wondered what 'Carlisle wall' was," she added. "Now I know."

Here the train stopped for dinner—"a regular meal"—giving them a little time to observe the castle and also an old church—"a splendid Gothic" —where Paley had preached. Then they were on again, and famous names sounding in their ears at the stops. Gretna Green—they knew about that—and they were in Scotland at last—Scotland, that to New England Calvinists was more truly the motherland than England herself.

"Ah," sighed Charles, who also had been reared on the Waverley novels, "how I wish Walter Scott was alive!"

The sun declined over Solway Firth, glimpses of which they caught from the train, and they talked about Redgauntlet and quoted from *Young Lochinvar,* and Harriet wondered "how many authors it will take to enchant our country from Maine to New Orleans, as every foot of ground is enchanted here in Scotland."

Their lamps were lighted, they could no longer see outside, so these lovers of congregational singing struck up Scotch tunes, lustily singing in the uproar *Auld Lang Syne* and *Bonnie Doon* and "Scots wha ha'," and *Dundee, Elgin,* and *Martyrs.*

"Don't get too much excited," warned Calvin.

"Mr. Stowe," said Harriet, "this is a thing that comes only once in a lifetime; do let us have the comfort of it. We shall never come into Scotland for the *first time* again."

The train stopped, and they heard the station-call, "Lockerbie." It was the real Walter Scott country now. Old Mortality himself was buried here. Then Harriet was aware of faces in the window and heard her name called out in a Scottish accent. She went to the door and dropped the window down, and a dozen hands stretched up to her, men's, women's, and children's. There was quite a crowd beyond, and everyone was calling, "Ye're welcome to Scotland."

After that, and far into the night, it was the same story at every stop, for the telegraph had apprized the folk of the authoress's progress. It was midnight when the train came to a stop in the station house at Glasgow, and Harriet stepped down only to see faces—faces everywhere—"earnest, eager, friendly faces, ever so many. Warm greetings, kindly words. A crowd parting in the middle, through which we were conducted into a carriage; loud cheers of welcome . . ."

They were in charge of Mr. Baillie W. P. Paton, who was to be their host in Glasgow. Baillie, Harriet explained to Aunt Esther, was the same as Councilman in an American city. They drove in a closed carriage through midnight streets, deserted. Once under a lantern Harriet's eyes caught a name—Argyle Street. Then, "a warm, cosy parlor," a "hospitable apartment," and "sleep fell over me for the first time in Scotland."

Next morning Harriet was so worn and weary that her Scotch breakfast of parritch, bannocks, and herring scarcely restored her. But she faced another trying day—a day that proved to be "a confused dream to me, of a dizzy and overwhelming kind." The Glasgow papers were trumpeting, "Her feet have pressed the soil of the fatherland, and she has breathed the air of the mother country." It began immediately after breakfast, when three little girls called to present an album of pressed Scottish sea-mosses. Harriet found the Scottish children "brilliant as pomegranate blossoms." She was seeing through rose-tinted glasses. Even the street urchins were pink and fat as Rubens' cherubs.

Letters—a mountain of them waiting for her. Charles worked most of the day, disposing of them. Invitations, flights of sentiment, advice, inquiries, pleas, suggestions, poems, presents of books, flowers, fruit. Deputations soliciting visits—from Paisley, from Greenock, from Dundee, Aberdeen, Edinburgh, even from Belfast in Ireland. Country homes put at her disposal, invitations . . . .

It was a little ridiculous, she thought, especially since the individual calling forth such an outburst "could be seen by the eye of sober sense to be altogether inadequate and disproportioned to it." Harriet meant it, when she wrote that remark to Aunt Esther. One could not be pretentious before Aunt Esther, but Harriet was genuinely humble.

Not until afternoon, however, did she feel the true weight of what the ecstatic Glasgow correspondents were calling "the acclamations of the nation." The Lord Provost of Glasgow himself called to take her in his "luxurious equipage" to see the Cathedral—and to give his city its first chance to view the celebrated guest at full length. The newspapers published the itinerary, as they usually did only for royal processions.

Sarah, her brother and son, Charles, the Patons, and their immediate party were in carriages bringing up the rear. At the Cathedral Harriet looked down over a crowd that blocked the entrance. It was Harriet's "first cathedral," and she devoured it. The crypt so interested her that "it was with difficulty that she could be got to retire from its precincts." Finally the neck-craning and the "sepulchral chill" grew unbearable, but Calvin and Charles kept climbing to see everything for her. A queue had already formed, as "many thousands" began to file past the visitors' book to see the divinity's actual signature and handwriting. Afterwards the Lord Provost drove her through the Saut Market, but she was too tired to remember anything about that tour.

As her "luxurious equipage" rolled homeward through the High Street, a moralist was wondering if Mrs. Stowe was "seeing with her eyes as well as hearing with her ears." Probably not, because "the lowest classifications are not visible excepting in their wynds and closes or in the neighborhood of whisky shops, spending the miserable pittance that they have either earned or begged for what they say is 'baith claes, meat, and drink' to them." Many were in dread lest the visiting handmaiden of God should discover something of Glasgow's drunkenness and degradation. "Talk of *Uncle Tom's Cabin*—and no man admires it more than I do," declared the moralist, "—there are more harrowing facts and circumstances and stories in this book which I hold in my hand (Testimony before the House of Commons on Juvenile Delinquency) than in any book I ever read of fiction or fact."

But perhaps Harriet *was* seeing a few things with her eyes. She wrote to Aunt Esther from Glasgow that she admired "ragged children on canvas much more than the same in nature."

Next morning she was so ill that her host called a physician. The doctor put Harriet to bed, denied her to all visitors, and even forbade her to look at her second day's accumulation of mail. But that evening she had to get up to attend a great public tea-party in her honour at the City Hall. The civic reception had attained such dimensions that only serious illness could be permitted to keep Harriet away from its principal functions. The rest had done her good, however; and when Dr. Wardlaw and his wife drove the Stowes to the meeting-place, it was the venerable and famous Scottish divine who caused the concern. He kept holding his hand over his heart and hoping ominously that he could get through the evening. (Actually, he was dead before Harriet could put her travel letters between book covers.)

They found the City Hall surrounded by an immense crowd, and Harriet preserved "a dim remembrance of a way being made for us." Within, the reception room was crowded with people important enough to be presented to Mrs. Stowe. The rest of the 2,050 persons lucky enough to secure tickets for the tea-party were in the great hall, waiting for their first glimpse of the lioness.

The table spread for Harriet and her party was in a small gallery at the front of the hall, where all the people could feast their eyes upon her. During the "chatting and enjoyment, while all were busy with the social meal," two thousand devotees of *Uncle Tom* reverently watched the wee

genius who had written the book that ranked next to the Bible with
Protestant Christianity. She seemed sunk in some profound and holy
thought. But really—for the deity was also a humourist—she was wondering
about the size of the pot it took to make tea for two thousand persons. It
must have been "the father of all tea-kettles." And she was wondering if,
"as is our good Yankee custom, old Mother Scotland had put in two thousand teaspoonfuls of tea for the company, and one for the teapot."

On Saturday Harriet's entertainers chartered a small steamer and took
her and a number of other invited guests for a sail down the Clyde to the
beautiful peninsula of Roseneath. Here she met one of the Duke of Argyle's
farmers, who told her he would walk six miles any day to see the author
of *Uncle Tom's Cabin.* He was a gigantic man; and, wrote Harriet, "when
I put my hand into his great prairie of a palm, I was as a grasshopper in
my own eyes."

But Harriet wanted to see more of the country and had only to express
the wish. Her hosts engaged a carriage and sent her home by land, along
the north bank of the Clyde. Through this beautiful countryside she made
a queen's progress. At every village "the butcher came out of his stall, and
the baker from his shop, the miller, dusty with his flour, the blooming,
comely, young mother, with her baby in her arms, all smiling and bowing."
The children gathered round her, she was "deluged with flowers." With
her and Calvin in the carriage were Dr. Robson and Lady Anderson. It was
Harriet's "first essay towards giving titles," and she made "rather an odd
piece of work of it, generally saying 'Mrs.' first and 'Lady' afterwards, then
begging pardon." Lady Anderson laughed and granted her "a general
absolution."

That evening Harriet was the guest of honour at a second tea-party in
the City Hall, of identical size with the former. Actually, this was an overflow party, made up chiefly by persons who had been unable to get tickets
for the first one; but it was held on Saturday night, tickets were sold at a
smaller price, and it was advertised as a workingmen's soirée to meet Mrs.
Stowe.

On this occasion Calvin distinguished himself. He had seemed oppressed
by all the noblemen and officials surrounding his wife and, in his replies
for her, had confined himself to lofty thoughts and august periods. Now,
at the Saturday-night "soiree," as if inspired by its proletarian label, he
launched forth in his best vein upon a speech on "Nobility," which was
widely quoted in the British press. Calvin humorously pooh-poohed coronets

and Norman blood, since every man traced his lineage to Adam. He concluded:

Now when I was a boy and had to get up at four o'clock in the morning and go down to the paper-mills and make the fires (tremendous cheering), I used to regret I could not go to the school with some of the other boys, who were blessed with wealthy parents, and I used to envy them because I could not go to the Academy. But my grandmother, a kind, good old lady, used to tell me to hope and persevere and work away, and something would turn up after a while. (Cheers.) And then she used to make me repeat—
First learn to write, then to indite,
And then a line of Latin;
And so by chance you may advance
To wear a suit of satin.
(Loud laughter and cheers.) And so I learned and got along and went ahead. (Cheers.) I have not got the suit of satin yet, but I 'spects Mrs. Stowe has. (Great cheering and laughter, amid which the learned Professor resumed his seat.)

On Sunday afternoon Calvin preached in Dr. Robson's church. On Sunday evening he occupied Dr. Wardlaw's pulpit, taking as his text, "Thy will be done on earth as it is in heaven." On Sunday evening Charles preached in the City Hall from the text, "Thy kingdom come." Did it remind Harriet of those joyous days when the crusading Beechers went migrating to the West, praying, singing, exhorting, and scattering tracts? Her entourage was again staffed to turn readily into a gospel caravan.

The invitation from Edinburgh had been impressive, and on Monday morning April 18, the Stowe party travelled to that city, a two hours' ride on the cars. Harriet had no fixed schedule or itinerary for her tour. She wanted to see as much of Walter Scott's country as she could, she wanted to visit Stratford-on-Avon, and she wanted to be in London in time for the "anniversaries" in May. Otherwise she was at the disposal of circumstances and her new friends.

Even the excitement of the past week had not prepared Harriet for Edinburgh's welcome to her. The fêting she received in Glasgow was only to have been expected, since Glasgow had invited her across the ocean and had arranged for her visit. Harriet could not suppose that crowds and huzzas and gifts would continue to make her tour a royal passage.

Yet the Edinburgh reception far outdid that of Glasgow in impressiveness. Whereas in Glasgow a mere baillie had met her at the station, in Edinburgh she was received by the Lord Provost himself, surrounded by the principal magistrates of the city. Ropes held back a great throng of citizens massed beyond.

After the formal presentation of the officials to Harriet and her party—and the presentation, too, of Mrs. Wigham, a wealthy Quakeress who was to be their hostess in Edinburgh—the Lord Provost took the Stowes into the official carriage and set out at once on a sight-seeing tour of the city. As the horses clattered forth, the station crowd set up a great cheer; and there were crowds everywhere to cheer Harriet—at the Castle, at the University, at Holyrood, at the hospitals, and along the principal streets—for her route had been published in advance, and she rode "amid shouts and smiles and greetings."

They passed Scott's monument, and Harriet "felt an oppressive melancholy." "Vanity, vanity," her good sense and her Puritan conscience were repeating to her. Her admiration for Walter Scott was boundless; in her heart, perhaps, she regarded him as the greatest of all writers; yet where was Walter Scott now? What a moment life seemed in the midst of eternity! For that matter, how momentary was art itself, in all its beauty! Scott had never heard for his work the acclaim now ringing in Harriet's ears. She was not letting the adulation turn her head.

The day exhausted her, and Tuesday she remained in seclusion. Mrs. Wigham called in Dr. Henderson, a celebrated homœopathic physician, and from that time on Harriet was to be a believer in the new system of medicine. Many were calling at the Wigham residence, content to leave their cards as a mark of respect, Harriet's "feeble health" having been advertised. So many letters that Charles, who rose "at all hours," was at them at six o'clock Tuesday morning to be able to answer all before the afternoon engagements. London invitations—the Duchess of Sutherland's for a levée in Stafford House, the Earl of Carlisle's to a dinner. Charles Kingsley wanted them out to Eversley in Hampshire for a visit. Two well-known dissenting clergymen of London, Mr. Binney and Mr. Sherman, extended the hospitality of their parsonages. That settled the problem of London accommodations. Harriet and Calvin accepted the proffer of Mr. Binney, whose parish was in Walworth, a southern suburb. Charles would go with Mr. Sherman, pastor of Surrey Chapel.

The official excuse for Harriet's presence in Edinburgh was to receive the Scottish National Penny Offering, the presentation of which took place Wednesday evening in the Music Hall. It was another "tea-party." So great had been the demand for tickets that determined Uncle-Tom devotees had paid "double the price at which they were issued." The doors were besieged before the hour of admission. Harriet, of course, attended, after a day of sight-seeing which had taken her to Craigmiller Castle, where Mary Queen of Scots had retreated after the murder of Rizzio. When the Lord Provost led Harriet to her gallery, the applause was deafening. She chose to regard the cheers as "Scotland's voice to America." The routine was becoming familiar. After the cake and fruit were passed (while the pipe-organ played *Old Hundred*), the Lord Provost presented the Rev. Mr. J. Ballantyne, who presented the Offering: a great silver salver on which were heaped one thousand gold sovereigns. This magnificent gift, contributed by Edinburgh and Glasgow people penny by penny, the parting with every one of which had been painful, made the Liverpool collection look puny; but its amount was £1,000 only as of April 20, 1853. The pennies were still coming in.

Scotland gave the Offering to Harriet without strings to spend for the benefit of American Negroes, but the salver was to be her own souvenir of the occasion. "A few ladies of Edinburgh" bought it for Harriet "in testimony of the high appreciation in which they hold her as a woman, as a Christian, and as the friend of humanity." It remained one of her most prized trophies of her tour.

The reproach of America for her sin became a little more fervid in this meeting than it had been in the former ones, and this led to a report in the United States—"paraded," as Calvin remarked later, "in the newspapers from Maine to Texas"—that during the proceedings the American flag was "insulted, torn, and mutilated." The only basis for such a story that Calvin could imagine was the fact that one American flag in the hall was so draped about its staff that only the stars were visible.

By this time Harriet had decided to see something of northern Scotland by accepting the invitations of the other two large Scottish cities, Dundee and Aberdeen. Accordingly, on the morning of April 21 she and her party were off on the long journey to Aberdeen, again in a first-class compartment that held just six passengers.

Harriet enjoyed this train-ride more than any other she took in Britain. Almost every station called up historical or literary recollections, and how strange it was to hear a station-master call out Bannockburn or Stirling or Perth! They caught a glimpse of Glamis Castle, scene of *Macbeth*. They were a merry group that day, joking and laughing, Calvin again presiding over the guide-book. The bracing sea air (or perhaps the homœopathy) greatly restored Harriet, nor was she again on her tour to suffer from the exhaustion that had been afflicting her. The rock-bound Scottish coast reminded her of the State of Maine, but she thought the Maine coast more beautiful, because it was wooded.

The Lord Provost of Aberdeen met them and drove them to the home of their host, Mr. Cruikshank, where they had time only for a hasty supper before proceeding to the hall in the County Rooms, where the throng was already assembled. "Deafening cheers saluted the honoured guest," said the contemporary account. "The meeting was refreshed by an excellent service of fruit, &c, &c." The Aberdeen greeting took the form of an "Address of The Citizens" and a purse containing £120. Professor Stowe responded to the Address and the Rev. Charles Beecher to the presentation of the purse.

Among the letters waiting for Harriet in Aberdeen was one from an eccentric who signed himself "The old Scotch Bachelor." This gentleman, a confirmed dissenter, advised Harriet, while being shown off as "a rare animal, arrived frae America, the wife that writ Uncle Tom's Cabin," not to forget to "speer at the Aberdeenians if it be true they ance kidnappet little laddies and selt them for slaves." And she was to "speer" at a certain judge, "if it be true that he flogget three laddies in the beginning o' last year, for the three following crimes: first, for the crime of being born of puir, ignorant parents; second, for the crime of being left in ignorance; and, third, for the crime of having nothing to eat." And she was to "speer" if there was a single school in all Scotland where helpless, homeless poor children could be fed and clothed at the public expense.

Next morning Harriet did some "speering" and discovered the industrial schools of Aberdeen which not only met Scotch Bachelor's objections but seemed worthy to serve as a model even to Boston, which in 1853 provided high-school education only for boys, but none for girls. Harriet sent to Catharine Beecher a full account of the Aberdeen schools to aid the latter in her educational work.

Early that afternoon the Stowe party left Aberdeen, a great crowd at the railway station seeing them off. They returned to Dundee by an inland route, and there were crowds at every station to greet the American authoress. At Dundee Harriet received the usual "Address" and "Offering,"

Calvin responding for her. Her baggage was growing heavy with gifts.

Next day, Saturday, April 23, after the usual morning spent in sight-seeing, the Stowe party took the cars early enough for Harriet to appear at the workingmen's soirée in Edinburgh in the evening. It was another vast meeting, with the customary address and response, and it ended Scotland's formal demonstrations in honour of Mrs. Beecher Stowe. There had been four consecutive evenings of packed halls, speeches, and cheers. On the Lord's Day Harriet rested in the quiet home of Mrs. Wigham.

But her strength and energy had returned to her fully. On Monday Calvin and Charles returned to Glasgow to address a temperance rally and receive an Address to Harriet from the students of Glasgow University. Harriet took the opportunity to lead a pious pilgrimage to Melrose Abbey, Scott's home at Abbotsford, and his grave in Dryburgh Abbey, on the Tweed.

It rained all day long, but Harriet tramped through it with determination and inspected every relic, every stone, and every inscription at Abbotsford, the poet's home, which, she said, "grew up like a bank of coral." She even made a poetical translation of Scott's Latin inscription on the grave of his favourite dog, Maida. She stood reverently at the grave in the ruined chapel of Dryburgh and plucked a sprig of ivy to press as a keepsake. Foot by foot she went over the ruins of Melrose Abbey, climbing "a ruinous, winding staircase" and going into ecstasies over the Gothic architecture. Owing perhaps to her *Baronial and Ecclesiastical Antiquities,* four volumes of proof engravings presented to her by an Aberdeen architect, she had developed a passion for the Gothic. A little later she would be calling Shakespeare's plays Gothic.

When, late in the day, they returned wet, cold, and hungry to their inn and saw the bright fire and the spread table and smelled the savour of the mutton-chops—such mutton, they agreed, as was unknown in America, "except," Harriet amended, "on the sea-coast of Maine"—they "voted poetry a humbug and damp, old, musty cathedrals a bore." Yet after tea the clouds showed signs of breaking, and Harriet proposed a visit to the Melrose ruins by moonlight. Scott had been fond of them in that illumination. She must see them as Scott described them.

The others, exhausted, longing only for their beds, were dismayed. Harriet must not attempt such a thing; she would overtax her strength, catch cold. But, having made up her mind, the little lady whose feeble health had so recently been making a nation worry was "sot in her ways."

"Nevertheless," she said to Sarah Beecher, "I am going back again tonight to see that abbey by moonlight. I intend to walk the whole figure while I am about it."

The first question was, would there be any moonlight on that date? They consulted a gentleman of Melrose who had been serving them as volunteer guide. He looked at his almanac and predicted moonrise at eleven o'clock. The hour was appalling, but Harriet occupied some of the interval by visiting the antiquary shops and picking up some Melrose relics for her collection.

When at fifteen minutes before midnight there was still no moon, they fared forth anyhow. But the moon had only been hiding behind the Eildon Hills, and at the abbey there was enough of it "to touch with a gloaming, uncertain ray the ivy-clad walls."

It was pokerish there, though, in the haunted abbey when the village bell tolled twelve. There was a rustling in the matted ivy, the two ladies uttered faint screams, and out of the tangle flew two disturbed rooks, rattling down some fragments of masonry. The tourists were groping up the ruinous stairway when a gust of rain beat into their faces and sent them scurrying back to the comfort of the inn.

When they joined Calvin and Charles in Edinburgh next day, Harriet felt satiated with celebrity. London, she knew now, would mean for her the same gaping crowds, the same crowded meetings, the same cheering and fêting. But she had a week before the London anniversaries would begin, and she decided to disappear from the public gaze for part of that time.

This she managed easily. Among the many prominent people who had offered her the hospitality of their homes was the wealthy and philanthropic Quaker, Joseph Sturge, of Birmingham. Birmingham was near Stratford-on-Avon, and she wanted to see Shakespeare's home, as Henry Ward Beecher had done on his tour. Harriet therefore wrote to Sturge asking to take sanctuary with him for a few days and "charging him on no account to let any one know of our arrival."

Pending the arrival of Sturge's good-natured consent, Harriet spent two days in and around Edinburgh about as she chose. On Thursday, April 28, —"a rainy, misty morning"—she was waving good-bye to the crowd in Edinburgh station and farewell to Scotland at the same time. But though temporarily out of the British panorama, her figure was looming over London, which the Scottish demonstrations had aroused to a fever of anticipation. Unable to dampen the popular enthusiasm with thunder, the *Times* resorted to satirical phrases. Harriet's imminent visit, that paper confessed, gave it "the least satisfaction."

What if Mrs. Stowe, whose fairy pen suggests so romantic an idea of the hand that guides the pen, the fair form that owns it, and the voice that must be still sweeter than the speechless instrument, should after all turn out something less lovely than the ideal! We have a suspicion that even Homer and Virgil are better hid in the mists of antiquity and would have gained little credit on British soil. How much better had Burns been no more than a name, particularly as the highest apotheosis of the man was a place in the Excise! Mrs. Stowe's portrait has already rather widely dispelled some agreeable, though, of course, unwarranted, illusions. But the portrait was a photograph, and copied on wood in an illustrated contemporary; and not even angelic beauty could survive that double ordeal. Now, however, we are to have the woman herself. . . .

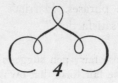

4

Lioness in London

Having no need for either rest or incognito, Sarah Beecher, William Buckingham, and little George Beecher proceeded directly from Edinburgh to London, where they sought out the Rev. Mr. Binney and secured lodgings near his parsonage, Rose Cottage, in Walworth, so as to be close to their distinguished relative.

The others descended at Birmingham, where Joseph Sturge met them at the station. They did not know him by sight, but tall Charles Beecher looked over the platform and recognized him at once "by instinct" assisted by the philanthropist's broad-brimmed Quaker hat. Mr. Sturge had been as good as his word, and there were no curious stares this time at Harriet. They supped with the Sturge family, and next morning the eminent Quaker drove them in his fly down to Stratford, that literary shrine not yet having been desecrated by the "whistling, whisking railroad cars."

At Stratford Harriet had a most satisfactory day-and-a-half, "doing" everything as thoroughly as she had done Abbotsford and Melrose Abbey. She took up cudgels for Shakespeare and, as a good Scotswoman now in sympathy, called Queen Elizabeth "a belligerent old Gorgon." She found evidence to satisfy herself that Shakespeare was a man of religious principle, that his father was a God-fearing citizen and his mother angelic, and guessed that he must have had a rigorous aunt to make him toe the mark. In short, she reconstructed the Shakespeare family as a sort of Elizabethan counterpart of the Litchfield Beechers. The souvenir sprig of mulberry she plucked for herself, she found out later, came not from Shakespeare's original tree but from a subsequent mulberry planted on the spot where Shakespeare's had grown. Harriet was fond of telling such little jokes on herself.

On Saturday she did Warwick Castle and, of course, Kenilworth, and then drove on to Lady Godiva's Coventry, where the weary tourists left the carriage to make its own way home, while they took the cars. In the luxurious Sturge mansion that evening Harriet met Elihu Burritt, the "learned blacksmith" from Connecticut, with whom she soon became so well acquainted that she was calling him Elihu.

On Sunday Harriet much wanted to attend church services but dared not for fear of being recognized. In the evening, however, she went with her host to call on the celebrated female Quaker preacher, Sibyl Jones, who came from Harriet's own Brunswick, in the State of Maine. Sibyl "had a concern upon her mind" for Harriet. "She desired to caution me against the temptations of too much flattery and applause and against the worldliness which might beset me in London." Next morning, May 2, Harriet relaxed her incognito enough to attend a private anti-slavery meeting in Birmingham and receive an "Address." Consequently, "a throng of friends accompanied us to the depot." Elihu Burritt was their travelling companion to London.

Whether her advent had been noticed, bringing the usual mob of the curious to the London terminal, we do not know. Harriet was growing so used to crowds that her London letters say little about them. But the Rev. Mr. Sherman and the Rev. Mr. Binney were there, the latter with the surprising information that there was barely time to drive to Walworth, dress, and return to the Mansion House for the Lord Mayor's dinner, at which Harriet was to be a special guest.

"What!" exclaimed our authoress. "The Lord Mayor of London, that I used to read about in *Whittington and His Cat?*"

An explanation of this impromptu and extraordinary honour for Harriet comes readily. The current Lord Mayor of London was a Dissenter and a member of Mr. Binney's congregation. Hearing, perhaps at the last minute, that the author of *Uncle Tom's Cabin* would arrive in London on the date of the Lord Mayor's annual dinner to the judiciary of England and, furthermore, be the house-guest of his own pastor, the Lord Mayor could not resist bagging the lioness thus providentially delivered into his hands, ahead of the Duchess of Sutherland, the Earl of Carlisle, and the other noblewomen and noblemen planning to sponsor her in London. To mask his lion-hunting a little, he gave it out that the judiciary dinner of 1853 would have an international literary cast. As England's literary representative he invited Charles Dickens.

At the dinner Harriet sat above the salt and opposite Mr. Dickens, who was perhaps not exactly relishing his position. He would have accepted it, however, if only to score on his friend Thackeray, who was pouring scorn on the Stowe dementia and especially upon the *Affectionate and Christian Address*. There was another guest, too, who was probably uncomfortable— the American Minister to the Court of St. James, Mr. Ingersoll, then secretly at work in the highest British circles to circumvent his country- woman's London triumph, if he could. He could not have been too cordial at the dinner, for Harriet barely mentioned his presence in her letter to Mary Perkins.

After the loyal toasts, the toast to the American Minister, and those to the chief dignitaries of British justice, came the one the guests had been waiting for. Mr. Justice Talfourd, himself the author of the tragedy *Ion,* proposed "Anglo-Saxon Literature." The learned justice alluded to two distinguished authors then present. The one was a lady who had shed a lustre on the literature of America, and whose works were deeply engraven on every English heart. The other was, of course, Mr. Charles Dickens, to whose works the learned judge paid an eloquent tribute.

In replying, Dickens uttered the most restrained praise of herself and *Uncle Tom's Cabin* Harriet was to hear publicly expressed in the course of her entire British visit. Mr. Dickens observed that, in returning thanks for the toast, he could not forget he was in the presence of a stranger who was the authoress of a noble book, with a noble purpose. He really should not call her a stranger, for she would find a welcome in every English home. And Dickens turned humorously to his troubles with a lawsuit amid the maze of British legal technicalities.

After the dinner Harriet had a few moments of what she called pleasant, friendly conversation with the novelist and his wife, and later Mr. and Mrs. Dickens drove down to Walworth to call on her. But Dickens' friendship was not one of the enduring ones Harriet brought from her London visit.

Rose Cottage, which Harriet called "a charming retreat," was, she dis- covered immediately, in an extremely unfashionable part of London. She learned this fact the first thing Tuesday morning, when Mrs. Follen called. The outspoken Boston lady told Harriet she should be in the West End. Everybody who was anybody in London lived in the West End. Mrs. Follen lived there, of course.

But Harriet maintained that she liked her suburb better. From her window she could see a meadow with grazing sheep and lambs, and

HARRIET BEECHER STOWE.

Authoress of Uncle Tom's Cabin.

From a Daguerreotype by Stevens, Andover, America.

Read & Co Lithographers 10 Johnson's Ct Fleet Strt

A BRITISH IMPRESSION

Of "portraits" like this, Harriet said, "They will be useful, like the Irishman's guideboard, which showed where the road did not go." (Page 369.)

London was smutty—"as smutty as Pittsburgh or Wheeling." It was a good hour's steady driving from Walworth to the West End, "so that my American friends of the newspapers," Harriet wrote to Mrs. Howard in Brooklyn, "who are afraid I shall be corrupted by aristocratic associations, will see that I am at safe distance."

Her friends of the American press, as they watched her phenomenal reception assume the aspect of a great, national, anti-American demonstration in England, were making other charges, the echoes of which were reaching Harriet in London. The alleged insult to the flag in Edinburgh was a sample. A story was circulating in the American newspapers that the Duchess of Sutherland, Harriet's chief patroness in London, had evicted the poor tenants from her Scottish estates, burning the cottages over their heads when they refused to leave. In one such cottage lay an old, bed-ridden woman, nearly a hundred years old. When her people protested against moving her, the Sutherland agent, as brutal a man as Simon Legree, replied, "Damn her, the old witch, she has lived too long. Let her burn." The blankets of the old woman's bed were on fire when she was carried out, and she died of shock within five days.

The Earl of Shaftesbury, from whose initiative had sprung the *Affectionate and Christian Address,* was also under heavy American fire. The New York *Observer* contrasted unfavourably his meddling officiousness with the quiet philanthropy of the late Lord Ashley, who had worked so effectively for British factory and colliery labourers and kept his nose out of other people's business.

Harriet had answers for all these canards. The flag incident, of course, was purely imaginary. The Scottish atrocities, granting that they had occurred, had all happened between 1811 and 1820, when the present Duchess was a girl, a member of the Howard family. She did not marry the Duke until 1823 and therefore could not have been even remotely responsible.

And actually no such atrocities occurred. The whole affair was investigated by the Commons, and the Duke of Sutherland was vindicated. In 1811 the overlords of Scotland began to abandon their feudal life and conform to the modern world. For the Duke of Sutherland it meant moving his retainers, who had been serving him as a military force, down from the infertile mountain tops to farms and seaside villages below, where they could lead independent lives. Inasmuch as the population of Sutherland was more than 21,000 souls, this was a vast undertaking. If old feudal cottages were burned, it was for sanitary reasons as much as anything else. As for the bed-ridden old woman, the accused agent had promptly sued the accuser for libel and had recovered damages.

Neatest of all was Harriet's retort to the *Observer's* comparison of Lord Ashley with Lord Shaftesbury, which, she wrote, "does not strike people over here as remarkably apposite," the "late" Lord Ashley and the Earl of Shaftesbury being one and the same person. When Ashley succeeded to the family estate, he took the name of Shaftesbury.

The charming retreat in Walworth proved no retreat for her at all. Harriet's stupendous entry into London as lioness of the Lord Mayor's dinner reverberated next morning in the press, and Mrs. Follen but pioneered a host of the wealthy and eminent whose carriages, day after day, threaded the drab reaches of the "Surrey side" to an obscure suburban manse. What a procession it was—the recent Prime Minister Lord John Russell and his lady, the future Prime Minister Viscount Palmerston and his lady, Lord Shaftesbury, the Duchess of Sutherland, the Duchess of Argyle, Dean Milman of St. Paul's, Archbishop Whately of Ireland, the daughters of the Archbishop of Canterbury (to invite the Stowes to Lambeth Palace), Thomas Babington Macaulay, Mr. and Mrs. Dickens, Sir Charles Trevelyan, Mary Howitt, Martin Farquhar Tupper.

On Tuesday evening the Stowes were dinner guests of the Earl of Carlisle, noting, as they drove up to Waterloo Bridge, the flaming, flaring gin shops, the number of which seemed to Harriet "absolutely appalling." They were all crowded, and she was shocked to see in them "multitudes of boys and girls of the age of my own."

It was strictly a family dinner party in which Harriet soon found herself —a Howard family dinner, the Earl of Carlisle and the Duchess of Sutherland being brother and sister. They had no intention of sharing their trophy with others in this preliminary gathering. Harriet here met for the first time not only Carlisle and the Duchess of Sutherland, her two principal sponsors, but also their sisters, Lady Dover, Lady Lascelles, and Lady Labouchere, and their cousin, the Earl of Burlington, heir to the Dukedom of Devonshire. There was a single outsider, Arthur Helps, the Queen's literary adviser, with whom Harriet had had correspondence. Perhaps this group of the nobility had felt a little doubtful of their ability to cope with the mighty intellect of the unknown and had invited the most brilliant man they knew to speak, if need be, the language of genius.

Next morning, May 4, Harriet made her first public appearance in London, at the Anniversary of the British and Foreign Bible Society. But of that, in a favourite locution of hers, more anon. On Thursday, May 5, Harriet visited the Dulwich Gallery, where she found herself disappointed in Claude Lorraine but won over to the fleshly Rubens, whose paintings of fat women she had always properly despised. The Edward Croppers had come down to London from Liverpool and that evening had the Stowes to dinner, where Harriet met Lord and Lady Hatherton, the Trevelyans, Lady Emma Campbell, the young Duke of Argyle's sister, and other notables. Her letters were beginning to look like pages from the *Peerage*.

On Friday morning a humble suppliant called at Rose Cottage. She was Miss Greenfield, a stout and unprepossessing black girl from Alabama, a freed slave. She had a natural but untrained voice and had given concerts in the United States as the "Black Swan." She had had no success in London, however, and came to petition the favour and help of the great authoress of *Uncle Tom's Cabin*.

The Deputation was equipped to handle just such cases. Charles Beecher sat down at Mr. Binney's piano and sounded a chord, and the Black Swan began to sing. Harriet was thrilled. Miss Greenfield had a magnificent voice and could sing in two ranges as she chose, tenor or soprano. While the impromptu concert was going on Mrs. S. C. Hall, an Irish journalist, called to offer Harriet the sanctuary of her country cottage. Mrs. Hall was so struck by Miss Greenfield's vocalizing that she volunteered to introduce the Swan to Sir George Smart, the Queen's musical director and quite the arbiter of London's musical world. Before night Mrs. Hall could send word to Harriet that Sir George, after hearing the coloured girl sing, had agreed to launch her in London. But the Swan had no gown suitable for such an appearance, and Harriet at once arranged to have one made for her—of "moire antique, trimmed with bugles." Ah, it was good to have the power to do such things for people!

The first week in London ended brilliantly on Saturday with the levée of the Duke and Duchess of Sutherland for Mrs. Harriet Beecher Stowe in Stafford House on St. James's Park, opposite Buckingham Palace—of which great event also, more anon.

Harriet's letters were not mentioning the London crowds. To hear their roar we must turn to the contemporary press. An amazed American journal reported that "the London *Times,* which cannot afford room for the speeches of Mr. Cass or Mr. Everett on the highest questions of international politics, publishes at full length a letter from Professor Stowe to Mr. McSymon, informing that gentleman and the world that Mrs. Harriet Beecher Stowe is indisposed." The *Times* was newspaper first and thunderer second, and Harriet was London's news. Like the others, the *Times* was charting her routes for the idolaters.

It was all proving too much for Professor Calvin Ellis Stowe. Human nature could not stand such worship as Harriet was receiving. The character of an angel could not come through it unscathed. He foresaw the wife of his bosom spoiled by it, rendered temperamental, conceited, dictatorial, short-tempered, a changed woman, their old domestic happiness lost. His spirits sank lower and lower. And he was going to be obliged to break his word to be back at Andover in time for the opening of the summer term in early June. He had cancelled his sailing on May 15th. What else could he do, with the Anti-Slavery Society, church organizations, and the Duchess of Sutherland arranging far into the future fêtes and soirées and other formal entertainments for Harriet, at which he would have to respond for her?

But even in his depression Calvin could not resist stunning the folks back in Andover with some of the incredible facts of the triumph—

I would rather be at Andover about my business than anywhere else in the world; & I am tired to death of the life I lead here. All that was anticipated by the newspapers, & ten times more, has befallen us. From the lowest peasant to the highest noble, wife is constantly beset, & I for her sake, so that we have not a moment's quiet. I have just refused to see three different persons, that I may get time to scribble this note.

At the Lord Mayor's, at Strafford House [sic], at Lord John Russell's, at the Duke of Argyle's, *we are the guests*,—& so at the Shaftesbury's, Carlile's, and other places that we knew of beforehand. Being at a dissenting minister's, in an unfashionable part of London, is no security. And the speeches that are constantly poured into poor wife's ears from all quarters, are enough to turn the strongest head. Lord Palmerston, the judges, the bishops, the literati, all speak the same language; and every distinguished man of every grade makes it a point to see her. J. P. Morley, Milman, Moncton Milnes, Tribler, Dickens have all called upon her with great apparent rapture; and old archbp. Whately seized her hand and said, "Now, I'll have this engraved on my tombstone." Even the archbp. of Canterbury has sent for us to Lambeth Palace; and this week and next are entirely occupied with visits of this kind. It [illegible word] & distresses me, for it is too mad.

The French papers received this morning say that the Paris reception will be altogether beyond the London, it will be *triumphal,* & all that. What shall a body do? I shall not go to Paris. I shall return to Andover, & I wish I were there now. Wife bears it all very well. She is gaining in health. She is meek, humble, pious, and loving, the same that she ever was. The Lord preserve her! Mr. Constable of Edinburgh yesterday offered her 10,000 dollars cash down to write a book for them, & half profits in all the sales besides.

If the Dutch beat the D———l, she beats the Dutch. But it makes me feel inexpressibly blue. The Lord keep our wits and save our souls!

Truly yours,
C. E. STOWE.

But wife was not being spoiled by it. Not even Archbishop Whately's extravagances could spoil her. The old archbishop tickled Harriet's sense of humour. He was like a character of her own West. "If he had been born in our latitude, in Kentucky or Wisconsin, the natives would have called him Whately and said he was a real steamboat on an argument." The archbishop was fond of puns "and odd turns of language." Perhaps there had been a twinkle in his eye when he spoke of his tombstone.

And it was no symptom of a turned head for Harriet to protest against the Egyptian plague of "portraits" of herself disfiguring the London shop-windows. She had as little vanity, perhaps, as any famous woman of her day; but her looks had always been something of a trial to her, and now she felt that she was at least entitled to what the Lord had granted her. But those English portraits—"I should think that the Sphinx in the London Museum might have sat for most of them." She was making a collection for Mrs. Howard, in Brooklyn. "There is a great variety of them," she wrote, "and they will be useful, like the Irishman's guideboard, which showed where the road did not go."

Harriet was learning something about women's looks in the sophisticated air of London society. In America women were old and withered at forty, when in England they would be just coming into full bloom. At forty-seven the Duchess of Sutherland was still a noted beauty. Harriet thought our superheated rooms might account for the difference, or the great quantities of hot biscuits and corn bread we ate, or, more likely, the necessity for an American woman to be everything in her house from confectioner, cook, and dining-room girl to hostess.

At any rate, in her adaptiveness she began to reflect in her own person the youthfulness of the patrician women surrounding her. Success was leaving its mark on her, physically. It was giving her a look of distinction, which she was never to lose. She thrived on the applause of London, she bloomed, she shed her years like magic. Even Calvin noticed it, though he thought it was recruited health. The London dressmakers were magicians, too, though, of course, a New England Puritan would not expose her neck and shoulders in an evening gown. Nevertheless, there could be fetching treatments of lace collars.

The sarcastic fear of the *Times* that deity in the flesh might be a dis-illusionment was without ground. Harriet's levée at Stafford House on Saturday afternoon was a private function yet one historically so important that Her Grace admitted representatives of the press. The *Daily News* reporter saw Mrs. Stowe then—"slim, sun-complexioned, active, intelligent, simply dressed, and perfectly self-possessed" as she was "petted and lionized by a whole bevy of duchesses and countesses who had been charmed by her marvellous book."

We can accept for our own this portrait of Harriet at the very pinnacle of her felicity and renown.

There had been news from home. An avalanche of advance orders, reaching a total of 58,000 copies, had held up the publication of the *Key to Uncle Tom's Cabin* for a few days. Northern reviewers had slipped their bridles in their praise for it, and Publisher Jewett could report a sale of 90,000 copies the first month. Another fortune in royalties would be awaiting Harriet on her return. And in England the *Key* attained at least a *succès d'estime*. Many speakers at the London Anniversaries referred to it in flattering terms, while the *Athenaeum* showed by quotations that "the nervous style, the scenic power, the pathos and the humour which made the fortune of the romance, are well preserved in these pages." The literary journal pronounced the *Key* "a most effective book."

Scurrilous pro-slavery editors in the States were railing at Harriet for having purchased a splendid "homestead" for herself at Andover with her Uncle Tom money, instead of devoting it to the cause of the slave, as consistency dictated. Her plumed knight, Henry Ward Beecher, stepped forward in his Star column to defend her. "No such disposition has been made of the avails of Uncle Tom's Cabin." To prepare the Stone Cabin the Seminary had merely borrowed the funds from Professor Stowe, who "can live in it while a professor at Andover, and, should he leave that post, can no more sell or control the disposition of it than of the Seminary chapel or the Seminary library."

And, Henry continued,

a word upon the pecuniary offerings to Mrs. Stowe, in England. It is well known to many that Mrs. Stowe has from the first desired to turn whatever influence this work might give her to the elevation of the African race. The plan which has been most in her thoughts has been a seminary in which persons of African descent may be thoroughly educated, not merely in literary and scientific courses but in practical arts by which they might secure and maintain a proper place in society. To the founding of such an institution she has determined to contribute much of her income, and the hope of securing greater interest for it was among the chief reasons for her tour. The generous contributions in money made to her in Great Britain are not understood by either party, but certainly not by Mrs. Stowe, to be for her own private and personal use, but to be employed for the education and elevation of the free colored people of the North.

While we are on this subject, let it be stated that the disposition of the "pecuniary offerings" remains a mystery. Harriet brought back from England almost $20,000 in gifts—the classic sum which Catharine Beecher always demanded for the endowment of a school—yet no academy or seminary for the coloured ever rose under Harriet's sponsorship, for all her good intentions. Nor did she ever render any account of her stewardship. At the end of her life she told the inquisitive Mrs. McCray, of Hartford, that she had used the British offerings "to educate several former slaves." But no available letter of hers nor any other record indicates the identity of a single person so educated. In contrast, after she had publicly befriended the Edmondson family, she continued to mention those protégés in her letters, even mentioning from abroad receipt of the news of the death of one of old Milly's children.

It seems reasonable to assume that Harriet, never a great head for accounts, soon mixed the British donations so hopelessly with her own funds that she lost track of them and let them slip through her fingers without knowing exactly where they went. During her successful years Harriet was noted for her generosity. No beggar or borrower could come to her with a plausible story and leave empty-handed. She was always ready to contribute handsomely to any visionary scheme for the benefit of every book she wrote—and she wrote many—was a "best-seller," she never became really a rich woman. Money got away from her almost as fast as she could earn it, and sometimes faster.

And Harriet might even have appropriated the British contributions to her own private use without too great a wrench to her conscience. Several of the purses had come to her without any stipulations whatever, and there can be no doubt that many of the contributors supposed they were giving their pennies to Mrs. Stowe personally. Morally she had every right to them. The total amount of the gifts was but a fraction of the royalties stolen from her by British publishers. Indeed, the London *Times* suggested that the ladies signing the *Affectionate and Christian Address* would have done better "to subscribe a neat purse of £20,000 or thereabouts and give it to the lady." Only, the *Times* mourned, "they had already spent their money in buying Uncle Toms."

There was a fellow-countryman of Harriet's in London that week in May—the Rev. Samuel Irenaeus Prime. It had been a trying winter for Mr. Prime. Conscious as he was of only rectitude in exposing the chicanery and callousness of Henry Ward Beecher and his sister, the whole affair had crashed down on his own head. As the New York *Observer's* mail grew heavy with the letters of irate readers cancelling their subscriptions, its editor found himself standing before a nation, branded as a man who would strike a lady. And the lady he had selected to strike—that nation's idol!

The *Observer's* influence dwindled, the *Independent's* as steadily swelled, but the militant Mr. Prime gave not an inch to *Uncle Tom* and the Beechers. By spring, however, he felt the need of a vacation. His health had become feeble. It was fairly easy for a clergyman in his position to secure a vacation in Europe, with expenses paid, by gaining appointment to one of the frocked delegations being sent to the London May Anniversaries. Mr. Prime looked about and found a vacancy on the delegation from the American Bible Society. He applied for the place and in due time received his credentials.

It is to be hoped that the voyage was healing to the shattered Mr. Prime, for he would need his strength to withstand a shock at the other end of it. With all England turning into a temple for the worship of Harriet Beecher Stowe, certain watchers on the ramparts noted the advent of the man whom Professor Stowe had been freely naming as the leader of the dark forces seeking to destroy the influence of *Uncle Tom's Cabin*. Perhaps the most

vocal of these sentries was the London *Morning Advertiser,* a newspaper
which then ranked almost with the *Times* in influence. When the good
ship *Devonshire* dropped anchor in London Pool, certain discreet friends
of Mr. Prime came out to meet him, bringing with them a copy of the
" '*Tiser,*" in which the church editor read this blast at himself:

> . . . How much our warning voice was needed is now proved by the
> fact that we may hourly expect to hear of the arrival on our shores of
> Rev. Samuel Prime, editor of the New York *Observer*—a paper which pro-
> fesses to be conducted in accordance with the principles of the most exalted
> piety. This man has been for years the most systematic and virulent of all
> the calumniators whom the Abolitionists of America have had to encounter.
> Had the venom of this pro-slavery divine taken effect, *Uncle Tom* would
> have fallen stillborn from the press, and Mrs. Stowe herself would have
> sunk under the load of calumny which her Rev. traducer heaped upon her
> head. . . .
>
> With a knowledge of the facts which our columns have been, and are this
> day again, the means of communicating to the British public respecting this
> pro-slavery Transatlantic divine, will the committee of the British & Foreign
> Bible Society persist in assigning Rev. Mr. Prime a part in the proceedings
> of Wednesday? We hope not. We cannot believe they will. . . .
>
> But it will not suffice that this Rev. Mr. Prime, the vehement advocate
> of slavery and the systematic slanderer of Mrs. Stowe and of all who, like
> that lady, seek to put down the gigantic evil, be excluded from the platforms
> of our religious meetings. He must be equally excluded from the evangelical
> pulpits of England. Any minister, no matter to what denomination he be-
> longs and however high may be his reputation for piety and devotedness in
> his Master's service, who opens his pulpit to a man who in his capacity of a
> preacher of the Gospel has for years been doing his best to uphold all the
> enormities of American slavery—will thereby render himself a partaker of
> the sins of this Transatlantic divine, so far as the question of slavery is
> concerned.

What was to be done? The hotter, or at least warmer, heads on Mr.
Prime's American welcoming committee were for calling a public meeting
to protest against this outrage on free speech and this insult to the United
States, but saner counsel prevailed. Precisely what happened is uncertain.
The correspondent of the anti-Tom *Christian Intelligencer* declared that
Mr. P. was stabbed in the back and that the British Bible Society rejected
his commission. The correspondent of the pro-Tom *Congregationalist*
crowed that Mr. Prime "backed out" and advised the American Bible
Society to inquire why he neglected his mission. Mr. Prime's own *Observer*

said he sent in his credentials only to have his letter ignored. News came to his ears, however, that "a body of men was organized to drive him from the platform, if he should appear." Mr. Prime was really anxious to meet the challenge, but "it was greatly to be regretted that his feeble health made it necessary for him to decline the public contest."

At any rate, he did not show up at the annual meeting of the British & Foreign Bible Society on Wednesday, May 4, in Exeter Hall, headquarters for most of the philanthropic and reform societies of England. (In an unguarded moment Macaulay had once spoken of "the bray of Exeter Hall," and the zealots had never forgiven him, though the historian's heart was with most of their reforms.) Nevertheless, the American delegation was complete. With happy inspiration, the Committee conferred on the 1853 anniversary a distinction no previous convention had known by seating Professor and Mrs. Stowe in the stead of the defaulting Mr. Prime.

Harriet went to Exeter Hall with Mrs. Binney. She arrived just as the Chairman, Lord Shaftesbury, was concluding his inaugural address. As she entered the hall and took her place on the platform for her first public appearance in London, the vast audience rose and remained standing until she seated herself, an honour ordinarily reserved for the Queen alone. When Rev. Mr. Binney proclaimed her a prophetess, he brought on Bedlam. Men jumped to their feet with shouts, women wiped the tears from their eyes, and the clapping of hands and stamping of feet rocked the building. On the platform the little object of such adoration remained apparently unmoved—smug, inscrutable, sphinxlike, acknowledging the acclamations with a faint bow, yet inwardly lapping it up as a kitten laps cream and in her heart passing all the praise on to her Maker, whose vicaress she knew she was. While somewhere in the outer darkness of London chafed her enemy, Irenaeus Prime, gnashing his teeth. Poetic justice had been done.

In writing to her sister Catharine about her party, or levée, in Stafford House, Harriet described that "most splendid of English palaces" even down to its carpets. Each room had its own colour-scheme, she discovered, though the predominating note was blue. The carpets helped carry this out. The colour-ground of each was "bedropped" with such fine figures as "to produce a mass of color of a certain tone, and not to distract the eye with a complicated pattern." This was a new idea to a New England village housewife of the 1850's.

A few minutes before eleven Harriet and Calvin arrived under the *porte cochère* of a mansion "not very showy in appearance." Two footmen in full Highland costume received them. Harriet then had only a confused idea of being passed from room to room by "an innumerable multitude of servants in livery, with powdered hair." At each entry the Stowes' names were called out, yet what astonished Harriet was that all these rooms and halls and passages were deserted. Nevertheless, the bewigged flunkies announced their names in all of them, as they did in the large drawing-room that proved to be their destination.

This room, too, was uninhabited, and the fact gave Harriet a chance to inspect an apartment which, she said, more perfectly suited her eye and taste than any she had ever seen before. It was not so much any particular splendour of furniture or dazzling display of upholstery as it was the room's "artistic, poetic air, resulting from the arrangement of colors and the disposition of the works of *virtu*." It was composed like a painter's picture. The Stone Cabin, which everyone found so charming, was going to feel the influence of this appraisal. "The great fault in many splendid rooms," Harriet told Catharine, "is that they are arranged without any eye to unity of impression."

The walls of this drawing-room were not papered but "covered with green damask, laid on flat, and confined in its place by narrow gilt bands." The furniture was all white and gold and upholstered in the same green damask. There was the green carpet of inconspicuous pattern, and in each window was a circular, standing basket, each with a growing bank of pale yellow primroses. Through the lace curtains Harriet could see a clipped lawn, on the borders of which were white lilac trees, just coming into bloom. The room was commanded by a large portrait, by Landseer, of the Duchess's children, and there was another Landseer portrait of Her Grace's oldest son, the Marquis of Stafford, in Highland dress at seventeen.

Then Her Grace appeared to welcome the Stowes, and Harriet thought her more beautiful by daylight than in the evening. She wore a white muslin dress with a drab velvet basque slashed with satin of the same colour. A gold and diamond net confined her hair in the back.

The Duke of Sutherland entered, and Harriet met him for the first time—"a tall, slender man, with rather a thin face, light brown hair, and a mild blue eye, with an air of gentleness and dignity. The delicacy of his health prevents him from moving in general society, or entering into public life." Harriet did not name his infirmity, but it was an almost total deafness.

The Duchess took Harriet to a little private boudoir, where the American visitor, rather daunted by the breeches and powder of the men-servants, confessed her ignorance of this sort of life and begged for any instructions she might need. Her Grace was all kindness and sympathy. She told Harriet she had only to be her own natural self and all would go well. A few friends were coming to lunch, some others would call afterwards, and Lord Shaftesbury would read a short address, which would require no answer.

Thus reassured, Harriet went out to meet the party in her honour. First to arrive were the various members of the family, reinforced now by the Marquis and Marchioness of Stafford, whom Harriet was meeting for the first time. Then the footman announced Lord and Lady Shaftesbury and Lord and Lady Palmerston, beautiful Lady Shaftesbury's parents. The Marquis of Lansdowne came next, and Harriet soon made a particular friend of him. He was a man of "about the middle height, with gray hair, blue eyes, and a mild, quiet dignity of manner." This wealthy nobleman had long been an Abolitionist.

Others were announced, and Harriet remembered Lord John Russell, Mr. Gladstone (then Chancellor of the Exchequer), and Lord Grenville, who Harriet thought resembled Longfellow. The butler spoke at the doors, and the Duke of Sutherland gave Harriet his arm to lead the party to the great dining hall. The repast to which they sat down, Harriet told Catharine, was called *lunch,* and she underscored the word. Lunch seemed to her to be "a less elaborate and ceremonious dinner. Everything is placed on the table at once, and ladies sit down without removing their bonnets." Children were admitted to the table, even when there was company. "It generally takes place in the middle of the day," wrote Harriet.

She found the table beautifully laid, the most striking adornment being two magnificent crystal vases filled with hothouse flowers and supported by wrought silver standards. Life-size silver doves perched on the edges of the vases, nestling among the flowers. On the wall opposite Harriet hung the Sir Thomas Lawrence portrait of the Duchess, with which American reproductions had made her familiar. She looked about the table and observed how youthful the men of England looked, too. Men were there, of sixty and seventy, whom she would have pronounced at first glance to be fifty. Why did Americans wear out so soon?

After lunch they ascended to the picture gallery by the most magnificent hall and staircase in Europe. Unable to converse with her tall, deaf partner, Harriet took in everything *en route*—the Rinaldi Sibyl, the Veronese frescos. She noted to Catharine that the gallery was forty feet wide and a hundred long. It was lighted by a coloured-glass dome. At night a ring of gaslights in the dome threw down a brilliant illumination "without the usual heat." Harriet noted two Murillos made familiar to her by the prints.

People began dropping in, until there were so many presentations she could not remember half of them. The vast gallery was packed when Lord Shaftesbury called for silence and read an address of welcome to Mrs. Stowe in behalf of the ladies of England. The reading took only a minute, after which the meeting became informal. Harriet greeted as many of the guests as she could. She had "a strange, mythological feeling" when talking with the legendary Lord Palmerston. A Quaker lady hung on her arm an old reticule in which had been carried the first anti-slavery tracts distributed in England. The Duchess of Sutherland informally presented to her a massive, gold slave-chain for a bracelet, on two of the ten links of which were engraved the dates of Britain's outlawing of the slave trade and of the emancipation of slaves in her colonies, and on a third the inscription: "We trust it is a memorial of a chain that is soon to be broken." A Cornish sculptor of cameos named Burnard gave Harriet a head of Wilberforce he had cut from the Westminster Abbey statue and begged from her the privilege of a sitting. She dubiously consented. Finally she and Her Grace slipped away to pay a short call on Lady Constance Grosvenor and meet her son, the richest young man in England, the future Marquis of Westminster. The future Marquis was not quite a fortnight old.

Thus ended Harriet's first week in London and the most glorious day in her almost forty-two years of life. She was within six weeks of her birthday. But she was far from appropriating all this homage to herself as a personal honour, choosing to regard it instead as the expression of the sympathy of the women of England for the plight of the slave.

The accounts of the diversions, as recited by Harriet in her letters, scarcely convey the rising roar of the mob, which by the end of her second week in London had reached the pitch of national dementia. So wrote the correspondent of the *Observer*. What had begun as an innocent, if foolish, fuss made by a people over an American lady who had made them laugh and cry, had ended as a Roman holiday, with Uncle Sam, the victim, being cudgelled over the slim shoulders of his gifted niece. Four decades of British envy and resentment of the United States rushed for the inviting outlet afforded by the rabble-rousing novel and the presence of its maker.

It was an orgy of national self-righteousness, a pharisaical debauch with few if any parallels in the history of nations. The daily "anniversary" in

Exeter Hall, no matter for what philanthropic purpose its society was organized, turned into a season of praise for *Uncle Tom's Cabin* and Mrs. Stowe and denunciation of her country for its sin. American slavery was the "awful crime" of the age. Its "inherent wickedness," "its evil per se," "the duty of immediate and unconditional emancipation," were phrases falling from the orators' lips. Extremists were urging English Christians to break off all relations with a country whose laws permitted Uncle Tom to be beaten to death and Cassy to be sold into a life worse than death.

The Yankee-baiting at length proved too much for the stomach of that old Natick boy, Calvin Ellis Stowe. After all, it was one thing to emancipate by act of Parliament a few thousand slaves in some distant and unrepresented West Indian colonies. It was quite another thing for a nation to break up a three-billion-dollar institution on which half its economic fabric was based. The Andover professor was finding it more and more "painful" to rise in whatever eleemosynary dock the evening afforded and confess his country's crimes. And at the very peak of the English fury for American reform, in the anniversary meeting of the British and Foreign Anti-Slavery Society, his patience broke, and Calvin Stowe, never noted for his tact, for once played a hero's part.

The Anti-Slavery anniversary was anticipated as the great public event of Mrs. Stowe's visit—the one meeting she was bound to attend. Never since the days of Clarkson and Wilberforce had there been such a demand for tickets to that annual meeting. Twenty-four hours in advance, people were forming queues at Exeter Hall. There seems to have been no police regulation of public assemblies in the London of 1853. On Monday evening (May 16) Exeter was shamefully overcrowded, four thousand persons having managed to squeeze themselves into the Hall to see their idol.

(There were discordant voices, however. Thackeray, who had seen both sides, was saying he would rather be a slave in America than a labourer in England, and a joke was running through the clubs, where the ribald were calling Stafford House "Aunt Harriet's Cabin.")

Harriet arrived at Exeter Hall after the meeting had begun. This time she was attended by the Duchess of Sutherland, Calvin having gone on ahead to sit on the platform. When Harriet stepped down into her private gallery, the almost palpable force of the applause that greeted her entrance shook her as a reed. There was a note of fierceness in it that made her tremble. She sat down, but the ovation continued. The great Duchess thereupon tenderly assisted the frail vessel of God's will to her feet and "supported" her while the four thousand shouted three immense huzzas.

As Harriet surveyed an ocean of faces billowing to the very ceilings of the auditorium, a woman fainted on the main floor, and a constable tried to force his way through to her. For just a moment it looked as if there might be an appalling catastrophe. "There were hoarse surgings and swellings of the mighty mass, who were so closely packed that they moved together like waves. Some began to rise in their seats, and some cried, 'Order! Order!'" The Duchess of Sutherland remarked, "I am afraid we are going to have one of our genuine Exeter Hall *'brays'*." Harriet admitted "feeling a good deal fluttered" inwardly, but the lady who could outface death during interminable cholera weeks in Cincinnati was equally thoroughbred. She sat composedly until the brief disturbance subsided.

The speeches that evening were the most painful Harriet, as an American, had ever heard, she told her father. The *Observer's* correspondent called them "nothing but downright, fanatical, unreasoning, blind, stupid, insane, unmitigated vituperation." When Lord Shaftesbury quoted from President Pierce's recent inaugural address the new Administration's pledge to enforce the Fugitive Slave Law, there was a storm of hisses and cries of "Shame! Shame!"

✓Perhaps it was this affront to his old classmate, Franklin Pierce, that made Calvin throw caution to the winds in his Response. Standing for once where his politic wife could not step on his toes, he informed four thousand auditors that England herself was responsible for American slavery, since England consumed four-fifths of the American slave-grown cotton. Had England insisted on free-grown cotton, American slavery would have fallen long ago. "Are you willing to sacrifice one penny of your own profits for the sake of doing away with this cursed business?" Calvin thundered. He had heard much talk about the conscience of the cotton-growers, but "has the cotton-consumer no conscience?" And it took courage to fling at such an audience the legal axiom—"The receiver is as guilty as the thief."✓

In retrospect Calvin wrote that his remarks "were heard by some with surprise and by others with extreme displeasure." One may well imagine so, though the press accounts of the meeting were reserved in statement. But the *Times* dropped its amused pose to mutter editorially that the Rev. professor's remarks were impractical; and the *Morning Advertiser,* which had virtually adopted the Stowes, turned savagely on Calvin, denouncing his speech as "an insult to the head and heart of the country, an outrage on Christianity itself, and especially unpardonable in a man placed in Prof. Stowe's circumstances." The *Observer's* London man declared that the Exeter Hall fanatics would throw the professor overboard, were he not the husband of Harriet Beecher Stowe. And Harriet, we can imagine, was patting the thick shoulders of her doughty spouse.

The Anti-Slavery Society had determined to give Mrs. Stowe a public soirée, and the earliest convenient day both sides could agree on was May 25. It made an interval of nine days, which Harriet filled with such entertainments and employments as her visit afforded. She attended no more "anniversaries," but Calvin spoke at one or two of them.

Assembled and alone for the first time since arriving in London, the Deputation went on a rollicking excursion to Windsor Castle. Calvin, having relieved his conscience at the Anti-Slavery meeting, was feeling his oats. Harriet was afraid he might burst out into madrigals. They dined merrily at the White Hart, and in the private apartments of the Castle (the Royal Family being away) they inspected a "baby's wicker wagon, with neat curtains and cushions of green merino," which Harriet pronounced "not royal, only maternal."

However, the day ended in a tiff. Calvin had a speaking engagement in town and kept prodding Harriet to leave. Finally she told him crossly to go on home, if he wanted to; she herself intended to find Gray's country churchyard, while she was in its vicinity. The indignant professor stumped back to the cars alone, but Harriet went on and found her churchyard, leaned on its wall, and recited the whole of the *Elegy*. That evening she learned that she had wept over the mute Miltons of the wrong cemetery. She should have gone to Stoke Pogis.

Harriet made an over-night visit to Playford Hall, where old Mrs. Clarkson, widow of the English emancipator, still lived. It was the oldest fortified house in England and "the only one that has water in the moat." Harriet was implicitly assuming the rôle of leader of the American Abolitionist movement, making this pious pilgrimage as a duty.

The venerable Archbishop of Canterbury had Harriet and Calvin to lunch at Lambeth Palace, where our indefatigable sight-seer dragged the entire company to the top of the Lollard's Tower. On the battlements the panting prelate admitted that it was the second time in his life he had been there.

Harriet sat to the crayonist Richmond for her portrait. Who was Richmond? "Not to know him," she wrote, "argues yourself unknown." In the West End, of course. The likeness he turned out was an effeminate chromo, but Harriet always loved it, fondly believing the talkative Richmond's assurance that it was the way she really appeared to the clairvoyant eyes of the artist.

At the Argyles' dinner she had a long talk with Mr. Gladstone, who looked remarkably young for one of such fame—"tall, with dark hair and eyes, a thoughtful, serious cast of countenance." At Lord John Russell's the company consisted almost exclusively of earls, baronets, and their consorts. The talk turned on fox-hunting, and Harriet learned that with these aristocrats shooting a fox was as bad as shooting a man. She listened with her usual sphinxlike gravity but was wickedly pondering the thought of the sensation she might cause if she told this noble circle about an old Indiana hunter she had known who retired to his bunk each night with his candle burning, then from the comfort of his bed shot out the light with his rifle. Richard Cobden gave the visitors a breakfast, and Harriet told the free-trade advocate of a Yankee farmer who was opposed to any tariff, because "they'd be sure to run the durn thing right through my farm." She also mentioned the Pennsylvania Dutchmen who still went to the November polls every fourth year in the firm conviction that they were upholding Ginral Jackson's administration.

From that breakfast Harriet went to Stafford House, where the Duchess was fulfilling her promise to introduce Miss Greenfield. Almost everybody who was anybody in English society attended that concert, except a great lady who lived across the park. The newspapers, however, mentioned Mrs. Stowe first, duly noting that the Black Swan's gown of black moiré antique trimmed with bugles was the gift of the distinguished authoress. To which Harriet added the details that the dress was "made high in the neck, with white-lace, falling sleeves." The Prussian Ambassador, Chevalier Bunsen, who monopolized Harriet that afternoon, was much struck by Miss Greenfield's double voice. And that evening, though tired, Harriet went with Charles to Exeter Hall to hear the London Sacred Harmonic Society sing Haydn's *Creation*. As she stepped into the gallery reserved for her, she was delighted to find there a beautifully bound copy of the score, inscribed to her.

At a luncheon given her by a "Miss R." in Oxford Terrace, Harriet again had that "strange, mythological feeling" when she met the silvery, ethereal Lady Byron, the lovely lady who had actually been the wife of Harriet's adolescent love—that wicked, romantic figure she could never shake from her literary imagination. Of all the friendships Harriet made in the British Isles, she valued this one most.

The visit culminated officially in Harriet's anti-slavery soirée in the famous social rendezvous known as Almack's, but which Londoners of late had been calling Willis's Rooms. The sale of tickets brought in nearly $1,000 in our equivalent, but the price of admission must have been low, for the place was crowded. Harriet stood at the head of the receiving line and met everybody. The Society through Joseph Sturge, its president, presented to Harriet an Address engrossed on vellum. Calvin responded.

Next day Calvin sailed for America. Harriet kissed him good-bye at the "station house" and departed immediately with her friend, the Duchess of Sutherland, to visit the House of Parliament, where she received unusual courtesies. A day or so later the Committee of the Anti-Slavery Society was approving a Minute—

> 827. Mr. Sturge stated, with reference to the Tribute to Mrs. Stowe for Anti-Slavery purposes, that the Committee had resolved to raise £2,000, if possible, and proposed making a more extensive appeal. The sum at present in hand was rather above £1,500.

This gift was double the amount of the National Scottish Offering. "It is humiliating," commented the Observer's man, "to every patriot here that any of our countrymen, and especially of our countrywomen, can thus receive alms at the hands of those who hate America and love to honor her who has made her country a byword in the world's mouth."

But it was not all pleasure during those final days in London. In her baggage Harriet had brought to England a piece of dress-goods—her "brown Chinese silk"—which she had bought in Boston but which she had been too busy to have made up before her departure from the United States. In London she inquired of her aristocratic friends for a dressmaker, and soon there appeared at Rose Cottage a deft, ingratiating lady who took Harriet's measurements and departed with the silk, perhaps sniffing a little to herself.

If there was one theme which could raise liberal British blood to the temperature inspired by slavery in America, it was the plight of the poor seamstresses in London. Within ten years Thomas Hood had stirred England with his Song of The Shirt in Punch.

O God! that bread should be so dear,
And flesh and blood so cheap!

What price flesh and blood in 1853? English needlewomen might starve in their hovels, but across the ocean likely black boys were bringing $1,500 on the New Orleans market. The benevolent Lord Shaftesbury had tried to do something for the seamstresses of the West End. He had secured the agreement of some of the principal dressmaking and millinery houses to limit the working day ("except rarely") to twelve hours, not to keep children working all night—again "except rarely"—and to abrogate labour on the Lord's day entirely. This was a considerable improvement upon conditions existing elsewhere in the metropolis.

While it was still growling over Professor Stowe's recriminations, the London *Times* heard something about the career of Harriet's brown Chinese silk, and for once that conservative journal stooped to what a later generation was to call muckraking. One morning it gave prominence to a letter purporting to be from an apprentice needlewoman but which Harriet suspected was of office composition. The writer informed the British public that Mrs. Stowe, whose heart beat with such sympathy for the oppressed, was having her dressmaking done in the vilest sweatshop of London, an establishment which let out its work to contractors, who worked their white slaves sixteen hours a day, six days a week, for pitiful wages. And the *Times* added its editorial plea to "the great philanthropist of her age" to "see if during her sojourn in England she can not extend a helping hand to her poor white sisters, who assuredly are in a more evil case than nine-tenths of the slave population in the Southern States of North America."

Harriet was much annoyed by this attack. That same evening she reproached Lord Shaftesbury, who had been telling her about his reforms.

"My dear lady," he replied, "this was not in one of my houses. I preside, you know, over the West End."

Harriet's first impulse was to keep silent, as she had under the *Observer's* attack, but the *Times's* exposé brought her a flood of letters, most of them from her followers, urging her to deny the accusation or explain it, saying that they were sure she must have meant well. Some cautioned her to be very careful where she sent her dressmaking in London.

Thus she was driven to reply to the *Times,* but her explanation was heart-warming to those who knew American village life. She had, of course, in her "sacred simplicity," been perfectly innocent in the whole transaction. Her previous experience with commercial dressmaking had been in Brunswick, "where the only dressmaker of our circle was an intelligent, refined, well-educated woman who was considered the equal of us all, and whose spring and fall ministrations to our wardrobe were regarded a double pleasure—a friendly visit as well as a domestic assistance. . . . I verily never thought but that the nice, pleasant person who came to measure me for my silk, was going to take it home and make it herself. It never occurred to me that she was the head of an establishment."

As for the *Times's* trumpet-call for her to take up the conflict for the needlewomen, Harriet could trade sarcasm for sarcasm. She would not think of doing such a thing, when that cause was evidently already in such able custody. "If the plantation hands had such a good friend as the *Times,* and if every overworked female cotton-picker could write as clever letters as this dressmaker's apprentice, and get them published in as influential papers, and excite as general a sensation by them as this seems to have done, I think I should feel that there was no need of my interfering in a work so much better done."

Calvin had left her the wise counsel to depart for the Continent as soon as possible. There is no guest who wears out a welcome so quickly as an official one, yet Harriet took nine more days to say her adieus.

She attended the Black Swan's public concert, under the ægis of Sir George Smart. "She comes out under the patronage of all the great names," Harriet wrote Calvin. All except that of the lady of Buckingham Palace. Finally, at a lunch given by the Milmans in St. Paul's deanery, Harriet met Thackeray. Mrs. Gaskell was also a guest. In spite of the scornful things he had been saying, Thackeray was courteous to Harriet and complimentary to her country, and she had a pleasant chat with him.

Her leaving was that of any obscure traveller, for she had said her farewells and withheld from the press the hour of her departure from London. On Saturday morning, June 4, she bade good-bye to the Binneys at Rose Cottage and drove with her party to "the great southwestern station house." There was no official delegation this time to help her entrain, nor even the usual crowd of the curious.

"Paris?" inquired an official voice at her cab's window.

"Paris—by Folkestone and Boulogne."

They were in their compartment, the guard locked the door. The wheels began to turn.

There had been an omission. The British public had idolized Harriet, the newspapers had printed columns about her, the nobility had knelt at her feet, cabinet ministers had hung on her words, prelates had breathed flatteries into her ears, the great in art and literature and philanthropy had vied to do her honour, but the British Queen had not received her.

There had been another omission, only less glaring. A past Prime Minister of Great Britain and two future ones had hobnobbed with Harriet during her visit, but the actual Prime Minister, Lord Aberdeen, had not received her—not even the day she visited the House of Lords in company with Aberdeen's Scottish neighbour, the Duchess of Sutherland.

That Harriet felt the royal and official snubs is indicated by the care she took to exclude any reference to them from her writings and, at the end of her life, from her son's biography of herself. Yet a hint crept into her final letter to Calvin from London. She was left at loose ends one afternoon. The Queen, having returned to town, gave a "drawing room," and all of Harriet's noble hostesses were in attendance. Mrs. Milman asked her if she had not had a curiosity to go, too.

"I confessed I had not. Merely to see public people in public places, in the way of parade and ceremony, was never interesting to me."

Strange words for one whose whole gorgeous month had been little but parade and ceremony—for one, too, who in no distant future would be revelling in the pageantry of the Vatican! Must we guess at the contention going on in the Palace beneath all the cheers and speeches and excitement over Mrs. Stowe? The Duchess of Sutherland was a close and valued friend of Queen Victoria, and we may take it for granted that she exerted every pressure to secure a royal audience for the famous visitor.

But there was something that weighed more heavily than Her Grace's pleading with the young Queen-Empress—Great Britain's foreign policy. For a bothered Administration in Washington it was bad enough to have the British aristocracy fawning on the author of *Uncle Tom's Cabin*. Garrison was rejoicing that Mrs. Stowe was making Abolition fashionable in the United States. Should there be any official recognition of her, the American public would take it as the British Government's endorsement of the Abolition movement in the United States.

No doubt the retiring American Minister to the Court of St. James, Mr. Ingersoll, dropped some such suggestion as this in the Foreign Office, whereupon Her Majesty's Government adopted a policy toward the embarrassing visitor.

However, we do not need to guess or infer. In August the new American Minister, James Buchanan, arrived in London to take up his duties. Soon he was writing privately to the Secretary of State, William Learned Marcy, that he was going out in society as a policy, since from the social gossip he could obtain information procurable from no other source. To a private letter to Secretary Marcy, dated 11th November, 1853, Minister Buchanan added this postscript:

> I have learned from a high titled lady that the Queen had absolutely refused to see Mrs. Stowe either at the Palace or the Duchess of Sutherland's; and that she had refused to attend the concert given at the latter place by the Black Swan, lest she might meet Mrs. Stowe there. My informant says, she remarked very sensibly that American Slavery was a question with which Great Britain had nothing to do.

Three years earlier an ignorant station-master in Pennsylvania was evicting Harriet from his tobacco-stained depot in the belief that she was a poor immigrant woman. Now chancelleries worried about her, diplomats intrigued, and governments acted to stem her influence upon the world. It was the high point in the most extraordinary success-story in our literary annals.

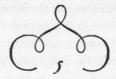

Harriet as Tourist

MRS. STOWE'S experiences on the Continent were not unlike those of any other tourist in the 1850's. The triumphal reception promised by the Parisian newspapers did not materialize. Her hostess, Mrs. Chapman, protected Harriet in her wish for obscurity; and she had been in Paris ten days when her brother Charles could still refer in his diary to "the few who know of her presence."

Maria Weston Chapman was a wealthy Boston woman who had taken up the cause of Abolition in its early days and had attained an influence in the American Anti-Slavery Society second only to that of Garrison. In 1853 she was living in Paris for the sake of her children's education, occupying the ground floor of the *hôtel* of the Marquis de Brige in the rue de Verneuil, Faubourg St.-Germain. Here Harriet, tired from her day's travel from London, sank down on a sofa in a cool, shadowy room, watched the play of leaves and flowers in the little garden on which her window opened, and sighed, "At last I have come into dreamland!"

The Louvre was within walking distance and attracted her first. While she had visited the Academy, the National Gallery, and other collections of paintings in London, Harriet felt that in Paris her time for "examining art" had really come. "Think of it! to one who has starved all a life, in vain imaginings of what art might be, to know that you are within a stone's throw of a museum full of its miracles, Greek, Assyrian, Egyptian, Roman sculptors and modern painting, all there!"

Among the painters she admired "great, joyous, full-souled, all-powerful" Rubens most and, though prejudiced against Medicis, thought that his allegorical treatment of the life of Marie de' Medici made him the Shakespeare of painting. But the single object she liked most in the Louvre was a head and armless torso then so little known in the United States that Harriet in her travel-book, *Sunny Memories,* needed to describe it as "a mutilated

387

statue which they call the Venus de Milon." This sculpture, she thought, cast even the Venus de Medici into the shadows. Though experts were then attributing the Venus de Milo to the period of Phidias, Harriet told her awed following, "I go a little further and ascribe her to Phidias himself."

Early in the visit she made the acquaintance of M. and Mme. Belloc, grandparents of the modern English writers, Hilaire Belloc and Marie Belloc-Lowndes. M. Belloc was a painter and Director of the Imperial School of Design. Mme. Belloc had made the best French translation of *Uncle Tom's Cabin.* M. Belloc begged the privilege of painting Harriet's portrait, and she sat many hours for him in his studio.

One day at the Bellocs' she met the celebrated French publisher Charpentier, who had issued Mme. Belloc's translation of *Uncle Tom.* He said he had considered a melodramatic American novel rather beneath the dignity of his conservative house, until he came upon Alfred de Musset, "the first intelligence of the age," reading it.

"What! you, too?" cried M. Charpentier.

"Say nothing against this book," replied the poet. "There is nothing like it. This leaves us all behind—all, all, leagues behind!"

The British and American ladies residing in Paris were, many of them, holding salons once a week in their drawing rooms. To Mrs. Chapman's salon came the ancient Count M., who told Harriet he had attended Judge Tapping Reeve's law school in his youth and considered her native Litchfield to have had the most charming society in the world. At Mrs. Putnam's salon Harriet met "Peter Parley," a fellow Connecticut Yankee just ending his service as United States Consul in Paris. At Lady Elgin's everybody was talking about spirit-rappings, as they had been also in London society. The theme was no novelty to the wife of vision-seeing Calvin Stowe. Harriet was growing used to hearing herself called Madame Besshare.

She plunged with Mrs. Chapman into shopping, "rummaging" the Palais Royal. She had indeed now attained a "suit of satin." At the Paris *octroi* Charles noted that the customs officer thumbed through "the fine silk and lace dresses" in his sister's trunk. Now under Mrs. Chapman's guidance Harriet went for a gown to the famous Mme. Roger, the Lanvin of her day. The legend was that Mme. Roger had once turned a duchess out of her *salons* because the haughty *cliente* failed to return the bow of M. Roger, the *couturière's* husband.

Sarah Beecher and her brother and son went on to tour Italy but Harriet and Charles remained to revel in Paris. Charles, after his years with the

Creoles of New Orleans, considered himself a good deal of a Frenchman. Harriet had a book knowledge of French but not yet the ear for it, and Charles did the interpreting. He reported that Harriet took to French cookery "like a duck to water." The brother and sister climbed the Arc de Triomphe, drove in the Bois evenings, visited the dubious entertainment of the Jardin Mabille in the Champs Elysées, where there were gaslights in the trees. There were many subsequent visits to the Louvre and to the Luxembourg gallery. Once Harriet and Charles hired a *calèche* and toured the circuit of the *grands boulevards*. Their carriage was halted by the state passage of Louis Napoleon, whose recent *coup d'état* had ended the Second Republic and made himself Emperor. The American pair saw him as "cold, stiff, stately, and homely" and noted that there were no cheers, no *vive l'Empereur!*

After eighteen days in this dreamland, they were off one morning (June 22) for Switzerland, going first by train to Chalons-sur-Saône, where they remained over night in the Hotel du Parc on the *quai*, occupying chambers with brick floors. Next morning they boarded a small steamboat and, with their Bradshaw's Continental Guide open, sailed down the Saône and Rhône to Lyons, where they put up at the Hotel de l'Univers. After a day here they boarded the diligence, which they had always supposed to be a creaking vehicle of about the comfort and speed of a prairie covered-wagon. To their surprise they found themselves bowling swiftly along macadam roads, drawn by four galloping horses, and by six when the road climbed.

"*I* call this travelling!" cried Charles.

So did Harriet. They found the passengers divided among five compartments, according to class. The American pair "set up housekeeping" in the first-class berline, right behind the first-class cubicle called the coupé. For the provident there was the omnibus compartment, in the rear. On the roof, behind the driver, was the banquette, and behind that the baggage-top, where, presumably, any deck passengers might ride. Frequent changes kept the horses always fresh, and their speed was such that they reached Geneva that evening, where their hosts, M. and Mme. Fazy, met them at the Messagerie. M. Fazy was owner and editor of the *Revue de Genève* and the leader of the Radical Party in Switzerland.

They could not have had better hosts. The Fazy residence was one of the largest and finest mansions in Geneva. The Fazys took them everywhere and introduced them to everybody. Here they remained for three delicious weeks, with one week taken out for an expedition to Mont Blanc and the

St. Bernard pass. On July 4 the rest of Harriet's party came up from Italy, and the Fazys took them in. Then Mrs. Chapman and two of her daughters arrived from Paris, and the Fazys had room for them, too.

One excursion out of Geneva took them to the village of St. Cergue, in the Jura range of mountains. There, while they took tea at the inn, the villagers discovered Harriet's identity and gathered round her. All had read *Uncle Tom,* and one mountain woman besought her, "Oh, madame, do write another! Remember, our winter nights here are very long." On the way down the great panorama of Mont Blanc, surrounded by a wilderness of snowy heights, was in full view to the south, across the lake—bathed in the carmine rays of the setting sun. It reminded Harriet of the Celestial City, with Mont Blanc its citadel, and she and Charles sang Charles's hymn, *New Jerusalem,* for the enjoyment of M. and Mme. Fazy and, no doubt, to the astonishment of the coachman.

One of the warmer pleasures of Harriet's new life came to her in Geneva, where her "Uncle Tom" money enabled her to buy for her beloved brother Charles, the musician, an Amati violin. Thenceforth with Charles it was not "my violin" or "my fiddle," but "my Amati."

On the trip to Chamonix and Mont Blanc Harriet and Sarah Beecher occupied the coupé in the diligence. In this narrow compartment Harriet thought she and her sister-in-law were like "the luckless fowls I have sometimes seen riding to the Cincinnati market in coupés of about equal convenience." The altitude gave the two women violent headaches, but it was worth it when they reached the niveous welter of heights at Mont Blanc, Harriet rejoicing in her familiarity with the Scriptures. Only "the great ground-swell of the prophets" could do justice to the Alps. "The everlasting mountains were scattered; the perpetual hills did bow."

Of course, they climbed to the Mer de Glace, Harriet, as many another traveller has since, waxing humorous over the stubbornness of the donkeys, which she always called mules. Hers was named Rousse, and "Rousse was gifted with one of those long India-rubber necks that can stretch out indefinitely, so that the utmost pulling and jerking only took his head along a little farther but left his heels planted exactly where they were before." She drew a picture of herself aboard the balky Rousse. The trails were so dizzy everybody's nerves were a little unsteady, though, Harriet added illuminatingly, "not by any means as much as on board a rail car at home."

From Chamonix they rode by *calèche* and "those mules" to Martigny, Switzerland, over a frightful road through the pass of the Tête Noir. In the scariest places William Buckingham and Charles would dismount and amuse themselves by "rolling avalanches" down the scoured escarpments. From Martigny they travelled up to the Great St. Bernard pass, the last hour over awful heights deep under snow which the July sun had so softened that the donkeys broke through. Harriet said the famous monastery smelled "of antiquity and dogs." For Calvin's benefit she enquired particularly about the St. Bernard dogs and drew a picture of one. She thought they must have some Newfoundland blood. On the way back she noted the universal filth, the universal affliction of goitre, and the many large-headed idiot children, locally called *crétins*.

From Martigny they travelled by carriage down the upper Rhône to Villeneuve, at the head of Lake Geneva. Chillon Castle was right outside Harriet's window. Byron memories again. A day here, and they returned to Geneva, where Harriet heard the interesting news that Sardinia (now Savoy) had adopted *Uncle Tom's Cabin* as the English reader in its schools. But she was growing homesick and wrote Calvin that she "had found no land, however beautiful, that can compare with home—Andover Hill . . . and an old stone house, brown and queer."

They left Geneva for good on July 18, travelling to Interlaken, entirely by private carriage, *via* Lausanne and Berne. Sarah and her little son elected to rest in the hotel at Interlaken, but the intrepid Harriet went on with Charles and William and a guide to ride on horseback to Lauterbrunnen and up to Grindelwald for a view of the Jungfrau. These were the scenes of *Manfred,* calling up more girlhood memories, but Harriet also had *Pilgrim's Progress* in mind. The Bernese Alps were the Delectable Mountains to her.

Swiss railroad construction was still so inadequate that they had to hire private carriages for the journey to Basle, where they met the German cars and efficiency. But Germany whirled by a homesick Harriet as a wearisome duty owed to her Germanophile husband. Trains and Rhine steamers whisked them from city to city—Strasbourg and its "dumpy" cathedral; Heidelberg, where the university savants hastened to greet Harriet; Frankfort, for a Goethe pilgrimage; Cologne, where Harriet was so homesick she nearly abandoned the rest of her trip.

They had their adventures. Harriet lost her basket of books in one station. Once in a mixed train compartment, Harriet, after jumping up to see a ruined castle, sat down in the wrong seat and crushed the beaver hat of a gentleman who for hours had been silent as a stone image but who now exploded in French and in a most ungentlemanly way. They understood no German, and in a Frankfort museum thought their guide was taking them to see Goethe's Bible. Instead, he conducted them to a cabinet in which reposed Goethe's *shoes*—"large as life—shoes without heels, great clumping, thick, and black." Harriet laughed aloud, and the female irreverence made the guide so "huffy" (as she wrote) he refused to show them anything else.

In Cologne Charles convulsed Harriet by pretending to regard seriously the bones in St. Ursula's church of the eleven thousand virgins slain for adhering to their vows of chastity. Charles remarked in the crypt that the Cologne virgins had evidently not known the Cologne water.

Then Leipzig, where Herr Tauchnitz entertained them; Dresden, where Charles thought the Italian nudes in the Art Gallery indecent, and Harriet criticized the Sistine Madonna because it contained the portrait of Pope Sixtus, whom she regarded as a homely man; Berlin, where she shopped; and, of course, these firm Protestants made the Lutheran pilgrimage to Wittenberg,• Erfurt, and Eisenach. August 17 found them crossing the German border bound for Antwerp, or, as the Latinized Charles, who scorned the German gutturals, exclaimed, "Ho, for Anvers!"

Antwerp‚ was obligatory. In 1853, not to adore Rubens was æsthetic heresy; and Longfellow had told Harriet that to see Rubens at his best she must visit Antwerp. She saw and capitulated. "Art has satisfied me at last, I have been conquered, and that is enough."

In Paris the Deputation broke up. The Rochester contingent, intending to stay abroad longer, went to a hotel. Harriet and Charles were guests of the Bellocs in their official residence in the Ecole Impériale de Dessin. Paris and "parquet floors" again! Harriet wanted to introduce them in America, but Mrs. Chapman told her that American ladies, who had to do most of their own housework, would never accept them, they required so much waxing. Paris and flowers! Harriet was studying the French arrangements of flowers, and to good purpose. Paris and the French people, whom Harriet now knew she liked "equally with the Scotch and English." This was a shocking thing for a prophetess of God to say to her American public; but she remembered Lafayette, and when fellow-countrymen repeated Voltaire's *mot* that the French were half tiger, half monkey, Harriet said it cut her to the heart. They were not all frivolous and sinful; she had found many God-fearing folk among them. She understood but could not approve the Continental Sunday, merely observing that the nations with the strictest Sabbaths were also the nations with the greatest liberty.

There was one important visit. The Bellocs took Harriet to see Pierre Jean de Béranger. The old song-writer was at breakfast and talked delightfully to Harriet for an hour. French conversation, she said, was like the gambols of a thistle-down or the rainbow changes in a soap bubble, at one moment so simple it seemed childlike to her and next moment frightening her a little, the shrewdness was so keen.

Saturday, August 27, found Harriet and Charles back in England, after a Channel crossing that laid everyone low. The emotional spree was over now, the Tom-mania gone, and Harriet, stopping with "our good friends, the L.'s," could devote four comfortable days to shopping and to a thorough inspection of Westminster Abbey. She then went on to do York Cathedral in order to compare the English Protestant minsters (to their advantage) with the Catholic fanes of the Continent.

There was an afternoon for Harriet at Castle Howard, seat of the Howard family, where Lady Carlisle showed her around, and three days at Leeds for an official reception and an "offering" of £100. There she and Charles were house-guests of Edward Baines, editor of the Leeds Mercury. The Lord Mayor of Liverpool telegraphed, asking Harriet if she would accept a public breakfast in his city. Feeble health enabled her to decline.

Nevertheless, the Lord Mayor met her at the Liverpool station on September 6, her last full day in England. The Edward Croppers took her and Charles to Dingle Bank, where she met an Irish delegation bringing to her a carved casket of bog oak lined with gold and filled with sovereigns, the Irish offering. Ireland mourned that she had cancelled her announced visit to the green isle.

And next morning the Lord Mayor of Liverpool was a guest at a private breakfast given Harriet by the Croppers. Many friends had gathered in Dingle Bank, and a large party accompanied Mrs. Stowe and her brother to the wharf, where they found a civic farewell committee and a final throng of civilians. The Rev. Dr. Raffles lifted his hands and, as women bowed and men bared their heads, prayed for the safety of Harriet Beecher Stowe while in peril on the sea. Her Liverpool friends and the civic committee went with her in the tender down the Mersey to put her safely aboard the S.S. Arctic. Her last impression of England was one of crowds lining the river banks, waving.

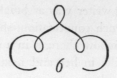

National Leader

ARRIET's first important act after her return to America was to come to an understanding with that other Abolition leader, William Lloyd Garrison. For she was a leader of abolition now, if not in her own mind *the* leader. What else had the British demonstrations meant, the homages paid her by the liberals of France, Switzerland, and Germany, the vast correspondence of her followers in the United States? Implicitly she assumed the cause of the slave as a personal stewardship.

But her Abolition and Garrison's were not the same. Garrison's was a political party, anti-church if not actually infidel. He was capable of such utterances as, "If public sentiment required it, the American clergy would burn the Bible tomorrow." Harriet's abolition was a common noun, representing the great world-wide desire aroused by her novel to free the slave. She could not countenance an abolition movement divorced from the Evangelical Christian church, or indeed one that was not as much a part of the church as missions and the Sunday School.

Never a demagogue for all his violent speech and deeds, Garrison welcomed support to his cause from any quarter. When such immense and unexpected aid came from *Uncle Tom's Cabin,* he held forth the hand of fellowship to the daughter of the man who in 1830 had had too many irons in the fire to help him. He invited Harriet to be guest of honour at the twentieth-anniversary meeting of the American Anti-Slavery Society.

It was an invitation Harriet could not accept, or at least without a public explanation; so one November day, after she had arranged her trophies in the Stone Cabin for effective display, she sat down at her desk before a quire of faintly ruled note paper and one of the new Uncle Tom's Cabin envelopes everybody was using, dipped her pen into the well of the allegorical silver inkstand her English friends had given her, and began a letter to Mr. Garrison.

(The back of the Uncle Tom envelope was covered with etchings of scenes from the novel, and, curving gracefully along the seal lines, ran two crossing mottoes: "All things whatsoever ye would that MEN should do unto you, do you so to them" and "Ye who take freedom from MEN, how will you answer it to God?" The two mottoes crossed on the common word *MEN* on the point of the flap.)

Harriet could adopt a somewhat lofty tone in her wary and elegant words of reproof to Garrison. The battle-scarred Saul of the *Liberator* had slain his thousands, but the female David of *Uncle Tom's Cabin*—and how often had the British orators likened her to David!—had brought low her ten thousands. Merely by running Mrs. Stowe's initials at its masthead as a stated contributor, though she had contributed nothing for nearly a year, the *Independent* was vaulting into the higher strata of newspaper circulations. She had a solid following of 150,000 readers, as the sales of her subsequent books were to show, whereas Garrison could probably not count 5,000 of his own.

The correspondence (which the *Liberator* published) was not remarkable, but it had one lasting result. In the course of it Harriet invited Garrison to Andover for a frank discussion, and in early December the zealot passed two days and a night under the roof of the Stone Cabin. Harriet found in the burning, humourless man a mind she could esteem and thereafter remained Garrison's friend and co-worker. At once she tried to arrange a reconciliation between him and Frederick Douglass, whom Garrison was calling an apostate. It is possible that she invited the coloured agitator to Andover, too. At any rate, she had an interview with him.

Before Christmas she was seeking Garrison's advice in spending some of her English sovereigns—the first disbursement of them which the record shows. Harriet proposed a course of anti-slavery lectures for Boston that winter, "similar to that in New York and Worcester." She nominated a list of speakers, expecting Garrison to add to it. Some of her nominations must have given him a wry smile, for they included several preachers undistinguished for labour in the abolition vineyard, one being Dr. Lyman Beecher, now in his seventy-ninth year. "It has been the wish of many of my father's friends that he should give an exposition of his views, and this will afford a *proper occasion.*"

Considering the size of the fund at her disposal, Harriet's contribution to the lecture course was none too generous. She offered to pay $25 to each lecturer, provided others would put up for the renting and lighting of halls.

"I would be willing to do *more,* if it is thought best," she wrote Garrison, "but I make it a general rule in using the money at my disposal to offer about half the expense, thus having some raised at home for each purpose. In short, I am willing to put $200 at disposal—*if necessary.*" But Harriet emphasized it that "Mr. Stowe offers to *give* his services for one lecture," and thought others might follow this example, since "the thing is of the nature of a charity."

Two books had awaited her approval and signature when she returned in September. John P. Jewett had made an abridgment of the novel for young readers, calling it, *A Peep into Uncle Tom's Cabin.* Willis P. Hazard, a Philadelphia publisher, had discovered that *Uncle Tom* was not Mrs. Stowe's first essay in slavery fiction. Previously she had written (probably for the *National Era*) a short story entitled *Uncle Sam's Emancipation,* a tale of a noble young master who manumitted his faithful black retainer out of principle. Hazard collected with this Harriet's *Earthly Care a Heavenly Discipline,* two of her *Letters from Maine* that had appeared in the *Era,* and the now famous article on the Beecher family "by An Alabama Man," whom Harriet seems to have forgiven, and asked Mrs. Stowe's permission to publish, under the usual terms. She gave it and by Christmas had two more volumes in the bookstores, gathering royalties for her.

Impressive as she had been to Andover the year before, Harriet returned from her European triumphs enveloped in something like the nimbus of a celestial being. Even Elizabeth Stuart Phelps, who could be critical of her in later life, admitted that by common consent she was "the greatest of American women." She was an awesome possession for a Massachusetts village. Harriet slipped at once into the rôle of Andover's *grande dame,* its Lady Bountiful, its world-travelled and sophisticated arbitress of all that was correct in human existence, the mainspring of its civic endeavour.

Perhaps the British worship had turned her head a little, though it was to be only a temporary lapse. "She never seemed to be of Andover," Mrs. Ward wrote, "or its life akin to hers." There must have been plenty of whispering about Mrs. Stowe and her grand ideas by Andover women with faces red from the kitchen stove. In fact, Andover, when it took thought, did not like her. In the words of Harriet's fair critic, "The privilege of neighborhood was but scantily appreciated."

There must always be some doubt whether the good folk of Andover really appreciated the magnitude of the reception their most celebrated citizen had received in England. To understand they must see the material evidences of the triumph—the Edinburgh salver on which had reposed a thousand gold sovereigns, the Irish bog-oak casket lined with gold, the great inkstand, the Duchess's gold slave-chain, the vellum "addresses," the books, the programmes, the trinkets Harriet had bought for herself, her many sketches—the museum of trophies she brought home with her. She arranged them all effectively and invited the Benevolent Society to hold its meeting at the Stone Cabin. Upon the curiosity of the ladies of Andover that invitation had the force of a command.

The twins, Harriet and Eliza Stowe, and little Georgiana were all attending Abbot Academy that year. Harriet and Eliza at seventeen are said to have been prepossessing young ladies, much prettier than their mother had been in girlhood. The Abbot legend is that they looked so much alike that they wore red and blue ribbons in school to distinguish themselves. They seem to have been feeling their new aristocracy. Eliza came back from a Boston shopping trip one day leading a spidery Italian greyhound, then the most fashionable of dogs. His name was Giglio. The girls were studying Italian and could ripple Giglio's name enchantingly.

And ten-year-old Georgie could presume upon her position as the child of her famous mother. Miss Charlotte Swift, one of the Abbot teachers, went into a classroom one day to reprove Georgiana for some infraction of the rules, but found the room deserted. A mouselike sound attracted Miss Swift's attention aloft, and there near the top of the tall stove-pipe, up which she had swarmed, clung the impish Georgie, shouting with laughter at her discovery.

Thus pleasantly 1853 slipped away, and at the turn of 1854 the snow fell beautifully on Andover Hill, the elms etched themselves upon a flawless sky, and from the front door of the Stone Cabin the common stretched away, pure and dazzling. Within all was kept snug by open fires of birch and beech. No more plebeian stoves for a wealthy authoress.

In our window-seats, unchilled, the scarlet geranium unfolds its flower, the scarlet heliotrope breathes its perfume. The queenly calla bears up its queenly leaves and milky blossoms, and hyacinths and narcissus slowly perfect their buds. The fire crackles and burns, sending its tongues of flames around the hissing logs. We are among the believers in the unveiled divinity of fire, and the scowling gnome of the air-tight has been banished our hearth.

God was in His heaven, and all was right with Harriet's world. *Uncle Tom's Cabin* was bringing the millennium—as the British could see so clearly from their distance. *Uncle Tom* was still marching on, though now the waves from his original splash in the literary sea were breaking on far shores. A missionary sent Harriet two translations published for Javanese readers. She heard of one in Hindoo, one in Armenian, one in Wallachian, one in a Hungarian dialect.

There were pleasant diversions that winter. One was the somewhat astonishing feat of procuring a portrait of Eliza Stowe, Harriet's predecessor in the conjugal bed. There were no models to copy. Eliza had lived before the day of Daguerre's chemical pictures and had never posed even for a family pencil. But in Boston lived a painter who had known Eliza and who indeed is said to have been in love with her himself. Calvin and Harriet met with this gentleman and by working with sketches evoked from their memories a likeness which satisfied them. Harriet paid handsomely for a large portrait in oils; and thereafter every year on Eliza's birthday she and Calvin sat for a season before the picture and brought back the sainted one's memory with reminiscences.

And that winter Harriet changed publishers—changed willy-nilly. John P. Jewett got into financial difficulties and sold out to the Boston house of Phillips, Sampson & Co. not only the copyrights of *Uncle Tom's Cabin,* the *Key,* and the satellite volumes but his contract with the author as well. The change was agreeable to Harriet.

Her literary work that winter was just enough to be pleasantly engrossing without any oppression to her health and spirits. There were her travel letters, which she had written with an eye to publication, to collect and two or three additional ones, to fill gaps, to be written from her notes. She was calling her travel book *Sunny Memories of Foreign Lands.* Calvin was preparing a heavy introduction for it, collecting the various addresses and his responses and editing them, with notes.

And Harriet resumed her contributions to the *Independent,* mounting happily to her pulpit in the first column with a series of short sermons on texts from the *Psalms.* Perhaps with the memory of some dappled Alpine scene in her mind, she called the series *Shadows on the Hebrew Mountains.* Thousands of American women were clipping and preserving her pious and gentle platitudes.

And then, suddenly and without warning, the South retorted to the hatred brewed in the North by *Uncle Tom's Cabin.* Backed by a sure majority in

Congress, the Southern leaders announced their intention to repeal the Missouri Compromise.

The Missouri Compromise had fixed, supposedly forever, the northern limit of slavery in the Louisiana Purchase at the 36th degree and 30th minute of north latitude, or, roughly, on the line of the present northern border of Arkansas as extended west through what is now Oklahoma. In 1820, when nobody but a few fur traders and adventurers had ever ascended the Missouri River, this concession seemed to the South a slight price to pay for the admission of Missouri, entirely north of the Compromise line, as a slave State.

But now the sod huts of the settlers were snuggling against the feet of the Rockies. The strip known as Kansas, lying west of Missouri between the 37th and 40th parallels, was already populous enough for statehood; and at the rate the Conestoga wagons were pouring across the Missouri, it would not be long before the vast region of Nebraska must be carved into States, each sending its two votes to the United States Senate. Such had become, under the ministrations of Harriet Beecher Stowe and others, the temper of the free States that each additional pair of votes were almost bound to be votes against slavery, unless the South could extend slavery into the new country. The Compromise thus suddenly, because of the westward migration, menaced the economic existence of the South, and the pro slavery leaders did not hesitate to tear it up, a scrap of paper.

There was another motive, not often mentioned in these days when novelists look fondly back upon slavery as a sort of lost Arcadia for the Negro race. The extension of the South's peculiar institution into Kansas and Nebraska would broaden the slave market and enrich the South by increasing the value of the slave property. By 1854 the breeding and exporting of slaves was getting to be a big business south of Mason and Dixon's line. It was a principal source of revenue for Virginia and only less so for North Carolina and Kentucky. At the gateways of these States the statistics of the slave traffic were kept in as cold blood as they were for livestock and tobacco. In two decades the prices of slaves had tripled, and in 1854 there were more than three million slaves in the United States. Should slavery occupy the Missouri Valley, the financial benefit to the South might be expected to mount to astronomical figures.

The repealer appeared in the Kansas-Nebraska Bill, to organize the Territories of Kansas and Nebraska. It was no cynical mandate, imposing slavery

upon the new units, but it granted each the right of self determination. The
fair words deceived no one. Kansas, where the first test would come, was
largely populated by Missourians. The Missouri slave-owners along the
Kansas border were violent and lawless men. It was taken for granted that
if the slave power could not win the Kansas election by honest votes, it
would do so by fraud and force.

The introduction of the Kansas-Nebraska Bill in January, 1854, fell on the
North with the impact of a physical blow. The five Abolitionists in Congress
—Senators Chase and Sumner and Representatives Giddings, Wade, and
Gerrit Smith—signed a manifesto which first signalled the danger to the
anti-slavery forces, but they spoke already in the accents of defeat.

> We shall resist it by speech and vote and with all the abilities which
> God has given us. Even if overcome in the impending struggle, we shall
> not submit. We shall go home to our constituents, erect anew the standard
> of freedom, and call on the people to come to the rescue of the country
> from the domination of slavery. We will not despair, for the cause of
> human freedom is the cause of God.

Abolitionists of the Garrison stamp were at once furious. Already saddled
with the obnoxious, though unenforceable, Fugitive Slave Law, they foresaw
another heavy set-back for their cause. And if the slave power could so
brutally break its word pledged in the Missouri Compromise, what was to
prevent the pro-slavery majority in Congress from legalizing slavery everywhere in the North? In the famous Lemmon case the Supreme Court had
already declared it to be any man's constitutional right to own slaves in a
free State. The Abolition nest in Boston buzzed angrily.

To Harriet Beecher Stowe, regarding herself as the custodian of the cause
of the slave, the news from Washington came almost as a personal assault.
Yet, unlike Salmon Chase and the others, she did not despair. She knew
exactly what to do to stop this attempt of slavery to extend its dominion,
and, secure in this knowledge, she used the strongest expression of defiance
the good folk of the 1850's employed. Harriet said, "We shall see."

Her faith in the power of the pulpit generally was as triumphant as
it was ever in the rightness of her own father himself. Unite the preachers
for a worthy end, and what could withstand them? Harriet should see, and
her action was important enough to find place in any compendious history
of those troubled times. She organized the preachers of New England,
Catholics and all, and sent them, heaven's Marines, to the rescue of poor

Africa, struck down by a Stephen A. Douglas and bleeding on the Senate floor.

Harriet proposed the plan, but Dr. Henry Martyn Dexter, the new editor of the *Congregationalist,* served as her public self. The preachers of Boston drew up the petition. Edward Beecher dropped everything for a fortnight or more to carry it out through Massachusetts and even into upstate New York. Calvin Stowe went out with a copy, old Lyman Beecher himself made a few calls, and Dr. Charles Lowell was active in Boston for the project. And Harriet's fingers were busy, writing letters to Dr. Bacon, the Rev. Mr. Streeter and other friends, enlisting their services.

The result was a swift and signal success. When the canvassers met together, they assembled a petition two hundred feet long and signed with 3,050 names, every one with a Reverend before it. Meanwhile, Harriet had sent her friend, Senator Charles Sumner, "a bulletin of the rising of the tide here in New England." Hold the fort, she told him in effect, the clergy is coming! She predicted "such an uprising of the country as never has been heard of since the days of the Revolution. A touch of that old altar-fire will do us no harm."

She enclosed to the Massachusetts Senator a copy of the petition and told him of the campaign to secure signatures. Writing under the date of February 23, she hoped "by the 7th of March (if possible, sooner) that a Committee from the clergy of all denominations will proceed to Washington, bearing with them the *united clerical protest of New England.*" All she wanted was time, which she trusted Sumner to secure for her movement "by every parliamentary device possible."

"We shall see," and Harriet underscored the words, "whether liberty is dead in this country or not. . . . Every pulpit in New England will be a battery against this iniquity." The Andover seeress, to whom nothing was impossible, urged Sumner to arrange "for the Committee of the Clergy themselves to appear in the House with the remonstrance," since "we want all the impressiveness possible given to the movement."

So much for Harriet's direct action to defeat the nefarious design of slavery. Meanwhile she had clipped short her series of sermonettes and mounted her rostrum in the *Independent* to deliver a ringing *APPEAL TO THE WOMEN OF THE FREE STATES OF AMERICA.* How the national legislature should act upon the Kansas-Nebraska Bill, she declared, was going "most vitally to affect the temporal and eternal interests not only of ourselves but of our children and our children's children for ages yet unborn." Women had been taught to "silence their voices" in national affairs; but in the face of such an issue every woman who did not "think it right to inflict on her neighbor's child what she would think worse than death, were it inflicted on her own," must set her influence resolutely against the iniquity proposed in Washington. The issue was not merely whether Kansas should be slave or free; it was whether the whole land should be laid under the curse of slavery. "Four years hence," Harriet predicted, "there may be slave depots in New York." Her clarion voice went on:

Women of the free States! the question is not, shall we remonstrate with slavery on its own soil? but are we willing to receive slavery into the free States and territories of the Union?

Shall the whole power of these United States go into the hands of slavery?

Shall every State in it be thrown open as a slave State? This will be the final result and issue of the question which is now pending. This is the fearful crisis at which we stand. And now, is there anything that the women of a country can do? O women of the free States! what did your brave mothers do in the time of our revolutionary struggle? Did not *liberty* in those days feel the strong impulse of woman's heart?

With this—and there was a whole column of it—Harriet had done all one frail woman could to protect her world-given mandate. And there can be no doubt that her muster of the clergy was effective. Senator Sumner seems to have had as much faith in it as Harriet herself. He was unable to secure for the ministerial Committee the privilege of the Senate floor, but he received the frocked delegation and its petition with a formal speech. "In the days of the Revolution, John Adams said, 'Let the pulpit thunder against oppression,' and the pulpits thundered. The time has come for them to thunder again."

In tangible results, however, Harriet's effort did little more than supply ammunition to Sumner, Salmon Chase, Joshua R. Giddings, Benjamin F. Wade, and Gerrit Smith, prolong the debate, and intensify its bitterness. The Southern legislators had their own clergy, which took a different view of the slavery question. At the end of May the Kansas-Nebraska Bill passed into law. The next step of the Abolitionists must be to attempt to control the Kansas election.

Sunny Memories came out in July, and three weeks later the *Independent* carried an item from its Boston correspondent saying that the book was selling at a surprisingly rapid rate, "if anything could surprise us in that line since the sale of 'Uncle Tom'." Actually, in view of the immense success of *Uncle Tom's Cabin* and the wide popularity of most of Harriet's subsequent books, *Sunny Memories,* though it ran into several editions, was a disappointment to the publisher. It did better in England, where a remembering people snapped up 40,000 copies as fast as the presses could roll them out, to see what their recent guest had said about them.

That summer Harriet made her first important expenditure of her royalties for her own benefit. She and Calvin bought a wood lot in the country near Andover. Nearly every well-to-do village family in New England in those days owned a wood lot, and the Stone Cabin, having banished the air-tight gnome its hearth, had especial need for one. Thereafter, a ride out to the wood lot was a favourite family excursion. Another prospering Beecher was also acquiring real estate. Henry Ward Beecher that summer bought a farm for himself at Lenox, Massachusetts.

For years his children had been urging Lyman Beecher to write the memoirs of his long and turbulent life. Now, at the close of his seventy-ninth year, too senile to write his autobiography with his own pen, or dictate it, or even marshal his memories coherently, he was at the Cabin taking part in a unique collaboration. Charles Beecher, who served as general editor in this family enterprise, had been through the mass of Dr. Beecher's papers and letters—"which he had never failed to date, year, month, and day"—and the daughters, Harriet and Catharine, the latter now a frequent visitor at Andover, filled in the gaps by asking the old man questions about his life. Thus primed, his memory began to flow, and the daughters took down his words as he uttered them, taking care to preserve his quaint Colonial cant, which probably sounded as strange in the ears of their generation as they do today in ours.

Harriet, who had probably suggested the plan, did most of the questioning and writing. She and Catharine and three of their brothers contributed chapters of reminiscences of their father; and thus, before the old Doctor's mind failed completely, they put together as entertaining an item as there is in the library of Americana. Catharine arranged for the publication of the *Autobiography* by Harper.

To run up to Andover to take part in the family dialogues, Charles Beecher had to tear himself away from an even more engrossing job at home in Newark, where he was helping his brother Henry select tunes and verses for the forthcoming famous and lucrative *Plymouth Hymnal,* first of the so-called "Gospel hymnals."

Through the generosity of Andover citizens, Abbot Academy had acquired a dormitory for the out-of-town girls; but in the early autumn of 1854 it was still a dormitory of bare walls and empty rooms. The Academy needed $2,000 to furnish it. By various innocent schemes the ladies of Andover had succeeded in raising several hundred dollars for furniture, but the goal of the campaign was still far away.

At this juncture some of the ladies thought of going to Mrs. Stowe, who was noted for her novel ideas, for advice. True, this was a good deal of an imposition. One had only to note the hacks that drove almost daily from the depot to the Stone Cabin, or listen to the postoffice gossip that Mrs. Stowe's mail was the heaviest in town, to be aware that she was a much-occupied woman. Still, she had always shown a willingness to engage in community affairs; and one afternoon a committee, headed by Mrs. Samuel Jackson, mother of Miss Susan, rang the front-door bell at the Cabin.

It was a bewildered committee that emerged from the interview. The busy authoress had not only been ready with a novel plan but had virtually taken the whole problem of the dormitory fund into her own hands. She had not so much suggested as decreed a great tea-party on a scale so vast that Abbot Academy's entire school-building must be turned over to it. Mrs. Stowe named a price of admission that made her visitors gasp. Fifty cents! There were a few faint demurrers, but the hostess overrode them.

The grand affair was given on September 29, from afternoon until what was for Andover late at night. Harriet's enthusiasm had by this time infected the whole town. Placards were up in Andover and the surrounding communities advertising the "festival and bazaar" and announcing that "Mrs. Harriet Beecher Stowe will preside." Male volunteers had stripped the academy building of desks and benches. Young theologians of the Seminary had visited the woods for evergreen boughs and the first sprays of autumn leaves with which to garland the walls. The wealthy Messrs. P. Smith and S. Lawrence emptied their conservatories to provide plants and cut flowers. Mrs. Lawrence sent her best silver and cut glass, as did also Mrs. Buck and Harriet herself. The boys of Phillips Academy climbed the trees in the school yard and hung up lanterns. Harriet said it all transformed the dingy old school building into a fairy palace.

The whole countryside turned out to attend. Cake and tea or coffee came free with the price of admission, but there were booths for the sale of oysters, ice cream, fruit, and the bazaar articles. However, the buggies were not rattling in that evening from Fry Village, Bradford, Lawrence, and even from Haverhill bringing people willing to pay fifty cents for the privilege of buying oysters or even that of listening to Charles Towne, of Salem, play the piano or the Lawrence Glee Club sing. They parted with their half-dollars to see Harriet Beecher Stowe, and they found her "presiding" in "Number Four" classroom, which had been converted into the coffee room. Harriet was wearing one of her best foreign dresses; and on her wrist, for all to see, was the "superb" gold slave-chain which, the reverent whisper went round, had been presented to her by Queen Victoria herself.

She had the Midas touch now. When the committee had counted the receipts, it could report: "The avails of the festival complete the sum of $2,000, considered sufficient for furnishing the hall."

The success of her festival seemed to fill Harriet with a new fervour. Theological Andover bore the reputation of being a dour Puritanical town— "a long street of houses with closed doors and window-blinds." Harriet, who at every service was in her front pew in the Seminary chapel, nevertheless saw no reason why religion and long faces had to go together. Perhaps Americans grew old so quickly because they took life too solemnly. She had herself eight years previously been advising Calvin from Brattleboro, and her father, too, to learn dancing. She determined to wake Andover up, and that fall and winter turned the Stone Cabin into a centre of merrymaking. Night after night its windows blazed for concerts, tableaux, and charade parties. One evening the twins gave a "levée" for the older girls of Abbot Academy, and nobody got home until half-past eleven! The trustees of an institution which until recently had operated a coffin factory as part of its spiritual discipline, shook their heads. It was vain to expect Professor Calvin Stowe to exert a husband's authority. Calvin could only exclaim in helpless admiration, "Wife beats the Dutch!"

The dialogues with Lyman Beecher ended in November with a family reunion at the Stone Cabin. Besides the visiting collaborators—the Doctor himself and his third wife, Catharine, and Charles—James Beecher, the Doctor's youngest son, was now in Andover. After a brief career at sea as sailor and officer on the China clipper ships, James was, at twenty-six, a student in the Theological Seminary, safe in the ministerial fold at last. With such a nucleus gathered, Edward and his wife came out from Boston, and at the last minute Henry Ward Beecher arrived.

It rained most of the time during the reunion, a rain that broke a long drought. Henry Ward Beecher had had a lecture engagement in Lynn, and in order to reach Andover the same night he had to hire a carriage and drive—a drive that continued into the small hours of Sunday morning. The wary Plymouth pastor did not give his enemies the opportunity to whisper about this clerical misdemeanour but came out boldly with it himself in the *Independent.* "A venerable father and mother, two sisters, three brothers—was it not worth such a ride to spend a Sabbath with them?" Henry was at his sultriest in describing Andover in its winter phase. "Trees do not die. They undress. They sleep in naked majesty." As for the weather, he apostrophized: "Rain away, then, full-breasted clouds!"

(A different sort of ride was just then taking place in another part of the world, as someone's blunder sent six hundred British brigadiers into a Crimean valley of death. Among them was the Hon. Frederick Leveson-Gower, cadet of the Scottish House of Sutherland.)

Catharine, who never regarded anything ever written by a Beecher as water over the dam, resurrected the *Miss Beechers' Geography,* revised it, and Phillips, Sampson & Co. brought it out that fall in a new edition. But this time the famous Mrs. Stowe's name appeared alone on the title-page, and the book itself was retitled, *Geography for My Children.*

Garrison was raising a fund to redeem a slave named Freeman. Harriet responded not with money but with "four *proof engravings* from Richmond's picture of me." She thought Garrison should get five dollars apiece for them, since "last week a gentleman in Hartford paid $5 for one of them towards the redemption of Miss Carrol's slaves." But Garrison or Freeman must peddle these art treasures as though they had come by them independently, since Harriet preferred not to appear to be selling them herself—Garrison would understand the difference.

Abolition took another defeat in Kansas, as bands of armed ruffians crossed the border from Missouri, seized the polls in the November election, and sent a pro-slavery delegate to Congress. However, the more important test would come in the spring, when the Territory would elect the legislature that would draw the constitution of the future State. Northern churches and newspapers began to urge young men to migrate to Kansas as anti-slavery settlers—stout-hearted young men, not afraid to handle Sharpe's rifles.

In her column Harriet was silent on the Kansas excitement. She contributed a poem widely quoted at the time—*Pilgrim's Song in the Desert*. She had been too hasty in promising to preside over a table at Boston's annual Anti-Slavery Christmas Fair and wrote to Anne Weston begging off, alleging "my husband's accident" for an excuse. The accident could not have been serious, for there is no other reference to it.

At Christmas Harriet perpetrated a famous joke on her neighbours. She set up her first Christmas tree and decked the Cabin with holly and coloured candles—"a growing innovation in our Puritan latitudes"—then invited the Seminary's faculty to a party. When the reverend professors unwrapped their packages, agog to discover what treasures their travelled hostess had parted with, they discovered that every present was a humorous one. It took the heavily masculine community some time to recover from that disappointment.

Thus on a merry note ended 1854, and no less tranquilly 1855 glided into Harriet's life. The "border ruffians" (who, the Abolitionists said, were led by Senator David R. Atchison, of Missouri) captured the spring election in Kansas. The free-state men, however, met and elected their own legislature, and the territory had two governments in armed conflict with each other. The North urged more immigration, and among those who responded were five tall sons of a farmer named John Brown, who lived at Mount Elba, New York, beside Gerrit Smith's Negro colony, plotting an invasion of Virginia.

In Brooklyn Plymouth Church communicants were heading up barrels of Sharpe's rifles, labelling them Bibles, and shipping them to Osawatomie and Topeka, where already the settlers were calling the new arm "Beecher's Bibles." The Plymouth pastor was shouting at a church meeting, "There is more moral power in one Sharpe rifle, so far as the slaveholders of Kansas are concerned, than in a hundred Bibles. You might just as well read the Bible to buffalos as to those who follow Atchison and Stringfellow; but they have a supreme respect for the logic that is embodied in Sharpe's rifles."

Harriet did not add her voice publicly to the uproar. Perhaps the ugliness of the times and the sudden glimpse they gave of war frightened her. In her *Independent* column she wrote of anything but the troubles in Kansas.

In 1854 one might have thought that Mrs. Stowe intended never to write anything more of serious weight. Still, she helped the family keep the printing-presses busy by revising her *Mayflower* for a new reprint by Phillips, Sampson & Co. Charles Beecher that year brought out *Pen Pictures of The Bible,* to which Harriet supplied an introduction. She wrote an introduction for *The Colored Patriots of The American Revolution,* by William C. Nell, a Negro.

But quite the greatest book event in the family that year was the publication in the late spring of *The Plymouth Collection of Hymns and Tunes,* compiled by Henry Ward Beecher, with prefatory credit to Mr. John Tundell and the Rev. Charles Beecher for the selection of the music. In this shelter Charles escaped the bludgeoning that is the lot of the anthologist but which was unusually severe in this instance because of the number of Henry's enemies. Moreover, many conservative churchmen disapproved of the lusty congregational singing which Henry was bringing into his church services. Henry defended his selections for columns of the *Independent's* space, as churches and Sunday Schools bought the new hymnal by the tens of thousands. Harriet gave the book a column of praise one week. Henry had included one of her compositions in it—her *Hymn,* beginning, "When winds are raging o'er the upper ocean."

In February Harriet had read Mr. Tennyson's new poem, *The Charge of The Light Brigade,* and almost simultaneously a touching letter from the Duchess of Sutherland in reply to Harriet's condolences at the death of Leveson-Gower in the Crimea. It was the Duchess's tragedy that she had never let her younger son know the full depth of her mother's love for him.

It made Harriet hug her Henry closer, when he came home for his vacations. She must never let that happen with this handsome son of hers. At sixteen Henry was growing to be a man—blond, athletic, and tall. Little Fred was undersized, like his mother. One more year at boarding school, and Henry would be ready for college. They were planning Dartmouth for him.

Of all her children Harriet felt now that Henry was her favourite. There was growing up "such a peculiar union" between them, as if they understood each other's unspoken thoughts. The boy must have wondered at the many times that summer his little mother ran her fingers through his bright curls and told him how she loved him. She gave him a handsome seal ring, of which he grew proud. A faint shadow rested on Henry. He had not experienced the phenomenon of conversion as yet. Still, he was trying to lead a Christian life and resist temptation and be a comfort to his parents. Harriet, at least, did not put too great a point on his unregenerate state.

At the reunion the year before, it was voted that the whole family must meet at the Stone Cabin on October 12, 1855, to celebrate Dr. Beecher's eightieth birthday. All made it except James, the sailor-brother, who, after a hasty graduation from the Seminary, had gone to Hong Kong to take charge of a seamen's mission. To show his agility to his clerical sons, the toothless patriarch of the clan leaped the bar fence enclosing the Seminary campus. Afterwards all ten of them went to a studio to have their group-portrait made by a new mechanical process called photography. It took a long pose to fix an image on a wet plate, but so used were these professionals to public appearance that there was not the slightest blurring of any figure nor in any face and pose the slightest look of self-consciousness. They all knew that this must be the last reunion, unless they met again at a grave-side, for Edward, who had always thought fondly of the West, was going back to it, having accepted a call to the Congregational Church at Galesburg, Illinois.

By this time Harriet's long period of literary hibernation was over, and she was incubating another novel. This, too, was to be on the slavery theme, partly because Phillips, Sampson & Co. wanted to bring out another anti-slavery story from her pen, and partly, no doubt, because it was patent to Harriet by this time that *Uncle Tom* alone was never going to persuade the South to manumit its slaves. On the contrary, Southern hatred of *Uncle Tom's Cabin* was more bitter than ever. A Mobile, Alabama, vigilance committee that winter ran out of town a bookseller named Strickland, caught handling the novel.

Senator Sumner rejoiced at the news of Harriet's new occupation. Catharine Beecher, in Washington to interest political leaders in her project for a women's normal school in Dubuque, Iowa, told Sumner about it, and he at once wrote, urging Harriet to press the work. "I feel it will act directly upon pending questions and help us in our struggle for Kansas, and also to overthrow the slave-oligarchy in the coming Presidential election. We need your help at once in our struggle."

As yet Harriet's ideas for the story were vague, beyond a general purpose to show the degrading effects of slavery upon the free white population of the South. Tentatively she was calling the novel *Canema,* the name of her heroine's Carolina plantation. Phillips, Sampson & Co. went ahead and took out a copyright for *Canema.*

Harriet began to write the novel, which became her *Dred: A Tale of The Great Dismal Swamp,* about the end of February, 1856. But first, she prepared a market for it, taking a column or more in the *Independent* to review a number of anti-slavery books she had been reading. As to anti-slavery fiction, Harriet proclaimed that "the use of the novel in the great question of moral life is coming to be one of the features of the age. A novel now is understood to be a parable—a story told in illustration of a truth or fact."

There were family affairs to take some of her attention as she wrote. With Edward now gone West, old Doctor Beecher cashed his Lane Seminary note and bought a house for himself in Willow Street, Brooklyn, to be near his famous son Henry for the rest of his days. William, least able and successful of the Beechers, having quarrelled with two previous congregations, quarrelled with a third and was dismissed by the Bethesda Church in Reading, Pennsylvania, the council putting full blame upon a faction of the parishioners. Harriet and Calvin found a charge for him at North Brookfield, Massachusetts.

But these were minor diversions; and even Senator Sumner's bristling speech on the "Crime against Kansas," in which he arraigned South Carolina and its Senator Butler, who was not present in Washington to reply, could not drag Harriet for long out of her reveries about her Bayard of a hero, Edward Clayton, and her heroine, Nina Gordon. All unaware was she that in Washington hot-headed young Representative Preston Brooks, of South Carolina, a relative of Senator Butler, was brooding to the point of insanity over what he regarded as Sumner's insult to his family.

One somnolent May afternoon, while Harriet in Andover was placidly advancing the love-story of Edward and Nina, in Washington the gavel of the President had just fallen to adjourn the Senate for the day. Senators were gathering up their books and papers, or chatting together in small knots. Senator Sumner sat alone at his desk, bent over a letter he was writing. Then down the padded aisle came Preston Brooks, and he carried a heavy cane. He approached the unconscious Sumner from behind, the stick rose and fell on Sumner's head with sickening force. Again and again Brooks struck, and Sumner slid from his chair and crumpled, senseless, to the floor. Brooks turned, stared defiantly around the startled Chamber, and stalked out, without a hand lifted to stop him. Then the marble corridors of the Senate end rang with confusion, as doors opened, men ran and

THE BEECHER FAMILY—1855

Thomas   William   Edward   Charles   Henry Ward

Isabella   Catharine   Lyman Beecher   Mary   Harriet

James

"It took a long pose to fix an image on a wet plate, but so used were these professionals to public appearance that there

shouted, colleagues and Senate employees bore the gory Massachusetts Senator to a couch in the cloakroom, and messengers clattered through the streets, galloping to fetch doctors.

Nothing since the great slavery contention began had created such excitement as the attack on Charles Sumner. For several days the Senator hung between life and death, nor did he ever recover completely from his injuries, but there was little or no sympathy for him on the slavery side. Legislators jeered that he was shamming at home. The junior Senator from Massachusetts denounced Brooks as a murderer and was instantly challenged to a duel from the opposite side. Preston Brooks became a national hero in the South. Admirers sent him dozens of walking-sticks. The House voted adversely against him, and he resigned, only to be back in his seat within a week, reëlected almost unanimously by his district.

The North's horror expressed itself in indignation meetings. Calvin Ellis Stowe presided over the one in Boston. Brooklyn's Sumner meeting was held in the City Hall itself, and even the New York *Journal of Commerce* for once printed anti-slavery addresses, though without comment. The principal speech was that of Henry Ward Beecher. From the City Hall Henry went back to his study, where he was contriving the most effective piece of propaganda to madden the nation since the appearance of his sister's great novel.

On Sunday morning, June 1, 1856, at the conclusion of his sermon and just before the closing hymn and benediction, the Rev. Henry Ward Beecher stepped reverently from his pulpit, as he was wont to do when about to say something not strictly connected with the sacred business of expounding God's word, to make a brief announcement. How far might a just man go in secular affairs on Sunday without desecrating the Sabbath? The Pharisees had asked Jesus that question on the Sabbath when He healed a man's withered hand, but His logic had confounded them. "Wherefore, it is lawful to do well on the Sabbath day." Henry then went on to tell his congregation about a young slave girl whose case had come to his attention. Her father, a white man of Virginia, was also her master, and he had sold her to go South, "for what purpose you can imagine when you see her." At this an audible gasp swept through the great auditorium. The unpredictable pastor of the Plymouth Church had brought in a slave girl and was evidently about to ransom her from the pulpit.

Henry told them how it came about. The Richmond trader, who bought

her from her master-father, pitied her for her fate, when he understood the
girl's piety and innocence. He offered to knock $100 off the price of $1,200
he had paid for her. A fellow trader—"so much of good is there in the
lowest of men"—had given her $100 more, and free-state men in Wash-
ington had contributed $500 to her. Her new owner had appealed to Henry
Ward Beecher for the rest. Henry had refused to do anything, unless she
were sent to New York; and the trader had permitted her to make the
journey into free territory on her parole to return her person to Richmond
or the balance of her purchase-price.

At this, Beecher stepped to the platform stairs and said, "Come up here,
Sarah, and let us all see you."

Plymouth Church had been built according to its pastor's ideas. The
pulpit was on a platform in the centre of the auditorium and was thus
surrounded on all sides by the pews. Four thousand persons had packed
into the church that morning, and Henry had held them breathless for an
hour with his sermon from Luke 10:27: "Thou shalt love the Lord thy God
with all thy heart, and with all thy soul, and with all thy strength; and thy
neighbour as thyself." But the silence of that hour was confusion compared
with the straining stillness within the church as a young mulatto woman,
neatly dressed, came up the carpeted steps to the platform and sank, half-
fainting with embarrassment, into a chair, her sleek head bowed, her hands
twisting together. She was comely—Henry's showmanship had made sure
of that before he ever embarked on any such enterprise. He had only to
speak above a whisper to be heard in the uttermost pews.

"This," he said, with a slight wave of his hand toward the shrinking
Sarah, "is a marketable commodity. Such as she are now put into one
balance and silver into the other. She is now legally free, but she is bound
by a moral obligation which is stronger than any law. I reverence woman.
For the sake of the love I bore my mother, I hold her sacred, even in the
lowest position, and will use every means within my power for her
uplifting."

Then Henry strode to the edge of his platform, and his eloquence began
to flash. "What will you do now? May she read her liberty in your eyes?
Shall she go out free? Christ stretched forth His hand, and the sick were
restored to health; will you stretch forth your hands and give her that without which life is of little worth? Let the plates be passed, and we will see."

Women were sobbing everywhere, men trumpeting into their handkerchiefs, as the wardens carried out the collection-plates. The youthful-looking

pastor of Plymouth, the Adonis of the American pulpit, stood watching, a faint, mystic smile on his lips, rolling, perhaps, in one palm some of the uncut rubies and emeralds his wealth was already enabling him to purchase. He loved the feel of precious stones and collected them passionately, carrying them in his pocket. Once he spoke:

"I see the plates are heaping up. Remember that every dollar you give is the step of a weary pilgrim toward liberty, and that Christ has said, 'Inasmuch as ye did it unto one of the least of these, ye did it unto me.'"

Here and there he could see a woman strip a ring from her finger and drop it into the plate, here and there one unpinning a brooch. Ah, this was success for a tongue-tied, backward boy who less than twenty years before had started his preaching career in a wretched river village in Indiana. Now, still young, he was one of the highest-paid professional men in the United States and, with his lectures, his rising salary, and his royalties, he was on his way to be a millionaire. He knew so well how to do this sort of thing—to throw the warm atmosphere of human life over a pious deed, thus making each donor feel doubly righteous in the giving.

As the plates went to the four thousand, Lewis Tappan—the same Lewis Tappan who had opposed Lyman Beecher and financed the rival Oberlin College—arose and announced that he and some friends stood ready to make up any difference between the amount of the collection and the sum required.

"Then, Sarah," cried Beecher, turning to the slave girl, "you are free now! You understand? Free!"

A great burst of applause filled the church, shocking to some. Henry let it subside, then spoke. "When the old Jews went up to their solemn feasts, they made the mountains round about Jerusalem ring with their shouts. I do not approve of an unholy clapping in the house of God, but when a good deed is well done, it is not wrong to give an outward expression of our joy."

Plymouth Church shook with the fervour of the closing hymn, but most of the audience would not leave until the collection had been counted. The guarantors were called upon for nothing. Henry's plea had brought in $783, besides the jewelry, thus not only completing Sarah's redemption but giving her something with which to start her new life.

It was a fatal fortnight for the United States that saw both the assault upon Charles Sumner and Henry Ward Beecher's sensational "slave auction." During those two weeks the Civil War moved appreciably closer.

That fortnight had an extraordinary effect upon Harriet Beecher Stowe's work. It found her half through the writing of an unhurried study of slavery as it affected the characters of various people in her story. Her anger over the attack on her friend caused her to drop this mood abruptly and— so flexible was her peculiar technique, so agile her faculty of improvisation— without abandoning the work she had already finished, or even revising it, to change the purpose of the novel entirely and turn it into a broadside of hate. It is probably impossible to point to any other historic piece of American fiction so influenced by a contemporary event.

Fired as she was by her new conception, Harriet took time to express her opinion of the Kansas troubles. John Brown had joined his sons in Kansas and, three days after Preston Brooks struck down Sumner, had led a band which massacred five pro-slavery men at Pottawatomie. The border posses were taking reprisals; and an Andover boy, who had joined the holy migration, wrote to his mother about the Kansas warfare. Harriet published this letter in her column in the *Independent,* adding her appeal to her anti-slavery sisters to aid the Kansas campaign in every way within their power.

In the midst of such stirring events—events which she, above all American women, could regard as her personal concern—Harriet finished writing her novel *Dred.* The result was the most curious of her works in fiction. Conceivably *Dred* might have been her masterpiece. It contains some of the best writing she ever did, and also a great deal of the worst. The manner of its composition was, of course, responsible for most of the faults. It is notable that the second part of the story, in which at last she felt herself borne by the inspiration which had carried her so triumphantly through *Uncle Tom's Cabin,* is the part that ruined *Dred* as a work of art. The deft sarcasms, the crushing ironies used so effectively in *Uncle Tom's Cabin* are gone, as Harriet's voice becomes shrill. She threw insults, being capable of such sentences as this:

> This time the blow felled Clayton to the earth, and Tom Gordon, precipitating himself from his saddle, proved his eligibility for Congress by beating his defenseless acquaintance on the head, after the fashion of the chivalry of South Carolina.

Had Harriet remembered an essay she had written for the *Independent* on gardening and its soothing effect upon the vengeful feelings of reformers, she might have struck out that final phrase.

On the other hand, there is no Negro character in *Uncle Tom's Cabin* so successful as Uncle Tiff in *Dred*. Uncle Tiff was the slave type to which the nostalgic Southern writers still love to return—the old retainer prouder of his "family" and more loyal to it than its white members themselves. And in some of the situations in *Dred* Harriet shows immense dramatic power, such as the one in which the aristocratic and dissolute Tom Gordon lusts after the wife of his mulatto half-brother Harry, who is also his slave, and informs Harry at the outset that he intends to take her. "The development of this theme," remarks John Erskine, "is as terrible as the old Websterian tragedy."

The character of Dred, whom Harriet adopted in midstream as the novel's "hero," is preposterous. When she made the transition in purpose for the novel, Dred was at hand as her implement, having already made a shadowy appearance in her pages—a swamp-dwelling fugitive conducting a single-handed vendetta against the white race. But when she brought this Negro, whose character was suggested to her by the red-handed Nat Turner, into the full light, she made him a major prophet, speaking the language of Sinai and the King James Version—and none knew better than Harriet how to imitate the resounding couplets of the Old Testament. As a credible character, however, Dred is as divorced from human reality as the statue of an Egyptian Pharaoh.

An amusing touch in *Dred* should be noticed. Harriet was feminine enough and still spiteful enough to pay in that novel her final respects to the abused Dr. Joel Parker, whom she had never forgiven. Introducing as a character the Rev. Dr. Shubael Packthread, "a minister of a leading church in one of the northern cities," she wrote of this gentleman:

> While other people look upon words as vehicles for conveying ideas, Dr. Packthread regarded them only as mediums for concealment. His constant study, on every controverted topic, was so to adjust language that, with the appearance of the utmost precision, it should always be capable of a double interpretation. He was a cunning master of all forms of indirection; of all phrases by which people *appear* to say what they do not say, and *not* to say what they *do* say.

In 1856 there could have been few of Harriet's readers who did not know what Northern minister was the original of Shubael Packthread.

As she drew near the end of *Dred* and saw how admirably she was duplicating the language of the prophets, Harriet became convinced that this novel was going to surpass *Uncle Tom's Cabin* both in literary quality and as a political document. Sacred as was to be its mission on earth, Harriet did not propose this time to lose her British royalties. Under the law, an author, to secure a British copyright, had to be on British soil when the application was made. Therefore, Harriet planned another trip abroad that would place her in London when *Dred* began to come from the American and English presses.

Her considerate publishers attended to the details, buying the tickets for Harriet and her party for the familiar old *Niagara,* sailing from Boston on July 30. Harriet had figured it out that she could finish her story just about in time. She could turn out twenty pages of manuscript each working day, and two of her pages made one page of type. A second volume of 260 pages (she had already written the first) would, she wrote Phillips, her publisher, "be enough to say my say out."

Once there was a rigid date for finishing her work, what had been merely an engrossing occupation for Harriet became a grievous burden. Her schedule made no allowance for illness or failures in inspiration. She had to turn out her twenty pages every day, except Sabbaths. The weather became hot. She was now a woman of affairs and had to give some attention to outside interests. Once, having some other business in Boston, she carried her latest instalment of manuscript in person to Phillips, Sampson & Co. In the office she felt faint and dropped into a chair, murmuring, "I am entirely exhausted."

William Lee, the junior partner, ran to the Tremont House and returned with a chilled bottle of champagne. Harriet drank a glass of it, then a second. She felt greatly revived. She told the solicitous partners that she had been overworking, dictating much of the story of *Dred* while walking the floor, keeping it up into the night. It amazed the publishers that she could do this. None of their other authors could. Mr. Emerson, whose *English Traits* they were to advertise on the flyleaf of the first volume of *Dred,* did not. Harriet told them that creating a story was for her like bearing a child. "It leaves me in as weak and helpless a state as when my babies were born."

After she left, the deferential partners—perhaps without consulting the daughter of the father of the Temperance movement in America—sent Harriet some bottles of Catawba wine. They may have worried a little about her reaction, but they got her answer within a fortnight, tagged to the end of a business letter. "I should like half a dozen more bottles of Catawba to support the hot weather and the long pull."

Harriet's dictation of *Dred* probably marked the advent of Eliza and Harriet, the twins, into their mother's professional work. These two girls, who were to devote their lives to Harriet, often served as her amanuenses in the future. This time they were to be handsomely rewarded for helping their mamma finish her book on time, for she was taking them abroad with her, to give them their finishing education in Paris. Handsome, blond, curly-headed young Henry Stowe was to have a few weeks of foreign travel before entering Dartmouth in the fall. Calvin Stowe would, of course, attend as the ostensible head of the journeying family, and this time Harriet had invited her sister Mary Perkins, of Hartford, to join the party. So it was going to be another Deputation.

As Harriet pressed the work on *Dred* that summer, a shadow lay on her heart. Her oldest and dearest friend, Georgiana May Sykes, was seriously ill. Georgiana had gone to Groton Point, Massachusetts, in the hope that the sea air might benefit her, but her letters about herself were not cheerful. Harriet arranged to have the publishers send the invalid the proof sheets of *Dred* as the pages were set in type.

That summer also, Harriet, for the first time in her life, so far as her letters show, was intensely interested in national politics. The Kansas dispute had riven the old Whig Party; and in June the anti-slavery Whigs, now calling themselves Republicans, convened in Philadelphia and nominated the glamorous Western adventurer, John C. Frémont, for President. Harriet became an ardent Frémont supporter and was convinced that he would win the election.

As was perhaps to be expected, Harriet underestimated the time it would take her to finish *Dred*. Sailing-day came, and she had still many pages to go. Phillips, Sampson & Co. had planned publication on September 1, but could only make the best of it. Harriet promised to work on the book at sea, if she could, but, remembering her last experience with the *Niagara*, told them not to count on it.

The ocean gods were kind to Harriet and *Dred*. On the third day at sea she wrote to Phillips—a letter no doubt to be transferred with the mail to any returning vessel spoken on the voyage—that they were having a prosperous run, "our sea smooth as glass," that she was steadily at work, and that, if the good weather continued, she would be able "to send back the needful" upon her arrival in England. The twins were "in high feather." The aristocratic Eliza had insisted upon bringing her Italian greyhound, Giglio, with her. The girls wanted Ma to tell Mr. Phillips, "We are having grand times, not sick at all."

Though the smooth weather held, Harriet was not quite able to make good her prediction. The *Niagara* dropped anchor in the Mersey on August 7, and six days later, in London, Harriet, good trouper that she was, had wrapped and addressed the final batch of manuscript and was writing victoriously to Phillips:

> *Io triumphe*—It's done!—& I send it. You may have it published as soon as you please. We shall have Dred out [in England] within ten days from this 13th of August. Congratulate me! I hardly thought I should do it, but it's done, & it *suits* me, & I hope it will suit you. Be sure and have Charles read the proof sheets & tell Mr. Ramsay that he must look after spelling and punctuation and verify the quotation from Wordsworth's sonnet of Toussaint l'Ouverture. I am worn to a rag but shall mend now rapidly. Write us all the *news*, do—and how *our* President's cause comes on. For the credit of our country, I hope he will succeed.

In her relief she was a little incoherent. She started to subscribe this note to the sedate Mr. Phillips "Affectionately," then caught herself, scratched out the *Aff,* and wrote over it, "Very truly yours."

Good news awaited Harriet in London. Her new publisher there was Sampson Low; and Mr. Low told her he was taking advance orders for *Dred* at the rate of a thousand a week. Sampson Low "fired," as Calvin said, on August 22, and in two weeks could point to a sale, including the advance orders, of fifty thousand copies. The *Times,* Harriet wrote, coughed and hemmed over it: the *Record* came down on it "with a cartload of solemnity," the *Athenaeum* was spiteful, and the *Edinburgh Review* was scornful, but the British public bought it. The English edition was bound in red cloth, and everywhere Harriet saw the shop windows full of "red Dreds." Sometimes, when the presses could not keep up, there were notices instead, reading,—

To Prevent Disappointment,
"DRED"
Not to Be Had Till, etc.

In one year the British circulation of the novel was 165,000 copies, and several pirated translations appeared on the Continent. "God, to whom I prayed night and day while I was writing the book, has heard me and given us of worldly goods *more* than I asked," was Harriet's pious comment.

In America, though the total sales for the first year were only 150,000, the success was relatively greater, according to population—vastly greater, when it is considered that for this anti-slavery novel Harriet had only the North for her circulation field. The 150,000 represented the following which Harriet could thenceforth rely upon to buy and read her books. An equivalent reader-following today would number about one million.

As in England, the reviews at home were disappointing to Harriet. Even the *Independent* was a little cool, wishing that "Mrs. Stowe had put at least one good clergyman in the novel." The attack on *Dred* generally was based on the allegation that it was "an onslaught upon the Christian religion," which, of course, it was not. The New York *Journal of Commerce* said that Harriet "unsexed herself" by ridiculing religion and rejoiced that "the keys of the Kingdom of Heaven are not committed to Mrs. Stowe."

But Harriet, watching the sales rise, seeing the New York *Saturday Evening Post* serialize *Dred* after book-publication, only remarked to Calvin, "Who cares what critics say?"

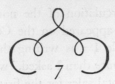

7

Strictly Confidential

HARRIET's second visit to England was marked by two interviews, both with women—small, delicate women, like herself, one elderly, the other eight years her junior. One interview forms as curious an episode as there is in Harriet's story, the other was destined to have a profound influence on her career and life. One of the women was Queen Victoria. The other was Lady Byron.

The Stowe party found London deserted after the August bank holiday—deserted, that is, by the aristocratic folk of Harriet's acquaintance. Everyone was in Scotland, and Harriet found two invitations to herself to fly thither as soon as her London business was accomplished. One was from the Duke of Argyle, the Duchess of Sutherland's son-in-law, to visit Inverary Castle; the other from the Sutherlands themselves in Dunrobin Castle in the far north.

Calvin Stowe's presence in London that summer seems to have been the legal necessity to remove, in that masculine era, any doubt of the validity of his wife's copyright. At any rate, no sooner had he arrived in England than he planned his return. He hoped to go by the Liverpool steamer, sailing August 30, but made the discovery that all the Liverpool boats were booked full until October 3. Pending an earlier opportunity to sail, Calvin decided to enjoy the Argyles's invitation with his wife.

They remained in London to see the red *Dreds* in the bookstalls and to attend to their shopping, and on August 28 departed for Scotland. Next day, in Glasgow, Calvin was writing to Professor Park, of Andover, that he had been able to book passage on the S.S. *New York,* sailing from that port on September 2, and would therefore be home in September after all.

"Yesterday," Calvin went on, "we had just the very pleasantest little interview with the Queen that ever was. None of the formal, drawing-room, breathless receptions, but just an accidental, done-on-purpose meeting at a railway station, while on our way to Scotland.

"The Queen seemed really delighted to see my wife, and remarkably glad to see me for her sake. She pointed us out to Prince Albert, who made two most gracious bows to my wife and two to me, while the four royal children stared their big blue eyes almost out of looking at the little authoress of 'Uncle Tom's Cabin.' Colonel Grey handed the Queen, with my wife's compliments, a copy of the new book. She took one volume herself and handed the other to Prince Albert, and they were soon both very busy reading. She is a real nice little body, with exceedingly pleasant manners."

Now either this letter was a complete fabrication, utterly at variance with the rugged honesty of Calvin E. Stowe, or else the public explanation of the same interview, which Professor Stowe would be making within two months in the American press, was false. Shortly after the disputed episode occurred, the Edinburgh *Witness* published the following item:

Among those assembled on Thursday morning at the King's Cross Terminus to witness the departure of the royal family for Scotland, was Mrs. Harriet Beecher Stowe. On the arrival of the royal party, Mrs. Stowe took the opportunity of presenting, through Colonel Grey, her new work, *Dred,* in two volumes just hot from the press. On learning that the fair authoress was present, both Her Majesty and Prince Albert came forward and gave her a gracious and friendly recognition, accepting the book with evident pleasure.

Proud of its leading contributor, the New York *Independent* picked up this item and reprinted it. From Andover Calvin Stowe at once wrote to contradict the truth of the paragraph; and his account of what really happened, if true, was enough to make a fellow-countryman blush today for the most representative American woman of the 1850's. The *Independent* found itself informed "from the highest authority" that—

Col. Grey invited Prof. and Mrs. Stowe to view the Queen's departure and courteously reserved for them a place on the platform directly facing the royal carriage. Just before the train started, Col. Grey informed Mrs. Stowe that *he* had procured a copy of "Dred" with a view of presenting it to Her Majesty. Mrs. Stowe objected to this, lest the Queen should suppose that the volumes came from the hand of Mrs. Stowe herself. Col. Grey, upon his own responsibility, presented the volumes to the Queen and informed her that the authoress was on the platform. The Queen came to the side of the carriage and bowed twice to Prof. and Mrs. Stowe, then spoke to Prince

Albert, who did the same. The train then started, Her Majesty and Prince Albert each having an open volume of "Dred". Mrs. Stowe was passive throughout; and the incident is honorable alike to the heart of Victoria and to the genius of our countrywoman.

Still Calvin was not satisfied with the way the *Independent* handled the denial. It had to be just right. Under date of October 13, 1856, he wrote again:

TO THE EDITOR OF THE INDEPENDENT.

Dear Sir:—There is still a mistake. Col. Grey did nothing but present "Dred" to the Queen and informed her of the presence of the author. All the rest was done by another gentleman official, whose name was not mentioned. No communication whatever passed between Col. Grey and Mr. or Mrs. Stowe. The whole matter of the presentation took us entirely by surprise. When we saw the book in the hand of the officer, we remonstrated, but to no purpose; and it all terminated very well, just as you say it did.

Truly yours,
C. E. STOWE.

Evidently, the episode was as honourable to the sweet will of Victoria as it was to her heart. In a public gathering Her Majesty might remark properly that the slavery question was America's own business, and that remark might take in Mr. Buchanan; but there is convincing evidence that Queen Victoria had adored *Uncle Tom's Cabin,* had agreed with its message, felt friendly toward its author, had an immense curiosity about her, and would have been delighted to receive her, had Harriet not been under her Government's frown. However, there was a limit to the dictation Victoria would take in her private affairs; and when there came an opportunity for her to steal a meeting with Mrs. Stowe, she took it.

This last statement is a conjecture, but one supported by the probabilities. Calvin Stowe would scarcely invent a story to tell Professor Park, his closest friend at Andover; and the gentlemen of Queen Victoria's household knew much better than to subject Her Majesty to any sudden and unwelcome confrontation. Moreover, Mrs. Stowe may have been a New England village woman, but she felt too strongly her dignity as an international figure to take a cat's look at a Queen.

We can be certain that the Kings Cross interview was arranged from the Palace. The Stowes were in London four weeks that August—quite long enough for them to have met socially Colonel Grey, or, more likely, the unnamed "other gentleman official," who learned that they were leaving for Scotland almost at the hour of the royal family's departure. When the arrangements were made, it is safe to assume that the Stowes were enjoined to regard the royal interview as strictly confidential, even to the point of denying, if necessary, that it ever occurred.

In his letter to Professor Park Calvin Stowe gave the true account of the incident. When he felt that Queen Victoria's honour was imperilled, the fat Andover professor stood up and lied like a gentleman.

The four weeks in London were long enough, too, to set the stage for Harriet's other interview, which was by far the more important one to her in its consequences. London was not quite deserted. Lady Byron was in town, trapped in her boudoir in Cambridge Terrace by the affliction of the lungs which would one day cause her death. Harriet had met Lady Byron only once during her previous visit, and then in a throng of people at a luncheon, but the two women had felt an instant affinity for each other. There had been an interchange of letters since, and in the interval each woman had learned something about the other from a common friend, whom Harriet designated as Mrs. ——, but who was, we know, the inquisitive Mrs. Follen.

Hearing that Lady Byron was in London, in reduced health, Harriet despatched a note to her, begging a meeting. By the same messenger Lady Byron returned her reply:

> My Dear Friend,—I *will* be indebted to you for our meeting, as I am barely able to leave my room. It is not a time for small personalities, if they could ever exist with *you;* and, dressed or undressed, I shall hope to see you after two o'clock.

It was *undressed*. Harriet found Lady Byron in bed, surrounded by books, pamphlets, periodicals, and letter-files. "Her sick-room seemed only a telegraphic station whence her vivid mind was flashing out all over the world." At sixty-four Lady Byron's silvery head seemed already to reflect the shimmer of the Gates of Light. Harriet remembered her slight, fragile form, her bright eyes, the graceful motions of her small, pearly-white hands.

During the August days following, their intimacy grew like a yeast-culture in a warm medium. Eager as Harriet was to enter the confidences of the wife of the man she had worshipped in her adolescence, the advances seemed to come from Lady Byron. Lady Byron knew all about Harriet's girlhood infatuation with Lord Byron. "I heard it from Mrs. ————; and it was one of the things that made me wish to *know* you." As soon as Lady Byron felt a little better, she had the entire Stowe party, including Mary Perkins, for lunch with her in Cambridge Terrace. Then there was an evening in Cambridge Terrace for just Harriet, Calvin, and Henry Stowe, and Lady Byron had in a few people to meet them, including (for young Henry Stowe's sake) her eccentric grandson, Lord Ockham, heir to the earldom of Lovelace, a physical giant who had taken a job as an iron-worker in the shipyard then building *The Great Eastern*. Before Harriet left London for Scotland, she sent Lady Byron a copy of *Dred*.

At his good luck in catching a boat so quickly, Calvin Stowe decided to forego his visit to the Duke and Duchess of Argyle. Harriet and the others therefore said good-bye to him in Glasgow and went on for a delightful week at Inverary Castle, a delightful week of travel up through the heart of the Highlands, and a third delightful week as guests of the Duke and Duchess of Sutherland in Dunrobin Castle.

At Dunrobin Harriet found a letter from Lady Byron, who had read *Dred* and was full of praise for it. "I know more than ever before how to value communion with you," wrote Lady Byron, subscribing herself, "Yours affectionately."

Dunrobin was near enough to Balmoral Castle for Harriet to hear news of the royal family. Guests were passing back and forth between the two centres of Scottish hospitality. The Duchess said to Harriet one morning at breakfast, "The Queen says she began *Dred* the very minute she got it and is deeply interested in it." Her Majesty was preferring it to *Uncle Tom*. She enquired for Mrs. Stowe and, particularly, for Professor Stowe, who seems to have made an impression on Victoria. There was something clandestine about such indirect messages, thrilling to Harriet, as if she and the Queen kept a secret between them. It was better than any formal presentation.

Their noble hosts made much of young Henry Stowe. The Duke gave him a Sutherland plaid, which the boy hung in his Dartmouth room as soon as he got back to America. Master Henry was a guest of honour at the tenants' dinner. He pledged every toast "in fair water," to the astonishment of the Duke's whiskey-drinking henchmen.

The Laboucheres were house guests at Dunrobin. Harriet had met them on her first London visit. Labouchere, an immensely wealthy man, held a Cabinet post; his wife, Lady Mary, the Duchess's sister, was of the Queen's household. This pair took a special fancy to Harriet at Dunrobin and invited herself and party for an October week-end at Stoke Park, their country place near Windsor Castle.

From Dunrobin the Stowe party went to Edinburgh for two weeks of visiting and sight-seeing, spent a day at Durham Cathedral, and on October 10 were at the railroad station in York to put Henry on the train for Liverpool and his boat. He was already overdue for the matriculation of his class at Dartmouth, and his mother felt that she should keep him from his studies no longer. She impressed it on him that few boys of his age had ever seen what he had already seen on this journey, or made more valuable friends. She kissed him fondly and sent him off with letters, her journal of the tour for Calvin's enjoyment, and a parting injunction "to do well and be a comfort." As the train moved out and she saw her sunny-headed boy leaning from the car window and waving back to her his last farewell, there was no presentiment in Harriet's heart.

Harriet, the twins, and Mary Perkins, went down to London, taking in Sherwood Forest and Oxford—"a mountain of museums, colleges, halls, courts, parks, chapels, lecture-rooms." They sent their baggage on ahead from York. At London, where they arrived late in the rainy evening of October 15, the Lows met them and took them out to their suburban home in Kentish Town. Next morning, "Confusion in the camp!" The baggage had not come, they had "not even a clean collar," and were engaged to take the train at two o'clock for Stoke Park and the Laboucheres' house-party. The twins wept with disappointment, and Harriet was incensed, forgetting the fate of Calvin's treasures when shipped by rail from Portland to Andover as she wrote scathingly, "I never saw such blind, confusing arrangements as these English railroads have."

Fortunately for Harriet, she had left some of her travelling wardrobe in London and had a suitable dress. After some frantic shopping for collars and handkerchiefs, she went on alone to Stoke Park, leaving the others to follow when they should have recovered their raiment. Stoke Park was a splendid, terraced Italian villa in the midst of a deer park. When Harriet saw her room, she "sat down in an easy chair before the fire and formed hospitable resolutions as to how I would try to make rooms always look homelike and pleasant to tired guests."

At lunch next day Harriet met young Lord Dufferin, the Arctic explorer, who had discovered a new island north of Spitzbergen. He had come over from Windsor with Lord Alfred Paget, both being gentlemen of the

Queen's household. The royal family had returned; and these gentlemen, Harriet reported, "brought news of the goings-on there." They brought something else—an invitation ("understood as a command") to the Laboucheres to dine that evening with Her Majesty. Presently the Laboucheres departed in state, Lady Mary "dressed very prettily in a flounced white silk dress with a pattern of roses woven round the bottom of each flounce," Labouchere in "breeches, with knee and shoe buckles sparkling with diamonds." Aunt Mary and the girls arrived just in time to see them go.

This abduction left the house guests and four or five others invited in, to their own devices at dinner. Harriet did not mind, however, when next morning Lady Mary told her about the royal party. The curious Lady of Windsor seems to have had a special motive in inviting the Laboucheres during Harriet's visit, for much of the talk at the Windsor dinner table was about American slavery and Mrs. Stowe's novels. The diners could have heard both sides, for one of the Queen's ladies was the Hon. Miss Murray, who had once written a book "not only exculpatory but even laudatory of American slavery." Time, however, and perhaps Mrs. Stowe's novels, had changed Miss Murray's opinions, and before Harriet left London she received from this lady a five-pound note, to be passed on to the free-state sufferers in Kansas.

After dinner Queen Victoria took Lady Mary Labouchere aside and, of course aware that every word would be passed on, "talked to her all about 'Dred,' and how she preferred it to 'Uncle Tom's Cabin,' how interested she was in Nina, how provoked when she died, and how she was angry that something dreadful did not happen to Tom Gordon." What delighted Harriet most, though, was that Her Majesty "inquired for papa and the rest of the family, all of whom she seemed to be well informed about."

So much could Queen Victoria do in recognition of Harriet Beecher Stowe, and a little more; for next day, when Harriet and Lady Mary were driving near Stoke Park, they met the royal carriage. They drew up beside the road, and the Queen "bowed graciously" to them as she passed. It was the crowning episode in what Harriet called "one of the loveliest visits I have made."

In London there was a note for her from Lady Byron. Lady Byron had made up her mind about Mrs. Stowe, but she approached her goal delicately. She feared there was but a slender chance of seeing her dear friend, since she was now in her country residence. However, she wanted to send £50 to the Kansas sufferers and asked Harriet's advice as to the safest channel.

Perhaps Mrs. Stowe herself would undertake the transmission of the money. Lady Byron's address was Oxford House, at Ham Common, two miles below Richmond.

Harriet replied with sentimental enthusiasm. She longed to see dear Lady Byron, having "so much to say, so much to ask, such need to be refreshed with a sense of a congenial and sympathetic soul." Accordingly, when, a few days later, Harriet and her sister, having left the girls with the Low family, were going by train down to Eversley, in Hampshire, they stopped off at Ham Common and had lunch with Lady Byron. Lady Byron asked Harriet if on her return she would stop again for a short visit, "as she had a subject of importance on which she wished to converse with me alone." Harriet promised.

They were going to Eversley to pay a visit to the Rev. Charles Kingsley, whom Harriet, for all their correspondence, had never met. Kingsley's *Alton Locke* and *Yeast* seem to have impressed Harriet more deeply than any novels of Dickens ever did. It was after dark when they drove up to the rectory door in a hack, and as they knocked Harriet felt her heart flutter. Kingsley himself admitted them, stammering a little in his speech. In the large, pleasant parlour, with its cheerful coal fire, Harriet "took a good view of him," finding him "tall, slender, with blue eyes, brown hair, and a hale, well-browned face, and somewhat loose-jointed withal. His wife is a real Spanish beauty."

And, Harriet continued, "how we did talk and go on for three days! I guess he is tired. I'm sure we were. He is a nervous, excitable being, and talks with head, shoulders, arms, and hands, while his hesitance makes it the harder." A polemist like Kingsley and the daughter of Lyman Beecher were bound to discuss religion and creeds. Somewhat to her surprise, Kingsley said that the thirty-nine Articles of the Church of England were the finest and broadest platform a man could stand on. Harriet had to admit that her husband thought them the best summary of doctrine he knew. It is possible that from this conversation sprang in Harriet's mind the train of thought that eventually took her out of Calvinism altogether and into the Episcopal Church.

Lady Byron had invited two other intimate friends, both women, to lunch that day. At the end of the repast, the hostess, who was having "one of her *well* days," took Harriet with her to a room where they would have privacy, leaving Mary Perkins to visit with the two other guests in the drawing-room. The early November night had long since closed in when Harriet and Lady Byron emerged from their conference. They had spent the entire afternoon together; and Harriet, still dazed and unable to collect her faculties of judgment, knew Lady Byron's secret of why she had left Lord Byron.

The reason Lady Byron gave for admitting Mrs. Stowe to her confidences was, for one of the former army of girls of two continents who had languished for the romantic poet, perhaps the greatest flattery Harriet ever heard from English lips.

"I think *you* could have understood him," Lady Byron said, with just this emphasis.

When she came to the "true cause" of her separation from Lord Byron, Lady Byron did not mince words. She used the word *incest*. Harriet thought her friend was going to faint after she said this, but Harriet herself did not feel faint. She had heard the story before—from Mrs. Follen, or Mrs. ————, as one prefers.

Lady Byron was not, she told Harriet, exposing the details of her married life with Lord Byron for the mere purpose of imparting scandalous information. She wanted Harriet's advice. Some publishers were about to bring out a cheap edition of the poet's works and in the promotion meant to revive the old story of Byron's having been driven to exile and death by the cold, mercenary heart of his wife. Should that wife keep silent any longer? Had not, in fact, her years of silence made her a party to the ancient falsehood? Then, too, Lady Byron believed that repentance and regeneration continued after death. Could Lord Byron's soul ever find peace, unless the great injustice were righted?

Impulsive, warm-hearted Harriet was for immediate disclosure, but she asked for time to think. She and Mary Perkins remained overnight with Lady Byron in Ham Common, though not to sleep. Harriet told Mary the whole story, and the two sisters sat up all night, talking it over. By morning the wicked, tragic, Calvinist poet, whom Lyman Beecher had so confidently thought he might have brought to grace, had become a Beecher-family possession.

Mary Perkins was so set against any disclosure of the incest story at all that she upset Harriet's confidence in her own judgment. Next morning, when they said good-bye to Lady Byron, Harriet said she would write later, when she had ripened her thoughts. It was six weeks later when, from Paris, she sent Lady Byron her considered judgment:

I would say, then, Leave all with some discreet friends, who, after *both* have passed from earth, shall say what was due to *justice*.

Harriet preserved a copy of this letter but with it no answer from Lady Byron designating *her* or any other person as the "discreet friend." Lady Byron, in fact, does not seem to have replied to this portion of Harriet's letter at all.

In Paris the four American ladies put up at the *pension* of Mme. Borione, at 19, rue de Clichy, at the foot of Montmartre, where they had a comfortable suite, consisting of a parlour and two bedrooms. They engaged a tutor and settled down for the winter to learn to speak and understand French. There were seventeen other boarders in Mme. Borione's *pension*, mostly Americans in Paris for study; but one was a talented English girl, Miss Durant, who was studying sculpture as a pupil of Baron de Triqueti, an artist of some note in Paris. Miss Durant took Harriet to Triqueti's studio, and the delighted *maître* insisted that his pupil must do a portrait at once of Madame Besshare-Stowe.

"But, my French lessons!" exclaimed Harriet.

"Ah, madame," said the gallant Latin, "we will teach you the French while you sit."

Thereafter Harriet climbed the Montmartre hill daily for her sitting, with incidental education.

"As usual," she wrote to Calvin, "my horrid pictures do me a service, and people seem relieved when they see me; think me even handsome 'in a manner.' Kingsley, in his relief, expressed as much to his wife, and, as beauty has never been one of my strong points, I am open to flattery upon it."

In the course of these sittings Harriet became intimate with the family of the Baron de Triqueti. The sculptor's oldest daughter, Blanche, was twenty—just the age of the twins. Mme. de Triqueti was English. The Baron, Harriet said, was "one of the loveliest men I ever saw." And Miss Durant's sculpture was lovely, too, everyone, and especially the twins, saying it was a perfect likeness of Harriet.

Besides having this social contact, Harriet spent one evening a week at the salon of her friend Mme. Belloc, another at the salon of Mme. Lanziel, and a third at that of Mme. Mohl, wife of the famous Orientalist and Sorbonne professor. At these gatherings she met the elite of French art and letters and one evening wondered aloud why she never encountered George Sand, who had said such nice things about *Uncle Tom's Cabin.* Mme. Belloc informed her that French ladies could not meet Mme. Sand, even though Mrs. Browning and Margaret Fuller had done so.

Harriet toyed with the idea of writing a book on French society and manners, and even collected some material for it. She resumed her letters to the *Independent,* displaying, after so few weeks in Paris, such a shrewd understanding of French character as to make one think she may have understood Southern aristocratic character, too, better than most critics gave her credit for.

In Kansas the border bands were avenging the Pottawatomie murders by murdering four of John Brown's sons, one after another; but to Lady Byron's gift was attached a proviso that none of the money should be spent for arms. Harriet forwarded it to Calvin, who presented it to the Kansas Committee, with due publicity in the *Independent.* "Having had the pleasure of a personal acquaintance with Lady Byron," Calvin wrote the editors, "I must say that her sympathy for the cause is to me more gratifying than any amount of pecuniary contribution could have been."

By the end of January Harriet and Mary had had enough of the fogs and frosts of a Paris winter. Harriet placed the girls in a Protestant boarding-school, and she and her sister travelled down to the warmer climate of Italy. They went from Marseilles to the Roman port, Civita Vecchia, by steamboat, and in the last night at sea were in a collision that sheared off one of the vessel's paddlewheels. The passengers, half-dressed, huddled in the cabin, as they waited two hours to learn the extent of the damage, before their minds' eyes the spectre of "the Naples boat," which had gone down after a similar collision a few nights before, the passengers trapped below by the fallen stack. Harriet and Mary sat in quiet calm, Harriet, however, for one, having small confidence in "the administration of the boat," resigned to the worst. "It was an inexpressible desolation to think that we might never again see those we loved. No one knows how much one thinks, and how rapidly, in such hours."

They remained three weeks in Rome, seeing everything. Then to Naples, Pompeii, and Herculaneum, and a climb up Vesuvius, where Harriet's guide steamed an egg for her in a smoking fissure in the crater. "It tasted of Glauber's salt and sulphur." Thence (from Naples) by boat, and "gloriously seasick," to Leghorn, and in to Florence for two weeks. There Harriet met the Brownings; and Mrs. Browning wrote to her friend, Mrs. Jameson, that she liked Mrs. Stowe better than she thought she should.

> I find more refinement in her voice and manner—no rampant Americanisms. Very simple and gentle; undesirous of shining or *posering,* so it seems to me. . . . She is nice looking, too; there's something strong, copious, and characteristic in her dusky, wavy hair. For the rest, the brow has not very large capacity; and the mouth wants something both in frankness and sensitiveness, I should say. But what can one see in a morning visit? I must wait for another opportunity. . . . Her books are not so much to me, I confess, as the fact is that she, above all women (yes, and men of the age), has moved the world—and *for good.*

Venice, Harriet thought, was the place where one really caught up with romance. In Milan she was convinced that Da Vinci's "Last Supper" *"was* the greatest picture the world ever saw"—not *is,* so little remained of it. Back to Rome for Holy Week, and "Papal Rome is an enchantress!" Then the sisters went to Paris.

At home the Supreme Court had decided that Dred Scott was only a piece of property, the *Independent* called on lovers of liberty to resist and wipe out the decision or "see light only beyond the storms of revolution and blood," and in Andover Calvin Stowe was worried. The New York *Times* had published a letter from its Paris correspondent, dated February 20, in which the statement was made that Mrs. Stowe was then in Paris, where she was planning to write an *Uncle Tom* for the downtrodden in white society. Mr. Phillips, the Boston publisher, wrote to Professor Stowe to learn if he had heard anything about such a book.

Calvin pronounced the story "all bosh." So far as he knew, Mrs. Stowe was in Rome on February 20. Now it was March 20, and Calvin informed Phillips that "one thing, however, is strange. Mr. Perkins, of Hartford, had a letter from his wife, dated Paris, Jan. 28, of the same purport with Mrs. Stowe's letter to me of the next day—*and since that we have neither of us had a word from either of them,* though, before, letters came regularly with every Liverpool packet. This I cannot account for, and I am awaiting with sincere anxiety the arrival of the next packet." No doubt the next packet brought good news, but Calvin's anxiety was justified. Not many American women gadded about Europe unattended in the 1850's.

In Paris in early May Harriet found the twins greatly improved in their studies and so enamoured of Paris that they begged to stay and come home with a party of friends, who were sailing in November. Harriet consented. She found in Paris also her brother-in-law, John Hooker, who had come to Europe in the interest of a client. He was planning a tour of Switzerland, and Mary Perkins decided to go with him. But Harriet was homesick now and decided to go on alone, even though, since the Mediterranean collision, she had a nervous horror of committing herself once more to the ocean. She booked passage on the *Europa,* sailing from Liverpool June 6.

In England she met Harriet Martineau for the first time, though the two had corresponded. At least Harriet thought it was the first time, but Miss Martineau believed that Harriet was the girl in the white frock and black silk apron she had seen in Ohio in 1835. "Your sister I knew well, and I have a clear recollection of your father. I believe and hope you were the young lady in the black silk apron." Harriet Martineau was praising *Dred* to the skies.

In London Harriet met John Ruskin, who took her out to Camberwell and showed her his gallery of Turners. After London she visited Mrs. Gaskell in Manchester, and of course there was a final day and night with the Croppers in the dear old Dingle. But in London she had called again on Lady Byron, and from Liverpool she wrote to that friend as follows:

> I left you with a strange sort of yearning, throbbing feeling—you make me feel quite as I did years ago—a sort of girlishness quite odd for me. I have felt a strange longing to send you something. Don't smile when you see what it turns out to be. I have a weakness for your pretty Parian things; and it is one of my own home peculiarities to have strong passions for pretty tea-cups and other little matters for my own quiet meals, when, as often happens, I am too unwell to join the family. So I send you a cup made of primroses, a funny little pitcher quite large enough for cream, and a little vase for violets and primroses—which will be lovely together—and when you use it think of me and that I love you more than I can say.
>
> I often think how strange it is that I should *know* you—you who were a sort of legend in my early days. That I should love you is only a natural result. . . . So, good-by, dear, dear friend, and if you see morning in our Father's house before I do, carry my love to those that wait for me; and if I pass first, you will find me there, and we shall love each other *forever.*

Harriet stepped on home soil barely in time to meet the shock of the greatest tragedy that ever fell on her life.

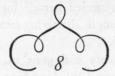

8

The Gathering Storm

IT WAS disappointing to Harriet not to find her son Henry at the Stone
Cabin to help welcome her after so many months of absence. There was
a letter from him instead, telling her that his Freshman examinations were
so near at hand he felt he should not spare the time for a trip to Andover
but should wait for the summer vacation.

His mother understood, knowing that her boy, in his fondness for her,
was making a real sacrifice for the sake of his studies. And Henry was as
proud of her as he was fond. Some of the Dartmouth boys had been
admiring his seal ring, telling him how handsome they thought it.

"Yes," said Henry, "and the best part of it is, my mother gave it to me."

Not every boy had a mother whose very presents were historic objects.
That spring, to his grief, Henry had fallen and cracked the ring—was it an
omen?—cracked it across the space where his name was engraved.

Only three, therefore, of Harriet's brood of six—Freddie, Georgie, and
Charley—were at home to make her greeting boisterous; and she thought
Fred looked rather peaked. Her impulse was to take Fred and go up to
Hanover, New Hampshire, to see Henry; but she reconsidered. Harriet
shared her age's belief in the medicinal properties of regional airs, and she
diagnosed Fred's trouble as an overdose of seacoast air. Since Harriet
thought that even Hanover shared this same atmosphere, she turned inland
with Fred, after less than a fortnight of the prose of resumed domestic life,
and sought an unspecified "water-cure establishment," which may, however,
have been at Matteawan, New York, where Henry Ward Beecher had just
bought a mountain farm. The undersized Freddie was now seventeen
years old.

Leaving him where mountain air could do its beneficent work, Harriet
went down to Brooklyn for a visit with her friend Susan Howard. She had
been there little more than a week when, the evening of Thursday, July 9,

433

1857, a telegram came for Mrs. Howard, who read it and with suddenly trembling hands and knees steeled herself for a dreadful scene with her guest. The telegram had brought shattering news. Harriet's son Henry was dead at Hanover—drowned.

At Dartmouth young Henry had gone in for aquatic sports, being a member of the crew that rowed the *Una* boat. Above the boat houses the Connecticut River came round a bend that was broad, deep, and full of strong currents. Only a strong swimmer could cross at this place; but for those of less endurance the currents had washed up in midstream a sand bar on which a spent swimmer could stand and rest. By using the sand bar that Thursday afternoon, Henry, his roommate, and another boy had swum to the Vermont side. On the return, Henry either misjudged the current or lost his landmark and in midchannel found himself below the bar and too exhausted to reach it against the stream.

The other two boys, standing on the sand, heard his cry for help and plunged in to the rescue. Henry's roommate found him, only to be gripped by the drowning boy and to sink with him. At the last moment, as if realizing that he was killing his friend, Henry let go, and both his companions managed to struggle to the New Hampshire shore. Their plight had been observed, and boats were on the way. College swimmers recovered Henry's body within fifteen minutes, but life was gone from it.

When Harriet came home, she found Henry's body in its casket and the Cabin filled with weeping classmates who had escorted it down from Dartmouth College. Harriet moved in a stricken daze. A year or so later in *The Minister's Wooing,* the novel inspired by this tragedy, she would be writing about the feelings of another mother, when she heard that her son was drowned at sea, and carrying her fictional mother to the gates of insanity. Harriet might easily have gone insane over the death of Henry, had she not by this time sufficiently liberalized in her philosophy the harsh doctrines she had imbibed in her childhood.

It had happened so suddenly there was no time to make permanent arrangements for Henry. The funeral was held Saturday, and the body was placed in the vault in the Old South Churchyard. On Monday Calvin and Harriet went up to Hanover to talk with their son's classmates and see his room, just as he left it, the Sutherland plaid on the wall, his books spread out. . . . "Every child that dies is for the time being an only one," Calvin told Harriet.

Andover Seminary had, too, as part of the laboratory equipment of its theological courses, its campus graveyard. On their return Calvin and Harriet picked out, as Harriet wrote to the twins in Paris, "a lot that is to be henceforth ours—

> 'Our just inheritance consecrated by his grave.' "

In time it was to be consecrated by Calvin's grave, too, and Harriet's. On the evening of August 24 they laid Henry to rest in this place, and Harriet wrote to the girls: "It seems selfish that I should yearn to lie down by his side, but I never knew how much I loved him till now."

Harriet for once in her life was ready to curse God and die. She said afterwards to Catharine it was as if a voice were saying to her, "You trusted in God, did you? You believed that He loved you! You had perfect confidence that He would never take your child till the work of grace was mature! Now He has hurried him into eternity without a moment's warning, without preparation, and where is he?" To the girls in Paris she was writing desolately, "As I walk the house, the pictures he used to love, the presents I brought him, and the photographs I meant to show him, all pierce my heart. I have had a dreadful faintness of sorrow come over me at times. I have felt so crushed, so bleeding, so helpless. . . ." One of the first things she had done was to take Henry's photograph to a Boston artist and have a portrait done in oils. Now it hung in the long, narrow parlour "as perfect almost as life," having "just that half-roguish, half-loving expression with which he would look at me sometimes, when I would come and brush back his hair and look into his eyes."

Harriet planted the grave with pansies, white immortelles, white petunias, and verbenas. She visited the grave every day, and Calvin often two and three times. Calvin said, "I am submissive but not reconciled." The two of them took little Charley and made a pilgrimage for Henry to Brunswick, stopping with the Uphams and visiting Getchell's mill and the old pond, Maquoit, Harpswell, and Middle Bay, where Charley, down among the rocks, caught a flounder with his own hand, "whereat he screamed loud enough to scare all the folks on Eagle Island." Peace was beginning to return to Harriet now, and in Brunswick she felt "very near the spirit land; and the words, 'I shall go to him, but he shall not return to me,' are very sweet."

Even grief so poignant and personal, occurring in the Beecher family, must be shared with the public. Henry Ward Beecher wrote touchingly in the *Independent* of Henry Stowe's death and burial, as half a nation sympathized and knew that the sudden silence over Andover sheltered a mother's breaking heart. In September Harriet resumed her columns in the *Independent.* She chose for the subject of her first article after the drowning of her son, Spiritualism.

WHO SHALL ROLL AWAY THE STONE?, was her title, and she left no doubt that she had been consulting spiritualistic mediums in an effort to communicate with Henry. But, if it was possible to roll away the stone from his grave, Harriet wanted it done by "an *unquestionable* angel, who executes no doubtful juggle by pale moonlight or starlight." If the raps and squeaks and tricks with tables and chairs constituted communion with the dead, "sadly and soberly we say we had rather be without it." As for the communications of spirits professing to describe things seen in the spirit world, "we can conceive of no more appalling prospect than to have them true."

"If," she continued, "the future life is so weary, stale, flat, and unprofitable as we might infer from these readings, one would have reason to deplore an immortality from which no suicide could give an outlet. To be condemned to such eternal prosing would be worse than annihilation."

These words have often been quoted as Mrs. Stowe's mature judgment against Spiritualism after she had gone into it thoroughly. Rather, they were her first impression as she entered the twilight of the séances. For many years thereafter she was going to experiment with the occult; and, though she made no public profession of adherence to the cult, her private letters show that she was more believer than sceptic.

There had been a home activity in the Stone Cabin that summer to draw Harriet's attention at times from her bitter bereavement. Charles Beecher had come up from Newark, bringing the completed manuscript of his father's *Autobiography and Correspondence,* and with him came the old Doctor himself and his wife, from Brooklyn, to hear Charles read the book aloud. "It is glorious, beautiful," Harriet wrote to Catharine.

And Harriet herself took part in a historic addition to the American scene that autumn. For some years a young man named Francis H. Underwood—the same Underwood who had given Harriet information for her *Key*—had been peddling in Boston the idea for an anti-slavery magazine of high literary quality. The two leading monthly magazines of the United States were then *Harper's* and *Putnam's,* neither of which published

anything on the slavery issue or indeed on any controversial subject. Underwood observed that some of the leading literary figures of the North—
Longfellow, Whittier, Dr. Holmes, and James Russell Lowell—were
Abolitionists, at least in sympathy, and argued that a militant anti-
slavery magazine, supported by such names, would become a signal success.

Underwood's enthusiasm failed to infect any men of means until the
vast triumph of *Uncle Tom's Cabin* showed that anti-slavery literature
could be profitable. The young journalist then went to Boston and succeeded in interesting John P. Jewett in his scheme. Before the thing could
be organized, however, Jewett's finances became involved, and he sold
his Stowe copyrights to Phillips, Sampson & Co. Underwood followed
them over to that office.

There he won the support of the junior partner, the same William Lee
who had rejected *Uncle Tom's Cabin* as a book for his house to publish.
This time it was M. D. Phillips who was dubious, although assured by
Longfellow, Holmes, and Lowell that they would support the magazine.
Meanwhile Underwood had met Mrs. Harriet Beecher Stowe in the
Phillips, Sampson & Co. office and imparted some of his enthusiasm to her.
Thereafter, when Harriet was in Boston she seldom let slip an opportunity
to urge Phillips to go ahead with Mr. Underwood's magazine.

In the autumn of 1857, after Lowell had agreed to serve as editor, if
elected by the staff, Phillips was about won over. He exacted a final condition, however. If the editors could get Mrs. Stowe's agreement to contribute a serial to the new magazine, he would consent to its publication by
his firm. Lowell and Underwood went out to Andover one October day
and called at the Stone Cabin. Harriet was momentarily absent, and Calvin
entertained the Boston gentlemen until her return. Years later one of
these visitors, probably James Russell Lowell, told Mrs. McCray, of
Hartford, about the meeting.

> The children were nearly all handsome and in every way attractive.
> They were full of animal life, too, and were dancing about with eager
> laughter and beaming eyes. I said something to Professor Stowe about their
> lively ways and ready speech; and he, with a look of deep pride, exclaimed,
> "Yes. Beechers, every one of them!" This was said quite naturally, as if there
> could be no question which side of the house their brilliant qualities came
> from. The self-abnegation rather touched me. I did not find it at all comic.

Calvin Stowe was by now thoroughly tamed by his wife's celebrity.
Still only in his middle fifties, he was already hinting of retirement,

giving the usual excuse of feeble health. The ambition which had burned
so hotly when he was the prodigy of Bowdoin, lay in cold ashes. Now that
Harriet's income made it possible, he asked only for hearty meals, a chair
in a warm place in winter and a cool one in summer, and no interruption
to his esoteric reading. He was soon to become that melancholy type, the
scholar who lives for research as an end in itself.

Lowell and Underwood left with Harriet's contract to write a serial
story for the new magazine and a sketch, which she had recently written
in her preoccupation with Henry's death, for the first number. She called
it *The Evening Veil,* and it was an allegorical treatment of the theme of
spiritual profit in bereavement. The magazine was then being called
tentatively, *The Orient,* Underwood's name for it. It was not until the
organization dinner at the Parker House a little later—a function quite
possibly attended by Harriet—that Dr. Holmes suggested the name, *The
Atlantic Monthly.* "No matter what the name may be when it is given,"
he remarked, "after the thing for which it stands manifests its quality,
then the quality will be transferred to the name. *The Atlantic* may mean
something or nothing; if you can make it a success, it will mean everything."

The Stock Market collapsed in October, sending the country into the
worst panic it had experienced since 1837. With unemployment almost
complete throughout the North, and New York facing a winter of soup
kitchens and State relief, such editorial leaders as Horace Greeley and
Henry Ward Beecher were whistling optimism. Harriet took the occasion
to speak out once more on public affairs, and her mood was not cheerful.
The nation could regard this stroke as the hand of God laid on a sinful
people. It was but a part of the turmoil and unrest everywhere.

The living had begun to demand her attention, and especially one
seven-year-old bundle of energy that romped in the Stone Cabin. For her
column Harriet wrote an article entitled *Our Charley,* full of advice for
mothers on how to entertain, instruct, and keep out of mischief their
seven-year-olds. So widely read was she now that "Our Charley" soon
became a generic name in the North for any irrepressible little boy. A
year later Harriet took this and several other papers on the same subject
and issued them as a slender volume under the title, *Our Charley.*

But she thought about Henry, too, and in February about that October
afternoon when—

Beneath the sunny autumn sky,
With gold leaves dropping round,
We sought, my little friend and I,
The consecrated ground.

She had planted crocus bulbs on the grave, and Charley had asked her if they would not die during the long, cold winter. She told him that in each bulb slept a living flower, which was but symbolic of the flower of immortality in that other form, lying deeper down. In February she transmuted this thought into a poem, *The Crocus.*

Harriet's *Evening Veil,* published unsigned in the first number of *The Atlantic Monthly,* attracted no attention; but to the third number she contributed *New England Ministers,* which was signed and in her best vein of realism. The *Atlantic's* publishers, editors, and contributors had inaugurated the custom of dining together once a month in the Parker House; and in those social gatherings in the winter of 1857-58 Harriet cemented with Oliver Wendell Holmes the most valuable friendship of her life. Of all the great people of literature who knew her, Dr. Holmes was always her greatest admirer and staunchest defender.

Holmes was carrying the *Atlantic* on his own shoulders that first year of its existence. With no distinctive fiction and with most of its factual articles published unsigned, the magazine was having a struggle to survive. Only the swift popularity of Dr. Holmes's *Autocrat of The Breakfast Table* bore it along. The second year, Holmes continued with his *Professor at The Breakfast Table,* and Harriet came in with her *Minister's Wooing,* and the two of them lifted the *Atlantic* safely out of the jaws of failure.

It may have been during this winter that Francis Underwood persuaded Mrs. Stowe to go with him to the National Theatre in Boston and see the stage performance of *Uncle Tom's Cabin.* The celebrated Mrs. Howard played "Topsy" and gave a superb performance; but the rest of the acting, Underwood thought, was poor. Harriet laughed and wept with the rest of the audience but said scarcely a word during the entire performance, nor did she ever tell Underwood what she thought of the play.

It was Harriet's first visit to a theatre but another count in Andover's indictment against her. The evangelical community was compressing its lips, too, at the white marble cross Harriet had erected over Henry's grave. The cross was a Popish symbol. Though Mrs. Stowe was always in her front pew at every chapel service, didn't she really have "Episcopalian leanings"?

In the midst of hard times and living on the edge of a volcano, at the moment dormant, the North picked up a new hysteria that spring, as a great religious revival swept the land. There had been nothing comparable since Colonial times. Harriet saw some of it in New York, where Protestant business men were neglecting their stores and offices to attend morning prayer-meetings, often conducted by Henry Ward Beecher. She had gone there during the Easter vacation with Calvin, who was on his way to Ohio, as a guest of Salmon P. Chase, now the Governor in Columbus. Chase was an unannounced candidate for the next Republican Presidential nomination. There was no doubt where the Stowes stood on that nomination. Professor Stowe was arranging for Governor Chase to deliver a great anti-slavery address at the coming church anniversaries in Boston. "You will ride triumphantly on the topmost wave," Calvin had written him. Harriet's mission in New York was to promote the endowment at Andover Seminary of a professorship of political science, the incumbent, of course, to be a strong anti-slavery man.

On the first anniversary of Henry Stowe's death his mother wrote for the *Independent* a poem, *Only A Year,* which must have filled many an eye with tears and gone into many a scrapbook as a clipping. Here are some selected stanzas:

> One year ago—a ringing voice,
> A clear blue eye,
> And clustering curls of sunny hair,
> Too fair to die.

> Only a year—no voice, no smile,
> No glance of eye,
> No clustering curls of golden hair,
> Fair but to die!

> The silent picture on the wall,
> The burial stone,
> Of all that beauty, life, and joy
> Remain alone.

> Where hast thou been this year, beloved?
> What hast thou seen?
> What visions fair, what glorious life?
> Where hast thou been?

The veil! the veil! so thin, so strong!
  Twixt us and thee—
The mystic veil! when shall it fall,
  That we may see?

Lord of the living and the dead,
  Our Saviour dear,
We lay in silence at thy feet
  This sad, sad year.

It was a changing world. Andover Seminary celebrated its semi-centennial in August, 1858, and in the midst of the ceremonies the news came that the two ends of the Atlantic Cable had been spliced in mid-ocean, and that Queen Victoria had flashed across the sea an instantaneous message of congratulation to President Buchanan. It was of special interest to Andover, since Samuel F. B. Morse was the son of a Seminary alumnus. There were shouts and cheers at the announcement, Harriet reported, and "the eyes of many filled with tears." Somebody struck up, "Praise God from Whom all blessings flow," and afterwards Dr. Hawes, one of the oldest alumni, offered a prayer of thanksgiving. That night there were bonfires and illuminations all over the land, North and South, and Henry Ward Beecher came down from "Mountain Rest" to address the jollification at Fishkill Landing.

Harriet's *Atlantic* article on New England's preachers held a significance beyond that of its text. It meant that she had begun to "compose" her serial story for the *Atlantic*—*The Minister's Wooing*. She was pursuing a study of the old Puritan clergymen; and the one she selected to be the hero of her love-story was Samuel Hopkins, of Colonial Newport, a saint in the Calvinistic galaxy only second to Jonathan Edwards himself. When she dared this, Harriet knew she was prodding a great many dry, theological bones. By a twist in history, she brought into her novel, by name and as an elegant sinner of the familiar Byronic stamp, Aaron Burr; and it was daring, too, in that prim age, for a daughter of the Beechers to devote part of her story to the attempt of Burr to seduce the novel's angelic heroine.

Lowell and Holmes and the other Boston lights she was meeting at the *Atlantic* dinners must have awed Harriet, for never before had she taken such pains with a story as she did with *The Minister's Wooing*. She claimed afterwards that she dictated it, but the novel shows many evidences of the etching tool which, it also shows, Harriet knew how to use if she chose. In sheer virtuosity *The Minister's Wooing* could compare favourably with any fiction of its day. John Ruskin wrote Harriet that the story was worth its weight in gold. Lady Byron, the friend of both authoresses, rated it above the current *Adam Bede*.

She began to write in June, and by December, when the first installment appeared, she was so far ahead of the printer that never was she to be hurried from that quarter. In fact, all during the autumn of 1858 she had been able to keep up her other interests. She contributed regularly to her column, and original poems from her pen spaced off from each other her rebuke to the American Tract Society for its pro-slavery attitude, her praise for the three Haitian Negroes who had won first prizes at the Sorbonne, her further articles about "Our Charley," and her occasional editorials on the slavery question. An October comet in the northwest seemed to symbolize the uneasy times, though it ushered in nothing but the quietest year in the great contention since the passage of the Fugitive Law. Harriet corresponded with Lady Byron on the possibility of regeneration after death. For her older children and their friends she organized the Picnic Club, which met regularly at the Cabin for music, stories, games, charades, and a collation. Business was getting better by January 1, 1859, when Harriet could welcome John Greenleaf Whittier as a fellow "stated contributor" to the *Independent*.

When by February Harriet had not heard from Mr. Lowell how he liked her new story, she interpreted his silence as disapproval. Highly sensitive now to criticism from this source, she wrote in trepidation for her editor's frank opinion about the work she was doing. Perhaps there was too much theology in the story to suit him. Lowell, who had not cared too much for either *Uncle Tom's Cabin* or *Dred,* now knew the Andover authoress well enough to speak to her as a brother, and his reply warmed Harriet through and through:

My Dear Mrs. Stowe,—I certainly did mean to write you about your story, but only to cry *bravissima!* with the rest of the world. I intended no kind of criticism; deeming it wholly out of place, and in the nature of a wet blanket, so long as a story is unfinished. When I got the first number in MS, I said to Mr. Phillips that I thought it would be the best thing you had done, and what followed has only confirmed my first judgment. From long habit, and from the tendency of my studies, I cannot help looking at things purely from an aesthetic point of view, and what *I* valued in *Uncle Tom* was the genius and not the moral. That is saying a good deal, for I never use the word *genius* at haphazard, and always (perhaps too) sparingly. I am going to be as frank as I ought to be with one whom I value so highly. What especially charmed me in the new story was, that you had taken your stand on New England ground. You are one of the few persons lucky enough to be born with eyes in your head,—that is, with something behind the eyes which makes them of value.

In characteristic fashion Lowell then went on to give Harriet a great deal of shrewd advice in her writing. "In the first place, pay no regard to the advice of anybody. In the second place, pay a great deal to mine." He ended this amusing letter with an encouraging pat on the back:

Only this I will say, that I am honestly delighted with *The Minister's Wooing;* that reading it has been one of my few editorial pleasures; that no one appreciates your genius more highly than I, or hopes more fervently that you will let yourself go without regard to this, that, or t'other. Don't read any criticisms on your story: believe that you know better than any of us, and be sure that everybody likes it. That I know. There is not, and never was, anybody so competent to write a true New England poem as yourself, and have no doubt that you are doing it. The native sod sends up the best inspiration to the brain, and you are as sure of immortality as we all are of dying,—if you only go on with entire faith in yourself.

In a different tone was Harriet's description of herself written in the very week she received Lowell's letter. Georgiana Stowe, now a keen, alert miss of sixteen, much in her mother's image at the same age, had been sent away that year to school. Harriet had been neglecting her, and Georgie wrote reproachfully. Harriet replied:

Why haven't I written? Because, dear Georgie, I am like the dry, dead, leafless tree and have only cold, dead, slumbering buds of hope on the end of stiff, hard, frozen twigs of thought, but no leaves, no blossoms, nothing to send to a little girl who doesn't know what to do with herself any more than a kitten. I am cold, weary, dead; everything is a burden to me. I let my plants die by inches before my eyes, and do not water them, and I dread everything I do, and wish it was not to be done, and so when I get a letter from my little girl I smile and say, "Dear little puss, I will answer it"; and I sit hour after hour with folded hands, looking at the inkstand and dreading to begin. The fact is, pussy, mamma is tired.

The mood must have been momentary, for Harriet was most active that winter and spring. She found time to intersperse between installments of the *Wooing* a series of sermonettes for her *Independent* readers on *The Higher*

Christian Life. The twins, pretty as ever at twenty-three but showing no signs of leaving spinsterhood, were nostalgic for Paris. Harriet packed them off in March with Miss Harriet Beecher, Henry's daughter, as travelling companion, promising to join them later in the year. She gave her blessing to Fred's plan to take passage with his friend Sam Scoville, of Brooklyn, in a sailing vessel bound for Europe. In May she wrote to Lady Byron about her plan to visit England in the summer to arrange for her British copyright of *The Minister's Wooing*.

As the proofs of each instalment of the story came back from the *Atlantic,* Harriet invited Professor and Mrs. Park to tea and read the chapters aloud to them. Professor Park approved of her treatment of Hopkins and even suggested a minor character for the story. Harriet was a writer who thrived on praise, and she thirsted for more than local approval. Sampson Low was receiving the *Atlantic's* proof-sheets and publishing *The Minister's Wooing* in London, uncopyrighted, in monthly parts. At some risk, perhaps, Harriet wrote to John Ruskin, commending her story to his attention. The great English critic's reply gave her another delightful letter to cherish. "Nothing can be nobler than the noble parts of it, nothing wiser than the wise parts of it, nothing more delightful than the delightful parts, nothing more edged than the edged parts."

The aging Lady Byron wrote pathetically of her eagerness to see Harriet once more. "The best flowers sent me have been placed in your little vases, giving life, as it were, to the remembrance of you, though not to pass away like them."

With such messages on her table, Harriet wrote the last words of *The Minister's Wooing* in July and was ready to sail on the S. S. *Asia* from New York on August 3rd. Before she left, however, she made a business change for herself. The times were getting better, but the financial storm had been severe, and one of the barks foundering in the ground-swells of the depression was the Boston house of Phillips, Sampson & Co. The firm did not fail until September, but Harriet must have known something in advance, because before her departure she arranged to have *The Minister's Wooing* published jointly by Derby & Jackson in New York and Brown, Taggart & Chase in Boston.

This time the entire family was to be abroad at once, except for Charley, who was entrusted to Andover friends for safekeeping. The twins and their cousin were waiting in Paris. Fred was at sea on a windjammer

eventually to be expected to reach Liverpool. With Harriet on the *Asia* went
Calvin and Georgie. Calvin described the first part of the tour to Charley
in a letter which shows why, when Professor Stowe was in the mood and at
leisure, one so often found a group of children clustered at his slippered feet.

Calvin wrote to his little son from "Castle Chillon" under date of
September 1:

We are all here except Fred and all well. We sailed from New York
in the steamer Asia, on the 3rd of August, a very hot day, and for ten days
it was the hottest weather I ever knew at sea. We had a splendid ship's
company, mostly foreigners, Italians, Spaniards, with a sprinkling of Scotch
and Irish. We passed one big iceberg in the night close to, and as the iceberg
wouldn't turn out for us, we turned out for the iceberg and were very glad
to come off so. This was the night of the 9th of August, and after that we
had cooler weather, and on the morning of the 13th the wind blew like all
possessed, and so continued till afternoon. Sunday morning, the 14th, we got
safe into Liverpool, landed, and went to the Adelphi Hotel. Mamma and
Georgie were only a little sick on the way over, and that was the morning
of the 13th.

As it was court time, the high sheriff of Lancashire, Sir Robert Gerauld,
a fine, stout, old, gray-haired John Bull, came thundering up to the hotel at
noon in his grand coach with six beautiful horses with outriders, and two
trumpeters, and twelve men with javelins for a guard, all dressed in the
gayest manner, and rushing along like Time in the primer, the trumpeters
too-ti-toot-tooing like a house afire, and how I wished my little Charley had
been there to see it!

Monday we wanted to go and see the court, so we went over to St.
George's Hall, a most magnificent structure, that beats the Boston State
House all hollow, and Sir Robert Gerauld himself met us and said he would
get us a good place. So he took us away round a narrow, crooked passage,
and opened a little door, where we saw nothing but a great, crimson curtain,
which he told us to put aside and go straight on; and where do you think we
all found ourselves?

Right on the platform with the judges in their big wigs and long robes,
and facing the whole crowded court! It was enough to frighten a body into
fits, but we took it quietly as we could, and your mamma looked as meek
as Moses in her little, battered straw hat and gray cloak, seeming to say, "I
didn't come here o' purpose."

That same night we arrived in London, and Tuesday (August 16th),
riding over the city, we called at Stafford House and inquired if the Duchess
of Sutherland was there. A servant came out and said the duchess was in
and would be very glad to see us; so your mamma, Georgie, and I went
walking up the magnificent staircase in the entrance hall, and the great,

noble, brilliant duchess came sailing down the stairs to meet us, in her white
morning dress (for it was only four o'clock in the afternoon, and she was
not yet dressed for dinner), took your mamma into her great bosom and
folded her up till the little Yankee woman looked like a small gray kitten
half covered in a snowbank, and kissed and kissed her, and then she took
up little Georgie and kissed her, and then she took my hand and didn't
kiss me.

Next day we went to the duchess's villa, near Windsor Castle, and had
a grand time riding round the park, sailing on the Thames, and eating
the very best dinner that was ever set on a table.

We stayed in London till the 25th of August, and then went to Paris
and found Harriet and Eliza and H. B. all well and happy; and on the
30th of August we all went to Geneva together, and today, the 1st of
September, we all took a sail up the beautiful Lake Leman here in the
midst of the Alps, close by the old castle of Chillon, about which Lord
Byron has written a poem. In a day or two we shall go to Chamouni
[Chamonix], and then Georgie and I will go back to Paris and London,
and so home at the time appointed.

But Calvin and Georgie did not go back to London alone, as the professor undoubtedly expected to do on September 1. Harriet, for some reason,
accompanied them and saw them aboard their steamer, then returned to
Switzerland for the twins, whom she had left in Lausanne. With them she
then departed immediately for Italy. In England, the land she had so recently
left, she spent two weeks with her husband and daughter, "travelling and
visiting," according to her biography which her son Charles wrote under
her direction. Assuming this statement to be correct, and allowing for
necessary travelling time, she was in Geneva and Switzerland from August
30th to the 18th or 19th of September, 1859.

Harriet's record that is available for research says not a word about those
three weeks beyond Calvin's statement that they were going to take a trip
to Chamonix. As a result, they form for a present-day biographer the most
tantalizing blank in her life-story. What happened to make her change her
mind about saying good-bye to Calvin and Georgie in Switzerland and
undertake the tiresome journey to London, with its dreaded Channel crossing? To visit English friends whom she had just visited? Or did Calvin's
sailing afford her an excuse to leave Switzerland suddenly? It is all conjecture; but of one or two facts we are certain. John Ruskin, whose marriage
had recently been annulled, was in Geneva; and Ruskin, who had previously
been only a friendly acquaintance of hers, in those twenty-one days formed

Courtesy of The Metropolitan Museum of Art

HARRIET BEECHER STOWE, ABOUT 1860

"I am a little bit of a woman . . . about as thin and dry
as a pinch of snuff." (Page 337.)

From a daguerreotype by J. J. Hawes

for Harriet Beecher Stowe an attachment that was warm indeed. Ruskin said she had made herself "cruelly pleasant" to him.

From Lausanne, which they left about October 10th, Harriet, the twins, and the Beecher cousin travelled "by easy stages" to Florence, "stopping at Lake Como, Milan, Verona, Venice, Genoa, and Leghorn." So easy were these stages that they took a month for the journey. In that month things happened in America important to Harriet professionally and as the mother of a son of military age. On October 20th *The Minister's Wooing* (with the final two installments yet to appear in the *Atlantic*) was published as a book in the United States, and on that same day the Boston publishing firm of Ticknor & Fields bought *The Atlantic Monthly* from its bankrupt ownership. Four days earlier, a Sunday morning, and almost exactly on the anniversary of the comet, Captain John Brown—"Osawatomie Brown"—with a handful of followers as addled as himself, surprised and captured the United States Arsenal at Harpers Ferry, Virginia. The tranquil year was over, and there was to be no more peace.

The first reaction of the North to John Brown's raid was one of horror and condemnation, as bulletins in the windows of the New York newspaper offices apprized the public of the progress of that excellent Army officer, Major Robert E. Lee, in his siege of the captured arsenal. Garrison and Whittier thought the raid had damaged the Abolition cause, but even in the first comment there was an undertone of justification.

John Brown held out in the arsenal until Tuesday and was then taken, sorely wounded, with what few of his men remained alive. Not one of the four million slaves he had expected to rise in rebellion came to his rescue. The South might still perhaps have held the affair to the importance of a minor incident soon forgotten, if it had treated "Old Brown," as Governor Wise, of Virginia, secretly wanted to do, with more lenity; but a South which had never forgotten the Nat Turner atrocities and which now did not know how far the plot might have extended among the slaves, was in no mood for temperate action. With Richmond under heavy military guard and troops on patrol in cities as remote from Harpers Ferry as Charleston and New Orleans, Brown was brought into court on a stretcher, tried and convicted in a few hours, and sentenced to death.

It was the trial rather than the raid that fanned the slavery dispute once more to white heat. The North in a few days elevated a blood-stained murderer and revolutionist to the eminence of its national martyr and hero, with Mr. Emerson making the address at the great defense meeting in Tremont Temple, and in New York the conservative Rev. Dr. Cheever predicting that the Harpers Ferry raid was "but the preliminary warning that God is about to take off his restraints from the ministers of vengeance and to let loose the avalanche." The fiery Joshua R. Giddings, of Ohio, justified John Brown's act in the Philadelphia meeting.

The South was matching extravagance with extravagance. In the Richmond *Whig* appeared an advertisement offering ten thousand dollars reward for the "safe delivery in Richmond," of Giddings, or five thousand "for the production of his head."

Because the Southern press was naming him as John Brown's accomplice, Frederick Douglass, the Negro Abolitionist, departed hastily for England, saying that that country was for him "a safer asylum than any afforded by the President of the United States," whom the Northern newspapers were calling, "Old Buck." In Washington a Quaker who expressed sympathy for Brown was arrested and bound over in $2,000 to keep the peace. Men were selling photographs of John Brown on Broadway for a dollar apiece, while in Charles Town, Virginia, at the gaol where the prisoner awaited his doom, was exhibited the rope that was to hang John Brown. It was made of South Carolina's long-staple cotton, and there was a placard—"NO NORTHERN HEMP SHALL HELP TO PUNISH OUR FELONS."

At 11 o'clock on the morning of December 2, as John Brown walked calmly to the gallows, tens of thousands of Northerners were meeting to pray, guns were booming a requiem in Albany, and when Yale College assembled for worship, the professors found that the undergraduates had hung the chapel with crepe.

While this excitement was going on at home, Harriet Beecher Stowe, the prophetess of war at home, was finding its close contact in Italy disillusioning. Napoleon III and his Sardinian allies had that summer crushed the Austrians at Magenta, near Milan, and driven them out of Lombardy. Harriet visited the battlefield and, in one of the shattered mansions, was disgusted when an Italian woman in the sight-seeing party began to gloat that the brick floors had been flooded with Austrian blood.

While the United States daily moved nearer one war, Harriet moved through another in northern Italy. Not until she reached Florence in November did she hear the news about John Brown at Harpers Ferry, and then she was at too great a distance to appreciate its importance. But a reign of terror had started in the South, as every village, it seemed, had its *vigilantes* to question strangers, expel citizens so rash as to send their children to Northern schools or to buy goods in New York and Boston, and tar and feather unfortunates suspected of the Abolition taint.

When Congress convened, the representatives of both sides openly carried pistols into the House sessions. For the first time Southern members began to threaten secession, if the new Republican Party should elect the President in 1860. One firebrand, denouncing the Abolitionists by name, shouted, "And if Henry Ward Beecher ever crosses the line into slave territory, you will find him hung high as Haman."

At last the Southern orators were crying out the real issue on which the war was to begin. It was no issue of the extension or abolition of slavery, and no question of the right of a State to secede from the Union. The South began to demand openly in Congress that the North suppress the whole anti-slavery movement or find itself merely a severed section of what had been the United States of America. Southern flesh and blood could endure the propaganda no longer, the abuse and recrimination it was receiving from the North; and a victory of the Republican Party in 1860 meant four more years of that torture.

One propagandist was not ready to quit. On New Year's Day Harriet Beecher Stowe in Florence viewed the world of 1860 for her *Independent* readers, and for the first time took public cognizance of the raid at Harpers Ferry, finding it part of a worldwide crusade for human freedom.

> Thus do all signs gather round this new year; and, when we hear from home, we find that in America the same demons of slavery are trembling and quailing before some advancing power. We hear here in Italy of a brave, good man who calmly gave his life up to a noble effort for human freedom and died in a way that is better than the most successful selfish life. We read of troops of soldiers to guard that one calm man—a whole country under martial law and yet not able to subdue the tremor caused by his great, quiet spirit. John Brown is a witness slain in the great cause which is shaking Hungary, Austria, Italy, France; and his death will be mightier for that cause than even his success. The cross is the way to the throne.

In Florence, Harriet and the girls had found Fred Stowe and Sam Scoville, who in their travels had picked up young Leonard Bacon, of New Haven, and also a youth named Porter, who was going to enter Andover Theological Seminary the next autumn after a year of foreign travel. Then, the day before Christmas, Harriet's wealthy Brooklyn friends, John T. and Susan Howard, and two of their children, Annie and John, arrived most unexpectedly, and Harriet could give a Christmas party that was a bit of New England on the bank of the Arno.

Harriet renewed her acquaintance with the Brownings that winter in Florence. Robert Browning gave her the material for a whole column in the *Independent* on the state of affairs in Italy. Elizabeth Barrett Browning no longer wondered if Mrs. Stowe's mouth were frank or her brow intelligent. The two eminent ladies had found a theme of absorbing mutual interest— Spiritualism. Calvin Stowe, in Andover, thought he was getting messages from the drowned Henry. A guitar in the Stone Cabin was strummed mysteriously, touched by no visible hand.

"I cannot think that Henry strikes the guitar," Harriet wrote him. "That must be Eliza. Her spirit has ever seemed to cling to that mode of manifestation, and if you would keep it in your sleeping-room, no doubt you would hear from it oftener."

But there had been an amazing coincidence. In the Stowes' *pension* in Florence was dwelling a Mrs. E., "a very pious, accomplished, and interesting woman, who has had a history much like yours [Calvin's] in relation to spiritual manifestations." She was "a very powerful medium," wrote Harriet, "but, being a very earnest Christian, and afraid of getting led astray, she has kept carefully aloof from all circles and things of that nature." Now this Mrs. E. also owned a guitar—a small, Florentine guitar, hanging on the wall of her parlour—and one Sunday, when Harriet was having lunch with Mrs. E. and Mrs. E.'s sister and feeling "as if Henry were close by me," the bass string of the guitar sounded "loudly and distinctly."

" 'Who struck that guitar?' said the sister. We both looked up and saw that no body or thing was on that side of the room. After the sister had gone out, Mrs. E. said, 'Now, that is strange! I asked last night that if any spirit was present with us after you came today, that it would try to touch that guitar.' A little while after, her husband came in, and as we were talking we were all stopped by a peculiar sound, as if somebody had drawn a hand across all the strings at once. We marveled, and I remembered the guitar at home."

What thought Calvin about that? Harriet thought that "spiritualism is a reaction from the intense materialism of the present age." In contrast to a previous opinion, she wrote Calvin: "We ought to enter fully, at least, into the spiritualism of the Bible. Circles and spiritual jugglery I regard as the lying signs and wonders, with all deceivableness of unrighteousness; but there is a real, Scriptural spiritualism which has fallen into disuse, and must be revived, and there are, doubtless, people who, from some constitutional formation, can more readily receive the impressions of the surrounding spiritual world."

Harriet did not mention that Elizabeth Browning had any part in these amateur séances; but that the English poetess knew about them and was much interested is indicated in a letter she wrote to her "dear Mrs. Stowe" a year later. "I don't know," she said, "how people can keep up their prejudices against spiritualism with tears in their eyes." As for Mrs. Browning herself, didn't her dear friend see "how I must want spiritualism above most persons?"

Harriet made new friends in Florence, among them Thomas Adolphus Trollope and his wife, whose home was a rendezvous for British and American writers. Although Thomas Trollope's mother had left Cincinnati before Harriet's arrival in that city, they could almost claim to be fellow Buckeyes and could, no doubt, laugh at Mrs. Trollope's old Bazaar, the wonder of the early West. One evening Harriet attended a large reception of international society held in an old palace on the Arno. Among the other guests were James T. Fields, the junior partner of Ticknor & Fields, of Boston, and his young second wife, Annie Adams Fields, and they were presented to the famous American authoress. In such a romantic setting, therefore, Harriet met her future publisher and the woman who was to be her most intimate friend during the remaining years of her life.

Mrs. Fields's description of this meeting is a comment on the utter reverence in which Harriet Beecher Stowe's countrywomen, and especially young women, held her at this time. As Mrs. Fields said, "We . . . saw her wrapped about, as it were, with a kind of sacred awe." Annie Fields, not yet twenty-six that Florentine evening, was a brilliant woman, already a shining figure in the Boston literary firmament and soon to become something of a dictator in it; but in the sudden presence of the little Andover authoress she became a trembling schoolgirl, abashed and uncertain of herself.

Future encounters, however, were warmer; and by the end of February, when they all travelled down to Rome together, Harriet and the Fieldses were fast friends. James T. Fields, besides being a publisher, businessman, and social ornament, was a poet, best remembered today for his *Ballad of The Tempest*, which begins with the familiar lines

We were crowded in the cabin,
  Not a soul would dare to sleep;
It was midnight on the waters,
  And a storm was on the deep.

With Fields, Harriet, always adaptable, stepped upon a special plane of communion, filling her letters to him with all sorts of odd pranks of the pen, a fact indicating that the poet-publisher was a man of puns and whimsical ideas.

The home newspapers were bringing Harriet much news of interest to her. Business was booming again, and the 1860 auction of Plymouth Church pews brought in nearly $30,000. The most coveted pew, No. 89, went for $280, and the trustees were talking about building a new church edifice to seat six thousand. Brother Henry Ward had made the address at a great woman-suffrage meeting in the Cooper Institute, going a little too far for Harriet, who still inclined more to Catharine's anti-suffrage views. That same week the Illinois lawyer Abraham Lincoln, who had attracted so much attention in 1858 in his campaign debate with Senator Douglas, also spoke in Cooper Institute and the New York *Evening Post* named him as a Republican Presidential possibility, though, of course, it was almost certain that Senator Seward would get the nomination. Brother Henry had auctioned another slave girl, Pink, from Plymouth pulpit, and in Boston Mrs. Follen was dead of pneumonia. Eunice Beecher had been badly injured in a runaway. Hoopskirts reached the height of fashion in New York that season, and they cost according to the number of hoops. The range was from eight to fifty hoops, with gradations between.

The publishers were reporting splendid sales of *The Minister's Wooing*. Secular reviewers had been good to it, but the novel had stirred up a mighty commotion among the religious editors. It is hard to realize today that *The Minister's Wooing* was almost as revolutionary in the religious life of the nation as was *Uncle Tom's Cabin* in its political life. It was a *coup de grâce* to the old absorption in dogmas and their cruel consistencies which had held the American people, or a large portion of them, since their ancestors came to this continent in order to develop those dogmas in peace. It marked the beginning of a more liberal and emotional type of religious observance.

In Rome, which they reached just in time to witness the Mardi Gras celebration early in March, Harriet and the girls took an apartment in the Via Gregoriana, sending out to a *trattorea* for their meals. With relations between the Vatican and the Italian Government at the breaking point, the Mardi Gras that year was more riot than *fête;* and Harriet was sorry she had taken her daughters out into the Corso when muddy bouquets were thrown into their carriage.

Two weeks later there were bloody riots in the Corso, and Harriet attended a Friday-noon mass and saw the Pontiff himself, "his great, light-brown eyes reminding us of a soft, sleek leopard's." A week later the Pope excommunicated King Victor Emmanuel, of Sardinia, and his court, and Harriet rushed to St. Peter's to see the historic edict tacked to the doors.

The Pope and the pageantry of Rome were fascinating her. She went into the noon mass again to study the Pontiff and wrote of the procession as the Pope left the church: "First, his lackeys all in crimson damask, then chamberlains in the rich old Spanish costume with velvet doublet and wide ruff, then cardinals in their violet-colored suits fit for the mourning of Lent, and, lastly, the mild old man with his round, calm face, his clear, lustrous hazel eyes, looking so fatherly as he blessed from right to left that one's heart longed to think well of him; and some stiff young Protestants of our acquaintance confessed to an inclination to kneel before him."

During the riots, William Wetmore Story, the most admired sculptor of his day, gave a dinner for Mrs. Stowe in his studio in the Barbarini Palace. She was brilliant that evening and presently was holding the entire company spellbound with her story of Sojourner Truth, "The Libyan Sybil."

Sojourner Truth was a famous character in the antebellum North. She was a tall, powerful, black Negress, a full-blooded African, perhaps slightly unbalanced, but gifted with a wild eloquence that made her a favourite speaker at the anti-slavery meetings. Subsisting on charity, old Sojourner travelled from State to State, a self-appointed abolition movement in herself.

After the success of *Uncle Tom's Cabin,* Sojourner felt that she had to see the white woman who had done so much for her race. The inopportune hour she chose to break in on Harriet found the Beechers holding a reunion in the Stone Cabin. It made no difference to the gigantic Negress. She told her story anyhow; and for an hour or more the Beecher children forgot it was their father's eightieth birthday as they listened to a barbaric eloquence which, Harriet thought, given the same culture, deserved the immortality of the words of St. Augustine or Tertullian.

At Story's dinner Harriet gave the company an account, in dialect, of the visit of the black woman who called herself "The Libyan Sybil." By bracing her shoulders and getting physically behind her chest-tones, the little authoress could give a tolerable imitation of Sojourner Truth's ringing barytone, and one so thrilling to William Wetmore Story, at least, that in subsequent gatherings he induced Harriet to repeat her mimicry. Before she left Rome Story showed her a plaster model of his Libyan Sybil as Harriet had inspired it. The finished statue attracted attention when exhibited in London in 1862 and remains as one of Story's masterpieces. There is a replica of it in the Metropolitan Museum in New York.

Harriet saw Holy Week and Easter in Rome and then bade farewell to her friends in the winter colony (which now included the Brownings) and with the Howards and the children, except Fred, started out on a tour of southern Italy. Fred and his friends, in fact, seem to have left the party in Florence to pursue their own ways. Fred's future was now settled. He had confided to his mother that he did not want to follow the family tradition into the ministry but wished to become a physician. Harriet knew just the man to advise him—Dr. Holmes, in Boston.

In Naples Harriet's room in the Hotel Crocella overlooked "a sea with a duck's-neck gloss," while opposite was Vesuvius displaying at night "a bed of great, live hickory coals, just raked and sparkling and blinking high up in air." They visited Castellamare, Sorrento, Salerno, Pæstum, Amalfi, and "old, voluptuous Capri." At Salerno a cold rain held them indoors for a day or two. To occupy the time, Harriet suggested that they all collaborate in writing a story.

With such a distinguished novelist in the party, of course none of the young people was willing to make the start. So Harriet, in almost no time, contributed a first chapter. The story sprang so ready-made into her head that she even brought in the name for it—*Agnes of Sorrento*. The first chapter introduced Agnes, a girl who sold oranges at one of Sorrento's gates.

When Harriet read this to the storm-bound travellers, they were dismayed, having expected nothing so fine as this as a pattern for their lesser gifts to follow. Mrs. Stowe must, of course, finish such a wonderful story herself.

On their slow journey back to Rome Harriet "composed" aloud more of this story to them in the diligence. In Charleston, South Carolina, the Democratic Convention was adjourning without agreement on either platform or candidate. From Rome our party went to Florence. In the Chicago Wigwam the Republican delegates were stampeding to Lincoln on the third ballot, as Harriet and the girls in Florence said good-bye to the Howards, who were going to "do" Milan and Venice.

(Lincoln's nomination was so unexpected that politicians in Washington at first thought the news from Chicago was a hoax. The disappointed Seward said afterwards that Lincoln for his nomination could thank *Uncle Tom's Cabin* and the spirit it had raised in the North.)

Before the end of May, Harriet, her daughters, and Miss Beecher were once more quartered in Mme. Borione's *pension* in Paris, and Harriet was writing to Calvin (May 28): "Since my last letter a great change has taken place in our plans, in consequence of which our passage for America is engaged by the *Europa,* which sails the 16th of June; so, if all goes well, we are due in Boston four weeks from this date."

What had been their plans? They must have been ambitious ones for further travel, since the change in them was great. Did they include another trip to Switzerland, perhaps to rejoin the Howards there—and perhaps for an eminent art critic at Geneva to talk nonsense to a staid New England matron eight years his senior, who had, moreover, a husband anchored to a distant American campus? Harriet closed her letter to Calvin with an unexpected sentence: "We will make a very happy home, and our children will help us."

While in London Harriet took time to go out to Ham Common and pay a last visit to Lady Byron. Lady Byron's appearance shocked her. "Her hands were like ice; her face was deadly pale; and she conversed with a restraint and difficulty which showed what exertion it was for her to keep up at all." Harriet hastily made another appointment. When she returned next time she found Lady Byron better, and they spent together "a long, still summer afternoon, in a garden."

At the end Lady Byron called her carriage and insisted on taking Harriet to the station herself. Near the end of the ride Harriet exclaimed that she had forgotten her gloves, and it was too late to go back for them.

"Never mind; take mine and I will keep yours," said Lady Byron.

"Oh, yes," Harriet murmured. "Thanks." But she did not put on the gloves.

Many years later, when Harriet was dead, they found the gloves—"a delicate drab" in hue—wrapped and preserved in tissue paper, together with a rosebud which Lady Byron had worn that day.

Harriet seems to have waited until almost the last minute before sailing to inform Mr. Ruskin of her abrupt departure, and then she neglected to give the name of her ship and its sailing-date. As a result, she was two days at sea when Ruskin replied to her from Geneva, hoping still that his letter might catch her in London, and Harriet did not receive it—forwarded by the senior Ruskin—until she had been at home some time. She preserved the letter and at the end of her life handed it over to her son for her biography.

Dear Mrs. Stowe:

It takes a great deal, when I am at Geneva, to make me wish myself anywhere else, and, of all places else, in London; nevertheless I very heartily wish at this moment that I were looking out on the Norwood Hills, and were expecting you and the children to breakfast tomorrow.

I had very serious thoughts, when I received your note, of running home; but I expected that very day an American friend, Mr. S., who I thought would miss me more here than you would in London; so I stayed.

What a dreadful thing it is that people should have to go to America again, after coming to Europe! It seems to me an inversion of the order of nature. I think America is a sort of "United" States of Probation, out of which all wise people, being once delivered, and having obtained entrance into this better world, should never be expected to return (sentence irremediably ungrammatical), particularly when they have been making themselves cruelly pleasant to friends here. . . .

I was waiting for S. at the railroad station on Thursday, and thinking of you, naturally enough—it seemed so short a while since we were there together. I managed to get hold of Georgie as she was crossing the rails, and packed her in opposite my mother and beside me, and was thinking myself so clever, when you sent that rascally courier for her! I never forgave him any of his behaviour after his imperativeness on that occasion.

And so she is getting nice and strong? Ask her, please, when you write, with my love, whether, when she stands now behind the great stick, one can see much of her on each side?

Ruskin went on to talk about Rome, the Pope, and Venice, continuing:

I've no heart to write about anything in Europe to you now. When are you coming back again? Please send me a line as soon as you get safe over, to say you are all—wrong, but not lost in the Atlantic.

*   *   *

I really am very sorry you are going—you and yours; and that is absolute fact, and I shall not enjoy my Swiss journey at all so much as I might. It was a shame of you not to give me warning before. I could have stopped at Paris so easily for you! All good be with you! Remember me devotedly to the young ladies, and believe me ever affectionately yours,

J. Ruskin.

A letter such as this would mean nothing today, and perhaps meant nothing in 1860 from a brilliant man noted for his startling expressions. Yet, read in the light of the usual reticences of the early Victorians, it was an extraordinary epistle. Calvin Stowe had never written one to his wife so warm in sentiment; and what other man of Harriet's acquaintance would have contemplated a trip from Geneva to London for the pleasure of a few hours with her? In all the record there is no whisper against Harriet's complete fidelity to Professor Stowe—unless that mysterious sentence about her change of plans in her letter of May 28 to Calvin indicates a previous rift of some sort, or perhaps remorse on Harriet's part at temptation momentarily entertained—and there is none in Ruskin's letter. The most suspicious reading of it merely indicates that the flirtation, if flirtation there was, was entirely on Ruskin's part, and that Harriet ran away from it.

She and her young charges were in the country in England recuperating before the ride to Liverpool when they all received a terrible shock. Annie Howard had died in Milan, after a short illness, and her parents were cancelling the rest of their tour. Young Hatty Stowe, who seems to have inherited something of her parents' hypochondria, took the loss of her friend especially hard. Who knew what seeds of death they might any of them have picked up in dirty, noisome Italy? As they took the train for Liverpool, Hatty had a fainting spell. She revived, but as the express was stopping at another station she suddenly cried out that she was dying and had to be taken into the air.

Harriet, in a great fright, Eliza, and Harriet Beecher got the stricken girl out, abandoning their baggage and even their hats in their haste. They took Hatty to a room in the station-hotel. Harriet thought her daughter was in her death agony. She called a doctor, who administered a "tonic," and the twin began to recover. Harriet telegraphed to hold the boat, if necessary, put her daughter on a stretcher, and they caught the next express in time for the sailing. At Liverpool they found their baggage waiting for them. It proved to be only hysteria after all. Next day, when Harriet was writing to Mrs. Howard from Cork, her daughter was on deck, a little wan but apparently as well as ever.

Mr. and Mrs. Fields were on board the *Europa,* and so were Nathaniel Hawthorne and his wife, ending their long residence in England. It was probably the first time that Harriet had met the Hawthornes, but both the Fieldses knew him well. The shy Concord recluse may not have relished the prospect of a voyage across the ocean with Harriet Beecher Stowe as a fellow-passenger. He had made an ungallant remark about the plague of female writers in the 1850's, and, though opposed to slavery, he disliked the anti-slavery agitation intensely. He had scoffed at the sincerity of the English demonstrations over Mrs. Stowe during her first visit.

But if Hawthorne had had Harriet especially in mind when he made his remark about America's female writers, he exempted her long before that voyage was over. There were fourteen days of it—fourteen days of perfect summer weather. Diffident at the start, Hawthorne at length "concluded to join the party." Harriet put herself out to be entertaining, Mrs. Hawthorne was full of New England lore and legend, Annie Fields was beautiful and witty, the suave Fields knitted their efforts together with his whimsicalities, and Hawthorne could listen to his heart's content. "Oh!" he exclaimed one evening, "I wish we might never get there."

But their ship and the Ship of State were moving inexorably on into violent waters. They arrived in Boston at the end of June to find that the Northern Democrats had nominated Douglas at Baltimore and the Southern minority Breckinridge. The *Independent,* though disappointed in the nomination of Lincoln—"if not Seward, we would have preferred Chase, of Ohio"—was neverthless supporting him, as was Henry Ward Beecher, that summer respectfully (but publicly) declining a Doctorate conferred upon him by his alma mater, Amherst College. With a Doctor of Divinity holding forth in every conspicuous pulpit, Henry regarded it as a distinction to lack that title.

The fatal significance of the Presidential campaign of 1860 did not at first impress itself upon Harriet, and she remained mute, as a lady should, on politics. She had been for her friend Salmon Chase, and the homely, homespun Abraham Lincoln did not commend himself to her strongly, after her contact with the civilized men of Europe. Her first thought on reaching home was for Fred and his ambitions. Oliver Wendell Holmes's *Elsie Venner* was running in the *Atlantic,* and on the pretext of praising this story Harriet wrote to Dr. Holmes, inviting him out to the Stone Cabin.

No doubt the Doctor accepted the invitation and discussed with his parents what to do about Fred. At any rate, Frederick William Stowe matriculated that fall at the Harvard Medical School, where Dr. Holmes taught Anatomy.

In August the Howards returned, bringing the body of their daughter, and after the funeral Susan Howard went up to Andover for a visit. Harriet returned with her to Brooklyn and spent the last exciting weeks of the campaign there. She caught a glimpse of the Prince of Wales on his visit to New York and wrote an enthusiastic column about him. She contributed a poem, *Lines to The Memory of Annie*. She engaged to compile a history of the career of *Uncle Tom's Cabin* in the world and wrote to her new friend, Annie Fields, in Boston for some information, ending her letter roguishly, "Drop me a line, as the fish said." Theodore Tilton, Henry's dearest friend and former secretary, "the brightest young man in New York," who was now managing editor of the *Independent* and would be its editor before he was thirty, wheedled from Harriet a promise to do a story for him that winter, or a short novel—"to run through four or five numbers." Serial fiction would be a new departure for the *Independent,* but Tilton was enterprising. Harriet remembered her "Maine story"—the one she wanted to write about Casco Bay and Brunswick. That would do for the *Independent.*

Not until November 1 did she speak of the political campaign in her column, and only then incidentally to her criticism of the recent convention of the Protestant Episcopal Church for evading the slavery issue. Nor did she mention Lincoln's name. "The Gospel of Christ," Harriet wrote, "is expounded at this day more truly in many of the political speeches of the Republican Party than in some pulpits and in some so-called religious papers."

By midnight on November 6 everyone knew that Lincoln had carried the entire North and was elected. In South Carolina the Governor announced that he was holding the State Legislature in session "to take action in the emergency." The emergency had come.

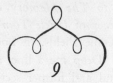

9

Harriet in Her War

THE North could not believe it, at first, nor understand it, as the most humanly understandable of our wars moved toward its start. Horace Greeley, bewildered as any, was telling the *Tribune* readers that nobody in the North could see the slightest reason for the South to break up the Union. "The grounds are so flimsy that few of us can believe they are put forth in earnest."

And it was true—there was no issue, or no immediate, critical issue of the kind that usually sends peoples into war. Lincoln was not pledged to put down slavery. The Democratic defeat was no defeat for any proposition to extend slavery's boundaries. Things were almost exactly as they had been, with even Kansas still standing at the door to statehood with her disputed free-soil constitution in her hands. The only difference was that there would now be in the White House a man opposed in principle to slavery and in control of the Government a party of the same opinion.

One magnetic sage of the North professed to see the thing clearly. The Sunday evening after election Henry Ward Beecher told four thousand solemnly nodding worshippers that Lincoln's victory had definitely ended the threat of a war which for ten years had seemed inevitable. Slavery, he predicted—and he was as right as prophets usually are—would now retreat to the deep South, as Virginia, Maryland, Delaware, Kentucky, and Missouri joined the company of the free States. "I hail their advent," said this Northern spokesman; "but if there are any that want to secede, we have nothing to say. We can stand it, if they can."

As for South Carolina, wasn't South Carolina always seceding about something? Back in 1832 South Carolina had seceded, or virtually so, over the tariff issue, and what had come of it? "We can stand it, if they can." The Plymouth pastor was speaking for thousands of his fellow

Northerners when he uttered that sentiment in that uncertain hour. South Carolina would be back, hat in hand.

The clairvoyant Mr. Beecher's sister Harriet, however, saw Lincoln's election as did the South, though from the opposite point of view. Much as the Republican platform left to be desired, the Republicans themselves were "for *stopping the evil,* and in this case to arrest is to cure." It was Harriet's restatement of the Abolition dictum that if you could stop the territorial spread of slavery, you would destroy the institution itself, which had to grow to live.

No one in the North seemed to see the compelling issue, which was sectional hatred roused by the propagandists, chief among them being Harriet Beecher Stowe. One section, its conscience smarting, had resolved to cut loose from the other and thus destroy the coercive force of an intolerable accusation.

There were at once scattered indications that what was going on in South Carolina and, quickly following, in Alabama, Georgia, and North Carolina, might not be entirely a display of childish temper. Colonel Colt's revolver factory at Hartford added a night-shift and began to turn out three hundred weapons a day—to fill Southern orders, it was said. Lights began to burn all night in the Sharpe rifle factory. Ships in Southern harbours were unloading consignments of the new French arm, the Minié rifle, which people on this side of the ocean called the Minny rifle.

The financial nerve felt it. A slowly sagging slave-market slumped at the election returns; and at Bruin & Hill's slave warehouse in Alexandria one could pick up for $800 a likely article that a year earlier would have fetched $1,500 on the block. Nearly half the value of the South's slave-property had vanished, at least on paper. And not entirely on paper for Virginia, which, the December trade statistics showed, in 1860 exported 12,000 slaves—5,000 by the Petersburg Road, 5,000 by the Tennessee Road, and 2,000 by other channels.

In Washington ten thousand Democratic job-holders were in a panic. (On election night a bomb had wrecked Republican Headquarters in the National Era Building.) Washington was astir with rumours, the most sinister being that Governor Wise, of Virginia, was plotting to seize the capital and prevent Lincoln's inauguration. In the Government offices treason sat in high places, as a trembling President looked on. Treasury orders were transferring federal cash to the New Orleans Mint. A Southern Secretary of War was gutting Northern arsenals and shipping the con tents to the arsenals of the South. As an item, during 1860 the War Department took 65,000 rifles from the arsenals of New York and Massachusetts alone and distributed them among the dépôts of South Carolina, Alabama and Louisiana.

As the legislature debated in Columbia, the name of a General Beauregard was coming into the dispatches from Charleston, but the North laughed with relief when the South Carolina delegation appeared as usual at the opening of Congress in December. There were gibes that the Southern fire-eaters did not follow their principles to the extent of forfeiting their congressional salaries and mileage accounts. Well-informed correspondents, however, were warning the Northern newspapers that the South Carolinians were on hand only to be able to walk out of the House and Senate chambers dramatically when their ordinance passed at home and thus make the secession emphatic.

And so it befell. The secession ordinance passed at Columbia, the South Carolina congressmen impressively shook the dust of the United States from their feet, and in Charleston General Beauregard moved into the Arsenal and found his forces plentifully munitioned. In Mobile a federal judge leaned from an upper window in the Customs House and announced to the crowd below: "The United States Court is adjourned forever!"

In the midst of other preoccupations Harriet Beecher Stowe paused only twice to glance at the political scene: once for her election psalm of praise, *What Hath God Wrought?*, and once, in December, to notice President Buchanan's message to Congress and his statement that the North was responsible for the South's fears of a servile rebellion. Harriet retorted that the *Marseillaise*, which South Carolina was singing as its secession song, might be helping to make the slaves rebellious. "They forget," she wrote, "who listens when they sing:

> 'O Liberty, can man resign thee,
> Once having felt thy generous flame?' "

With sarcasm heavy for her, Harriet declared that it could not be that revolutionary song which caused unrest among slaves, or the South's assurances to them (in public speeches) that Lincoln was likely to break their chains, nor the barbarisms of slavery, nor the lynching parties. "No, none of these tend to servile insurrection—not a bit of it. It's the North, the wicked, truculent, horrid North, who are constantly declaring things they have no business to, in sermons, magazines, poems, and speeches."

But she had other things to occupy her. One was a correspondence that autumn on Spiritualism with Robert Dale Owen, whose *Footfalls on the Boundary of Another World* was attracting attention in occult circles. Harriet wrote Owen, "You will regard this letter, I trust, as between ourselves." She was not going to expose publicly her receptive attitude toward a cult which most of her public considered as heathen as devil-worship.

Out of her European experiences she had brought a definite purpose to preach home-beautification to America, and inaugurated it with a "parable" in her column, *The Deacon's Dilemma.* She wrote two or three poems on the hereafter and took up that bothersome story she had promised Mr. Tilton. In its December 6th issue the *Independent* announced for 1861 "Mrs. Harriet Beecher Stowe's *New Story,* 'The Pearl of Orr's Island,' a Story of the Coast of Maine." The *Independent* was boasting of a gain of 20,000 subscribers in 1860, raising its total circulation above 200,000. Only the weekly *Tribune* could beat that.

Harriet's *Pearl* began with the first issue of the newspaper in 1861. Now she had saddled herself once more with *weekly* installments, forcing her, to her annoyance, to neglect her *Agnes of Sorrento,* which she expected to start in the *Atlantic* in May and simultaneously in the *Cornhill Magazine* in England. However, after the Christmas holidays, she persevered and by the middle of January was able to put the first installment of her Italian story into the hands of James T. Fields, who now, Lowell being about to step down, had assumed to all purposes the editorship of the *Atlantic Monthly*. Fields had evidently wanted more of the story written before he scheduled its publication; but Harriet explained that she had been under the necessity of getting herself "out of the immediate pursuit of the Independent," and that Fields could rely upon having "three numbers ahead" in May.

She had taken time, too, to "reread my little darling, for whom I have a peculiar love." She meant the part of the story she had written in Italy for the girls. "Authors," she went on, "are apt, I suppose, like parents, to have their unreasonable partialities. Everybody has—and I have a pleasure in writing 'Agnes of Sorrento' that gilds this icy winter weather. I write my Maine story with a shiver, and come back to this as to a flowery home where I love to rest." And a careless Harriet thought it best, at this the start of their professional association, to inform her friend of one of her auctorial peculiarities. "My manuscripts are always left to the printers for punctuation, as you will observe. I have no time for copying."

Her friend Jamie Fields, when he read the first chapters of *Agnes,* was not much impressed by Harriet's endorsement that the story had been conceived and begun on the scene. As diplomatically as he could, he suggested that it might be better to do another New England story for the *Atlantic,* instead of her little darling. A depressed authoress took the suggestion home to a council of her husband and daughter Eliza, "who are both pretty good judges. Their advice decides me that it is better to go on."

Harriet had good reasons for her decision—at least, the good, feminine reasons of a lady whose mind was already made up. The *Atlantic* had been publishing several New England stories, and there was danger that "the Novo-Anglo dialect might be run into the ground." Then, too, she was writing a Yankee story for the *Independent,* and she was bound to borrow back and forth. "People might say that there was overmuch at once of the same kind of thing." She added the clincher: "Mr. Stowe has read over my Italian story and says it is as good as anything I ever wrote, and advises me to finish it.

"Therefore, let us cross the Rubicon. The story will not discredit your paper and, if it be not immediately *ad captandum,* has in it materials of great power. At any rate, it must be written."

Who was Fields to dispute such a dictum, when uttered by the most popular of his magazine's contributors? As she was often to do, when she wanted to carry a point with the *Atlantic,* Harriet addressed this letter to Annie and James Fields jointly, no doubt expecting the adoring Annie to act as her friend at court. Actually, the playful author addressed it (inside the envelope) to "Mr. and Mrs. Meadows," accompanied by a pen sketch of grass and daisies growing. And on the reverse of the folded sheet she wrote: "To Sweet Fields beyond the swelling flood."

Fields privately grimaced and published *Agnes of Sorrento* as a serial, paying Harriet $200 an instalment plus "half share of profits in book form." And if the story did not discredit the *Atlantic,* it was as poor a piece of fiction as that magazine ever printed in its early years under a celebrated name. *Agnes* appears now to have been a piece of snobbery on Harriet's part. Italy was the literary fashion. George Eliot, the Brownings, and John Ruskin were writing about Italy; so even was Hawthorne. An Italian novel therefore seemed to Harriet to place her so securely within that rarefied circle.

On the other hand, Harriet's *newspaper* serial, *The Pearl of Orr's Island,* which she slighted, neglected, improvised to suit her convenience, and treated generally as her ugly duckling, turned out to be one of her literary swans. Whittier preferred it above all Mrs. Stowe's other works. He wrote to her once, "When I am in the mood for thinking deeply, I read *The Minister's Wooing.* But *The Pearl of Orr's Island* is my favorite. It is the most charming New England idyll ever written."

Harriet knew the people of Casco Bay better than she knew the peasants of southern Italy.

As she wrote on two novels at once, Harriet could glance up and see the war-clouds gather, though she did not recognize them as such. In Washington "Old Buck" had put loyalty back into the War Department and Major Anderson, the commandant at Fort Moultrie at Charleston, could at the beginning of the year occupy Fort Sumter without risking a charge of insubordination. The new Secretary reinforced and provisioned the officer and his command.

Alabama was understood to be fitting out a gunboat. Georgia voted secession and started a column of State volunteers toward Fort Pickens at Pensacola, Florida. The city of Vicksburg was stopping all steamboats on the Mississippi and examining them for cargo and personnel. The slave market was in a panic, the price of plantation hands dropping to $435 in South Carolina. So many customs houses were closed that Southern sea trade had almost stopped. Louisiana voted secession and seized the Federal Mint, with $389,000 in silver bullion. New York newspapers were speaking of "the revolting districts," as the Governor of Maine tendered to a deaf President Buchanan all the resources of his State in men and money to maintain the Union. A bewildered and suddenly sobered North, losing a good deal of its invective, was turning toward a "compromise" that was really surrender in that it contained a guarantee against any further meddling by the North with the slavery issue. It never got beyond the talking stage, however.

Buchanan had intrusted to General Winfield Scott the duty of seeing to it that Lincoln's inauguration took place; and by February 4 the old Mexican War hero had turned the capital into an armed camp, with almost the entire Army bivouacked in the city's open spaces. By this time the Southern volunteers had become "Rebels" in the Northern press. On February 11 Abraham Lincoln bade farewell to a tearful crowd at Springfield and began his slow progress eastward, with precautions taken that his train was not ambushed, and the Montgomery convention (on February 8) named Senator Jefferson Davis President of the Provisional Government of the Southern Confederacy.

Amid these stirring preparations, Harriet's only recorded utterance is a letter to Dr. Holmes, praising the closing chapters of his *Elsie Venner* and telling him not to mind too much an attack made on him by a religious newspaper. The Doctor was in the black books of the orthodox for having cut away from the Calvinist faith of his fathers.

Buchanan went out, confessing his own weakness by declaring that Lincoln had no alternative but accept the war. But would Lincoln accept it or pursue the same policy of avoidance? He left no doubt in his first Presidential utterance, saying on that March 4 from the Capitol steps, "In your hands, my dissatisfied fellow-countrymen, and not in mine, is the momentous issue of civil war." It was conciliatory but firm, and the *Independent* said: "The night has been dark and wild, but now the Pilot is on board, the skies are bright, and the ship is steady under her helm."

The Republicans were in, and Harriet at once appealed to Senator Sumner in behalf of her brother William's application for the postmastership at North Brookfield, Massachusetts. "Are we," she asked sarcastically at the end of her letter, "still living in the United States—or in the Northern Confederacy? We are waiting to know." She probably expressed the unterrified opinion of many a Northern village and town on that day. John Brown had unwittingly done his side a disservice. The spectacle of this man and his score of followers frightening the South into arms and holding it so for six weeks convinced the North that the Southerners were cowards. In war it is a major blunder to underestimate your enemy; but the South was making the same mistake about the Yankee shopkeepers.

With North Carolina and Tennessee voting in March against secession, perhaps there might be no war after all. Against that fact came the dark prediction from Washington that Virginia would be out and the national capital in the hands of the Confederates within six weeks. Baltimore mobs were gathering nightly around hotels frequented by Northerners. Lincoln moved with deliberation. He notified Jefferson Davis and Beauregard that he was sending a supply ship to Major Anderson and that if this vessel were fired on, he would exert all the power of the Federal Government to defend it. Beauregard's answer was to open fire on Fort Sumter.

All Friday night, April 12-13, boys cried extra editions of the newspapers through the streets of New York, and next morning men looked at each other and, in a sense of utter unreality, said, "The war has begun." Sumter's flag came down on Sunday; and that evening Henry Ward Beecher, who was to raise it again, cried to his Brooklyn congregation, "I hold that it is ten thousand times better to have war than to have slavery."

Next day President Lincoln called up 75,000 state militiamen "to enforce order and repossess American property." Fort Pickens at Pensacola was already under siege. As late as April 15 the Connecticut arms factories were working night and day on Southern orders, though a munitions manufacturer on the Hudson had refused to ship any more supplies to the South. The *Independent* had named it "The Civil War." Everyone knew that a call for volunteers must soon come, and companies and regiments were forming. One of the first to reach a Boston recruiting office was Frederick William Stowe, medical student and namesake of a King of Prussia. Undersized, like his mother, and, like her, possessed of a lion's courage, Fred enlisted for his mother's war in Company A of the 1st Massachusetts Volunteer Infantry, which was as close to the front rank of the volunteer army as one could get.

It was all too much for Harriet Beecher Stowe in Andover, trying to write two novels at once, watching her country break up over the issue she had made her own, and sending her son away to fight for her cause. She had to abandon one of the serials, and she chose to drop her *Pearl,* offering Tilton the alternative propositions of winding up the story with a brief synopsis or of postponing the conclusion until the times should quiet down. Tilton elected the latter, and Harriet wrote him, for publication, one of those plausible letters of hers—

Dear Mr. Tilton: With this number ends Part First of "The Pearl of Orr's Island." Part Second will be ready to appear in the autumn, and will extend through the year.

In order to give the story the finish and completeness I wish, it will be necessary for me to revisit those scenes once more and see them in their summer glory. Time has somewhat dimmed my recollection.

I hope to be able to write the second part amid the very scenes, and under the shadow of the very pine trees, which first suggested the idea.

Very truly yours,
H. B. STOWE.

Having done this, Harriet wrote an editorial for her column, urging the North not to take the crisis too lightly. The Massachusetts militia had been fired on in Baltimore, and Harriet warned her people that some of the boys now enlisting might never return. "But," she said, "this is a cause to die for, and—thanks be to God!—our young men embrace it as a bride and are ready to die." Harriet wrote:

> There is one direction where we can scarcely look for the tears that blind us. When we see the wholehearted, unselfish devotion of our Northern people, we thank God that we have a country. We thank God for mothers that cheer on their sons, for young wives who have said *go* to their husbands, for widows who have given their only sons. It is our solemn belief that since the Proclamation of the President there has been in this country more earnest, unselfish heroism, more high-minded self-devotion, in one week than in years of ordinary life.
>
> If war be an evil, it is a less evil than many others and one attended by many and high forms of good. We wake to the higher aims of a land that has lost for a little her love of gold, her love of a peace that was full of wrongs and shames,
>
>> "Horrible, hateful, monstrous, not to be told,
>> And hail once more the banner of battle unrolled.
>> Though many a light shall darken, and many shall weep
>> For those that are crushed in the crash of jarring claims,
>> Yet God's just wrath shall be wreaked on a giant wrong,
>> And many a darkness into the light shall leap
>> And shine in the sudden making of splendid names,
>> And noble thought be freer under the sun;
>> For the peace that was no peace is over and done."

Actually, though, Harriet, like many in the North, did not think the war would be a long or a difficult one. How could it be? With the God of justice riding on the Northern banners, how could the forces of darkness prevail? The dubious Lincoln seemed to be doing all right in Washington. He had issued his call for three-year volunteers on May 3, and the same day Theodore Tilton wrote a poem, *The Great Bell Roland,* which was being reprinted by the thousands and distributed among the regiments in training. So far it was largely the *Independent's* and the Beechers' war—and Lincoln's. Plymouth Church was contributing two companies to the "Brooklyn Phalanx," equipping them at congregational expense. The boys in their new uniforms attended church on the evening of April 28, and Henry Ward Beecher gave them a special address.

Henry said he would "consent" to a compromise of the struggle, as follows: "Hang the ringleading traitors, suppress their armies, give peace to their fields, lift up the banner, and make a highway in which every true American citizen, minding his own business, can walk unmolested; free the territories, and keep them free." It was a scrambled platform, but the emphasis was upon the existing restriction of travel, which incidentally restricted the lecturing activities of popular Northern preachers. He told the Brooklyn boys, "And if you fall in the struggle, may some kind hand wrap round about you the flag of your country, and may you die with its sacred touch upon you." Henry sent two of his sons into the war and secured the chaplaincy of the Brooklyn Phalanx for his youngest half-brother, James Beecher.

Andover assumed a martial appearance. Ninety of the theological students had formed themselves into the "Havelock Grays." The boys of Phillips Academy were too young for war, most of them, but not for home defense; and, as the ladies of the campus sewed red braid on blue flannel shirts to make uniforms, the Phillips Guard shared with the Havelock Grays the great common in front of the Stone Cabin for drills and manoeuvres. The young men of the town were training as the Andover Light Infantry; and all day long under the campus elms one heard the rataplan of drums and the far-off whistling of fifes.

On the Tuesday before Harriet's fiftieth birthday the Seminary presented a flag to the Havelock Grays, and Harriet made a *gala* of it, composing a "banner-hymn" for the occasion (to be sung to the tune of *America*) and after the ceremonies inviting officers and men into the Cabin for coffee and a collation.

The flag had been raised over Phillips Hall when, as Harriet wrote, "the drums of the Andover Light Infantry were heard approaching. The company was coming to salute the flag. The officers of the Havelock Grays and of the Phillips Guard then marched to meet them and conducted them with honor onto the esplanade in front of the buildings, where various complicated military evolutions were executed with great precision."

Finally they assembled at the far end of the Common and came marching down toward the faculty families assembled as reviewers in front of the Stone Cabin—marching spread out in echelon, the Grays flanked by the Andover Light Infantry and the Phillips Guard. As they drew near, the watchers became aware that these young soldiers, of town and gown alike, were singing—a new, thrilling song nobody had heard before. They caught the words—

John Brown's body lies a-mould'ring in the grave,
John Brown's body lies a-mould'ring in the grave,
John Brown's body lies a-mould'ring in the grave,
  As we go marching on.
Glory, glory, hallelujah!
Glory, glory, hallelujah!
Glory, glory, hallelujah!
  His soul's marching on.

A little later Massachusetts troops would swing down Broadway to the beat of this song, which had sprung almost spontaneously out of their training-camps, and tens of thousands on the sidewalks and packed into doorways and windows would take up the melody and sing with the soldiers and weep and laugh and slap backs. Still later Julia Ward Howe would hear it on a Washington parade-ground and awake in the night inspired to write worthier words for the stirring march. Her lines were sublime; but their meter, substituting a prancing iambic for the thudding spondees of the army folksong, turned a battle-chant of Visigoths into a Sunday-School tinkle.

It was a time of illusion, and Northern hearts were high. McClellan was gathering his army on the Potomac, and soon the blow would be struck. A few of these boys might be expected to fall, but it would be in a noble cause and they would embrace death like a bride. Whenever she could, Harriet was going into Boston to see Fred. At the end of the war she looked back on these unstricken days with disillusioned eyes. She was appealing to Senator Sumner in behalf of a man who had been Fred's comrade in Company A, 1st Mass. V. I. He had had an honourable career in the war, reaching the rank of Captain, but his ambition was humble—a mere clerkship in the Boston Postoffice. Harriet was sure Sumner would intercede for him, "since this seems to be a case which will appeal to the heart of a Massachusetts man. But a mere handful of that brave First ever came through the War. I used to go every week to see them at their Armory when they first enlisted, little dreaming for what earnest and bloody work they had gone in and how few of them should ever return."

But there was an immediate disillusionment. Lincoln's first act after the fall of Fort Sumter was to declare a blockade of all Southern harbours, and it was in effect an order closing the cotton mills of England. At once British public opinion surged up against the North. The Queen's proclamation of neutrality virtually recognized the belligerency of the Confederate States of America. The British press began to tell the public that the success of the American Rebellion was assured. The *Saturday Review* declared that "the revolted provinces are beyond the reach of invasion." The North seemed to have no friend in England. Even Lord Shaftesbury, whose own hand had penned the *Affectionate and Christian Address,* made a statement sympathetic to the South.

Harriet refused to believe it. Had the vast British reception to her, nay, to *Uncle Tom's Cabin,* nay, to the cause of the slave, been hollow and insincere after all, a mere chance to blackguard the United States cheaply, as Harriet's enemies had charged at the time? She did not believe it and wrote for her column an apology for the English people, saying that the Southerners had long been planning their *coup d'état,* as she called it, and to that end had kept agents in London to feed the British public with false propaganda. But she felt sure that once the English realized that the war was over slavery, the North would have their complete support, "even that of the London *Times.*"

But when steamer after steamer brought only news of a strengthening of pro-Southern sentiment in England—the London *Anti-Slavery Reporter* attacking the North, Exeter Hall silent, Shaftesbury swayed by his "monarchical proclivities"—the scales dropped from Harriet's eyes. "O England, England!" she cried. "What, could ye not watch with us one hour?" It is probable that nothing that occurred in the Civil War—the reverses to the Northern armies, or even the fate of her own son—affected Harriet so deeply as the realization that in her British reception she had been duped. "But be it so," she announced resolutely; "though all the world deny us— though we stand alone, yet in God's strength we of the free States of the North will fight this battle through to the end. While there is a brick in our chimneys, a tile on our roofs, a drop of blood in our hearts, every man, woman, and child of us are of one mind to give it all to this cause."

Harriet was in New York when she wrote this contribution. She had been eating July strawberries "big as peaches" on Henry's mountain farm at Peekskill and had gone on to visit the Howards, at 100 Hicks Street in Brooklyn. Her daughter Hatty was with her. Henry Ward Beecher's new brownstone house was on the East River, and from his study window the pastor could see all the water-borne traffic. One day at noon Henry rushed into the Howards' home to announce that the Sound steamer *Common-*

wealth had just passed down the river. They all knew that on the *Commonwealth* was the 1st Massachusetts, bound at last for the South.

Harriet, Hatty, Eunice Beecher, and Fred's friend, Sam Scoville, took a carriage to Fulton Ferry and reached Jersey City to find the First disembarked and having a luncheon of sandwiches and lemonade in the vast Jersey City depot among its multitude of tracks and platforms. The public was excluded, but the magic name of Stowe procured "a bit of printed satin" which admitted them. After some search they spied Fred at a distance, and Sam went leaping across the tracks to fetch him. "Immediately afterwards," Harriet wrote Calvin, "a blue-overcoated figure bristling with knapsack and haversack, and looking like an assortment of packages, came rushing towards us."

In spite of his martial beard and equipment, so few years had it been since he was a little boy that Harriet had to restrain an impulse to wipe his face with her handkerchief before she kissed him. Was it liquor she smelled on his breath? No matter; Fred was a soldier, and people were being generous to the "boys." Somewhat hysterically Harriet and Eunice insisted on giving Fred their handkerchiefs, and then they stuffed his haversack full of oranges, a greater luxury then than now.

For two hours they stayed with Fred in the depot, while the regiment's band played, the soldiers sang, some of the companies drilled, and the crowd, jammed against the iron fence of the gallery, cheered and waved handkerchiefs. The family in Andover were taking Fred's soldiering rather casually. Neither his father nor his sisters came in the few miles to bid him good-bye when he left for the front. He felt mighty lonesome, he told his mother, there on Boston Common, which was crowded with fathers, mothers, wives, sweethearts, sisters and brothers at the official farewell to the First, some laughing, many tearful. Fred seemed to be the only soldier without a friend. But this visit made up for everything—such a special visit from such a special mother. The whole regiment was watching.

But the trains were backing in, bugles were sounding, companies falling in. Fred escorted his visitors to the gate, meeting on the way the regimental chaplain, Mr. Cudworth, whose handsome black eyes and hair were set off by the white havelock so many of the early volunteers affected. The chaplain wore a sword, and Fred touched it and asked playfully, "Is this for use or ornament, sir?"

"Let me see you in danger, and you'll find out," was the answer.

That was the spirit of this army. When even its men of God practised a

FREDERICK WILLIAM STOWE

"Undersized, like his mother, and, like her, possessed
of a lion's courage, Fred enlisted for his mother's war
in Company A of the 1st Massachusetts Volunteer Infantry, which was as close to the front rank of the
volunteer army as one could get." (Page 467.)

muscular Christianity, who could prevail against it? Harriet had been forced to carry on this visit the burden of continuing with *Agnes of Sorrento*. To "Blessed Friend Fields" she sent from New York an instalment of unusual length, complaining, "Your type-setter is a devouring monster." She liked the instalment herself, "though nobody in these stormy times will ever stop to read it."

At the opening of July there were events to draw one's attention even from the stormy times and one's literary task—Mrs. Browning's death in Florence, and in Cambridge the shocking accident to Mrs. Longfellow, who was burned to death when making wax seals for her children. The Lincoln Administration chose the *Independent* as the official organ for the publication of the Acts of Congress, as then required by law. The *Independent* was claiming 250,000 readers.

But as McDowell marched south from Washington and the death blow was about to fall on the insurrection, it was impossible to keep one's eyes off the armies. On Sunday morning, July 21, the whole North knew that the skirmishes were now over and that the great issue was being joined at Bull Run. At Andover Mrs. Stowe assumed the spokesmanship of the Federal forces and in church passed to the clergyman the following note to be read from the pulpit:

> The prayers of this congregation are requested for our Army on the eve of battle; & for the relatives of those who have already fallen.

And that afternoon—while the trivial incident of a runaway team of artillery horses was throwing the raw Northern levies into panic and rout at Bull Run—Harriet sat penning a long, patient, open letter to Lord Shaftesbury, showing him with every proof she could muster that it was not a war of politics or a war of a majority to coerce a reluctant minority, but a war to free the slave.

Fred Stowe behaved so well in the débâcle that he was promoted to a sergeancy. Bull Run was a profound disillusionment, and the first impulse was to blame Lincoln, in whom the Eastern editors now discovered that they had never had any too much confidence, anyhow.

The discouragement did not last. After Bull Run Harriet secured (through Sumner) a furlough for Fred and had her soldier boy at home for a fortnight. Fred told her that the morale of the Army was good and that next time it would give a better account of itself. Bull Run had been a sort of accident; the troops had not yet really been welded into an army at that time. Small, courageous Fred was a real soldier. He went back to Washington and in almost no time was commissioned a second lieutenant in the Massachusetts Heavy Artillery, at Fort Runyan, with his own mount. But the promotion cost money—$250 for a lieutenant's outfit—and Fred applied to his mother for it. Where were the *Uncle Tom* royalties now, or the thousands she had brought back from England? Harriet asked Fields to send the money to Fred, in the first of a long series of letters to the *Atlantic* office, beseeching small payments.

So before the summer of 1861 ended, the military prospects once more looked rosy; but a propagandist in Andover, who had been assuring the British public that it was a war to end slavery, still had reason to be indignant with Abraham Lincoln. What was Lincoln doing to end slavery, as the North had a right to expect? What was anyone doing—except Frémont, who as fast as he captured the Missouri plantations freed the slaves by military edict? Butler at Old Point Comfort was accomplishing the same result but by another, and more legal, method. He was declaring captured slaves to be contraband of war. The term offended Harriet, though she welcomed the liberation.

But Frémont's glorious act—"at last," Harriet exulted, "a blow has been struck which finds an echo in the heart of a whole nation. The hour has come, and the man!" She continued:

> Fremont does not call the slave contraband of war. That position, advantageous and ingenious in its day, is now abandoned for higher vantage ground. Fremont does not even speak of the slave as property. He makes the just distinction: the *property* of the traitors he declares confiscated, their slaves, if they have any—free. There we have it, fair and square. Out goes his banner! down goes his glove! and, if anyone does not like it, let him try conclusions sword with sword—that is all!

Lincoln did not like it and tried conclusions first with a statement disavowing Frémont's act, saying the general had exceeded his authority, and, a little later, to the stunned amazement of the ultra-Abolitionists, with an executive order relieving Frémont of his command. Calvin Stowe was so indignant that he wrote to Salmon P. Chase about it; and, since Chase, as a member of Lincoln's Cabinet, shared some of the guilt for this crime, the letter lacked a good deal of Professor Stowe's old cordiality.

Hon. S. P. Chase.

My Dear Sir:—I do not know that you have either time or inclination to listen to a word from the common people; but I wish you could hear the cries of surprise, indignation, disgust, and contempt, which now everywhere find utterance at the removal of Fremont. The feeling is frightfully earnest.

McDowell lost the battle of Bull Run and was made Major General. Patterson spent millions of money, proved himself a traitor or an imbecile, and was allowed to retire without censure. Stone by his carelessness or incapacity murdered hundreds of our best young men at Ball's Bluff, and is officially excused.

Stringham and Butler took Hatteras, the only success we have had in the East; and Stringham is immediately dismissed and Butler sent to New England. Fremont was driving the enemy before him, his officers and soldiers were enthusiastic in his behalf; and in the face of the enemy and on the eve of victory he is superseded, as if he were a Benedict Arnold.

Our Government gives rewards to defeat and shame, and punishes success and honor. Imbecility and treachery are sure of favor; fidelity and energy are equally sure of hostility and disgrace.

I have always had entire confidence in your capacity and honor; I have regarded yours as the steadiest and soundest brain and the purest heart in the Cabinet; and I cannot do otherwise than write you this brief note.

Very truly and sadly yours,
C. E. STOWE.

That this letter also represented Harriet's opinion of Lincoln and his Administration in the autumn of 1861, there can be no doubt. Henry Ward Beecher was also silently fuming; though that thinker was mentally rattling around on the war issues, having recently preached from Plymouth pulpit (to the shock of Dr. Cheever, when he read it in London) that it was no war for emancipation, since the President lacked constitutional power to end slavery.

But Henry's sister was preaching immediate emancipation, the first voice of consequence lifted for it since the outbreak of hostilities.

Now is the time—the accepted time. Now emancipation can be given as a gift; by-and-bye it will seem to be wrung out as a cowardly expedient. Let the people petition the Government! Let them demand that this mighty weight shall be cast into our scales now!

Let the President of the United States proclaim that all men shall hereafter be declared free and equal, and that the services of all shall be accepted, without regard to color. Some are shocked at black regiments:

they are shocked too late. The question is not, shall there be black regiments, but, shall they fight on our side or on the side of our enemies? One of the returned Massachusetts men testifies to having fought with a company of black soldiers in the Confederate Army, and they fought like tigers. Perhaps they fought under promise of emancipation—for that very freedom which we had power to give them and did not give. We may rest assured that if we delay till we alienate the blacks, the enemy will find means to turn them against us effectively, as they have done hitherto. Who dug the trenches and raised the masked batteries before which so many Northern men lie dead? The negroes. Why were the Southern forces fresh and ours weary? They had the negroes to do their hard work.

Despite the Orr's Island tradition that Mrs. Stowe wrote most of her story of *The Pearl* there on the spot, it seems unlikely now that she was able to visit the scenes of the novel again, as she promised her readers in the spring. At any rate, she was either in Andover or Brooklyn all during the spring and summer of 1861, and she spent much of the autumn in Andover completing her *Agnes of Sorrento* so as to be able to send a copy to England "before steamers begin to make winter voyages." This she accomplished so expeditiously that in the *Independent* of November 21 she was able to publish in her column "A CARD," announcing the resumption of "Part Second" of *The Pearl of Orr's Island* on December 1st and apologizing to her readers for the delay:

Who could write on stories that had a son to send to battle, with Washington beleaguered, and the whole country shaken as with an earthquake? Who could write fiction, when fact was so imperious and terrible, in the days of Bull Run and Big Bethel? But the author has labored assiduously on her literary engagements, and if she must commence a month or two later in the autumn than she expected, it is no greater delay than the war has caused everywhere in every department of business. The readers will see by this frank statement that there has been no intention of dealing unfairly with them.

Harriet, however, had, during these shaking events, been able to write on the story of *Agnes of Sorrento*, which, she was still insisting, was her masterpiece. She was annoyed, therefore, when Mr. Tilton, simultaneously announcing the Second Part of *The Pearl of Orr's Island*, called it "MRS. STOWE'S GREAT STORY, said to be the best which this renowned author has ever written," and rebuked the young editor's presumptuousness with another "card" which she ran at the head of the renewed story when it appeared December 5.

That a story so rustic, so woodland, so pale and colorless, so destitute of all that is expected ordinarily in a work of fiction, should be advertised in the columns of *The Independent,* as this was last week, as "Mrs. So-and-so's *great* romance," or with words to that effect, produces an impression both appalling and ludicrous.

It is as if some golden-haired baby who had touched her mother's heart by singing—

"Jesus, tender shepherd, hear us!"

should forthwith be announced with flaming playbills to sing in the Boston Theatre as the celebrated Prima Donna, Madame Trottietoes!

We beg our readers to know that no great romance is coming—only a story pale and colorless as real life and sad as truth.

In other words, Mr. Tilton should understand that Madame Trottietoes had gone to the *Atlantic* and the *Cornhill* and not to his weekly newspaper. Mr. Tilton could not have been too upset by the reproof, for at the moment great changes were occurring in the office of the *Independent.* The old editorial board, which had served since the paper's founding, was retiring, and Henry Ward Beecher was stepping in as editor-in-chief. In noticing the realignment the new editor announced in his grandest manner: "Theodore Tilton will remain and labor in a sphere where he has begun to achieve a most honorable reputation:—of whom we may not speak more, such are the ties of personal affection between us, lest it seem an imputed egotism."

The old year had ended with the death, of "gastric fever," in England of the Prince Consort, and a new one opened with a sickening reiteration from Washington of the sentence: "All quiet on the Potomac." The editorial guns were barking at McClellan and his inactivity; but in March came the first really heartening news the North had received. That barefooted Grant boy, who used to watch the Ohio River steamboats at Point Pleasant, near Ripley, had grown up to be a thick-set, cigar-chewing, whiskey-drinking, ruthless and efficient soldier, and in ten February days he took both Fort Henry and Fort Donelson, commanding the Tennessee and Cumberland Rivers. He continued his successes in March, taking Nashville,

CRUSADER IN CRINOLINE

while, farther west, the capture of New Madrid wiped the Confederacy out of Missouri.

But the war had to be won in the East, if it were to be won; and in March Lincoln listened to the criticisms and replaced McClellan with Halleck, Grant's superior in the West, as commander-in-chief. At the same time he reinstated Frémont and, with western Virginia forming a separate and loyal State, put him in command of the Mountain Department. It was what the editorial strategists had been demanding. Men of action now headed the armies, the "decisive battle" was near, and one could regard the war as nearly over.

Watching the drama, Harriet Beecher Stowe found herself once more in the uncomfortable seat she had occupied when writing *Uncle Tom's Cabin*. No matter how stirring or depressing the news, her desk and pen were always waiting for her as she kept up with a hungry printing-press in New York, waiting to devour all she could write every week. The almost inevitable happened. In March a cold got her "in claw," and she missed an edition. Mr. Tilton made the usual apology for her.

In April, while the "decisive battle" still held off in the East, Grant gave the Ohio, Indiana, and Illinois volunteers their first bath of blood at Pittsburg Landing and Shiloh. The North claimed it was a victory, though Beauregard, outnumbered, was able to conduct a strategic retreat. Harriet had completed *The Pearl of Orr's Island* and had seen that novel and her *Agnes of Sorrento* both published by Ticknor & Fields in June, and still there had been no battle that would bring peace. When it came in July it was a disaster for the Army of the Potomac on the Chickahominy, and the editorial fire-eaters of the North struck furiously at the National Administration.

Calling for a draft of 1,000,000 men and also for immediate "Military Emancipation" of the slaves, Henry Ward Beecher despaired of the future as long as "the President is more interested in politics than in prosecuting the war.

"What has Mr. Lincoln's education done for *him* more than ours for us to fit him to judge of military affairs?" demanded Editor Beecher. "We have a Country. We have a Cause. We have a People. Let all good men pray that God gives us a Government!"

Harriet Beecher Stowe knew the reason for the Northern misfortunes and in her column joined the chorus. "How long must this people wait in their hardness and impenitence, with this great arrear of crime and injustice unrighted? The time has come when the nation has a *RIGHT* to demand, and [Brother Henry to the contrary notwithstanding] the President of the United States a right to decree their [the slaves'] freedom; and there should go up petitions from all the land that he should do it. How many plagues must come on us before we will hear the evident voice, 'Let this people go, that they may serve me!' Must we wait for the tenth and last? Must we wait till there be not a house where there is not one dead?"

But the long-suffering man in the White House, worried about his border States, wondering if a general emancipation might not bring the greatest horror of modern times, was unmoved. And the tide of volunteers flowing southward did not share the Beechers' views, as they sang:

> We are coming, Father Abraham,
> Three hundred thousand more.

Lincoln was not alone in the North in fearing that emancipation might bring a black reign of terror in the South; though some, like Mrs. Stowe, had worked themselves to a pitch of fanaticism where they did not care if it did.

The retreat of the renamed Army of Virginia in August and the loss of its supplies to Stonewall Jackson brought from the prophetess another lamentation: "Never was a nation harder pressed by God's Providence. The voice, *Let this people go,* has been as evident to us as to the old Egyptians; and every refusal has been followed by defeat and plague, till the most Egyptian of Egyptians are now hurrying and pressing, 'Up, get ye out, or we be all dead men!'" And Harriet urged the nation to turn to prayer to make Lincoln "obey the voice of the Lord."

But Pope turned on his pursuers on the old battlefield of Bull Run. Fred Stowe was with that Army; and as Longstreet's artillery was cutting the Federal flank to ribbons, Fred's apprehensive mother was in Andover writing of the war's disillusionments.

Another editorial voice in New York was even more irritating to the White House than Henry Ward Beecher's or his sister's. Horace Greeley's criticisms of the President's slavery policy were so severe that the *Herald* was demanding that Greeley be arrested and imprisoned. It paid Greeley then to be an enemy of the Administration. Lincoln sent him a statement of his war aims—the policy he followed steadfastly to the end of the war—and the exclusive publication of that letter in the *Tribune* was one of the notable newspaper "beats" of the war. It contained a famous paragraph:

My paramount object in this struggle *is* to save the Union and *is not* either to save or destroy Slavery. If I could save the Union without freeing *any* slave, I would do it; and if I could save it by freeing *all* the slaves, I would do it; and if I could do it by freeing some and leaving others alone, I would also do that. What I do about Slavery and the colored race, I do because I believe it helps to save this Union; and what I forbear I forbear because I do *not* believe it would help to save the Union. I shall do *less* whenever I shall believe what I am doing hurts the cause, and I shall do *more* whenever I shall believe doing more will help the cause.

Harriet was rash enough to answer Lincoln in her column, paraphrasing his words as she imagined they would have been written, had Christ been in the White House. Her statesmanship was lamentable:

My paramount object in this struggle is to set at liberty them that are *bruised* and *not* either to save or destroy the Union. What I do in favor of the Union, I do because it helps to free the oppressed; what I forbear, I forbear because it does not help to free the oppressed. I shall do less for the Union whenever it would hurt the cause of the slave, and more when I believe it would help the cause of the slave.

Monomania could not go much further. Harriet mourned: "Alas, our sons will be slain not because our God was cruel, but because He was good; not because He was angry with them, but because our Commander-in-Chief would hold them in the very way of God's thunderbolts, in the whistling path of His glittering spear."

Then, just when Harriet despaired of the White House, a recalled McClellan turned back the invading Confederate Army at Antietam Creek (only his over-caution preventing the victory from being decisive), and Lincoln decided that the time had come to do more for the slave and, as a result, more for the Union cause. Under his extraordinary war-powers (as Henry Ward Beecher had insisted) he issued the text of an Emancipation Proclamation, "as a fit and necessary war measure for suppressing said rebellion." He announced his intention to sign this proclamation and put it into effect on the first day of January, 1863. Thus, if the Confederates had any real reason to believe that emancipation would be followed by the butchery of the women and children of the South, they had three months in which to make up their minds to surrender and prevent it.

The Proclamation took the extreme Abolitionists by surprise, and its reception was mixed. Some, like Henry Ward Beecher, shouted for joy.

Henry printed it in his newspaper under the caption, "THE MOST IM-
PORTANT PAPER EVER PUBLISHED IN *THE INDEPENDENT*."
Others, like Harriet Beecher Stowe, were suspicious. Harriet thought it was
too good to be true. Did Lincoln really mean it?

Another decision, relatively as profound, had been taken that year in the
Stowe household. Calvin Stowe was sixty years old and was putting into
action, no doubt with his wife's complete consent, his long wish to retire.
He knew more perhaps than any other living American about the historical
origins of the Biblical texts, and it was in him to write the standard and
definitive work on that subject. If the indolent man could only be induced
to do it! His professorial duties (and feeble health) had always offered him
a convenient excuse to delay the start. After retirement he would have only
the feeble health.

At the August commencement exercises Professor Stowe announced his
resignation, to take effect at the end of the next collegiate year. It meant
a great change for the family. For one thing, they would have to give up
the Stone Cabin, which belonged to the Theological Seminary. Would they
remain in Andover? Harriet does not seem even to have considered it. She
had few close friends there—only the Park family. As Mrs. Ward was to
write delicately, the privileges of neighbourhood with the famous Mrs.
Stowe were but scantily appreciated.

But Harriet was a Connecticut woman and never one of Massachusetts.
Except for North Brookfield, where William Beecher was postmaster and
preacher too, the one New England place where she could settle and be
near her kindred was Hartford. At Hartford she would have her sisters
Mary Perkins and Isabella Hooker, and Harriet had always liked Hartford,
the first city of any size she had ever known. She could do as she pleased,
for her family revolved around her, husband and all, like satellites around
a sun. The twins, in fact, at twenty-six were becoming confirmed old maids,
living only to serve their famous mother. They were housekeepers, secre-
taries, and amanuenses for her, and imitated her to such an extent that
even their handwritings were alike. Hatty and Eliza wrote many of their
mother's letters for her, *and signed them*—letters many of which are preserved in libraries today as genuine autographs. The laboratory examination
of the great collection of Mrs. Stowe's letters in the Huntington Library
in California shows that they are in three hands, though they look alike to
the inexpert eye.

Harriet remembered a beautiful grove on the bank of the Park River in Hartford, where she, when she was a girl attending Catharine's Female Academy, used to go for rambles with poor Georgiana May. At the beginning of October, 1862, Harriet went down to Hartford to see it. The grove was still there, about as she remembered it. To be sure, the city had now stretched out and swallowed it—it was within the city limits—there were some factories operating at no great distance from the grove, and perhaps the water in the Park River was not quite so pure as it had once been; but the price was not high, and Harriet bought it then and there—"four acres and a half of lovely woodland," as she wrote Annie Fields upon her return to Andover. It meant building a house, but Harriet had always adored building operations. She had enjoyed every minute of the work of remodeling the Stone Cabin. So, that autumn and winter she spent much time planning a mansion such as she thought a successful authoress ought to have.

Lincoln's pledge to free the slaves at New Year's, unless the South sued for peace first, gave Harriet the opportunity to appeal once more for the support of British public opinion, now so overwhelmingly with the South that it could blink the construction of a Confederate Navy in British shipyards. How could she previously have argued with her former idolaters that the war was being fought to end slavery, when the silence at the White House shamed and stultified her? But now (if Lincoln meant it) the issue was in the open at last—the Southern forces fighting to perpetuate slavery, the Northern to abolish it. Harriet could speak, and hold her head high.

There was a final arrow left in her quiver, one of her sharpest. All these years since the winter of 1853 there had been in Harriet's study that monument to a nation's insincerity, *The Affectionate and Christian Address of Many Thousands of Women of Great Britain and Ireland to Their Sisters, The Women of The United States of America,* in which the ladies of England (vicariously through Lord Shaftesbury) had reproachfully called upon the cisatlantic "Sisters" to rise and end the shameful crime of American slavery.

What were these same British ladies—562,848 of them by actual count of their signatures—now themselves doing to help end American slavery, in which great sin they had acknowledged with grief and shame their heavy share? They were countenancing the construction in England and Scotland of gunboats for the Confederate Navy, in violation of the Queen's proclamation of neutrality. They were arguing that the Southern States had as much right to rebel against the Union as had the original colonies to rebel against England. They were asking how long the South had to maintain independence before earning recognition by the British Government. And what was Lord Shaftesbury doing—the gentleman who had composed the *Affectionate Address?* Lord Shaftesbury was arguing that the Emancipation Proclamation was no genuine act of abolition at all, in that it would free the slaves only in the revolted regions, but was actually a bribe offered to the South to come back into the Union and preserve its peculiar institution.

Harriet had received this document as spokeswoman for America, but had done nothing about it. Now she had an inspiration. She would make a public answer to the *Affectionate and Christian Address.*

But first, after apprising James T. Fields of her purpose to contribute her *Reply* as an article for the *Atlantic,* Harriet had to make sure that President Lincoln meant to sign the Proclamation on January 1. "I am going to Washington to see the heads of Departments myself and to satisfy myself that I may refer to the Emancipation Proclamation as a reality and a substance not to fizzle out at the little end of the horn," she wrote Fields on November 13, "as I should be sorry to call the attention of my sisters in Europe to any such impotent conclusion. I start for Washington tomorrow morning, and mean to have a talk with 'Father Abraham' himself, among others."

Harriet took her daughter Hatty with her, and also "Our Charley," now a fine boy of twelve dressed in a sort of Andover modification of the Scotch costume, a jaunty feather stuck into his plaid turban. They stopped over in Brooklyn for about a week with the Howards, where Harriet found time to write the first two-thirds of the *Reply.* "I would willingly send you the first part for the press before I leave for Washington," she told Fields, "but think it best, on the whole, to wait till I see how things lie there and then send all together."

In Washington Harriet's first thought was to find her son Fred, now a First Lieutenant of the Infantry and stationed in a neighbouring camp. He was overjoyed to see her—"as loving and affectionate as a boy can be," Harriet wrote home—and her maternal eye took in the fact that he had grown heavier. Army life was agreeing with him. Nothing would do Harriet but that she must have this bronzed soldier-boy of hers with her in her Washington hotel. Fred thought it was impossible to arrange it on such short notice; but Harriet visited a colonel in one fort and a brigadier-general in another and at the end of the day triumphantly bore off Fred in her carriage, a forty-eight-hour pass in his tunic. " 'Oh!' he exclaimed in a sort of rapture, " 'this pays for a year and a half of fighting and hard work.' "

Harriet described to Calvin the scene that evening: "Imagine a quiet little parlor with a bright coal fire and the gaslight burning above a centre-table, about which Hatty, Fred, and I are seated. Fred is as happy as happy can be to be with mother and sister once more." Since this mother of his could work miracles with the Army, Fred had a complaint to make. He had grown impatient with so much garrison duty with the infantry and wanted more dangerous service, preferably in the cavalry, which was always sure of seeing action. Harriet agreed with him. She wrote a letter or two; and before his mother's visit ended a week later Fred had a captaincy and was attached to the staff of General Siegel, in the field.

Early in her visit Senator Henry Wilson, of Massachusetts, took his famous constituent to the White House to see Lincoln. Harriet brought little Charley along, so that he might say that he had met the war-time President. Lincoln received them in one of the small rooms of the White House, which he used for his office and study. As Harriet put her hand into the President's great knotted one, no doubt once more she felt as a grasshopper in her own eyes; and Lincoln must have been surprised at the diminutive size of the Titaness who had influenced his nomination.

"So this is the little lady who made this big war?" he exclaimed, as the family story has it.

In the grate a fire of cannel-coal was sputtering and jetting smokily. Lincoln went to it and warmed his hands, rubbing them together.

"I do love a fire in a room," he said. "I suppose it's because we always had one to home."

It has been said, though perhaps figuratively, that the interview lasted a "brief hour." Though Mrs. Stowe never reported directly what the conversation was, undoubtedly she told the President of her intention to reply to the *Affectionate and Christian Address* and received his approval; and Lincoln, in turn, without question assured her of his intention to sign and issue the Emancipation Proclamation on New Year's Day. He must, though, have told her of some of the difficulties besetting his course and of the pressures and influences upon him resisting the proposed order, for Harriet, though she left the interview convinced of Lincoln's good faith, was not completely assured that he could carry out his intention. She told Fields that in writing her *Reply*, "I have noted the thing as a glorious expectancy."

Washington then was, as Harriet wrote afterwards, "one great hospital of wounded soldiers." The conversation turned on the amount of time Lincoln spent in the churches and public buildings visiting the war casualties hospitalized there.

"Mr. President," Harriet asked him, "where do you ever find time to dine?"

"Well," said Lincoln, and Harriet found "something irresistibly quaint and pathetic in the odd, rustic tone in which this was spoken," "I don't exactly, as you say, *dine*. I just browse round a little, now and then."

Whatever Harriet Beecher Stowe thought of President Lincoln before this interview—and her "Father Abraham" in her letter to Fields had been a sarcasm—she left it his firm supporter. Even had he failed to issue the Emancipation Proclamation, she would have understood and condoned his failure. As Lowell had told her, she was one of the few born with eyes in her head, and those eyes looked straight into Lincoln's soul and knew its sweetness and honesty and greatness. Responsible critics, in whose camp Harriet had been dwelling, were calling the President an ape, a satyr, and a stupid blockhead; Harriet remarked, "Even the ass can kick safely and joyfully at a lion in a net." This was her only meeting with the Emancipator; but within two years after the assassination of Lincoln she wrote of him a biographical tribute which, if uncritical, has not often been surpassed in pathos.

Little Charley, who had been reared on eastern college campuses, could not get over Mr. Lincoln's homespun expressions.

"Ma," he exclaimed excitedly, when they reached the cold November air outside, "why does the President say 'to home' instead of 'at home'?"

His mother answered him in the words of Paul: "Though I be rude in speech yet not in knowledge; but we have been thoroughly made manifest among you in all things."

From the White House Harriet went to her hotel and there in two days completed her *Reply to The Affectionate and Christian Address*, signing it "in behalf of many thousands of American women" the evening of Thursday, November 27, 1862, which was Thanksgiving Day.

The *Reply*, which spread over some eight or ten pages of the January

Atlantic, was Harriet's ablest editorial utterance on slavery. She was a mistress of sarcasm, and the inconsistency of British public opinion gave her immense opportunity to use her talent, yet she restrained her pen and kept the *Reply* in tone temperate, sad, and straightforwardly reproachful. Perhaps the contact with Lincoln had sweetened her. Yet at the end she could not resist one ironic touch. After reciting her evidence that the war was being waged to end slavery and sorrowfully listing the numerous instances of British unfriendliness towards the North, she lifted bodily and without quotation marks one of the paragraphs of the *Affectionate and Christian Address* and used it for her own concluding one:

We appeal to you as sisters, as wives, and as mothers, to raise your voices to your fellow citizens, and your prayers to God, for the removal of this affliction and disgrace from the Christian world.

It was an eloquent and powerful document she turned out. John Bright wrote Harriet from England in the spring that there it had "covered some with shame, compelled many to think, and stimulated not a few to act," while in Parliament "now nobody says a word in favour of recognition, or mediation, or any such thing." The North received the *Reply* with acclaim. Even Hawthorne, who detested the war and its disturbance to the meditations of a recluse, wrote Harriet his congratulations. "If anything could make John Bull blush, I should think it might be that; but he is a hardened and villainous hypocrite. I always felt that he cared nothing for or against slavery, except as it gave him a vantage-ground on which to parade his own virtue and sneer at our iniquity."

By December 13 Harriet was back in Andover. Days passed, Christmas came and went, and there was still no sign of weakening in the White House. The British press was recoiling from the savagery of an Administration that could precipitate by executive order the bloodiest massacre in modern history, but Boston went ahead with plans for a New Year's Emancipation Jubilee, to be held in the Boston Music Hall at 3 o'clock in the afternoon. Though it was not strictly a prayer service, Harriet decided to attend.

The year 1862 had ended in a streak of unusually springlike weather, and New Year's Day was mild and calm, with the sun shining and the pavements and sidewalks dry. At the Music Hall Harriet took a modest seat in the balcony. She heard Mr. Emerson read his poem. She heard Zerrahn's orchestra play the Beethoven overture, the chorus sing Mendelssohn's *Hymn of Praise,* and Mr. Dresel perform on the Chickering grand. Then came the intermission. The packed auditorium was buzzing with talk and movement, when a gentleman in formal attire came out to the middle of the deserted stage and held up his hands. The audience did not need the usual volunteer admonitions to become quiet, for the air was pregnant with impending history.

"Ladies and gentlemen," he shouted into the abrupt hush, "the telegraph has just brought the news from Washington that the President has signed, and the Emancipation Proclamation is now coming in over the wires."

At the word *signed* a demonstration exploded and drowned the rest of his words. The whole audience was on its feet, cheering and waving, and the noise was like granite, solid and unrelieved. Harriet, hidden away by the taller celebrants around her, was as excited as any, clapping her hands and cheering, too. Lincoln had done it! In the jostling her hat was knocked awry and her shawl half-pulled from her shoulders. That blessed man in Washington!

She became vaguely conscious that her name was being called in the uproar—"Mrs. Stowe! Mrs. Stowe!" People knew she was there and were calling to see her, this woman who had put down slavery. "Mrs. Stowe! Mrs. Stowe! Mrs. Stowe!"—the cries swept nearer, and now those around her were calling her name, and a circle was widening out, and people were smiling and bowing and pointing to the balcony rail. Fingers touched her shoulders and impelled her. She went to the rail and looked down, and everyone else was looking up and shouting and waving. She could only bow and dab her eyes with her handkerchief.

Thus in great triumph ended the cycle that had begun with her vision in a Brunswick church. The play was over, the curtain falling, and the star would never hear such salvos for herself again.

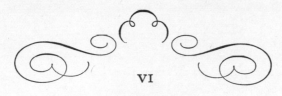

VI

HARTFORD

1864-1896

The Later Hartford Home

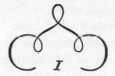

Harriet in Mr. Lincoln's War

WITH the signing of the Proclamation Harriet passed her war over to the custody of Mr. Lincoln in Washington. Her work, and *Uncle Tom's,* was finished. The slaves were free, at least in theory, and—though, to be sure, nearly a million of them remained in bondage in the loyal States and regions—the curse that had followed the Union arms was dissipated. Harriet's responsibility was ended, and she could with confidence entrust the cause to the hands of Lincoln, which she now knew were safe ones. She withdrew from the *Independent,* though without announcement, and spoke no more in public on the issues, becoming merely one of a hundred thousand Northern mothers with boys at the Front, enduring the suspense until victory and peace should come.

She had scarcely returned to Andover after the Jubilee concert when she had to go down to Brooklyn again and this time take the family with her. In the words of Henry Ward Beecher, "The old oak finally fell." At five o'clock in the afternoon of Saturday, January 10, 1863, at the age of 87, Dr. Lyman Beecher, "his face illuminated by a solemn and divine radiance, softly and tenderly, without even a sigh, passed to the everlasting rest." For a year he had been tottering about the Brooklyn Heights neighbourhood, a fragile, transparent, mortal shell and little else, his mind all but gone, his speech reduced to incoherent sounds.

Though awake, he was virtually in a coma out of which they could rouse him occasionally and catch something like a flash of his old spirit. Harriet was particularly successful in accomplishing this. One day, in November, when the old Doctor sat staring at nothing with expressionless eyes, she tried the experiment of pronouncing several names to him slowly and distinctly—names of his former friends: "Taylor—Edwards—Cornelius." His sounds suddenly crystallized into words.

"Oh, I know them all," he said. His power of speech faded, but with

491

an effort he collected it again. "One more thing let me say—they are all gone, gone! I am left alone . . . alone . . ."

It was an awful thing to hear a voice come from that darkness.

Even the war seemed to recede for a few days as New York and New England renewed their memory of "the most-quoted man since Franklin." Lyman Beecher was buried at his birthplace, New Haven, beside his beloved fellow-heretic Dr. Taylor, the Rev. Leonard Bacon, D.D., conducting the service.

It was impossible for his children to mourn a man who had passed to a life so much happier for him than the one he had quitted, and on the way home Harriet and the twins stopped in Boston for a spree of shopping, visiting, and concert-going. On February 10 Harriet was back in Andover writing to Annie Fields, "We have all subsided quietly after our Boston dissipation, and Eliza sits by me making up the new dress she bought." Choleric Britishers were sending to the London papers their retorts to Mrs. Stowe's *Reply*. Had Annie seen the letters in *Punch?* Harriet found them "very funny." A quick response had been a great meeting in Liverpool to express sympathy for the Union cause. The flood was rising—"all over England the President's Proclamation going by acclamation!"

Harriet's plans for the new Hartford house were completed that spring. It was a curious creation. In general architectural type it might perhaps be called Tudor, though Tudor without the half-timbering. Harriet seems to have taken a good many ideas for it, as Walter Scott did his actual materials, from the ruined abbeys of Scotland. No doubt she thought the general effect was Gothic.

But even the house-plans scarcely offered Harriet an escape that year. The war was weighing on her, so heavily that, except for one more article for the *Atlantic,* she did no writing at all in the spring and summer of 1863. Fredericksburg was followed by Chancellorsville; and it seemed that the prophetess, in predicting that success would follow the Union arms once they had shaken off the curse of slavery, was a false one. But then came Gettysburg, and the tide of the Confederacy at last began to ebb. Fred was with Meade's Army, and for a week after the great battle they did not hear from him. Then Calvin Stowe took from his postoffice box an envelope with a Gettysburg cancellation stamp, and his hands shook when he realized that it was addressed in unfamiliar writing. He tore it open and read:

Gettysburg, Pa., Saturday, July 11,
9:30 P.M.

Mrs. Stowe.

Dear Madam,—Among the thousands of wounded and dying men on this
war-scarred field, I have just met with your son, Captain Stowe. If you have
not already heard from him, it may cheer your heart to know that he is in
the hands of good, kind friends. He was struck by a fragment of a shell,
which entered his right ear. He is quiet and cheerful, longs to see some
member of his family, and is, above all, anxious that they should hear from
him as soon as possible. I assured him that I would write at once, and,
though I am wearied by a week's labor here among scenes of terrible suffering, I know that, to a mother's anxious heart, even a hasty scrawl about her
boy will be more than welcome.

May God bless and sustain you in this troubled time!

Yours with sincere sympathy,

J. M. Crowell.

Crowell, they afterwards ascertained, was an Army chaplain. The family
legend is that upon receipt of this letter Professor Stowe, in a sort of
panic, left for Gettysburg on the first train out of Andover, but only to get
as far as Springfield, where, in the railroad station, he lost all his money to
a pickpocket. There is no record of any of the family having gone to see
Fred at this time. The wounded officer remained in the care of the Army
hospitals until the late autumn, when he secured his discharge for
disability.

Vicksburg fell on the last day of Gettysburg, and the back of the
Confederacy was broken; but, with Chattanooga following Chickamauga,
it was a bloody and anxious summer and fall, with fluctuating fortunes
for both flags. The war was outstripping in slaughter anything ever known.
Tales of atrocities poisoned the home fronts, North and South. In Tennessee the black plantation hands fled in terror before the invading
Yankees, who were supposed to wear horns; and in July the death on a
parapet of Fort Wagner of young Colonel Robert Gould Shaw, the Harvard
graduate commanding the first coloured regiment raised in the North,
gave Boston a new hero. The story went that when Boston asked for
Shaw's body, the reply came back that it was impossible to comply with
the request. "We have burned him with his niggers." A Mrs. Anna
Waterstone wrote a poem about it which Harriet must have circulated. In
the New York Public Library there is a signed copy of the poem in Mrs.
Stowe's autograph.

But a more dreadful picture of war and its effect on the gentlest souls is reflected in a letter which Harriet wrote on the last day of July, 1863, in response to a sympathetic note from her friend, the Duchess of Argyle. The year was proving for her, she said, "one long sigh, one smothering sob." "I thank God," she added, "that we have as yet one or two generous friends in England who understand and feel for our cause."

The Duchess in her letter must have told her some of the stories of Northern brutalities which the English were repeating, for Harriet wrote:

> Why do the horrible barbarities of *Southern* soldiers cause no comment? Why is the sympathy of the British Parliament reserved for the poor women of New Orleans, deprived of their elegant amusement of throwing vitriol into soldiers' faces and practicing indecencies inconceivable in any other state of society? Why is *all* expression of sympathy on the *Southern* side? There is a class of women in New Orleans whom Butler protects from horrible barbarities, that up to his day have been practiced on them by these so-called New Orleans ladies, but British sympathy has ceased to notice *them*. You see I am bitter. I am.

Harriet was bitter, too, about that "pious humbug," Exeter Hall, and about Lord Shaftesbury and the other erstwhile Abolitionists who had deserted her cause.

> It is the moment when every nerve is vital; it is our agony; we tread the winepress alone, and they whose cheap rhetoric had been for years pushing us into it now desert *en masse*. I thank my God I always loved and trusted most those who now *do* stand true—your family, your duke, yourself, your noble mother.
>
> I have long known *what* and *whom* we had to deal with in this, for when I wrote "Uncle Tom's Cabin" I had letters addressed to me showing a state of society perfectly *inconceivable*. That they violate graves, make drinking-cups of skulls, that *ladies* wear cameos cut from bones and treasure scalps, is no surprise to me. If I had written what I knew of the obscenity, brutality, and cruelty of that society down there, society would have cast out the books. . . . I wish *them* no ill, feel ·no bitterness; they have had a Dahomian education which makes them savage.

If a Harriet Beecher Stowe could believe such things as this, what must have been the beliefs of less enlightened minds!

Another scion of the family had fallen at Gettysburg, grievously wounded

—Lieutenant Frederick Beecher, son of Brother Charles, who since 1857 had held the Congregational pastorate at Georgetown, Massachusetts. Troubles heaped up on Charles all at once. Even as Gettysburg was being fought, the Essex North Conference was trying the Rev. Charles Beecher for heresy. He believed in Evolution and the preëxistence of souls and Christian spiritualism and preached and wrote about all three.

Frederick Beecher was the oldest son of his parents, and Charles was sorely tempted to let his heresy trial go by default and hurry to Gettysburg, but was dissuaded by his wife. The news of the great battle came at the beginning of a long-remembered heat-wave. Poor Mrs. Beecher had to go alone to find her boy, while Charles remained in torrid Massachusetts "to fight," as Harriet said, "the beasts at Ephesus." (Though Lieutenant Beecher's wound was considered fatal at first, he lived to join the regular Army after the War and in 1868 was killed when with Forsythe's Scouts, fighting Indians at Beecher Island, Colorado, which was named for him.)

The verdict went against Charles, but his church refused to accept it and withdrew from the Conference. His enemies next secured the appointment of a church council to consider a motion to "disfellowship" not only the Georgetown Congregational Church but the Rev. Charles Beecher as well, which would end Charles's career in the Calvinistic pulpit. To save his congregation from the burden of such a trial, Charles resigned his pastorate and prepared to face the disfellowship charges alone.

At this point the clanswoman at Andover went into action for her next-to-favourite brother. With the weight of her prestige behind them, she wrote letters to numerous New England churchmen of influence, urging them to take up the cudgels for Charles in the coming Council. Particularly, she wrote to her friend Dr. Bacon, of Yale, and as usual when defending her family, she used vigorous language—

> The persecution against my brother Charles conducted by an unscrupulous minority in his church, who used for their purposes the various passions and prejudices of his ministerial brethren, has at last proceeded to a length that flesh and heart can endure no longer, and he has resigned his parish—as I view it, to save his life.

Harriet spoke of the "unscrupulous steadiness" of Charles's enemies, their "intriguing," their terrorist methods. "Shall my father's son," she demanded, "by all allowed to have been a faithful, conscientious minister, be cast from the ministry by such a course as this?" In another letter she called those enemies "moles and bats."

Her appeals were successful. The Council exonerated Charles of heresy and restored him and his church to good standing. Simultaneously, Brother Henry Ward Beecher was in England quelling those riotous meetings and making those famous addresses which made Lincoln designate him to raise the flag again over Fort Sumter—"for without Beecher in England there might have been no flag to raise." Frederick Beecher and Fred Stowe were in Army hospitals after Gettysburg. A Beecher was always appearing on some battlefront, literary, political, ecclesiastical, or actual. It must have been about this time that Dr. Bacon (who liked them) made his famous remark that "this country is inhabited by saints, sinners, and Beechers."

That summer or fall Harriet's contractor broke ground for the new mansion in Hartford, and the prospective châtelaine, spending much time now with the Perkinses, could retreat from the war into her plans for its embellishment. Was it to be a house or a home? Harriet made the distinction, and it gave her an idea. She wrote to James T. Fields proposing a series of *House and Home Papers* for the *Atlantic,* or rather, announcing it to him, for she sent along the manuscript of the first paper, which she called *The Ravages of a Carpet*. The series was to run through "six, eight, ten, or twelve numbers."

Modern critics have sometimes complained of the banality of the subjects which Mrs. Stowe picked for her writing. In writing on home beautification in the 1860's she was striking a new note in this country. The *House and Home Papers* were immensely successful both in the *Atlantic* and between book covers later. *Atlantic* readers found much of the flavour of the *Autocrat* in them. The book and subsequent volumes on the same theme which Harriet wrote, some in collaboration with Catharine Beecher, blazed a trail along which would presently come the first of the American household magazines and that Nineteenth Century movement which took the name of "The House Beautiful."

Harriet wrote the first two of her "papers" in Hartford in October and November, 1863. She had been suffering a good deal that year from a facial neuralgia. In Hartford she had found a physician with a galvanic battery, and, being one ever ready to try any new quirk in medicine, took electrical treatments for it, with such beneficial results that on November 3 she could write Fields: "I feel more like myself than I have for some time and shall soon forward the second no., which will be entitled, 'Homekeeping versus Housekeeping.'"

"Tell Mrs. Fields," she said later in this letter, "that my house with *eight* gables is growing wonderfully. I go over every day to see it. I am busy with drains, sewers, sinks, digging, trenching, and above all with manure! You should see the joy with which I gaze on manure-heaps, in which the eye of faith sees Delaware grapes and d'Angoulême pears, and all sorts of roses and posies, which at some future day I hope you will be able to enjoy."

But the mention of *eight* gables reminded her of something. "Do tell me," she asked Fields, "if our friend Hawthorne praises that arch-traitor Pierce in his preface [to *Our Old Home*], and your loyal firm publishes it. I never read the preface and have not yet seen the book; but they say so here, and I can scarcely believe it of you, if I can of him. I regret that I went to see him last summer. What! patronize such a traitor to our faces? I don't believe Annie knew you were out when you did it. But I haven't read it."

(As a historical fact, Fields had objected when Hawthorne proposed to dedicate his travel-book to his friend Franklin Pierce, who was opposing Lincoln and the war and making himself extremely unpopular with the Northern radicals, his old classmate Calvin Stowe included. Fields told Hawthorne that such a dedication would "sink" his book. Hawthorne replied: "If the public of the North see fit to ostracize me for this, I can only say that I would gladly sacrifice a thousand or two of dollars rather than retain the good-will of such a herd of dolts and mean-spirited scoundrels." Hawthorne's friends believed that the criticism he received on his dedicatory letter helped bring about his untimely death the following spring.)

From Hartford Harriet went to New York in November on a special mission. The wound in Fred Stowe's ear had never healed entirely, and he wrote to his mother suggesting that he ought to get out of the Service. A letter from her to Secretary of War Stanton quickly brought Captain Stowe's honourable discharge for physical disability. Meanwhile, Fred had come up to Brooklyn on a leave of absence, and while the volleys were crashing at Chattanooga, Harriet went to New York to meet him and bring him home.

Home was still the Stone Cabin; for, while Calvin Stowe had not been connected with the Seminary since summer, the family had made an arrangement to occupy the Cabin until the Hartford house was ready for them. But there was a greater anxiety than Fred's wound for them all that winter. The young veteran had become an inebriate. The family story is that his open wound made him suddenly susceptible to alcoholic poisoning. This he did not know until, at a home-coming banquet given to him in Andover one glass of wine made him drunk. After that he could not control his craving for liquor.

Whether we accept this story or regard Fred Stowe as a victim of what is now called shell-shock, he grew into a besotted drunkard, reeling home day after day and scandalizing the pious Seminary community. His Aunt Isabella Hooker, in a private diary kept some years later, made the assertion by implication that Fred's debauches would end in attacks of delirium tremens; but at that time "Sister Belle" was on the outs with Harriet, and her remark may have been mere spite. How Professor Stowe and the other children reacted to Fred's drunkenness we do not know; but the unfortunate young officer's mother, at any rate, defended him and condoned his weakness and wasted thousands in her effort to cure him of his vice.

When Henry Ward Beecher returned to New York that fall after his triumphs in England, it was to find himself out of the editorship of the *Independent* and his friend and protégé, Theodore Tilton, then aged twenty-eight, in. Shortly before his departure one of his chief female worshippers, the beautiful Lucy Maria Bowen, died. She was the wife of Henry C. Bowen, founder of Plymouth Church and owner of the *Independent;* and on her deathbed she told her husband something that made any further friendship or business association between him and Henry Ward Beecher impossible.

Harriet Beecher Stowe, of course, knew nothing about the true cause of her brother's retirement from the *Independent,* but the fact made it certain that she would never again contribute to that journal. As a result, 1864 is almost a blank year, so far as the existing record shows her attitude toward the war. Even her private letters contain few references to the great struggle. Her own maternal pledge withdrawn from the Army, she seems to have done her best to close her eyes and seal her ears to the carnage and thunder by throwing herself into her professional work.

It made 1864 a busy year for her, and it was otherwise an eventful one in her life. It was the year that saw her family's removal to the Hartford riverside mansion, which she was calling (whenever she remembered to)

"Oakholm." Once away from the Calvinistic shades of the Andover campus, she went frankly into the Episcopal fold in Hartford. The elegant twins, Hatty and Eliza, had already joined the Episcopal Church; and that year, too, saw the engagement of the pretty and sprightly Georgie, now twenty-one, to a young Episcopalian clergyman, Henry F. Allen.

It was not only a psychological necessity which drove Harriet to her writing-desk. She was pouring money into the new Hartford house at a rate absolutely appalling to Professor Stowe, now for the first time in his life completely severed from a salary roll and with his master-work still a vague project. The financial prospect, however, did not disturb his wife. In January she signed a contract with the highly moral *Watchman & Reflector* journal for a series of biographical sketches to be published under the categorical title of *Men of Our Times*. The *W. & R.*, as Harriet invariably abbreviated the long name, paid handsomely for these articles; and even amid the upset of moving she applied herself so diligently to these and to her *House and Home Papers* for the *Atlantic,* that at the end of the year she could report with complacence to Fields that she had earned $2,400 with her pen.

This was not bad, even for a successful writer at that time. It was more than Hawthorne made. And, of course, the figure did not by any means represent all of Harriet's income. Her books continued to sell—especially *Uncle Tom's Cabin, The Minister's Wooing,* and her *Pearl of Orr's Island*—and there always seemed to be some new by-product of *Uncle Tom's Cabin* to bring in revenue. That year it was what she called a "toy book Uncle Tom," which a firm of Philadelphia publishers got out. Harriet had no fears for the future.

From this time until the end of her active life Harriet was to be besieged by visitors. She was uncommonly gracious about receiving strangers and often generous in her responses to their pleas. She dreaded to rebuff visitors or hurt their feelings, yet she was forced to develop a technique for disposing of them quickly. A later contemporary described it. She would listen to the visitor's story with "her cordial smile and shining, soulful eyes," make her reply, and then "she would terminate the interview by rising and saying 'Goodbye,' with a clasp of the hand and an honest look into the eyes."

Harriet had acquired so many possessions, animate and inanimate, that moving to "Oakholm" was a strenuous business. It occurred during the last week in April, the Stowes' tenancy of the Stone Cabin expiring May 1; and Harriet seized the occasion to have one of her prostrate spells. She wrote to James T. Fields on May 1—her first letter from the new house: "I came here a month ago to hurry on the preparations for our house, in which I am now writing, in the high bow-window of Mr. Stowe's study, overlooking the wood and river. We are not moved in yet, only our things, and the house presents a scene of the wildest chaos, the furniture having been tumbled in and lying boxed and promiscuous."

Not the least of the difficulties of moving must have been the transport of the family's dogs. This memoir has been rather neglecting the dogs, but there had been a steady succession and growing multitude of them, and also a steady mortality. At each demise there was a canine funeral, with all the requisite pomp and circumstance. Indeed, it was said that the subsequent tenant of the Stone Cabin was puzzled at the number of mysterious mounds in the back yard. Enlightenment came when "Our Charley" Stowe returned with his mother that summer for a brief visit. Charley at once raced behind the house to see the graves of his lost playmates.

Before Harriet could unpack her pictures and knicknacks, there was a trouble for her to contemplate in Brooklyn. One of her friend Susan Howard's sons, Joseph Howard, Jr., rather fancied himself as a writer. Harriet liked Joe and in 1861 had secured a commission for him to furnish a biographical sketch of Frémont to the *Atlantic*. But Joe Howard was a stock manipulator; and on May 18, 1864, when better men of his age than he were falling by thousands in the Wilderness, and a nervous stock-market was ready to snatch up any rumour, Howard used his literary talent to forge an Executive Proclamation in which Lincoln purported to call for a draft of 400,000 fresh troops and to appoint a day of fasting and prayer. Joe had his one-day panic and his profits, and also a visit from the Secret Service, and presently found himself in Fort Lafayette, a Federal prisoner.

It would never do to allow even a friend of the Beechers to suffer for his sins. Henry Ward Beecher went to Washington and saw Lincoln. The Emancipator was also a politician—and it was not going to affect the Union cause whether Joseph Howard was 'punished or went scot-free. He handed Henry Ward a note to carry to Secretary of War Stanton: "I very much wish to oblige Henry Ward Beecher." Joe was released, but the brief scandal ended any ambitions Henry may have been entertaining to secure the Republican Presidential nomination for himself that autumn. Years later Joe Howard returned the favour by writing a biography of Henry Ward Beecher.

That summer Our Charley arrived at the ripe age of fourteen and announced himself ready for a life on the bounding main. Harriet indulged him, securing for him a berth in the crew of a Boston sailing-vessel bound for the Mediterranean. With the coastal waters full of gunboats, blockade-runners, and commerce-destroyers, a present-day mother might be pardoned for exclaiming, "What *was* she thinking of!" but Harriet regarded it calmly, writing to Annie Fields in July: "I have had to fit out 'Our Charley' for sea. He has gone proud and glorious as a foremast hand to Malaga and Sardinia on the 'Mountain Wave'."

By the end of July Harriet had packed Charley off and so settled the house that she could leave for Rye Beach on the northeast coast and "get a little strength from the sea." There she would have "nothing to do but write and write, write and forward these chats as fast as possible, and then keep right on till *all* are done." One thing that had kept her so busy in Hartford was Fred. She wrote to Mrs. Fields, "I have had to nurse and care for poor Fred, whose wound is still open, and who suffers constantly." On no existing paper did Harriet ever write about Fred's other infirmity. She permitted her son to say in her biography, in speaking of Fred: "The cruel iron had too nearly touched the brain of the young officer, and never again was he what he had been."

That year Harriet began to contemplate the work which, next to her *Uncle Tom's Cabin*, was to be her chief contribution to American literature. It was a loosely strung together collection of old New England legends and stories, weird and otherwise, based on the boyhood experiences of Calvin Stowe in Natick, Massachusetts. The stories, in fact, which for years Calvin had been telling his wife and children. The novel was to be entitled *Oldtown Folks* and could be considered with its sequel, *Oldtown Fireside Stories,* as a single *opus*. Whittier compared the Oldtown stories favourably with those of Chaucer and Boccaccio.

In 1864, however, the novel was still only an idea. Harriet's British outlet, the *Cornhill Magazine,* was not interested in a series on home-beautification, but it did want fiction from her. Tentatively she promised to give them a new serial for 1865, and during her visit to Boston she mentioned the fact to Fields, since she would expect the *Atlantic* to serialize the story simultaneously. Later in the year she amplified: "It [the story] is to be of New England life in the age after the Revolutionary War and before railroads had destroyed the primitive flavor of our life—the rough, kindly, simple, religious life of a Massachusetts town in those days when the weekly mail stage was the only excitement. It is something I have been skimming and saving cream for for many years, and I have a choice lot of actors ready to come onto the boards."

Still later in the fall, however, Harriet changed her mind about writing the story immediately, having decided to go on for another year with the popular *House and Home Papers*. "I could prepare my story for your magazine," she told Fields, "but I do not feel that the public mind is just now in a state for a story. It is troubled, unsettled, burdened with the war. The home nest is everywhere disturbed, and the birds consequently flutter around that. . . . The story would be amusing and funny but have no practical bearing. Home is the thing we must strike for now, for it is here we must strengthen the things that remain."

Georgiana May Stowe had a real beau that summer. The young, handsome, elegant, erudite, and well-to-do Rev. Henry Allen, rector of the Episcopal Church in Stockbridge, in the Massachusetts Berkshires, near the New York State line, was making the long journey to Hartford at frequent intervals to see Georgie—so frequent that Harriet could usually now send her manuscripts by him to Fields, as the young suitor stopped off in Boston on his roundabout way home, and no longer have to trust the mails. The courtship looked serious.

At twenty-eight Hatty and Eliza were consecrated to perpetual maidenhood. With a mooning, absent-minded mother and a helpless father, somebody with sense had to take charge of that family, and the inseparable twins made it a joint partnership. Georgie was the fieriest and most individual of the Stowe children. There were many who thought she inherited her mother's genius and might have made a name for herself in literature, had she been less frivolous. In Boston, where she later lived for many years, her wit was famous. Once at a dinner-table she found Mr. Longfellow at her right. In shaking open her napkin, she flipped its enwrapped roll to the floor. Longfellow at once offered her his. "Oh, Mr. Longfellow!" she cried. "I couldn't think of accepting the rôle of a poet." When the extravaganzas and musical shows began to visit Boston, the comedians used to take their scripts to Mrs. Allen to have her enliven them with jokes taking off the élite of Boston society.

Harriet must have been observing Georgie's tactics in courtship when she wrote: "My youngest [daughter] was busy as yet in performing that little domestic ballet of the cat with the mouse, in the case of the most submissive youth of the neighborhood." Certainly the Rev. Henry Allen was to be a most submissive husband, and a most complacent one. Nor did Harriet and her "little senate of girls" remain long that summer at Rye Beach. Mid-August found them at Northampton, Massachusetts, which, one can only note, is much nearer to Stockbridge than is Rye Beach. On one occasion when young Mr. Allen took material for Harriet to Boston, Georgie accompanied him. When the girls wanted shopping money in Boston, rather than supply them from her purse Harriet was finding it less painful to give them orders on Ticknor & Fields. Her letter dated Northampton, August 16, Harriet ended with the request, "Will you please hand to Mr. Allen $20 on my account?" At the bottom of the page appears the notation: "Rec'd twenty dollars, August 17, 1864. G. M. Stowe."

On that date, therefore, we can assume that Georgie and Henry Allen were engaged. They set the wedding for a day in August, 1865, by which time Harriet expected Oakholm to be at its best, outside and in.

Like all new houses, it seems, built since the beginning of time, Oakholm was costing a great deal more money than its owner had expected to spend. By the autumn of 1864 the drain on her resources began to worry the easygoing and confident Harriet, and she began to press for writing engagements as she never had before.

Madame Demarest, whose fashion magazine was a rival of *Godey's Lady's Book,* was planning to add a literary department to her publication and made Mrs. Stowe an offer to become its leading contributor. Madame Demarest sent Harriet a prospectus of the new and enlarged magazine, and Harriet discovered that the publisher also planned a new family or domestic department. The House-Beautiful movement was beginning.

It gave Harriet an idea, and she sent to Fields what now seems the amusing proposal to add a regular household department to the *Atlantic.* She would conduct this, she said, for $200 a month, which was the price she would have received for the now postponed serial-story.

Fond as he was of Mrs. Stowe, and appreciative of her value to his magazine, Editor Fields could not quite agree to turn the *Atlantic* into a housekeeping journal on her suggestion. Her manoeuvring nevertheless brought her the benefit she wanted. She did not get her household department in the *Atlantic;* but to keep her as his contributor "sole and only" Fields doubled to her the price he had been paying for her *House and Home Papers.*

And late in the year there came an unexpected addition to her income. Ticknor & Fields announced a new juvenile magazine, *Our Young Folks,* starting in January, 1865; and Howard Ticknor (with Fields's consent) signed Harriet as its first contributor. Thereafter for a number of years Mrs. Stowe's story or sketch always led off *Our Young Folks,* which was eventually absorbed by *St. Nicholas Magazine.* Harriet did not receive much for these contributions—$50 apiece at first—but she enjoyed writing for children, and eventually her work gave her four profitable juvenile books: *Queer Little People, A Dog's Mission, Daisy's First Winter,* and *Little Pussy Willow.*

But, with Petersburg under siege, Sherman laying an empire in ruins from Atlanta to the sea, and the Confederacy's western Army moving towards destruction at Nashville, the war would obtrude—and especially in Brooklyn, where Harriet spent the week of the election with Henry Ward and Eunice Beecher, after that event subscribing herself in a letter, "Yours for Old Abe and the Union." The North was seething over the treatment of Union prisoners at Andersonville and Libby Prisons; and, despite the exorcising power of the great Proclamation, the people were enduring Harriet's "tenth and last plague," with scarcely a door unvisited by the Destroyer.

Harriet had to get out her *Atlantic* piece for January in Brooklyn; and, instead of continuing her pleasant discussions of housework, servants, the entertainment of company, and good taste in dress, she wrote about her land's misery.

She told Fields: "I have sent my New Year's article, the result of one of those peculiar experiences which sometimes occur to us writers. I had planned an article gay, sprightly, wholly domestic; but as I began and sketched the pleasant home and quiet fireside, an irresistible impulse *wrote for me* what followed—an offering of sympathy to the suffering and agonized whose homes have forever been darkened. Many causes united at once to force on me this vision, from which generally I shrink, but which sometimes will not be denied—will make itself felt."

But there was happiness in Hartford:

"Our Charley" came home all right for Thanksgiving, stocky and manly, with the same boy's face, but with hands so spread with hard work that they look twice too big for him. He had a real hard voyage, the vessel going short-handed out of port and losing several men at Caglieri in consequence of a mutiny; so that Master Charles had to do a full man's work, taking his turn at the wheel with the others and steering the ship in dark, stormy nights in midocean. They had a stormy passage from Malaga to Caglieri and were thrown on their beams' ends and tossed about fearfully. The ship was old and leaky, so that the sailors all said she would never get home. On the whole, he was glad to see home again, and yet I can not see that the radical passion for the sea has much abated; only he wants to study and rise in his "profession," as he still calls it. Unfortunate is the hen who hatches a duck, but she must make the best of it. He is now going to the commercial college, and I should not wonder if he should want to try again by spring.

But Charles did not prove to be a duck. He forgot the sea, went on to Harvard in due time and then to Heidelberg, and finally followed the footsteps of his father and grandfather into the Congregational ministry.

At Oakholm that first winter of the new home's existence, it was almost possible—except for the heartache that was Fred Stowe—for a busy authoress to put the war out of her mind. It was sullenly inactive that winter, as if Grant, like the prize-fighter who has battered his foe into helplessness, dreaded to finish the bloody business he had begun. Visitors were now driving out to a grove on the Park River—missionaries to the Dakota Indians wanting letters of introduction to Senator Sumner, who, Harriet trusted, was "not even at this hour of the day weary in well-doing"; Quaker ladies doing a splendid charity in visiting the prisons and hospitals.

But with her "Chimney Corners" (as she was now calling the *House and Home* articles) and her stories for *Young Folks,* with her constant visitors, with her conservatory and camellias and her humming-bird, her indolent, gluttonous husband, sunk in research, her sailor-boy, studying for his "profession," her little senate of girls, busy now with a trousseau, and with the problem of Fred, Harriet waited through the long, final night to see the dawn of peace.

Late in March, 1865, Grant stirred and resumed his "hammering." With Lee's Army starving and exhausted, it was like slugging a dying man. On April 9 Lee surrendered at Appomattox Court House, and the Confederacy collapsed.

Harriet reread *Uncle Tom's Cabin.*

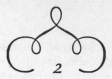

Heyday of a Career

IT HAD been the Beechers' war at the beginning, and a Beecher rang down its curtain when, to the joy and pride of the clan, the Administration designated Henry Ward to make the address at the raising of the Stars and Stripes over Fort Sumter on the fourth anniversary of its striking. Henry went down on a gunboat, accompanied by Garrison, Theodore Tilton, and several of the chief men of the Plymouth Church congregation, and, on the afternoon of April 14, stood on a heap of stones and delivered one of his forensic masterpieces. His words still seemed to be echoing through the stricken and patrolled streets of occupied Charleston, across the bay, when Booth's bullet ended the life of Abraham Lincoln in Washington.

The news of the assassination seems to have stunned Harriet Beecher Stowe into complete silence. We have now no record of any words of hers spoken at the time, but within a month she was writing for her "Chimney Corner":

> The kind, hard hand that held the helm so steadily in the desperate tossings of the storm, has been stricken down just as we entered port; the fatherly heart that bore all our sorrows can take no earthly part in our joys. His were the cares, the watchings, the toils, the agonies, of a nation in mortal struggle; and God, looking down, was so well pleased with his humble faithfulness, his patient continuance in well-doing, that earthly rewards and honors seemed all too poor for him, so He reached down and took him to immortal glories . . . The eyes are yet too dim with tears that would seek calmly to trace our Abraham Lincoln's place in history. He has been a marvel and a phenomenon among statesmen, a new kind of ruler in the earth. There has been something even unearthly about his extreme unselfishness, his utter want of personal ambition, personal self-valuation, personal feeling.

Yet, though Harriet could accept the fact, she could not soon forgive the agents of God's will. Three years afterwards, she wrote a biography of Lincoln, devoting one-tenth of it to an account of the assassination. She set down the names of all the alleged conspirators named in the indictment, and argued at length for the personal guilt of Jefferson Davis. "Whether or no Jefferson Davis and his fellows in the rebel government were actually aiding and abetting in this particular crime, it has not been unjust or unnatural to suspect them of it."

Indeed, at this time, though Henry Ward Beecher was endorsing President Johnson's proclamation of amnesty to the erstwhile rebels, Harriet went along with the rest of the family (and with all the radical Republicans of the North) in crying for vengeance. The North, forgetting that the Confederate armies had been starving, too, could not forget Andersonville and Libby Prisons; and there was a widespread belief that the Confederate Administration had been in a plot to burn New York and other Northern cities through hired incendiaries. Harriet vented all her hatred and vindictiveness in a Chimney Corner article called *The Noble Army of Martyrs,* writing it in May, 1865, and sending it to Fields with the following endorsement:

> The article . . . is an account of the martyrdom of a Christian boy of our own town of Andover, who died of starvation and want in a Southern prison [Salisbury] on last Christmas Day; and it gives me a chance to speak what I burn to say of Robert Lee and Jeff Davis.

She urged that this article be advanced and published immediately in the *Atlantic,* so that she might send copies to influential politicians, writing to Fields:

> There is a false, mawkish, pseudo-talk of humanity and magnanimity to these cruel assassins, Davis and others, which [sic] I have resolved to do what *I* can to bring up the more legitimate objects of pity—the hearths and homes which this wretch has desolated.

The *Martyrs* article was no less unrestrained. Harriet believed the most ferocious stories of the Southern prison camps—stories of deliberate torture, it being "the infernal policy of the Rebel Government either to wring from them [the prisoners] an abjuration of their country, or by slow and steady draining away of the vital forces, to render them forever unfit to serve in her armies." When the prisoners were starving, "the Rebels . . . brought in delicacies to tempt their appetite, hoping thereby to induce them to desert their flag." Her angry pen wrote on:

> If General Lee had been determined *not* to have prisoners starved or abused, does any one doubt that he could have prevented these things? Nobody doubts it. His raiment is red with the blood of his helpless captives. Does any one doubt that Jefferson Davis, living in ease and luxury in Richmond, knew that men were dying by inches in filth and squalor and privation in the Libby Prison, within bowshot of his own door? Nobody doubts it. It was his will, his deliberate policy, thus to destroy those who fell into his hands. The chief of a so-called Confederacy, who could calmly consider among his official documents incendiary plots for the secret destruction of ships, hotels, and cities full of peaceable people, is a chief well worthy to preside over such cruelties; but his only just title is President of Assassins, and the whole civilized world should make common cause against such a miscreant.

It was a prettier Harriet who turned from such vengeful thoughts to a domestic event which could dispute for a distracted mother's attention even with her grief for Lincoln and her hatred of Robert Lee. Georgiana Stowe and her fiancé, Henry Allen, suddenly decided to be married in June instead of August, as they had originally planned. The decision threw the household into confusion, as Oakholm was still far from being as presentable as its owner wanted it to be on such a grand occasion. Harriet told the Fieldses about it at once; and as a result Georgie received in mid-May, a full month before the event, the first of her wedding-presents. It was a set of Hawthorne's works, specially bound for the bride and bridegroom. Harriet wrote back to her editor and publisher:

> Many thanks on the part of our Psyche and myself about or anent the welcome present of Hawthorne. Nothing could be prettier, more lastingly beautiful—the first adjective belonging, you observe, to the getting up; the second to the contents.
>
> The wedding is indeed an absorbing whirlpool, but amid it all I have the next C. C. [Chimney Corner] in good train and shall send it on tomorrow or next day. As to the artist you speak of [no doubt he who drew Harriet at her writing-table, gazing into the conservatory], could he not, and you, wait till after the wedding day, the 14th of June, when all that remains of me will be at his service, and I will receive him with gladness.

But, Harriet reminded him, though her *House and Home Papers* was out as a book, there had never been any contract signed; and Ticknor & Fields had not rendered her any account at all since January, and here it was the 18th of May.

Harriet seems to have admired the uniform edition of Hawthorne—in white bindings, we discover later—above all of her daughter's wedding-presents. It gave her an idea, too. One of the Foote cousins, Miss Katy, was to be married on July 20; and Harriet proposed to have a set of her own works, "bound in a style like the Hawthorne," among her relative's presents. She listed the titles for Fields:

> Uncle Tom's Cabin.
> Mayflower.
> Sunny Memories.
> Minister's Wooing.
> Agnes.
> Pearl.
> House and Home Papers.

It became a standard wedding-present for Harriet to give. Thereafter, when any favoured young lady of Harriet's acquaintance or kindred walked to the altar, she was pretty sure to have on her table of presents a uniform set of Stowe, bound in white.

Her letter of June 18 contained another interesting item:

> One thing more—in the spring I left at Kinnard's a great, gold bracelet given me by the D. of S——, to have certain dates engraved on it. They were to send it to me by express. I have never heard from it. Will you be so kind as to inquire for me what has become of it, and ask them to send it back to me?

The dates were those of the abolishing of slavery in the District of Columbia and the Emancipation Proclamation. The bracelet was not lost, for later Harriet had engraved on another link of the gold chain the date of the ratification of the Thirteenth Amendment, forever ending slavery in the United States.

That fall Harriet began to press once more to improve her income. For her "sole and only" services in 1865, Fields had doubled his rate of payment to her and permitted her to finish her contract with the *Watchman & Reflector*. She now thought it was not enough, informing Fields:

This year I shall feel obliged to ask you to remit that portion of our contract, in respect of this one fact, that the high prices make the liberal terms you offer in fact less than I used to have, as a hundred dollars buys only fifty dollars' worth of anything. I do not ask, however, any increase from you, only to allow me to make use of what time remains over and above the supply of my agreement with you, to gain something from other papers.

The Watchman & Reflector have been always remarkably honorable and gentlemanly in their treatment of me, and are anxious to have six pieces for the coming year, for which they offer so good a sum that I would like to accept.

Fields must have concurred, for we find Harriet contributing regularly to the *Atlantic* in 1866, and going right on with her condensed biographies for the *W. & R.* Otherwise, in the record we catch only occasional glimpses of her that fall and winter.

Harriet befriended a novice in letters that autumn, a Miss Josephine Ruggles, and seems to have secured for her at least a brief appearance in the *Atlantic's* pages with a short serial story of New England life. Georgie and Henry Allen visited her the last week in October. Her Chimney Corner papers were published that year as a book bearing the title, *Little Foxes;* and Harriet wrote Fields, just before Christmas, "The bundle of Little Foxes came to hand, and I am charmed with the getting up. It is very nicely executed; and the foxes, scampering off in front, refreshingly lively." She began to collect her poems for publication by a somewhat reluctant James T. Fields, a poet himself. So many pious women had written Harriet in praise of her poetry that she never doubted its high quality. Her verses were, in fact, her only writings of which she was at all vain.

The final half of the year 1865 brought about a great change in Harriet's attitude toward the South. As the immediate memories of the war faded and her feet grew accustomed to the paths of peace, she lost most of her vindictive animosity toward the former enemy and began to advocate a policy of conciliation, being one of the few "ultras" who did. Even her brother Edward disagreed with her. In particular, she opposed the granting of immediate suffrage to the freedmen, writing to the Duchess of Argyle:

We all know that the state of society at the South is such that laws are a very inadequate protection, even to white men. Southern elections always have been scenes of mob violence *when only white men voted.*

Multitudes of lives have been lost at the polls in this way; and if against their will negro suffrage was forced upon them, I do not see how anyone in their senses can expect anything less than an immediate war of races.

If negro suffrage were required as a condition of acquiring political position, there is no doubt the slave States would grant it—grant it nominally, because they would know that the grant never could or would become an actual realization. And what would then be gained for the negro?

In this Harriet was following the lead of Henry Ward Beecher, who was making a great many enemies for himself by counselling "lenity" toward the defeated South. Theodore Tilton, who represented the vengeance-seekers, was running at the masthead of the *Independent* a new slogan: "The slave a man; the man a citizen; the citizen a voter." Horace Greeley was calling Henry an apostate.

But Harriet said of Henry, "I cannot but think it is the Spirit of Christ that influences him."

Calvin Stowe had now been retired nearly three years, and his wife thought it was high time for him to be making a start with that work to which he was supposed to be devoting his uninterrupted leisure. It took diplomacy to move Calvin toward a task so formidable in prospect, but that spring Harriet managed it. In a conspiracy with her, Fields sent the Professor an offer to publish such a book as only he could write. In the enthusiasm roused by the unexpected letter, Calvin actually sent Fields the title for his proposed masterpiece—*The Origin and History of the Books of the Bible*. "Do," Harriet begged Annie, "ask your husband to announce it, so he may feel contented, for I fear otherwise he may get swamped with lecturing, &c." Twice previously Harriet had seen Calvin start forth on grand book projects, only to drop them after short spurts of industry. This time, however, to her not altogether convinced gratification, he kept on, though complaining of ill health and threatening to run down like an unwound clock.

Someone had to bestir himself to feed the sumptuary appetite of Oakholm, and if not Calvin directly, then Calvin indirectly. That summer (1866), therefore, Harriet took up again, in her mind, the New England story she had for so long been skimming and saving cream for. The milk from which she skimmed was her husband's reservoir of reminiscences of his boyhood in Natick. She spent a month with Georgie and Allen in beautiful Stockbridge—a month devoted "to the recollections and quietudes necessary for the imaging in the waters of what is to appear," as she phrased it to Fields. "I must dream and weave a while in peace and stupidity. What do you say to 'My Grandmother's Kitchen' for the title?"

Eventually these reveries produced strokes of Harriet's pen, though strokes that did not entirely satisfy her. Again she was adopting a masculine pseudonym for herself, another alliterative one—Horace Holyoke—in order to tell the story in the first person. Horace Holyoke was, of course, Calvin Stowe. Harriet made only indifferent progress with it that autumn, though by midwinter she could report "a pretty good pile of manuscript." Fields was not to suppose that she was indolent or was putting off the novel in order to write pot-boilers for other publications. "This story grows even when I do not write. I spent a month in the mountains in Stockbridge *composing* before I wrote a word."

Fond as he was of the lady, the gentle Fields grew exasperated with the author and her ready explanations. There had been no word of fiction by Harriet Beecher Stowe in *The Atlantic Monthly* since the concluding ones of *Agnes of Sorrento* in 1862, and even a Mrs. Stowe could not hold her popularity forever with Chimney Corner chats. Fiction, not factual writing, was her *forte*. To spur her on, therefore, Fields, when in February, 1867, he sent her the contract for the New England story, firmly wrote September 1 into it as the date when the manuscript should be delivered. Harriet returned the contract, with a horrified answer:

> I am so constituted that it is absolutely fatal to me to agree to have any literary work done at certain dates. I *mean* to have this story done by the first of September. It would be greatly to my pecuniary interest to get it done before that, because I have an offer of eight thousand dollars for the newspaper use of the story I am planning to write after it.
>
> But I am bound by the laws of art. Sermons, essays, lives of distinguished people, I can write to order at times and seasons. A story *comes,* grows like a flower, sometimes will and sometimes won't, like a pretty woman. When the spirits will help, I can write. When they jeer, flout, makes faces, and otherwise maltreat me, I can only wait humbly at their gates, watch at the posts of their doors.

And, as usual, she had her own way about it. But Fields had a right to be impatient with her. Annie Fields testified after Harriet's death that her husband advanced Mrs. Stowe $10,000 against *Oldtown Folks* before he at last got the completed manuscript from her.

Harriet did not mention what newspaper had offered her $8,000 for another story (which, incidentally, she never delivered), but in all probability the offer was made by Robert Bonner, owner and editor of the New York *Ledger,* for whom Henry Ward Beecher was that winter writing his one novel, *Norwood,* for serialization. In January, 1867, Harriet visited in Brooklyn and at that time heard all about Henry's work for the *Ledger.* And it is likely that she met Bonner at that time.

Not exactly *all* about Henry's work for the *Ledger.* She heard about his magnificent contract with Bonner—$25,000 for the serial, which was an unheard-of price for an editor to pay for a serial-story in that day. But Henry would tell her nothing about what he was writing for the *Ledger,* beyond the fact that it was "a New England story." "Henry is like me— busy," Harriet wrote Fields. "All [meaning *both*] New England stories. Neither of us sees the other's, and we give only dim outlines of what we are trying to do." Is there a note of pathos in that statement? She repeated it in a subsequent letter: "He [Henry] has been tugging along through the sandhills, like me, neither of us showing our work to the other."

It must have been Henry who fixed the mutual prohibition, for Harriet was always only too ready to read her work in manuscript to anyone who would listen, and particularly to her admiring relatives, and she coveted Henry's admiration above all the rest. Was Henry Ward Beecher, who had never previously written a word of fiction in his life, actually afraid of being plagiarized by his sister, who, whatever one may think of her art and technique, was one of earth's greatest story-tellers? He was exactly that, for Harriet had always confessed to her susceptibility to the "influences" of other people's work. Holmes's *The Guardian Angel* was then running in the *Atlantic,* and Harriet would not read it, writing Fields: "I deny myself, because he is so fine and subtle that I might imbibe and absorb influences from him that I am not aware of."

It throws a sudden light on the relations between Henry Ward Beecher and Harriet Beecher Stowe. The loving, loyal Harriet seems never to have been aware that her pyrotechnic brother was jealous of her. Why should he not have been—he, the family's least promising member, its stone the build- ers rejected, arriving in early manhood at fame, wealth, and position beyond the dreams of his famous father, only to have a sister surpass him in celebrity?

There is plenty of evidence to support the supposition. Henry was among the last to read *Uncle Tom's Cabin,* the book which in his lordly, patronizing way he had promised his shabby sister to scatter like the leaves of Vallom- brosa; and in the chorus of extravagant praise which followed its publication,

Henry's voice was not heard. It became increasingly difficult for Harriet even to see Henry, he who was so available, at least in profession, to everyone else. To meet and talk with Henry and hear his views became a rare and prized privilege for her, and she would travel many miles for it. Invitations to visit him in Brooklyn became infrequent, after her first fame. Usually she stopped with the Howards in Brooklyn; and one of her pathetic reasons for cultivating the friendship of Susan Howard was that Susan would write her and tell her what Henry was doing. Harriet seldom got more than a brief note from her brother, who, as events were to show, wrote too many letters to others for his own good, and too voluminous ones.

When Henry became editor of the *Independent,* one of his first acts was to evict Harriet from the first column and occupy that conspicuous position himself with his editorials and Star papers. When at first people charged Henry with having written *Uncle Tom's Cabin* himself, he denied it, but with an enigmatic smile; just as he smiled enigmatically when asked about the truth of the story that during the darkest hours of the war Lincoln, enveloped in his shawl, sought him out one night for a season of prayer. And now Henry was receiving $25,000 for a single serial. What was the paltry $2,400 paid Harriet by her *Atlantic* for twelve instalments of a story, compared with that? Didn't it argue that potentially—excepting always for the phenomenal and lucky *Uncle Tom's Cabin*—Henry Ward Beecher was a ten-times greater novelist than his sister? At any rate, Henry did not intend to have her steal any of his fire—though, of course, he could tell Harriet that he would not want inadvertently to take any of her incidents, either. It was better to keep the two growing novels severely apart.

When *Norwood,* for all its huge price, fell flat as a novel, Henry's wit had a ready answer. He had written it, he said wryly, to prove that he could not have written *Uncle Tom's Cabin* and thus give the quietus to that old story.

Early in the autumn of 1866, two young Connecticut farmers, veterans mustered out in Florida, came home with glowing accounts of the possibilities of growing cotton in that State. Land was going for a song—a dollar an acre for the best—and the ex-slaves provided an abundance of cheap farm labour. With only their service back-pay, they had rented during the past year the thousand-acre "Laurel Grove Plantation" on the west side of the St. Johns River, near Orange Park, not far down from Jacksonville. There, however, their money had run out, and, unable to hire help, they had not been able to develop much of the plantation; and now they had come North to try to interest other "comrades," with money, to join their enterprise.

They had secured one willing to go, another young veteran who indeed had no money to invest but who could supply a wife able to cook and keep house for them all. At this point poor Fred Stowe, who couldn't keep out of barrooms, heard their story. The tanned and stalwart farmers scarcely could regard this undersized, dissipated city man as a partner; but Fred told his mother about it, and she was at once enthusiastic. The upshot was that she agreed to finance the Laurel Grove operation herself on terms which we do not know, but which undoubtedly secured to herself an adequate interest in the enterprise and placed Fred in charge as superintendent. Before winter came, Fred went down to Florida with the other three.

Calvin and Harriet had decided that a healthful, outdoor life, combined with the responsibility of watching the investment and making a success of the plantation, might straighten Fred out. But Harriet would not have been the daughter of Lyman Beecher—the same Lyman Beecher who had called it a speculation when once he sold his house for more than he paid— if she had not found higher moral grounds than that to justify her investment. She wrote Charles:

My plan . . . is not in any sense a mere worldly enterprise. I have for many years had a longing to be more immediately doing Christ's work on earth. My heart is with that poor people whose cause in words I have tried to plead, and who now, ignorant and docile, are just in that formative state in which whoever seizes has them.

Corrupt politicians are already beginning to speculate on them as possible capital for their schemes and to fill their poor heads with all sorts of vagaries. Florida is the State into which they have, more than anywhere else, been pouring. Emigration is positively and decidedly setting that way; but as yet it is mere worldly emigration, with the hope of making money, nothing more.

Calvin Stowe continued to assemble and arrange his notes and work on his book that summer, to such good purpose that by early autumn Harriet could tell "Friend Fields" that "Mr. Stowe at last is ready to begin, or have you begin, *to print,* and desires me to send you the inclosed as what he designs for one volume, which he says he is ready to put right through the press." By *print* Harriet usually meant *set in type.* "The Old Testament, he says, must be left for next year, in a separate volume." Harriet went on to give Fields instructions on how to manage the difficult Professor. Fields must have followed directions, for on October 18, 1866, Harriet wrote him:

Mr. Stowe and I shall come to Boston next week. He will bring two-thirds of the volume ready for the printer and engage to furnish the other third as fast as it is needed. . . . In regard to Mr. Stowe, you must not scare him off by grimly declaring that you must have the *whole manuscript complete* before you set the printer to work. You must take the three-quarters he brings you and at least make believe begin printing, and he will immediately go to work and finish up the whole; otherwise, what with lectures and the original sin of laziness, it will all be indefinitely postponed. I want to make a crisis, that he shall feel that *now* is the accepted time, and that this must be finished first and foremost.

Thus did a scheming and clear-sighted wife manoeuvre the most indolent, procrastinating, neurasthenic, temperamental, scholarly and likeable husband in the world into producing a masterpiece for the theological library. Fields kept a severe countenance in the comedy, and by the end of the winter Calvin had been beguiled into writing the rest of it, the Old Testament part, and both were issued as a single work in 1867. Its success surprised everyone except Harriet. The book returned its author $10,000 in royalties, and Calvin Stowe had justified his retirement.

Simultaneously Harriet had been prosecuting a book project of her own. She had exhumed and collected all her poems and sent them to Fields, as instructed. Then she waited. Finally Fields told her his house could not publish them in 1866, alleging business reasons. Then, insisted Harriet, bring them out early in 1867. Fields weakly suggested that she might want to give them first "a critical revision." The small Hartford battleship steamed relentlessly ahead. Very well, she replied, "print" them and send proofs, and she would manage the critical revision on the proof-sheets. Before the winter was over she got her volume of verses, *Religious Poems*.

"When the book is published," she wrote to Annie Fields, "I want Mr. Fields to send one to Dr. Holmes and one to Longfellow from me." Harriet was then on the eve of leaving for Florida. "And will you, dear friend," she asked Annie, "write 'From the author' on the blank leaf?"

Calvin's burst of energy that winter carried him by sheer momentum headlong into another book. The war and its aftermath had brought a boom to the subscription-book industry—the buggy of the book-agent was as conspicuous on the dirt roads as the wagon of the pedlar who exchanged kitchen tinware for rags and old iron—and Hartford had become the nation's subscription-book centre.

CALVIN STOWE IN HIS SEVENTIES

"The success of this work [*Origin and History of the Books of the Bible*] brought the author into his final phase—Calvin the Patriarch and Sage." (Page 166.)

Harriet described the development to Fields. "You must know, then, that Hartford is getting to be an immense publishing mart. Two or three publishing houses in agency business are here, driving their presses and making their fortunes. Witness the palace of Case on the corner of Asylum Avenue, which you so much admired when here."

The Hartford Publishing Company approached the Rev. Prof. C. E. Stowe, D.D., for a quick subscription book that spring. Not only did the Professor have a reputation as a witty and popular speaker, but he also bore a magical name. In the hands of a fast-talking book agent, a work by C. E. Stowe might almost pass for an utterance by the famous Harriet herself. The bait was glittering. The Professor had only to throw together a book of excerpts from his old sermons and lectures and be assured of drawing royalties on 100,000 copies. Any book the company handled sold 100,000. Pessimistic about his *Origin and History,* still seeing the roof of the poorhouse looming above the next hill, Calvin agreed to do it.

With this capture made, the representative of the Hartford Publishing Company boldly climbed to the top of Olympus and solicited an agency book from the great authoress herself. He addressed a willing listener, and chiefly because Harriet had the text for such a volume ready at hand – her biographical sketches in the *W. & R.* Jamie Fields was showing little interest in publishing them between covers. The Hartford book man left the Park River villa that February day with the contracts of both celebrities in his pocket.

There was one small fly in this new ointment. The company man had glanced over the material and told Harriet there was not enough of it. The book agent at the front door needed an attractive title, a well-known author, and a fat volume to make the farmer think he was getting his money's worth. Harriet thought she saw the way out, writing to Fields for permission to use "the Chimney Corner articles I have still remaining."

Twenty-four hours later, however, Harriet discovered that she had put herself into strait harness. From Oakholm the book-agent man had gone to his office to explore his own resources, discovering in his bins eighteen engraved portraits of contemporary celebrities. The list of these he took to Mrs. Stowe and told her to fit them with biographies. Her Chimney Corner papers would be entirely out of key, as filler.

Harriet was dismayed. She had written only a dozen of the biographies for the *Watchman & Reflector,* and some of those, the book-agent man told her, would have to be filled out with more details. It meant "scratching up" so much new material that Harriet said she could never get the book done for publication that spring. Then, said the book man, it would be better to bring it out in the fall, and have a sure success.

The figure *100,000* danced before Harriet's eyes, and she agreed to assume the new burden, writing Fields that she would not need his waiver, after all. She minimized the extra labour entailed in her Hartford project, declaring that she intended to keep right on with the New England story, and leaving the impression that she would work on the biographies at odd times when her fictional inspiration would not come. But the long-suffering Fields read between her lines, and in fact her Hartford contract resulted in another long postponement of the story on which he had already advanced so much money.

At one of the portraits supplied by the Hartford publishers Harriet balked. It was that of Henry Ward Beecher. The book man argued that a biography of America's greatest preacher by his sister, America's greatest novelist, would be the best selling point about her book. Harriet firmly shook her head. Finally the publisher offered her $1,000 cash, apart from her royalties, for Henry's biography, and that argument overcame her scruples.

To anticipate, the subscription book delayed the New England story, and the story delayed the subscription book; and it was not until the spring of 1868 that the Hartford Publishing Company could issue *Men of Our Times*. Its title-page was a sales-talk in itself:

MEN OF OUR TIMES;

or

LEADING PATRIOTS OF THE DAY

Being Narratives of the Lives and Deeds of

Statesmen, Generals, and Orators,

including

BIOGRAPHICAL SKETCHES AND ANECDOTES

of

LINCOLN, GRANT, GARRISON, SUMNER, CHASE, WILSON, GREELEY, FARRAGUT, ANDREW, COL-FAX, STANTON, DOUGLASS, BUCKINGHAM, SHERMAN, SHERIDAN, HOWARD, PHILLIPS AND BEECHER.

By

HARRIET BEECHER STOWE,

Author of Uncle Tom's Cabin.

Beautifully Illustrated

WITH EIGHTEEN STEEL PORTRAITS.

Pile commitments upon herself as she would, Harriet was not going to be cheated out of a trip to Florida. Fred was writing her from Laurel Grove about flowers and birds and warm sunshine—he himself was wearing white linen—and Harriet, who had been rhapsodizing for years about the New England winters, and even writing two novels simultaneously in one of them, made the discovery that cold weather "torpified" her brain. She was like Henry, who had said to her that very winter, "My thoughts never run free till the sap begins to rise in the trees; winter months freeze me." For writing, Harriet wanted *warm* weather, and not to be in the state of a 'froze and thawed' apple." Winter weather and cold, she realized now, had always been a sort of nightmare to her.

She could not get away when she planned, but a wintry snap late in February, which left her "like a frost-bitten plant," only strengthened her determination. She left early in March and it does not seem to have occurred to her that it took courage to go deep into a land where for fifteen years hers had been the most hated of all women's names.

Harriet went to Charleston from New York by boat and on the way painted some fans for Annie to sell at the Boston fair for the benefit of the suffering Cretans, whose latest revolution had just been crushed by the Turks. "They need in spots a little rubbing with fine white sandpaper," Harriet told Annie, "to take off some little spots and soils they have acquired in the work, but unluckily I have not a bit with me and must trust them to you. Make them do the Cretes all the good you can."

The South in winter was all she had dreamed. "Here I am in Charleston! Could I tell you one-half what I have seen and see! Room fragrant with violets, banked up in hyacinths, flowers everywhere, windows open, birds singing!" And only the 13th of March! Those eyes of hers that could see were taking in something else, too. "Dear soul," she confided to Annie, "I wish you could know of the sorrow and suffering I see, among people that one can not help pitying. Yet a brighter day is breaking both for *white* and black." Harriet believed whatever her eyes told her, and she was not afraid to change her mind. Certainly these people did not look like vitriol-throwers.

At Charleston she got a boat that went up the St. Johns. The three or four weeks she spent at Orange Park completely won her heart for Florida as a winter residence. The fact that she could, in about a week of travel, step from winter into May utterly charmed her. She had never quite believed it until she experienced it herself; and she was to spend much time for a good many years to come trying to convince other Northerners, though with scant success, that they had a winter paradise at their doors.

It was in the cut-over pine woods known as the scrub; and the St. Johns, four or five miles broad at the bend, was like an inland sea running through it. The floor of the woods was white sand, and there were sloughs and streams choked with evergreen shrubs and trees. Enormous liveoaks, half-smothered in gray Spanish moss, lined the banks of the big river. The woods were full of deer and bear and smaller game.

Orange Park received its mail at Mandarin, a settlement on the other bank of the St. Johns River; and since the mail arrived only once a week, on the steamer from Charleston, it was the custom to row or sail across to get it. Harriet went once with Fred in a rowboat and discovered Mandarin, a village settled largely by people from England, under what were and still are perhaps the largest liveoak trees in America—trees with overhead spreads of one hundred and thirty-five feet and with trunks seven feet in diameter. A white, sandy road muted the sounds of hoofs and wheels. Along the river, on the rise above the sedgy margin, extended a board walk between masses of Cherokee roses. A long wharf ran out to the steamboat landing at deep water, and there were shorter wharves for the sailboats of the residents of the water-front.

There Harriet saw, for sale, a place which utterly captivated her. Under one of the largest liveoaks was a small house—"a very comfortable cottage," she called it in one letter; in another, "a hut"—but its door and windows looked northward down one of the broadest and straightest corridors of the St. Johns twelve miles to Jacksonville at the other end. In the rear clearing, between the river-bank oaks and "a great, wild park" of them, following the road behind, was an orange grove, the produce of which, she learned, brought in $2,000 annually at the wharf in front. The golden globes, studded like Christmas ornaments into the glossy green foliage, were a temptation beyond Harriet's power to resist. In March, when she first saw it, the orange blossoms, appearing simultaneously with the ripened fruit, were loading the air with perfume, while mocking-birds, cardinals, and towhees burst their throats in the hedges. Harriet had not dreamed of such loveliness in this country. It was a fairy grotto; it was Sorrento.

But she did not buy it immediately, trying first, upon her return to Hartford in May, to induce her brother Charles to take it. She had her eye on a more modest place, having on it "five large date palms, an olive tree in full bearing, besides a fine orange grove," though seemingly with no house. Even such beauty could not quite be its own excuse for being, and Harriet must link its enjoyment with a heavenly purpose, writing to Charles:

I am now in correspondence with the Bishop of Florida, with a view to establishing a line of churches along the St. Johns River; and if I settle at Mandarin, it will be one of my stations. Will you consent to enter the Episcopal Church and be our clergyman? You are just the man we want. If my tasks and feelings did not incline me toward the Church, I should still choose it as the best system for training immature minds such as those of our negroes. The system was composed with reference to the wants of the laboring class of England, at a time when they were as ignorant as our negroes now are.

Charles Beecher, though a heretical mystic, was not ready to change his affiliation, however, even at the appeal of his beloved sister. His mental honesty had once caused him to step off the path into the Calvinistic ministry, though it might break his father's heart; and now, no less conscientiously, he would not yield to Harriet. Nevertheless, she so interested him in Florida as a place to live that he went down there, explored all the inhabited regions, and bought a plantation for himself at Newport, on the St. Marks River, on the Gulf side not far from Tallahassee.

Harriet therefore bought the place she had recommended to Charles, though whether that summer, through Fred's agency, or the following winter, when she again went to Florida, we do not know.

Upon her return to Oakholm in the spring of 1867 a conscience-stricken Harriet plunged into work—first, however, for the sake of some ready money, writing a short fiction story for the *Atlantic*. She thought it "rather an original one." She paused, too, to dispatch her "sea baby Charley" on another voyage, but then took up her New England story with such energy that on July 13 she could write Fields that she was "ready next week to begin printing." "My girls say that this is going to be my best work, and, as they wouldn't listen to a stupid thing from the best friend they had in the world, I am somewhat encouraged that the world at large may find it readable."

Apparently having forgotten the imminence of her delivery-date in her contract with the Hartford Publishing Company, she forged ahead on the New England story, reporting to Fields August 8 that she had fourteen chapters done. (This, as it proved, was about one-quarter of the story.)

A week later she sent in the first 130 pages of the manuscript, revised and corrected, with the following note:

> Here goes the first of my nameless story, of which I can only say it is as unlike everything else as it is like the strange world of folks I took it from. There is no fear that there will not be as much matter as in "Uncle Tom's Cabin"; there will. There could be an endless quantity, if I only said all I can see and think that is strange and curious.
>
> I am disappointed, too, that it is not done; but it is of that class of things that cannot be commanded. As my friend Sam Lawson (vide MSS.) says, "There's things that can be druv, and then agin there's things that can't," and this is that kind, as had to be humored.

Charley got home from his second voyage that month, convinced that sailoring was not the profession for him. "Done with the sea, thank heaven!" commented Harriet. He was going now to prepare for Harvard. Calvin's subscription book was out—and selling at the rate of four hundred copies a day. "Of course, he likes that." Harriet solicited a review of it in the *Atlantic* by her new friend Mary Abigail Dodge, now writing successfully in Boston under the name of Gail Hamilton. Gail, who was a sister member of the staff of *Our Young Folks,* visited at Oakholm for a few days in mid-August.

The Hartford book man grew impatient; and Harriet dropped work on the New England story for a while to appease him. Then her conscience smote her, and she took up the work for Fields; and so she kept shuttling from one to the other through the dog-days and far into the autumn.

Money, money—she grasped for it everywhere. With Calvin's subscription book selling 400 a day, his *Origin and History of the Books of the Bible* going, too, and her own royalties on past books steady, still she needed more. There had not been a penny's return yet from the thousands she had put into Laurel Grove Plantation, Oakholm was as expensive to maintain as ever, and now she was buying an orange grove. Harriet had set up at least one trust fund for herself in Boston and possibly took the money from this to buy the Mandarin place. To one of her letters to Fields that autumn, she added: "I have received from your bookkeeper the cheque for One Hundred Twenty-eight, as well as the Two Hundred from yourself. There is Fifty due on the last 'Young Folks,' which, if sent, makes accounts all straight." A few days later she wrote to Fields: "I have a story half done, and, though I am at present in a great hurry, I will look it up and finish it and send it to you. If it suits you, you can have it for the usual price you have paid for my monthly articles. I write it just now, because I want a little of the ready."

But the Hartford Publishing man grew so insistent for his book that Harriet had to turn to the more gentlemanly Jamie Fields, who at least would not lose his temper, and beg off.

Fields, of course, had to comply, though, as Annie revealed after Harriet's death, "both author and publisher required all the tender regard they really had for each other and all the patience they possessed to keep in tune." For "they," read "Fields." It bothered Harriet not a whit. At once she was appealing to the Fieldses for help in writing her biographies. She was going to trouble Dear Friend Fields (whom for brevity she was thereafter going to address as D.F.F.) to forward the enclosed note to Garrison *"exactly where he lives,* I do not know whether in Boston or Roxbury," since "I want to get one or two special bits of information out of him." To pad out her *W. & R.* sketch, of course. And Annie certainly wouldn't mind looking up for her that speech to the Massachusetts legislature which Governor Andrew regarded as his favourite. But, though working "like a dray horse" on *Men of Our Times,* she assured Fields: *"My own book* instead of cooling boils and bubbles daily and nightly, and I am pushing and spurring like fury to get to it."

But the gentle Mr. Fields was not to be entirely flattened by this small Juggernaut and, when she came into Boston for a day, informed her that, since the novel was still so indefinite, he must have a Stowe book to publish immediately. There were those Chimney Corner papers. She had said she would not permit book publication of them until she had given them a drastic revision. Fields thrust them into her hands and told her that at any rate she must prepare them, even though the work delayed the subscription book. She went to Hartford and in a few days returned them.

In December, two months after she broke off work on the novel, she wrote to Annie Fields: "The book is almost done, hang it! but done *well* and will be a good thing for young men to read, and young women, too, and so I'll send you one. You'll find *some* things in it, I fancy, that I know and you don't about old times before you were born, when I was a-'hush-my-dear'-ing in Cincinnati." And Harriet's postscript was: "The book will be all done before Christmas."

It was, for all we know to the contrary, and thus ended what had perhaps been the most strenuous year in Harriet's life. The Hartford book man's predictions had been too optimistic; but *Men of Our Times* did sell to 50,000 copies and so repaid her for the trouble it cost.

After this excitement and that of the Christmas holidays, Harriet turned once more to the New England story, which, incidentally, she had now named *Oldtown Folks*. But she resumed none too diligently. Things easily distracted her attention from her own work. One was a real annoyance. Harriet had made her sketch of Governor Andrew, Massachusetts war governor, which she had written largely on data supplied by Annie Fields, do double duty, selling it as an article for the *Watchman & Reflector,* which published it in its issue of January 2, 1868. Later Harriet got a letter from the deceased Governor's brother, saying that her sketch was full of errors and she must not think of publishing it in her Hartford book until she had consulted Edwin P. Whipple, critic and biographer, and a close friend of the late Governor. Where was Whipple? Harriet asked. Well, Whipple was away on a lecture tour; he would be back "by and bye."

"This to me," exclaimed Harriet indignantly to Fields, "about a thing stereotyped and just going into print!"

Presumably, since the Hartford publishers were not going to bring out the book until the roads had settled after the spring thaws, it was satisfactorily adjusted. At any rate, the sketch of Governor Andrew appeared in *Men of Our Times*.

After all of Harriet's assurances and promises to Fields, it was really outrageous of her to go down to Florida again that year, and stay three months, during which time she wrote not a word on *Oldtown Folks* or anything else. She had her usual excuse of bad health—a perpetual cold, her lungs touched. She was determined to go.

This time she took Charley with her—Charles, now a stripling of 18, preparing to enter Harvard in the fall. They left at the end of February, travelling overland this time, and making a stop in Washington, where Harriet accepted the invitation of Judge John C. Underwood and his wife to attend the State Constitutional Convention at Richmond as their guest. Underwood was a Virginia Abolitionist who had remained loyal to the Union and received a Federal judgeship from Lincoln as his reward.

In Richmond Mrs. Underwood showed Harriet a photograph of her daughter Alice. Harriet was so struck by the young lady's appearance that, unseen, she wrote her a note, telling her that she inferred from her picture and her mother's words that "you are a bright, whole-hearted, little Union maiden and going to give your whole heart and soul to the great and glorious future which the true *Union* shall open before us all." It was the beginning of a long friendship, and a long correspondence, between Harriet and Alice Underwood, who became one of Harriet's chief idolaters.

Harriet and her son travelled into the deep South as guests of the Government, riding as passengers on a military train from Aquia Creek, a town on the Potomac below Alexandria, to Charleston, South Carolina. There was further disillusionment awaiting Harriet in the southern city about whose inhabitants she had spoken so disrespectfully in *Dred*. The news of her coming had been published in Charleston; and a young man in civilian dress, who had, however, been a major in the Confederate Army, met Harriet at the station and introduced himself. His mother, who would not take no for an answer, had sent him to bring Mrs. Stowe and her party to her house to be her guests while they waited for the St. Johns River boat.

Wondering at this unexpected invitation, Harriet accepted; and she and Charley entered the carriage with the ex-major and were driven to one of the fine old houses of Charleston, the black coachman visibly swelling with importance at having such a famous passenger. They went in, and the major introduced them to his mother and two sisters. Both sides covertly sized each other up. The little Yankee war-maker was not, at any rate, an ogress in appearance—and Harriet saw no Union scalps.

"I suppose, Mrs. Stowe," said the white-haired hostess, "you would like to know why we so much wanted you to come." She then told Harriet that during the war, when the men were away, she and her daughters had moved inland to the greater safety of Columbia, the State capital. When that city was sacked and burned by the Union troops, a band of drunken Yankee privates invaded their house and began to ransack it. One of the daughters was seriously ill. The mother ran to the door and screamed. A Union colonel was passing. He ran into the house with drawn pistol and drove out the looters. Then he said to the mother, "Madame, if it will make you feel safer, I can move my quarters into this house and protect you during the occupation."

"That man, Mrs. Stowe," said the hostess, "was Colonel Robert Beecher, your nephew."

This mother had given a son to the war, too; and presently Harriet was weeping over the boy's last letter as bitterly as she ever wept over any

Northern soldier's letter from camp, prison, or hospital. It was this letter which was most disillusioning; for the boy had been a divinity student when the call came, studying for the Presbyterian ministry. Fatally wounded, he scrawled a few lines to his mother, telling her that he was laying down his life joyfully for God and truth as against injustice and oppression. After reading that Harriet knew these people had not used Yankee skulls for drinking goblets.

Disillusionment continued on the *Dictator,* the little steamer that took them from Charleston to Mandarin. Its short, bristling, red-faced skipper, Captain Atkins, had been as fiery a Rebel as there was below the Mason and Dixon Line. He had been a blockade-runner; and no doubt in his earlier days he, too, had repeated the poetic injunction to ol' Harriet Beecher Stowe to go, go, go. But now, having the lady herself under his protection, he exhibited, as Charles Stowe remembered, "an almost pathetic solicitude for Mrs. Stowe's comfort and safety." So, Harriet may have been wrong when she made her bitter remark in *Dred* about Carolina chivalry.

There is not a word from Mrs. Stowe during the three months she spent on the St. Johns River in 1868; but two subsequent letters of hers indicate what subjects occupied her to the exclusion of her writing. The cottage at the orange grove was much too small to serve her family as a winter residence, and it is probable that she began to enlarge it that spring. In a letter to George Eliot written some years later she told how the place grew.

The other letter brings up a darker theme. Harriet wrote it soon after her return to Hartford in the late spring or early summer of 1868. As if afraid to tell James T. Fields directly that she had done nothing for months with *Oldtown Folks,* she addressed her plea for herself to the tender heart of Annie Fields.

> I want to see you. I have a long story to tell you of *what* has prevented my going on with my story, which, you must see, would so occupy all the nerve and brain force I have that I have not been able to write a word, except to my own children. To them in their needs I must write chapters which would otherwise go into my novel. But if Mr. Fields will have patience, I want to have time to write it *when* I can write well, and without my mind distracted with something else. . . .

This letter gains all its pathos from what it does not tell. It was not just another of Harriet's glib excuses, when she had been delinquent in her tasks. The "something else" was real. Harriet in her pride would put nothing on paper about Fred and his drunkenness, even in a letter to Annie; but that was what she wanted to tell Annie about. During those three months in Florida, Fred had at last broken her heart.

She found the Laurel Grove Plantation completely demoralized. Away from the restraints of home, Fred, who was supposed to be managing it, had become a wretched, nerve-shaken alcoholic, stupefied most of the time. But it was not entirely the fault of his habits that the plantation venture had failed. None of the Yankee farmers knew much about growing cotton and still less about managing Negroes as demoralized as their former masters by their liberation. Charles Stowe, who saw Laurel Grove that year, said it looked to him like "a free boarding-house for a gang of lazy negroes." Harriet had put $10,000 into it, and it had yet to market its first bale of cotton. What cotton had been harvested—at a cost much higher than its selling price—mildewed for want of proper storage; the army worms got the rest on the stalk.

Harriet had courage and energy for anything, and it seems probable that she first attempted to reorganize the plantation herself. Otherwise, she would hardly have remained so long away from her husband and daughters. But though she knew something about growing flowers, she must soon have realized that the management of a cotton plantation was beyond her abilities. She withdrew her support from Laurel Grove, at any rate, and took Fred North with her in June.

She had by no means given Fred up for lost. If by some means she could keep her boy away from liquor until he was thoroughly sober, she felt certain that his own will would sustain him after that. A long sea voyage for him suggested itself; but it would never do to let Fred go alone. His father must be with him, to guide and protect him. Harriet went back to Hartford firm for the plan, though it must have taken all her persuasion and tact to move fat Calvin, now in his 67th year, out of his easy chair and into the perils and discomforts of the sea. She accomplished it, though, and on July 27 wrote to Annie Fields: "My Rabbi and Fred have gone to the Mediterranean—in a sailing vessel, for the benefit of being at sea."

Then Harriet prepared for a visit of the Brooklyn Howards, in August.

After the Howards left, Harriet really got down to business, resisting Annie's invitation to visit for a few days at Manchester-by-the-Sea, where the Howards now maintained a summer home. She was now "sole custodian" at Oakholm, "Mr. Stowe being in France, or on the way, and the girls with Georgie in Stockbridge."

Planchette boards had been introduced, and people were beginning to play with them. Harriet was getting remarkable results from one, and asked Annie, "Have you heard of any of the dealings and doings of 'Planchette'?" But with that question she retreated with pen and quires into the silences, not to emerge until the day before Christmas, when she reported to Fields that "the end [of *Oldtown Folks*] is in plain sight," although "there is still a great deal to be done to bring it out worthily, and I work upon it steadily and daily. I have never put so much work upon anything before."

But she exasperated her impatient publisher by informing him that she had been gathering some "really very extraordinary materials for the Planchette article," though, of course, "I don't want to have to write it now, when I am driving so hard upon my book." She broke the news, too, about "my new paper, 'The Hearth & Home.' I say mine, because I have a sort of editorial connection with it." Her sort of connection was the position of co-editor, with Ik Marvel. Their associate editor was Mary Mapes Dodge, later to become godmother and editor of *St. Nicholas Magazine*. Harriet told Fields that for her first contribution she was preparing a series of articles on learning to write, "designed to be helpful to a great many beginners, especially among women, who are endeavoring to help themselves to competence by writing."

Harriet engaged a secretary to help her, and thus the new connection (which, in fact, she gave up after a few months) did not hold back the story much. At the end of the year she sent Fields two more chapters together with a note ("per sect.") thanking him for his encouraging words, which she really needed, and hoping he would continue to read and not find the story dull.

Before Christmas Calvin brought Fred home, little improved by his trip. He had sobered up during the voyages but was still unable to withstand the temptations of the shore. It changed Harriet's plans. Had Fred straightened himself out, she had intended to make him manager of her Mandarin orange grove. Now that was impossible; and in January, 1869, Harriet went down to Guilford to see her second cousin, Spencer Foote, who, like many a Civil War veteran, was still unsettled in any permanent business or profession.

We have to guess that on this visit Harriet made her relative an offer, which he accepted, for him to go down to Mandarin and operate the orange grove in some sort of partnership with her. At any rate, Foote moved himself and his family to Mandarin that winter and for a number of years thereafter resided in the Mandarin cottage, taking complete charge of the orange business and for some time serving the village as postmaster. Presumably Fred Stowe went South with him, for never again do we hear of Fred at Hartford.

In her fifty-eighth year Harriet was at the top of her physical and mental powers. She could write a masterpiece of fiction, conduct a weekly department in a farm journal, gather spirit-writings from her Planchette, accept the tragedy of her son's life and work to mollify it, rule her family, arrange her business affairs, shrug off heavy financial losses, and still retain her poise and judgment and be her own good-humoured, gay, and willful feminine self. She was wonderful that year. In one of her letters to Fields she inserted a sentence so unexpected as to be ludicrous, when contrasted with her lifelong claims of fatigue and prostration—"I have worked so hard that I am almost tired."

So, she worked on like a dray horse, and on February 3 could report that she was turning out the story at the rate of fifteen pages a day, "and so hope soon to see the end"; and on February 17 announce with relief, "I do hope tomorrow to send the end of my story." This time she estimated correctly. It was done.

As she approached the end of this story, which she had begun so irresolutely and then had trifled with and neglected for so many months and years, Harriet had no doubt of its merit or its ranking among her works. She placed it next to *Uncle Tom's Cabin,* as did later many of her literary friends, Whittier in particular. John Erskine regrets that *Oldtown Folks,* with its companion story, *Poganuc People,* are not still on the American reading list. It was again a question of a British copyright. Harriet had not bothered to copyright either *The Minister's Wooing* or *The Pearl of Orr's Island* in England, but *Oldtown Folks* was different. She wrote Fields:

The book must be *copyrighted* in England.

It is not for profit but *protection,* I say it.

It is of the last importance to me that all the publishing houses in England shall *not* have the power to print *garbled copies.*

Now *when* shall the day be.

You will have the whole copy in hand by Monday.

I can spend next week with you, if needful, to hurry matters on, though I would rather be here, as better for my health.

The book is a success and will be. I know it.

Write me at once.

The law had been changed. A foreign author could now obtain a valid British copyright, if he stood on British soil anywhere at the moment his publisher was taking out the copyright in London. For an American author Canadian soil was most convenient, though few American authors went to the trouble. But Harriet was determined. "I want the thing brought along," she told Fields, "so that when it is done, I shall have to spend the least possible time in Canada. We must use the Ocean Telegraph in fixing the time." In another letter she elaborated: "My plan is send all [the proof-sheets] we can, and the last in manuscript, and then wait till Low telegraphs its receipt in England. Then I set out for Canada and stay there till he telegraphs its copyright completed."

As Fields read the concluding chapters of *Oldtown Folks,* he became excited about it. There had never been much said about serialization in the *Atlantic*—the tale, at first, seemed too slow-paced and episodical for that—but now Fields was sure he wanted it for his magazine, even though, because of the story's great length, it would take two years to serialize it. He therefore offered Harriet the flat sum of $6,000 for serial rights here and in England and for all book rights for one year after book publication.

It was much the largest sum the *Atlantic* had ever offered her for anything, and it tempted her. The money all in hand at once—no risks—the greater part of her Florida losses reimbursed to her. But her faith in *Oldtown Folks* was complete, and she preferred to gamble on it, declining Fields's offer in a letter which contains her only known statement of her earning ability as an author.

My Dear Mr. Fields:—There are several objections to the plan you propose. In the first place, as to the success of the book *as* a book. It is more to me than a story; it is my resume of the whole spirit and body of New England— a country that now is exerting such an influence on the civilized world that to know it truly becomes an object.

But the Atlantic has on the part of *my* people (i.e., the orthodox) prejudices to encounter that would predispose them to look suspiciously on it, more than even by the fact of its being by a Beecher.

Dr. Holmes has stung and irritated them by his sharp, scathing irony and keen ridicule; and, after all, they are not ridiculous, and the estimate of New England life and principles and orthodoxy, as dramatically set forth, must be graver and wider than he has revealed it.

Under all the drollery that is to be found in it, this book will be found to have in it the depths of the most solemn tragedy of life, and I shall make it my means of saying many things which I hope will be accepted pacifically on all sides. It will answer my purpose better to be read at once in a book. To spend two years in getting my story before the world, before half of my friends will read or judge, would not suit my views.

As to profits, I understand your offer as amounting to this—you give me $6,000 for the use of the book here and in England, for I do not consider the sale of any year worth counting, after the first.

Now, I am just offered $2,000 by an English paper for a weekly story that should run through one year—of about half the length of this—and an American paper offers me $4,000 for the simultaneous issue in America, and then I am to have the disposal of the profits in book form in both countries afterwards.

I made on *The Minister's Wooing* in America alone, $7,500, and in England, $4,000. On *Dred* I made $10,000 in England, and an equal sum in America.

Now, however times may have changed, I cannot suppose but what, with a book *better* than either of the two, I may make quite as much as you offer. Is it not so?

I think, if you try your prettiest in the lawful arts and means of the trade, that you may make a large sale of this book. I think it is a book that will bear some effort to sell it largely—but all these things cannot be told. I know that nothing has ever moved me more powerfully and deeply.

When Harriet said, "I *know* it," in predicting a book's success, it behooved a publisher to take heed. She had said it of Calvin's history of the Bible, and now the returns from that work were permitting her to finish her New England story without worrying about money. She was right about *Oldtown Folks,* too, which proved to be her greatest success since *Dred.* The American public bought 25,000 copies before August 1, it took three editions to satisfy the British demand, and, for all its Yankee dialect and solecisms, it went into numerous translations across the Channel. At home, Harriet's rustic story-teller, Sam Lawson, became a household familiar, though his name has faded from today's memory.

With this success Harriet Beecher Stowe, at fifty-eight, stood at the very top of her prestige and fame. It was a lofty plateau she had trodden for seventeen years, but the descent was steep.

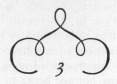

3

Catastrophe

Far from being worn out by the effort to finish *Oldtown Folks* and get away to Florida, Harriet at once resumed writing on the same theme. Jamie Fields's desire to serialize the novel in the *Atlantic* had given her an idea. Since he wanted Oldtown atmosphere in his magazine, Harriet could supply it *ad libitum*—or, say, in a set of twelve short, complete stories, at her regular rates, which would make just a year's work. *Oldtown Folks* had by no means exhausted Calvin's store of yarns about his native Massachusetts town.

Harriet must have kept herself employed on them even while on the Charleston boat; for, on March 2, 1869, when she had barely had time to reach Mandarin, she sent Fields the *second* of the tales, together with her title for the series—*Oldtown Firelight Stories*.

> The origin is this: there was an amount of curious old Natick tradition that I could not work into "Old Town Folks" without making the book too bulky, and still that has great attractions for my imagination.
>
> Just for the sake of diverting myself and making myself laugh and dream, I am writing these out. I do not know how far a series of Yankee stories told in Yankee dialect may do, but to me it is very fascinating to write it. I send you by this mail the second of the series. The third is to be a story of the Indian wars, and the fourth of the witchcraft. Then, there are some of pure fun, like the adventures of old Father Homer, of Newtown.
>
> Do you want to engage the set for the Atlantic? I write more readily for the Atlantic, and the *set* ought to go into the same periodical.

Fields did want the set; and thus, later in 1869, the reading public was getting its Oldtown from two sources simultaneously: Harriet's own orthodox from the book, the Unitarians, Transcendentalists, and infidels from *The Atlantic Monthly*. Incidentally, the defiant pride in Harriet's "*my* people (i.e., the orthodox)" in her letter to Fields is the only indication in her record she ever gave that Dr. Holmes's flings at the religion of his father hurt her feelings.

There had been a change in Fields's office that winter. Since the death of his partner, in 1863, he had still been carrying on the business as Ticknor & Fields; but now he had taken in James R. Osgood and formed the firm of Fields, Osgood & Co. There had come into the office, too, an accommodating young man from Ohio, Mr. Howells, who could translate Harriet's Italian quotations for her, or even put them into tolerable English verse, if requested.

In contrast to conditions at the Laurel Grove cotton plantation a year earlier, Harriet found her Mandarin place a scene of activity. Spencer Foote and Fred Stowe were planting more orange trees and also transforming the property into a general fruit farm by setting out peaches, lemons, and grapes. Harriet bought a box of lemons in Jacksonville, and her son saved and planted the seeds. They germinated surprisingly well, and next year poor Fred could show his mother two hundred fine lemon seedlings of his cultivation—the only constructive thing, perhaps, he ever did in his life. Spencer Foote, being a smart Yankee, was already capitalizing the famous name of the grove's owner. In the packing shed hung new stencils for painting on the fruit boxes:

ORANGES
from
HARRIET BEECHER STOWE
MANDARIN
FLA.

The original "hut" had been enlarged so that it now had at least "a small parlor," which Harriet kept filled with roses and wildflowers, though "this spring is an unusually cold and late one." "I took a drive yesterday through the pine woods to a cracker's cottage," she wrote to Fields early in April. "There were two rose-bushes before the door that I think must have had a hundred full-blown roses each, all growing out of white sand. We came away with our hands full of different kinds of roses, pomegranate blossoms, and other matters of that kind. We stopped in the woods and added a handful of little white Florida lilies."

Before she left Mandarin that spring a contractor, employed by the Freedmen's Bureau, was erecting on the road behind her house, the framework

of a school building for Negro children. Harriet was constituting herself the
Board of Education. "I shall start a school here," she informed Annie Fields,
"and shall want a little help from your northern education funds to sustain
a teacher."

Through the mail Harriet received the surprising news that James and
Annie Fields were about to depart for Europe. Having now a partner to
look after business at home, Fields could enjoy a long-deferred vacation
and see some foreign authors besides. Harriet remained in Mandarin to put
into execution plans for enlarging the cottage to accommodate the whole
family the following winter, then left in time to be in Canada on May 15th.

According to the custom then, book-critics on both sides of the Atlantic
were reviewing *Oldtown Folks* in advance of publication for the general
reader. "The 'Nation' has come out with a wild, mad *rave* about 'Old
Town Folks'," Harriet wrote to Annie in London, "the general drift of
which is that there is nothing in it, not a character, and never was in anything I ever wrote, and that they are tired and sick of it, and vote it a bore.
There's criticism for you!"

But she was a veteran in the taking of abuse and could regard the *Nation's*
attack good-humouredly.

In Hartford, Harriet found cards for the usual June wedding whose
nuptial table must display a set of Stowe, bound in white. In Fields's absence
Mr. Osgood attended to it for her this time. In Boston, she told Mr. Osgood
to be sure to send a review copy of *Oldtown Folks* to the *Banner of Light,*
the organ of Spiritualism in America. There was a great deal of the supernatural in *Oldtown Folks,* as there was bound to be in any veracious story
of the boyhood experiences of that psychic phenomenon, Calvin Stowe.

Then Harriet went on to Canada for her enforced legal visit. There would
be a boring week in a hotel room, and she looked over the Boston book-
stores for reading-matter. A new title caught her eye—a book just issued by
Harper & Brothers. It was called, *My Recollections of Lord Byron.* It was
anonymous; but in lieu of a signature on the title-page, Harpers had
printed a quotation from the review of the London *Athenaeum:* "The long-
promised work of the COUNTESS GUICCIOLI."

Harriet returned from Canada with her feelings whipped into a mighty
rage. At least, she had convinced herself it was rage. As a modest and pious
woman in 1869, she could plead a special interest in *My Recollections of
Lord Byron,* which was not, however, a book that a Professor Park would

permit on his table at Andover, or a Dr. Bacon at New Haven. Everybody knew of old Countess Guiccioli, the last mistress of Lord Byron. For years she had been one of the notorious sights of Paris, parading herself in the Tuilleries Gardens for the benefit of English and American tourists— bewhiskered, frock-coated American gentlemen tourists who, on the boats going home, would wink and whisper and slap their legs and haw-haw mysteriously when exchanging their experiences in Paris.

But la Guiccioli's book about Byron contained none of those details which the leg-slapping gentlemen, and perhaps Harriet, expected to find. As Harriet read on through a most dull and banal work, her indignation mounted as she discovered that it was a long attempt to prove that the ruin, exile, and untimely demise of the brightest genius the world ever knew were entirely due to the cold, mercenary heart of Lady Byron.

The effrontery of it! This vile woman, this strumpet fouling the name of Lady Byron—a slug on the petals of a damask rose! And when the *true* story could so triumphantly acquit Harriet's dearest English friend of blame and so eternally consign Byron to the execration of civilized society! "Leave all," Harriet had advised the widow of Ham Common, "with some discreet friends, who, after both have passed from earth, shall say what is due to justice."

The hour had come for justice to receive its due. To be sure, Lady Byron had not exactly designated Harriet as the discreet friend; but surely that departed saint would have wished Harriet to crush with the truth the charges of the Countess Guiccioli. Or so a New England mother in Zion, whom fame and travel had sophisticated, persuaded herself and returned from Canada determined to tell in *The Atlantic Monthly* the story of Lord Byron's incest, as Lady Byron had told it to her.

Calvin begged her to change her mind, but she was used to his fears. Osgood was apprehensive but stood in such awe of Harriet Beecher Stowe that her command was fiat with him. The one man who might have saved her was James T. Fields, and he was in Europe. Harriet would listen to no one else, not even Dr. Holmes.

Harriet was headstrong, and her obstinate determination in itself argued a complex motive deeper than the ostensible one of clearing Lady Byron's reputation. She swept away obstacles and invented her justification. She had waited patiently, she informed her public, for the proper persons in England to answer the Guiccioli charges and had only been drawn to speak herself when convinced that no answer would come from that source. Actually, not more than six weeks elapsed from the time Harriet picked up the Guiccioli book until she had written her long article for the *Atlantic, The True Story of Lady Byron's Life*. The one fact she could plead was that the Guiccioli memoirs had been out some time in England before their publication in New York.

Harriet reiterated that the Guiccioli book was sweeping the English-speaking world and re-enslaving the youth under the power of "that brilliant, seductive genius, from which it was hoped they had escaped." But this statement was not true, either, for the reviewers were treating the Countess Guiccioli and her "revelations" with light contempt, and the book had little appeal except to the prurient, who searched it for salacious details. There were no such details in it. Actually, it was little more than a rewriting of other people's biographies of Byron, with gluttonous quotations from the poet's works to prove his nobility of soul. The charge of Lady Byron's hard-heartedness was nothing new. It was the story that had been accepted from the beginning.

But Harriet was snatching for reasons to justify her foolhardy act. Whether she recognized it or not, a small, selfish voice was whispering to her that in telling this unsavoury story she was proclaiming to the world the glamorous, stupendous fact that she, Harriet Beecher Stowe, had been the bosom friend of Byron's wife and widow, the sharer of her most intimate secrets.

She wrote her article with an indirection unusual for her. Not once did she say that Lady Byron told her the story. That story had "long been perfectly understood in many circles in England," and "by a singular concurrence of circumstances, all the facts of the case, in the most undeniable and authentic form, were at one time placed in the hands of the writer of this sketch, with authority to make such use of them as she should judge best." The public might guess who gave the authority. Nor did Harriet once mention the name of Augusta Leigh, Byron's half-sister. It was, "a secret, adulterous intrigue with a blood relation, so near in consanguinity that discovery must have been utter ruin and expulsion from civilized society." Only once did Harriet graze an identification, quoting Byron's last, incoherent words at Missolonghi—"My sister—my child!"

The twins made copies of the manuscript, and Harriet showed them to some of her friends, whose shock must have expressed itself in remonstrances which made Harriet cautious, for on June 23 she wrote to Osgood:

I think, on the whole, as this article is very important and will probably make a good deal of sensation, that I should have time quietly to revise the proof-sheets, and therefore we had better calculate it for the September number. In that case, it will come out in the middle of August, which will be a good time for the reading public.

Please send the proof-sheets as fast as they can be printed, as I want to correct them as soon as possible. I should like to have Dr. Holmes see them, and I shall write to him today on the subject.

The delay would give Harriet opportunity to change her mind, though there was little likelihood that she would. In her letter to Holmes, after relating her reasons for writing the exposé, she said:

"When you have read my article, I want, *not* your advice as to whether the main facts should be told, for on this point I am so resolved that I frankly say advice would do me no good. But you might help me, with your delicacy and insight, to make the *manner of telling* more perfect; and I want to do it as wisely and well as such a story can be told."

Thus advised, Holmes did not seek to dissuade her, but does seem to have urged her to be more specific about her authority for the story. On June 28 Harriet wrote to Osgood:

It has been thought by my friends that the communications in my article on Lady Byron are so extraordinary and will make such a sensation both here and in England, that it will be necessary to authenticate them by publishing precisely how I came by this information. I therefore send you this, which I want printed as a kind of postscript, on the end of the article.

The postscript was a brief statement of Harriet's memorable afternoon with Lady Byron at Ham Common. And having despatched this to the *Atlantic,* Harriet and the family retreated for rest to Mrs. Soule's boarding house on an island off Westport Point, Massachusetts, in Buzzards Bay.

Annie Fields wrote that, in publishing her Byron story, "Mrs. Stowe felt her message as from the Most High." But, though Harriet had been engaged in God's work, she expected her usual tribute from Mammon, writing to Osgood in July, "Please send me a cheque on New York for the Lady Byron article, directed to Westport Point, as usual." Well was it for her that her enemies never saw this letter. One of the harshest accusations brought against Harriet in the uproar which soon followed was that she had lost her money and saw her popularity declining and so turned to writing pornography to recoup her fortunes.

Harriet expected the Byron article to stir up a sensation but was scarcely prepared for the hurricane it caused. Late that year Dr. Holmes wrote John Lothrop Motley: "We have had three storms this autumn: first, the great gale of September 8, which I recognized while it was blowing as the greatest for fifty-four years, for you remember that I remember *the* September gale; second, the Byron whirlwind, which began here and swiftly traveled across the Atlantic; and third, the gold-storm, as I christened the terrible financial conflict of the last week."

The first puffs came from England, *Macmillan's Magazine,* in which Osgood had arranged for the publication of the Byron article, appearing a few days before the *Atlantic* in Boston. The British press at once attacked the article and its author so savagely that the American correspondents in London sent dispatches about it by the ocean telegraph. Harriet's first impulse was to fight back, as she had when attacked formerly, writing to Osgood about "the infamous course of such papers as the Times in persisting in believing the story of an avowed libertine against that of a pure, noble woman, whose whole life shows not one record of duty unfulfilled."

Then came the *Atlantic* and the American blast; and all the vilification Harriet had ever received for *Uncle Tom's Cabin* and *Dred* and her treatment of Joel Parker was but a whisper beside the roar of anger that went up from one end of the country to the other. "The most unsparing and pitiless criticism and brutal insult," her son Charles called it later. While editors and critics were exhausting their most scathing adjectives to characterize Harriet's act, *Punch* in England and *Harper's Weekly* in the United States were cartooning her as an evil old frump, armed with an umbrella, and swarming up the noble statue of Byron to sully its marble with mud. No American woman, before Harriet's time or since, ever received such a castigation.

Had it been only her old enemies who seized this opportunity to beat down her reputation once more, it would have been easier for her to endure; but those journals that had been her friends, and her chief friends, joined in the outcry against her. No friendly voice was lifted for her, or no influential one. Justin McCarthy, then in the United States, wrote for Harriet's own *Independent* an attack above which Theodore Tilton put the caption: *MRS. STOWE'S LAST ROMANCE.* Its unrestraint was typical:

The Bettmann Archive

Now then, old gal, if you want to make yourself conspicuous, you had better go elsewhere, and not leave your dirty marks there.—From *Fun Magazine*, 1869.

A TYPICAL ATTACK ON MRS. STOWE FOR HER BYRON EXPOSE

"'The most unsparing and pitiless criticism and brutal insult,' her son Charles called it." (Page 538.)

There is a sentence in Macaulay's essay on Byron which has been so often quoted, and is likely just now to rise to so many lips again, that I am almost ashamed to cite it here; and yet it is temptingly, terribly appropriate. "It is not every day," says Macaulay, explaining in language of bitter eloquence the outcry against Byron, "that the savage envy of aspiring dunces is gratified by the agonies of such a spirit and the degradation of such a name." In our day, however, we have reformed on the rude condition of things described by Macaulay. The abominable stories which only "aspiring dunces" then rejoiced in, and which they only whispered about in congenial atmospheres of scandalous gossip, are solemnly endorsed and affirmed today by a most distinguished woman, and are printed and circulated by a most respectable publisher.

Moreover, I do not know that any one in Macaulay's time had learned how to make money out of such abominations. See how we manage things now! An authoress of reputation gets hold of a disgusting story about Byron —a story which, true or false, is revolting and obscene. She sells it to a publisher; and for weeks before its appearance the press is inundated with little preliminary puffs, whetting and goading on the meanest curiosity on the part of the public. The coming disclosures are advertised, announced, heralded, trumpeted everywhere; and, of course, the result is a splendid success. A story which would have suited and delighted the taste of a Borgia family-circle is sent into every household in the United States; and the circulation of the magazine is thereby made enormous. Well might Macaulay call the scandalous gossipers of his day aspiring dunces. Dunces indeed! They had not the brains to see that they might have made money out of their garbage. Perhaps, however, the publishers of that day lacked courage. Perhaps, too, the authoresses of that day had not discovered that the cause of morality is served by the publication of an infamous accusation, utterly unsupported by evidence, against a dead man; and that the best way to stop the circulation of an author's books is to startle the whole world by an appalling story of which he is the guilty hero.

McCarthy went on to say indignantly that he, for one, did not believe a word of the story. Not that he doubted that Lady Byron told it; but it should have occurred to Mrs. Stowe that Lady Byron must have been out of her head to confide to a relative stranger something she had hidden from her own family.

She [Mrs. Stowe] was evidently ready to believe anything. Her rapturous enthusiasm for Lady Byron rendered her childlike in her incapacity to doubt or criticize. Mrs. Stowe, as we all know, has a weakness for ladies of title. She fairly melts, dissolves away, like Mrs. Pendennis, into her pocket handkerchief, over Lady Byron. If Lady Byron had told her that she lived with her husband twenty years, instead of two, the simple devotee would have believed it all.

All the critics had pounced on that palpable error in Harriet's article, the Byron marriage having lasted only one year. Justin McCarthy concluded: "I do not think that Mrs. Stowe has done much to serve the memory of her friend, and I know she has done much to injure her own fame."

The *Independent* itself said:

> It is with regret that we employ the columns of a journal in which Mrs. Stowe has been a familiar contributor and in which one of her novels received its first publication, to utter a protest against her recent and horrible tale concerning Lord Byron. Startling in accusation, barren in proof, inaccurate in dates, infelicitous in style, and altogether ill-advised in publication, her strange article will travel round the whole literary world and everywhere evoke against its author the spontaneous disapprobation of her life-long friends.

If a friend could say that, what were her enemies saying? Harriet was utterly confounded. She had expected a sensation, but she had also expected to be believed. "Proof! Proof!" everyone seemed to be screaming at her; but she had given them her proof. Lady Byron was her proof. Not one of these hateful critics was questioning her veracity in reporting Lady Byron's words, yet all kept demanding proof of the story. It was beyond Harriet's comprehension of her sainted friend's character even to grant as a possibility that Lady Byron, in thirty years of jealous brooding over the wreck of her marriage, might have built the whole legend of incest on a few evidences innocent in themselves. Harriet never did admit that possibility. At the end of her days she still believed the story true, and maintained to Mrs. McCray that she had never regretted her publication of it.

In her first dismay Harriet was uncertain what course to take to defend herself. As the violence of the editorial assault increased, she thrust her head into a familiar sandpile, maintaining, perhaps with no small degree of truth, that she was not reading the diatribes of her critics. It would have been hard for anyone, man or woman, to read such an indictment of one's character, mentality, and motives as that penned by Justin McCarthy.

"At first, I thought the world's people must have all lost their senses— or I," Harriet wrote to Susan Howard. "*Could* that account be called uncalled-for?"

In the first uproar Osgood sent her a bundle of hostile clippings, begging her to do something about them. She replied:

It appears to me that the best thing to be done in the premises is *not* just at this moment for me to come out and write more, but for somebody to make an article, say, for the Tribune out of what Macmillan's says.

The fact that a magazine of that standing and respectability in England is willing to take the responsibility of giving it to the public and expressing itself *glad* to do so, shows that in England there is both knowledge and belief abroad in society.

I wrote yesterday for Charles Follen's address. [The son of the late Mrs. Follen, who told Harriet the incest story originally.] Years ago I heard him make the remark that there were documents in Chancery that proved the paternity of that child. I want to get his address and communicate more directly with him.

The course the American papers take is trying. As my health is not good and I am trying to avoid all excitement, I do not read at all upon the subject. The wild and distracted calling on me for proof, utterly ignoring the only kind of proof that I have to give, shows that the public is yet not in a proper state to weigh anything.

Nobody ever called for *proof* from any of the numberless writers who reported their conversations with Lord Byron.

The proofs will probably eventually come out; but my belief is founded simply on Lady Byron's known character—a character remarkable for truthfulness, accuracy, self-control, patience, and, above all, conscientiousness.

When such a person makes statements to me of facts which came under her immediate observation, I ask no other proof. Reliable human testimony is the only proof of facts which we rest on, in anything.

I cannot be mistaken in this, that Lady Byron asserted that the intrigue was not only acknowledged by Lord Byron but *defended* and persisted in.

The course of the papers surprises and grieves me. They are not as good as I thought them.

You must have patience and keep quiet. The nine-days' wonder will die out in time, and the truth will come out.

I shall return your notices by next mail. I am at present in a feeble state of health and unable to write more.

Osgood had reason to be uneasy. *The Atlantic Monthly* was taking a ferocious bludgeoning along with Mrs. Stowe. Its subscribers were dropping away by the hundreds. Ellery Sedgwick, a recent editor, told Mrs. Stowe's grandson that the Byron exposé almost wrecked the *Atlantic*. "The result was appalling." When James T. Fields got home and saw the havoc, he was so angry that Harriet dared not write to him for several months, transacting her professional business with Mr. Osgood.

At least, such an experience showed one who were one's true friends—with even George Eliot writing Harriet more in sorrow than anger, "For my own part, I should have preferred that the Byron question should never have been brought before the public, because I think the discussion of such subjects is injurious socially. But with regard to yourself, dear friend, I feel sure that, in acting on a different basis of impressions, you were impelled by pure, generous feeling."

Susan Howard remained steadfast, and Harriet wrote to her: "It is worth while to have a *storm* of abuse once in a while—for one reason, to read the Psalms. . . . 'The eternal God is thy refuge, and underneath thee are the everlasting arms.' . . . It's worth while to have trouble, to have friends stand by one as mine do by me. Depend upon it, the spirit of the Lord didn't pitch me into this seething cauldron for nothing, and the Son of Man walketh with me in the fire. Eternal right and justice are with me, and I shall triumph by and bye on the other side of the river—and here, too."

Then came a letter which Harriet could read and exclaim with the Psalmist, "Why do the heathen rage, and the people imagine a vain thing?" It was from Oliver Wendell Holmes, in whose eyes Harriet was always the perfect woman, nobly planned; and the Doctor was standing firmly at her side—

My Dear Mrs. Stowe: I have been meaning to write to you for some time, but in the midst of all the wild and virulent talk about the article in the *Atlantic,* I felt as if there was little to say until the first fury of the storm had blown over.

I think that we all perceive now that the battle is not to be fought here, but in England. I have listened to a good deal of talk, always taking your side in a quiet way, backed very heartily on one occasion by one of my most intellectual friends, reading all that came in my way, and watching the course of opinion. And first, it was to be expected that the Guiccioli fanciers would resent any attack on Lord Byron, and would highly relish the opportunity of abusing one, who, like yourself, had been identified with all those moral enterprises which elevate the standard of humanity at large, of womanhood in particular. After this scum had worked itself off, there must necessarily follow a controversy, none the less sharp and bitter, but not depending essentially on abuse.

The first point the recusants got hold of was the error of the two years which contrived to run the gauntlet of so many pairs of eyes. Some of them were made happy by mouthing and shaking this between their teeth, as a poodle tears round with a glove. This did not last long. No sensible person could believe for a moment you were mistaken in the essential character of a statement every word of which would fall on the ear of a listening friend like a drop of melted lead, and burn its scar deep into the memory. That Lady Byron believed and told you the story will not be questioned by any but fools and malignants. Whether her belief was well founded there may be positive evidence in existence to show affirmatively. The fact that her statement is not peremptorily contradicted by those most likely to be acquainted with the facts of the case, is the one result so far which is forcing itself into unwilling recognition. I have seen nothing, in the various hypotheses brought forward, which did not to me involve a greater improbability than the presumption of guilt. Take that, for witness, that Byron accused himself, through a spirit of perverse vanity, of crimes he had not committed. How preposterous! He would stain the name of a sister, whom, on the supposition of his innocence, he loved with angelic ardor as well as purity, by associating it with such an infamous accusation.

Suppose there are some anomalies hard to explain in Lady Byron's conduct. Could a young and guileless woman, in the hands of such a man, be expected to act in any given way, or would she not be likely to waver, to doubt, to hope, to contradict herself, in the anomalous position in which, without experience, she found herself?

As to the intrinsic evidence contained in the poems, I think it confirms rather than contradicts the hypothesis of guilt. I do not think that Butler's argument, and all the other attempts at invalidation of the story, avail much in the face of the acknowledged fact that it was told to various competent and honest witnesses, and remains without a satisfactory answer from those most interested.

The letter helped clear Harriet's head of its confusion. The Doctor was showing her that her case might be proven without complete reliance on Lady Byron's story; and Harriet made up her mind to prove it, even though it meant writing a book. She would tell in every detail her pertinent conversations with Lady Byron (and this time mince no words), ransack Byron's works for utterances corroborative of her thesis when read in the light of understanding, collect what all the poet's biographers had said about his marriage, and add to these the new depositions and arguments which the discussion had brought forth in England, and which *Macmillan's Magazine* was sending to her. When she had done this, she thought, she would have a brief to convince the most sceptical.

A promised visit with Catharine Beecher late in September to a girls' reform school at Providence, Rhode Island, took Harriet's mind off the controversy for a few days, and she returned to Hartford her old self. She could even give her attention to other business affairs, one of which was pressing. Since the first of the year she had been serving as co-editor of the weekly agricultural and household weekly, *Hearth & Home,* contributing regularly, but had never yet received a penny in payment. By the beginning of October the publishers owed her the neat sum of $5,000. As usual, when in difficulty she appealed to her publisher—this time, Mr. Osgood—for advice. His obliging counsel was probably to write them a stiff letter, demanding her money, and at the same time to retire publicly from her editorship. On October 16 Harriet wrote to Osgood:

I have had a letter from Bales. [The almost illegible word is possibly Bates]. He gives in. The fact is, I suspect they are hard up. I shan't be hard and stiff with him. "Lordy Massy, these 'ere pouts ain't to blame for bein' fish." If he'd-a told me that, I'd-a helped him. Pray don't let anybody know anything agin him.

You see, five thousand dollars is a great deal, and they can't pay it, and don't want to say they can't. Neither are any great [illegible word], as I know of; but then I want the *item* started, because I don't want those all over the country who are taking it simply for my part, to be disappointed, you see. It isn't fair to them.

And Harriet enclosed the text for her item, which Osgood was to put in the papers:

We understand that Mrs. Stowe is going to Florida to spend the winter with her family, and will not continue the editorship of Hearth & Home after the 31st of October.

"Something like this," Harriet said. "Items are generally best, short and to the point. The going south may give a general idea of retiring, and indeed, when this Byron matter is out, I shall want a little rest. I read the first part last night to my husband and family."

Already she had the book clearly mapped out in her mind:

I want a book the size of "Chimney Corner"—printed handsomely. As there will be much quoting of documents, which I want to have in a markedly different type, I propose that they be put in leaded in smaller type. But first, choose a good, clear, plain type for the *documents,* so that nobody may skip them as fine print, and then have a larger type for my own words.

The documents are the very marrow of the thing, and every care must be taken to make them flash clearly on the eye at a glance. The first part will be about one-fourth of the book; and, as I said, it is very important. The title of this part is:

WHY HAVE I TOLD THIS STORY?

It will come like an avalanche. I *feel* how it is coming.

Harriet intended to have this book impregnable to any attack and to that end engaged the eminent New York jurist, David Dudley Field, to act as her legal adviser. Field strongly urged her to come to New York, so that her argument might unfold from day to day under his watchful eye. It was an imposition to ask the Howards to put her up for such a length of time, and Eunice Beecher evidently showed no eagerness to extend hospitality, so Harriet arranged accommodations for herself in the home of Dr. George H. Taylor, at 69 West 38th Street, which was then well up-town.

But Judge Field only served as the head of a battery of legal, literary, and historical counsel, including Harriet's two brothers-in-law, Thomas C. Perkins and John Hooker, of Hartford, both lawyers. Harriet arranged with Osgood to send proof-sheets to a list of some fifty persons (later reduced to twenty) who had consented to read the text critically. Never was an author more thoroughly assisted in a work.

Harriet went to New York after the middle of October and buckled down to her task. The Fieldses were back, and Harriet probably had more than an inkling of what Jamie Fields thought and said when he viewed the havoc wrought in the *Atlantic* office. The guilty culprit in New York took thought and addressed her next business letter not to Mr. Osgood, as customarily, but to "Messrs. Fields & Osgood. Gentlemen." In it she slipped a pathetic feeler: "Please write me what Mr. Fields says on the subject, if anything."

But only a grim silence came from James T. Fields, and Harriet resumed addressing her almost daily letters to "Mr. Osgood."

The storm still blew, and the attacks on Harriet kept up, especially in England. "This is war to the knife," she wrote Osgood. "The enemy are perfectly unscrupulous." The scurrilous cartoons of herself, which she could not help seeing, the bewildering intricacy of her task, the constant interviews with Dudley Field and others, combined with the necessity for speed in the writing, began to tell on her. She grew nervous and irascible.

The proof-sheets from Boston were a continual irritation. Her argument was so complex that she could scarcely get along without the printed record of her past work before her, yet the proofs, it seemed, were forever getting delayed or lost in the mails.

On one occasion the postoffice "fussification" lost a package of her manuscript altogether and, to her immense tribulation, she had to write it anew. When her next consignment was ready, she caught a train for Boston and delivered it by her own hand. "If anything should happen to it," she wrote Osgood in advance, "it seems as if I never could get it all together again." After that she used Adam's Express.

Eventually Harriet showed signs of breaking down under the strain, and the clan rallied to help her. Dr. Taylor found his house invaded by an army, as the carriages of lawyers and critics clattered to his door, Adam's Express men brought and took away bundles, and the postman staggered in under heavy loads. Calvin Stowe came down from Hartford to write notices for the press and perform any other services he could. Henry Ward Beecher called every day to soothe, read copy, and advise. Isabella Hooker, in New York cementing a baleful friendship with Victoria Woodhull and Tennie Claflin (their common bond was Spiritualism, in which Isabella claimed mediumistic powers), moved in to act as Harriet's secretary during the final days.

Harriet could not make up her mind about a title for the book. At first she had been calling it, *The Vindication of Lady Byron,* though as the writing went on it became more and more evident that a truer title would be, *The Vindication of Harriet Beecher Stowe.* Indeed, she almost confessed as much in December, when she decided on a change of title to *The True Story of Lady Byron Established.* Her original *Atlantic* article had borne the title, *The True Story of Lady Byron's Life.*

Then, at last, after ten feverish weeks, the book was finished, or so nearly finished that the Stowes could be at home in Hartford for Christmas. But before she left New York, Harriet, the only time in her career she ever did such a thing for a book of hers, solicited a favourable criticism of it from an influential newspaper. She wrote to Horace Greeley, of the *Tribune:*

Dear Mr. Greeley: When my Vindication of Lady Byron appears, may I ask it as a favor of *you* to read it and write *yourself* whatever may be said of it in your paper?

I ask you to read, knowing that for a man of your engagements really to read a book in this whirling New York is something of an effort.

I ask this, because from the Memoirs of Margaret Fuller I some time ago became aware of your deep feeling for woman; and from your own Auto-biography I see how deep is your sense of the real sacredness of family life.

This story as I have related it touches the roots of many things. It was perhaps a mistake in me to put it forth in the simple, unsupported form I first did, because the American press, being under the influence of a tradi-tional Byron mania and largely manned by Englishmen, prejudiced the cause at once. My object in this book is to take the case into the court of History and have justice done to the memory of one of the noblest of women.

I consider Lady Byron's story as a type of the old idea of woman: that is, a creature to be crushed and trodden under foot whenever her fate and that of a man come in conflict. She had a wider, a stronger, a deeper mind than her husband. Had she been in a man's form, she might have con-trolled and guided the thought of England; but all has been wrecked, crushed, hidden, in her history as wife of a wicked reprobate. Her life was a silent sacrifice, and it is further exacted that her historic name should be forever blasted.

But I only ask of you a patient reading of my book, and you will then see *why* I wrote it—why, being her friend, I could not *but* have written it and believe in justice.

What I have remarked in our American papers on this subject is: 1st, An ignorant, violent commitment to the man's side before examination; 2nd, A steady ignoring the points made by leading English papers who supported it, and a one-sided habit of publishing only what makes against it.

What I now fear is that, having waited till this late hour to get a calm, fair hearing, I may be again drowned in a tempest of clamors unworthy of our nation. I therefore ask you as father of your paper, as an early friend to woman, as a man that has stood for the perpetuity and purity of the family state when attacked by ignorant reformers, and as a representative American, to *do justice* to this cause in your paper.

Only justice, I ask. Nothing is so beautiful or in such good taste as justice.

Ever yours,
H. B. Stowe.

Back again in Hartford at the end of the year, the book that had uprooted him finished, except for a few details, Calvin Stowe expressed his relief as follows to a now friendly James T. Fields:

When we get quite through—and I want to see "Medora Leigh," an-nounced by Bentley, claiming to be an autobiography clearing up the Byron mystery—I say, when we get quite through, then I will sing:

Te Deum laudamus!
Laus Deo!
To Thee doxai.
Amen and Selah!

About this whole affair, I feel as old Eleazar Bacon, of Natick, did after the great Equinoxial gale of 1817. "I hope to Massy the sun will never cross the Line agin in *my* day, if he is a-going to make *sich* a devilish piece of work on't."

We must do the matter up brown, now we are in for it, and all will be well. So says Madam, who does not feel able to write herself.

They must have got their hands on a copy of *Medora Leigh* that same day and could regard it as nothing less than a Godsend, Calvin writing in astonishment next day to Fields:

Have you seen "Medora Leigh," edited by that contemptible Charles Mackay and just published by Bentley? If it is intended as a defense of Lord Byron, as it purports to be, it is the most wonderful instance of what the old theologians called "judicial blindness" that has appeared for a long time. The whole narrative of Medora Leigh confirms and more than confirms all that Mrs. Stowe and Lady Byron have said. Medora was that child of sin, born of incestuous adultery, the daughter of Byron and his half-sister, Mrs. Leigh; and she knew it and speaks accordingly.

Simultaneously Harriet was dashing off a preface for her book, which was now in its plates, ready for printing—a preface beginning, "Since this work has been in type, a confirmation of the story has been presented in a most singular manner," and ending with the sentences:

The story confirms the whole account given by Lady Byron, so that the whole thing may now be regarded as settled.

Except for its value as a document, it is not worth reading, being the maunderings of a vicious, unprincipled being, incapable either of love or gratitude.

Strange to say, the infatuated man who edits this story makes it a *text* for a—
"Vindication of Lord Byron."
We rather call it a comment on the text, "There is no darkness or shadow of death where the workers of iniquity may hide themselves."

Then, next day—it was January 1, and Harriet dated her letter to Fields, "New Year's. Wish you a thousand, each happier than the last"—she withdrew and suppressed the preface, "as the book is so far printed." She had "concluded *not* to have any allusion to the Medora Leigh story in it." Perhaps Harriet decided that she was retailing enough filth in the body of the book as it was, without adding to it any account of Medora's sexual promiscuity.

Or perhaps Calvin gave *Medora Leigh* a second reading and decided that he was the one chargeable with judicial blindness. (And "contemptible" and "infatuated" were harsh adjectives to apply to the London correspondent of the New York *Times* and the foster father of Marie Corelli.) Medora Leigh's so-called autobiography had been kicked about the Fleet Street offices for years without finding a publisher with a stomach stout enough to sponsor it. The renewal of the Byron controversy made it a pertinent contribution, Charles Mackay offering it as a refutation of Mrs. Stowe's charges. And well he might. The ignorant, wayward Medora boasted that Lord Byron was her father but naively divulged the fact that it was Lady Byron who told her the story of her paternity.

So it all came back to Lady Byron, who was, as one chose to think, either a noble martyr suffering in silence under one of the greatest injustices the world ever knew, or a garrulous, slightly mad, old lady living under an hallucination.

Harriet's book, which came out in January, 1870, under its final title, *Lady Byron Vindicated,* did nothing to break that deadlock. It adduced no new proof but was merely her *Atlantic* paper amplified, filled in with more detail and more argument from circumstances. It brought no converts into her camp, it alienated none already there. Her personal influence with the press availed her little. As the *Independent* said, "However much she might have bettered the execution of this poorest of all her performances, the data themselves, even in the most skillful hands, could not be made to converge into a proven case."

Less friendly critics went over *Lady Byron Vindicated* with mental microscopes, ravening for slips or admissions with which they could crush the sanctified Mrs. Stowe. It is remarkable that none discovered the astonishing fact that much of the book's argument—the more important part for Harriet personally—was based on a misrepresentation of fact, and a deliberate one. Not one critic or enemy ever found it, and Harriet died with her guilty secret intact. But in her business correspondence with her publishers, now available for research, her deception stands revealed.

It is a little cruel to Harriet's memory to cite here the paragraph in her book with which she first introduced her violation of the commandment, for it was one of her typical preachments on telling the truth:

What interest have you or I, my brother and sister, in this short life of ours, to utter anything but the truth? Is not truth between man and man and between man and woman the foundation on which all things rest? Have you not, every individual of you, who must hereafter give an account of yourself alone to God, an interest to know the exact truth in this matter, and a duty to perform as respects that truth? Hear me, then, while I tell you the position in which I stood, and what was my course in relation to it.

Harriet meant the position she stood in when she wrote her exposé for *The Atlantic Monthly*. Having thus, so to speak, lifted her hand and taken the oath, Harriet proceeded with her prevarication:

> A shameless attack on my friend's memory had appeared in the *Blackwood* of July, 1869, branding Lady Byron as the vilest of criminals, and recommending the Guiccioli book to a Christian public as interesting from the very fact that it was the avowed production of Lord Byron's mistress. . . . Its statements . . . were being propagated through all the young reading and writing world of America. . . . I saw these foul slanders crystalizing into history uncontradicted by friends who knew her personally, who, firm in their own knowledge of her virtues and limited in view, as aristocratic circles generally are, had no idea of the width of the world they were living in, and the exigency of the crisis. When time passed on and no voice was raised, I spoke.

This was not the only place in her book where Harriet named the article in *Blackwood's Magazine* as the incitation of her sensational outburst in the *Atlantic*. Far from it. She repeated the essential statement again and again and devoted a chapter to the *Blackwood* article itself, as demonstrating why it was her duty to answer it, when no one else did. In fact, she made it her main ground for justifying herself in writing the original exposé, and in a book of which her own justification was at least the co-purpose.

With so many snarling at her heels, it is strange that nobody noticed the one clue she left exposed. Critics picked at such flaws as her misspelling of Miss Milbanke's name and her inaccurate statement that the Byrons' married life had lasted two years, but never once saw that in her *Atlantic* paper, which, she cried so passionately in her book, she had written in answer to the review in *Blackwood's,* she did not mention that review at all.

The explanation is, of course, that when she wrote her dreadful gossip for the *Atlantic,* she did not know of the *Blackwood* review. It had not yet been published. Harriet's business correspondence shows by a dated letter that she had placed her manuscript in Osgood's hands as early as June 23,

1869. She could not possibly have seen the July *Blackwood's* much before the middle of July.

After the *Atlantic* came out with the exposé, to her dismay and bewilderment she found herself arraigned before the bar of public opinion as a scandal-monger and breaker of confidences. The worst of it was, with almost every critic asserting that Lady Byron herself would never have stooped to answer the Countess Guiccioli, she had no honest ground to stand upon. The sands of her great popularity were slipping away beneath her feet, and she was desperate. She could not tell her public the truth, which was that she had rushed out with her scandal in order to flatter her own vainglory.

Then could she thank her stars that she had ordered Osgood to hold her article for the September *Atlantic* and not publish in the August number, as they had first intended; for meanwhile the July *Blackwood's* had reached the United States, and *Blackwood's* was a magazine of great influence upon American thought. Of course! Harriet was not answering the Countess Guiccioli, either, in the *Atlantic,* but was replying to *Blackwood's,* to prevent a perversion of history. She did not need to mention to the upright David Dudley Field that she had written her Byron article in June. Only two men, if they took thought and the pains to look into the file of correspondence, knew the truth—James R. Osgood and William Dean Howells—and they would never betray her.

Whatever the truth or falsity of Harriet's charges against Lord Byron, her publication of them was a disaster for her career. Never again would she stand alone as the supreme female figure in the American scene. She had disillusioned her following, which henceforth would realize that she was only common clay, after all, like any other woman. For years the Byron scandal would remain as a bad taste in the public's mouth, largely accounting, without doubt, for the rapidity with which Harriet's fame and memory declined. Today with the millions the most conspicuous and influential American woman of the 1850's and 1860's is but a name—the author of *Uncle Tom's Cabin*—she who deserved to be remembered for so much else.

It was the *Independent* which pronounced the sentence of dethronement—that *Independent* she had helped to greatness:

> Mrs. Stowe's ill-advised disclosure . . . has inflicted a wound not only upon her reputation but upon her happiness. So, even though she has judged others too harshly, let her not be judged too harshly herself. Whatever has been her misstep in the present instance, she can not thereby lose her standing among the best and greatest women of her country.

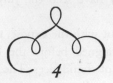

4

Afternoon of a Career

Soon after January 1, 1870, Harrite closed the draughty, expensive house on the Park River and with her husband and twin daughters, Charley now being in Harvard, retreated to her Mandarin orange grove, where she hoped to be beyond earshot of the uproar she had created with her Byron revelations.

Just before New Year's she had fallen from a step-ladder, hurting her head, and the accident delayed her start a few days. But the fall was the least of the troubles besetting her. That winter Harriet faced the fact that Oakholm had been a dreadful mistake. The slums of Hartford had crept out to the estate and had even gone past it, and Hartford factories were rapidly turning the lovely stream into such a sewer that the city renamed it Hog River. As she closed her place for the winter, Harriet resolutely placed Oakholm with the real-estate brokers with instructions to sell it for whatever they could get, then departed in the fervent hope that she would never have to reoccupy it.

Though Harriet was still adding to it, the house at Mandarin was now large enough to accommodate them all comfortably, while affording quarters to Spencer Foote and his wife and child. Since it was evident that henceforth they were going to shuttle back and forth between Florida and the North, the twins, Hatty and Eliza, struck a bargain together. Hatty undertook to serve as housekeeper at Mandarin, taking charge of everything while Eliza enjoyed her leisure. Eliza was to be housekeeper in the North and had rather the better of the deal in that the family usually spent some summer weeks at mountain or seaside resorts. The arrangement gave Hatty the Mandarin garden. She brought down most of the plants that had been in the Oakholm conservatory and also planted the seeds of annual flowers, phlox drummondi and nasturtiums always among them. The broad verandah, built around a huge liveoak, suited Calvin to a T. After looking the place over, he ensconced himself there with a basket of books and a rocking-chair which he could move with the sunshine and was thereafter not to be budged, except for meals and his bed. He left such things as picnics, excursions, and sails on the river to his younger and spryer wife. At sixty-eight he was about as round as a human being could get, weighing 250 pounds.

Harriet at once resumed work on her *Oldtown* short stories, "writing them as a pure recreative movement of mind to divert myself from this stormy, unrestful present." She told Annie Fields: "There may be twelve, or there may be less, according as they run or as the spirits from the vasty deep hand them up," and Harriet would finish the series "at the terms named." Mr. Fields had objected to the series title, *Firelight Papers*. "Suppose we call them, *Oldtown Fireside Stories,*" suggested Harriet, and that was the name they received.

That winter the Mandarin ménage began to take on its permanent form. It is probable that Harriet then engaged the three Negro servant girls who remained in her employ so many years. They were Laura and Tesia Summerall and Felicia Primus Zeigler. Old Aunt Felicia was still alive in Mandarin when the materials for this book were being gathered. She remembered that Mrs. Stowe paid her $12.50 a month, which was a fabulous wage for a Florida Negress right after the war, and high anywhere. At various times Harriet took all three of these girls north with her in the summer, though never all at once. Harriet bought a flea-bitten mule named Fly in Mandarin, and engaged Felicia's cousin Frank to take care of the stable and help around the yard and fruit groves.

Next door to the Stowes, the houses not far apart and separated only by a hedge, lived C. G. Crane and his family. His daughter Gussie, then a little girl, became a favourite of Harriet, who took her north one spring later on, to spend the summer with the Stowes in Hartford. As Mrs. Nicholl, Gussie Crane was also still alive to contribute from her memory of the Stowes to this narrative. She remembered, for instance, that it was a common occurrence, when the Cranes were at breakfast, for the famous neighbour to enter their dining-room in a brown study, gaze absently at the pictures on the wall or through the windows, speaking not a word and oblivious of the presence of the Crane family. Then, in complete silence, Harriet would leave, and next the Cranes would see her sauntering along the board walk on the river-bank, still lost in reverie.

It is probable that it was that winter that Harriet invested in more Mandarin property, purchasing thirty acres of the old Fairbanks grant—river

frontage a short distance upstream from the orange grove. This was one of
the few investments Harriet ever made that turned out well for her. She
sold off this land later in lots—one to Eunice Beecher, who thereafter made
a practice of coming to Mandarin for March—and from a property that had
cost her $200 she realized $7,000, she told Mrs. McCray. She used the money
to buy a parsonage for her son Charles, when he became pastor of the
Windsor Avenue Congregational Church, in Hartford.

By the end of the winter the cottage had grown to such size that it could
accommodate guests. "Mr. and Mrs. Howard are making us a visit," Harriet
wrote to Fields on March 21. "I wish with all my heart you and Annie were
here to hear our birds sing and smell orange blossoms and eat oranges. We
are having heavenly weather. When we have friends here, then only do we
really fully enjoy our place, and some time, I hope, we shall see you."

But in a scrambling, dollar-grabbing age when a winter vacation for a
businessman was regarded as sheer lunacy, John T. Howard was not in
Mandarin for the orange blossoms or the heavenly weather. He had brought
down a business proposition for Mrs. Stowe to consider. A bankrupt religious weekly, known as the *Church Union,* could be taken over for its
debts; and Howard and his sons were forming a syndicate to pick it up.
Henry Ward Beecher was coming in, and with enthusiasm, writing, "If
wisely managed, I think there is money in it; and if it does succeed, there
will be a good deal of money." Henry was to be editor, though "with a
bishop's, not a curate's, place"; by which he meant that he would lend his
prestige and contribute leading articles to the paper but that the actual editorial labour would have to be done by someone else. Joe Howard was
undertaking the managing editorship. At Henry's suggestion, the name of
the paper was to be changed to *The Christian Union.* (Its ultimate name
would be *The Outlook.*)

The Howards wanted Harriet's financial and editorial participation in the
venture. Joseph Howard had, in fact, already taken it up with her by mail.
As to putting her money into it, she had replied: "I have invested thirty-four
thousand dollars in various ways, none of which can give me any immediate
income." It is difficult to say now what these investments were; whether
Harriet was referring to the money she had put into Oakholm and the
orange farm, or to her "trusts," which her letters occasionally mentioned.
Probably she was including the orange grove in her statement, for she
wrote, "My investment in this Southern place is still one whose returns are

ELIZA

HARRIET

THE STOWE GIRLS

"Calvin's twin daughters must bear the names of *both* his wives. So, the twins were rechristened Harriet Beecher and Eliza Tyler Stowe, and Harriet Beecher and Eliza Tyler Stowe they remained to the end of their long, gentle, virgin lives." (Page 192.)

in the future." However, Harriet managed to find money to put into the *Christian Union*—several thousands, the family story has it, from which she never received any return. This unfortunate outcome seems unlikely, since her brother Henry, in 1876, sold his *controlling interest* in the paper for $10,000.

However, the immediate demand of the promoters was more for Harriet's pen than for her purse. She was still the most popular novelist in America, unless this Byron unpleasantness was injuring her more than her friends thought. Just as the founding of the *Atlantic Monthly* had once depended upon Mrs. Stowe's promise of a serial, so now the antecedent of the *Outlook* was hesitating at birth until it could win a similar promise, and it was worth a trip to Florida to secure it.

Except that since finishing her *Oldtown Folks* Harriet had given no thought to the plot of another novel, her promise was not hard to obtain. Harriet became as enthusiastic as Henry Ward for the *Christian Union*. She liked the catholicity of the name, writing to Joseph Howard: "Every denomination has its paper; but there is a yearning after a centralizing point, a point where all shall feel themselves *one*. That feeling is the one to which a new religious paper may address itself with mighty power." As to the promised serial, "My mind is bubbling and boiling, and I think of so many stories I could write that I don't settle upon any."

It was hard for Harriet to conceive a novel without a social purpose, and she was at first terribly tempted to choose a theme close at hand. Her letter about it to Joseph Howard suggests something of the wretchedness of her mother's heart that winter and spring as she contemplated the wreck of what had been her brave and gallant Freddie. "There is a misery—a desolation—an anguish deeper than that of the slave; there is a cause where every good soul ought to be roused—but how to do it? Temperance stories have been thick as pigweed in rich land. I think I see how a better one could be written, but am not sure yet."

The theme was too personal with her, and she put it aside. She thought of writing about the slaves once more—the freed slaves now—but nothing would "compose." "I have a desire, a longing, to express myself once more on a certain subject," she wrote, "but a story ought to *grow* out of one's heart like a flower." Meanwhile in New York the deal had gone through, and the managing editor of the *Christian Union* came out with the announcement of a new serial by Harriet Beecher Stowe as one of the attractions of the paper's first year. The advertisement provoked Harriet, who knew what such fixed commitments meant to her in expenditure of physical and nervous force. She wrote Howard:

> Therefore, I ought to be thinking what to write. On looking back to the time when "Uncle Tom's Cabin" came forth, I see myself then a woman with no particular capital of reputation, driven to write then, as now, by the necessity of making some income for family expenses. In this mood, with a mind burning with the wrongs of slavery, I undertook to write some loose sketches of slave life in the "National Era," and out of that attempt grew "Uncle Tom's Cabin." If there had been a grand preparatory blast of trumpets, or had it been announced that Mrs. Stowe would do this or that, I think it likely I could not have written; but nobody expected anything, nobody said anything, and so I wrote freely. Now what embarrasses me is to be announced as an attraction—to have eyes fixed on me and people all waiting.

Howard at once struck the announcement out of the *Christian Union,* though listing Mrs. Stowe as a contributor. Her letters to Howard continued to show her concern over her finances. For such a paper as the *Christian Union* she would have been glad to write for nothing, but unfortunately she had arranged no income for herself that year. If she promised the serial, could Howard guarantee her a certain amount of money every month? Would he permit her to write on religious subjects? Would he accept articles from Professor Stowe on Biblical themes, paying for them at *her* rates? Howard assented to everything, and presently, while waiting for a plot to take form in her mind, Harriet was writing for the *Christian Union* on Florida, on the Negroes, on Spiritualism, on mild New Testament texts or texts from the Psalms—what Elizabeth Cady Stanton was later to call "Mrs. Stowe's heavy Scripture lessons." But Mrs. Stanton was not calling them that in 1870. In her own short-lived woman-suffrage journal, *The Revolution,* she was advertising Harriet Beecher Stowe as a contributor and an attraction to subscribers.

From his Mandarin rocking-chair Calvin Stowe wheeled into action with *The New Testament. and Its Completeness, The Last Twelve Verses of Mark—Their Genuineness,* and *Retribution in A Future Life A Living Idea with The Ancients.* The Beechers had a family organ once more. Henry resumed his Star papers on the front page; his weekly Friday *Lecture-Room Talk* was becoming the most popular feature of the new publication. The most methodical and faithful contributor was Eunice, who never missed an edition with her *Motherly Talks with Young House-keepers*. Poor old Catharine Beecher, now seventy and, after a life of disagreeable usefulness, reduced to the position of Professor of Domestic Economy in Dr. Dio Lewis's Advanced Physical Culture School at Lexington, Massachusetts, contributed an occasional article on some educational subject. Edward Beecher, now retired and living in Brooklyn, came in with theological discussions. Thomas K. Beecher, already scandalizing the Ministerial Union of Elmira by drinking beer, playing cards, and holding Sunday evening services in the Opera House, and who that year was to pronounce the marriage benediction over Samuel Langhorne Clemens and Olivia Langdon, wrote on current topics.

As a group, the Beechers were never more famous and popular than in 1870. Under their combined influences the circulation of the *Christian Union* grew much more rapidly than that of the *Independent* ever had—nearly a hundred thousand new subscribers the first two years. Meanwhile J. B. Ford & Co., its publishers, a concern organized in the first place to bring out Henry Ward Beecher's *Life of Jesus The Christ,* was taking on other Beecher books—Henry's *Sermons* and *Lecture-Room Talks,* Thomas's *Our Seven Churches,* and *Principles of Domestic Science,* a collection of Catharine's writings which Harriet obligingly signed as collaborator. Now, having added Mrs. Stowe's future volumes to its list, J. B. Ford & Co. advertised itself, "Printers and Publishers to the Beecher Family."

Exhausted as her work on *Lady Byron Vindicated* undoubtedly left her, Harriet's powers of recuperation were now great, and her pen flew that winter as she contributed almost weekly to the *Christian Union* and pursued her *Oldtown Fireside* series for the *Atlantic* so assiduously that by May 10 she had forwarded five of the stories and was reporting to Fields, "I shall have the sixth ready soon." At the same time, one guesses, she was managing to do some work on a novel she had started the summer before at Westport Point—that serial she had promised "an American paper" for $4,000. It turned out to be her *Pink and White Tyranny.* Harriet's available letters are so silent about this story, which was published the following year in Boston, that one can only surmise when she found time to write it.

Fields had sent her the first book by a new and vivid Western writer—*The Luck of Roaring Camp and Other Sketches,* by Francis Bret Harte. "Have read two," Harriet wrote. "They are good. I have an unsanctified hankering for slang. About all the originality of the world is in it, though you must cradle and gold-wash for it in a mess of trash; but this book, so far, has just enough to be racy without being disgusting."

She told Fields she was starting on an excursion up the St. Johns, *"the most magnificent river in America."* Perhaps she was going in her neighbour Crane's sailboat, the *Nellie Thorn.* She was most fond of sailing on this small schooner-yacht, and always sought to make a day of it, appearing early in the morning at the Crane's dock with the twins and a heavy picnic-hamper. The Professor, however, was not to be dragged along on these jaunts but remained on his porch where, Harriet reported to the readers of the *Christian Union,* his red skull-cap served mariners as a sort of daytime lighthouse.

In a spanking breeze, the *Nellie Thorn* heeling well over, Harriet, when she found herself on the lee side of the boat, was wont to raise herself up on her hands "to lighten her side." Hatty and Eliza, who imitated their mother in everything, did the same. Captain Crane assured them it made no difference in their weight whether they perched on their hands or based themselves in their seats more conventionally, but he could never make a logical Harriet believe it. Mrs. Nicholl's memory retains a picture of the trio thus solemnly elevated on their hands and glancing apprehensively at the water racing past so near the top of their rail.

Harriet told Fields that she expected to be home in Hartford about the first of June.

I hate to leave my calm Isle of Patmos, where the world is not, and I have such quiet, long hours for writing. Emerson could *insulate* himself here and keep his electricity. Hawthorne ought to have lived in an orange grove in Florida.

You've no idea how small you look, you folks in the world, from this distance. All your fusses and your fumings, your red-hot, hurrying newspapers, your clamor of rival magazines! Why, we see it as we see steamboats fifteen miles off—a mere speck and a smoke. If I had my way wholly, I wouldn't come North at all, but am holden by a house that must be lived in half the year.

Still, there was one worldly commodity that one could use even on the Isle of Patmos. "If you will send me a cheque for the three last [*Fireside Stories*] together," Harriet suggested to Jamie, "I'll be even with it, P.P. You don't know what that means, you old heathen you—confess now! Well, it means, Providence permitting."

Fields responded promptly, and in her acknowledgment Harriet wrote:

I am leaving the land of flowers on the 1st of June with tears in my eyes, but, having a house in Hartford, it must be lived in. I wish you and Annie would just come and see it—the H. house, I mean. You've no idea what a lovely place it has grown to be—and I am trying to sell it as hard as a snake to crawl out of its skin. Thus on, till reason is pushed out of life. There's no earthly sense in having anything—Lordy Massy, no!

She was not sending him her sixth *Fireside* story, *The Ghost in The Cap'n Brown House,* from Florida after all, delaying it "till I can go to Natick and make a personal inspection of the premises and give it to you *hot.*"

Two young men who had joined the Stowes in Mandarin that spring were Henry Ward Beecher's son William and his friend, Frank Howard. They were amateur naturalists and spent most of their time shooting and stuffing birds. They planned to remain a year in Florida, hunting and perhaps doing a little missionary work among the Negroes. Frank Howard was not well. He was thin and hollow-chested and had a persistent cough.

When at the beginning of June the Stowes packed themselves, bag, baggage, and six bird-cages, off for the North, there was one member of the throng on the wharf who watched the steamboat's departure with unfathomable emotions. Fred Stowe had secretly made up his mind to disgrace his parents no longer. A little later he left on one of his mysterious trips to Jacksonville and Charleston but soon returned and began to pack his belongings. He told the Mandarin people that he had signed on a sailing vessel for a voyage around the Horn.

Mrs. Nicholl remembers that Fred spoke about Chile as being a land of opportunity. For all his failings he was popular with the neighbours, and nearly everybody in Mandarin went to the wharf to say good-bye to him. Not one of them ever saw him again. Before sailing he must have written to his mother, telling her of his purpose, for a little later, in a letter to Mrs. Howard, Harriet expressed the anxious hope that Fred had found a safe and seaworthy ship.

Fred did not debark in Chile but kept on to San Francisco, where he at once succumbed to the temptations of the shore. Friends he had made took him to a hotel. He eluded them and disappeared in San Francisco, never to reappear. The police could find no trace of him. The San Francisco water-front was a tough place in those days. It was months, of course, before Harriet learned this, and months more before she could bring herself to realize that she would never have her erring soldier-boy again.

But as her son was walking out of her life, her first grandson entered it. Early that summer Georgie Stowe Allen was brought to bed of a male child whom Harriet described as "very pretty, very gracious and good, and his little mamma and he are a pair." As Annie Fields had predicted, Harriet was "being first lady-in-waiting on his new majesty." In fact, she was transported with happiness, almost always mentioning "my one brave little grandson" in her letters that summer and fall.

Simultaneously had occurred another event which, if not such a blissful one, was at any rate a relief. "We have sold out in Hartford," Harriet wrote to Mrs. Fields on August 4, 1870. To move Oakholm, however, she had had to consent to a ruinous sacrifice. When the papers were signed for the transfer, she could look at the smoke-blackened gables of her Park River mansion and at her venture in Florida cotton-growing and write off a total loss to herself of something like $35,000.

"I am thinking of setting up my tent in Cambridge," she told Annie. Henry Allen was about to leave Stockbridge for a Boston parish, and, with Charley now a student in Harvard, it meant that the family would be together again. However, Harriet did not long hold her ambition to join the Cambridge intellectuals. Before the end of August Catharine Beecher was chosen Principal of the Hartford Female Seminary, the school she had herself founded nearly a half-century before. The Hartford *Courant* announced: "She will be aided by Mrs. H. B. Stowe, as soon as she has completed certain literary engagements," and it was promised that Professor Stowe would lecture at the school on Biblical Literature. It may have been her desire to aid her elder sister, who had been a second mother to her, that determined Harriet to remain in the city of her childhood.

Annie Fields had, as usual, invited Harriet to visit her that summer at Manchester-by-the-Sea, and, as usual, Harriet had had to decline. Her pen was flying ahead on *Pink and White Tyranny,* as it had to do, if she were to enable Joseph Howard to fulfil his promise to the readers of the *Christian Union* to produce a Stowe serial for them that year. Immediately after her arrival from the South, she had gone down to New York to talk to him about her writing plans and while she was there figured indirectly in one of the more curious episodes of her life.

She found New York clicking its tongues over the action of Henry

CATHARINE BEECHER

"Firm, self-opinionated, domineering, goaded
by an eternal unrest into vast and noble,
though scattered, purposes." (Page 57.)

Ward Beecher in marrying a dying man to a divorced woman with whom he had been living in sin. The dying man was Albert D. Richardson, a member of the *Tribune* staff, and the divorcée was the former wife of Daniel McFarland, who had shot Richardson and was in gaol for it. It was a city sensation, and Henry was being sharply criticized for his gratuitous act. Harriet stepped forward to defend him, writing for the *Christian Union* a sermonette called *Christ and Woman,* in which she justified Mrs. McFarland's adulterous life, or at least excused it as Christ excused Mary Magdalen's.

(In the same issue of the *Christian Union* appeared a disapproving review of a new type of juvenile book, *Ben, The Luggage Boy,* by Horatio Alger, Jr., and news of the sudden death of Dickens.)

It is probable that on this visit Harriet found the inspiration for the serial she was going to write for the *Christian Union.* For years now she had been in and about printing offices. She had been a familiar in the editorial rooms of the great *Independent* during that journal's most stirring days, and now she entered the offices of the equally exciting *Christian Union* as a proprietor. The smell of the pressroom had become part of her existence; no woman of her day knew more than she about Park Place. She decided to do a newspaper story.

✓ With that central theme she could discuss, in terms of her "pictures," about anything she chose, since journalism touched everything. She could satirize hypocritical editors and newspaper-owners, pay her respects to the critics, work in something of that theme her Fred had suggested to her— the virus of drink in a young man's blood—and particularly she could hold up to scorn that current phenomenon, "the new woman," and not only the more respectable Anthony-Stanton type but also the type represented by those sister hussies, Victoria Woodhull and Tennessee Claflin, now so scandalously advocating free love in their new *Weekly.* In sum, the most advanced of Manhattan females, vintage 1870, who could invade a pure young bachelor's bedroom, perch on his easy chair, hang her polonaise over the arm, and expose a booted ankle and a portion of well-fleshed calf above as she chucked him under his chin-whiskers and solicited his subscription to her paper, *The Emancipated Woman.* The fact that Victoria Woodhull had thoroughly enslaved the mind of Harriet's own sister Isabella subtracted nothing from her malice. ✓

All through the heat of a blistering summer she toiled at Hartford (presumably still occupying Oakholm), getting ahead with *Pink and White*

Tyranny, "composing" her newspaper story, dashing off an occasional story for *Our Young Folks,* and never failing to write her weekly piece for the *Christian Union,* which, she knew, was for her, as an owner, like putting money in the bank. Yet this was not enough for her necessitous greed, and on August 14 she actually took up another project with James T. Fields:

Dear Mr. Fields: Where are you and what? Are you alive or melted? Is there anything left of you and the divine Annie? How are my affairs coming on? When will "Pussy Willow" [the juvenile serial she had written for *Our Young Folks*] appear? And when will you be ready to get up "Fireside Stories"? I think you should have some artists at work on the stories you have already in hand. [There were six by August 14, and she would need ten or a dozen for a book.] Illustrations well got up will make a book that will sell immensely on the cars and everywhere and, combined with authentic New England traditions, will make quite a rush. Moreover, it will keep "Old Town Folks" afloat and going. . . . How soon could you get it out, if you had all the printing matter in hand?

What made it so timely was that Natick, immensely flattered by *Oldtown Folks,* was going to hold a grand celebration in October, with its most celebrated native son, Professor C. E. Stowe, as principal speaker. As part of the festivities Natick intended to conduct what was perhaps the first "pilgrimage" ever given in an American town. All the places celebrated by Harriet in *Oldtown Folks* were to be thrown open to the inspection of the crowds expected in from Boston and elsewhere.

But perhaps Harriet was merely wasting this letter. Perhaps Mr. Fields was dead and buried. Perhaps the hot weather had killed him. "If so, tell us how you find things, and whether there is or not anything in Spiritualism." A gentleman had been making a goose of himself in the *North American* by explaining rationally the alleged manifestations of spirits. "Tell that to the Marines!" said Harriet. "It is quite too late in the day to tell it to sensible folks who have seen as much as I have, and as you have or Annie has, for all you keep still about it—like the rest of us. That cock won't fight." And Harriet informed her friend that she expected to spend two months in Boston in the fall and "could get up my 'Oldtown' book in good order in that time."

It may have been in the torrid summer of 1870 that Harriet suffered a mishap which gives us one of our most amusing glimpses of her at the peak of her fame and self-assurance. In Boston, while mentally trying to populate her newspaper story with interesting figures, she met casually Thomas Bailey Aldrich, the editor of *Every Saturday,* and his young wife, who was already the mother of bouncing twin boys. After the meeting Harriet, who had become a remorseless character-hunter, remembered the journalistic couple, and especially looked back at Mrs. Aldrich with a raptorial eye. In their brief encounter, however, she had not had time to study her literary prey sufficiently.

The Aldriches were spending the summer in the ancestral seaside cottage at Portsmouth, New Hampshire, the editor commuting daily to Boston. One sultry evening, upon his return from the city Aldrich announced to his wife, "We are, *nolens volens,* to have a visitor, 'o'ermaster it as you may.' This morning Mrs. Harriet Beecher Stowe came to the office and without preamble said, 'I should like to make you and Mrs. Aldrich a little visit; the personality of your wife strongly attracts me.'" Furthermore, the determined authoress informed Aldrich that it would be convenient for her to come to Portsmouth the next day.

Poor Mrs. Aldrich was terror-stricken. It was enough to have to entertain single-handed for some hours the great woman of America, without the knowledge that it was one's attractive personality which had brought about the visit and that therefore one would be up for inspection. Furthermore, to judge by Mrs. Stowe's writings, she was one who thought and conversed almost exclusively in the terms of exegetical theology, a subject in which Mrs. Aldrich felt herself singularly unversed. Her husband promised to bring home with him next evening a visitor who could meet Mrs. Stowe on her own ground, and further suggested, since the weather was so hot, that his wife make some of her delicious claret cup for the great lady's refreshment.

Next morning, after her husband's departure, Mrs. Aldrich was still trembling, and, as she mixed the claret cup, kept wondering what made a personality attractive and what she must do not to disillusion her daunting guest. In her preoccupation she poured into the mixture far more claret than the recipe called for.

It was nearly noon when Harriet arrived, gasping with the heat. The train had been late and crowded, and the authoress was wilted and thirsty. Mrs. Aldrich put her in an easy chair in a window overlooking the sea, removed her bonnet, put a fan into her hand, and then brought from the ice-chest a pitcher of the claret cup, placing it with a goblet on the table at

Harriet's elbow. Then Mrs. Aldrich left to attend to some of her household duties.

When she returned half an hour later to see how the visitor was getting along, she discovered that the pitcher was empty, and Mrs. Stowe was complaining about conditions. The room seemed to be unsettled, having fixed itself at an angle of forty-five degrees. The sea was turning, too, and everything was in a blue mist. Did they, Harriet asked, often have such sudden fogs at Portsmouth? She felt like lying down, but the sofa had attained such momentum she was afraid to venture it. To Harriet's eye, the sofa was misbehaving as badly as any berth she ever occupied at sea.

Mrs. Aldrich assisted her to the couch, in later years describing the rest as follows:

> In the days of the 60's, women still wore hoops or reeds in their skirts; and, in lying on the sofa, Mrs. Stowe's skirts, like Hamlet's words, "flew up," revealing very slender ankles and feet encased in prunella boots, the elastic V at the sides no longer elastic, but worn and loose. The stockings were white, and the flowery ribbon of the garter-knot was unabashed by the sunlight.

What was to be done? Harriet had dropped into a profound sleep, and as the afternoon hours passed Mrs. Aldrich began to worry, for her husband had promised to come home early, bringing theological aid. It would never do to have the celebrated Mrs. Stowe discovered in such an undignified posture. Mrs. Aldrich found a light, silk scarf and, tiptoeing to the sofa, attempted to drape it over Harriet's bottom hoop.

The touch awoke Mrs. Stowe. She sat bolt upright "and with dim, reproachful eyes asked, 'Why did you do it? I am weak, weary and worn as I am. Let me sleep.'" Mrs. Aldrich suggested that her clothing needed rearranging. "The negative was firm and decisive. 'I won't be any properer than I have a mind to be. Let me sleep.'"

Mrs. Aldrich prevailed upon her guest to drink a cup of coffee, and that restored her. At dinner the hostess overheard Harriet telling the other guest that "the heat of the day and the motion of the train had produced a strange dizziness which she had never experienced before."

When she left next morning Harriet said to Aldrich: "I am always like a spider that is puzzled where to attach his threads for a web. You and Mrs. Aldrich unknowingly gave me a *motif* for a story." She turned to Mrs. Aldrich. "There is so much positive character in this little lady that I could not resist the desire to put her in a book. But I had come to the end of the bridge, and there was need to meet my heroine again." She kissed her hostess good-bye and added comfortingly, "But she is not you—not just you —but a type of you."

Mrs. Aldrich rather resented being used as a character in fiction, even Mrs. Stowe's fiction, and cried a little about it afterwards. Whether Harriet had the Aldriches in mind when writing her newspaper novel, *My Wife and I,* it is impossible to say; but certainly in Eva Henderson Mrs. Aldrich recognized no portrait of herself, nor did she ever find herself depicted in any of Mrs. Stowe's stories.

All was grist that came to Harriet's mill those days. The *North American* article gave her an idea, and she wrote an oblique and noncommittal defense of Spiritualism so long that it ran through four numbers of the *Christian Union* in September. The Germans were besieging Paris, and there is a hint of some disagreement about the sudden war in the Stowe household. That unrepentant Germanophile, Calvin Stowe, took an unpopular position by penning for the *Christian Union* an article in defense of the Prussians, while Harriet wrote to Mrs. Fields:

> My Dear Soul:—You are always a dear, sweet angel and wanting to do all you can to bring in the Kingdom, can't you start something in Boston for the poor, starving French peasantry whom this war has ruined? There is a fair to be holden for them in New York that begins about the 15th [November]. Can't you start one in Boston? I will do all I can to help, if you will only begin.

Harriet had been unable to get to Boston that autumn, after all. Instead, she spent the two months, at least, in Stockbridge with Georgie and Henry Allen, Calvin and the twins with her, it seems, the indications being that the Stowes vacated Oakholm at the end of the summer. Fields had been complaining about Harriet's neglect of them. He had not written entirely in jest. He had something special to tell her, and it was that at the end of the year he intended to retire from the *Atlantic* and from the publishing business, to devote the rest of his active life to writing and lecturing. After that, Harriet's professional world would never be the same. As Fields's final editorial act, he placed in the December, 1870, number of the *Atlantic* Harriet's sixth *Oldtown Fireside* story, *The Ghost in The Cap'n Brown House.* Not for nearly eight years would a contribution of hers appear in that magazine again.

Despite Harriet's enthralment to work, there had been too many inter-ruptions in the form of new grandsons to admire and sad mansions to vacate, and she was nowhere near the end of *Pink and White Tyranny* when Joseph Howard demanded his serial for the *Christian Union*. Harriet bowed to the inevitable and accepted the most driven year of her life, as the *Christian Union* announced:

> Next week will be commenced a characteristic serial of modern life and society by Mrs. H. B. Stowe. She calls it, "My Wife and I," a title which, as she justly says, embodies the oldest form of *christian union* known. It treats of many of the special themes which agitate our day and generation.

My Wife and I began in the November 12 issue, and Harriet subtitled it, *Harry Henderson's History*. Since it was an autobiography in form, again she was writing in the guise of a man.

My Wife and I was a great success from the start. After its book-publication Harriet remarked that only *Uncle Tom's Cabin* had brought her more letters from readers. At the end of the year 1870, when seven instalments of the story had appeared, the *Christian Union* was obliged to get out a supplement containing all the back chapters for the benefit of new subscribers attracted by the much-discussed serial. "Although thousands of each number were printed in anticipation of the demand for back num-bers, the list has exceeded all probabilities and all calculations." When the story ended in the autumn of 1871, the *Christian Union* had a circulation of nearly 90,000, at least half of which had been added by the serial.

My Wife and I delighted the ears of the generation of 1870-71. A light, satirical, fast-moving fiction of the times, it was a novelty, as up-to-the-minute as croquet, *bouffante* skirts, flat, broad-brimmed bowler hats, or that ditty the young bloods of Manhattan were at the moment roaring:

> If an engine meet an engine
> Coming round a curve,—
> If it smash both train and tender,
> What does it deserve?
> Not a penny paid to any,
> Far as I observe.

It was smart, slangy, sophisticated, and could scarcely have been more timely; for New York was in the first of its great surges of physical expansion. New York was no longer just a big town in the East but the metropolis, the centre of business and amusement, if not yet of culture, and its mazes had become a fascinating scene for fiction stories. That winter, with Isabella Beecher Hooker issuing her famous "Declaration and Pledge of the Women of the United States concerning their Right to and their Use of The Elective Franchise," there was no topic commanding more attention than woman-suffrage. And New York, where Susan B. Anthony and Elizabeth Cady Stanton were publishing their *Revolution* and the Claflin sisters their less sedate *Weekly,* was the fountain-head of the movement.

This was the New York Harriet gave her readers in *My Wife and I*—the materialistic, corrupt, cynical, feverish, glamorous New York—and she gave it to them, in her own expression, *hot.* She gave them Broadway. She gave them Bohemia and elegant society. She gave them The New Woman, and not only the scandalous Woodhull-Claflin type nor the firm-chinned Anthony-Stanton grenadiers, but the intelligent girls who were just then beginning to step out and make careers for themselves—careers other than the time-hallowed one of lady-writer. This was the New York her country readers expected, and she gave it to them deftly.

Mrs. Stanton, whose own hand was none too light, would sneer at Harriet's heavy Scripture lessons, but she could have brought no such complaint against the impudent opening of *My Wife and I:*

> I trust that Miss Anthony and Mrs. Stanton, and all the prophetesses of our day, will remark the humility and propriety of my title. It is not *I and My Wife*—oh no! It is *My Wife and I.* What am I, and what is my father's house, that I should go before my wife in anything?

Thus sounding a sarcastic theme-note, Harriet kept on; and, if what she produced was not the greatest novel of its day, it was the best weekly serial, and it represented Harriet Beecher Stowe at the peak of her virtuosity. It betrays nothing of the strain under which it was written, for hers by now was a well-practiced pen. The loose, slipshod writing and bad construction that marred some of her greater novels are little in evidence in *My Wife and I.* Its plot was trite, even in that day. The Rev. Mr. Alger was writing the same plot for boys. Harry Henderson is the poor but brilliant New Hampshire youth who comes to New York, makes a success in journalism, and wins the hand of the city's fairest and—it was Mrs. Stowe writing the story—saintliest society maiden.

When *My Wife and I* appeared as a book, Harriet presented it with a foreword disclaiming that any of her characters were drawn from living persons. It was perhaps the first time that now familiar notice had ever appeared in an American novel. She had need to make her disclaimer emphatic, for already the newspapers were pointing to certain resemblances. For instance, Audacia Dangyereyes (a name Harriet might have hyphenated, Dang-yer-eyes) manifestly might be taken for a composite portrait of Victoria Woodhull and Tennie Claflin; and the rampant Claflin sisters would not shrink from another lawsuit, especially one in which they appeared as plaintiffs asking damages. Some professed to see in the character of Mrs. Stella Cerulean a likeness of Elizabeth Cady Stanton. With Lib Tilton pouring her dreadful nonsense about Henry Ward Beecher into the ears of Susan Anthony, Mrs. Stanton's closest friend, as Harriet knew from Sister Belle, Mrs. Stanton herself was in no mood to take the backwash of any Beecher.

Despite Harriet's distaste for the woman-suffrage leaders, she by this time truly believed in equal political rights for women. Her one confidant high in the movement was Thomas Wentworth Higginson, now of Boston. To him she wrote in May, 1871, a letter which reveals her adherence to the cause— a letter which, unfortunately, though dated, bears no sender's address. Its final paragraph is important:

> I shall come to Boston Thursday and be at the Rev'd E. Hale's for a week and hope to see you and her [Mary A. R. Livermore, editor of *The Woman's Journal.*] I would like to *tell* you some things I cannot write.

It is not hard to guess what those things were—with the New York suffrage organization giving signs of turning itself into a prosecuting agency for the disgrace and ruin of Henry Ward Beecher. As early as the preceding year Harriet must have heard what Theodore Tilton was whispering in New York—that story so impossible for a sister to believe who knew her brother's purity but which nevertheless was raising in Henry's heart a fear so terrible that he could think of suicide. If that story were made public, even as a baseless charge! After Henry had married the adulterous Richardson to his paramour, Harriet had seen then something of the ferocity of her brother's enemies.

Was their time coming now? At any rate, to meet the possible emergency, Harriet was making all the influential allies for Henry she could. That year and almost all of the next the distressing state of affairs in New York hung as a weight on the Beecher clan. It threatened to make a rift in that once compact phalanx, for Isabella Hooker was hearing Susan B. Anthony's version of the Tilton story, and believing it. And to a degree Thomas K. Beecher, of Elmira, another of Harriet Porter's children, sided with Isabella.

Another trouble began for Harriet that year, an intimate one and always to be poignant. During the winter Georgie Allen, the funny little mother of Harriet's grandson, Freeman, fell ill with a nervous affliction which Harriet in a letter described as a "sudden and utter prostration with nervous sleeplessness and such depression of spirits as made her, so gay and buoyant, a distress to look at." Georgie's physician confidently administered morphine to relieve his patient's misery, with an aftermath not unusual in those days. The family thereafter kept Georgie's condition a close secret.

In the spring of 1871 Harriet finished her *Pink and White Tyranny* and thus shook some of her burden from her shoulders. Roberts Brothers, of Boston, published the novel in July, advertising an advance sale of 10,000 copies. It meant no rest for Harriet, however, for, with *My Wife and I* only a little more than half completed, she at once began writing Oldtown stories for the book Osgood was going to publish for her. At the withdrawal of his partner, Osgood had reorganized the publishing house as James R. Osgood & Co.

On June 14 Harriet paused in the midst of such labours to realize that she was sixty years old. Later, when she had resumed her column in the *Christian Union,* she wrote about how it felt to approach the portals of old age:

> Heads that we remember glossy with youthful curls are snow-white. Those that we remember as young men have become old men. The caravan is moving, moving, the first rank continually disappearing. And where are we? Waiting by the river!—waiting for the postman's knock, whether it come at eventide, or cock-crowing, or in the morning.

Being foot-loose now, at the onset of hot weather Harriet fled with her family to the White Mountains and there made such progress (though she did miss the August 2 issue of the *Christian Union* with the instalment of her serial) that by August 16 she could report to Osgood that his book of *Fireside Stories* was practically ready for him.

The "week or two" it was going to take Harriet (on August 16) to finish *My Wife and I* stretched into nearly three months before she wrote the concluding words, and those words were a postscript promising her readers a

sequel to her popular Broadway story. Her pen kept on and completed the
last story for her *Fireside* series; and then, from New York, where possibly
she had gone to deliver her final instalment to the *Christian Union,* Harriet
wrote to her twin daughters:

> I have at last finished all my part in the third book of mine that is to
> come out this year; to wit, "Oldtown Fireside Stories," and you can have
> no idea what a perfect luxury of rest it is to be free from all literary en-
> gagements of all kinds, sorts, or descriptions. I feel like a poor woman I
> once read about—
>
> > "Who always was tired,
> > 'Cause she lived in a house
> > Where help wasn't hired,"
>
> and of whom it is related that in her dying moments—
>
> > "She folded her hands
> > With her latest endeavor,
> > Saying nothing, dear nothing,
> > Sweet nothing forever."
>
> I am in about her state of mind. I luxuriate in laziness. I do not want to
> do anything or go anywhere. I only want to sink down into lazy enjoyment
> of living.

Sweet nothing forever, and the weary sexagenarian luxuriated in laziness
during the remaining six weeks of 1871, merely turning out a two-part
Thanksgiving fiction story for the *Christian Union* and another two-parter,
The First Christmas of New England, for her paper's illustrated, pale-green
Christmas number, and making her business arrangements for the future.
In its annual prospectus the *Christian Union* said: "The single fact that
Mrs. Stowe, after finishing one brief outside engagement, is to give her
exclusive services to the *Christian Union* during the year 1872, will be the
best kind of news to all interested in the paper," which was now claiming
"a very large circulation." The "publishers to the Beecher Family" advertised *My Wife and I* as "the success of the season."

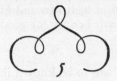

Harriet in a Storm

HARRIET had a special purpose for being in Brooklyn that fall and winter, one so influential upon her that for the first time in her life she could miss Christmas with her own family. The nightmare that hung over Henry, and over all who loved Henry, seemed to be approaching some sort of crisis, as Isabella Beecher Hooker threatened to indict her half-brother publicly for having seduced Elizabeth Tilton. The brothers and sisters were now regarding Bella as eccentric. Actually, she was quite mad.

For Sister Belle was now hugging to her heart a great secret, a secret so vast and awful that she could not yet impart it to her own husband and children. Only one other person knew it—Victoria Woodhull, who, in fact, had told it to Isabella in the first place. Victoria possessed mediumistic powers (she was president of the American Association of Spiritualists), and Victoria had obtained it from On High.

It was this: the Millennium was close at hand. The whole world would soon become a single matriarchy—a "maternal government," as Isabella called it—and she, Isabella Beecher Hooker, of Hartford, Connecticut, was to rule it as vice-regent of Christ—"with Him to usher in the millennial day." Bella kept whispering to herself her title—"*the* inspired one."

But now "the inspired one," no doubt on evidence which, if inadmissible in any court, was conclusive with Sister Belle, had become convinced of the guilt of Henry Ward Beecher. Nay, she *knew* he was guilty; and, knowing it, was she not making herself *particeps criminis* by not coming out with the truth? She turned to her brother, Thomas K. Beecher, in Elmira, for advice, and he replied with a letter strongly urging her to hold her tongue:

> You have no *proof* as yet of any offense on Henry's part. Your testimony would be allowed in no court. Tilton, wife, Moulton & Co. *are* witnesses. Even Mrs. Stanton can only declare hearsay. So, if you move, remember that

you are standing on uncertain information, and we shall not probably ever get the facts—and I am glad of it. If Mr. and Mrs. Tilton are brought into court, nothing will be revealed. Perjury for good reasons is, with advanced thinkers, no sin.

Whereby Father Tom, as he was to be known in Elmira, definitely declared himself outside the company of the advanced thinkers.

But Isabella was getting her instructions from a higher authority than the Rev. Thomas K. Beecher, who, though wise, was mortal; and one day a half-frantic Henry Ward Beecher rushed to Frank Moulton, the go-between who was supposed to be trying to settle the Beecher-Tilton affair without open scandal, but who from this distance of time seems to have served principally to muddy waters already roiled enough. Henry thrust a letter into Moulton's hands and told him to read it.

"What do you think of the condition of a man who gets such letters as this from a member of his own family?" cried the Plymouth preacher. "What is to be done? Is there no end of trouble and complication?"

It was a letter from Isabella, and it contained these sentences:

I can endure no longer. I must see you and persuade you to write a paper which I will read, going alone to your pulpit and taking sole charge of the services.

It was well for Henry's peace of mind during the next few weeks that Harriet was in Brooklyn. Every Sunday, morning and evening, Harriet went to Plymouth Church and sat in a front pew, waiting for Isabella. Belle held her older half-sister in great awe; and Harriet, small and physically weak as she was, knew she could handle Sister Belle, if the latter appeared and tried to shock the Sabbath hush of the church by shouting her sensational charges.

Theodore Tilton himself went to Hartford and saw Mrs. Hooker, who, in her fiftieth year, was still a handsome and vibrant woman. What Theodore said to her—and on the witness stand later he refused to testify what he said—must have had more weight with Isabella than her spirit-messages; for, after his return, Moulton told Henry that there would be no more danger from that quarter. And Moulton, as a witness under oath, testified for Tilton. He said Tilton had silenced Mrs. Hooker by "charging *her* with adultery."

Her vigil on the Plymouth ramparts over, Harriet assembled her family in mid-January and went down to Florida. While still on the watch, Spiritualism had again engaged her attention. Her own paper, the *Christian Union*, had given Robert Dale Owen's new book, *The Debatable Land between this World and the Next*, what she regarded as an entirely inadequate review. She wrote to the author to tell him how disappointed she was, "and Henry is no less so. He took some pains to indoctrinate the writer, but the result was very unsatisfactory."

Harriet herself was "delighted with the calm and philosophic spirit shown in the work." She promised Owen a discussion of it *"in extenso"* from her own pen, and also said, "I shall take some pains to get the book read by leading minds in England, particularly by Mrs. Lewes *(Adam Bede)*, with whom I correspond."

Harriet was as good as her word and wrote for the *Christian Union* more than two columns about *The Debatable Land*, and as soon as she was settled in Mandarin she kept her promise and commended Owen and his books to George Eliot, to whom she had not written for two years, alleging "two years of constant severe work" as her excuse.

> Years ago, in Naples, I visited Mr. Owen for the first time, and found him directing his attention to the phenomena of spiritism. He had stumbled upon some singular instances of it accidentally, and he had forthwith instituted a series of researches and experiments on the subject, some of which he showed me. It was the first time I had ever seriously thought of the matter, and he invited my sister and myself to see some of the phenomena, as exhibited by a medium friend of theirs who resided in their family. The result at the time was sufficiently curious, but I was interested in his account of the manner in which he proceeded, keeping records of every experiment with its results, in classified orders. As the result of his studies and observations, he has published two books, one, "Footfalls on The Boundary of Another World," published in 1860, and latterly, "The Debatable Land between This World and The Next." I regard Mr. Owen as one of the few men who are capable of entering into an enquiry of this kind without an utter drowning of common sense, and his books are both of them worth a fair reading. To me they represent a great deal that is intensely curious and interesting, although I do not admit, of course, all his deductions, and think he often takes too much for granted.

But George Eliot was unmoved by her epistolary friend's obvious, for all its reservations and evasions, attempt at proselyting. She replied:

> When I am more at liberty I will certainly read Mr. Owen's books, if he is good enough to send them to me. I desire on all subjects to keep an open

mind, but hitherto the various phenomena, reported or attested in connection with ideas of spirit intercourse and so on, have come before me here in the painful form of the lowest *charlatanerie.* Apart from personal contact with people who get money by public exhibitions as mediums, or with semi-idiots such as those who make a court for a Mrs. ———, or other feminine personages of that kind, I would not willingly place any barriers between my mind and any possible channel of truth affecting the human lot.

Harriet wrote ecstatically to Annie Fields: "Very sweet note from dear Mrs. Lewes. Can't she be got to come to America? England wears her out." Harriet was beginning to assume a personal intimacy with George Eliot, whom, however, she had never met in person. Their long-distance acquaintance had begun when in January, 1870, Harriet had ventured to write, commending her *Oldtown Folks* to George Eliot's attention. Calvin took a hand in it. The great English novelist, whose *Middlemarch* was that year running in *Harper's Weekly,* must be brought to see the light. In his dancing, Chaldaic hand, Calvin presumed on his wife's acquaintance to indite a brief note to George Eliot, who had declared in her letter that the American medium, Hume, then creating a *furore* in London, was, in her opinion, a perfect fraud.

Mrs. Lewes:—I fully sympathize with you in your disgust with Hume and the professing mediums generally.

Hume spent his boyhood in my father's native town, among my relatives and acquaintances, and he was a disagreeable, nasty boy. But he certainly has qualities which science has not yet explained, and some of his doings are as real as they are strange. My interest in the subject of spiritualism arises from the fact of my own experience, more than sixty years ago, in my early childhood. I then never thought of questioning the objective reality of all I saw, and supposed that everybody else had the same experience. Of what this experience was you may gain some idea from certain passages in "Old Town Folks."

The same experiences continue yet, but with serious doubts as to the objectivity of the scenes exhibited. I have noticed that people who have remarkable and minute answers to prayer, such as Stilling, Franke, Lavater, are for the most part of this peculiar temperament. Is it absurd to suppose that some peculiarity in the nervous system, in the connecting link between soul and body, may bring some more than others into an almost abnormal contact with the spirit-world (for example, Jacob Boehme and Sweden-borg), and that, too, without correcting their faults or making them morally better than others? Allow me to say that I have always admired the working of your mind, there is about it such a perfect uprightness and uncalculating honesty. I think you are a better Christian without church or theology than most people are with both, though I am, and always have been in the main, a Calvinist of the Jonathan Edwards school. God bless you! I have a warm side for Mr. Lewes on account of his Goethe labors.

Goethe has been my admiration for more than forty years. In 1830 I got hold of his "Faust," and for two gloomy, dreary November days, while riding through the woods of New Hampshire in an old-fashioned stage-coach to enter upon a professorship in Dartmouth College, I was perfectly dissolved by it.

Sincerely yours,
C. E. STOWE.

Harriet in her reply tactfully dropped the discussion, saying merely: "My poor Rabbi!—he sends you some Arabic, which I fear you cannot read. On *diablerie* he is up to his ears in knowledge, having read all things in all tongues, from the Talmud down."

Though delighted to receive a letter from the fabulous Professor Stowe, George Eliot was unconvinced by it. She replied diplomatically (to Harriet):

> Pray give my special thanks to the Professor for his letter. His hand-writing, which does really look like Arabic—a very graceful character, surely—happens to be remarkably legible to me, and I did not hesitate over a single word. Some of the words, as expressions of fellowship, were very precious to me, and I hold it very good of him to write to me that best sort of encouragement. I was much impressed with the fact—which you have told me—that he was the original of the "visionary boy" in "Old Town Folks"; and it must be deeply interesting to talk with him on his experience. Perhaps I am inclined, under the influence of the facts, physiological and psychological, which have been gathered of late years, to give larger place to the interpretation of vision-seeing as subjective than the Professor would approve. It seems difficult to limit—at least limit with any precision—the possibility of confounding sense by impressions derived from inward conditions with those which are directly dependent on external stimulus. In fact, the division between within and without in this sense seems to become every year a more subtle and bewildering problem.

Professor Park, of Andover, would have agreed with George Eliot. He thought Stowe's visions were due to a diseased condition of the optic nerves. At any rate, as Calvin moved into his 70's, his visions became even more vivid. Once Harriet missed a train in Hartford and, having some time to wait for the next, returned to her home to get some papers she had forgotten. As she entered the study she vaguely observed Calvin reading at the window, but, being in one of her absent-minded fits, she said nothing to him but went to the desk and rummaged through it. When she had found what she wanted, she turned and spoke to her husband. Calvin's jump bounced his spectacles on his nose.

"Goodness, Hattie!" he exclaimed. "Was that you? I thought I was having a vision."

As he neared the brink of eternity, Calvin began having encounters with the Devil. Charles Stowe was then studying in Germany, and the Devil took a mean advantage of a man who had already lost three sons tragically. As Calvin told the story to a Hartford clergyman, the Devil tempted him night after night, coming in the guise of a horseman and yelling that Charley was dead, then questioning the father's faith.

"But I was ready for him last night," Calvin said. "I had fortified myself with passages of Scripture. I found some things in *Ephesians* which were just what I wanted, and when he came last night I *hurled* them at him. I tell you, it made him bark like a dog, and he took himself off. He won't trouble me again."

Harriet took to Florida that winter a literary project that would pleasantly occupy her spare time, keep her name regularly in the *Christian Union,* and give James R. Osgood the book she had promised him. Actually, she had promised him a novel, but she had need to give her imaginative faculty a long rest. What she wrote was a series of travel-articles about Florida under the title of *Palmetto Leaves.*

This was probably the first promotion-writing for Florida ever done, or the first sustained writing of the sort. Except what it might read in an occasional traveller's letter in the New York or Boston papers, the North knew nothing about Florida. In *Palmetto Leaves* Harriet, besides giving an intimate glimpse of her own life at Mandarin, painted a picture of Florida as a tropical paradise which remained as the Northern impression until railroads and the motor car opened up the State as a winter playground. At the end of the winter Harriet wrote to Annie Fields that 14,000 Northern tourists had been through that year, many of them no doubt drawn southward by the *Palmetto Leaves* in the *Christian Union.*

A new phase of life was opening for Harriet that winter. At some point in her peregrinations in the autumn, a man named Williams, representing the American Literary Bureau of Boston, made her a proposition to put her on the lecture-platform, with a programme of readings from her own works. The idea terrified her, but the financial offer was tempting, and she had not rejected it categorically. In January Williams began pressing her for a decision. Harriet wrote to Annie from Mandarin, describing her indecision.

> I have put off replying to Mr. Williams, because I felt extremely uncertain what I could do, and, as the Yankees say, didn't know what to do nor to don't. My state in regard to it may be described by the phrase, "Kind o' love to—hate to—wish I didn't—want ter." I suppose the result will be that I shall not work into their lecture system.

James T. Fields, himself a popular lecturer now, replied to this, strongly urging her to accept for the sake of the easy revenue the lyceum circuits offered. She therefore agreed, but with the reservation that her tour must end in time for her to get back to Mandarin, now her only home, before Christmas.

Williams had booked her for forty readings during September, October, and November, 1872, in as many New England halls. It was frightening to one brought up never to open her lips in public, and in the midst of her trepidation came the sad news from Hartford that Thomas C. Perkins was dead. "The blow has fallen!" she wrote to the Howards. "My dear brother has left us. Nowhere in the world had I a truer friend. It is a blow that strikes deep on my life and makes me feel that it is like ice breaking up under my feet. Those who truly love us, and on whom we can at all times depend, are not many; and all my life he has been one of these."

As the day approached when she must start her reading tour, her nervousness increased. She was not to "open" in Boston after all, but in Springfield, Massachusetts, and on a date which a present-day impresario might not have chosen for a début of a highly paid but untried entertainer. It was Friday, September 13.

"Where will you be in September?" she asked Mrs. Fields. "I am then to read in Boston, and would like, if you were there, to take up under your shadow the 26th and 28th of September. It seems to me that it is a little too early for Boston, isn't it? Will there be anybody in town then? I don't know as it's my business—which is simply to speak my piece and take my money."

Next day she sent Annie her schedule—Friday the 13th at Springfield, Monday the 16th at Lynn, Tuesday the 17th at Salem. "Now it has occurred to me that, should you still be in Manchester and all things right, this would give me an opportunity to spend a day or two with you. If not, I would like to go somewhere by the seaside to some quiet house. I have a sort of indefinite idea that Lynn and Salem are both accessible easily from Manchester."

The Fieldses duly invited her to Manchester-by-the-Sea, but it was a sad Harriet who arrived there Saturday noon, September 14, having arisen at five o'clock in the morning in Springfield to catch her train. Friday the 13th had not been her lucky day, for she felt that she had failed in her début. She had been full of stage-fright, her voice lost its power, and she had not held her audience. It was like her, though, not to accept her failure as defeat. She was a mime, an actress by nature, and she knew she had only to read as she had spoken and entranced the studio parties in Rome, and she would win. Lynn and Salem were better, restoring some of her confidence; and then came September 26, and she was at the Fields's house at 148 Charles Street, Boston, gathering her resolution for the afternoon encounter with an audience in the dreaded Tremont Temple.

In her 60's Harriet's hair had not only turned white but had become short. As a joke for Annie, she stood before her mirror and brushed her usual curls into a high pompadour above her broad brow, then called her friend to her bedroom. As Annie entered, Harriet struck an attitude.

"Now, my dear, gaze upon me," she said. "I am exactly like my father, when he was going to preach." And Harriet waggled her forefinger in Dr. Beecher's best-known gesture. Of what followed Mrs. Fields wrote:

It was easy to see that the spirit of the old preacher was revived in her veins, and the afternoon would show something of his power. An hour later, when I sat with her in the anteroom waiting for the moment of her appearance to arrive, I could feel the power surging up within her.

That reading was a great success. She was alive in every fibre of her being. She was to give portions of *Uncle Tom's Cabin* to men, women, and children who could hardly understand the crisis which inspired it, and she determined to effect the difficult task of making them feel as well as hear. With her presence and inspiration, they could not fail to understand what her words had signified to the generation that had passed through the struggle of our war. When her voice was not sufficient to make the audience hear, men and women rose from their seats and crowded round her, standing gladly, that no word might be lost. It was the last great leap of the flame which had burned out a great wrong.

Annie Fields must have waited until this triumph was scored before imparting news which struck into Harriet's heart like a knife. Two weeks earlier, addressing a convention of Spiritualists in Boston, Victoria Woodhull had made a public charge that Henry Ward Beecher was guilty of adultery with the wife of Theodore Tilton. Every newspaper in Boston had a reporter at the convention, but not one mentioned the sensational accusation. The *Journal* merely said: "Prominent New York clergymen were personally accused of the most hideous crimes."

But hundreds had heard it and were repeating it; and not even Frank Moulton, if indeed he ever intended to, could now suppress the scandal.

Knowing Henry as she did, Harriet believed not a word of the accusation. The Woodhull was but a female of that world of devils which hated Henry and was trying to cast him from his spiritual eminence. None of the Boston papers had taken the charge seriously, and Harriet dismissed the whole unpleasant episode from her mind. Or pretended to.

Harriet went on with her readings, and after Tremont Temple there was no doubt of their success. She had gained full confidence in her power to hold an audience, and this little, white-haired woman, with her cameo profile and the aura of greatness she carried needed only that. She expanded her repertory, and besides Eva and Topsy and *Uncle Tom* scenes gave her hearers samples of Cap'n Kittridge, from *The Pearl of Orr's Island* and stories of *Oldtown,* of which *The Minister's Housekeeper* was her favourite, this being entirely in Sam Lawson's rustic dialect, beginning, "Wal, you see, boys, 'twas just here—Parson Carryl's wife, she died along in the forepart o' March," etc. She also read *Laughing in Meetin',* a story she had contributed to the *Christian Union* in June.

Her first swing brought her back to Boston and the Fieldses on October 3, and she wrote to Calvin: "Have had a most successful but fatiguing week. Read in Cambridgeport tonight and Newburyport tomorrow night." The spectacle of his elderly wife gallivanting around New England and exposing herself to death from train accident or cold in order to earn bread for the family, threw Calvin Stowe into profound melancholy. The old man's dependence on Harriet, especially now that he was homeless and merely bestowed upon such relatives and friends as would receive him, was pathetic. He knew that he would not live to see the end of her tour.

As she had always done, Harriet tried to laugh him out of his hypochondria, writing him from Westfield, Massachusetts: "Now, my dear husband, please do *want,* and *try,* to remain with us yet a little longer, and let us have a little quiet evening together before either of us crosses the river. My heart cries out for a home with you—our home together in Florida. Oh, may we see it again!"

But Harriet was finding the lyceum circuit a good deal of a trial. She would, she told Calvin, give up the effort, "but that my engagements have involved others in heavy expense, and, should I fail to fulfill them, it would be doing a wrong."

Harriet's itinerary next took her into Maine. She dreaded Bangor, as lonesome and far-away, but her experiences there turned out to be the pleasantest of her tour. All of northern New England was gripped that fall by an epidemic among horses, and in many communities the quarantine regulations forbade the driving of horses in the streets. It was that way in Bangor, but the Mayor walked a long distance to bring Harriet flowers and tell her that he was to be chairman at the reading. How strange it was to find Newman Smyth, whom as a little boy she had taught in her home school in Brunswick, when she was struggling to write *Uncle Tom's Cabin,* now a full-fledged minister in Bangor. It "rained tremendously" that evening, and everyone had to walk, besides, but she had "an excellent audience." Some had travelled fifty miles to see her, for Maine claimed as its own the author of *Uncle Tom's Cabin.* A child named Eva was presented to her, another named Harriet Beecher. A deaf, old lady shook her hand, and Harriet wondered if she had heard any of the reading.

"Bless you, no," the good soul replied. "I came jist to see you. I'd ruther see you than the Queen."

Dull hours alone in hotels were something to be dreaded by one haunted by fears for a threatened brother. To fill her idle time with another interest, Harriet projected for the *Christian Union* a series of sketches of women of the Bible. As she travelled that fall, putting up with poor food, wretched train accommodations, and lonely hotel rooms, there came regularly from her pen *Martha and Mary* (in two parts), *Sarah the Princess, Hagar the Slave,* and so on. After November 2 she had special need to concentrate on them; for on that date Victoria Woodhull, balked

by the daily press, spread the Beecher-Tilton story, with embellishments
supplied by her imagination, through most of the edition of *Woodhull &
Claflin's Weekly*. Next day one could get $40 for a single copy of the
Weekly, and the Federal District Attorney had clapped Victoria and her
sister, Tennessee Claflin, into the Ludlow-Street gaol for sending obscene
matter through the mails.

And yet, nothing else happened in this miasmic Brooklyn nightmare.
Tens of thousands of tongues were clacking over the scandal, and there
was not a word in the *Christian Union* to indicate that its editor had taken
the slightest cognizance of the assault on his character—no libel action
against *Woodhull & Claflin's Weekly,* no denial from the Plymouth pastor.
Strangely, press and public waited for Theodore Tilton to deny the story,
but there was only silence from that quarter.

A few, however, thought it should be Henry Ward Beecher to speak out,
and among them was Henry's half-brother Thomas. Isabella Hooker had
written immediately to him: "At present, of course, I shall keep silent;
but truth is dearer than all things else, and if he will not speak it in some
way, I cannot always stand as consenting to a lie." Father Tom replied:

> I respect Mrs. Woodhull, while I abhor her philosophy. She only carries
> out Henry's philosophy, against which I recorded my protest twenty years
> ago. Of the two, Woodhull is my hero, Henry my coward.

Harriet knew nothing then of this exchange. She gave her readings,
wrote about her Bible heroines, and carried on. Back to Hartford for a
brief visit with Mary Perkins (though not with Calvin, who was probably
stopping at this time with the Allens in Cambridge), and then Harriet
was off on the final swing through Connecticut and Rhode Island that
would complete her reading-tour.

She was a good trouper. The work had been hard, disagreeable, and even
risky, but it had also been profitable. As she settled her accounts with Mr.
Williams of the lecture-bureau, she signed for another reading-tour for the
autumn of 1873—one to take her into the West she had left twenty-three
years before.

Harriet's quick visit to Hartford in November had probably been for
the purpose of inspecting a house there that had been offered for sale. She
was beginning to see that her plan would not do, to maintain only the

Florida home and spend the summers visiting friends and touring the resorts in the North. It was unfair to her "poor, good man," who was getting too old to be dragged around in such fashion. And when in December Calvin fell sharply ill—the first serious illness of a long and complaining life—Harriet, stricken in conscience and fearing that she might have killed her husband, acted at once and acquired a permanent home in Hartford.

Whatever her other resources at this time, forty "readings" at what was certainly a minimum of $250 each, provided the money. The house she bought was at No. 1 Forest Street, in Hartford; and it seems certain she purchased it before she took the convalescent Calvin south at the end of December, because, when the family returned in the late spring, the house was ready for them, redecorated according to Harriet's specifications. She wrote to her brother Charles: "We have bought a pretty cottage there [Hartford], near Belle," who was not yet in Harriet's bad books.

"Pretty cottage" was scarcely an apt description of the four-square house of the type which prospering merchants and professional men throughout the North were building for themselves on the shady streets of towns and smaller cities. It had bay windows, a *porte-cochère,* sliding walnut doors, and plenty of small but high-ceilinged rooms on three floors. The surrounding grounds were small, but large enough for Harriet to put down the wickets of a fashionable croquet set in back.

The back of Harriet's property coincided with the side line of the grounds around the fine house which Samuel and Livy Clemens had just built for themselves on Farmington Avenue. Mr. Clemens, under the name of Mark Twain, had written a funny travel-book, *The Innocents Abroad,* which had brought him money and fame, but his *Tom Sawyer* was still three years in the future. A greater luminary than he, Charles Dudley Warner, lived at the corner of Forest Street and Farmington Avenue; but Mrs. Stowe, in 1873, was the most distinguished of the three neighbours. Proud Hartford called the neighbourhood "the Nook Farm literary colony."

Calvin's recovery from his illness was as abrupt as its onset, and Harriet was gratefully enabled to accept, for the pair of them, an invitation to spend Christmas with Annie Fields's brother, in Framingham, Massachusetts. On Christmas Day she wrote to Annie: "On Friday of this week Charles and I shall take our patient to New York on our way south." In New York they would stop with Henry; and, Harriet enjoined Annie, "If you see the Devil's tail forking out at any rat-hole, don't fail to hit it a clip."

One had been forking out at a Boston rat-hole, where Victoria Woodhull

and her sister, released in bail and capitalizing on their notoriety, attempted
to make a public appearance but were unable to rent an auditorium. "I am
delighted that Boston has fought the good fight with those obscene birds
so manfully," Harriet wrote to Annie. "There was a quiet uprising, not
noisy but effective. Mrs. Claflin said Gov. Claflin [not related to the Claflin
sisters] went to the Hall and, remonstrating with the committee, said that
they might as well have the undressed women of North Street on the stage
there; and he found afterwards that the man who *hires the women* and
runs the thing was listening to him. I fancy she gave it up, for they did
not speak in Boston, as I am told. It was admirably done, and done without
saying a word about them in the papers; and they can't get it."

There was a piece of gossip about The Woodhull in Framingham; and
Harriet's relation of it rankled with a tribeswoman's hatred of her enemy:

> Did I tell you that here in Framingham lives the wife of that Colonel
> Blood whom this wretched woman has seduced and infatuated to be her
> tool and slave? Mrs. Blood is a lovely, dignified, accomplished woman,
> with a daughter twelve years of age. Her husband, she tells me, was a
> young man of one of the best families in St. Louis, had served with honor
> in the Army, was in good position and with every prospect of rising in
> the world, perfectly correct in all his habits, and devoted to her and her
> child. This Woodhull woman set up in St. Louis as clairvoyant physician,
> and Blood consulted her as to his wife's health. Immediately this wretch
> set her eye on him and never left practicing every diabolical art till she
> really got him to give up his family—his position, his prospects in life, his
> wife and his child—to follow her in a life of infamy, as he has been doing
> ever since. Mrs. Blood is connected with one of the first families here, much
> beloved and respected, and great sympathy is felt for her. She bears her
> sorrow with a quiet dignity that wins universal respect.
>
> She is very lovely in person and manners, and one wonders what Devil's
> spell can have taken away a man from such a woman. I do hope that this
> pending trial will land The W. in the penitentiary. If it would shut her
> in and him out, there might be some hope for him.
>
> * * * *
>
> In reply to what you said, Tilton *does* deny the story in the most indig-
> nant manner and threatens suit against anybody that dares repeat it. But all
> parties advise that no public notice be taken of a slander from such a
> source. You see what a precedent it would be, if women of that class could
> throw into the community such stories about respectable people and call
> on them to disprove them. What man or woman would be safe from the
> most loathsome persecution? The impending trials of Woodhull & Co. will
> be answer enough to everything from that source.

Meanwhile Harriet's professional pen had been busy. Greeley died early in December, and she wrote nearly three columns about him in the *Christian Union*. She contributed her usual Christmas and New Year's stories to her paper's illustrated holiday editions. In its prospectus for 1873 the *Christian Union,* now claiming "the largest circulation of its class in the world," announced that "Harriet Beecher Stowe's new story, a sequel to 'My Wife and I,' will probably be commenced next fall." Two new writers were to appear with serials: Louisa M. Alcott, whose *Little Women* and *Little Men* were safely on the shelf of juvenile classics, and Edward Eggleston, whose *Hoosier Schoolmaster* had recently achieved great success. To every new subscriber the *Christian Union* was giving away as a premium a beautiful oleograph entitled *Runaway and Her Pets,* "to which Mrs. Stowe has added a charming little poem:

"'Nursing, watching, cooing, with tireless tenderness;
Motherhood and womanhood in her babe's caress.'"

Whether Harriet gave the *Christian Union* any definite promise to have her sequel that year, she did nothing about it when she reached Florida. She was tired, she had made a great deal of money by her readings, and probably felt that she deserved a rest. She continued with her Bible women, contributed an occasional "Palmetto Leaf," and for the rest basked in the Florida sunshine and invited her soul. She could hardly bring herself to write a letter. It was really "dear nothing, sweet nothing" for her that winter. In a contribution dated January 20, a paper describing her life at Mandarin, she wrote: "Our next sensation is the *City Point* stopping at the wharf, all flags flying, and William C. Bryant on board!"

With her passion for entertainment, Harriet was forever organizing picnics and parties in Mandarin. Sometimes it was a charade party, sometimes a private theatrical production on an open-air stage, and every now and then she sponsored square-dancing in the rebuilt schoolhouse, with music by some local fiddler. As he regained strength Calvin held religious services in the schoolhouse Sunday mornings for the coloured element, and in the afternoon preached to the whites.

Jacksonville discovered in the Stowe orange grove an attraction for sightseers that could be capitalized. The daily steamboat out of Jacksonville, making the local river-stops, was the *Mary Draper*—"the buzzing little *Mary Draper,*" Harriet called her. The owners of the *Mary Draper* began to sell 75-cent, round-trip excursion tickets from Jacksonville to Mandarin, assuring patrons of a glimpse of America's most famous authoress; and the daily crowds that thereafter disturbed the privacy of the Stowes became something of a national scandal.

Calvin Stowe, sitting comfortably with his Goethe on the porch, was particularly irritated by the daily throng rumbling in over the long, wooden pier and scattering over the grounds. One woman brazenly stepped up on the porch and introduced herself, adding significantly, "But I would have preferred to meet Mrs. Stowe."

"So had I, Madam," retorted Calvin. "So had I—a thousand times."

All that winter Charles Beecher kept urging Harriet to come over and see his roses and pecan trees at Newport, on the Gulf Coast. Under the carpetbag government of Florida Charles, perhaps through Harriet's intervention in Washington, held the post of State Superintendent of Agriculture and Public Instruction; but Charles was no carpetbag adventurer himself. His plantation at Newport was a permanent undertaking with him; he gave the State an able administration, and was held in high esteem in near-by Tallahassee, even by those who disapproved of his politics. It was probably owing to his influence that Tallahassee the next year gave a public reception to the once detested Harriet Beecher Stowe.

Charles operated his Newport plantation as an experimental farm, and there first showed Floridians how to grow Irish potatoes successfully—by planting them in the fall and harvesting in January or February. Planted in the warm weather, they grew all to tops. He also served the Federal Government as volunteer weather observer at Newport.

Because of Calvin's condition, however, Harriet could not make the visit that year. In January Osgood had brought out her *Palmetto Leaves*. Harriet waited until the last moment, which was May 19, 1873, then sent Charles a copy of her new book and "my parting love. If I could either have brought or left my husband, I should have come to see you this winter. The account of your roses fills me with envy.

"We leave on the 'San Jacinto' next Saturday, and I am making the most of the few charming hours yet left; for never did we have so delicious a spring. I never knew such altogether perfect weather. It is enough to make a saint out of the toughest old Calvinist that ever set his face as a flint. How do you think New England theology would have fared, if our fathers had landed here instead of on Plymouth Rock?"

She and her family reached New York on May 27, and Harriet

remained there ten days, giving half a dozen readings in and near the metropolis for a New York lecture bureau. Then she had the money for the summer vacations.

Harriet divided her summer between Hartford, where she was putting her new house in order, and Twin Mountain House, the famous White Mountain resort, where she saw her brother Henry Ward Beecher, and did no writing at all, not even letters. Henry sent to the *Christian Union* a Star paper from Twin Mountain House, extolling the region as a refuge for sufferers from hay fever. Thus patronized, the hotel began to advertise conspicuously in the Beecher paper. Harriet was back in Hartford before the end of September, writing to Mrs. Fields: "I am going to travel in the West all the month of October."

She referred to her 1873 reading-tour, about which we know little more than what she wrote at its end in a letter to her son at Harvard. Because of the difficulties of this trip, and its distances, her lecture manager, Mr. Saunders, accompanied her to keep smooth her path. Harriet left her girls—nearing forty, Hatty and Eliza were still, as they were always to be, "the Stowe girls"—to close the Forest Street house and take their father to Florida early. She was not going to risk her poor, good man in any more New England Novembers.

Harriet told Charley she gave readings in Chicago on two successive evenings, but there must have been a good many engagements ahead of those. Her journey from Chicago to Cincinnati in a stifling train was harrowing. The West was not commending itself to her in 1873 any more strongly than it had in the 30's and 40's. That same George Beecher who had as a child travelled with her on her first trip to Scotland was now a man domiciled in Cincinnati. She sent him a telegram from Chicago; but, of course—something that could never have happened in the East—he did not receive it, and so there was no hospitable home waiting for her with open doors, no rooms engaged at all; and George's boarding-house was full. It was nearly midnight when Harriet crawled into a hotel bed, "with every nerve aching from fatigue. The next day was dark and rainy, and I lay in bed most of it; but when I got up to go and read, I felt only half rested, and was still so tired that it seemed as though I could not get through."

However, the Cincinnati she had left so many years before gave her "a most sympathetic audience." It must have been a memorable experience for her auditors, to most of whom she was but a name, a legend, to gaze at last upon her frail, magnetic figure, marvelling that the miracle she wrought stemmed from their own smoky bank of the Ohio. "They all seemed delighted and begged me to come again. The next day George took us for a drive out to Walnut Hills, where we saw the seminary buildings, the house where your sisters were born, and the house in which we afterwards lived. In the afternoon we had to leave and hurry away to a reading in Dayton." Which was all Harriet had to say about the city in which she had spent the eighteen drabbest, most significant years of her life.

Harriet went South that year by train, taking her sister Mary Perkins with her and stopping for a week or ten days, early in December, in Washington to give her final public readings. They were to be the last ones she would ever give, her experiences in the West having convinced her that the work was too severe for one of her age and constitution.

In New York she had made certain business arrangements. During the summer she had done some work upon her sequel to *My Wife and I*. She had at least "composed" its story in outline, and she had selected its name —*We and Our Neighbors*.

On her tour she had resumed writing sketches of the women of the Bible, turning out *The Witch of Endor, The Daughter of Herodias, The Woman of Samaria,* and so on. They had been popular with pious readers, and in New York she signed a contract with Ford & Co. to bring them out as a six-dollar subscription book, "with art illustrations," under the title, *Women in Sacred History*. Some years later, when the book-agents had exhausted their market, Harriet condensed it as *Bible Heroines,* and it enjoyed a second success in the bookstores. Ford & Co. were advertising that the editions of *My Wife and I* had reached 50,000 copies.

"I am very much gratified," she wrote the company from Florida that winter. "An English novelist has purloined my title and published a 'My Wife and I' in Queensland. The title was a good hit, more shame to him for stealing it. When you advertise again, there is no harm in saying how many you have sold. I like people to know it for very many reasons."

One can guess the reasons. The success of *My Wife and I* was a complete retort to those critics who had predicted that Mrs. Stowe's *Lady Byron Vindicated* would ruin her popularity.

The Brooklyn nightmare continued to exhale its maddening vapours. The District Attorney had dropped the indictment of Woodhull and Claflin, and those outrageous sisters were pursuing a vigorous campaign to ruin Henry Ward Beecher. Victoria Woodhull hired Cooper Union Hall and before an immense meeting repeated her charges in full. *Woodhull & Claflin's Weekly* kept a standing editorial head: *BEECHER, TILTON, BOWEN.* From Troy, New York, was being issued a scurrilous paper dealing exclusively with the scandal. Everybody knew about that scandal, everybody talked about it, and all over the country newspaper editors, pious church-goers many of them and addressing readers who were church people and who wanted to believe in Henry Ward Beecher, were demanding why in the name of God someone on high did not utter the word "False" about the Woodhull charges.

Henry Ward Beecher did not utter it, either from his pulpit or in his Friday-evening Lecture-Room Talks. The *Christian Union* did not utter it. Theodore Tilton did not utter it. There was only silence from those quarters. Yet Yale University revealed its opinion by engaging Henry to continue his lectures on preaching to the Yale "theologs"; and Plymouth Church, when Harriet was in Brooklyn that November, met and dis-fellowshipped Theodore Tilton.

Harriet and Mary Perkins went down to Washington, where Harriet had an experience which remained long in her memory. When her readings were first advertised in the capital, her friends Judge and Mrs. John C. Underwood wrote, inviting her to be their guest in that city. She accepted for herself and sister. While Harriet was at the Underwoods', the judge died one night in his sleep. Harriet was a tower of strength on such occasions. She had at her fingertips all the consolations of Scripture; and it must have been a solace to the widow, too, to read in the *Christian Union* in January a page obituary and eulogy of Judge Underwood signed by Harriet Beecher Stowe.

For once in her life Harriet that winter worked ahead on a serial with no printing-press snatching the sheets of copy from her hand, and must have completed the writing of most of *We and Our Neighbors* before its first instalment appeared in the *Christian Union* in May. At any rate, she seemed to spend a fairly idle year while it was running in the paper, and there were no missed editions.

In April Harriet made her long-promised visit to the plantation of her brother Charles at Newport, Florida, not far from Tallahassee. Tallahassee made an occasion of it, driving its distinguished Yankee visitor to see what sights there were and tendering her an official dinner, after which she stood on the steps of one of the public buildings and shook hands with several hundred people who wanted to meet her.

On May 1 she wrote to her son: "Strawberries and blackberries are over with us; oranges are in a waning condition, few and far between. Now we are going North to begin another summer and have roses, strawberries, blackberries, and green peas come again." It was an early departure for them; but the *Christian Union* was about ready for her serial, and she did not want to trust her manuscript to the mails for such a distance.

Harriet went home from New York and remained most of the summer in her Forest Street house, working on the final chapters of *We and Our Neighbors* to the exclusion of all else. It was well for her during those weeks that she had an occupation that could absorb all her thoughts, a world of her imagination into which she could retreat completely, for the Beecher-Tilton scandal had gone into its most bewildering phase. Its repercussions reached England, where George Eliot, a little uncertain how Harriet was regarding the whole thing, wrote her friend a cautious letter of sympathy.

I can not, dare not, write more in my ignorance, lest I should be using unreasonable words. But I trust in your not despising this scrap of paper which tells you, perhaps rather for my relief than yours, that I am always in grateful, sweet remembrance of your goodness to me and your energetic labours for all.

The letter reached Harriet that summer just when her heart was heaviest for Henry, her worry for him greatest. She did not answer it for two years.

What a morass the scandal had become, as discussion churned and puddled it, and original issues all but disappeared! Before nine-tenths of the God-fearing, Theodore Tilton now stood as a scoundrel who had coerced a confession from an innocent wife in order to tear down his former patron whom he envied and had tried unsuccessfully to outrival, whereas Henry Ward Beecher was a noble martyr enduring the slander in silence to protect the Church and the fair name of a woman. If indeed Tilton's purpose was not blackmail—though Dr. Richard Storrs, pastor of the great Brooklyn Church of the Pilgrims and Henry's former friend and associate on the *Independent,* had adopted Tilton's cause and was demanding that Congregationalism cast out Plymouth Church for supporting its pastor. And Elizabeth Cady Stanton was writing that the financial "rings" of New

York were supporting Beecher and blackening "every one who dared to hear or tell the most astounding scandal of the 19th century!"

There is no space here for any attempt to make clear the position and actions of Theodore Tilton in a sensational muddle which few at the time ever understood. The Beecher version is that Tilton, his head turned by success, grew insanely jealous of his former protector, invented the story of adultery out of whole cloth, and, when he failed privately to force Henry Ward Beecher's resignation from his pulpit and his editorship, attacked him openly to bring about his ruin. Those on the opposite side contended that Tilton had a real grievance, but, being a devout churchman, tried at first to bring about a private settlement, lest a public airing of the affair should shatter Evangelical Christianity in the United States. Only when Beecher's powerful friends tried to ruin Tilton, according to this view, did he in self-defence publish his charges and drag his adversary into court.

Whatever Tilton's motives were, the scandal made a field-day for the atheists and scoffers. With the populace almost as frantic as the principals, even P. T. Barnum's new "Great Roman Hippodrome," on Madison Avenue between 26th and 27th Streets, forerunner of an institution that would be conspicuous in American life after the Beecher scandal was forgotten, could scarcely compete for interest with the greatest free show the country had ever known. Every Sunday overflow crowds milled at the doors of Plymouth Church merely to catch a glimpse of the famous accused, while the auditorium within was packed with lip-licking strangers intent upon catching the slightest word whereby "the greatest preacher the world has seen since St. Paul preached on Mars Hill" might betray his trouble.

Isabella Hooker gave the New York newspapers her correspondence with her brother Thomas, and the door at No. 1 Forest Street closed to her. The clan was forever riven. Dr. Bacon, of New Haven, taking a hand and in a public letter denouncing both Tilton and Francis Moulton as scoundrels—Tilton replying privately with an enormous letter, setting forth his version of the entire affair—Dr. Bacon daring him to publish the letter and risk the consequences. Tilton published it—and nothing happened. Or not the criminal-libel case the public expected. Instead, Henry entered a general denial before a committee of his congregation, which he appointed to investigate the charges. Then, Lib Tilton stultifying Mrs. Stanton by suddenly taking her children and leaving her husband, announcing that she intended to stand by her Pastor! A bewildered public could not understand it; nor could Henry Ward Beecher when, his Committee having thrown

HENRY WARD BEECHER

(At the Time of the Famous Beecher-Tilton Scandal)

"Every Sunday overflow crowds milled at the doors of
Plymouth Church, while the auditorium within was
packed with lip-licking strangers intent upon catching the
slightest word whereby 'the greatest preacher the world
has seen since St. Paul preached on Mars Hill' might betray his trouble." (Page 590.)

out the Tilton charges, his enemies only jeered the more savagely that he had hand-picked his own jury. The distracted man crept to Mrs. Moulton (as she testified under oath) and told her: "I have a powder at home on my library table which I have prepared, which I shall take, and shall sink quietly off as if going to sleep, without a struggle."

Amid such a commotion, with the newspapers of the country that summer carrying little else than the developments of the scandal, Harriet wrote the last chapters of *We and Our Neighbors*. She ended her work at the end of August, received a short visit from Alice Underwood, and then fled with Mary Perkins to Twin Mountain House, where she knew Henry would soon be driven by his hay fever. He had, in fact, written that he wanted to see her there. Soon he came, despairing and shaken, to weep out his misery on this loyal bosom.

Still, the sisters, Harriet and Mary, could not learn much from Henry, question him as they would. He knew little himself. He had adopted the familiar Beecher subterfuge of not reading anything about the case—only such paramount things as his church Committee found it necessary to bring to his attention. His plea was that he could not divide his thoughts between his personal tragedy and his duty to God and his flock. His sisters scolded him for having been too Christlike for his own good. One could overdo even in abiding by the Golden Rule.

Harriet felt that she had to tell somebody outside the family exactly what she thought of the whole terrible affair, and for her confidant she selected Dr. Leonard Bacon, whose intercessions for Henry had shown such an understanding spirit. At the same time, she did not want to be drawn into the noisome business herself. In 1870 she had stood bound to something like this same stake, and she wanted no more of the experience.

"Now, dear Doctor," she wrote to Bacon, "as I know God made you a gentleman before he made you a clergyman, I entrust this note to you, trusting that you will in no way or shape allow it to get into the press. Have no faith in man—let nobody have it to look at—but let me have the satisfaction of speaking my mind to one of my father's friends without fear. I want you to know how I feel about this matter, that is all." And Harriet reinforced this injunction with a postscript: "I am peculiarly situated and must beg that you will not, without consulting me, compromise me in any way before the public about this affair."

Thus throwing herself upon Dr. Bacon's compassion and honour, Harriet wrote to him:

From the knowledge I have always had of the magnanimity of your nature, I have always supposed you to feel on this subject as a just and generous man ought to feel. Now that I at last see by what devilish ingenuity the two conspirators have continued (while binding my brother to honorable silence) to lay this hideous story before one and another influential person in society, I can but wonder at the good providence which has saved him.

That your sagacity three years ago detected the *real* archtraitor, the conspirator who taught Tilton refinements of art unknown before, is like what I have always known of you. You saw at that distance of time the exact spot where the Devil lay, as it has but recently been made manifest to my brother and the Committee.

Read in this light, how generous was your tribute to my brother before the theological class last spring!

You then said that it was a fault in him that he permitted "evil men to know too much of him." But at the time he first became interested in Tilton, he [Tilton] was *not* an evil man. He was a fair and hopeful son, an Absolom; and Henry set his heart on him. When Moulton sought him out and obtruded his management upon him, he was so free [?—this much erased and interlined passage in the autograph letter is obscure] as appeared plausible; and the recommendation he had in Henry's eyes, was that Tilton promised to submit to him, and Moulton boasted that he could save him. He (Henry) could only keep the madman from setting the house on fire and destroying himself and others, and therefore Henry trusted him [Moulton]. But it is my brother's nature, coming straight down to him from his father before him, to give a simplicity of love and trust to a fair-spoken man professing friendship which exposes him to treachery. My father was again and again betrayed by men whom he had trusted in just such an enthusiasm of friendship.

And now, dear Doctor, I confess ingenuously that I felt somewhat impatient at the time of your articles in the "Independent"; but, since I see the secret game that Moulton and Tilton were playing, I am glad, for one, that you forced them to show their hand. The snake has fairly been drawn out of his hole at full length, and *you* have struck at him the most telling blow that has been struck yet. Your article led Butler to this movement for a compromise—which has failed, and which shows the weakness of the enemy.

Three weeks after Dr. Bacon received this letter, the *Christian Union* published its first reference to the Beecher-Tilton scandal. It was a contribution entitled *Bearing False Witness,* and it was a defense of Henry Ward Beecher against the charges now so widely circulated. It was signed, "By a Widely-Known Clergyman."

Harriet wrote another letter from Twin Mountain House. Her faith in the church was triumphant as ever. If a church congregation acted in some dispute or issue, that action must be conclusive upon public opinion. She therefore proposed that Plymouth congregation tender Henry a great welcome home after his vacation and thus demonstrate the faith of his people in his innocence.

But the reception did not still the storm, and to get away from the scandal Harriet fled with her family to Florida at the end of October, the earliest she had ever arrived in Mandarin. When in December Theodore Tilton brought an alienation suit against him, Henry Ward Beecher must have breathed deep with relief. At any rate, this would bring the long nightmare to an end. The linen would all be washed out now, in public, but in an orderly court, under oath, and no more innuendoes and raised eyebrows. For the first time he broke his silence in the *Christian Union,* and in a leading editorial, which he signed with his name, he uttered a defiance of his enemies and promised the public that there would be no compromise.

Neither side wanted a postponement, and the case came to trial in the Brooklyn City Court early in January, 1875. There were days of recess because the ice had stopped the East River ferries, and the New York attorneys could not get across. Before it ended—in disagreement—spring had turned into summer, and a juror had fainted from the heat.

For Harriet the six months were a period of such agony and suspense that she wrote not a word professionally, except for one small sermonette reciting the consolations of the Lord for one going through an ordeal. All she could do was endure and wait for the semi-weekly mail to bring the newspapers, which were running pages of the *verbatim* testimony. The whole festering mess was spread before the public to read; and "nothing," said the *Sun,* "since the outbreak of the Civil War has excited such intense interest all over the United States."

Susan Howard was Harriet's great solace in this time—Susan, who was present and could give her more intimate, sympathetic impressions than the hard appraisals of the courtroom reporters. For the new journalism—essentially the journalism of today—was coming into its own at the Beecher trial, the objective newspaper reporter supplanting the subjective "stated correspondent." Dana was already at the *Sun,* and the Chicago *Tribune* was making its everlasting reputation in its handling of the case.

"I have been quite unwell for two days, and no letter comes!" Harriet cried in one of her letters to Mrs. Howard; and in another: "Faithful friend, cease not to write, for your letters are as cold water to a thirsty soul." She scarcely noticed it when in April *We and Our Neighbors* came to an end in the *Christian Union* and Ford & Co. published the book with advance sales of 17,000 copies. They went North early that year, but the dreadful trial was still in progress, and Harriet did not linger in Brooklyn.

The Beecher-Tilton scandal was the last great dramatic episode in the life of Harriet Beecher Stowe—and it was a part of her life almost as much as if she had been the victim of the slander. "This has drawn on my life, my heart's blood," she wrote to George Eliot the next year. "He [Henry] is myself. I know you are the kind of woman to understand me when I say that I felt a blow at him more than at myself." The affair, too, meant for Harriet and all of them a readjustment of the family relationships. For the Beecher clan split on the question of Henry's guilt, and the line of cleavage was between Roxana Foote's children and those of Harriet Porter; although James, the youngest son, now preaching to mountaineers in an Adirondack wilderness, paid no attention to the case and probably took Henry's innocence for granted.

Edward Beecher, now living in Brooklyn, was one of Henry's chief captains in the struggle. Mary Perkins was as staunch for Henry as Harriet herself. The ineffective Brother William, now retired and living with his married daughters in Chicago, did not count. Charles kept out of it, though he was so much like Harriet and Henry in temperament that he probably remained loyal; but Isabella and Thomas, having taken a public stand with Henry's enemies, had cut themselves off from Henry Ward Beecher and Harriet Beecher Stowe, and probably from Mary Perkins.

The homeless, old Catharine Beecher (she was seventy-five), took care not to express her opinion, whatever it was, aggressively and thus remained friendly with both sides. After four months of administration she had resigned as Principal of the Hartford Seminary, a complete failure, and faced a future of living as a semi-independent pensioner upon her brothers and sisters. When the passions roused by the conflict had somewhat abated, Catharine essayed the rôle of peacemaker.

Though the scandal itself and its effects upon Harriet are part of her life-story, it is not incumbent upon her biographer to enter any opinion on Henry's guilt or innocence. However, it is only fair to state that of the civil jury which disagreed, nine members voted for Henry's innocence, while three held out to the end for his guilt. Harriet told George Eliot afterwards that the foreman of the jury had been offered during the trial a bribe of $10,000 to vote against Henry. The jury reported and was discharged on July 2, 1875. The trial had cost Henry Ward Beecher $118,000. The opinion of Plymouth Church was expressed five days later when the Trustees voted their pastor a salary of $100,000 for the year 1875, "live or die."

The most damning piece of evidence against Henry brought into the trial was his signed confession that his relations with Mrs. Tilton had been improper. His reply, maintained through severe cross-examination, was that he had signed the confession without reading it. The paper had been drawn up by Francis Moulton, and Henry had supposed it was only an agreement whereby he and Theodore Tilton could live at peace with each other. Sceptics fairly shouted their incredulity at this statement, saying that no man as successful as Henry Ward Beecher in his professional and business life could have been so childish. Yet in this narrative we have seen how similarly careless he was in handling his sister's side of the Stowe-Parker controversy, how equally full of trust in the benevolence and good faith of his fellow men. It was entirely in his nature to have signed the confession without reading it.

Since the civil case had ended inconclusively, the public clamour continued for a definite decision. Accordingly a great Church Council was called to re-examine the million words of testimony offered in the trial and to hear any new witnesses who might come forward. Hostile writers then and since have asserted that this was but another jury packed in favour of Henry Ward Beecher; but Lyman Abbott, examining the case dispassionately some years afterwards, wrote that the Council "included many men of strong prejudices against Mr. Beecher on theological grounds, and some men full of suspicions engendered by the trial and public reports." Yet the Council exonerated Henry without a dissenting voice.

Furthermore, William A. Beach, Tilton's chief of counsel, who had believed Beecher guilty when he took the case, asserted publicly later that, as the trial progressed, he felt "that we were a pack of hounds trying in vain to drag down a noble lion." And Justice Neilson, who had presided at the trial, also presided over the public dinner which Brooklyn tendered Henry Ward Beecher on his seventieth birthday. Thus, though the ungodly and the preacher-haters would to the end of their lives believe Beecher to be a lecherous hypocrite, the weight of legal authority rested firmly on his side. There was no doubt where his sister Harriet stood. She wrote to George Eliot:

> He is of a nature so sweet and perfect that, though I have seen him thunderously indignant at moments, I never saw him fretful or irritable—a man who continuously, in every little act of life, is thinking of others, a man that all the children of the street run after, and that every sorrowful, weak, or distressed person looks to as a natural helper. In all this long history there has been no circumstance of his relation to any woman that has not been worthy of himself—pure, delicate, and proper—and I know all sides of it and certainly should not say this, if there were even a misgiving. Thank God, there is none; and I can read my New Testament and feel that by all the Beatitudes my brother is blessed.

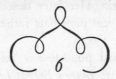

Rainbow at Night

THE emotional ordeal of the trial left Harriet's mind so limp she did no writing that summer. She was at the Twin Mountain House in September in time to meet her vindicated brother. They talked everything over; and Henry told her that he intended to take a more active part in the editorial direction of the *Christian Union*. Lyman Abbott would become his assistant, and Horatio King, of Brooklyn, was coming into the reorganization, as publisher. Henry wanted Harriet to continue to write for the paper; and when, at the end of September, the publisher's statement announced these changes, it added:

> MRS. HARRIET BEECHER STOWE
> will continue to write exclusively for the *Christian Union*. Arrangements
> have already been made for a Thanksgiving as well as a Christmas story
> from her pen. She will also be a frequent contributor to other departments
> of the paper.

Charley Stowe had been graduated from Harvard that spring. Greatly to his father's approval, he wanted to continue post-graduate studies in Germany. Early in the fall they saw him aboard a steamer bound for Europe and the University of Bonn.

Harriet dutifully contributed her Thanksgiving story, a four-part fiction serial with the title, *Deacon Pitkin's Farm*. For her Christmas contribution she sent up from Mandarin a short, Biblical dramatic sketch in six scenes— *Christ's Christmas Gifts*. But she was tired and no longer wanted to write anything. Sweet nothing forever! Her wants were becoming simple; and she had many books in print, each adding its bit of royalty, to support them. Charley's expenses in Germany were not heavy. Harriet herself in 1875 began to grow old-fashioned. *We and Our Neighbors* was her last fling in the up-to-date. Fashion moved by her as she adopted for herself a sort of standard costume, like Queen Victoria. Her later descendants found her perpetual bonnets and shawls and conical petticoats rather eccentric among the shirt-waists and sailor hats of the 1890's.

Early in January Ford had published a collection of her short stories under the title of one of them, *Betty's Bright Idea*. Harriet sent an advance copy to Dr. Holmes for a Christmas present. But she was thinking again that winter about Spiritualism. Calvin had been "wading through" eight volumes of *Die Christliche Mystik,* by Professor J. J. Görres, of the University of Munich, and finding much curious lore in them. What Harriet wrote next to Oliver Wendell Holmes represented what we may take as her final judgment on spirit-communication.

> I have long since come to the conclusion that the marvels of spiritualism are natural, and not supernatural, phenomena—an uncommon working of natural laws. I believe that the door between those *in* the body and those *out* has never in any age been entirely closed, and that occasional percep-tions within the veil are a part of the course of nature, and therefore not miraculous. Of course, such a phase of human experience is very substantial ground for every kind of imposture and superstition, and I have no faith whatever in mediums who practice for money. In their case I think the law of Moses, that forbade consulting those who dealt with "familiar spirits," a very wise one.

Time was slipping by her, and how swiftly she was brought to realize in February, when she was writing to Osgood, who had now taken in H. O. Houghton as his publishing partner. Plymouth Church was setting up its Mayflower Mission in the Brooklyn slums, and Henry was bringing in James Beecher from his mountain parish to take charge of it. The church was to hold a great fair in March to raise money for the Mayflower Mission, and Harriet could think of no donation for herself to make more appropriate than two dozen autographed copies of her *Mayflower*.

Was that book out of print? she asked Osgood; and, if so, wouldn't it be a good idea to issue a new edition to go with her other works? Then she remembered something, and added this postscript: "I trust you are keeping an eye out about renewing the copyright of Uncle Tom." *Uncle Tom* was the great event in her life, and this splendid existence which was hers and which still seemed new to her, dated from that book. But twenty-five years had almost passed since *Uncle Tom* first shook the world, and now she must renew the copyright if she expected to continue to enjoy the royalties from its still steady sale. Time slipped by.

In March, 1876, Harriet wrote her long letter to George Eliot, reciting the history of her association with Henry Ward Beecher from the cradle through his recent victory over the powers of evil. *Daniel Deronda* was running in *Harper's,* and Harriet informed her unseen friend: "Your ancient admirer, who usually goes to bed at eight o'clock, was convicted by me of sitting up after eleven over the last installment of 'Daniel Deronda,' and he is full of it." Before they left Mandarin that spring, George Eliot had replied: "Please offer my reverential love to the Professor, and tell him I am ruthlessly proud of having kept him out of his bed."

It was a time for philosophy that happy and restful winter. Harriet told George Eliot, "I feel myself at last as one who has been playing and picnicking on the shores of life and has waked from a dream late in the afternoon to find that everybody, almost, has gone over to the beyond. And the rest are sorting their things and packing their trunks, and waiting for the boat to come and take them."

At the early date of April 24 Harriet was packing her mundane baggage and waiting for the Charleston boat. The family arrived in New York on May 2, and Harriet stayed in Brooklyn the rest of the month visiting with the Howards and with Henry and Eunice Beecher.

That same month of May, 1876, Isabella Beecher Hooker returned to her Hartford home and began in a dark, secretive way to keep a diary. It was no ordinary diary written in vanity or for amusement or for any of the other reasons that impel people to keep diaries. There had never been any other diary with the purpose of this one. A great and awful day was close at hand when the trumpets of the Lord would sound and Isabella Hooker would be seated in glory and majesty on the world's matriarchal throne. On that day she would leave behind a poor, humdrum, bedazzled family, and she was writing her diary to inform them then how authentic was her title and how thoroughly forewarned she had been of the celestial *coup d'état.*

Once before she had tried to impart her great secret to her husband, John Hooker, as modest and conventional a lawyer as ever walked home through Hartford's streets for his noonday dinner, but had been unable to compass it. She had written him, "I dare not tell you all that I see in the future and know is to come to pass shortly. I would not put it on paper, even if I had time and strength. God knows it, and that is enough—but be sure that *woman's hour* has come." And she wrote, "I find such loving and supporting friends who *believe* that I am raised up to strike this last blow for freedom."

And, still later: "I am every day touched by indications, trivial in themselves, that I am called to a great and holy work whereof no one can prophesy the end."

These letters had been written some years earlier. Now, in the spring of 1876, she had thought of a way whereby she might dare to put her secret on paper—in a confidential diary, to be read by her husband and children *after* the great event. On the cover she warned off the prying eyes of others in words which a superstitious mind might interpret as a curse.

This demented document would have no place in these pages, except that Isabella was sane enough about the ordinary details of existence; and so her chance comments in the diary on Harriet and Henry and Catharine Beecher throw a considerable light on the Beecher family at this time. Her first entry, dated May 11, contains the following, which tells something about the relations of Mark Twain, then writing his *Tom Sawyer,* and the Hartford Beechers:

> Just now Mr. Clemens and Livy called, with Mr. and Mrs. Fuller, of New York, and seemed carried away with the study, which is one memento of our travels. I showed Livy the vases that were associated with her dear father, close by my mother's.

In the same entry there is a reference to Victoria Woodhull, the clairvoyant friend who first told Isabella of her divine call.

> I cannot resist the conviction that the meeting of Victoria and myself in Washington was full of significance, and that she has much to do with the development of my future.

Isabella's spiritual "control" was her mother, Harriet Porter Beecher. Isabella possessed no portrait of her mother, but she did have "an angel of lilies," which was "an engraving brought me by Sister Hattie the first time she went abroad." Isabella could substitute this for her mother's picture and, by concentrating upon her, receive her revelations from the other world.

Harriet had returned to Hartford on June 1, and at the end of July Catharine Beecher arrived for her usual summer visit with the Stowes. On August 5, which happened to be Belle's thirty-fifth wedding anniversary, she entered in the diary:

> John was moved to write this week to Mrs. Stanton on the letter to Professor Phelps which Sister Catharine gave me to read.

This was a letter written by Harriet to the President of Andover Seminary and, apparently, one criticizing Elizabeth Cady Stanton for her hostile activities during the uproar of the scandal. Isabella's entry continued:

> Mrs. Stanton's reply this week is so noble, and I am glad he [John Hooker] has entered the lists as her champion. At first I wondered that he should have consented to talk with Catharine, at her request, as he did one day, and when she was very unreasonable and excited. But I soon saw that he was probably guided, for wise reasons—and so in his letter to Mrs. S., of which I should not have approved, if I had known he was writing. I shall be interested in watching developments, but I take no part; and when Catharine said to me, "Belle, weren't you comforted by Harriet's letter to Professor Phelps?", I said, "Catharine, I will not answer a question from you concerning Henry," and then invited her kindly to come into the other room.

Belle's spirits had assured her that the day would dawn when Henry would come on his knees to her, begging her forgiveness, and she confidently awaited the hour of reconciliation. On the morning of August 7 she awoke to find herself communing with her mother and lay in bed for an hour until the communication was broken off. Later in the morning Catharine called. Belle had to go out to mail a letter; but Catharine said she was tired and would lie on the sofa. Then Belle, remembering the "influence" of the early morning there, took Catharine to her own bed, adding the comment in her diary: "I feel that my dear mother remembers Catharine with love and wants to help her to meet her own dear mother and Mr. Fisher." Though Catharine Beecher was seventy-six years old, the family still remembered her broken romance with Professor Fisher. The diary entry gave the aftermath:

> She came down refreshed and asked me to come up that evening and play croquet with her and Harriet. I promised, wondering at the request but determined to meet it cordially; and now I see the influence, for they have not asked me before, though playing constantly.

Isabella, however, seems to have doubted the genuineness of the influence after all, or perhaps she had an inkling that Sister Harriet's welcome would not be quite so cordial as Catharine, strong-headed as ever in her old age and urging peace within the clan, insisted. At any rate, Sister Belle did not attend the croquet match, pleading weariness and sending her son Ned with her regrets.

On Sunday, August 13, Isabella brought in a medium and held a séance in her house. The spirits of various relatives attended: Lyman Beecher "in prayer," "my mother, Mother Hooker, Father Hooker . . . and then Fred Stowe, whom we all thought Louis Spencer being scalped by Indians (but it was delirium tremens, no doubt)."

At a September séance (Mrs. Roberts, medium) the spirit of Lord Byron told Belle to take a letter from Mrs. Roberts' pocket. "It proved," Isabella wrote, "to be from Lady Byron to Mrs. Stowe. This was on —— [the dash is Isabella's]; and when I told him I should not give it to my sister, he said, with a curious, scornful look passing over her [the medium's] face, he knew very well I would not."

This document, for what it is worth, throws the only light we have on Mrs. Stowe's summer of 1876. When next we hear from Harriet herself, it is autumn, and she is in Florida writing to Charley at Bonn about what a rough passage they had coming down.

Almost to her astonishment, Harriet found herself that winter entrapped in the meshes of another serial story. In New York she had transacted some important business. For one thing, she had arranged with Ford (now Fords, Howard & Co.) to bring out for the Christmas trade a collection of her religious writings under the title, *Footsteps of the Master.* (Counting collaborations with Catharine, it was her thirtieth book.) Then, too, Henry had sold his interest in the *Christian Union,* and, no doubt, Harriet's along with it, and at the end of the year was turning over the editorship to Lyman Abbott.

The reorganization was amicable. Henry Ward Beecher was in his sixties, and, after the long strain of his trial, felt that he should not try to do so much in the future. (He was having dizzy spells and feared a stroke, and, besides, he still had to write the second volume of his *Life of Jesus the Christ,* for which he had accepted $25,000 as an advance of royalties.) It may well have been that as part of the bargain the new owners demanded another serial by Mrs. Stowe. She had the nucleus of something that might do —a four-part Christmas story she had already written for the paper, *Dolly's First Christmas Day,* which was, in fact, a fictionized account of her own discovery, as a small child in Litchfield, that the Episcopalians celebrated a day called Christmas. She proposed to expand this into a complete novel.

Thus, while most novelists are autobiographical in their earlier works, Harriet reserved her fictional autobiography for the nostalgia of her old age.

The brain and imagination that had already produced so much, still held another great story; for the novel that resulted, *Poganuc People,* takes rank with her major works. She herself was Dolly, the "odd little girl" of the story. *Poganuc People* held much of the charm of *Oldtown Folks,* and it is today invaluable as an authentic picture of New England village life in the early decades of the Nineteenth Century.

She did not press the writing of *Poganuc People,* for the *Christian Union* did not begin its serialization until the end of the year 1877, and it was not a long novel in comparison with others she had written. However, the days of impromptu magazine publication, when popular authors wrote their instalments week by week or month by month, were over. Editors now insisted upon complete manuscripts in hand before beginning publication.

There was no hint of age or weariness in Harriet's pen when, in February, 1877, she defended Florida in the New York *Tribune.* A correspondent had written to that paper complaining that Yankee tourists and settlers in Florida exposed themselves to ill-treatment by the natives. Harriet wrote an emphatic denial of the charge:

> I came down to Florida the year after the war and have held property in Duval County, on the St. Johns River, ever since. In all this time I have received not even an incivility from any native Floridian.
> Duval County is largely settled by northern people who have come here since the war, and I have yet to learn of any act of disobligingness or incivility as happening to any northern settler on the part of native Floridians. So far as they are to be observed in this county, the Floridians are a remarkably quiet, peaceable, and honest set of people who believe in the Apostolic injunction, "Study to be quiet and mind your own business."
> It is quite true that they had at first no very warm love for northern settlers, but they have always treated them justly and fairly. That they should prefer to associate with themselves and not with strangers was but natural. It is true also that there was after the war a good deal of bitter feeling, that people who had lost property and grown poor were sore and uncomfortable, and that it was not a pleasant thing for people who had always owned slaves to give them up and go to work themselves; but this feeling has never, so far as we know, expressed itself in any way to prevent settlers from being made comfortable in their midst.

Those same sore and uncomfortable people were even then on their knees praying that the Electoral Commission would decide the disputed 1876 election in favour of Tilden and end the Reconstruction; but Harriet, as unquestioning a Republican as the followers of Lincoln were ever to be, rejoiced when the Commission, dividing on party lines, seated Hayes. On Inauguration Day she wrote to Alice Underwood in Washington:

We have shared the political anxiety. Today, I suppose, it will be happily ended, and tomorrow morning will dawn on R. Hayes the newly elected President of the United States. I hope his reign may be one of *real* reconstruction, that the North and the South may at last come to understand and esteem one another *for what they are,* and that there may be what there has never been before—a *real* Union. I hope the distinction between North and South may at last fade out in the real, genuine unity of free society.

Otherwise it was a silent year for Harriet, as she wrote along on her *Poganuc People.* The next glimpse we have of her comes through a pair of malicious eyes. In January, 1878, an engaging young Kentucky writer, "Sylvia Sunshine" (Amanda M. Brooks), attended church one Sunday morning in Jacksonville. She wrote of it:

Mrs. Harriet Beecher Stowe is here today from her home in Mandarin, for the purpose of attending church. Dr. Stowe, her husband, accompanies her, as he preaches. When they both entered the Southern Methodist Church a slight rustle was heard in the congregation, and a few persons left the house. Mr. and Mrs. Uncle Tom were more than a Sabbath dose for some of the Jacksonville community. Harriet B. has no resemblance to a perpetrator of discord or scandal, or one who has swayed the divining rod of Abolitionism with sufficient potency to immortalize herself with many coming generations, or probed the private life of a man who, during the period of his checkered existence, never carved out virtue for his shrine. Three snowy curls on each side of her face gave her a matronly look, and her stout-built frame, well covered with flesh, a substantial appearance.

The service was opened by a very long prayer from Dr. Stowe, after which he preached a purely orthodox sermon on the subject of godliness. Mrs. Harriet had confidence in the ability of her husband, she knew the discourse would be right without her vigilant eye, and she went to sleep. Like other sleepers, she nodded naturally; her digits were concealed beneath kid covers, and thrusting at no one. She looked the picture of content, and was no doubt dreaming of that far-off, beautiful country where those who create dissensions and stir up strife can never enter.

Time was slipping by for Harriet, and how it marred people—families! Life began so beautifully for all, so hopefully! Young families were like groups of saplings, each one strong and lovely and perfect; then orchard or grove grew up, and there was not a tree uncrippled by wind or lightning stroke, scarcely a leaf not distorted by hail or blight or sting of insect. It had been that way with the Beechers, starting out so young and brave and noble; and now Tom an enemy, Isabella throwing in with the evil-minded, and Henry, Christlike as ever but forever marked by the great trouble.

Other people's families—Frank Howard dead in young manhood of consumption; and that trouble Joe Howard had been in, during the war. Harriet's own family—Fred, a drunkard, and gone; Georgie, leading her brilliant, brittle life in Cambridge, burning her candle at both ends, consorting with stage people, keeping her admirers at bay. Even a mother as tolerant as Harriet might think Georgie took too much wine. And Georgie had never come to see Mandarin!

And now in the late winter of 1878 a shocking trouble for them all—one of Harriet's favourite nephews, Mary Perkins's son-in-law, a rich and supposedly upright citizen of Hartford, a confessed defaulter and gone to prison! Harriet wrote frankly about it to Alice Underwood, who had met the Perkinses when visiting Harriet in Hartford.

Life was taking its toll of them. On May 12, 1878, Catharine Beecher died suddenly of an apoplectic stroke at the home of her half-brother, Thomas K. Beecher, of Elmira. It was the first break in the phalanx since George was killed so many years before. Perhaps it was as well for Harriet that she was a thousand miles away and could not attend the funeral, thus being spared the embarrassment of meeting Tom. But she felt as if a mother had been taken from her.

They went North that spring in time to meet Charley, back from Bonn and ready for ordination—and simultaneously announcing his engagement to Miss Susan Munroe, of Cambridge, whom he had met when a student at Harvard. James R. Osgood was going to Europe, one of his projects being to secure materials for a history of *Uncle Tom's Cabin* in its world career.

Poganuc People, in the *Christian Union,* was showing that Harriet's pen had not yet lost its power or popularity. Indeed, Osgood & Houghton were so impressed with its quality that they outbid the Fords, in New York, for its book publication; and now that nice Mr. Howells, who had been so kind about translating Harriet's Italian quotations, had become editor of *The Atlantic Monthly,* and that fall he invited Harriet to contribute again to the magazine.

It was quite like old times, and Harriet fell to work with considerable enthusiasm. Before she left Hartford for Florida in the autumn of 1878 she turned out two short stories for the *Atlantic—The Parson's Race Horse* and *A Student's Sea Story*. But it was a final jetting of the flame. In the languorous air of Florida it died out, never to revive again. During the next two years she wrote sporadically for the *Christian Union* a few unimportant stories and sketches, but the two *Atlantic* stories constituted her last significant work in fiction. However, *A Student's Sea Story* was one of Harriet's best short stories. In subsequent editions of her works, Houghton, Mifflin & Co. added it to the end of her *Oldtown Fireside Stories*.

Poganuc People was out as a book at the end of 1878, and Harriet as usual sent a copy to Dr. Holmes. He sent her a note of acknowledgment, and she replied:

Dear Doctor:—I wish I could give to you and Mrs. Holmes the exquisite charm of this morning. My window is wide open; it is a lovely, fresh, sunny day, and a great orange tree hung with golden balls closes the prospect from my window. The tree is about thirty feet high, and its leaves fairly glisten in the sunshine.

* * * *

I feel with you that we have come into the land of leave-taking. Hardly a paper but records the death of some of Mr. Stowe's associates. But the river is not so black as it seems, and there are clear days when the opposite shore is plainly visible, and now and then we catch a strain of music, perhaps even a gesture of recognition.

The land of leave-taking; and in England Mary Ann Evans, better known as George Eliot, had just taken her leave of George Henry Lewes. Harriet wrote her friend one of her letters of condolence. It was not until April that George Eliot replied:

My Dear Friend:—I have been long without sending you any sign, but my heart has been going out to you and your husband continually as among the chief of the many kind beings who have given me their tender fellow-feeling in my last earthly sorrow. When your first letter came, I was unable to read any letters, and did not for a long time see what you had sent me. . . . Thank you for telling me that you have the comfort of seeing your son in a path that satisfies your best wishes for him. I like to think of your having family joys. One of the prettiest photographs of a child that I possess is one of your sending to me. . . .

It was the last letter Harriet ever received from George Eliot.

A FAMILY GROUP AT MANDARIN

Eliza Mrs. Stowe Charles Stowe Prof. Stowe Eunice Beecher Hatty

"I hate to leave my calm Isle of Patmos, where the world is not." (Page 558.)

But while her generation was going, another was fitting into its place; and on May 26 Charley and Susie Munroe were going to be married. "I wish you could see our roses," Harriet wrote to Mrs. Fields. "Everything is coming in bloom—roses, lilies, and a carnival of flowers—and we have to pull up stakes and go to the chill North so as to be ready for the wedding. Well, so goes life!" And Harriet told Annie: "Georgie has taken a house at Nahant for the summer. Isn't that nice? She is much better."

Charley was a comfort to his parents—the only one of their four sons who proved to be that—going along, as he was, in the path they would have chosen for him—and successfully, for the bridal pair were going to live in Saco, Maine, where the Rev. Charles had secured his first ministerial charge.

Harriet spent most of the summer of 1879, she wrote Annie Fields later, getting the young couple settled in their new parsonage, but she found time to write a few stories for the *Christian Union*. An uneventful year followed. At the end of 1880 both Annie and Jamie Fields brought out books of their verses. Much as Harriet loved Annie Fields, she did not like Annie's verse, which was much too subtle and shaded and indefinite for an elderly lady who preferred beefsteak and potatoes in her literary ration; and Harriet, too, had reached an age when she did not mind telling Annie, though delicately, what she thought. She wrote from Hartford on December 2, 1880; and, for all its affectionate tone, the letter must have wounded Annie, who would probably have preferred the unqualified praise of Harriet Beecher Stowe for her poetry to that of any other person.

James T. Fields's book was his *Ballads and Other Verses*. Harriet found it waiting for her when she reached Mandarin; and she needed its note of cheer, for she found something else, too, not so pleasant. One of those periodical freezes, which were to extinguish orange culture in northern Florida until hardier varieties of trees brought it back again, was long over-due in the St. Johns River country; and in December, 1880, it came. When Harriet stepped off the boat, she wept at the destruction. Her whole orange crop was gone—and it was not only the loss of the beauty of the fruit and the pleasure she took in it, but also the loss of a revenue on which she had come to rely.

She had heard that James T. Fields was coming back to be editor of the *Atlantic* again. That *would* seem like old times. It was about the *Atlantic* that she wanted to consult him, in her New Year's letter. One from whom they had all taken leave during 1880 was George Eliot, two years after the death of Lewes, and married at the end to their mutual intimate, J. W. Cross.

I thought of writing an article on George Eliot for the "Atlantic." I have quite an interesting series of letters from her. They show her to be so fine and noble. The only hesitation is one of delicacy.

Do you or Annie know whether any marriage ceremony of *any* kind passed between her and Mr. Lewes? We Americans are perfectly willing to accept, if there was, even though the laws of England would not. Do you know anything about this Mr. Cross? Would he return my letters to me, if I wrote for them? And would you write?

Fields could give her no assurances of any marriage, and perhaps for that reason, perhaps from lassitude, she dropped the subject.

On a June morning in Hartford Harriet opened her eyes to the fact that she had stepped into "the long valley of age," as Annie Fields said. She was seventy. In November she was writing to Annie from Mandarin:

I am come to those years where I may hope before long to join that circle of friends beyond the river, that is every year growing larger and more inviting. All the companions of my early youth, with but here and there an exception, are there—and some of my children. Of four sons, but one is now living—living here, I mean. I trust to find them all again.

She had reason to write to Annie in that vein, for Jamie Fields had gone to join the circle, too. It was part of Harriet's grief that she had never been able to induce him and Annie to visit her in Florida.

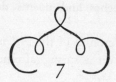

7

Happy Birthday

IT WAS a delightfully consistent touch that the nation should celebrate Harriet Beecher Stowe's seventieth birthday on her seventy-first. Harriet herself had always been just about that far from complete accuracy in her own dates and spellings, and now history had its little joke with her and paid her back in kind.

The *Atlantic's* observance of the seventieth birthdays of its original contributors was becoming something of a national institution. John Greenleaf Whittier had had his on December 17, 1877, and Oliver Wendell Holmes had followed in 1879. (The *Atlantic* indeed erred slightly in the date of the Doctor's celebration, giving him his "breakfast" on December 3, 1879, whereas he had reached his seventieth milestone on August 29. Although her correspondence makes no reference to it, it is probable that Harriet took in the Holmes Breakfast in Boston on her way to New York to catch the Charleston boat.)

Whittier's birthday celebration in 1877 had set the pace. Whittier was a bachelor, and the *Atlantic* gave him a "stag" dinner. In the advance publicity one seems to detect the hand of a press-agent, though, of course, such a functionary was not known then by that name. At any rate, a story coursed through the pages of the American newspapers to the effect that the lady contributors to the *Atlantic,* thus inconsiderately excluded from the party, were in revolt. Mrs. Stowe, Harriet Prescott Spofford, Gail Hamilton, "H. H." (Helen Hunt Jackson), Rebecca Harding Davis, Louisa M. Alcott and a few others had entered into a conspiracy. Each, though not invited to the Whittier Dinner, sent a note of regrets; and each note contained the intimation that the lady contributors were about to found a new, all-women magazine to give competition to the *Atlantic.* According to J. C. Derby, a voluminous writer on the literary and publishing world of that period, the threat had the *Atlantic's* owners a little worried. They were not quite certain if it was a joke. At any rate, the publicity focused attention on the venerable Quaker poet, and the speeches and poems delivered and recited at his dinner were national news.

One can imagine the old cronies of the *Atlantic* sitting over their coffee-cups at the Parker House on a spring afternoon in 1882, gossiping and exchanging reminiscences.

"Now, there's Hattie Stowe down in Hartford," one would say. "Isn't she getting along towards seventy?"

Dr. Holmes was quite certain that she was. The Doctor would be seventy-three that summer, and he had always been under the impression that he was three years older than Mrs. Stowe. Furthermore, since his head was a repository of odd facts about everybody, he knew that her birthday was June 14th. Accordingly, a letter was dispatched, probably to Florida, and in due time came the reply that the lady addressed would not deny the impeachment. She would be seventy years old on June 14, 1882—and she could keep the mental reservation, "at least." Harriet, too, may have felt a little piqued that the *Atlantic* had overlooked the true date. Since she was no longer a contributor, she had too much pride, or vanity, to notify the magazine in advance of her seventieth birthday. However, she had been through too many emotional crises in her life to be upset by a trivial slight like this, and she accepted the honour in the spirit in which it was offered.

It seems probable that Mr. Houghton, for one, suspected or knew that Harriet was more than seventy. On the great day he acted as master of ceremonies, and he opened the formal proceedings with the words: "We are come together again to celebrate a birthday, but what is the number of the birthday we will not too closely inquire." However, the introduction made no impression upon Dr. Holmes. The Doctor had become quite deaf in his old age, and he remained firm in the conviction that Mrs. Stowe was just seventy.

Whittier's celebration had been a dinner, Holmes's a breakfast, but the first lady contributor to be honoured (Julia Ward Howe's turn would come later) must have a garden party. Harriet's friend, ex-Governor Claflin, of Massachusetts, offered his beautiful summer home at Newtonville, west of Boston, for the occasion. The affair was announced—everybody of importance in the American literary scene invited—several hundred invitations.

Some of these invitations implied duty for the recipients. As the foremost "occasional" poet of America and also as an old and intimate friend of Mrs. Stowe, Dr. Holmes, for one, would be expected to produce something special. The Doctor had never for one moment since 1852 doubted the authenticity of the inspiration behind *Uncle Tom's Cabin*. That a New England village housewife could in one divine effort pick up the universal tongue and speak evenly and with the same effect to all mankind was to him one of the great miracles of our history. The Doctor had an exalted theme with which to work. He knew that the Alexanders and Caesars and Napoleons came along through the ages oftener than the Homers and Shakespeares and Mrs. Stowes.

So one day, in plenty of time before the occasion, the Doctor sat down with his scratch-pad and pen and an idea, and he wrote down a title—*At The Summit*. He followed this with the lines:

> Sister, we bid you welcome—we who stand
> On the high table-land . . .

Not bad for a start! The Doctor thought of old age as a plateau attained. How good the air was up here, cleaned of the mists of passion, of the fogs of prejudice and dusts of strife and battles! Here one could really fill his lungs; here one could see the great verities in perspective and truly evaluate life at last. The Doctor kept on with the theme, and in time could read his completed poem:

AT THE SUMMIT

> Sister, we bid you welcome—we who stand
>   On the high table-land;
> We who have climbed life's slippery Alpine slope
> And rest, still leaning on the staff of hope,
> Looking along the silent Mer de Glace,
> Leading our footsteps where the dark crevasse
> Yawns in the frozen sea we all must pass—
>   Sister, we clasp your hand.
>
> Rest with us in the hour that Heaven has lent
>   Before the swift descent.
> Look! the warm sunbeams kiss the glittering ice;
> See! next the snowdrift blooms the edelweiss;
> The mated eagles fan the frosty air;
> Life, beauty, love, around us everywhere,
> And, in their time, the darkening hours that bear
>   Sweet memories, peace, content.

Thrice welcome! Shining names our missals shew
    Amid their rubrics' glow;
But search the blazoned record's starry line,
What halo's radiance fills the page like thine?
Thou who by some celestial clew couldst find
The way into the hearts of all mankind,
On thee, already canonized, enshrined,
    What more can Heaven bestow?

As the Doctor read this over, perhaps his old eyes brimmed as he thought once more of the miracle of that little, homely, shabby country woman who had found the celestial clew—still as homespun as ever in her tastes and expressions, still, for all her travels and honours, as rustic as one of her own characters in *Oldtown Folks*. The poem was good. By George, it was too good for a picnic—and its solemnity would be out of key. Dr. Holmes decided to sell *At The Summit* to the *Atlantic* and write something else more in keeping with lawns and shade, silk hats, parasols, and lemonade.

Something more in the comic spirit. What was it old Archimedes said about a lever big enough, and he could move the world? Δὸς ποῦ στῶ καὶ τον κοσμον κινήσω. Capital! Hattie Stowe had found the lever that was only hypothesis with Archimedes, and she had moved the world with it, too. And the στῶ, spelled out, of course, *sto,* in English letters, afforded the Doctor a learned pun. He kept on with the idea and produced this:

If every tongue that speaks her praise,
For whom I shape my tinkling phrase,
    Were summoned to the table,
The vocal chorus that would meet,
Of mingling accents harsh or sweet
From every land and tribe, would beat
    The polyglots of Babel.

Briton and Frenchman, Swede and Dane,
Turk, Spaniard, Tartar of Ukraine,
    Hidalgo, Cossack, Cadi,
High Dutchman and Low Dutchman, too,
The Russian serf, the Polish Jew,
Arab, Armenian, and Mantchoo
    Would shout, "We know the lady!"

Know her! Who knows not Uncle Tom
And her he learned his gospel from
    Has never heard of Moses!
Full well the brave, black hand we know
That gave to Freedom's grasp the hoe
That killed the weed that used to grow
    Among the Southern roses.

When Archimedes, long ago,
Spake out so grandly, "*Dos pou sto*:
    Give me a place to stand on,
I'll move your planet for you now,"—
He little dreamed or fancied how
The *sto* at last should find its *pou*
    For woman's faith to land on.

Her lever was the wand of art,
Her fulcrum was the human heart,
    Whence all unfailing aid is.
She moved the earth! Its thunders pealed;
Its mountains shook, its temples reeled;
The blood-fed fountains were unsealed,
    And Moloch sank to Hades.

All through the conflict, up and down,
Marched Uncle Tom and Old John Brown—
    One ghost, one form ideal.
And which was false, and which was true,
And which was mightier of the two,
The wisest sibyl never knew,
    For both alike were real.

Sister, the holy maid does well
Who counts her beads in convent cell,
    Where pale devotion lingers;
But she who serves the sufferer's needs
May trust the Lord will count her beads,
    As well as human fingers.

When Truth herself was Slavery's slave,
Thy hand the prisoned suppliant gave
    The rainbow wings of fiction;
And Truth, who soared, descends today
Bearing an angel's wreath away,
Its lilies at thy feet to lay
    With heaven's own benediction.

That other first-class occasional poet, Mr. Whittier, was also a close friend of Mrs. Stowe—they had a common interest, unshared by the hard-headed Dr. Holmes, in Planchette writing—and he, too, was exceptionally inspired in his birthday verses to her:

> Thrice welcome from the land of flowers
> And golden-fruited orange bowers
> To this sweet, green-turfed June of ours,
> To her who in our evil time
> Dragged into light the nation's crime
> With strength beyond the strength of men
> And, mightier than their sword, her pen;
> To her who world-wide entrance gave
> To the log cabin of the slave,
> Made all his wrongs and sorrows known
> And all earth's languages his own!
> Welcome from each and all to her
> Whose Wooing of the Minister
> Revealed the warm heart of the man
> Beneath the creed-bound Puritan,
> And taught the kinship of the love
> Of man below and God above;
> To her, whose vigorous pencil-strokes
> Sketched into life her Oldtown Folks;
> Whose Fireside Stories, grave or gay,
> In quaint Sam Lawson's vagrant way
> With old New England's flavor rife—
> Waifs from her rude, idyllic life—
> And racy as the legends old
> By Chaucer or Boccaccio told.
>
> To her who keeps through change of place
> And time, her native strength and grace
> Alike where warm Sorrento smiles
> Or where, by birchen-shaded isles
> Whose summer winds have shivered o'er
> The icy drift of Labrador,
> She lifts to light the priceless Pearl
> Of Harpswell's angel-beckoned girl—
> To her at three-score years and ten
> Be tributes of the tongue and pen;
> Be honor, praise, and heart-thanks given,
> The loves of earth, the hopes of heaven!

Ah, dearer than the praise that stirs
The air today, our love is hers!
She needs no guarantee of fame,
Whose own is linked with Freedom's name.
Languages after ours shall keep
Her memory living, while we sleep;
The waves that wash our gray coast-lines,
The winds that rock the Southern pines
Shall sing of her; the unending years
Shall tell her tale in unborn ears.
And when with sins and follies past
Are numbered color-hate and caste,
White, black, and red shall own as one
The noblest work by woman done.

The invitations for June 14, 1882, read: "From 3 to 7," and some two hundred guests were assembled at "The Old Elms," as Governor Claflin's country seat was named, when the collation was served. Elizabeth Stuart Phelps was present; and in her memoirs she described it as an occasion when "literature did honor to the foremost woman of America." Miss Phelps added: "The one or two exceptions, of the school which does not call *Uncle Tom's Cabin* literature, were scarcely missed."

Her statement was somewhat exaggerated; for, though the company which attended the garden-party was distinguished, there were a good many conspicuous absentees. Yet the party was brilliant enough. Besides Holmes, Whittier, and Miss Phelps, there were present: Lyman Abbott, Bronson Alcott, Thomas Bailey Aldrich, Arlo Bates, Rose Terry Cooke, William Dean Howells, Lucy Larcom, Frank B. Sanborn, President Alice Freeman of Wellesley College, and many lesser luminaries. Frances Hodgson Burnett came all the way up from Washington for the party. The widowed Annie Fields was in Europe that spring, but she sent a poem.

Among those who sent regrets were Mark Twain, Louisa M. Alcott, Henry James, John Hay, Julia Ward Howe, Francis Parkman, Murat Halstead, President Eliot, Thomas Wentworth Higginson, Mary Mapes Dodge, Rebecca Harding Davis, and Wendell Phillips. James Russell Lowell sent a letter from the Legation in London.

The Beecher family turned out, too. Edward, Henry Ward, and Charles were there, as was Mary Perkins and—almost a member of the family—John Tasker Howard, of Brooklyn. The irrepressible Isabella Hooker lugged her husband up from Hartford, indicating that by this time, perhaps, bygones had been let to be bygones. We may be sure, however, that Eunice Beecher did not speak to Isabella, nor did Henry Ward Beecher, either. Brother William, in Chicago, sent regrets, as did Thomas K. Beecher, from near-by Elmira. His letter held a bitter note:

> The Uncle Tom which the children of the author first knew regrets his inability to share in the festivities of the 14th inst., to which you invite him.

There is no mention of the twins in the list of guests, but the rest of the Stowe family was there—Calvin, Georgiana Allen and her husband, and Charley and Susie, down from Saco, Maine. With them came Susie's parents from Cambridge—Mr. and Mrs. Charles W. Munroe.

Houghton, Mifflin & Co., as Calvin undoubtedly remarked, did the thing up brown. On the lawn they had erected a large marquee and had imported from Boston the Germania Band and the Beethoven Club, and also Mrs. Humphrey Allen, as soloist. With such musical resources, Harriet would probably have preferred a good, rousing hymn to the tra-la-las of any Madame Thingumbob.

Dr. Holmes was "a happy boy all day," Elizabeth Phelps reported; but Miss Phelps concentrated her light on Harriet, who that day "had dignity, repose, and a certain dreaminess and aloofness of manner characteristic of her," blended with an air of peace and happiness. At five o'clock the company assembled in the marquee, Harriet taking a modest chair well back on the platform.

It was like old-fashioned times, when Henry Ward Beecher rose to respond for his sister, after Mr. Houghton's address of welcome.

Henry, as if a little in awe of this literary and critical audience, made a graceful and witty speech in response. It was on this occasion that he made his remark that he had written *Norwood* to prove he could not have written *Uncle Tom's Cabin*. But at the end he relapsed into his more treacly manner:

> Of course, you all sympathize with me today, but, standing in this place, I do not see your faces more clearly than I see those of my father and mother. Her I only knew as a mere babe-child. He was my teacher and my companion. A more guileless soul than he, a more honest one, more free from envy, from jealousy, and from selfishness, I never knew. Though he thought he was great by his theology, everybody else knew he was great by his religion. My mother is to me what the Virgin Mary is to a devout Catholic. She was a woman of great nature, profound as a philosophical

thinker, great in argument, with a kind of intellectual imagination, diffident, not talkative—in which respect I take after her—the woman who gave birth to Mrs. Stowe, whose graces and excellences she probably more than any of her children—we number but twelve—has possessed. I suppose that in bodily resemblance, perhaps, she is not like my mother, but in mind I presume she is most like her. I thank you for my father's sake and for my mother's sake for the courtesy, the friendliness, and the kindness which you give to Mrs. Stowe.

Whittier, though present, was too infirm to read his own lines effectively and Frank Sanborn performed the service for him. Next, Dr. Holmes arose and, before reading his poem, he told the audience how he became acquainted with *Uncle Tom's Cabin*. He was engrossed in Dickens' latest novel but opened the much-discussed *Uncle Tom* out of curiosity to see what it was like. He read a few paragraphs, then laid aside his Dickens and read the American novel through its last page before he did anything else.

Adeline Dutton T. Whitney, of Boston, a voluminous but now forgotten writer of verse and children's books, read a poem. Dr. Holmes read Elizabeth Stuart Phelps's poem for her. It was Georgiana Stowe Allen's turn; and Georgie, with her queer-looking eyes, rose and handed her manuscript to her rector-husband to read. Georgie's poetical effort was no worse nor better than any of the other offerings, except those of the two masters. Annie Fields's poem was entirely undistinguished. Charlotte F. Bates's began:

> England has Eliot, France has Sand, to show:
> America, her Harriet Beecher Stowe.

John T. Trowbridge, a poet best remembered today for his *Darius Green and His Flying Machine,* read a poem written for the occasion. It was *The Cabin,* and it was published later in the *Youth's Companion.* Three or four guests, Edward Beecher one of them, made brief speeches, and then the programme seemed to hesitate. The day was gone when a woman might not with propriety speak at a public gathering—and the Chairman had hinted that Mrs. Stowe might be induced to speak. Now the hand-clapping continued until she consented to step forward on the platform; and as she did so, every one rose, and all remained standing while Harriet delivered the only speech she ever made in her life.

Many eyes had been wet that day at the beauty of the tributes, but the one who seemed the least moved was Harriet Beecher Stowe. She had accepted the honour as imperturbably as she had received the vast ovations of Scotland and London. She was, in fact, beginning now to withdraw within herself—obeying that instinct which cropped out in so many of her later letters, which no one was to show to anybody, lest she be drawn into public controversy—beginning to assume her final phase as the inscrutable sphinx of Hartford, whom even her own children scarcely knew. Long before Harriet Beecher Stowe died, she had become to the young, oncoming generations a vanishing figure of the past, she was so silent at the end, so immobile.

Now, as she faced the last audience she would ever face, her voice was calm and so strong and clear it carried easily to all the two hundred people in the marquee. She said:

I wish to say that I thank all my friends from my heart—that is all.

She hesitated here, as if she would stop with that, then suddenly went on:

And one thing more—and that is, if any of you have doubt, or sorrow, or pain—if you doubt about this world—just remember what God has done. Just remember that this great sorrow of slavery has gone—gone by, forever. I see it every day at the South. I see these people growing richer and richer. I see men very happy in their lowly lot; but, to be sure, you must have patience with them. They are not perfect, but have their faults, and they are serious faults in the view of white people. But they are very happy, that is evident; and they do know how to enjoy themselves—a great deal more than you do. An old Negro friend in our neighbourhood has got a new, nice two-story house, and an orange grove, and a sugar-mill. He has got a lot of money, besides. Mr. Stowe met him one day, and he said, "I have got twenty head of cattle, four head of hoss, forty head of hen, and I have got ten children—*all mine, every one mine.*" Well, that is a thing that a black man could not say once; and this man was sixty years old before he could say it. With all the faults of the coloured people, take a man and put him down with nothing but his hands, and how many could say as much as that? I think they have done well.

A little while ago they had at his house an evening festival for their church, and raised fifty dollars. We white folks took our carriages, and, when we reached the house, we found it fixed nicely. Every one of his daughters knew how to cook. They had a good place for the festival. Their suppers were spread on little white tables with nice clean cloths on them. People paid fifty cents for supper. They got between fifty and sixty dollars and had one of the best frolics you could imagine. They had also for supper ice-cream, which they made themselves.

That is the sort of thing I see going on around me. Let us never doubt. Everything that ought to happen is going to happen.

The invited absent sent numerous letters of praise for Mrs. Stowe, and some of these were read aloud to the company. Rutherford B. Hayes wrote from Fremont, Ohio. John W. De Forest, the Civil War historian, "put Mrs. Stowe at the head of all living American novelists." Edward Eggleston spoke of the kindness she had always shown to younger and less famous writers. One letter was unexpected. It was on the letterhead of the New York *Observer,* and it said:

No lady has done more by her pen to make a distinctively American literature than Mrs. Stowe, and every true American is proud to know that among women there is no name in letters more widely known to fame than hers. With many thanks for your invitation, I am very truly yours,

S. Irenaeus Prime.

The land of leave-taking was a land of peace-making, too.

Two letters came from the South. From New Orleans George W. Cable, himself a Confederate veteran, wrote:

To join friends in rejoicing over the continuance on earth of one who has earned the gratitude of two races of humanity, is greater than the measure of my cup. I can only send you: Blessings on the day when Harriet Beecher Stowe was born.

And from Atlanta came this from Joel Chandler Harris:

I owe a great deal, in one way and another, to the author of *Uncle Tom's Cabin.* In 1862, when quite a youngster, I chanced to get hold of a copy of the book, and it made a more vivid impression upon my mind than anything I have ever read since. It may interest you to know that I read it on the plantation where Uncle Remus held forth, and within a stone's throw of where ex-Secretary Seward taught school, when he was a young man.

When the party ended, most of the guests lingered to say something personal to Harriet, while Mr. Howells gathered up all the poems and letters and reports of speeches, to be published in a special supplement to the July *Atlantic.* It was the only supplement the *Atlantic Monthly* had ever published.

In the August *Atlantic* appeared Dr. Holmes's poem, *At The Summit.* There was no title hint or editorial note referring it to Harriet; but she who was called "Sister," in the Doctor's lines, needed no identification with the American public.

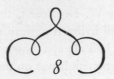

8

"And Now I Rest Me"

HARRIET'S seventieth birthday had made her think about her biography—
the record of her life she should leave to posterity. She wrote to her
son Charles:

> I have been going over and arranging my papers with a view to sifting
> out those that are not worth keeping and so filing and arranging those that
> are to be kept, that my heirs and assigns may with the less trouble know
> where and what they are.

Her scheme of sifting was a curious one, for it consisted largely in dis-
carding references to some of the most dramatic and tumultuous incidents
of her life. The only motive for this that can be ascribed to her is that of
modesty, for there was nothing in these memories unpleasant to her or
which need bring a blush to her cheeks. Passions were burned out now,
hatreds forgotten. One could almost feel compassion and forgiveness for
Theodore Tilton, exiled to Paris and playing chess with an ex-President in
the Café de la Régence.

Who cared about the past quarrels and triumphs and defeats of an old
woman dwelling in the Land of Beulah, whence one could see the Celestial
City? Why rake up the old feud with Joel Parker and Irenaeus Prime, or
the intrigue that kept Queen Victoria from receiving her formally? Why
expose her own anguish during her brother's ordeal? Why reveal her
private tragedies, her thousand and one personal joys and sorrows? It was
vanity to think that anyone cared. She even preferred to suppress the episode
of her Byron exposé, but could not quite dare do that, since now her name
was linked with Lord Byron's in public remembrance almost as closely as
it was with Uncle Tom's. However, that incident could be kept to a bare,
brief statement. For the rest, she must include in her biography every bit of

writing she had ever committed to paper that tended to lead people to
Christ and heaven at last. She went on, to Charley:

> I cannot describe the peculiar feelings which this review occasions.
> Reading old letters, when so many of the writers have gone from earth,
> seems to me like going into the world of spirits—letters full of the warm,
> eager, anxious, busy life that is *forever* past. My own letters, too, full of
> by-gone scenes in my early life and the childish days of my children. It is
> affecting to me to recall things that strongly moved me years ago, that
> filled my thoughts and made me anxious—when the occasion and emotion
> have wholly vanished from my mind. . . . The romance of my youth is
> faded, it looks to me now, from my years—so *very* young. Those days when
> my mind only lived in *emotion,* and when my letters never were dated,
> because they were only histories of the *internal.* But now that I am no
> more, and never can be, young in this world, now that the friends of those
> days are almost all in eternity, what remains?

Perhaps Georgie, after the birthday party, felt she had been neglecting
her famous mother a little of late. At any rate, Harriet and Calvin, in the
late summer or early autumn of 1882, made an extended visit to the Allens
in Cambridge—their first for several years. Harriet wrote to Charley in
Saco that his father was enjoying his proximity to the Boston Library and
was reading the life and diary of John Quincy Adams, in a dozen volumes or
more. Harriet was reading them, too, and it gave her a chance to recall to
Charley some of the events of a war he only vaguely remembered.

"All, all are gone," she wrote. "All that raged; all that threatened; all
the cowards that yielded, truckled, sold their country for a mess of pottage;
all the *men* that stood and bore infamy and scorn for the truth—all are
silent in dust. The fight is over; but eternity will never efface from their
souls whether they did well or ill, whether they fought bravely or failed
like cowards. In a sense, our lives are irreparable."

They had to go South early that autumn to take part in a great event at
Mandarin. On November 4, 1882, on a site donated by Harriet from her
Fairbanks purchase on the river-front, the new rector, Rev. C. M. Sturgess,
dedicated the Mandarin Church of Our Saviour. The low, wooden church
still stands there and serves a secluded parish, which has installed a memorial
window, by Tiffany, to the Stowes. It bears the quotation from Harriet's
hymn:

> In that hour, fairer than daylight dawning,
> Remains the glorious thought, I am with Thee.

By the summer of 1883 Calvin Stowe had at last eaten himself to the edge of the grave. It had taken him eighty-one years to do it, and his case could scarcely serve to point a dietitian's moral. He fell dangerously ill that summer, and the doctor pronounced his malady Bright's disease. He recovered in time to go South with his family as usual; but he knew his condition was incurable and that it was only a question of waiting for the end.

During his illness, Harriet thought again of her biography. She intended to leave one to the world, but equally she intended that no outsider should write it. There were too many suppressions in her material to be entrusted to the good faith of a stranger. Others were thinking that her biography should be written. Thomas Wentworth Higginson knew a capable woman in Boston who would be just the one for the work. He wrote to Harriet, recommending his candidate. Harriet replied:

> Will you be kind enough to say to the lady that all the matter necessary for that purpose has been placed in care of my son, Rev'd Charles E. Stowe, and of my son-in-law, Rev'd H. F. Allen, who in good time will write such things as ought to be written.
>
> I would much prefer that no other attempts be made. Will you kindly so represent it to your friend?

Harriet had no presentiment that the winter of 1883-1884 would be her last at Mandarin. The doctor said her husband might linger on for some years, his strength was keeping up well, and certainly the orange grove and his sunny porch made the best place for him in winter. The trees had recovered from the freezing and were as beautiful as ever. Harriet's own health was none too good during the early part of the winter. But the climate had its effect, and by March she was much like her former self.

Jewett, the publisher, had told J. C. Derby, who had constituted himself historian of the American publishing business, that Mrs. Stowe, when she brought *Uncle Tom's Cabin* to him for publication, had no confidence in the book's success. Harriet, forgetting how pleased she and Calvin had been not to be enticed into buying a half-interest in the book, accepting a royalty arrangement instead, retorted in replying to Derby:

> What Jewett says about Uncle Tom is false. I was not altogether such a fool as he represents, although I confess I was surprised at the *extent* of the success.
>
> The last edition of Uncle Tom has an introduction written by me, con-

taining perhaps some things that you might find of service in your proposed book. I am writing with all windows open and orange trees in bloom visible from all, and hear from the North today: "Our trees are loaded with ice."
What a country!

At the end of their southern sojourn that year Harriet wrote to Mrs. Howard that she and Calvin had never "enjoyed each other's society more than this winter. His mind is still clear and bright, and he is competent as ever to explain a text or instruct me in the merits of a verse." But they could not stop off in Brooklyn this year, or ever again. "While my husband lives," Harriet said, "I cannot visit and leave him, neither can I take him. He requires personal attentions that only a wife ought to render. At our home in Hartford everything is arranged with reference to his comfort, and he *is* perfectly comfortable, but my friends must come there to see me. I cannot leave him to go to them."

Yet, back in that home, Calvin seemed to improve; and as late as August 26, 1884, Harriet expected "that, D. V., we are going South again the last of November." She wrote this to Annie Fields, who, after a long silence, had told Harriet she had been thinking of her and wondering where she was and what she was doing. And wasn't she coming to Boston? Harriet answered: "Whether we go to Boston or not is not yet decided, but, I trust, if you are passing this way, you will set some definite day when we may expect you, and I will certainly be at home."

Annie decided to go to Hartford. Her friend was getting old—seventy-three that year—and she was no longer the indefatigable trip-taker and visitor she had been. Annie did not want to lose touch with her and went down to Hartford for a day or two, taking Sarah Orne Jewett with her—Sarah Orne Jewett, who modern critics say received the torch of New England realism from Harriet Beecher Stowe's hand. With them they bore gifts—Miss Jewett's new novel, *A Country Doctor,* and a new edition of Annie's book of verses which Harriet had read (without too much approval), *Under the Olive.*

While pleasant, the visit with Sarah Orne Jewett did not strike Harriet as momentous or historical. The Nook Farm section of Hartford was building up, and No. 1 Forest Street had become No. 49. From there Harriet wrote to Annie Fields on September 24—the last letter to Annie we have:

How many delightful memories your short, little visit brought back to me! I must thank you, too, for bringing Miss Jewett. I have just finished reading her book, having been delayed in indulgence to Mr. Stowe's eagerness to read it. It is not only interesting and bright but full of strong and earnest thought. The conversation between the two doctors is full of gems from the deepest mines of thought. Will you give her my love and thanks for the book, which will always be a treasure to me.

I cannot write much nowadays. Let me thank you for sending me "Ida," made doubly precious by Ruskin's preface and notes. He traveled a week with me and my daughters in the Alps, and made a special pet of my Georgie. He is an original, but one of the most delightful of men, and a true Christian whom I hope to meet hereafter. I do wish he would visit America, but have no hope of it.

With best love to you and Miss Jewett, I am ever

The same old friend,

H. B. Stowe.

P.S.—Did I write my thanks for "Under The Olive?" If not, accept them now. Do remember the invitation to you and Miss Jewett to come to us in Florida the last part of February and onward.

Though Harriet "could not write much nowadays," she published her final book that year. It was *Our Famous Women,* a book-agent proposition put out by one of the Hartford companies. Harriet, however, did little more for this book than allow her name to appear as author, though she told Mrs. McCray that she prepared two biographical sketches for it: one, of her sister Catharine, and the other, of her friend Mrs. A. D. T. Whitney, the Boston poetess.

As late as September 24, 1884, Harriet had expected to go to Florida for the winter; but when the time came for departure, Calvin felt too feeble to attempt the trip. Harriet would not leave him, and so for the first time in years the Mandarin house remained unoccupied during the winter months.

Faithful as she was in her care of him, Calvin's condition deteriorated rapidly that winter, and he became too great a burden for his seventy-four-year-old wife to bear alone. In January Harriet wrote to Mrs. Howard:

I am watching the slow sinking of my dear husband under an incurable disease, and only praying now that he may be spared pain. I do not feel strength within me to see him suffer.

I have many things to be thankful for: a comfortable home, with every convenience for the care of the sick; two daughters, who relieve me of every household care; and a trained hospital nurse, who knows how to do everything and *does it* with neatness, order, and efficiency. So I live day by day. I feel myself rather weak and weary, not with physical labor, for of that I have none—but you know all about it, just how it would be. Please ask Henry to write me a few lines that I can read to my dear husband. His mind is clear, and I read all my letters to him; and nothing would please him more than a few lines from Henry, whom he always loved peculiarly, from the time he was a student onward.

The châtelaine of the "Old Stowe Place," as Harriet said her orange grove would one day be known, must have suspected that she would never return to it, and that winter made efforts to bring Charley to Hartford. What influence an eminent Episcopalian could bring to bear upon a Hartford Calvinist congregation it is hard to say; but it could not have been entirely coincidence that in the spring of 1885 the Rev. Charles Edward Stowe, of Saco, Maine, received and accepted a call to the pastorate of the Windsor Avenue Congregational Church in Hartford, not two miles north of his famous mother's house.

Then ensued for two elderly people in Forest Street a season of placid waiting during which they learned to look upon the approaching Messenger with a friendly and even twinkling eye. The following summer (1885) Harriet wrote to Dr. Holmes:

My dear husband is slowly and gradually sinking under Bright's disease. I am thankful that the passage downward is mostly painless, though sure. He is longing to depart to a higher rest; or, as you said to have inscribed on his grave:
"Not Finis, but End of Vol. I."

It was a birthday letter for Dr. Holmes—August 29, 1885. In tearing the daily sheet from her "Whittier Calendar," Harriet noted the anniversary, and the lines:
Long may he live to sing for us
His sweetest songs at eventime!

She told the Doctor, "I could not resist the impulse to let you know how warmly I think of you."

Thus a wife kept her courage up and joked with her dying husband about his tombstone; but it was not always easy for her.

Calvin was tarrying yet a while, though by the following June it was evident that the end was near. At its Commencement, Yale College was inducting Timothy Dwight into its presidency, and among the notables invited to attend was Calvin Ellis Stowe, D.D. Harriet replied formally that Professor Stowe would be unable to attend, "being confined to his room by an incurable illness." Just as the sun set on August 6, 1886, the old Professor died, murmuring, "Peace with God! Peace with God!" Henry Stowe's grave at Andover had consecrated "their just inheritance" for his parents. Had it been left to Harriet, she would probably have given her husband the middle grave in the broad cemetery lot; but the twins and Charley had taken charge, and they knew what would be in proportion. They placed their father on the other flank, opposite Henry, leaving the commanding central position still unoccupied. Thus as he slept in death, awaiting the final trumpet call, Calvin Stowe remained what he had been in life, a celebrity's husband.

The great ship of life, in Harriet's metaphor, ploughed ahead, leaving in its wake a few vanishing bubbles of praise or lamentation—and more and more the bubbles of her own lamentation. Another galaxy rose as her half-brother James lay dead by his own hand in an Elmira sanitarium—the same James who as a toddler had made friends with the pigs in Cincinnati's streets. Harriet had hardly known James, however, for he had grown up while she was raising her own family, and as an adult he had always been at sea or in China or the wilderness, or commanding his coloured regiment in the war.

No reference in her letters now about a winter in Florida. Her books brought an old woman and two middle-aged spinster daughters a sufficient income. Harriet sold all her Mandarin property except the orange grove, and turned the money over to Charley, so that he might buy a house for himself and his family in Hartford. He and Susie had presented her with two grandchildren—Lyman Beecher and Leslie Stowe—but there would never be another matchless Freeman Allen. It was Grandma now in Hartford, not first grandmother-in-waiting to His Majesty.

Calvin's death was a warning to Harriet that if she intended to prepare her biography, she must be about it; and that winter she and the Rev. Charles sorted and discarded and arranged, and Charles made a start with the writing. Harriet played with the idea of making it an autobiography, with some such title as *Pebbles from the Shores of a Past Life*. Charley, of course, must do the actual work.

The great ship was sailing over a new grave the first week in March, 1887, when Henry Ward Beecher, struck down by the apoplexy he had always feared, lay dying in a Brooklyn Heights house before which Isabella Beecher Hooker paced the sidewalk up and down and gave appalling interviews to the reporters keeping the death-watch. Eunice Beecher herself had slammed the door in Isabella's face, when at the news she had rushed down from Hartford. Her own brother—dying—and she was not permitted to say a last word to him!

Isabella's actions made almost as great a sensation in New York as the death of the great preacher itself. But the family was unrelenting, and Isabella was even denied permission to attend the great public funeral as a mourner. Isabella had imparted to no one her secret necessity to see her half-brother before he went—that she knew from her spiritual influences that Henry wanted to ask her forgiveness and tell her she had been right. The graying veterans who mounted guard in Plymouth Church during the lying-in-state were not there entirely for pomp. They had incidental orders not to permit Mrs. Hooker to make a scene. Late at night, Isabella took a place at the end of the queue of 50,000 persons which had been moving through the church since morning, and was permitted to gaze for the last time on the face of her brother. The cold, pale lips did not move.

Thomas K. Beecher appeared at the funeral services but refused to ride in the cortège to the cemetery. Presumably Harriet attended, though she left no record of the experience. She could not regard the passing of her brother as an ordinary death, referring to it in a subsequent letter to Mrs. Howard as "Henry's exaltation." A maelstrom of bubbles ascended from this grave; but, a little later, there was a quieter seething as Georgiana Allen succumbed to the disorder that had racked her for years. Harriet seemed to bear all these blows with equanimity. How could she, at seventy-six, mourn at such partings, when they merely meant that she would not have to wait in eternity for her dear ones? No woman's faith in the nearness and reality of heaven was ever more complete than hers.

From this time until her death, the picture of Harriet Beecher Stowe is contributed largely by others than herself. Her pen seldom even wrote letters any more. Since the 1870's she had retired so completely from the public scene that, except with her neighbours in Hartford, she had become something like a national myth or legend. Now and then the public was surprised when some newspaper item or magazine article brought the information that old Mrs. Stowe, who wrote *Uncle Tom's Cabin,* was still alive in Hartford.

(People were still reading her *Uncle Tom's Cabin,* however. At the end of 1887 Charles Stowe looked over a royalty statement and noted that 12,225 copies of the novel had been sold since May.)

At the end of October, 1887, Miss Frances E. Willard, having presided over a convention of the Women's Christian Temperance Union at Bridgeport, Connecticut, went up to Hartford expressly to visit Harriet. Miss Willard was shy about such things, having only once before in her life solicited an interview with a celebrity. That was with Longfellow, to whom Elizabeth Stuart Phelps introduced her. With Miss Willard now was Mrs. J. G. Parsons, of Hartford, a friend of Harriet's, and "this temptation was too great. The creator of Uncle Tom and Little Eva was within reach, and I would depart from my wise and righteous rule just once."

So, "having received the gracious consent of the most celebrated American woman of history," Mrs. Parsons and Miss Willard drove out to Forest Street. A maple tree flamed with autumn colours in the front yard. It was "a tasteful, lilac-colored, wooden house of medium size. Three well-to-do cats, one yellow, one tortoise, one black, and all handsome, had dignified positions on the walk, the porch, and the rug before the door, respectively." Miss Willard wrote:

> The bell was promptly answered by a plump colored maid who evinced uncertainty as to the whereabouts of her mistress. A voice from upstairs called out, "I am at home—I *am* at home," and we were shown into a pleasant study with bookcases, easy-chairs, writing-table, and many photographs, the largest being of Henry Ward Beecher, evidently taken just before his last illness, the hair snow-white.
>
> A little woman entered, seventy-five years old, decidedly under-size, and weighing less than a hundred pounds. She was very simply attired in a dress of black-and-white check, with linen collar and small brooch; her hair, which had once been brown, hung fluffily upon a broad brow and was bound by a black ribbon in front and gathered in a low knot behind. Her nose is long and straight, eyes dimmed by years, mouth large and with the long Beecher lip, full of the pathos of humanity's mystical estate. This is what time has left of the immortal Harriet Beecher Stowe.

In the course of the conversation Miss Willard mentioned that Harriet was a famous pedestrian. Harriet said she learned the value of walking many years before at a water-cure establishment at Brattleboro, Vermont. "I go out in the morning," she said, "and again in the afternoon, making from five to seven miles daily. If I am not feeling well, I can usually walk it off; or, if not, I sleep it off, going to bed by eight o'clock."

Harriet was proud of a photograph of Master Freeman Allen. "He is so handsome that he is not vain," she said, "and the way of it is this: he has heard himself called handsome since his earliest recollection and thinks it is some quality belonging to all boys."

Miss Willard told Harriet about her own mother, and Harriet sent love. She said: "I love everybody. As I walk alone in the fields and along the streets, meeting many who speak a friendly word to me, I rejoice to think how much I love them and every creature that God has made."

She did not mention that it was a cultivated virtue with her. She did not tell her visitor how in girlhood she had struggled against her natural tendency to dislike people and think harshly and critically of individuals, until she had made love her guiding principle. True, her life had not always exemplified her ideal, but love for humanity and its members had nevertheless remained its creed. Now, on the threshold of her dotage, love was all in all with her.

Harriet could dismiss professionally even the president of the W.C.T.U. When, as she thought, the interview had lasted long enough, she suddenly rose and, as Miss Willard reported, "took me by the hand, saying earnestly, 'God help you. God be with you.' I kissed the dear old wrinkled hand that in its strength had written *Uncle Tom's Cabin;* she gave a kind good-bye to each of us, and we went our ways."

Another who had opportunity to observe Mrs. Stowe at the end of her life was her neighbour, the Rev. Joseph H. Twichell, pastor of the Asylum Hill Congregational Church. Twichell said that among her books Mrs. Stowe had "a priceless library of 'Uncle Tom' literature, including copies of most of its thirty-seven translations." He went on:

> There are relics also of a more private sort. For example, a smooth stone of two or three pounds' weight, and a sketch, or study, on it by Ruskin, made at a hotel on Lake Neufchatel where he and Mrs. Stowe chanced to meet; he having fetched it in from the lake shore one evening and painted it in her presence to illustrate his meaning in something he had said.

Another observer was Florine Thayer McCray. Mrs. McCray was a journalist and a newcomer to Hartford, having recently taken the editorship of the *City Mission Record,* which was published in that city. Mrs. McCray had independent means, and was, according to the family memory of her, which is hostile, a rather vulgar, pushing person. She dressed emphatically and was fond of driving, manwise, a smart turnout, having hands that could hold a spirited horse shying at an "ordinary" which some striped-blazered young man was pumping along, or at one of the new, solid-tired "safety" bicycles, which even children were beginning to ride.

At any rate, Mrs. McCray pushed herself into the confidence of Mrs. Stowe, and so firmly that when in the autumn of 1887 she asked the celebrated authoress for permission to write a sketch of her life, Harriet readily consented. Harriet knew what life-sketches were. She had written many a one in her time.

But Mrs. McCray was not content with a mere oral authorization. She wanted it in writing. Harriet might have had a few doubts about the necessity of this, but finally accommodated as follows, under date of December 11, 1887:

Dear Friend:—You are quite welcome to write the sketch you propose. I believe that all the material for such an one is quite at hand and at your disposal.

Yours very truly,
H. B. Stowe.

Mrs. McCray put this note away, carefully.

Meanwhile, work on the real biography began in earnest that autumn. In October Harriet wrote to her old brother Edward in Brooklyn:

Charley told me that he has got all written up to my twelfth or thirteenth year, when I came to be under sister Catharine's care in Hartford. I am writing daily my remembrances from that time. You were then, I think, teacher of the Grammar School in Hartford . . .

I feel about things now as I do about the things that happen in a hotel, after my trunk is packed to go home. I may be vexed and annoyed, but what of it? I am going home soon.

So she sat beside her trunk, and wrote her little daily quota of memories, and received her callers, and obligingly sent her autographs (along with pious texts), and thought about that Jesus she would meet when she got home, writing in a letter:

I am come to that stage of my pilgrimage that is within sight of the River of Death, and I feel that now I must have all in readiness day and night for the messenger of the King. I have sometimes had in my sleep strange perceptions of a vivid spiritual life near to and with Christ and multitudes of holy ones; and the joy of it is like no other joy—it cannot be told in the language of the world. What I have then I *know* with absolute certainty, yet it is so unlike and above anything we conceive of in this world that it is difficult to put it into words. The inconceivable loveliness of Christ!

The year 1888 was one of waiting for Harriet. The biography progressed slowly, with her uncertain assistance—and Mrs. McCray, too, was taking plenty of time with the material, it seemed, for one who merely wished to get a few facts for a sketch. Still, Mrs. McCray would not want to miss anything really salient, and she had to defer to the Rev. Charles Stowe, who kept large sections of the file for weeks at a time, awaiting his opportunities to write.

It had to be an inclement day indeed that could keep Harriet from her walks, and in the proper seasons she was agile enough to climb or crawl under fences to search the fields for wildflowers. Often the morning walk took her to Charley's parsonage, two miles away. She had always been fond of building and in her elderly leisure became an ardent specimen of that genus of idlers whom a modern generation has dubbed "sidewalk superintendents." She told the Rev. Mr. Twichell proudly, "I keep track of all the new houses going up in town, and I have talked with the men who are building most of them."

One of the joys of her waiting was Sabbath worship. Confirmed Episcopalian though she was, she was ending her days as a communicant in the church of her fathers. It meant no change of heart or creed for her. She was merely attending Charley's church.

Another winter came to the watcher beside the River, and it brought news of the death of her old Mandarin neighbour, C. G. Crane, and a letter from his widow, saying that the Mandarin church was having a hard struggle to survive. It was felt that if money could be found and a rectory built, the parish then could keep up with the rector's salary. A new system of raising money for charity had been devised—the chain-letter—and Eva Crane wanted to know if Harriet would compose one for the Mandarin parish.

Harriet not only did so but authorized its circulation over her signature. Each recipient was asked to contribute ten cents and send two copies of the letter to friends, adding a serial number to the letters. When the serial number reached 15, all recipients were to close the scheme and send no other letters. Harriet added:

PLEASE TAKE NOTICE.

Anyone refusing to join in the scheme is requested to return this paper *immediately* to Mrs. Crane, for only in this way can she know that the chain is broken.

It means only ten cents to each person, but yet a break in the chain entails *a serious loss to the church.*

In the spring of 1889 a composer named J. F. Petri set one of Harriet's poems to music, and Harriet wrote him a letter of thanks. "With increasing years I find an ever-increasing joy in music, and a sense of gratitude toward every maker of sweet songs." The biography came along famously that year. Almost at the last moment Harriet remembered all the letters she had written to Charles Sumner and wrote to Edward L. Peirce, Sumner's literary executor, asking to have them back. Whether Peirce complied or not, the letters, at any rate, did not get into the biography.

There came a day in September when Charley could bring her the final page of manuscript and say, "Ma, it's finished." In her own copperplate hand, which still failed to show any senile tremor, Harriet wrote a brief preface, saying of her son's work, "It is the true story of my life, told for the most part in my own words, and has therefore all the force of an autobiography." She closed the preface with the words of Valiant-for-Truth, of *Pilgrim's Progress:*

I am going to my Father's; and, though with great difficulty I am got hither, yet now I do not repent me of all the troubles I have been at to arrive where I am.

My sword I give to him that shall succeed me in my pilgrimage, and my courage and skill to him that can get it.

It was her true valedictory to the world she had shaken, for she wrote these sentences almost at the very end of her lucid existence on earth. Within a few weeks she was smitten by a brief, acute illness—Mrs. McCray called it a stroke—and, though she made a physical recovery, she was never the same after that.

Harriet's emotions seemed to have burned themselves out long before, but in the autumn of 1889 she showed that she was still capable of a good, soul-stirring rage. Near the end of the year appeared Florine McCray's *Life-Work of the Author of Uncle Tom's Cabin,* and Harriet knew why her energetic friend had spent so much time over the file of materials. It was no sketch she had turned out but a full biography, a volume of 450 pages; and, though she had not beaten the authorized biography into the market, she was in the same market, and with a much livelier, more entertaining book than Charles Stowe's diplomatic and uninspired work. As her authorization, Mrs. McCray reproduced Harriet's note to her, in her own handwriting.

At this piece of literary perfidy Harriet was so indignant she read Mrs. McCray's book everlastingly into the family Index, where indeed it still remains. In her rational periods later she told anyone who asked that the McCray *Life-Work* was unauthorized, unreliable, and misleading, if not actually false. Annie Fields, to whom Harriet's wish was law, evidently did not deign to glance at Mrs. McCray's biography of Mrs. Stowe before writing her own a few years later. She might have done so to her advantage; for Mrs. McCray had made good use of her materials, and her accuracy, if not her ethics, was unimpeachable.

For a while, however, it seemed as if Harriet might have no more rational periods. After her illness her mind failed so rapidly that on January 29, 1890, Hattie Stowe could write to a Boston gentleman who had solicited an interview with her mother, "Intellectually she is not now above a child of two or three years."

But she recovered, at least partially, and during her more lucid intervals nobody knew her own mental condition better than she did herself. "My mind wanders like a running brook," she wrote to Susan Howard, "and I do not think of my friends as I used to, unless they recall themselves to me by some kind action. I have written all my words and thought all my thoughts, and now I rest me in the flickering light of the dying embers— a rest so profound that the voice of an old friend rouses me but momentarily, and I drop back again into repose."

Thus had she studied her father in his dotage, as she now studied herself.

So Harriet Beecher Stowe came up to her eightieth birthday, an event important enough to be noticed by the newspapers. But, as we would say today, she had a bad press on that occasion. It had become critical fashion to cry down Mrs. Stowe and all her works. In the *Independent*—what had been Harriet's own *Independent*—Maurice Thompson, remembered now as the author of *Alice of Old Vincennes,* had this to say about her:

> *Uncle Tom's Cabin* was the output of a very inferior artist. Mrs. Stowe is famous, and her novel has had a great triumph, but it is a mediocre piece of sensational romance, and more than mediocre, viewed from a just,

critical point of view. It represents no life that ever was. Its style is crude, sentimental, and violently sensational; there is not a single really lifelike character in it. She sketched in most exaggerated lines and with the falsest colors the most stupendous fact of American history. There was just enough terrible truth in her book to make its mass of untruth effective with weak and sentimental readers. Its effect was not due to her art but to the conditions she criticized, and the policies and politics she aided. Her style was of that flamboyant kind grateful to the crude, popular, and vulgar taste. She made hysterical folk have fits, and politicians caught up her hysterical wail and made the very most of it.

Maurice Thompson, however, was a prejudiced critic. Though Indiana born, he was reared and educated in the South and served in the Confederate Army. Yet here was a Northern item:

MRS. STOWE'S DECLINE

The eightieth birthday of Mrs. Harriet Beecher Stowe was almost unnoticed by the public. The reports say she has passed into her dotage. Their tone is almost contemptuous.

What change has come over the attitude of the public toward the author of "Uncle Tom's Cabin"? The memories of that book are not yet dead. Its influence is abiding. On the stage its story still moves to tears.

We incline to think that Mrs. Stowe's crusade against Lord Byron hurt her deeply in popular regard. She came forward with a nauseating scandal at a time when Byron's genius had placed him among the classics of literature, and when the question of his moral character was interesting to none but lovers of gossip. She broke the confidence which, as she said, Lady Byron had reposed in her and wantonly smirched the dead. If her tale was true, that was all the more reason for burying it in profound silence. If it was false, her offense was rank.

The result was that people came to regard her less as the creator of Uncle Tom than as the purveyor of this disreputable dish of tittle-tattle. The masterly work which she had accomplished went for nothing, demolished by the unsavory work which she had attempted. If she sought notoriety in the Byron scandal, she paid for it dearly. She fell into an unhonored old age; and the newspapers, recording her eightieth birthday, declare her to be out of her mind and jeer at her achievements.

Such shafts could not reach Harriet now; and besides, not all the critics felt that way about her. Kirk Munroe was estimating her place in history:

ᐧ Not only does she stand in the foremost rank of famous women of the world, but, in shaping the destiny of the American people at a most critical period of their history, her influence was probably greater than that of any other individual. Charles Sumner said that if *Uncle Tom's Cabin* had not been written, Abraham Lincoln could not have been elected President of the United States.

Of course, the abolition of slavery was not, and could not be, accomplished by any one person. It was the result of the united efforts of Mrs. Stowe with her wonderful book, of Garrison with his *Liberator,* of Whittier with his freedom-breathing poetry, of Sumner in the Senate-chamber, of Wendell Phillips with his caustic wit and unanswerable arguments, of Frederick Douglass with his convincing tales of personal wrong, of Gamaliel Bailey with his *National Era,* of Theodore Weld, the pioneer Abolitionist, of James Birney, and of a host of other heroic workers, besides the thousands of brave souls who cheerfully offered their lives on the battlefield; but the greatest and most far-reaching of all these influences was that of *Uncle Tom's Cabin,* the work that ranks but fourth in point of circulation among all the books of the world.

She had her friends still, and they loved her for what she was. One to whose "crude, popular, and vulgar taste" Uncle Tom had appealed, was Oliver Wendell Holmes, who, since her great party, had always written her on her birthdays and sometimes in between. Mrs. Storrs Seymour, of Litchfield, never forgot to send Harriet birthday flowers from her mother's grave or Judge Reeve's old garden. Miss Philena McKeen, who for many years now had been head of Abbot Academy in Andover, wrote in May, 1892, asking Harriet for an autographed copy of *Uncle Tom's Cabin* for the school's new library.

In the winter of 1893 Dr. Holmes, now eighty-four, wrote her to inquire after her health. Harriet was in her right mind on February 5, the day she answered that letter—

My Dear Friend Dr. Holmes:—Your more than kind—your most charming, really lovely letter of January 31 was to me the profoundest surprise and the greatest pleasure I have had in many a day—I might say, year. That you should remember and think of me and write me so at length, with your own hand, too, is a kind courtesy and an honor that I sincerely appreciate.

I must tell you, my dear friend, if you do not know it yourself—and I say it not to flatter but because it is true—your lamp burns as brightly as ever. The oil in it has not run low, leaving but a feeble gleam, as mine has done. Your noble and beautiful lines to our friend Whittier show no diminution of mental power, but only the sweetness and richness of many summers.

I am glad to know how you pass your time, and that you have such a peaceful, cheerful, happy life. That you make others happy I know, for your presence always was like sunshine.

As to myself, there is not so much to tell as of you. I am passing the last days of my life in the city where I passed my schoolgirl life. My physical health, since I recovered from the alarming illness I had four years ago, has been excellent, and I am almost always cheerful and happy. My mental condition might be called nomadic. I have no fixed thoughts or objects. I wander at will from one subject to another. In pleasant summer weather I am out of doors most of my time, rambling about the neighborhood and calling upon my friends. I do not read much. Now and then I dip into a book much as a humming-bird, poised in air on whirring wing, darts into the heart of a flower, now here, now there, and away. Pictures delight me and afford me infinite diversion and interest. I pass many pleasant hours looking over books of pictures.

Of *music* I am also very fond. I could not have too much of it, and I never *do* have as much as I should like. The street bands, even organs, give me great pleasure, but especially the singing and playing of my kind friends, who are willing to gratify me in this respect.

I make no mental effort of any sort; my brain is tired out. It was a woman's brain and not a man's, and finally from sheer fatigue and exhaustion in the march and strife of life it gave out before the end was reached. And now I rest me, like a moored boat, rising and falling on the water, with loosened cordage and flapping sail.

I thank you much for your kind words regarding myself. Blessed I have been in many ways, in seeing many of the desires of my heart fulfilled, and in having the love of many people, as has been made manifest to me in these my declining years. Sorrows also I have had, which have left their mark on my heart and brain.

But they are all passed now. I have come to the land of Beulah, which is heaven's borderland, from whence we can see into the gates of the celestial city; and even *now* all tears are wiped from my eyes.

Thanking you again and again for your great kindness in writing and letting me know of your friendship and regard for me,

I am most sincerely your friend,
Harriet Beecher Stowe.

It was almost her last letter, and she had never written a more beautiful one or one so pathetic. A woman's brain, she apologized for her confused mental condition, and not a man's! And she had never had enough music! Two old, old comrades, keeping in touch with each other before the last great adventure!

Her last letter, written June 15, 1893, thanked Mrs. Seymour, of Litchfield, for a birthday bunch of heartsease "from the dear old garden in Litchfield." "My eighty-second birthday was made very bright and happy by the kindness of my friends and neighbors, who called to see me bringing with them lovely roses and still more lovely words of kindness and friendship." The last scrap of her writing we have is her autograph, spelled out in full—"Harriet Beecher Stowe"—and dated March 23, 1894. The handwriting is still firm and legible.

After that the mists closed in around her. There lived on her street Charles W. Burpee, a middle-aged, dignified gentleman who had been a colonel in the Civil War. One summer evening after tea, attired in his regimentals, he was passing the Stowe house on his way to his G. A. R. meeting when out rushed little, old Mrs. Stowe and embraced and kissed him, calling him, "Fred." The embarrassed colonel disengaged himself and held her off until one of the twins came out and rescued him. The twin led a bewildered mother back into the house. Wasn't that Fred? She had been sure it was Fred.

Thereafter it became one of her obsessions that Fred was coming home again. She was going to see her boy once more! An incorrigible early riser, she would be up, dressed, and out at the crack of dawn, returning about the time the others arose, bedraggled and soaked with dew, but with an armful of wildflowers with which to deck the house for Fred. She became too great a problem for the "Stowe girls" to handle, and they engaged for her a stalwart, Irish nurse, whose arms were as strong as her heart was tender. The little, stooped Mrs. Stowe and the big Irish girl who accompanied her became a familiar pair in the neighbourhood.

The safety bicycles, which now had pneumatic tires, were becoming numerous in the streets. Some evenings there were gala parades of them under the vocal carbon arc-lights of Farmington Avenue, with jingling bells and Japanese lanterns hung to their handlebars. One day Harriet stopped a little girl with a bicycle and had her demonstrate exactly how to mount and dismount. The nurse had to dissuade her charge from trying it herself.

When Harriet's mind left her finally, there came a rapid change in her physical appearance. Her teeth were gone, and her hollow cheeks and the collapsed look of her face suggest now that it had become dangerous to allow her to wear false teeth. The broad, firm mouth became an indistinct line, and more and more she resembled that transparent mortal shell which had for a space detained the soul of Lyman Beecher.

The lady who had sat so solemnly at the great, solemn tea party in Edinburgh and wondered if Mrs. Scotland had put in an extra spoonful of tea for the pot, had always had a strong streak of mischief in her. Now, out of the control of sanity, it took alarming forms. A ministerial conference in Hartford sent the usual committee out to Forest Street to read the usual address to Mrs. Stowe. She sat thoughtfully through the brief ceremony, then arose and went forward, as if to shake hands with the chairman, but suddenly darted around and began to drum a tattoo with her fists on his broadcloth back.

One of her delights was to plot craftily to escape from the nurse. When she managed it, great was her glee. If they lost her, they were apt to find her wandering in her slippers through Mark Twain's house, or playing the piano in Charles Dudley Warner's and singing *Love Divine* in her cracked voice.

What a vast life hers had been, and for one who in her thirties had had the premonition of early death! When she came into the world candles guttered in sconces, gentlemen wore knee breeches and queues, and the war which was to end that epoch had not yet begun. She had seen in Litchfield women brought to church, riding on pillions. In Hartford she had seen the stage-coaches depart for New Haven or Boston and the post-riders come in from New York with bulging saddle-bags. One of the morning duties of a small schoolmistress had been to take a penknife and sharpen quills for her pupils.

Now through those same Hartford streets electric trolley cars groaned and whined and filled snowy winter nights with strange lightnings. Her occasional business letters now came in green characters impressed on the paper by an office machine called the Caligraph typewriter. In neighbouring Springfield a Mr. Duryea had piloted over the cobbles an explosive contraption propelled by a gasoline engine and called a horseless carriage.

Her life had spanned the gulf between the two most widely separated centuries in human history, and spanned it importantly.

But Harriet knew nothing of Mr. Duryea and his machine, for that last year was blank for her. Even when Oliver Wendell Holmes died, the fact made no impression on her. In Chicago an eloquent Nebraska Congressman

HARRIET BEECHER STOWE: b. 1811; d. 1896

(From the Hall of Fame bust, by Brenda Putnam)

"Prophet and priestess! At one stroke she gave
A race to freedom, and herself to fame."
(Page 641.)

was telling the Democratic National Convention that it should not crucify mankind upon a cross of gold, but Harriet knew nothing of Mr. Bryan or of the fact that it was her eighty-fifth birthday. She lay in bed now, an ashen ember in the heart of which a spark of life barely glowed.

How stubborn the spark was! The Irish nurse was alone with her the evening of July 1, 1896, when at midnight almost, she opened her eyes. As the nurse came to give her medicine, the poor, disfigured mouth tried to smile, and she said, "I love you." Then she closed her eyes again, and with no more trouble than that, to anyone, went on to meet others she had loved long since, and lost awhile.

P. S.

ON FRIDAY, July 3, 1896, they buried Harriet Beecher Stowe in the Andover Chapel cemetery between the graves of her husband and son. The mound of new earth and the graves of C. E. Stowe and Henry E. Stowe were banked deeply with green boughs and brier roses.

With the funeral party from Hartford had come the Rev. and Mrs. Charles E. Stowe, the Misses Harriet and Eliza Stowe, the Rev. Charles Beecher and his daughter, Mrs. Isabella Beecher Hooker and her son, Dr. Hooker, Mr. Freeman Allen, Mrs. James T. Fields, Miss Sarah Orne Jewett, and several others, including a representative from Brunswick, Maine, which claimed the deceased for her *Uncle Tom's Cabin* and *Pearl of Orr's Island*— Mr. G. F. Dunning, a member of that Dunning family which was no longer launching and sailing its wooden ships to the ends of the earth.

("Father Tom" Beecher, of Elmira, was too feeble to attempt the journey. William was buried seven years gone in a far-away Chicago, now engaged in tearing down its World's Columbian Exposition. Edward had died in Brooklyn during the year. Catharine, Henry, and James were gone. Mary Perkins at ninety-one was too intent upon her ambition to round out her century to attend a funeral or even to notice much the passing of her sister. Hattie gone? Well, they couldn't all be long-lived—and Mary's will took a fresh grip on mortal existence.)

From Florence, Italy, the Rev. Henry Allen cabled pink waterlilies. Mrs. Fields's floral offering was purple fleurs-de-lis. On the casket was a wreath presented by Negroes of Boston. It bore a card: "The Children of Uncle Tom."

Only four pallbearers—Professor Churchill, Principal Bancroft, Professor Moore, and the Rev. Dr. Selah Merrill—carried the coffin to the grave; but it was not heavy. Professor Egbert Smyth conducted, and read Mrs. Stowe's hymn, *Still, still with thee*. The throng sang *Nearer, my God, to Thee*. The Episcopal burial-service was said.

A little later Harriet's three surviving children erected over her grave a sturdy cross of granite imported from Scotland. It was a replica of a cross of ancient Ionian design she had admired at Inverary Castle, seat of the Dukes of Argyle.

Harriet, whose faith in the African race was great, had noted the artistic talents of the coloured people. Already that race had produced a good poet; and Harriet had always inspired poetry, some of it excellent. In the *Century Magazine* for November, 1898, appeared the following sonnet:

HARRIET BEECHER STOWE
By Paul Laurence Dunbar

She told the story, and the whole world wept
    At wrongs and cruelties it had not known
    But for this fearless woman's voice alone.
    She spoke to consciences that long had slept:
Her message, Freedom's clear reveille, swept
    From heedless hovel to complacent throne.
    Command and prophecy were in the tone,
    And from its sheath the sword of justice leapt.
Around two peoples swelled a fiery wave,
    And both came forth transfigured from the flame.
    Blest be the hand that dared be strong to save,
And blest be she who in our weakness came—
    Prophet and priestess! At one stroke she gave
    A race to freedom, and herself to fame.

SOURCES

In General:

Inasmuch as this book was written for reading enjoyment, I have not interrupted the text with reference marks and footnotes. This is not to say I could not have done so. Although Mrs. Stowe's life falls astonishingly into the form of fiction and holds much of the flavour of a novel, imagination has had small part in the preparation of this biography. In the preceding pages there is no important statement of fact unsupported by an adequate reference, and few unimportant ones. Even a life-record as voluminous and detailed as Mrs. Stowe's, however, shows gaps in its continuity. When I have bridged such gaps by guess, I have nearly always indicated so in the writing. Now and then, when the inference has been so obvious as to be self-evident, I have permitted myself an unqualified statement of what is really a supposition, but these instances are rare in the text, and they never concern anything important. Whenever I have had to reconstruct by reasoning any important episode in the subject's life, I have given my conclusions in the form of an argument, with which any reader is entitled to disagree.

Few famous American lives have left so broad a track of themselves, reckoned from the cradle to the grave, as Harriet Beecher Stowe's. Most of our celebrities were not born to fame, and so the periods of their childhood remain obscure. Mrs. Stowe was born into a family already famous, a family of gifted and alert people who wrote an abundance of letters and preserved them. In consequence, we have a month by month, and almost a week by week, record of the childhood of Mrs. Stowe. When she came into adolescence and young womanhood, she fell in with the family habit of writing many letters; and because her letters were profound or jolly, and because she was the daughter of Lyman Beecher, her relatives and friends kept them, and they exist today.

From the date of her marraige in 1836 until almost the end of her active life, Mrs. Stowe was at various times connected with newspapers as a correspondent, and her frequent contributions, like those of our modern columnists, were apt to be autobiographical. Moreover, since during her great days almost everything she did was "news," her own papers reported frequently upon her movements and activities. The files of the Cincinnati *Journal*, in the 1830's, those of the New York *Independent* from 1852 to 1860, and those of the *Christian Union* from 1870 to 1876, are mines of information about Harriet Beecher Stowe. She wrote three autobiographical books: *Sunny Memories in Foreign Lands,* which tells of her first trip abroad; *Palmetto Leaves,* an intimate picture of her life in Florida, and *Poganuc People,* a novel of her childhood in Litchfield, Conn. She contributed several autobiographical chapters to the so-called *Autobiography of Lyman Beecher.* Of her *Life,* by her son Charles Edward Stowe, which appeared in 1889, she said in a foreword: "It is the true story of my life, told for the most part in my own words, and has therefore all the force of an autobiography."

These sources—the newspaper files and the autobiographical writings—have, with the letters, supplied the bone and sinew and most of the flesh of this narrative. To them should perhaps be added, as a major source, Annie Fields's *Life and Letters of Harriet Beecher Stowe,* published in 1898; but since Mrs. Fields kept closely to the 1889 *Life,* reprinting sections of it, her book has been used here principally as a check for dates, etc. I have, however, used Mrs. Fields's personal impressions of Mrs. Stowe and have also relied largely on her book for Mrs. Stowe's letters to Susan Howard, which are important. I have found of value, also, the centennial (1911) biography by Charles E. and Lyman Beecher Stowe and the biographical studies of the Beecher family in the latter's *Saints, Sinners and Beechers.*

For the rest, I have had access to half a hundred or more books, most of them contemporary with Mrs. Stowe's life, containing sketches of her or anecdotes or reminiscences in which she figures, and some thirty-five magazine articles of similar date and character. When any of these have furnished material, their names appear in the chapter reference-summaries which follow. I should mention one valuable contemporary biography, Florine Thayer McCray's *Life-Work of The Author of Uncle Tom's Cabin* (1889), a book which Mrs. Stowe detested.

THE LETTERS:

A special word about the hitherto unpublished letters used in this biography. I have, of course, made full use of all previously published letters of Mrs. Stowe, but in addition I have found about 175 unpublished letters, written mostly by Mrs. Stowe but including a few written by her husband, C. E. Stowe, or by her sister, Catharine Beecher, and closely related to her life-story. This is rather more than the number hitherto published. Furthermore, I have had access to the original autograph letters used by Mrs. Fields in her *Life and Letters of Harriet Beecher Stowe.* In quoting from these letters Mrs. Fields was highly selective. In her intimate correspondence Mrs. Stowe was often roguish and mischievous; and Mrs. Fields, as if in fear of detracting from the dignity of her revered and lately deceased friend, omitted a great many of these characteristic touches and a great deal, too, of material of a private and personal nature which, she evidently felt, it was not proper for the public to know. As a result, to the extent that she omitted the human elements from the letters she dehumanized her friend's memory. As a further point, Mrs. Stowe was careless about dating her letters, and it often takes close study to determine their approximate dates. This study Mrs. Fields did not give them, frequently bunching together letters that were chronologically far apart. Her very quoted excerpts, therefore, gain point by appearing in their proper order. As a result of all these facts, the amount of hitherto unpublished epistolary material that has gone into this biography is even more impressive than the figure of 175 letters indicates. Actually I have worked from 249 manuscript letters and have discarded about twenty-five more as unimportant or inscrutable.

The chief repository of Stowe letters today is the Henry E. Huntington Library, at San Marino, California, near Pasadena. Considerable collections are in the Library of Congress, Yale University Library, Harvard College Library, and the Boston Public Library.

REFERENCE SUMMARIES BY CHAPTERS

LITCHFIELD: 1. The Blessed Village. The materials from which this chapter was written were taken from the following: *Autobiography of Lyman Beecher,* hereinafter referred to as *Autobiography;* C. E. Stowe: *Life of Harriet Beecher Stowe,* hereinafter referred to as *Life;* Henry Ward Beecher: Two "Star Papers" in the New York *Independent* for September 17 and September 24, 1857; E. D. Mansfield: *Personal Memories;* Paxton Hibben: *Henry Ward Beecher;* Mae Elizabeth Harveson: *Catharine Esther Beecher, Pioneer Educator;* Alice Morse Earle: *Two Centuries of Costume in America;* Annie Fields: *Life and Letters of Harriet Beecher Stowe,* hereinafter to be referred to as *Life and Letters;* C. E. and L. B. Stowe: *Harriet Beecher Stowe* (the 1911 *Life*); *Atlantic Monthly Supplement* for July, 1882; John P. Foote: *Memoirs of The Life of Samuel E. Foote;* Edward F. Hayward: *Lyman Beecher;* and Alain C. White: *History of The Town of Litchfield, Connecticut: 1720-1920.*

LITCHFIELD: 2. Entry into Israel. *Autobiography* and *Life.* Emily Noyes Vanderpool: *More Chronicles of A Pioneer School;* Catalogues of Miss Pierce's School for 1816, 1817, 1818, and 1819; John P. Brace's "Miscellanies" for 1819, 1820, 1821, 1823, and 1824; Harveson: *Catharine Esther Beecher, Pioneer Educator;* Foote: *Memoirs of The Life of Samuel E. Foote;* White: *History of The Town of Litchfield.* The remark that Mrs. Stowe and the New England Puritans lived "in an Israel of their own" was made by "A Carolinian" in an article, *The Political Crisis in The United States* in the *Edinburgh Review* for October, 1856, quoted in the New York *Independent* of February 19, 1857. Mrs. Stowe's reference to herself as "an odd little girl" is in a letter to James T. Fields, dated Feb. 13, 1870, now in the Huntington Library.

HARTFORD: 1. A Boyless Girlhood. The materials for this chapter come principally from the *Autobiography* and *Life,* with supplementary details from Harveson: *Catharine Esther Beecher;* McCray's *Life-Work;* Fields: *Life and Letters;* Foote: *Memoir of Samuel E. Foote;* Charles Theodore Greve: *Centennial History of Cincinnati and Representative Citizens;* Mansfield: *Personal Memories;* H. W. Beecher: *Bowdoin Street Church,* an editorial in the New York *Independent* of May 15, 1862; Cincinnati *Chronicle,* Nov. 17, 1832; and Cincinnati *Daily Gazette* of Feb. 22, 1833. The "jolly" letter to Mary Dutton is postmarked "Hartford, May 25" and shows the notation in another hand: "H. E. Beecher, 1830." It is in the Yale University Library. Two other manuscript letters in the Yale Library have been used here for their facts, both from

Catharine E. Beecher to Mary Dutton and dated Feb. 8, 1830, and Sept. 4, 1831.

CINCINNATI: 1. London of The West. Cincinnati Directories for 1829 and 1831; file of the *Western Monthly Magazine,* June-December, 1833; file of the Cincinnati *Gazette* for 1833; Greve's *Centennial History of Cincinnati;* Charles Frederic Goss: *Cincinnati, The Queen City;* Mansfield's *Personal Memories;* Frances Trollope: *Domestic Manners of The Americans;* Katherine Morris Lester: *Historic Costume;* Carl Kohler: *A History of Costume.*

CINCINNATI: 2. First Adjustments. *Autobiography* and *Life;* Mansfield: *Personal Memories;* Goss: *Cincinnati, The Queen City* (which notes the publicity value of Dr. Beecher to Cincinnati); Greve's *Centennial History;* McCray's *Life-Work;* "An Alabama Man": *Some Account of Mrs. Beecher Stowe and Her Family,* from *Littell's Living Age* for Dec. 1, 1852, reprinted from *Fraser's Magazine;* Nathaniel Wright: Memorial address, *Lyman Beecher,* before the Second Presbyterian Church and Society of Cincinnati, April 28, 1872; *Western Monthly Magazine* for June, August, and September, 1833; Cincinnati Directory for 1831; Cincinnati *Chronicle* for Nov. 24, 1832; Cincinnati *Gazette* for Nov. 28, 1832, and July 25 and 29, 1833; and the Cincinnati *Journal* for Jan. 4, Feb. 1, March 8 and 22, April 5, 12, and 19, May 10 and 17, August 2, 9, 16, 23, and 30, and Sept. 13, all in 1833. Rev. Thomas Brainerd's recollections of Dr. Beecher, quotations from which appear in this chapter, are published in *Autobiography,* Vol. II, pp. 529-535. Two manuscript letters, now in the Yale Library, have been used in this chapter, both from Catharine E. Beecher to Mary Dutton and dated Feb. 3 and Feb. 15, 1833.

CINCINNATI: 3. The Literary Clubs. *Life;* Semi-Colon Club Papers, in the Historical and Philosophical Society of Ohio; E. D. Mansfield: *Memories of Daniel Drake, M.D.;* also Mansfield's *Personal Memories;* Foote: *Memoirs of Samuel E. Foote;* Mary Macmillan: contribution to Goss's *Cincinnati, The Queen City;* Greve: *Centennial History;* and W. P. Trent and John Erskine: *Great American Writers.*

CINCINNATI: 4. End of Spinsterhood. The body of this chapter comes from the *Autobiography,* the *Life,* and the files of the Cincinnati *Journal* for 1833, 1834, and 1835. The references to that weekly are so numerous that they will not be listed here, since there is scarcely an issue which has not supplied something. From the *Journal* come many of the details of the revolt of the Lane students under Theodore Weld, the correspondence between Calvin Stowe and John Rankin, the obituaries of the first Mrs. Stowe and the second Mrs. Lyman Beecher, the interesting digests by "H" of Professor Stowe's exegetical lectures, and many dates useful for the chapter. Only less important as sources are the files of the *Western Monthly Magazine* for the same years plus 1836. The following numbers have supplied information used here: May, October, and December, 1833; April, May, July, and December, 1834; March, May, July, and November, 1835; and January and December, 1836. Other citations are from Greve's *Centennial History,* Goss's *Cincinnati* (Mary Macmillan's contributions), the 1834 Directory of Cincinnati, and H. B. Stowe: *The Mayflower;* W. C. Beecher and S. Scoville: *Henry Ward Beecher, a Biography;* Harveson: *Catharine*

Esther Beecher; B. F. Morris: *Life of Thomas Morris;* Paul R. Grim: *The Rev. John Rankin, Early Abolitionist,* a thesis presented to Ohio State University and published in the *Ohio State Archeological and Historical Quarterly* for July, 1937; J. Hoby: *The Baptists in America;* Cincinnati *Gazette,* July 8, 1835 (for the Meek-Phillips case); and H. W. Beecher: Two Star Papers in the New York *Independent* of October 5, 1854, and October 25, 1855.

CINCINNATI: 5. Suitor and Husband. References: L. B. Stowe: *Grandfather* (MS); Catherine Gilbertson: *Harriet Beecher Stowe;* Mansfield's *Personal Memories;* Nehemiah Cleaveland: *History of Bowdoin College;* Louis C. Hatch: *The History of Bowdoin College;* C. E. Stowe: Introduction to Mrs. Stowe's *Sunny Memories of Foreign Lands;* J. T. Winterich: *Books and The Man;* Cincinnati *Republican* for January 6, 1836. The account of C. E. Stowe's boyhood and his psychic experiences are taken from his letters and writings in the *Life.*

CINCINNATI: 6. Brush with Slavery. Goss's *Cincinnati* and Mary Macmillan's contributions to same, Greve's *Centennial History of Cincinnati,* the *Autobiography* and the *Life;* C. E. Stowe: *Prussian Education,* a pamphlet published in Cincinnati in 1836; the *Western Monthly Magazine* for April, 1836; a.l.s. from Catharine E. Beecher to Mary Dutton, April 12, 1836, now in the Yale Library; ditto undated but written later the same year, also at Yale; Stephen B. Weeks: *Anti-Slavery Sentiment in The South,* in *Publications of The Southern History Association,* April, 1898; Winterich: *Books and The Man;* Hart: *Salmon Portland Chase;* Beecher and Scoville: *Henry Ward Beecher;* Hayward: *Lyman Beecher;* Harveson: *Catharine Esther Beecher;* Semi-Colon Papers; Cincinnati Directory for 1836; *Cincinnati Chronicle* for February 11, 1837; and the *Cincinnati Journal & Western Luminary* for December 3, 1835, and in 1836 the issues of Jan. 7 and 14, March 31, April 14, May 12, 19 and 26, June 2 and 28, July 21, August 4 and 25, Sept. 1 and Dec. 1.

CINCINNATI: 7. Hard Times. *Life* and *Autobiography,* Greve, Foote's *Memoir,* McCray's *Life-Work,* Harveson's *Catharine Esther Beecher,* Cincinnati Directory for 1839-1840, Beecher and Scoville's *Henry Ward Beecher,* and Charles Cist: *Cincinnati Miscellany,* October, 1845; C. E. Stowe: *Report on Elementary Public Instruction in Europe made to the 36th General Assembly of the State of Ohio, December 18, 1837* (Harrisburg: 1838); letters from Catharine E. Beecher to Mary Dutton dated May 21 and August 10, 1838, and February 13 and March 11, 1839, all in Yale Library; a.l.s. by H. E. Stowe to Mary Dutton, undated but with contemporary notation, "H. E. B. Stowe, Dec., 1838," also in Yale Library; Cincinnati *Daily Gazette* for Feb. 21, 1837; Cincinnati *Chronicle* for April 29, 1837, and Sept. 28, 1839; and the Cincinnati *Journal & Western Luminary* for Feb. 15 and 23, March 8, April 5 and 26, May 18, July 6 and 27, Aug. 3, Sept. 21, Oct. 5, 12, 19, and 26, and Nov. 9, all 1837, and Jan. 11, May 15, Aug. 14, Sept. 18, and Dec. 24, in 1838. The controversy between Alcott and Catharine Beecher is reported in the Cincinnati *Journal & Western Luminary* of Dec. 24, 1838, which reprints the charge of plagiarism against McGuffey's *Fourth Reader* from the *American Annals of Education,* August, 1838, and Miss Beecher's reply in the Cincinnati *Daily Gazette.*

CINCINNATI: 8. The Drab Years. *Life, Autobiography,* Greve's *Centennial History,* Cist's *Cincinnati Miscellany* for May and October, 1845, Hayward's *Lyman Beecher,* Harveson's *Catharine Esther Beecher,* Mansfield's *Personal Memories,* Winterich's *Books and The Man,* McCray's *Life-Work,* and C. E. Stowe: *Letter to R. D. Mussey,* pamphlet, Cincinnati, 1843, and *The Religious Element in Education,* address before the American Institute of Instruction, published in Boston in 1844; J. C. Derby: *Fifty Years among Authors, Books, and Publishers;* G. A. and H. W. Wheeler: *History of Brunswick, Topsham, and Harpswell;* a.l.s. by H. B. Stowe to Sarah Pierce, May 8 [1845], in the Litchfield Historical Society, and another to Mrs. T. P. G. Bannister, with the minute, "Rec'd Sept. 25, 1845," in the Yale Library, Aldis Collection, pasted in a first-edition copy of *The Mayflower;* a.l.s. by C. E. Beecher to Mrs. Judge Cushman, Troy, N. Y., in the Litchfield Historical Society; sundry numbers of the Cincinnati *Weekly Gazette* for 1849; New York *Independent* for May 29, July 5, and October 11, 1849, and April 4, 1850; and the Cincinnati *Daily Gazette* for May 10 and 16, June 14, 19, and 28, July 2, 5, and 8, 1849. The original of the slave-dealer's handbill quoted in this chapter is in the Historical and Philosophical Society of Ohio, in Cincinnati.

BRUNSWICK: 1. Immigrant Woman. *Life,* Cleaveland's *History of Bowdoin College,* Hatch's *History of Bowdoin College,* Winterich's *Books and The Man;* Newman Smyth: *Recollections and Reflections;* John Clair Minot: *Maine's Contribution to Literature* in *The Maine Book;* John Erskine: *Leading American Novelists;* Robert P. Tristram Coffin: *Kennebec: Cradle of Americans* and *Captain Abby and Captain John;* H. B. Stowe: *Earthly Care a Heavenly Discipline;* autograph letter from C. E. Stowe to Prof. E. A. Park, Sept. 18, 1850, now in the Boston Public Library; and the New York *Independent* for May 10 and Oct. 17, 1850, and Jan. 2 and 9, Feb. 6, 13, 20, and 27, and March 13, 1851.

BRUNSWICK: 2. Woman of Carthage. *Life, Autobiography,* McCray's *Life-Work,* Erskine's *Leading American Novelists,* Trent and Erskine's *Great American Writers,* Hatch's *History of Bowdoin College,* Smyth's *Recollections and Reflections,* Winterich's *Books and The Man,* Harveson's *Catharine Esther Beecher,* and Levi Coffin: *Reminiscences;* Ludwig Lewisohn: *Expression in America;* Josiah Henson: *Father Henson's Story;* E. P. Parker: *Harriet Beecher Stowe,* in *Eminent Women of The Age;* H. B. Stowe: *Uncle Tom's Cabin;* the file of the weekly *National Era* from May 8, 1851, to April 1, 1852, inclusive; the *Independent* for April 17 and 24, May 8, and all issues for July, 1851, and for March 4, 18, and 25, 1852. Autograph letters signed: one from C. E. Stowe to Prof. Park, dated Sept. 22, 1851, now in the Boston Public Library; one from H. B. Stowe to Mrs. Sarah J. Hale, Philadelphia, Pa., dated November 10 [1851], now in the Huntington Library, miscellaneous collection, marked HM; one from H. B. Stowe to an unnamed correspondent, dated May 19, 1875, relating to Henson as the prototype of Uncle Tom, now with the Historical and Philosophical Society of Ohio. The "women-of-Carthage" letter from Mrs. Stowe to Dr.

Bailey, dated March 9, 1851, is a typewritten copy, made in 1888, of the lost original, and is among the Garrison Letters in the Boston Public Library.

BRUNSWICK: 3. Success Story. *Life;* C. E. and L. B. Stowe: *Harriet Beecher Stowe;* L. B. Stowe: *Saints, Sinners and Beechers;* Winterich's *Books and The Man;* McCray's *Life-Work;* Harveson's *Catharine Esther Beecher;* Erskine's *Leading American Novelists;* Hattie Tyng Griswold: *Personal Sketches of Recent Authors;* Elizabeth Stuart Phelps (Ward): *Chapters from A Life;* Anonymous: *Mrs. Harriet Beecher Stowe,* in the *Abbot Academy Bulletin* for April, 1930; Sarah Stuart Robbins: *Old Andover Days,* quoted in *The Story of Essex County,* edited by Scott H. Paradise and Claude M. Fuess; *The Andover Magazine,* undated but probably 1895, only one issue of this magazine having ever been published; article on *Uncle Tom's Cabin* in London *Times Literary Supplement,* July 8, 1926; *Littell's Living Age* for July 10, 1852; *Independent* for April 1, 8, 15, 22, May 13, 20, 27, June 3, 10, 24, July 8, 15, 22, 29, Aug. 19, Sept. 9, 23, and 30. Also a.l.s. by H. B. Stowe to Tappan & Whittemore, dated Brunswick, June 25 [1852], in Harvard College Library, pasted in first Christmas edition of *Uncle Tom's Cabin ex libris* William Lambert Richardson.

ANDOVER: 1. Harriet in Battle. New York *Observer* for Sept. 23 and 30 and Oct. 7, 1892; *Independent* for Sept. 30 and October 7 and 14, 1852. A.l.s. by Henry Ward Beecher to the Rev. Joel Parker, D.D., dated Oct. 9, 1852, in the Historical Society of Pennsylvania, Simon Gratz Collection.

ANDOVER: 2. First Woman of America. *Life and Letters, Life,* McCray's *Life-Work, Autobiography,* Parker's *Eminent Women of The Age,* Winterich's *Books and The Man,* Erskine's *Leading American Novelists,* and Van Wyck Brooks: *The Flowering of New England;* N. D. Hillis: *The Battle of Principles;* David W. Bartlett: *Modern Agitators;* Katharine Thompson: *Literature in Essex County,* in *The Story of Essex County,* edited by Paradise and Fuess; Stephen B. Weeks: *Anti-Slavery Sentiment in The South,* in Publications of The Southern History Association, April, 1898; *The Affectionate and Christian Address,* in the Connecticut Historical Society, Hartford; Littell's *Living Age* for October 16, 1852, January 22 and March 26, 1853; New York *Times* for Oct. 30, 1852; *Times* (London) *Literary Supplement* for July 8, 1926; and the *Independent* for October 7, 14, 21, 28, Nov. 11, 18, 25, Dec. 9, 16, and 23, 1852, and Jan. 6, 27, Feb. 10, 24, and March 24, 1853. Manuscript letters: C. E. Stowe to Prof. Cleaveland, Oct. 23, 1852, in Boston Public Library; C. E. Stowe to Charles Sumner, Dec. 21, 1852, and on same letter, H. B. Stowe to Sumner, in the Sumner Papers, Harvard College Library; H. B. Stowe to Charles Sumner, undated, but after letter of Dec. 21, in Sumner Papers, Harvard Library; H. B. Stowe to Mary Dutton [1853?], in Yale University Library; H. B. Stowe to Lord Denman, Jan. 20, 1853, in Huntington Library, marked HM but in J. C. Clawson Collection of letters by Mrs. Stowe.

ANDOVER: 3. Queen of Scots. H. B. Stowe: *Sunny Memories of Foreign Lands;* C. E. Stowe: Introduction to same; *Life,* McCray's *Life-Work; Independent* for April 7, 14, 21, 28, May 5, 12, 19, 26, 1853; New York *Observer* for April 28, 1853, which reprints London *Times'* editorial on Harriet Beecher Stowe.

ANDOVER: 4. Lioness in London. Mrs. Stowe's *Sunny Memories* with Prof. Stowe's Introduction; McCray's *Life-Work;* H. W. Beecher: Star Paper in the *Independent,* May 26, and another in the issue of June 2, 1853; quotations from the British press are taken from them as republished in the New York *Independent* and the New York *Observer* May 26 and June 2, 9, 16, and 23, 1853, which issues have also supplied other material; New York *Herald* for May 2, 1853; Minute Book of the British and Foreign Anti-Slavery Society, London, Vol. III, from photostat copy in the Library of Congress. Autograph letters: Charles E. Stowe to Albert C. Bates, April 5, 1898, transmitting the "Affectionate and Christian Address" to the Connecticut Historical Society; C. E. Stowe to Rev. E. A. Park, dated London, May 10, 1853, at the Boston Public Library, Chamberlain Collection; James Buchanan to William Learned Marcy, Secretary of State, dated November 11, 1853, in the Library of Congress, Marcy Papers, Vol. 43.

ANDOVER: 5. Harriet as Tourist. *Sunny Memories, Life,* McCray's *Life-Work,* Hayward's *Lyman Beecher, Independent* for July 14, 1853.

ANDOVER: 6. National Leader. *Life, Autobiography,* McCray's *Life-Work,* Erskine's *Leading American Novelists,* Derby's *Fifty Years among Authors, Books and Publishers;* two books by Mrs. Stowe: *Uncle Sam's Emancipation* and *Mrs. Stowe's First Geography;* Philena McKeen: *History of Abbot Academy;* Elizabeth Stuart Phelps: *Chapters from A Life;* Wm. C. Nell: *The Colored Patriots of The American Revolution;* anonymous paper, *Mrs. Harriet Beecher Stowe,* in the *Abbot Academy Bulletin* for April, 1930; H. W. Beecher, Star Paper in the *Independent* for Nov. 16, 1854; and the following other issues of the *Independent:* Jan. 5, 12, 19, 26, Feb. 2, 9, 16, 23, Aug. 3, Oct. 12, Dec. 5 and 26, 1854, Jan. 16 and 23, Feb. 15, May 10, June 14 and 28, Aug. 9, Sept. 6, Nov. 1, and Dec. 27, 1855, Jan. 31, Feb. 7, 14, 21, May 1 and 29, June 5, 12, 19, and Sept. 18, 1856. Autograph letters: seven from H. B. Stowe to W. L. Garrison, dated [Nov.], Nov. 30, Dec. 19, Dec. 22, undated but in December after Christmas, all in 1853, Feb. 18, and Nov. 23, 1854, these letters being among the Garrison Papers in the Boston Public Library; also from the same collection a letter from Mrs. Stowe to Miss Anne Weston, dated [Dec.] 16, [1854]; H. B. Stowe to Charles Sumner, dated Feb. 23, 1854, in the Sumner Papers at Harvard Library; C. E. Stowe to Mr. Phillips, dated Andover, June 11, 1856, with postscript signed H. B. S., in the Chamberlain Collection, Boston Public Library; from the same collection, unaddressed note initialed H. B. S. to [Phillips], with postscript by C. E. Stowe, undated but written about the same time as preceding; from the same collection, H. B. Stowe to Mr. Phillips, with postscript by C. E. Stowe, dated Andover, July 13 [1856]; same collection, H. B. Stowe to Mr. Phillips, marked [London] posted Aug. 15, 1856; same collection, C. E. Stowe to Mr. Phillips, dated London, Aug. 18, 1856; and H. B. Stowe to Mr. Phillips, dated Steamer Niagara, Thursday, July 31 [1856] in the Historical Society of Pennsylvania, A. G. Coffin bequest.

ANDOVER: 7. Strictly Confidential. *Life,* McCray's *Life-Work;* C. E. Stowe's public explanation of the "royal interview," in the *Independent* of Oct. 9 and 16, 1856; C. E. Stowe on the gifts of Lady Byron and Miss Murray to the Kansas sufferers, *Independent,* Nov. 20 and 27, 1856; a.l.s. by H. B. Stowe to Mrs. Livermore, undated, but written in the early 1870's, in T. W. Higginson's scrapbook of women's autographs, in the Boston Public Library; H. B. Stowe's travel letters in the *Independent* of Jan. 22 and April 23, 1857; a.l.s. by C. E. Stowe to Mr. Phillips, dated Andover, Mar. 20 [1857], from the Chamberlain Collection, Boston Public Library; E. B. Browning: *Letters.*

ANDOVER: 8. The Gathering Storm. *Life,* McCray's *Life-Work,* Fields's *Life and Letters,* Derby's *Fifty Years among Authors,* Erskine's *Leading American Novelists;* H. B. Stowe: Introduction to *The Minister's Wooing;* H. W. Beecher: Star Paper, on the death of Henry Stowe, *Independent,* July 16, 1857; Gail Hamilton: *Letters.* The following additional issues of the *Independent:* 1857— Sept. 3 and 24, Nov. 12; 1858—Jan. 28, Feb. 18, March 11 and 25, July 22, Aug. 12 and 26, Sept. 2 and 30, Oct. 7, Nov. 4, Dec. 9 and 30; 1859—Jan. 6 and 13, March 17, May 19, Sept. 15, Oct. 20 and 27, Nov. 3, 10, 17, 24, Dec. 1, 8, 15 and 22; 1860—Jan. 12 and 19, Feb. 9 and 16, March 15, April 5, 12, 19, 26, May 3, 10, and 24; June 14, July 12 and 19, Aug. 23, Oct. 16 and 25, Nov. 1, 8 and 15. Letters: two from C. E. Stowe to S. P. Chase, dated Andover, January 25 and March 30, 1858, in the Library of Congress, Chase Collection; H. B. Stowe to unnamed correspondent, dated April 14 [1858?], in Boston Public Library; H. B. Stowe to Mrs. Park (with unsigned line by Prof. Park), undated but written in 1859, in Boston Public Library, Chamberlain Collection.

ANDOVER: 9. Harriet in Her War. *Life, Life and Letters,* C. E. and L. B. Stowe's *Harriet Beecher Stowe,* L. B. Stowe's *Saints, Sinners and Beechers,* Phelps's *Chapters from A Life,* Erskine's *Leading American Novelists,* Laura E. Richards and Maud Howe Elliott: *Julia Ward Howe, 1819-1910;* H. B. Stowe: *Abraham Lincoln,* in *Men of Our Times.* The following issues of the New York *Independent:* 1860—Nov. 15 and 22, Dec. 6, 13, 20 and 27; 1861—Jan. 3, 17, 24, 31, Feb. 7 and 21, March 7 and 14, April 4, 11, 18, 25, May 2, 9, 30, June 6, 13, 20, July 10 and 17, Aug. 1 and 29, Sept. 5 and 12, Oct. 10, Nov. 21 and 28, Dec. 5, 19, and 26; 1862—Jan. 2, Feb. 20, March 13 and 20, April 10, July 10 and 31, Aug. 7, 21, 28, Sept. 4, 11, and 25. The Boston *Transcript* for Jan. 2, 1863. The following autograph letters: H. B. Stowe to Robert Dale Owen, dated Andover, Dec. 8, 1860, in the Historical Society of Pennsylvania, Dreer Collection; H. B. Stowe to J. T. Fields, dated Andover, Jan. 16, 1861, in the Huntington Library; H. B. Stowe to J. T. Fields, dated Bath [England] [1860], in the Huntington Library; H. B. Stowe to "Mr. and Mrs. Meadows" [Fields], undated, but written shortly after Jan. 16, 1861, in the Huntington Library; two from H. B. Stowe to Charles Sumner, dated Andover, March 15, 1861, and Hartford, April 13, 1866, both in the Sumner Papers in Harvard College Library; H. B. Stowe to J. T. Fields, dated Peekskill, Friday [1861], in the Huntington Library; autograph by Mrs. Stowe, dated July 21, 1861, in the Boston Public Library, Chamberlain Collection; H. B. Stowe to Charles Sumner, dated Andover, Aug. 6, 1860, in the Sumner Papers, Harvard Library; H. B. Stowe to J. T. Fields, dated Aug. 25 [1861], in the Huntington Library; H. B. Stowe to J. T. Fields, undated but written in 1861, in the Huntington Library; C. E. Stowe to S. P. Chase, Nov. 6,

1861, Chase Papers, Library of Congress; H. B. Stowe to Mrs. Fields, Andover, Oct. 20, 1862, Huntington Library; H. B. Stowe to J. T. Fields, Hartford, Nov. 13, 1862, Huntington Library; H. B. Stowe to J. T. Fields, dated Washington, Nov. 27, 1862, in the Huntington Library; H. B. Stowe to Charles Sumner, Andover, Dec. 13, 1862, in the Sumner Papers, Harvard Library.

HARTFORD: 1. Harriet in Mr. Lincoln's War. *Life,* McCray's *Life-Work,* Hayward's *Lyman Beecher,* L. B. Stowe's *Saints, Sinners and Beechers, Independent* for Jan. 8, 15, and 29, 1863. Autograph letters: H. B. Stowe to Mrs. Fields, Andover, Feb. 10, 1863, at Huntington Library; H. B. Stowe to J. T. Fields, Andover, March 10 [1863], at Huntington Library; H. B. Stowe to Dr. Leonard Bacon, dated Hartford, Oct. 19, 1863, in Yale University Library; H. B. Stowe to J. T. Fields, Oct. 27 [1863], in Huntington Library; H. B. Stowe to J. T. Fields, dated Hartford, Nov. 3, 1863, in Huntington Library; H. B. Stowe to Secretary Stanton, dated New York, Nov. 27, 1863, in Stanton Papers, Library of Congress; H. B. Stowe to J. T. Fields, March 2 [1864], in Huntington Library; autograph by H. B. Stowe, dated Andover, March 5, 1864, in Yale University Library, Aldis Collection; H. B. Stowe to J. T. Fields, undated but written in 1864, in Huntington Library; H. B. Stowe to J. T. Fields, May 1 [1864], in Huntington Library; H. B. Stowe to J. T. Fields, dated Hartford, June 3, 1864, in Huntington Library; H. B. Stowe to Mrs. Fields, dated Andover, July 26 [1864], in Huntington Library; H. B. Stowe to Mrs. Fields, dated Tuesday morning [1864], in Huntington Library; H. B. Stowe to J. T. Fields, dated Northampton, Aug. 16, 1864, in Huntington Library; H. B. Stowe to J. T. Fields, dated Hartford, Sept. 8 [1864], in J. T. Fields's Autograph Book, in Harvard Library; H. B. Stowe to Charles Sumner, dated Hartford, Sept. 10, 1864, in Harvard Library, Sumner Papers; H. B. Stowe to J. T. Fields, undated but written in September, 1864, in Huntington Library; H. B. Stowe to J. T. Fields, undated but written in 1864, in Huntington Library; H. B. Stowe to "Atlanticus" [Fields], dated Brooklyn, Nov. 9, [1864], in Huntington Library; H. B. Stowe to Mrs. Fields, Nov. 29, 1864, in Huntington Library; three letters from H. B. Stowe to J. T. Fields, dated Oakholm, Dec. 9, 1864, Hartford, Dec. 29, 1864, and Hartford, Jan. 4 [1865], all in Huntington Library.

HARTFORD: 2. Heyday of a Career. *Life, Life and Letters,* McCray's *Life-Work,* Erskine's *Leading American Novelists.* The following autograph letters: H. B. Stowe to J. T. Fields, May 18 [1865], Huntington Library; H. B. Stowe to J. T. Fields [May 25, 1865], Huntington Library; H. B. Stowe to J. T. Fields, dated Oakholm, June 18, 1865, Huntington Library; H. B. Stowe to J. T. Fields, Sept. 8 [1865], Huntington Library; H. B. Stowe to Mrs. Fields, dated Hartford, Oct. 18, 1865, Huntington Library; H. B. Stowe to J. T. Fields, dated New York, Nov. 29 [1865], in Huntington Library; H. B. Stowe to J. T. Fields, dated Hartford, Dec. 19 [1865], Huntington Library; H. B. Stowe to J. T. Fields, dated Hartford, 27 [Jan., 1866], Huntington Library; H. B. Stowe to J. T. Fields, Feb. [13 or 14] [1866], Huntington Library; H. B. Stowe to Mrs. Fields, undated, but 1866, Huntington Library; H. B. Stowe to J. T. Fields, undated, but 1866, Huntington Library; H. B. Stowe to J. T.

Fields, dated Hartford, Oct. 18 [1866], Huntington Library; H. B. Stowe to J. T. Fields, dated Hartford, Dec. [1866], Huntington Library; H. B. Stowe to J. T. Fields, Jan. 20 [1867], Huntington Library; H. B. Stowe to J. T. Fields, dated Hartford, Feb. 8 [1867], Huntington Library; H. B. Stowe to J. T. Fields, Feb. 9, 1867, Huntington Library; H. B. Stowe to J. T. Fields, dated Hartford, Feb. 19 [1867], Huntington Library; H. B. Stowe to Mrs. Fields, dated Hartford, Feb. 26 [1867], Huntington Library; H. B. Stowe to Mrs. Fields, dated Charleston, March 13, 1868 [should be 1867], Huntington Library; H. B. Stowe to J. T. Fields, undated, but 1867, Huntington Library; H. B. Stowe to J. T. Fields, dated H., July 13 [1867], Huntington Library; H. B. Stowe to J. T. Fields, undated, but summer, 1867, Huntington Library; H. B. Stowe to J. T. Fields, Aug. 8 [1867], Huntington Library; H. B. Stowe to J. T. Fields, Aug. 16, 1867, Huntington Library; H. B. Stowe to J. T. Fields, dated Stockbridge, Sept. 3 [1867], Huntington Library; H. B. Stowe to Mrs. Fields, dated Hartford, Oct. 21 [1867], Huntington Library; H. B. Stowe to J. T. Fields, undated, but 1867, Huntington Library; H. B. Stowe to Mrs. Fields, dated Hartford, "Nov. 21 or 2 or something" [1867], Huntington Library; H. B. Stowe to W. L. Garrison, Nov., 1867, Garrison letters, Boston Public Library; H. B. Stowe to J. T. Fields, undated, but 1867, Huntington Library; H. B. Stowe to Mrs. Fields, dated "Monday morning, Somewhere in December, 1867 (for sartin)," Huntington Library; H. B. Stowe to Alice Underwood, dated Richmond, Va., March 6, 1868, in Underwood Papers, Library of Congress; H. B. Stowe to Mrs. Fields, July 27, 1868, Huntington Library; H. B. Stowe to J. T. Fields, undated, but 1868, Huntington Library; ten letters from H. B. Stowe to J. T. Fields, two undated, but written in 1868, one undated but written in October, 1868, one dated Oct. 19 [1868], two undated but written in 1868, one undated but written in Dec., 1868, one dated Hartford, Dec. 24, 1868, and one dated Hartford, Dec. 28, 1868, all in Huntington Library; H. B. Stowe to Mrs. Fields, dated Hartford, Aug. 17 [1868], Huntington Library; H. B. Stowe to J. T. Fields, undated but 1869, Huntington Library; H. B. Stowe to Mrs. Fields, undated, but written from Guilford in Dec., 1868 or Jan., 1869, in Huntington Library; five letters from H. B. Stowe to J. T. Fields dated Hartford, Jan. 19, 1869, Hartford, Feb. 3, 1869, Hartford, Feb. 10, 1869, Feb., 1868 [should be 1869], and Feb. 16 [1869], all in Huntington Library; H. B. Stowe to Mrs. Fields, dated Hartford, Wednesday, Feb. 17 [1869], Huntington Library.

HARTFORD: 3. Catastrophe. *Life,* McCray's *Life-Work,* Harveson's *Catharine Esther Beecher;* the *Independent* for Aug. 26, 1869, and Jan. 20, 1870. The following letters: H. B. Stowe to J. T. Fields, Mar. 2, 1869, Huntington Library; H. B. Stowe to J. T. Fields, dated Mandarin, April 8 [1869], Huntington Library; fragment of letter from H. B. Stowe to Mrs. Fields, marked April, 1869, Huntington Library; H. B. Stowe to Mrs. Fields, dated Hartford, May 9 [1869] Huntington Library; five letters from H. B. Stowe to J. R. Osgood, contained in bound scrapbook *"ex libris* John L. Clawson," indexed under Miscellaneous Papers, and dated Hartford, June 9, 1869, undated but written in June, 1869, Hartford, June 23, 1869, Hartford, June 28, 1869, and Hartford, June 30 [1869], in Huntington Library; H. B. Stowe to J. R. Osgood, dated West Port Point, July 6 [1869], in Harvard Library; H. B. Stowe to J. R. Osgood, dated West Port, July 13 [1869], Huntington Library, Clawson Collection; H. B. Stowe to J. R. Osgood, dated Stockbridge, Aug. 24 [1869], Huntington Library, Clawson Collection; H. B. Stowe to J. R. Osgood, undated but 1869, Huntington Library, Clawson Collection; H. B. Stowe to Fields & Osgood, dated Hartford, Sept. 15 [1869], Huntington Library, Clawson Collection; H. B. Stowe to J. R. Osgood, dated Providence, Sept. 17 [1869], letter owned by Leslie B. Cooper, Garden City, L. I., photostat copy in New York Public Library; the following from the Clawson Collection in the Huntington Library: H. B. Stowe to Field [sic] & Osgood, dated Hartford, Sep. 23, '69; H. B. Stowe to J. R. Osgood, dated Saturday, Oct. 16 [1869]; H. B. Stowe to J. R. Osgood, dated New York, 69 West 38 St. [1869]; H. B. Stowe to J. R. Osgood, two undated letters written in fall of 1869; H. B. Stowe to J. R. Osgood, dated Monday morning [1869]; two letters from H. B. Stowe to J. R. Osgood, undated but written Oct. 19 and Nov. 16, 1869; and H. B. Stowe to J. R. Osgood, dated Friday, Nov. 19 [1869]; H. B. Stowe to J. R. Osgood, undated, but with notation, "Rec'd Nov. 29" [1869], Yale Library, Aldis Collection; three letters from Isabella Beecher Hooker to Fields, Osgood & Co., dated New York, 29 Nov. [1869], undated but Nov. 29, 1869, and dated New York, Dec. 2 [1869] all in the Huntington Library, Clawson Collection; H. B. Stowe to "Gentlemen," dated N. York, Dec. 6 [1869], Huntington Library, Clawson Collection; H. B. Stowe to J. R. Osgood, dated New York, Dec. 8 [1869], Huntington Library, Clawson Collection; H. B. Stowe to Mrs. Fields, undated but late 1869, Huntington Library; H. B. Stowe to Horace Greeley, dated Brooklyn, Dec. 19, 1869, Miscellaneous Papers, Ford Collection, in the New York Public Library; C. E. Stowe to J. T. Fields, with postscript by Mrs. Stowe, dated Hartford, Conn., Dec. 29, 1869, Huntington Library, Clawson Collection; C. E. Stowe to J. T. Fields, dated Hartford, Conn., Jan. 1, 1870, Huntington Library, Clawson Collection; MS of suppressed preface to *Lady Byron Vindicated,* in Clawson Collection, Huntington Library; H. B. Stowe to J. T. Fields, dated "New Year's" [1870], in Clawson Collection, Huntington Library.

HARTFORD: 4. Afternoon of a Career. *Life,* McCray's *Life-Work,* Harveson's *Catharine Esther Beecher,* Mrs. Stowe's *My Wife and I;* Anon.: *John Tasker Howard and His Wife,* privately printed, 1909; Miss Mary B. Graff's Mandarin notes; personal recollections of Mrs. H. F. Nicholl; Mrs. T. B. Aldrich: *Crowding Memories;* issues of the *Christian Union* as follows: 1870—April 23, May 7, 21, 28, June 11 and 18, Aug. 20, Sept. 3, 10, 24, Oct. 1 and 8, Nov. 5 and 12, Dec. 31; 1871—Jan. 11, April 5, July 5, Aug. 2, Nov. 1, 8, and 29, Dec. 6 and 25; and Jan. 1, 1873. The following letters: H. B. Stowe to J. T. Fields, dated "New Year's" [1870], Clawson Collection, Huntington Library; H. B. Stowe to J. T. Fields, dated Mandarin, Feb. 13, 1870, Huntington Library; H. B. Stowe to Mrs. Fields, dated Mandarin, March 9, 1870, Huntington Library; H. B. Stowe to J. T. Fields, March 21, 1870, Huntington Library; H. B. Stowe to J. T. Fields, [May, 1870], Huntington Library; H. B. Stowe to J. T. Fields, dated Mandarin,

May 10, 1870, Huntington Library; H. B. Stowe to Mrs. Fields, dated Northampton Depot, Aug. 4, 1870, Huntington Library; H. B. Stowe to J. T. Fields, dated Hartford, Aug. 14 [1870], Huntington Library; H. B. Stowe to Mrs. Fields, dated Stockbridge, Nov. 4, 1870, Huntington Library; H. B. Stowe to T. W. Higginson, dated May 24, 1871, Higginson Autographs, Boston Public Library; H. B. Stowe to J. R. Osgood, Aug. 16 [1871], in Theatrical Division, Harvard Library; H. B. Stowe to Mr. Wood, Aug. 20, 1871, in New York Public Library.

HARTFORD: 5. Harriet in a Storm. *Life, Life and Letters,* McCray's *Life-Work,* Paxton Hibben's *Henry Ward Beecher;* Anon.: *Pictures from Florida,* in *Scribner's Magazine,* Nov., 1875; Silvia Sunshine: *Petals Plucked from Sunny Climes;* the 1911 *Life;* L. B. Stowe's *Saints, Sinners and Beechers.* The letters of Isabella Beecher Hooker and Thomas K. Beecher relating to the Beecher-Tilton affair come from undated clippings of the New York *Sun* in the New York Public Library. The following issues of the *Christian Union:* 1872—Jan. 24, Feb. 7, 14, 21, 28, March 13, 20, 27, May 8, 15, 29, June 26, July 24, Aug. 7, 14, 21, Sept. 11, Oct. 2, 16, Dec. 11, 18; 1873—Jan. 1, 22, March 12, May 14, July 9, Sept. 17, Oct. 22, Nov. 26; 1874—Jan. 7, May 6, 13, 20, Sept. 23, Oct. 7, Dec. 23; 1875—April 7, 14, July 7. Letters: H. B. Stowe to Robert Dale Owen, Jan. 4, 1872, from Dreer Collection, Historical Society of Pennsylvania; H. B. Stowe to Mrs. Fields, Feb. 6, 1872, Huntington Library; H. B. Stowe to Mrs. Fields, dated Mandarin, March 2, 1872, Huntington Library; H. B. Stowe to Mrs. Fields, March 16, 1872, Huntington Library; H. B. Stowe to Mrs. Fields, dated Mandarin, April 30 [1872], Huntington Library; H. B. Stowe to J. R. Osgood, dated Mandarin, May 14, 1872, in Miscellaneous Letters, Huntington Library; H. B. Stowe to Mrs. Fields, dated Mandarin, June, 1872, Huntington Library; H. B. Stowe to Mrs. Fields, dated Twin Mountain House, Aug. 20 [1872], Huntington Library; two more from H. B. Stowe to Mrs. Fields addressed from Twin Mountain House and dated Aug. 21 and 27, 1872, in the Huntington Library; H. B. Stowe to Mrs. Fields, Nov. 22, 1872, Huntington Library; H. B. Stowe to Mrs. Fields, dated Framingham, Christmas Evening, 1872, Huntington Library; H. B. Stowe to J. T. Fields, Feb. 13, 1870, Huntington Library; H. B. Stowe to Mrs. Fields, dated Hartford, April [Sept.]? 24, 1873, Huntington Library; H. B. Stowe to Mr. Brelsford, dated Mandarin, May 9, 1873, in Historical and Philosophical Society of Ohio; H. B. Stowe to Mrs. Underwood, dated Hartford, Nov. 10, 1873, from Underwood Papers, Library of Congress; H. B. Stowe to Mr. and Mrs. Fields, Jan. 29, 1874, Huntington Library; three letters from H. B. Stowe to Alice Underwood, dated Aug. 22, 25, and 27, 1874, from Underwood Papers, Library of Congress; H. B. Stowe to Dr. Leonard Bacon, dated Twin Mountain House, Sept. 9, 1874, from the Bacon Letters, Yale University Library; H. B. Stowe to Alice Underwood, dated Mandarin, March 12, 1875, Underwood Papers, Library of Congress.

HARTFORD: 6. Rainbow at Night. *Life, Life and Letters,* 1911 *Life,* L. B. Stowe's *Saints, Sinners and Beechers,* Hibben's *Henry Ward Beecher,* Miss Graff's historical notes on Mandarin, Silvia Sunshine's *Petals Plucked from Sunny Climes.* The *Atlantic Monthly* for October, 1878, and January, February, and May, 1879.

The issues of the *Christian Union* of Oct. 7, Nov. 3, 10, 17, 24, and Dec. 15, 1875. The manuscript diary of Isabella Beecher Hooker, with the Historical Society of Connecticut. Letters: H. B. Stowe to Mrs. Fields, Aug. 30, 1875, Huntington Library; H. B. Stowe to J. R. Osgood, Feb. 6, 1876, in the Slack Collection, Marietta College Library; H. B. Stowe to Alice Underwood, April 24, 1876, Underwood Papers, Library of Congress; H. B. Stowe to Editor, New York *Tribune,* dated Mandarin, Feb. 8, 1877, in the Ford Collection, New York Public Library; three letters from H. B. Stowe to Alice Underwood, dated March 4, 1877, March 11 and April 16, 1878, in the Underwood Papers, Library of Congress; H. B. Stowe to J. R. Osgood, dated Hartford, July 26, 1878, in Miscellaneous Letters, Huntington Library; three letters from H. B. Stowe to Mrs. Fields, dated July 30 and Aug. 2, 1878, and April 28, 1879, in the Huntington Library; H. B. Stowe to Alice Underwood, dated Hartford, Nov. 12, 1879, Underwood Papers, Library of Congress; H. B. Stowe to Mrs. Fields, dated Hartford, Dec. 2, 1880, Huntington Library; H. B. Stowe to Mrs. Fields, dated Mandarin, Jan. 1, 1881, Huntington Library; H. B. Stowe to Alice Underwood, dated Mandarin, May 27, 1881, Underwood Papers, Library of Congress; H. B. Stowe to Mrs. Fields, dated Mandarin, Nov. 30, 1881, Huntington Library.

HARTFORD: 7. Happy Birthday. The *Atlantic Monthly* (Supplement) for July, 1882, and for August, 1882; Elizabeth Stuart Phelps's *Chapters from A Life,* J. C. Derby's *Fifty Years among Authors, Books and Publishers.*

HARTFORD: 8. "And Now I Rest Me." *Life,* 1911 *Life,* Lyman Beecher Stowe's *Saints, Sinners and Beechers,* McCray's *Life-Work,* Hibben's *Henry Ward Beecher,* Miss Graff's Mandarin historical notes; J. H. Twichell: *Mrs. Stowe in Hartford,* in *Authors at Home,* edited by J. L. and J. B. Gilder; Frances E. Willard: *Harriet Beecher Stowe at Home,* in *The Chautauquan* for February, 1888; George C. Boswell, editor: *The Litchfield Book of Days;* Hattie Tyng Griswold: *Personal Sketches of Recent Authors;* Kirk Munroe: *Harriet Beecher Stowe,* in the 1889 edition of *Lives and Deeds of Our Self-Made Men;* H. B. Stowe: Preface to the *Life;* Philena McKeen: *History of Abbot Academy;* Van Wyck Brooks: *New England: Indian Summer.* Letters: H. B. Stowe to T. W. Higginson, Oct. 19, 1883, in Higginson Autographs, Boston Public Library; H. B. Stowe to J. C. Derby, dated Mandarin, March 11, 1884, Clawson Collection, Huntington Library; two from H. B. Stowe to Mrs. Fields, dated Aug. 26 and Sept. 24, 1884, both in Huntington Library; H. B. Stowe to O. W. Holmes, Aug. 25, 1885, in the Library of Congress; H. B. Stowe to Yale University, dated Hartford, June 23, 1886, from T. Dwight Miscellaneous Papers, Yale University Library; H. B. Stowe to O. W. Holmes, Oct. 29, 1886, Library of Congress; H. B. Stowe to Mrs. C. G. Crane, March 17, 1889, in the possession of Jack V. Nicholl, Mandarin, Fla.; H. B. Stowe to J. [or I.] F. Petri, May 19, 1889, in Harvard Library; H. B. Stowe to E. L. Peirce, Jan. 13, 1889, in Harvard Library; Miss H. B. Stowe to Mr. Secor, Jan. 29, 1890, in Harvard Library; Z. C. to Miss Gould (containing copy of opinion of Maurice Thompson of *Uncle Tom's Cabin*) in E. P. Gould's annotated copy of the *Life,* in the Boston Public Library; H. B. Stowe to O. W. Holmes, Feb. 5, 1893, in the Library of Congress; H. B. Stowe to Mrs. S. O. Seymour, June 15, 1893, in Miscellaneous Letters and Autographs in the Litchfield Historical Society; autograph "Harriet Beecher Stowe," dated March 23, 1894, in the E. J. Wendell Bequest, Harvard College Library. Henry Drummond's comment on Mrs. Stowe is from an unidentified newspaper clipping pasted in E. P. Gould's annotated copy of the *Life,* in the Boston Public Library. The newspaper clipping, *Mrs. Stowe's Decline,* is in Random Papers, Vol. 37, p. 157, in the Litchfield Historical Society. Paul Laurence Dunbar's sonnet, *Harriet Beecher Stowe* appeared first in the *Century Magazine* for November, 1898.

INDEX

ABBREVIATIONS: HBS for Harriet Beecher Stowe.
UTC for *Uncle Tom's Cabin.*
CES for Calvin Ellis Stowe.
HWB for Henry Ward Beecher.
LB for Lyman Beecher.